Windows® Server 2003: The Complete Reference

Kathy Ivens
with Rich Benack, Christian Branson, Kenton Gardinier,
John Green, David Heinz, Tim Kelly, John Linkous,
Christopher McKettrick, Patrick J. Santry, Mitch Tulloch

McGraw-Hill/Osborne

New York   Chicago   San Francisco
Lisbon   London   Madrid   Mexico City
Milan   New Delhi   San Juan
Seoul   Singapore   Sydney   Toronto

The McGraw·Hill Companies

McGraw-Hill/Osborne
2100 Powell Street, 10th Floor
Emeryville, California 94608
U.S.A.

To arrange bulk purchase discounts for sales promotions, premiums, or fund-raisers, please contact **McGraw-Hill**/Osborne at the above address. For information on translations or book distributors outside the U.S.A., please see the International Contact Information page immediately following the index of this book.

Windows® Server 2003: The Complete Reference

1234567890 DOC DOC 019876543
ISBN 0-07-219484-7

Publisher
Brandon A. Nordin

Vice President & Associate Publisher
Scott Rogers

Acquisitions Editor
Tracy Dunkelberger

Project Editor
Elizabeth Seymour

Acquisitions Coordinator
Athena Honore

Copy Editor
William McManus

Proofreader
Pat Mannion

Indexer
Valerie Perry

Computer Designers
Apollo Publishing Services
Tara A. Davis
Carie Abrew

Illustrators
Lyssa Wald
Melinda Lytle
Michael Mueller

Series Design
Peter F. Hancik

This book was composed with Corel VENTURA™ Publisher.

Information has been obtained by **McGraw-Hill**/Osborne from sources believed to be reliable. However, because of the possibility of human or mechanical error by our sources, **McGraw-Hill**/Osborne, or others, **McGraw-Hill**/Osborne does not guarantee the accuracy, adequacy, or completeness of any information and is not responsible for any errors or omissions or the results obtained from use of such information.

I'd like to thank all the talented people at McGraw-Hill/Osborne who worked so hard to bring this book to you, with special homage to Tracy Dunkelberger and Athena Honore, who were directly involved in every step of this book's creation. Picture me delivering a loud and enthusiastic round of applause as I give special thanks to the technical editor, David Heinz, for his expertise, and a standing ovation for copy editor Bill McManus for his extremely skillful work.
I owe Chris Cannon, Microsoft's Product Manager for Servers, more than I can ever repay, for providing explanations, information, and an incredible amount of patience (all delivered with a much appreciated sense of humor). Brandi Muller of Waggener Edstrom Strategic Communications was a life saver whenever I needed information.
—Kathy Ivens

This chapter is dedicated to my loving wife, Connie, for all her support in my career and in our marriage.
—Rich Benack

This is dedicated to my wife, Tanya. You always thought I'd reach the stars.
—Christian Branson

For my wife, Deborah, whose patience and support are neverending sources of strength; and for my sons Andrew and Brandon, who never cease to inspire me.
—John Green

Dedicated to all the technology workers who have helped create the fantastic computing environments we enjoy today; who endure the pain and complex learning curves of new technologies in extremely short timeframes and apply them to business problems we face today.
—Tim Kelly

To my parents.
—John Linkous

Dedicated to my wife, Karyn Santry, and children, Katie, Karleigh, and P.J.
—Patrick J. Santry

About the Author

Kathy Ivens has been a computer consultant and author since 1985. She has written and contributed to more than forty books, and hundreds of magazine articles. She also writes the Reader Challenge for *Windows 2000 Magazine* (formerly known as *Windows NT Magazine*).

Expert Contributors

I owe a deep debt of gratitude to a number of experts who shared their knowledge and writing skills to make this book accurate and useful to readers.

Rich Benack is a security support engineer with Microsoft Product Support and Services (PSS). He provides virus and computer intrusion support to Microsoft customers as well as technical support in securing Microsoft products. He is also a Major in the United States Air Force Reserve working for the Department of Defense CyberCrime Center (DCCC). At the DCCC, Rich provides forensics support and technical analysis on Microsoft-related forensics issues. Rich has a B.S. in Mathematics from the University of Illinois at Urbana as well as a B.S. in Computer Information Management from the College of St Mary in Nebraska. He has earned an M.S. in Geography with a specialization in Remote Sensing and computer mapping from the University of Nebraska at Omaha. Rich also has advanced blackbelts in Tae Kwon Do and Hap Ki Do.

Christian Branson has been a Systems Engineer for 12 years. He worked for Microsoft Product Support Services for six years as a support professional and a lab engineer. He has also been a network administrator in San Antonio's largest hospital system, and a field support engineer as a contractor to the Army. He lives in Dallas with Tanya, his wife of 24 years, and their son, Ian.

Kenton Gardinier, MCSA, MCSE, and CISSP, is a senior consultant with Convergent Computing. He has designed and implemented technical and business driven solutions for organizations of all sizes for over 10 years. He is an author of numerous books (his latest is *Windows Server 2003 Unleashed*), print magazine articles, and online articles on computer technology. In addition, he speaks on technology issues at conferences nationwide.

John Green, MCSE and MCDBA, is a former member of the Windows and .NET Magazine lab and author of numerous magazine articles. He is president of Nereus Computer Consulting.

David Heinz has been involved in computer systems management for eight years. He has worked for several small businesses and for Micron Technology as a systems manager. He is a columnist at www.myitforum.com. He lives in Las Vegas with his family and can be reached at dheinz99@yahoo.com.

Tim Kelly is a technology leader for a major credit card processing company. He leads the development and implementation of a new process management web application for customers in multiple vertical industries, based on the Microsoft .NET development environment and Windows 2000/Windows 2003 platforms. He worked for three years with Microsoft (1998-2001), at the time of the rollout of Windows 2000 and assisted multiple corporate customers with Active Directory implementations, Exchange 2000 implementations, and transitions from Windows NT 4.0 to Windows 2000 technologies. He has worked extensively in the electronic commerce and highly available web applications space for the last five years, and counts as his specialties IIS, Microsoft Clustering Technologies, Microsoft SQL Server availability, Active Directory, and core networking technologies. He is a graduate of the University of Idaho (B.S.), and Auburn University (M.B.A.) and has 10 years experience in the technology field. When not having fun losing hair to new technology, Tim enjoys family time with his wonderful wife, Lynn, and sons Russell and Jackson. He also enjoys jumping out of perfectly safe airplanes.

John Linkous is president of Technology Workflow Solutions, LLC (www.techworkflow.com), an end-to-end technology integration vendor. He specializes in integrating a broad range of technologies, including operating systems, messaging products, relational and object-oriented database systems, vertical market products, and enterprise management solutions across multiple platforms. His company's clients include organizations in the financial services, healthcare, aerospace, and food service industries. When John's not in a plane, train, automobile, or data center, he lives in suburban Philadelphia, PA. He can be reached at jlinkous@techworkflow.com.

Christopher McKitterick received his M.A. in writing from the University of Kansas. He has a B.A. in English, with minor concentrations in writing, astronomy, and psychology. He has been a technical writer, developmental editor, and documentation manager at Microsoft in the Windows Division for nearly five years, and also has numerous fiction, poetry, essay, nonfiction, and miscellaneous publications to his name. Chris is currently teaching technical communications at the University of Kansas, has taught astronomy and fiction writing, directed observatory and planetarium programs, built nearly 100 telescopes, and is an expert on restoring automobiles. Chris chairs the Theodore Sturgeon Memorial Award for best short science fiction of the year; has served as a juror for the John W. Campbell Memorial Award for best science fiction novel of the year; and works with the Center for the Study of Science Fiction (http://www.ku.edu/~sfcenter/index.html).

Patrick J. Santry, MCT, MCSE, MCSA, MCP+SB, A+, i-Net+, CIW CI, is an independent consultant specializing in Web-based solutions using Microsoft .NET technologies. Patrick is a contributing author and technical editor of several books and magazine articles on Microsoft technologies.

Mitch Tulloch, MCSE, Cert.Ed., is a consultant, trainer and author of more than a dozen computing books including *Administering IIS4, Administering IIS5, Administering Exchange Server 5.5*, and *Administering Exchange 2000 Server*, all from McGraw-Hill/Osborne. He is also the author of the *Microsoft Encyclopedia of Networking*, now in its second edition, and the upcoming *Microsoft Encyclopedia of Security*, both from Microsoft Press. Mitch has also developed university-level IT courses and written feature articles for industry magazines like NetworkWorld. He can be reached through his website, www.mtit.com.

Contents

Acknowledgments

Special thanks to Andy Erlandson, the director of PSS Security, for his support in allowing me to work on this book. Thanks to my coworkers on the PSS Security team for all your technical help. I would also like to thank Dave Poole, Director of the DoD Cyber Crime Institute (DCCI), for his support while I was with the DCCC.

—Rich Benack

First and foremost, I would like to thank Kathy Ivens. This opportunity would not have come my way without her. My thanks to my wife, Tanya, and son, Ian, for their support. I love you both. This would not be complete without naming those who allowed it to happen: Thanks to Sean Johnson, Dallas Lab group manager, and Matt Loschen, National Lab Manager.

—Christian Branson

Over the years I have been extremely lucky to work with a great group of people who allowed me to grow and become better in my field. While I know I may forget many, those that loom large are Thomas Stewart for forcing me to learn to program, Dave Spray for trusting me to catch on when I was not too sure I would, and Jean for pushing when I needed to be pushed. I love you.

—David Heinz

Thanks to the extremely professional McGraw Hill/Osborne staff, especially Athena Honore, and Dave Heinz.

—Tim Kelly

I'd like to thank Kathy Ivens for her fantastic help, and for mentoring me throughout the development of this book. I'd also like to thank VMWare Corporation for their excellent Workstation and GSX Server products, without which this book would have been tremendously more difficult to write.

—John Linkous

Introduction

Windows Server 2003 is the new and improved version of Windows 2000, offering new features and functions that make administration of your network efficient and easier. If you're moving to Windows Server 2003
from Windows NT, learning about Active Directory, Group Policies, and the other management features may seem overwhelming at first, and in fact, the learning curve can be quite consuming. This book helps you put the concepts and tasks you need to understand into an orderly pattern, which will shorten your learning curve.

Is This Book for You?

This book is written for network administrators, IT professionals, and power users. Throughout the book, the authors assume that the reader is familiar with basic networking issues and jargon. In addition, all directions for performing tasks assume you're logged on to your network with administrative permissions.

We wrote this book for the people who bear the responsibilities for managing Windows networks. You can translate "managing" to include deployment, configuration, and day to day administration.

The
Complete
Reference

Chapter 1

Introducing Windows Server 2003

1

W indows Server 2003 is an evolutionary step from Windows 2000, and it offers a lot of features that were on my "wish list" as I worked with Windows 2000. For administrators currently running Windows 2000 networks, deploying this new version of Windows won't present an onerous learning curve, because the basics haven't changed very much. For administrators currently running Windows NT networks, this fine-tuned version of Microsoft's corporate operating system is so filled with administrative tools and controls that you've run out of reasons to stay with NT.

Windows Server 2003 Editions

Windows Server 2003 is available in the following four editions:

- Windows 2003 Standard Server
- Windows 2003 Enterprise Server (32-bit and 64-bit versions)
- Windows 2003 Datacenter Server (32-bit and 64-bit versions)
- Windows 2003 Web Server

In this section, I'll present an overview of the distinguishing features for each version.

Standard Edition

Windows Server 2003 Standard edition is suitable for most network chores. It supports four-way symmetric multiprocessing (SMP), and 4GB of RAM. You can use Standard edition for Network Load Balancing (but not for Cluster Services) and for Terminal Server hosting.

In a large organization, this edition is perfect for file services, supporting Distributed File System (DFS), Encrypting File System (EFS), and Shadow Copies. You can also use Standard edition for Remote Installation Services (RIS), and for web services. This edition can run all network management services, .NET application services, and multimedia. You can use Standard edition as an all-purpose server for departmental and small-site locations. For small organizations, Standard edition works well in any role, from providing file and print services, to acting as a domain controller.

Enterprise Edition

Enterprise edition is "muscled up" to meet all the needs of businesses of all sizes. It supports eight-way SMP, 32GB of RAM in the 32-bit version, and 64GB of RAM in the 64-bit version. It supports server clusters, handling up to eight nodes.

Its ability to scale makes it a good choice for any role in a large organization, offering a solid base for applications, web services (especially if you need web clusters), and infrastructure management.

Enterprise edition replaces Windows 2000 Advanced Server.

Datacenter Edition

The powerhouse of the Windows platform, Datacenter edition supports 32-way SMP in the 32-bit version, and 64-way SMP in the 64-bit version. It can handle 64GB RAM in the 32-bit version, and 512GB RAM in the 64-bit version. Eight-node clustering is built in. As with its Windows 2000 version, Datacenter is available through OEMs who participate in the Datacenter program, and who provide support.

Web Edition

This new Windows product is built to develop and run a web site. It includes IIS 6.0, and other components that let you host web applications, web pages, and XML web services. You cannot use Web edition to run web server farms that require clusters. Nor can you install any network management services, such as Active Directory, DNS services, or DHCP services. Web edition is not available as a retail product; you must purchase it preinstalled from an OEM, or from a Microsoft System Builder partner.

Brand New in Windows Server 2003!

If you've been running your enterprise on Windows 2000, you'll find a lot of new features, some of which are subtle improvements on existing features, and others that are brand-spanking new. If you've been running a Windows NT enterprise, because you adopted a "wait and see" attitude about Windows 2000, the new features in Windows Server 2003 should reassure you that upgrading provides more power to your users, and to you as an administrator. In this section, I'll present an overview of the versions and new features available for Windows Server 2003. Detailed instructions for using the features mentioned here are found throughout this book.

New Remote Administration Tools

Windows Server 2003 offers several tools that make it easier for you to manage servers and domains remotely. You can view, change, or troubleshoot server-based services, and domain settings, from your own workstation. In addition, you can delegate specific tasks to other members of your IT department, and let them manage aspects of your enterprise from their own workstations, or from a help desk center.

RIS Now Deploys Servers

Previously, RIS was only available for client/workstation versions of Windows. With Windows Server 2003, you can use the new NET RIS functions to roll out all versions of Windows Server 2003 except Datacenter.

Remote Desktop

Remote Desktop was actually introduced in Windows 2000, when Microsoft divided Terminal Server into two distinct applications: Administrative mode and Application mode. Administrative mode provided two free Terminal Server licenses on a server, so that administrators could access the server to perform administrative tasks. Application mode provided the standard Terminal Server tools for running applications on a server.

Now, in Windows Server 2003, Terminal Server is used only for running applications, and a new component, Remote Desktop for Administration, is built in to the operating system. Because it's a component, and not a separate application, there are no licensing issues, so as many administrators as you care to designate can manage your Windows Server 2003 computers remotely.

The client-side software (called Remote Desktop Connection) is built in to Windows XP (the client member of the Windows Server 2003 family). For versions of Windows earlier than XP, you can install the client-side software from the Windows Server 2003 CD, or from a network sharepoint that contains the Windows Server 2003 installation files.

Configuring a server for remote access takes only a few mouse clicks. All Windows Server 2003 servers have a local group called Remote Desktop Users Group, to which you can add users and configure security. See Chapter 3 for a full discussion of setting up and using Remote Desktop for Administration.

Remote Assistance

Your help desk personnel will tell you that often the best way to help a user is to go to the user's workstation (or send someone else). Sometimes the problem is just too complicated to walk a user through the solution, and sometimes the user needs detailed instructions that would take forever if you have to wait for the user to find the appropriate dialogs or menu options. Remote Assistance provides a way to work on a remote user's computer without leaving your own desk. Remote Assistance works in either of two ways:

- A novice user requests help from an experienced user.
- An experienced user provides help to a novice user without receiving a request for help.

When a support person connects to a user's machine with Remote Assistance, the support person can view the user's screen and even use his own mouse and keyboard to control the user's computer. To add to all of this convenience, Remote Assistance provides a chat feature and a file exchange function. To use Remote Assistance, the following criteria must be met:

- The computers must be running either Windows Server 2003 or Windows XP.
- The computers must be connected over a LAN or the Internet.

This means your support personnel who are working on Windows XP workstations don't have to go to a Windows Server 2003 computer to provide assistance to users.

Requesting Help   A user working at a computer running Windows Server 2003 or Windows XP can request help from another user running Windows Server 2003 or Windows XP. Remote Assistance requests are enabled by default in Windows XP, so any users running Windows XP can request assistance from any experienced user running Windows Server 2003 or Windows XP. On computers running Windows Server 2003, you must enable the Remote Assistance feature in order to request help.

A group policy is available for enabling and disabling requests for Remote Assistance, on both the domain/OU level and on the local Windows Server 2003/Windows XP computer. You can find the policy at Computer Configuration\Administrative Templates\ System\Remote Assistance.

Note   *To open the local group policy editor, choose Start | Run and type **gpedit.msc**.*

If the group policy is not configured, you can enable or disable the feature in the System Properties dialog (right-click My Computer and choose Properties). Move to the Remote tab and select the option Turn on Remote Assistance and allow invitations to be sent from this computer. Click Advanced to open the Remote Assistance Settings dialog, in which you can do the following:

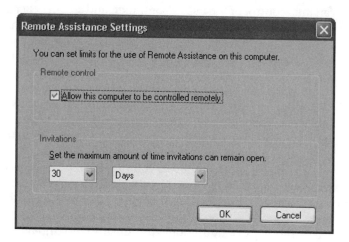

- Enable or disable the remote control feature.
- Set a limit for the amount of time a request for assistance is valid.

Note   *If the group policy is enabled or disabled, instead of Not Configured, it takes precedence over the settings in the System Properties dialog.*

To request help, take the following steps:

1. Click Start and choose Help and Support.
2. In the right pane, click Remote Assistance, which is under Ask for Assistance in Windows XP, and under Support Tasks in Windows Server 2003.
3. Click Invite someone to help you.

The system opens Outlook Express or Outlook, depending on which application is the default e-mail program, to send the request. The requesting user enters the recipient's e-mail address, or opens the address book to select the recipient.

Caution   *If you're not using Outlook or Outlook Express, the process fails. This feature doesn't work with any other e-mail software, including the popular Eudora.*

If both users are working at computers running Windows XP, and both users are also signed in to Windows Messenger, the requesting user can use an instant message, instead of e-mail, to request help.

Once the Remote Assistance connection is made, the support person (the invitee) has access to the computer of the user (the inviter). If the user gives permission, the support person can take control of the user's computer, and perform any task that the user could perform. (Not only must the user specifically give permission, but group policies, or the settings in the System Properties dialog, must support the "take control" feature.)

Offering Help Without an Invitation   A user doesn't have to go through all the steps in the GUI to request help—she can pick up a telephone (or yell down the hallway) to contact your help desk. Then, the support person can directly connect to the user's computer with the Remote Assistance feature. In fact, the support person can use this direct connection feature to connect to a computer even if no request (e-mail or verbal) for assistance exists. Because accessing another computer can be a risky activity, the process fails unless you've enabled the feature with a group policy.

The group policy is called Offer Remote Assistance, and you can enable it on a local computer by opening the local GPE (enter **gpedit.msc** in the Run dialog) and expanding the console pane to Computer Configuration\Administrative Templates\System\Remote Assistance.

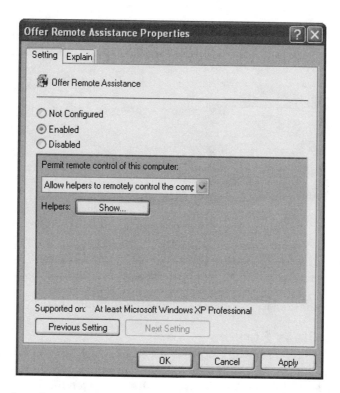

Specify whether the remote user can take control of the computer or merely view the screen. Then click Show, and add the names of groups or users who can access the computer with Remote Assistance. Use the format *Domain\UserName* or *Domain\ GroupName*.

 Offer Remote Assistance doesn't work unless the Solicited Remote Assistance policy is also enabled.

Even with the policy enabled, when a support person attempts to connect to a user's computer, the user must give explicit permission in order to complete the connection. The support person takes the following steps to establish a Remote Assistance connection:

1. Click Start and then click Help and Support.
2. In the Support Tasks section, click Tools.
3. In the left pane, click Help and Support Center Tools.

4. Click Offer Remote Assistance.

5. Enter the name, or IP address, of the target computer, and click Connect.

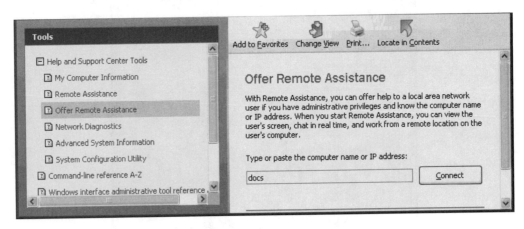

No Browse button exists, so you must know the computer name or IP address.

Manage Headless Servers

Remotely administered server support is a new feature that lets you install and manage *headless computers,* which are computers that lack monitors, VGA display adaptors, keyboards, or mice. Many companies have hundreds, or even thousands, of servers, and it isn't unusual to find "server rooms" filled with rows of computers.

Computer manufacturers now build computers that contain BIOS sets that let the computer boot, without error, in the absence of basic components such as input devices or video controllers. (This is the beginning of the end of our favorite BIOS message: Keyboard error, press F2 to continue.)

Installing headless servers means you don't have to spend money for keyboards, monitors, or mice, or even for KVM switches and cable. Even more important, you don't have to worry about providing the desktop real estate to hold all those hardware components.

New Active Directory Features

Windows Server 2003 introduces new features and functions to AD and the Group Policy Editor. Of course, if you're coming to Windows Server 2003 from Windows NT, all the AD and group policy features are new to you. You can learn about AD in Chapter 19 and group policies in Chapter 22, so in this section, I'll simply present an overview of some of the new features.

New Ways to Navigate and Manage Active Directory

It's now easier to find and manipulate AD objects. The search functions are improved, so finding what you need is not just easier, it's also faster. The search capabilities depend, of course, on the amount of information you enter when you're setting up AD objects. For example, if you enter information about a user's work environment (department, division, name of manager, and so on), you can search on those filters.

To manipulate objects in AD, you can select multiple objects simultaneously and modify their properties in one fell swoop. Additionally, you can drag and drop objects between containers. This is a nifty way to add users (or groups) to a group.

Administrators can now impose AD quotas to limit the number of objects a user, group, or computer can own. Domain Administrators and Enterprise Administrators are exempt from quotas.

You can redirect the default location for user and computer accounts. Moving these accounts from the Users and Computers containers into OUs means you can apply group policies.

You can now create a DC by restoring a backup from an existing DC. This is an incredibly efficient way to deploy a domain (see Chapter 18 for details).

Saved Queries

Active Directory Users and Computers now sports a Saved Queries folder in the console pane, and you can use it to create, save, and edit queries. This eliminates the need to design custom ADSI scripts that perform queries on AD objects. Saved queries are a quick way to access a set of directory objects when you need to manipulate or monitor them. You can copy your customized queries to other Windows Server 2003 DCs on the domain.

Creating a saved query starts with right-clicking the Saved Queries folder and choosing New | Query. Name the query and, optionally, provide a description.

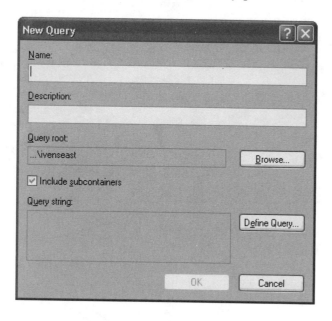

Then, create the query using the tools in the New Query dialog. Click Browse to select the container you want to use as the query root.

Click Define Query to define a common query based on Users, Computers, or Groups (you cannot mix and match the object type).

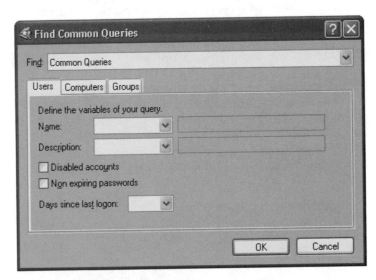

Application Directory Partitions

An application directory partition is a directory partition that is configured for limited replication, replicating data only to specific DCs. After replication, each of the participating DCs holds a complete replica of the partition.

Both applications and OS services can store data in an application directory partition, and the only restriction is that an application directory partition can't contain security principals. Most of the time, an application directory partition is created by an application, which manages the partition in addition to storing its data in the partition. However, administrators can use the Ntdsutil command-line tool to manually create application directory partitions, or manage partitions created by applications.

An application directory partition can be a child of a domain directory, or of another application directory partition. For example, if I create an application directory partition named AppsA as a child of my ivenseast.com domain, its DNS name is appsa.ivenseast .com, and its distinguished name is dc=appsa, dc=ivenseast, dc=com. If I then create an application directory partition named AppsB as a child of the first application directory partition, its DNS name is appsb.appsa.ivenseast.com and its distinguished name is dc=appsb, dc=appsa, dc=ivenseast, dc=com. You can see that the hierarchical logic of these partitions makes it easy to manage them.

You can also establish an application directory partition as the root of a new tree in an existing forest. For example, ivenseast.com is the root of the only domain tree in my forest. I can create an application directory partition with the DNS name appsc and the distinguished name dc=appsc. This application directory partition isn't part of the same tree as ivenseast.com; instead, it's the root of a new tree in the forest.

 You cannot make a domain directory partition a child of an application directory partition.

The benefit of this feature is obvious: it reduces replication traffic across the forest. Additionally, you can replicate data only to DCs where the data is useful to the users who connect to those DCs, which means intersite replication can be drastically reduced.

Improved Replication

Windows Server 2003 has changed the way the AD database and the global catalog are replicated, using a new paradigm called *linked value*. When attributes change in the global catalog, only the changes are replicated. For example, after changes, individual group members are replicated, instead of treating the entire group membership as a single replication unit. In addition, new algorithms make replication processes faster and more efficient, working across multiple sites and domains within forests.

Rename AD and Domains

Windows Server 2003 lets you change a domain's DNS and NetBIOS names. Previously, renaming a domain required you to create a new domain, and then migrate all the existing domain objects to the new domain. This new feature is a welcome addition to administrators in companies that are involved in mergers and acquisitions. In addition, this is a great tool for administrators who decide to separate the internal infrastructure from the Internet by creating separate DNS names (a good security scheme).

Availability and Reliability Improvements

We're all trying to get to "four nines," and Windows Server 2003 introduces some tools to help.

Automated System Recovery

Floppy disk–based recovery procedures have become more and more difficult to implement in Windows. The last "workable" (and I use the term loosely) floppy disk recovery process was the Emergency Repair Disk (ERD) in Windows NT 4. Windows 2000 also provided a way to create an ERD, but the size of the data files made it almost useless.

Automated System Recovery (ASR) is a floppy-based recovery tool, but unlike the ERD, the ASR is linked to a related backup of the files required to start Windows. You can store this backup on a local tape drive or a locally attached removable disk. See Chapter 26 for details.

Emergency Management Services

Emergency Management Services (EMS) provides a mechanism to manage servers when the operating system is not functional. When a server is operating normally, you can manage it remotely with the regular administrative tools provided with Windows Server 2003. Remote management of servers with these tools is called *in-band management*, or working with an *in-band connection*. In-band connections include NICs, modems, ISDN, and other familiar devices.

When an in-band connection is unavailable, you can use EMS to access and administer a Windows Server 2003 computer. This is referred to as working with an *out-of-band connection*, which doesn't even require operating system network drivers. You can even use an out-of-band connection to troubleshoot a server that isn't fully initialized and functioning. Most of the time, you can do this remotely, as long as the server is equipped with out-of-band hardware (headless servers fit this description). In fact, the only time you ever have to travel to the server is when you need to install hardware.

EMS works in terminal text mode, not the GUI, so you can use this tool with a wide range of communication media (the most common are serial ports), through standard out-of-band tools such as terminal emulators. Of course, this also means you can use EMS with other platforms, such as UNIX and Linux.

User State Migration Tool

When you're deploying Windows Server 2003 as an upgrade, the User State Migration Tool (USMT) captures existing settings, files, and documents. You won't have to reconfigure those settings.

Program Compatibility

Windows Server 2003 offers two tools designed to help you run legacy software: the Compatibility Wizard, and Program Compatibility Mode. These tools are especially useful for in-house programs that have hard-coded references to Windows versions (alas, an all-too-common programming paradigm).

The wizard walks you through the steps required to test a program for Windows version compatibility. When the compatibility mode is set (for example, the program is most compatible with Windows 9x), the program will start in that mode every time. You can also run the Program Compatibility Wizard on the setup file for a program.

Program Compatibility Mode performs a similar task, but omits the wizard in favor of working directly on an executable file. In Windows Server 2003, all executable files have a new Compatibility tab in the Properties dialog (see Figure 1-1). You can use the options to adjust the Windows version, video settings, and security settings. Chapter 3 has detailed instructions for getting the most out of this feature.

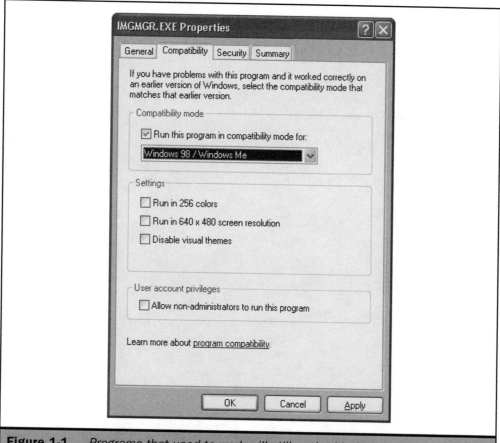

Figure 1-1.   *Programs that used to work will still work with the tools on the Compatibility tab.*

Volume Shadow Copy Service

A volume shadow copy is a point-in-time replication of a document folder. You can configure the service to create a set of copies, which is the current state of every document in the folder (including documents currently in use). Each set is discrete, bearing the date and time of its replication. As users modify documents, they can retrieve previous versions of those documents from the shadow copy. This is better than simple backups for large, important documents that are worked on by multiple users. (See Chapter 16 for more information.)

Resultant Set of Policies

One of the most frustrating aspects of Windows 2000 is the fact that I, like many other administrators, eventually lost track of the policies I imposed on computers and users. The group policy user interface doesn't provide any way to determine what you did. Windows Server 2003 includes a nifty tool called Resultant Set of Polices (RSoP) that lets you see the effect of policy settings on computers and users. Finally, I have a way to debug policies when users complain about inappropriate restrictions, or slow boots due to too many policies. Even better, RSoP has a "planning mode" that shows you the effects of policies before you apply them.

Chapter 2

Installation

Windows Server 2003 offers several methods for deploying the operating system throughout the enterprise. Before you start, however, you need to document your current network configurations, and plan the method and timing of the upgrade. Planning and preparation are the linchpins to a successful deployment of Windows Server 2003, whether you're rolling out one server, one hundred, or one thousand. You need to make sure your hardware, network configuration, and applications will accept the new operating system without interrupting your company's productivity.

Hardware Requirements

No operating system runs properly if it's installed on an underpowered machine, or on a machine with unsupported hardware. Windows Server 2003 places some significant minimum requirements on hardware. Table 2-1 describes the hardware requirements for all editions. You'll find that the "minimum required" specification is woefully inadequate for real-world applications, so recommended values are included, too.

Hardware Compatibility List

Microsoft's Hardware Compatibility List (HCL) provides an extensive list of vendors' products, including systems, clusters, disk controllers, and storage area network (SAN) devices. To be included on the HCL, vendors must certify the fact that their hardware supports Windows Server 2003.

The HCL is part of Microsoft's Windows Hardware Quality Labs (WHQL) group. Look for the current HCL at www.microsoft.com. In addition to reassuring administrators of hardware compatibility, inclusion in the HCL means you'll find drivers included in Windows Server 2003. This is especially important for systems that use a custom HAL, such as symmetric multiprocessing (SMP) hardware, or for systems that use complex disk controllers.

Symmetric Multiprocessing Hardware

Symmetric Multiprocessing (SMP) hardware has been supported by Microsoft since the earliest versions of Windows NT. SMP (sometimes called *tightly coupled* multiprocessing) lets the computer share two or more processors, with each CPU sharing memory and I/O.

Clustering Hardware

A server cluster is a collection of computers that are closely tied together, running a common group of applications, and appearing to the network as a single, cohesive system. The computers in a cluster are physically tied together through high-speed interfaces, and use special software to provide support for clustering the operating system and applications.

	Web Edition	Standard Edition	Enterprise Edition	Datacenter Edition
Minimum Processor Speed (x86)	133 MHz (550 MHz recommended)	133 MHz (550 MHz recommended)	133 MHz (550 MHz recommended)	133 MHz (550 MHz recommended)
Minimum Processor Speed (Itanium)			1 GHz	1 GHz
Number of Processors Supported	2	4	8	32
Minimum RAM (x86)	128MB (256MB recommended)	128MB (256MB recommended)	128MB (256MB recommended)	128MB (256MB recommended)
Minimum RAM (Itanium)			1GB (2GB recommended)	1GB (2GB recommended)
Maximum RAM (x86)	2GB	4GB	32GB	64GB
Maximum RAM (Itanium)			64GB	512GB
Minimum Disk Storage (x86)	approx. 2GB	approx. 2GB	approx. 2GB	approx. 2GB
Minimum Disk Storage (Itanium)			approx. 4GB	approx. 4GB

Table 2-1.   *Windows Server 2003 Hardware Requirements*

Windows Server 2003 natively supports two types of clustering:

- **Microsoft Clustering Services (MSCS)**   Requires tightly coupled hardware and provides redundancy, failover, and shared applications and data across the cluster. MSCS is available only on Enterprise and Datacenter editions.

- **Network Load Balancing (NLB)**   Provides a way to balance IP traffic across multiple servers. Unlike MSCS, NLB doesn't provide for failover of applications or data. NLB is available in all editions of Windows Server 2003.

In addition to NLB and MSCS, Windows Server 2003 can support a third type of clustering, Component Load Balancing, which allows COM+ objects to be load-balanced across multiple systems. However, this method isn't native in Windows Server 2003, and requires the purchase of Microsoft Application Center 2000.

 See Chapter 24 to learn about clusters.

When selecting hardware for a clustering solution, keep the following in mind:

- Through the use of a new quorum resource called Majority Node Set, MSCS no longer requires a shared quorum device. This means you can create a server cluster with no shared disks (although the traditional cluster quorum mechanism is still available).

- MSCS has been optimized for storage area network (SAN) devices.

- Unlike NLB in previous versions of Windows, NLB now supports multiple network interface cards (NICs), allowing load balancing across multiple subnets and allowing NLB systems to function as proxies or firewalls.

When selecting hardware for a clustering mechanism, especially MSCS, it's important to ensure that the server hardware and the physical interconnections between servers and disks are supported by the operating system. Microsoft provides a list of Windows Server 2003–compatible hardware clusters on the HCL.

Plug and Play Support

Microsoft's client and server operating systems have supported the Plug and Play (PnP) standards for detecting devices and installing corresponding drivers for some time. Windows Server 2003 continues this support. You can use a variety of PnP devices with the operating system, including both PCI and ISA bus cards.

If you have non-PnP devices in your system, Windows Server 2003 can use them. However, you must ensure that the resources used by the device don't conflict with each other, or with the reserved resources in the computer's BIOS. If you're already using one or more non-PnP devices in an earlier version of Windows, and these devices are working correctly, it's probable that the devices will continue to behave nicely. However, you should document those devices, including the current I/O address range(s), memory address range(s), IRQ, and DMA channel (if applicable). This information might be useful later, when you're configuring or reconfiguring devices in Windows Server 2003.

ACPI Issues

Advanced Configuration and Power Interface (ACPI) is currently the standard for the way PC-compatible hardware communicates with the system BIOS. Windows Server 2003 supports ACPI, but it may not support older systems that use older Advanced Power Management (APM) methods. Be sure to check the HCL to avoid problems.

Developing a Deployment Plan

Installing a new operating system into a production network is not a trivial effort. Before you install or upgrade your first computer to Windows Server 2003, thoroughly test the operating system in a lab environment, and have a clear, documented path of the steps you need to take to deploy and control the operating system into your production environment. This documented path is your deployment plan.

There are no hard and fast rules about content or length, but any good deployment plan should be extremely detail oriented. Begin with basic information about your current infrastructure and environment, the way your company is structured, and a detailed map of your network, including protocols, addressing, and connections to external networks (such as inter-LAN links and Internet connectivity). In addition, your deployment plan should identify the applications used in your environment that might be affected by the introduction of Windows Server 2003. This includes multitier applications, web-based applications, and all components that will run on the Windows Server 2003 computer(s).

Once the components of your environment have been identified, the deployment plan should address the specifics of your installation, including the specification of your test environment, the number of servers that will be deployed, and the order of deployment. Last but not least, your deployment plan should include the steps you need to perform in the event that something goes wrong; developing contingencies to counter potential deployment problems is one of the most important aspects of the planning phase.

If you're having trouble identifying the full range of hardware, applications, and data used in your enterprise, see if your organization has a business continuity plan that includes IT resources. Many IT shops maintain a disaster recovery plan that identifies specific steps that will be taken to restore servers in the event of a natural disaster, and this can be a great location of information regarding current hardware platforms, application versions, and locations of critical business data.

While a document created with a word processor is fine for the written deployment plan, if your environment is large or if you plan on deploying Windows Server 2003 computers over a period of time, consider tracking the progress of your deployment using a good project management software product such as Microsoft Project.

Your deployment plan should include a list of everyone directly involved with the deployment process, and their roles. This lessens the likelihood of tasks being duplicated or, worse, not being completed at all.

Document the Hardware

Determining whether your hardware will even support the fairly beefy requirements of Windows Server 2003 is critical before you begin your installation. Because there are so many requirements that affect compatibility with the operating system, you need to document all existing systems on which you plan to install or upgrade the OS. Based on this analysis, you may find either that you need to upgrade components like RAM, CPU, and disk space to support Windows Server 2003, or that the computer must be replaced.

A hardware inventory sheet, on which you list the hardware specifications of your candidate servers, can help you to identify any upgrades or hardware replacements you need to make before deployment. Table 2-2 is a sample of a hardware inventory sheet used to collect information about two candidate systems that are to be upgraded to Windows Server 2003.

Use the information you collect in the hardware sheet, together with the information in the "Hardware Requirements" section earlier in this chapter, to develop a hardware upgrade or replacement strategy for your Windows Server 2003 installations.

Document the Network

Documenting network information in your deployment plan involves surveying every aspect of networked communication in your organization. This includes not only physical networking equipment, such as network adapters, cabling types, routers, switches, and hubs, but also protocol configuration information, geographic sites, and logical topology.

To communicate with other hosts on your network, your Windows Server 2003 computer must utilize a compatible network addressing scheme, and must have

Computer	Server15	Server22
Current Operating System	Windows NT 4	Windows 2000 Advanced Server
Current Role	Domain controller (PDC)	Member server
Primary Function	PDC, print server	Database server
RAM	512MB (PC133 SDRAM)	2GB (PC2100 DDR)
CPU	1.2 GHz Pentium III	2.0 GHz Pentium 4
Disk Storage	40GB IDE (RAID-0)	18GB SCSI (RAID-5)
Network Interfaces	10/100 Mbps, (1) 1 Gbps	10/100 Mbps
HAL Architecture	Non-ACPI uniprocessor	ACPI multiprocessor
Upgrades	Add second 1.2 GHz Pentium III CPU Upgrade to latest BIOS Add 512MB RAM	Upgrade to latest BIOS

Table 2-2.   *Sample Hardware Component Inventory Sheet*

a unique name. For the TCP/IP protocol, this includes documenting your current subnets, available static IP addresses in each subnet, available DHCP servers, and DNS namespaces. For network names, you should document the method your organization uses to name servers on the network.

Windows Server 2003 installs TCP/IP as the default and only protocol (on clean installations). Other protocols can be bound to the same network adapters, however, allowing you to (for example) run IPX/SPX to communicate with a NetWare network.

Your deployment plan should identify any connectivity between internal physical networks, as well as connections to other metropolitan area networks (MANs) and wide area networks (WANs). Documented features should include connection type, bandwidth, and the type of data that travels across the link.

Regardless of whether you plan on upgrading your domain controllers to Windows Server 2003, documenting your current domain structure will provide you with a good overview of how individual Windows Server 2003 computers will fit into your network. It will also allow you to more easily see the upgrade path of your domains and domain controllers, should you be upgrading them as well.

Document the Software

Document your applications, including the name of each application running on each server, current versions (including patch levels), and a brief description of the software's function. Also, in addition to more obvious business applications, make sure that you include major services, such as SQL Servers, and less visible components, such as third-party services and software management tools.

Document the Legacy Components

The term "legacy" is just a quaint way of saying "obsolete," and it is a term that refers equally to hardware, applications, protocols, and data. Legacy components usually serve an important purpose across the enterprise, and there is often a good reason why the legacy component hasn't yet been eliminated or replaced. As it pertains to the installation of Windows Server 2003, legacy components might include:

■ Certain ISA or PCI cards, such as proprietary SNA cards for mainframe connectivity or encryption host adapters, which are not supported by the operating system. If these devices currently work on a Windows NT or Windows 2000 server, there's no guarantee that their device drivers will work with Windows Server 2003.

■ Older mass storage controllers, or controllers with a downlevel BIOS that are not supported by the operating system. For example, if you've ever tried to get an older version of a DEC/Mylex DAC960 RAID controller working with Windows 2000, you know firsthand the kind of frustration this can cause!

- Older 8-bit and 16-bit applications based on DOS or Windows 3.*x*. Although Windows Server 2003 goes to great lengths to maintain backward compatibility with older software, not every program will run correctly with this operating system.

Prepare for Problems

In the real world, bad things happen. Even the best deployment plans don't take into consideration every possible problem that you might encounter when introducing Windows Server 2003 into your environment. Perhaps a critical application was missed when gathering information about the network, and the application fails to run on Windows Server 2003. Or maybe an early ACPI BIOS is causing bizarre behavior on one of your freshly upgraded domain controllers. Regardless of the specific problems you may encounter, it's important to identify the potential risks associated with each stage of your deployment, and include contingencies in your deployment plan. You need to ensure that you have a way to back out of the current stage, preferably by restoring the environment to its previous state.

Risk can be handled either by taking problems into consideration before they happen or by dealing with them after they happen. Of course, it's not possible to document every possible thing that can go wrong with your deployment and develop a contingency to counter it. But, by including a list of potential problems and their solutions at each stage of your deployment plan, you can proactively eliminate a lot of work, including those terrible "it's 2 A.M. and I've been here 18 hours and my server won't work and I don't know how to fix it" pangs of fear that occur when something goes horribly wrong.

Obviously, backing up everything is a prerequisite for deploying a new operating system, but restoring backups shouldn't be your only contingency plan. You should make sure to include contingencies in your deployment plan for events such as incompatibility with the hardware and applications included in your plan, and failed third-party drivers.

Complete the Preinstallation Tasks

In this section, I'll go over a checklist of some of the tasks you should complete before you begin the installation process.

Disconnect UPS Devices from Serial Port

During the setup phase of Windows Server 2003, the setup utility scans the system for connected hardware. Unfortunately, UPS cables attached to a serial port can cause the setup utility to hang. To prevent this, if you have a UPS attached to your computer via the serial port, remove it until the Windows Server 2003 installation process has completed.

Know the Location of Files on the Windows Server 2003 Installation Media

The Windows Server 2003 installation CD-ROM contains all the files that you'll need to create and manage installations of the operating system throughout your enterprise. Because there are a lot of installation files and deployment tools on the media, you should be familiar with the location of files on the CD-ROM. Table 2-3 lists the contents of the installation media (this table refers to the 32-bit installation media only).

Directory	Contents
\	AUTORUN.INF: Launches SETUP.EXE when the CD-ROM is installed on a Windows-based computer with the Autorun feature enabled. README.HTM: Contains information regarding compatibility and installation. Uses many of the files in the \DOCS folder. SETUP.EXE: Launches the setup program for Windows Server 2003. Can only be used on Windows-based computers.
\DOCS	Release Notes. This includes last-minute information, troubleshooting steps, and compatibility information.
\I386	The installation files for the Windows Server 2003 operating system, including the WINNT.EXE and WINNT32.EXE setup programs. Also contains several subfolders with utilities.
\I386\ADMT	Active Directory Migration Tool 2.0 (ADMT), which is used to migrate data between Windows NT 4 and Windows Server 2003 domains.
\I386\COMPDATA	Compatibility data for applications and hardware. This is used when running the hardware and software compatibility checker.
\I386\DRW	Dr. Watson troubleshooting tool.
\I386\LANG	Language files used with Windows Server 2003 applications.

Table 2-3.   *Files on the Windows Server 2003 Media*

Directory	Contents
\I386\SYSTEM32	Session Manager subsystem, used for starting user sessions.
\I386\WINNTMIG	Migration DLLs used when migrating to Windows Server 2003.
\I386\WINNTUPG	Upgrade DLLs used when upgrading to Windows Server 2003.
\PRINTERS	Printer drivers and supporting DLLs.
\SUPPORT\TOOLS	DEPLOY.CAB: Windows Server 2003 Corporate Deployment Tools. This compressed archive contains tools for deploying the operating system, including SYSPREP, the Setup Manager, and several .chm help files. GBUNICNV.EXE: Utility to convert character values from the Chinese national standard for text encoding (GB18030-2000) to the internationally accepted Unicode format. MSRDPCLI.EXE: Remote Desktop Client, for use with Terminal Services. NETSETUP.EXE: Network Setup Wizard. SUP*.*: Support tools for managing everything from disks and files, to Active Directory objects, peripherals, and system security.
\VALUEADD\MSFT\ FONTS	Additional TrueType fonts.
\VALUEADD\MSFT\ MGMT\CIMV2R5	Managed object format (MOF) file that can be compiled to provide extended attributes to the common information model repository (CIM) of Windows Management Instrumentation (WMI).
\VALUEADD\MSFT\ MGMT\DOMREN	Domain rename tool. Used to rename domains that are running in the Windows Server 2003 domain functional level.
\VALUEADD\MSFT\ MGMT\IAS	Windows NT 4 Internet Authentication Service (IAS) snap-in for MMC.

Table 2-3.   *Files on the Windows Server 2003 Media* (continued)

Directory	Contents
\VALUEADD\MSFT\ MGMT\PBA	Phone Book Administrator program.
\VALUEADD\MSFT\ NET\TOOLS	TTCP.EXE: Previously part of Windows Resource Kits, this tool is used to generate raw TCP or UDP data.
\VALUEADD\MSFT\ USMT	User State Migration Tool (USMT), used to migrate a user's profile and applications from one system to another.

Table 2-3. *Files on the Windows Server 2003 Media* (continued)

Understanding Installation Models

Windows Server 2003 can be installed in many different scenarios, from installing a single copy of the operating system on a computer with a new, unpartitioned hard drive, to upgrading a previous version of a Windows operating system. In this section, I'll discuss the most common scenarios—or installation models—for the operating system.

Upgrades vs. New Installations

Windows Server 2003 supports both new installations and upgrades. If you have a computer with a functioning operating system, and the hardware is compatible with Windows Server 2003, you're likely to consider upgrading the computer. However, you should be familiar with the advantages and disadvantages of both models before you begin installing Windows Server 2003.

Upgrades   In-place upgrades preserve existing settings, including user and group accounts, profiles, shares, services, and permissions. Files and applications installed on the system are preserved, including registry settings, desktop icons, and folders. However, this does not mean that these applications are necessarily compatible with Windows Server 2003.

If you're upgrading Windows 2000 servers, the decision might be made on the basis of ease of implementation. For example, if you've deployed a Windows 2000 Server to serve a complex application developed in-house, and you don't have an easy way to rebuild the application's components, upgrading can be a lot easier since it will retain the services, registry settings, and other components of the application that may have been "tweaked" but not thoroughly documented.

On the other hand, if your Windows 2000 server was previously upgraded from Windows NT 4 (which may have been originally upgraded from Windows NT 3.51), consider a clean installation. Each subsequent upgrade preserves components from the previous operating system, and these components may have an adverse effect on the stability and performance of your Windows Server 2003 installation.

Clean Installations   In a clean installation, there are no remnants of the previous operating system, such as extraneous registry settings, services, folders, or files. Clean installations ensure that all of your Windows Server 2003 computers match a certain baseline.

Winnt.exe vs. Winnt32.exe

Winnt.exe and Winnt32.exe are the venerable names for the 16-bit and 32-bit installers used throughout the Windows platforms. These two utilities provide a rich set of command-line options for installing and upgrading computers, including unattended installations, dynamic update support, complete installation logging, and support for Emergency Management Services. Depending on your installation method for Windows Server 2003, you may use one or the other to install the operating system on your computer.

- Winnt.exe is a 16-bit program, and is only used to perform clean installations of Windows Server 2003.
- Winnt32.exe is a 32-bit program, and can be used to perform either clean installations or upgrades from a compatible version of Windows.

Many of the command-line parameters of these applications are similar. Both provide parameters to assist in unattended installations. Both support accessibility options. Both allow you to specify commands to run after the setup of Windows Server 2003 is complete.

However, because Winnt32.exe is a 32-bit program that supports upgrading from previous versions of Windows, it offers several additional commands to support features such as Dynamic Update, Emergency Management Services, and installation logging.

Using Winnt.exe

Winnt.exe is a 16-bit binary, and will not run on 32-bit operating systems. The program can be run on a computer running an older Windows version, for a clean install (not an upgrade).

The following parameters are available:

/s:sourcepath specifies the location of the Windows Server 2003 source files. The *sourcepath* value can be in the form of a drive path (D:\i386) or a UNC (\\INSTALLSVR\i386SOURCE). If you're pointing to a UNC, you must have connectivity to the network resource.

/t:tempdrive places temporary files on the drive specified by *tempdrive*.

/u:answer_file is used for unattended installations (see the section "Unattended Installation," later in this chapter). *Answer_file* is the answer file that sends

information to the setup program, eliminating the need for a user to enter the information manually. This parameter requires the /s parameter.

/udf:id [,*UDB_file*], used for unattended installations, passes Setup an identifier used to specify how a Uniqueness Database (UDB) file will modify the answer file. Values in a UDB file override their counterparts in an answer file, allowing unique setup information to be used when installing the operating system, without specifying every required parameter. If you don't specify the filename of a UDB file (a path to either a drive or a UNC), Setup will prompt you to point to a file named $UNIQUE$.UDB.

/r:*folder* specifies a folder to be installed after Setup is complete. The folder and its contents remain on the system after installation is complete.

/rx:*folder* specifies a folder to be copied to the computer. After Setup is complete, this folder is deleted.

/e:*command* specifies a command (or program) that will execute after Setup completes. This command executes in the context of the local system.

/a enables installation of accessibility options.

Using Winnt32.exe

Winnt32.exe is the 32-bit binary Setup program, which you can use for a clean install or on a computer that is currently running Windows 95 or higher. However, although Winnt32.exe can be run on a legacy version of Windows, it can't upgrade all versions. Winnt32.exe can only be used to upgrade certain downlevel versions of Microsoft server operating systems. You can, however, run Winnt32.exe from a nonupgradable platform (such as Windows 98) for the purpose of completely overwriting the current OS, or performing a dual-boot installation.

The following parameters are available:

/checkupgradeonly checks the computer for compatibility with Windows Server 2003. The results are displayed onscreen, and you have the option of saving the results. The default file name is %SYSTEMROOT%\UPGRADE.TXT.

/cmd:*command* specifies a command to execute after the computer has restarted (after Setup has gathered all configuration information, but before the final phase of Setup completes). This command runs in the context of the local system.

/copydir:*folder_name* specifies that you would like to create a folder in the location where the Windows source files are installed.

/copysource:*folder_name* specifies a folder that will be copied to the computer during installation. After Setup is complete, this folder is deleted.

/debug[*level*]:[*filename*] instructs Setup to create a debug log during setup, corresponding to one of five levels of detail:

- ■ 0   Includes only severe errors
- ■ 1   Includes all errors
- ■ 2   Includes all errors and warnings
- ■ 3   Includes all errors, warnings, and information
- ■ 4   The most detailed logging level, and includes all errors, warnings, information, and other detailed information

/dudisable instructs Setup to disable Dynamic Update during execution. This forces Setup to use the original Windows Server 2003 source files. This command overrides the value of the [DUDisable] parameter in the UNATTEND.TXT file.

/duprepare:*pathname* instructs Setup to download Dynamic Update files from the Windows Update web site. In this way, clients can install updated source files, without the need to download them separately.

/dushare:*pathname* specifies a location (either a path to a drive or a UNC) where you previously downloaded files from Dynamic Update using the /duprepare parameter. When you run this parameter on a computer on which you will install Windows Server 2003, the updated source files are used for installation.

/emsport:{com1 | com2 | usebiossettings | off} instructs Setup to either enable or disable Emergency Management Services (EMS). EMS allows you to remotely manage a server in situations where a server may not be functioning correctly.

/emsbaudrate:*baudrate* specifies the baud rate for EMS when operating through a serial port. The value of the *baudrate* parameter can be 9600, 19200, 57600, or 115200. This parameter is not applicable to 64-bit installations, since EMS cannot be made to use a serial port on IA64-based hardware.

/m:*folder_name* instructs Setup to first look for updated or replacement files in an alternate location. If the files are present in the specified location, they will be used instead of the files from the default source media location.

/makelocalsource instructs Setup to make a copy of all source files to the local hard drive. This parameter is typically used when you know that you will not have access to the source files later on in the installation process.

/noreboot instructs Setup to not reboot the computer after copying files.

/s:*sourcepath* specifies the location where Windows Server 2003 source files can be found. The *sourcepath* value can be in the form of a drive path or a UNC (assuming you have network connectivity).

/syspart:*drive_letter* instructs Setup to only copy installation files to the specified hard drive, and mark the disk as active. When the computer is restarted, it will begin with the next Setup phase. This parameter requires the /tempdrive parameter, and it cannot be used on computers that are currently running Windows 95, Windows 98, or Windows Me. This parameter is not available on 64-bit installations.

/tempdrive:*drive_letter* places temporary files on the specified drive, and installs Windows on that drive. If this parameter isn't specified, Setup locates a suitable drive.

/udf:id[,*UDB_file***]**, used with unattended installations, passes an identifier used to specify how a Uniqueness Database (UDB) file will modify the answer file. Values in a UDB file override their counterparts in an answer file, allowing unique setup information to be used when installing the operating system, without specifying every required parameter. If you don't specify the filename of a UDB file (either a path to a drive or a UNC), Setup will prompt you to point it to a file called $UNIQUE$.UDB.

/unattend instructs Setup to upgrade your previous Windows server operating system, provided that it is upgradeable. Setup will automatically download Dynamic Updates, and will include these files when upgrading the operating system. All settings are copied directly from the previous installation, so there is no user action required.

/unattend[*num***]:[***answer_file***]** instructs Setup to perform a new installation using the unattended setup mode, with the following meanings:

- *num* specifies the number of seconds that Setup will wait after copying files, before it reboots the computer.
- *answer_file* is the full path to the UNATTEND.TXT file (drive or UNC) that will be used during Setup to provide installation information.

Installing from CD

The Windows Server 2003 CD is probably the easiest installation method, since it doesn't require any additional hardware or networking support. In addition, CD-ROM installations are generally faster than other installation methods because they rely on high-speed bus I/O transfers between the CD-ROM and the CPU, instead of relying on slower network connections that are used in other installation methods.

Booting to the Windows Server 2003 CD

The Windows platform has supported bootable CD-ROM media for many years, and Windows Server 2003 continues to provide this simple and useful installation method. In order to boot from the CD, you must be using a CD drive that supports the ISO 9660 El Torito extensions for bootable media, and the computer's BIOS must be set to use the CD drive as the first bootable device.

This method can only be used for a new installation of Windows Server 2003, not for upgrading a previous version of Windows.

Running Setup.exe from CD

You can use this method if you already have a Windows operating system installed on your computer and you want to either upgrade the operating system (if it is a supported upgrade path) or install Windows Server 2003 as a separate operating system (dual-boot configuration). Insert the CD into the drive, and if AutoRun is enabled, a GUI launcher opens, providing you with a menu of options. If AutoRun isn't enabled, double-click Setup.exe on the CD.

Installing from an MS-DOS Boot Disk

Installing Windows Server 2003 from an MS-DOS boot disk is a viable option only if you are installing a new copy of the operating system. This method can't be used to upgrade an existing operating system installed on the computer.

There are two primary reasons why you might want to use this ancient, but effective, method to install Windows Server 2003. One is that you have a CD drive that can't boot, and the other is that you want to dual-boot Windows Server 2003 on a computer that is already running an operating system that is unable to execute any of the Windows Server 2003 setup programs, such as Linux or FreeBSD.

In either case, you can use an MS-DOS boot disk with CD support to access the CD drive, and then run Winnt.exe to install the operating system.

 Unlike Windows NT and Windows 2000, Windows Server 2003 does not include or support boot disks.

Creating an MS-DOS boot disk is a simple task (you can even prepare one from a Windows 9x system). The disk must contain the MS-DOS boot files, DOS drivers for most IDE, ATAPI, and SCSI CD-ROM drives, and tools for creating disk partitions, including Fdisk and Format. It should also have the Smartdrv.exe disk-caching program, which will significantly decrease the installation time of Windows Server 2003 during the first phase of Setup, when it's copying files to the system drive. To be effective, make sure that Smartdrv.exe is called after Mscdex.exe in the Autoexec.bat file of the boot floppy; for example:

```
@echo off
a:\mscdex.exe /d:mscd0001
a:\smartdrv.exe
```

Before you can use the MS-DOS boot disk to start the installation of Windows Server 2003, you must make sure that you have some disk space for the setup program to use. While the setup program that runs when you boot directly from the CD drive is capable of creating disk partitions, the stand-alone setup program Winnt.exe program is not capable of doing so. If you try to install Windows Server 2003 after booting with the MS-DOS boot disk and you don't have any available formatted FAT16, FAT32, or NTFS disk partitions, the setup program will inform you that no disk space is available, and your only option will be to quit the setup process.

To get around this limitation, you need to create a disk partition that can store the temporary Windows Server 2003 setup files. This partition should be a primary partition and made active. It needs to be big enough to hold the setup files (about 1GB is a good estimate), but it doesn't necessarily have to be the boot partition or the system partition once the operating system is installed. However, it makes the installation and management of Windows Server 2003 a lot easier if the partition is both the boot and system partition; this means it should be at least big enough to hold the fully installed operating system (2GB minimum for 32-bit $x86$ systems, and 4GB minimum for 64-bit Itanium systems). The partition can contain any supported Microsoft file system, including FAT16, FAT32, or NTFS. To create the partition, you can use any tool that writes compatible partition tables, including the Fdisk and Format tools on the MS-DOS boot disk.

Once you've created the boot disk and verified that you have a FAT or NTFS partition available, boot the computer on which you want to install Windows Server 2003. Your CD-ROM drive should appear as a system drive, and you can then execute \i386\Winnt.exe to begin the installation process.

Using Network Sharepoints

Because the installation of Windows Server 2003 is file-based, almost any media can be used for installation, including network shares on other Windows-based computers. You can use a sharepoint to centralize the installation files for either on-the-fly installations or automated unattended installation. To perform an installation from a network sharepoint, the target computer must contain a Microsoft operating system that's able to provide network connectivity.

To install Windows Server 2003 from a remote network share, connect to a network resource containing the source files and run Winnt.exe or Winnt32.exe.

Using Logon Scripts and Batch Files

You can use logon scripts (both command files and WSH scripts) or manually executed batch files to kick off Windows Server 2003 installations. While not technically an automated installation method (since, on its own, a batch file can't provide the Windows Server 2003 Setup program with installation information), you can use the logon scripts or batch files to pass commands to Winnt.exe and Winnt32.exe in order to perform unattended installations. (See the sections "Using Winnt.exe" and Using Winnt32.exe," earlier in this chapter, for detailed information on parameters.)

Automated Installations

Automated installations of Windows Server 2003 let network administrators quickly and easily install the operating system across the enterprise. More importantly, these installations are extremely consistent, since during the automated installation process each computer utilizes the same setup and configuration information, and the same installation files.

Another key advantage to automated installations is that they eliminate most of the interaction with the setup process; as a result, users with relatively little technical knowledge of the operating system can perform Windows Server 2003 deployments. With a properly designed automated installation method, the entire process can be reduced to booting with a floppy disk, or double-clicking a desktop icon.

Choosing an Automated Installation Type

Automated installations are supported under Windows Server 2003 using the following three methods.

- Unattended installation
- SYSPREP installation
- Remote Installation Services (RIS)

Each method has advantages and drawbacks. Tools are available on the installation media to implement each of these methods.

The basic idea behind automated installations is that you provide the Windows Server 2003 setup program with a significant amount of information about your computer ahead of time so that, during the installation process, this information can be automatically merged with the installation. Because automated deployments work in this way, it's extremely important to know almost everything about your installation before the deployment, including the number and location of servers being deployed, networking configuration options, naming conventions, and installed services.

In addition, each of the automated installation methods requires you to carefully and thoroughly weigh factors such as network bandwidth availability and installation time. Typically, network administrators find that more than one automated installation method can work in their environment; however, there's usually just one method that suits the environment best.

Two key concepts define the basic function of automated installations:

- **Image-base installations**   Replicate a fully configured Windows Server 2003 master computer onto one or more other systems. SYSPREP is an image-based installation method, and RIS can also perform an image-based installation.

- **Answer file–based installations** Use a text file to configure the target Windows Server 2003 computers. The text file contains answers to the questions the setup program would ask a user who was installing the program interactively, such as computer name, licensing mode, and network settings. Unattended setup is an answer file–based installation method, and RIS can also be an answer file–based installation method.

Table 2-4 provides a quick overview of the considerations for the three automated installation methods.

Consideration	SYSPREP	RIS	Unattended Installation
Can be used for new installations?	Yes	Yes	Yes
Can be used for upgrades?	No	No	Yes
Requires high bandwidth?	No	Yes	No
Ideal for homogeneous hardware?	Yes	Yes	No
Ideal for heterogeneous hardware?	No	No	Yes
Requires TCP/IP?	No	Yes	No
Supports static TCP/IP addressing?	No	No	Yes
Supports custom HALs?	No	No	Yes
Limited to NICs that support PXE, or are supported by the Remote Boot Configuration Tool?	No	Yes	No
Easily supports nonstandard mass storage controllers?	No	Yes	Yes
Requires Active Directory?	No	Yes	No
Requires DHCP?	No	Yes	No
Supports preinstalled applications that rely on Active Directory?	No	Yes	Yes
Supports automated installation of preconfigured domain controllers?	No	Yes	Yes

Table 2-4. *Quick Reference for Determining an Automated Installation Method*

Consideration	SYSPREP	RIS	Unattended Installation
Supports automated installation of Certificate Services?	No	Yes	Yes
Supports automated installation of Clustering Services?	No	Yes	Yes
Third-party application support in installation method?	No	Yes	Yes
Can be used with Windows Server 2003 Web Edition?	Yes	No	Yes

Table 2-4.   *Quick Reference for Determining an Automated Installation Method (continued)*

Note   *Both SYSPREP and RIS can only be used to perform new system installations. They cannot be used to upgrade a computer to Windows Server 2003. Unattended installation is the only automated installation method that can be used to upgrade an operating system.*

As you can see in Table 2-4, many different factors must be weighed to determine the best automated installation method for your organization. Some additional considerations for specific environments that may affect your decision include the following:

- **Bandwidth**   RIS installations always require high bandwidth, since by definition the images are installed from across the network. SYSPREP installations and unattended installations can also require high bandwidth if the SYSPREP image file or operating system source files are located on a network share. However, SYSPREP and unattended installations can also use files from local media, such as a CD-ROM or local hard drive.

- **Architecture support**   When using SYSPREP or RIS with the RIPREP option, the target computer must use a HAL that is compatible with the source computer. Table 2-5 lists the cross-compatibility of the default HALs that are supported by Windows Server 2003.

- **NIC hardware support**   To use RIS, one or more network adapters in the target computer must support the Intel Pre-Boot Execution Environment (PXE) standard, or the NIC must be supported by the RIS boot floppy disk that is created using the Remote Boot Floppy Generator Tool (RBFG.EXE). The RIS boot floppy disk supports only a specific, limited list of PCI-based network adapters, and cannot be modified to support additional NICs.

HAL Name	Description	Supported Computer Architectures
HAL.DLL	Non-ACPI Programmable Interrupt Controller (PIC)	Non-ACPI PIC ACPI PIC Non-ACPI APIC uniprocessor and multiprocessor ACPI APIC uniprocessor and multiprocessor
HALAPIC.DLL	Non-ACPI Advanced Programmable Interrupt Controller (APIC) uniprocessor	Non-ACPI APIC uniprocessor ACPI APIC uniprocessor
HALMPS.DLL	Non-ACPI APIC multiprocessor	Non-ACPI APIC uniprocessor and multiprocessor ACPI APIC uniprocessor and multiprocessor
HALACPI.DLL	ACPI PIC	ACPI PIC ACPI APIC uniprocessor and multiprocessor
HALAACPI.DLL	ACPI APIC uniprocessor	ACPI APIC uniprocessor
HALMACPI.DLL	ACPI APIC multiprocessor	ACPI APIC multiprocessor

Table 2-5.   *HAL Compatibility Considerations for Automated Installations*

■ **Mass storage controllers**   If the target computer uses a mass storage controller that isn't listed in the default device information (.inf) files for Windows Server 2003, and you're using an image-based installation method, you will need to configure a special Mini-Setup portion of the installation. Because of this additional step, unattended setup may be a better installation option.

■ **Network protocols and services**   RIS requires the TCP/IP protocol, DNS, DHCP, and Active Directory to be running on your network (however, DNS and DHCP services do not have to be the versions provided by Microsoft). SYSPREP installations and unattended installations can use other protocols such as IPX/SPX, and don't necessarily require DNS or Active Directory unless the image you're installing on the target computer requires them.

■ **Clusters**   In a cluster of servers, machines should have identical configurations, except for network addressing. SYSPREP-based installations can be an incredibly efficient method in this situation, since all systems will be guaranteed to have the exact same file set and versions. It's important to remember, however, that Network Load Balancing (NLB) cannot be implemented in the SYSPREP image. NLB must be set up and configured on each system independently after the imaging process.

■ **Applications and services**   If you plan on distributing applications as part of an image-based installation method, you must thoroughly test how these applications perform on a machine prepared with SYSPREP or RIS with the RIPREP option (reviewed later in this chapter). When using SPSREP or RIPREP, unique information about the computer, such as TCP/IP configuration, machine SID, and other information, is wiped clean during the imaging process. For this reason, applications that rely on Active Directory services should not be installed on a SYSPREP image. Instead, they should be installed after the target computer has the SYPREP image applied. This limitation with SYSPREP and RIPREP also means that these methods cannot be used to install Active Directory, Certificate Services, or Clustering Services on the target computer, although a computer imaged with one of these two methods can have any of these services installed after its initial configuration.

■ **TCP/IP subnetting**   RIS requires the TCP/IP protocol, and works by relying on DHCP to provide IP addressing information to RIS clients. If you plan on using RIS as an automated installation method, and target computers are located on a different TCP/IP subnet from an available DHCP server, you will need to configure your router to forward DHCP packets between the DHCP server and the target computers. Also, if the RIS server is located on a different subnet than the target computer, you will also have to configure your router to relay DHCP packets to the RIS server. This is usually accomplished by modifying the IP Helper table of the router to include an entry for the RIS server, or by modifying the DHCP relay provider.

Clearly, there is a lot of information to digest before you can make a cogent decision about the most effective automated installation method for your organization. It's also important to remember that there may not be just one solution that's right for you—for example, in a large organization with multiple geographic locations, it might make more sense to use a combination of different automated installation methods to leverage the value of different amounts of bandwidth between locations. If you choose an efficient method that meets the requirements of your environment, you'll find automated installations to be a fast, efficient, and uniform way of deploying Windows Server 2003 computers in your organization.

Unattended Installation

As an answer file–based installation method, unattended installation (also referred to as *unattended setup*) works by using an answer file to provide the Windows Server 2003 setup program with information required for installation. In addition, unattended setup can provide any needed custom hardware drivers, and can even install applications without user intervention after the operating system setup is complete. Unattended installation is initiated with the Winnt.exe and Winnt32.exe setup programs:

- Use Winnt.exe to install a new operating system
- Use Winnt32.exe to upgrade an existing operating system

Creating the Distribution Folder

The first step in preparing an unattended setup is to create a distribution folder. The distribution folder contains the source operating system files, third-party drivers, patches and upgrades, and other components that you will install on the target computer. A distribution folder can exist on almost any media, including a network share, a CD, other removable media, or a local hard drive partition.

To create a distribution folder, either manually copy the files and other components you need to the source folder or use the Windows Setup Manager (included in the \SUPPORT\TOOLS\DEPLOY.CAB file on the Windows Server 2003 CD) to create the folder for you.

At a minimum, the distribution folder needs to contain the entire \i386 folder (or \ia64 folder, for 64-bit installations). This folder can simply be copied to the root of the network share or automated setup media. If you need to distribute additional software with the original source media, such as Service Packs and custom drivers, create a folder named OEM in the \i386 folder of the distribution folder. The following items can be added to the OEM folder (note that all files and subfolders in these locations should follow the 8.3 naming convention):

- **\$OEM$\$$**   This folder holds any updated system files that replace existing files. The files in this directory are copied into the Windows Server 2003 installation folder, and the structure of files in the OEM\$$ folder must precisely match those in the installation folder. For example, if you want to replace the file C:\WINNT\SYSTEM32\DRIVERS.CAB with another version, you must place the updated version in the distribution folder \i386\$OEM$\$$\SYSTEM32.

- **\$OEM$\$1**   Similar to the \$OEM$\$$ folder, files placed here will be copied verbatim to the target computer. However, unlike \$OEM$\$$, these files and folders will be placed in the root of the drive on which Windows Server 2003 is installed.

- **\$OEM$\\*drive***   Files and folders placed in this folder will be copied verbatim to the root of the drive letter on the target computer specified by *drive*. For example, files placed in \$OEM$\E will be copied to the root of the E: drive on the target computer.

■ **\OEM\textmode**   This folder contains device drivers, HALs, and other hardware-dependent files that are used during the text mode setup phase of Windows Server 2003. These files should be referenced in a TEXTMODE.OEM file (covered later in this section).

Applying Service Packs

If you're installing Windows Server 2003 after one or more Service Packs have been released, you can apply the Service Pack to your distribution folder. This means target computers immediately receive the updated files during installation (this is referred to as a *slipstream* installation). To apply a Service Pack to your distribution folder, download the Service Pack executable from the Microsoft Update web site. Expand the Service Pack by running the Service Pack's executable name with the –x parameter. This expands the files in the Service Pack to a folder that you will be prompted to specify. Once completed, update the distribution folder with the expanded Service Pack files with the following command:

[sp_drive]:\[sp_path]\update.exe –s:[ds_drive]:\[ds_path]

where:

sp_drive and *sp_path* represent the path to the expanded Service Pack files

ds_drive and *ds_path* represent the path to the distribution folder

Applying Mass Storage Controller Drivers

Using other automated installation methods, applying mass storage controller drivers from sources other than the Windows Server 2003 setup media can be a nightmare. Fortunately, unattended setup provides an easy way to manage nonstandard drivers. Using the special \OEM\textmode folder, you can specify one or more mass storage controller drivers to be used during the driver identification process of Setup.

To add these drivers, copy the driver file to the \OEM\textmode folder. You should have at least one .sys file (the driver) and one TXTSETUP.OEM file (description file provided by the driver's vendor). Once these files have been copied, edit the TXTSETUP.OEM file and replace the path referencing the location of the driver files at the end of each line with a period.

Next, modify the UNATTEND.TXT file to include the [MassStorageDrivers] entry. For each driver in the TXTSETUP.OEM file, create one line in this section. The finished code looks like this:

```
[MassStorageDrivers]
"[name of driver from txtsetup.oem]" = "OEM"
```

You also need to add a line to the [Unattended] section of the UNATTEND.TXT file, as follows:

```
[Unattended]
OEMPreInstall = Yes
```

Applying Updated Plug and Play Drivers

Using the special \$OEM$\$1 folder in the distribution share, you can specify additional Plug and Play drivers to be available when installation clients enumerate their hardware during installation. Copy the drivers to any subfolder location under \$OEM$\$1, and then modify the OEMPnPDriversPath entry in the UNATTEND.TXT file to point to the driver location, using the root of \$OEM$\$1 as the base. For example, if you create the folder \$OEM$\$1\Drivers\NIC\MegaNIC in the distribution share, add the following lines to the UNATTEND.TXT file:

```
[Unattended]
OEMPnPDriversPath = \Drivers\NIC
```

This ensures that the drivers copied to this folder are included when the installation client searches for Plug and Play drivers during device enumeration.

Creating an UNATTEND.TXT File

UNATTEND.TXT is the name of the answer file that is used during unattended setup. The answer file provides information that would be entered by the person installing the operating system through the GUI. The UNATTEND.TXT file provides key information such as ownership, regional settings, third-party drivers, and other data that is required to install the operating system. By providing information in the UNATTEND.TXT file, you can partially or fully automate your unattended setups.

Although the file is usually referred to as UNATTEND.TXT, you can actually name it anything you like. The file is typically installed in the root of the distribution folder. In addition to manually creating an UNATTEND.TXT file, you can create a new file or modify an existing one using the Windows Setup Manager, included in the \SUPPORT\TOOLS\DEPLOY.CAB file on the Windows Server 2003 installation media.

Running the Unattended Installation

You can use Winnt.exe or Winnt32.exe to kick off an unattended installation. Following are some common scenarios, in the form of syntax, that demonstrate how flexible unattended installations can be.

```
winnt32 /unattend:5:unattend.txt /s:\\installsrv\dist
```

launches unattended setup using the file UNATTEND.TXT, found on the network share \\installsrv\dist, and waits five seconds after files are copied before rebooting the computer.

```
winnt /u:unattend.txt /s:d:\i386 /e:c:\dcpromo
```

launches unattended setup for a new installation using the file UNATTEND.TXT, found on the local CD-ROM drive in the \i386 folder, turns on accessibility features during setup, and launches the DCPROMO.EXE program.

SYSPREP

For many years, system administrators have used the process of *cloning* a computer—a binary copy of the operating system, registry, and applications, and all files and other structures on the computer's hard drive—to duplicate a replica of one computer onto another. This process is incredibly useful, because it allows one or more computers to be configured in very little time, with no need to enter licensing information.

Unfortunately, disk cloning has an Achilles' heel. The fact that it duplicates everything on the disk means that the subtle information that must be unique between computers, such as the TCP/IP address, security identifiers (SIDs), and other values, is also duplicated. While this isn't a big problem for older Microsoft operating systems such as Windows 95, it's a serious problem with a complex operating system like Windows Server 2003. Although a number of tools exist that do an excellent job of compensating for some of these values that must be unique, such as SysInternals' (www.sysinternals.com) NewSID, these tools don't really provide any way to customize the cloned image.

SYSPREP not only automates the assignment of unique information to cloned images, but also provides customized information for each installation made from a cloned image. Using SYSPREP, you can easily merge custom build information such as computer name, domain name, product licensing, and even product activation information into a cloned Windows Server 2003 installation.

The SYSPREP program and its supporting tools (including the Setup Manager program) are located in the \SUPPORT\TOOLS\DEPLOY.CAB file on the Windows Server 2003 CD.

Preparing the Master Image

Before you can deploy a customized image using SYSPREP, you must prepare a master image that contains the fully configured copy of Windows Server 2003 that will be copied to the target computers. Building a master image is a very detailed process. Because every file and device configuration on the image you are creating will be used on one or more target computers, it's critical that the master image contain the right components—no more, no less.

Start by identifying all the Windows Server 2003 components you want to install on the master image computer. Remember that whatever gets installed on the master computer will be copied to all target computers.

Network Protocols   Your image must include TCP/IP, but you may also have to include legacy protocols such as IPX/SPX and NetBEUI. Remember that you should target all of the components on the master computer image to fit the "least common denominator" rule. This means you should only install components that will apply to all target computers.

For example, let's assume you're using SYSPREP to distribute your master Windows Server 2003 image to 20 different target computers. Two of those computers will function as bastion hosts (or *gateways*) to a legacy NetWare environment, which requires the IPX/SPX protocol. In this case, you don't want the extra overhead of IPX/SPX on all of your target computers. Instead of installing IPX/SPX on the master image, rely on a custom SYSPREP.INF file (discussed later in this section) to provide custom network protocol settings to the computers that require the IPX/SPX protocol.

Windows Components   Windows components are the components you can select in the Windows Components section of the Add or Remove Programs Control Panel applet. Use the least common denominator rule to install only those services that are needed by all target computers.

Because SYSPREP removes customized information about the master image before it is copied to the target computers, services that are tightly coupled with Active Directory *cannot* be installed on the master image. This includes Clustering Services and Certificate Services. In addition, you cannot make the master computer a domain controller before it is imaged.

Applications   You can save a significant amount of time installing software applications to target computers by installing them on the master image. Applications will transfer their files, registry settings, desktop icons, and other components to the target computer, completely bypassing the need to run third-party setup programs.

Another advantage to installing applications to the master image is that you can eliminate the need to log on with a privileged account on the target computer. Since applications are installed by you on the master image, presumably using an account with local administrative privileges, there should be no need for a user to log on locally to a target computer using a privileged account once the SYSPREP setup has been completed. This is extremely useful when you're shipping a target computer to a remote office and you want to lock down the server and minimize user interaction onsite.

Remember, however, that the limitation on Active Directory, Clustering Services, and Certificate Services still applies when installing applications on the master computer. If an application relies on any of these services, you should install that application on target computers *after* the SYSPREP installation (fortunately, this too can be automated using SYSPREP).

System Patches   System patches both improve the performance of your Windows Server 2003 operating system and eliminate potential security threats. Microsoft's most important operating system patches are released as either *hotfixes* (patches that correct a specific behavior) or *Service Packs* (a large number of hotfixes released together in a single package). Installing patches on the master image eliminates the need to install them separately on individual target computers, and guarantees a minimum patch level for all target systems. You should only install patches that are known to work with all software that you plan to deploy on target computers.

Custom Environment Settings   In many organizations, custom backgrounds, wallpaper, and icons are used to provide a uniform image and user experience across the enterprise. If your organization has a company logo, for example, this can be copied to the master image.

Service Startup State   Because services take up memory and provide entry points into your server, carefully consider which services are activated by default.

Third-Party Device Drivers for Plug and Play Hardware   You must install third-party device drivers if one or more target computers have hardware that is not present on the master image computer, and the driver for the device is not present in the Windows Server 2003 DRIVERS.CAB file.

Unlike network protocols, Windows components, and applications, you should *not* follow the least common denominator rule when installing drivers for target computer hardware. You can copy drivers to the master image computer and, because of the nature of PnP, only the relevant drivers will actually be installed. You can copy drivers for non-PnP hardware to the master image as well; however, these devices will need to be manually installed on the target Windows Server 2003 computer. You can copy these drivers to any location on the drive; a file called SYSPREP.INF will point Windows Server 2003 to the correct folder to find third-party drivers.

Performing the Installation

After you have identified the components that will be required for the master computer and all target computers, you can build the master image by installing Windows Server 2003 and all the components you've identified. The master image can be installed using any installation method. In fact, if you plan on making several iterations of your master image to get it just right, you can use the unattended setup installation method to ensure a consistent build each time. You can simply modify the .inf file for the unattended setup to add or remove components and applications.

After the Windows Server 2003 setup process completes its final reboot, you should log on using a local, privileged account before running SYSPREP. By default, the local Administrator account is the only account that meets this criterion. This will give you all the control you need to install applications and drivers, and customize the environment. You should avoid using a domain account, since the profile for any domain account will be orphaned after SYSPREP runs.

Install SYSPREP on the Master Computer

The SYSPREP program consists of several required files, all of which must be copied to the %SystemDrive%\SYSPREP folder of the master computer (usually C:\SYSPREP):

- Sysprep.exe is the actual SYSPREP executable program, and prepares the master computer for reimaging to a target computer by stripping out customized information such as computer name, network address information, and product registration.

- Setupcl.exe generates new security identifier (SID) values for the target computer, and must be in the same folder as Sysprep.exe.

- Factory.exe is a program that is used to support SYSPREP in a special Factory Mode, which is reviewed later in this section ("Running SYSPREP in Factory Mode").

In addition to these mandatory files, there are several other files optionally involved in the SYSPREP process that can enhance and automate the installation process:

- Sysprep.inf is an optional text file, similar to an .ini file, that contains customized information to be applied to the target computer, such as network configuration, domain membership, and product registration and activation. This is a completely optional file, but if it is used, it will partially or fully automate the installation of Windows Server 2003 on the target computer during the Mini-Setup phase of SYSPREP.

- Winbom.ini is an optional text file (the "bom" in the filename stands for "bill of materials") used when running SYSPREP in Factory Mode. Unlike the other required and optional SYSPREP files, Winbom.ini does not need to be installed in the %SystemDrive%\SYSPREP folder. See "Running SYSPREP in Factory Mode," later in this section, for details on using this file.

- Setupmgr.exe, the Setup Manager, is a powerful optional utility that will automatically copy the required SYSPREP files to the %SystemDrive%\SYSPREP folder for you, and also provides an easy-to-use GUI for developing a Sysprep.inf file. If you use the Setup Manager to develop a Sysprep.inf file, there's no need to manually copy the SYSPREP mandatory files to the %SystemDrive%\SYSPREP folder.

All of these files, except the customized Sysprep.inf and Winbom.ini files, are found in the \SUPPORT\TOOLS\DEPLOY.CAB file on the Windows Server 2003 CD.

Creating Sysprep.inf

It's not necessary to create a Sysprep.inf file in order to use SYSPREP. However, it can greatly reduce, and even eliminate, user interaction during installation. When the target computer is rebooted for the first time after the master computer image is installed, a special reduced-input *Mini-Setup* stage is launched, which requires the person installing the target computer to answer questions about the customization of the computer, such as network settings, regional settings, and domain or workgroup membership. However, if a Sysprep.inf file is present in the %SystemDrive%\SYSPREP folder, the Mini-Setup will use the values in this file.

Sysprep.inf is a text file that is very similar in syntax and layout to the UNATTEND .TXT file used in the unattended setup method. The file is broken into sections, and each section provides a set of parameters and values that are used when installing the master image on a target computer. There are a huge number of individual entries available, and many are the same as the entries in UNATTEND.TXT. However, for the sake of brevity, only the commonly used entries are presented in Table 2-6.

Section	Entry	Allowed Values	Description
[Display]	Xresolution	Any integer >= 640	Horizontal resolution in which Windows Server 2003 starts.
	Yresolution	Any integer >= 480	Vertical resolution in which Windows Server 2003 starts.
[GuiRunOnce]	n/a	Any command, enclosed in quotes	For each line in the [GuiRunOnce] section, SYSPREP executes the command in the context of the logged-on user.
[GuiUnattended]	AdminPassword	Any valid Windows Server 2003 password, enclosed in quotes	This value becomes the local administrator password.
	AutoLogon	Yes or No	Tells SYSPREP to automatically log on to the computer after the first reboot, using the value of AdminPassword.
	AutoLogon	Any integer	Tells SYSPREP how many times to log on to the computer using the specified AdminPassword.
	OEMSkipRegional	0 or 1	When set to a value of 1, instructs SYSPREP to skip the regional and language options page in the Mini-Setup stage. Regional information can be included in the [RegionalSettings] section of the Sysprep.inf file.
	OEMSkipWelcome	0 or 1	When set to a value of 1, instructs SYSPREP to skip the Welcome screen at the beginning of the Mini-Setup stage.
[Networking]	n/a	None	Specifies network identification information.
[Identification]	JoinWorkgroup	Any valid workgroup name	Identifies the workgroup name to which the target computer will belong.
	JoinDomain	Any valid domain name	Identifies the domain the target computer will be joining. If you specify this value, you can also specify the DomainAdmin and DomainAdminPassword entries.

Table 2-6.   *Commonly Used Sysprep.inf Data Items*

Section	Entry	Allowed Values	Description
	DomainAdmin	Any valid domain administrator username	Identifies the username that will be used to join the target computer to the domain. This account must have the right to add computers to the domain.
	DomainAdminPassword	Valid password for the user identified in DomainAdmin	Identifies the password of the user specified in DomainAdmin.

Table 2-6.   *Commonly Used Sysprep.inf Data Items* (continued)

For a complete overview of all the sections and entries available for Sysprep.inf, see the Windows Pre-Installation Reference help file, located in \SUPPORT\TOOLS\DEPLOY.CAB on the Windows Server 2003 CD.

 Setup Manager allows you to generate a preconfigured Sysprep.inf file that is customized based on your responses to questions presented in the Setup Manager GUI.

Eliminate All User Interaction

If you want to extend the entries in Sysprep.inf to completely automate the Mini-Setup portion of the target computer, and eliminate all user interaction, you must complete, at a minimum, the sections of the Sysprep.inf file described in Table 2-7.

Section	Entry
[GuiUnattended]	OemSkipRegional = 1
	AdminPassword
	TimeZone
[UserData]	FullName
	OrgName
	ComputerName
	ProductKey

Table 2-7.   *Entries Required to Eliminate User Interaction During Installation*

Section	Entry
[Networking]	No entries are needed for this section; however, the section name must be present in the SYSPREP.INF file in order to specify entries in the [Identification] section
[Identification]	JoinWorkgroup (if joining a workgroup)
	JoinDomain (if joining a domain)
	DomainAdmin (if joining a domain)
	DomainAdminPassword (if joining a domain)
[LicenseFilePrintData]	AutoMode = PerServer (if using Per Server licensing)
	AutoUsers (if using Per User licensing)

Table 2-7. *Entries Required to Eliminate User Interaction During Installation (continued)*

Using the entries I've discussed, along with some others that aren't fully described here, here's a simple Sysprep.inf file that installs Windows Server 2003 with no user interaction:

```
[GuiUnattended]
OemSkipRegional = 1
AdminPassword = "W1k1d@L337!H4x0r"
TimeZone = 027
[UserData]
ComputerName = WEBSERVER01
FullName = "Network Administrator"
OrgName = "Widgets International, LLC"
ProductKey = "00000-19095-ABCDE-FGHIJ-KLMNO"
[Networking]
[Identification]
DomainAdmin = Administrator
DomainAdminPassword = "!p074zz1um%"
JohnDomain = WIDGETINT
[LicenseFilePrintData]
AutoMode = PerServer
AutoUsers = 100
```

Specifying Alternate Mass Storage Controllers

Generally, you should use SYSPREP as an installation method only in situations where the master image computer and all target computers use the same, or very similar, hardware. However, in certain situations, you may have a target computer that uses a slightly different mass storage controller than the master computer (perhaps due to the use of a different chipset). Fortunately, the Sysprep.inf file can force a target computer to re-enumerate its mass storage controllers. The correct driver is selected through Plug and Play. To enable this feature, the following entry must be in the [Sysprep] section of the file:

```
[Sysprep]
BuildMassStorageSection = Yes
```

This entry tells SYSPREP to populate the [SysprepMassStorage] section of the same Sysprep.inf file, and install the driver for each of these mass storage controllers into the critical device database. You can then populate the [SysprepMassStorage] section of your Sysprep.inf file by running Sysprep.exe with the –bmsd switch (discussed later in this section).

 Fully populating the [SysprepMassStorage] section of the SYSPREP.INF file will result in a significantly longer SYSPREP setup time on the target computer. If you know the specific mass storage controllers available on all target computers, it's a good idea to delete all but these entries from the [SysprepMassStorage] section before you make the final master image.

Adjusting Partition Sizes

When you copy the master image to a target computer, you may find that the target computer has significantly more disk space than the master computer. While most disk cloning products can automatically adjust partition sizes for you to ensure that Windows Server 2003 takes up the full size of available space, some products will not do this for you automatically. In this case, you can use the following entry in SYSPREP.INF to force Windows Server 2003 to extend the partition to fill all unpartitioned space that immediately follows the partition on which the operating system is installed:

```
[Unattended]
ExtendOemPartition = 1 value
```

where *value* is an optional size, in megabytes, by which you would like to increase the size of the partition.

There are a few important caveats to using the entry. First, you are only able to extend NTFS partitions. This entry will be ignored if the partition type of the image you're restoring to the target computer is based on the FAT file system. Also, since you're expanding the partition size, the target computer's hard drive must be at least the same size as the master image computer. The partition you want to expand must have unallocated space. You cannot extend into space that is taken up by any existing partition. Finally, you can't allocate the entire space of the disk, because this entry never allocates the last cylinder of the hard disk, to allow dynamic disks to work properly.

Running Programs after SYSPREP Is Finished

In addition to providing customized system information, SYSPREP can install software and run programs on target computers after the installation of Windows Server 2003. There are frequently times when you'll want to do this. For example, applications cannot be installed on the master image computer if these programs rely on Certificate Services or Clustering Services or integrate with Active Directory, yet you may want these programs installed automatically immediately after SYSPREP is complete. You can use Sysprep.inf to kick off most commands, including program installers, batch files, Windows Scripting Host scripts, and the commands necessary to create a domain controller.

To run a program after the target computer has completed the installation of Windows Server 2003, create a new section in the Sysprep.inf file called [GuiRunOnce]. In this section, create one entry for each command you want to run. Each command must be on a new line and must be enclosed in quotes. The following sample section installs Active Directory on the target computer, and then runs a Microsoft Installer–based setup program. In this example, the files Setup.msi and dcpromo_answer_file must exist in the C:\Installers folder of the target computer.

```
[GuiRunOnce]
"c:\windows\system32\dcpromo /answer:c:\installers\dcpromo_answer_file "
"c:\windows\system32\msiexec c:\installers\setup.msi"
```

[GuiRunOnce] works by modifying the HKEY_CURRENT_USER\Software\Microsoft\Windows\CurrentVersion\Runonce registry key, and adding each command to this value. Each command runs synchronously, which means the commands are processed in order, and the next command doesn't execute until its previous command finishes.

An important limitation of the [GuiRunOnce] section is that programs run in the context of the logged-on user. If the user logging on to the server doesn't have the necessary privilege to run a command in the [GuiRunOnce] section, the command will fail (although subsequent commands will try to execute.) Because [GuiRunOnce] runs in the context of the locally logged-on user, this also means that any programs that write profile-specific information for only the current user will not be available to other users who log on to the computer.

If you want to run privileged commands on the target computer after the installation of Windows Server 2003, and you know that the first user logging on to the computer *doesn't* have the necessary privileges to execute these commands, there is an alternative to [GuiRunOnce]. Create a \i386\OEM folder in the SYSPREP program folder and add the following entry to the SYSPREP.INF file (this assumes your system drive is C:):

```
[Unattended]
InstallFilesPath = C:\Sysprep\i386
```

Next, create a plain text file named Cmdlines.txt, which is similar to the [GuiRunOnce] section of the Sysprep.inf file. The file contains one section called [Commands], and each entry in this section is a command surrounded by quotes. For example, the following Cmdlines.txt file kicks off a Visual Basic Script file, then starts a setup program to run in quiet mode:

```
[Commands]
"wscript c:\scripts\cleanup.vbs"
"c:\installers\setup.exe -quiet"
```

There are two advantages to using the Cmdlines.txt method of running programs after SYSPREP is complete. First, the commands in the file are run *before* the final SYSPREP reboot (as opposed to *after* the final reboot, in the case of [GuiRunOnce]). This means the commands are executed in the privileged context of the local system. The second advantage is that any profile-specific information is written to the HKEY_USERS\.Default profile, so that any user who logs on to the target computer will get this information copied to their local profile the first time they log on to the computer.

There are also a few disadvantages to using Cmdlines.txt:

- MSI packages (using Msiexec.exe) can't be installed, because Cmdlines.txt executes before the final SYSPREP reboot. At that point, the Microsoft Installer service is not fully functioning. Use [GuiRunOnce] instead, or repackage the MSI file into a format that doesn't rely on the Microsoft Installer service (for example, a Microsoft Systems Management Server [SMS] package).

- When Cmdlines.txt executes, there is no network connectivity. Any programs that rely on a network connection or resource will fail.

Caution *SYSPREP cannot be used to automate any input or user interaction that is required for commands in the [GuiRunOnce] section or in the Cmdlines.txt file. If a program in one of these two locations requires input (for example, entering a serial number or clicking an OK dialog button), the user will be required to enter this information. Fortunately, many programs and scripts can be modified to silently install with no user interaction. Alternatively, you can package an application into a format that requires no interaction, such as a Microsoft Installer (MSI) package or an SMS executable package.*

Executing Sysprep.exe

After Windows Server 2003 has been installed on the master image computer, and your Sysprep.inf file is complete, run Sysprep.exe to wipe machine-specific information from the computer.

The Sysprep.exe and Setupcl.exe files must be located together in the %SystemDrive%\ SYSPREP folder to work. If you're using a Sysprep.inf file to provide setup and configuration information to the target computer, this file must also be located in the same folder.

Sysprep.exe has numerous parameters to customize the way it runs on the target computer. The syntax is

```
SYSPREP -command
```

where *command* is the action you want the program to take. (Some of the commands are designed for use exclusively with the special Factory Mode of SYSPREP.) The commands you can use are described next.

-activated   If you are running SYSPREP in Factory Mode, and you have already activated Windows Server 2003, this switch allows you to specify not to reset the grace period for product activation. This option is used before you use the –reseal command in Factory Mode.

-audit   If you are running SYSPREP in Factory Mode, this command will reboot the computer without generating new SIDs, and without processing any commands in the [OEMRunOnce] section of the Winbom.ini file.

-bmsd   This command requires that the BuildMassStorageSection = Yes entry exists in the [Sysprep] section of Sysprep.inf, and a [SysprepMassStorage] section also exists in the file. Provided that these requirements are met, when SYSPREP runs with this command, it will populate the [SysprepMassStorage] with the PnP IDs of all mass storage devices that are natively supported by Windows Server 2003. You can then manually remove the entries you won't need for clients.

You can also use this command when you want SYSPREP to build the [SysprepMassStorage] section of the Sysprep.inf file on the master computer— for example, if you know that one or more target computers use a different mass storage controller than the master computer. This command will only populate the [SysprepMassStorage] section of the Sysprep.inf file; it will not remove the master computer's customized information, it will not generate new SIDs, and it will not shut down the computer. This command must be used by itself. You cannot use it with any other SYSPREP commands.

-clean   This command eliminates unused mass storage drivers added to the Sysprep.inf file by the [SysprepMassStorage] section. It also removes any unused devices created by Plug and Play.

-factory   Initiates the special Factory Mode of SYSPREP. This command restarts the computer and places it in a network-enabled state; however, the Mini-Setup portion of the SYSPREP process will not be started. Once Factory Mode has been enabled on the master computer, the computer can be cloned to an image. This image is then restored on a target computer, at which point the Sysprep.inf file can be modified to perform additional steps, or additional drivers for devices such as mass storage controllers can be added to the image. Once all Factory Mode tasks are completed, SYSPREP is run with the –reseal command to complete the process and prepare the system for Mini-Setup stage.

-forceshutdown   This command forces SYSPREP to shut down the computer after installation. This command can be used when the computer's ACPI BIOS doesn't shut down on its own after SYSPREP completes its process.

-noreboot   This command instructs SYSPREP not to shut down or reboot the computer after it has completed. Normally, you should use this command only for testing purposes, because if you modify the master computer after SYSPREP has run, the master image may not install correctly.

-nosidgen   By default, SYSPREP generates new SID information for each target computer. However, if you're only making a single copy of the master computer, and the original master computer will be decommissioned or reimaged, you can use this command to make sure that SYSPREP doesn't generate a new SID on the target.

-pnp   This command forces the Mini-Setup portion of SYSPREP to completely enumerate all PnP devices in the computer. You should only use this command if the target computer has legacy ISA PnP devices. The full enumeration process adds a significant amount of time to the SYSPREP process on the target computer.

-quiet   This command forces SYSPREP to eliminate the display of onscreen confirmation messages.

-reseal   When a target computer is in Factory Mode, and after all additional changes have been made to the image, this command prepares the computer for final imaging. Sealing is the last step of the Factory Mode process.

While you can run any of the SYSPREP parameters from the command line, the SYSPREP program also has a GUI that gives you access to most SYSPREP features, including Factory Mode settings. To enter the GUI mode of SYSPREP, run Sysprep.exe without any parameters.

Once SYSPREP starts, it executes the parameters that were passed on the command line (or, if it's in GUI mode, it will perform the actions selected in the interface). Depending on the commands passed to SYSPREP, execution time may take anywhere from a few seconds to several minutes. Once completed, SYSPREP automatically shuts down the computer if it is ACPI-compliant. Otherwise, you're informed when the computer can be safely shut down.

Cloning the Master Image to a File

Since Microsoft doesn't (yet) provide or sell any software for performing this step, cloning the master image requires a third-party piece of software. There are a number of excellent cloning products on the market, including Symantec Software's *Ghost*, PowerQuest's *Drive Image*, and NovaSTOR's *NovaDISK*. Most third-party commercial cloning software allows you to clone the master image to a variety of media, including another disk partition, network shares, CD-R/CD-RW, or one of the writable DVD standards.

Restoring the Master Image to the Target Computer

The process used to restore the master image varies depending on the software you used to create the image. Check the documentation for the imaging software you use for detailed instructions on how to restore the image file. Note that most third-party imaging programs can automatically handle some differences between master and target computers, such as different hard disk sizes. However, no imaging software can install more data onto a disk than will fit, so make sure your target computer has adequate disk space to hold the files from the master image that's restored by your imaging program.

Launching the Mini-Setup Stage

When a computer that has been restored with a SYSPREP image boots for the first time, the following steps are executed, unless they are provided for in a Sysprep.inf file:

1. Plug and Play detects all compatible system hardware. Normally, this process takes about three to five minutes to complete. However, if the [SysprepMassStorage] section of the Sysprep.inf file is fully populated, this process can take considerably longer (up to 45 minutes!).

2. You are prompted to accept the Windows Server 2003 End-User License Agreement (EULA).

3. You are prompted to specify your name and organization.

4. You are prompted to join a workgroup or domain.

5. You are prompted to specify the server's regional settings, such as language, currency type, and time zone.

6. You are prompted to specify Telephony API (TAPI) information, such as area code.

7. You are prompted to specify the network protocols, services, and addressing.

8. The SYSPREP folder is automatically deleted.

9. The computer restarts, and the logon dialog appears.

At this point, Windows Server 2003 has been successfully installed on the target computer. You can log on to the computer just as you would any other Windows Server 2003 computer, and you can further modify the computer by installing additional software or updated drivers.

Running SYSPREP in Factory Mode

Factory Mode is a special feature of SYSPREP that allows administrators to maintain a single base image for all Windows Server 2003 computers, regardless of the differences in hardware (provided, of course, that they share a compatible HAL). When you create a master computer image in Factory Mode, and restore it to a target computer, the target computer will not automatically load into Mini-Setup mode. Instead, Factory Mode processes another file similar to the Sysprep.inf file, called Winbom.ini. Winbom.ini lets you specify information specific to the machine, such as additional applications or updated mass storage controller drivers. Once the Winbom.ini file has been processed on the target computer, you can prepare the computer again for the Mini-Setup portion of SYSPREP by using the –reseal command.

Remote Installation Services (RIS)

Windows Server 2003 supports a third automated installation method, Remote Installation Services (RIS). RIS is somewhat of a hybrid between automated setup using an UNATTEND.TXT file and SYSPREP.

RIS works by using a partition on a Windows Server 2003 host computer that is set up as a RIS server. The RIS partition on this server contains one or more Windows Server 2003 images, along with optional files that modify these images during the installation process.

Although all client installation files in RIS are called "images," they can actually be file-based (called *flat images*), similar to unattended setup; or they can be true binary images (called *RIPrep images*, after the utility used to create them), similar to SYSPREP.

After images are created on a RIS server, target computers (clients) connect to the RIS server and install the image across the network onto their local hard drive. Clients do not need to have a local copy of the installation media or the image, and unlike SYSPREP, no third-party imaging software is required to create or install the image on target computers. (However, RIS is capable of deploying images created by third-party cloning software.)

RIS Requirements

Although RIS is a very flexible method for installing Windows Server 2003, there are some stringent requirements for using it, as follows:

- RIS relies on clients connecting to a dedicated RIS server. However, to do this, the clients must have a network adapter that either supports the Intel Pre-Boot Execution (PXE) remote-boot standard or is supported by the Microsoft RIS Boot Disk. The RIS Boot Disk is a bootable disk that can be created using RIS, and supports network connectivity to the RIS server. The RIS Boot Disk supports a limited number of network adapters; however, support for additional adapters cannot be added to the disk. As a result, if the network adapter in your target computer does not support PXE, and is not supported by the RIS Boot Disk, you cannot use RIS as an automated installation method.

- RIS requires a disk partition on the RIS server to hold the RIS images, and this partition must use the NTFS file system. The RIS partition cannot use EFS, and the RIS partition cannot be on the system boot or root partition. The RIS partition cannot be addressed as a DFS share.
- The RIS service must be installed on the RIS server. The RIS service can be installed from the Windows Server 2003 installation media.
- The RIS server must meet the minimum hardware requirements for the edition of Windows Server 2003 that is being installed to clients, and the server should have a high-speed connection to all clients (such as 100 Mbps Ethernet).
- The RIS server cannot be a multihomed computer.
- TCP/IP must be running on the RIS server.
- DHCP, DNS, and Active Directory must be available for the network and domain on which your RIS server and clients reside, although they don't need to be running on the RIS server itself. The DHCP server does not have to be a Microsoft DHCP server; however, if it is, it must be authorized.
- RIS can only be used with the Standard, Enterprise, and Datacenter editions of the Windows Server 2003 product.

Installing the RIS Server

Installing a RIS server is the first step to enabling RIS installations. If RIS isn't already installed on your RIS server, the service can be installed using the Windows Components section of the Add or Remove Programs applet in Control Panel. Once installed, the RIS Setup Wizard guides you through the steps to configure your RIS server.

RIS File Location   The Setup Wizard prompts you for the location of RIS partition and image files. The RIS partition does not have to be exclusively dedicated to RIS; instead, clients access it through the UNC *ris_server_name*\RemoteInstall. You must select an NTFS partition for the location of RIS server files, and this partition cannot be the boot or root partition of the server.

Enable RIS   To enable RIS immediately on the server, select the Respond to Client Computers Requesting Service check box. You can manually start RIS responding to clients later, if you would prefer to first create RIS images.

To allow RIS to only respond to prestaged clients, select the Do Not Respond to Unknown Client Computers check box. When checked, only client computers that have been prestaged will be allowed to install an image from the RIS server. Prestaging simply means that the client computer's unique GUID, based on the MAC address of the NIC, has been populated in Active Directory.

Locate Files for Initial Image   The Setup Wizard prompts you to enter the location of the Windows Server 2003 installation files that will be used to create the first image on the RIS server. You can later modify, replace, or delete this image. These files will be copied to the \RemoteInstall share created on the RIS server. The files can be located on physical media, such as the CD, or on a network share.

Name the Directory for the Initial Image   The Setup Wizard prompts you to enter the name of a directory where the files will be installed. This directory will be created in the \RemoteInstall share created on the RIS server. The directory name should be descriptive enough to determine the operating system (for example, WIN2K3_STANDARD). The directory name does not need to conform to the 8.3 naming convention.

Enter Friendly Description and Help Text   Entering a friendly description and help text allows you to provide a more thorough description of the RIS image. The description and help text are presented to clients when they select an image to install on the target computer. If you have a large number of RIS images available for installation, these values can greatly assist in differentiating between them.

After you've completed the Setup Wizard, assuming that you selected the Respond to Client Computers Requesting Service check box, your RIS server is now able to serve the Windows Server 2003 image to clients. The following three services are enabled on the server to service client requests:

- **Remote Installation (BINLSVC)**   This is the service that listens for requests from RIS clients that are using either a PXE-enabled NIC or the RIS Boot Disk. It is responsible for sending images to clients and, if the clients are not prestaged, creating their computer accounts in Active Directory.

- **Trivial File Transfer Protocol Daemon (TFTPD)**   This service is responsible for transferring the initial setup files required by RIS to the client computers. Both PXE-enabled network adapters and the RIS Boot Disk support this protocol. The most important file that TFTPD sends to the client is Startrom.com, which bootstraps the client computer and then allows the user to initiate a RIS installation.

- **Single Instance Store (SIS)**   This service reduces the overall amount of space used on the RIS server, by eliminating multiple copies of the same file. If SIS finds more than one copy of a file on the RIS partition of the RIS server, it keeps one copy and creates links to the other copies. In this way, multiple images that share a lot of the same files can be created on a RIS partition, without taking up as much space.

Managing RIS Servers

RIS servers control almost all aspects of image installation and distribution, including availability, security, and installation features. Fortunately, there are a variety of tools you can use to manage your RIS servers and ensure that your installations are fast and effective.

Managing RIS Server Properties with Active Directory   RIS is managed through property pages within objects in Active Directory. To access the RIS property pages for a RIS server, open the Active Directory Users and Computers snap-in, navigate to the container holding the RIS server, right-click the server, and select Properties. You can set the following options for the RIS server from the Remote Install properties page:

- **Client Servicing**   This specifies whether the RIS server responds to all clients requesting service or only to prestaged clients. If you select the Respond to clients requesting service option, RIS will response to any client computers requesting an image (this is also how you enable the RIS server if you initially did not check this option when running the RIS Installation Wizard). If you select the Do not respond to unknown client computers option, the RIS server will only respond to prestaged clients. For information about prestaging RIS clients in Active Directory, see "Prestaging Computers," later in this section.

- **Verify Server**   This option launches a wizard that checks the consistency of the RIS server by verifying settings and configuration. If key RIS files are missing, you're prompted to provide the Windows Server 2003 installation media. The Verify Server option is only available if you are logged on locally to the RIS server or connected through Remote Desktop.

- **Show Client**   This option allows you to search the Active Directory for RIS clients. A dialog box displays, showing a list of client computers (both prestaged and not) along with their globally unique identifier (GUID).

- **Advanced Settings**   These settings allow you to finely control how client computers respond to the RIS server. The subfeatures of this option include:

  - **Automatic client computer account naming format**   This allows you to specify a naming convention for client computers, so that this information doesn't have to be entered by the person executing the installation at the target computer. To ensure name uniqueness, you can use the following parameters:

Parameter	Substituted Value
%First	First name of logged-on user
%Last	Last name of logged-on user
%Username	Network logon name of user
%MAC	MAC address of target computer's network adapter
%#	Inserts an incremental number that is tracked by the RIS server

In addition, you can insert a number after the percentage sign in any of the preceding values to specify the number of digits. For example, the naming format "%1First%7Last%MAC" would yield a computer name of "JHAMILTO0030628AC74D", assuming the user installing the target computer is named John Hamilton, and the MAC address of the first NIC in the client is 00-30-62-8A-C7-4D.

■ **Active Directory location of client computer accounts**   Identifies the container in which prestaged target computer accounts are found, and the container in which computer accounts for nonprestaged target computers are created.

Manage RIS Server Properties Using Risetup   The Risetup utility is a command-line tool designed to allow you to manage and automate aspects of your RIS server, such as images. The syntax is

risetup [/add] | [/check] | [/auto *filename.inf*]

where:

/add tells Risetup to add a new installation image on the RIS server.

/check performs a test to validate that the RIS server is functioning properly, identifies and fixes most problems related to RIS servers not functioning correctly, and reauthorizes the RIS server in Active Directory.

/auto *filename.inf* tells Risetup to configure the server automatically, as defined by the file filename.inf. This file defines the configuration of the RIS server in a manner similar to the RIS Setup Wizard, but doesn't require any administrative interaction.

Here's a sample .inf file for the Risetup /auto parameter:

```
[Version]
Signature = "$Windows NT$"
 [Risetup]
RootDir = "e:\RemoteInstall"
Source ="z:\InstallSource\i386"
Directory = "WIN2K3_STANDARD"
Description = "Windows Server 2003 Standard Edition"
HelpText = "Base image for all servers in the Philadelphia office."
Screens = "overwrite"
Architecture = "x86"
Language = "English"
```

These entries are rather self-explanatory, and all are mandatory within the .inf file. A few entries need some further explanation:

■ **[RootDir]**   Identifies the drive and directory where the RIS files are located. This is the folder that is shared using the \RemoteInstall sharename. If RIS is already installed, and you have run the Setup Wizard to specify the location of the RIS folder, then this path must remain the same (you can't change this entry to move the location of the RIS folder). The path must be a local drive, not a UNC, and the maximum number of characters in the path and folder name is 127.

- **[Source]** Identifies the location of the installation media from which to create an installation image. The path to the files can be either local or a UNC, and can be up to 260 characters.

- **[Directory]** The directory that will be created in the RIS server's \RemoteInstall share to hold the files of the image. This name can be up to 39 characters.

- **[Description]** The short descriptive name of the image. It can be up to 65 characters in length.

- **[HelpText]** The longer descriptive name of the image. It can be up to 260 characters in length.

- **[Screens]** Identifies the action that will be performed on existing .osc files when installing the image; .osc files contain text that is displayed on the screen of the target computer during installation of the RIS image. The three values allowed are overwrite, backup, and leavealone.

- **[Architecture]** Specifies the processor architecture for the image. This can be either "x86" for 32-bit CPUs or "ia64" for 64-bit Itanium family processors. RIS will not let you install an image on the wrong processor.

Managing Access to RIS Services

If you are deploying RIS in a large enterprise, you'll likely want to limit both the number of computers that can install an image through RIS and the people who can install an image on these computers. There are several ways to accomplish this.

Using Group Policy to Manage Access Group Policy Objects (GPO) is an Active Directory feature that allows an administrator to delegate permissions throughout the enterprise. By using the Active Directory Users and Computers snap-in, you can limit the level of access that an organizational unit (OU) has to RIS services. Right-click the OU to which you want to delegate or limit RIS access, and choose Properties from the shortcut menu. Then select the Group Policy tab. Drill down to the User Configuration\ Software Settings\Remote Installation Services container and double-click Choice Options. You can then enable or disable access to any of the following four RIS features, or leave them unconfigured to inherit policy:

- **Automatic Setup** Verifies that the GUID for the client computer has been prestaged. If so, it keeps the existing computer account. Otherwise, it creates a computer account using the name policies specified for RIS.

- **Custom Setup** Allows users to specify their own computer name, along with the location of the computer account in the Active Directory tree.

- **Restart Setup** Allows a user to resume setup if the previous attempt failed.

- **Tools** Toggles the display of any additional tools that you have installed for RIS client computers.

Prestaging Computers

By allowing only computers that are prestaged to use your RIS server, you are eliminating the possibility of any domain user installing an image onto a computer. Allowing any computer to install your images has serious ramifications, including licensing and management issues. If you can, consider prestaging all of your client computers.

To prestage a client, use the Active Directory Users and Computers snap-in. Navigate to the container where you want your client computer accounts to be located, right-click and select New, and then select Computer. In the New Object dialog, enter the computer name that will be assigned to the computer, then click Next. Check the This is a managed computer check box, enter the GUID of the computer, and click Next.

The GUID typically contains the MAC address of the NIC, with a string of characters (often zeros) at the beginning. The computer's GUID can often be found in the system BIOS, and vendors frequently print the GUID on or inside the system case. Once your client computers have been prestaged, and you have configured the RIS server to not respond to unknown client computers, only prestaged clients will be able to use your RIS server.

Setting Image Permissions

In addition to using GPOs to limit users' rights within RIS, and prestaging clients to limit the computers that can install using your RIS server, you can also limit the specific images to which a user has access.

To limit access to a specific image, follow these steps:

1. Open the Active Directory Users and Computers snap-in.
2. Navigate to the container containing your RIS server, right-click, and select Properties.
3. Move to the Remote Install tab.
4. Click Advanced Settings, then click the Images tab.
5. Select the image to which you want to limit access, and click Properties.
6. Click Permissions, and select the Security tab.
7. Specify the users who can or can't have access to the image. (If the image is a flat image, you only need to set permissions on the image's Ristndrd.sif file.)

Creating Flat RIS Images

Creating a flat RIS image involves identifying to the RIS server the location of operating system installation files. These files are copied to the RIS server and can then be selected for installation at a client computer (assuming that the user has permissions to run RIS, and has appropriate permissions for the image file).

To create a new flat RIS image, follow these steps:

1. Open the Active Directory Users and Computers snap-in.
2. Navigate to the container that holds the RIS server, right-click the server, and select Properties.

3. Move to the Remote Install tab.

4. Click Advanced Settings, then click the Images tab.

5. Click Add to launch the RIS Setup Wizard.

6. Select Add A New Installation Image, and click Next.

7. Enter the path to the Windows Server 2003 setup files (for example, D:\i386 if you're copying from CD-ROM) and click Next.

8. Enter a name for the folder that will store these source files on the RIS server, and click Next.

9. Enter a friendly name and help text to describe the image, and click Finish.

The source files are copied to the image directory on the RIS server. During the process of copying these files, the RIS server creates a file called Ristndrd.sif. This file, like the UNATTEND.TXT and Sysprep.inf files, identifies custom information about the installation that gets merged with the source files when they're installed on the client. In this way, Ristndrd.sif completely automates the installation of the image on the client. Ristndrd.sif is a plain text file, and can be further edited to provide additional configuration information beyond the basic information that the RIS server knows about the image. You can also use the Setup Manager to create a .sif file. Once a .sif file has been created, it can be associated with multiple images. The Windows Server 2003 Corporate Deployment Kit (located in the \SUPPORT\TOOLS\ DEPLOY.CAB file) contains extensive information on customizing the Ristndrd.sif file.

Using RIPrep RIS Images

Similar to SYSPREP, RIS allows you to create an image of a computer that has been preconfigured and preinstalled with applications and custom drivers. The utility used to perform this function within RIS is called RIPrep (Rprep.exe). RIPrep has some advantages over SYSPREP, most notably that it doesn't require computers using the same image to be identical, or even use the same mass storage controller (however, they are required to share a compatible HAL).

To create an image with RIPrep, you must be a member of the local Administrators group on the computer that will be used to create the image, and you must have permission to write to the RIS folders (\RemoteInstall) on the RIS server.

RIPrep cannot be used to create an image for a 64-bit IA64 architecture system. If you want to use RIS to install images on IA64-based Windows Server 2003 computers, you must use flat images.

Create the Image   Similar to SYSPREP, begin the process of creating a RIPrep image by acquiring a baseline system that closely matches the hardware of all target computers that will use the image. Install Windows Server 2003, along with any custom drivers, applications, and other files that you want made available to all target computers using the image.

When you create the baseline image, only use a disk partition, and make the partition size as small as you can while still accommodating space requirements for the operating system, application files, the paging file, and other components. RIS will use the entire size of the partition to determine the minimum size of client partitions; if you make a baseline image containing 20GB of files but use a 120GB disk partition, you won't be able to use the image on clients with drives less than 120GB in size. For a review of components that can be installed on the RIPrep image at this stage, see "Preparing the Master Image" in the "SYSPREP" section, earlier in this chapter.

Run the Remote Installation Preparation Wizard   After the image is created, run Riprep.exe, which copies the image to the RIS server and prepares it for installation on target computers.

The wizard requires you to enter customized information for the image, including the name of the RIS server (which will default to the RIS server from which you are running Riprep.exe), the name of the folder on the RIS server in which you would like to install this image, and a friendly description and help text for the image.

Note	*RIPrep may inform you that it is unable to stop certain services that should be stopped in order to complete the image installation process. If you encounter this error message, you should try to manually stop these services. If stopping these services fails, or if the services can't be stopped due to dependency requirements, you can still continue the RIPrep process.*

After the replication process has completed, the image is added automatically to the list of operation system installations that are available to client computers on the RIS server. Similar to SYSPREP, images created using RIPrep are only usable on target computers that share a compatible HAL. Other hardware does not need to be identical between the computer on which the RIPrep image was created and target computers, since the RIS client installation process fully enumerates any Plug and Play devices to ensure that the correct drivers are installed.

When creating an image using RIPrep, a Riprep.sif file is created in the directory on the RIS server where the image is created. This file, similar to the Sysprep.inf file, identifies custom configuration information about the client computer. Like the Ristndrd.sif file used in flat images, this file can be edited to suit the requirements of your remote installation. The Windows Server 2003 Corporate Deployment Kit (located in the \SUPPORT\TOOLS\DEPLOY.CAB file) contains extensive information on customizing the Riprep.sif file.

Installing RIS Images on Client Computers

Once images have been created, the process of actually installing a RIS image to a client computer is fairly simple. If the client computer has a PXE-enabled network adapter, and the client is located on the same network segment as the RIS server, you can simply turn on the computer. Otherwise, if your client computer's NIC doesn't support PXE, you can create a RIS Boot Disk. Remember that the RIS Boot Disk only supports a limited selection of network adapters; if your NIC doesn't support PXE, and isn't supported on the RIS Boot Disk, you can't use RIS to install images on the client computer. To create a RIS Boot Disk, from any computer, launch the Disk Boot Generator (Rbfg.exe) from the RIS server, and click the Create Disk button.

 Although your network adapter may support PXE, your BIOS may not be configured to select the PXE adapter as a boot device. If you know your adapter supports PXE, and you are unable to get the computer to boot into RIS, verify that your PXE adapter is configured as the first boot option in ROM.

When the PXE adapter or Remote Boot Disk starts, the user is instructed to press F12 to begin the installation process. The user takes the following steps to install the operating system:

1. Enter a valid username and password. The account must be in the same domain as the computer account (if prestaged). If the computer is not prestaged, the account must have permissions to add computers to the domain.

2. Enter the domain name. This is the fully qualified DNS domain name (ivenseast.com), not the NetBIOS name (ivenseast).

3. Choose a Setup Option. Depending on how GPOs are configured for the RIS server, the user may have access to these options: Setup; Custom Setup; Restart a Previous Setup Attempt; Maintenance; and Troubleshooting Tools.

4. Enter computer name and directory path. This is only required if the user chooses Custom Setup in the previous step.

5. Select the image you want to install. Depending on how ACLs are set on the RIS server, the user may not have access to all the images available on the server.

6. Install the image. Depending on the size of the image and its feature sets, as well as the network connectivity speed and traffic saturation between the client and the RIS server, this may take a lot of time. If information such as company name, registered username, and product key are not provided in the image's Ristndrd.sif file (for flat images) or Riprep.sif file (for RIPrep images), the user is prompted for this information.

The
Complete
Reference

Windows Server 2003

Chapter 3

System Basics
for Servers

If you're moving to Windows Server 2003 from Windows 2000, you'll find few major changes in the way the operating system works, or in the way you manage your enterprise. The differences between managing servers running Windows 2000 and Windows Server 2003 aren't substantial—you'll just find some new features that make your job easier.

However, if you're moving to Windows Server 2003 from Windows NT 4, you have a lot of new information to absorb—and you'll learn about the new paradigms and new features throughout the chapters in this book.

In this chapter, I'll present an overview of the Windows Server 2003 basics—the stuff you need to know about in order to take advantage of the features and tools you have at your disposal.

Manage Your Server

After installing Windows Server 2003, the Manage Your Server page automatically opens every time you boot the computer. Microsoft introduced this tool in Windows 2000, and the Windows Server 2003 version is just terrific! As you can see in Figure 3-1, this window contains a plethora of utilities for configuring server roles, and managing the services you provide to users with those roles.

Note *You can also open this page by selecting Manage Your Server from the Start menu.*

Configure Your Server Wizards

You can use the wizards that spring from the Manage Your Server tool to configure a Windows Server 2003 server for a specific role, or multiple roles (a separate wizard exists for each role). The wizard walks you through the installation of the components required for the services you want this server to provide to your users.

Note *The Configure Your Server Wizards are not available in Windows Server 2003 Web Edition.*

Launch the wizard by clicking Add Or Remove A Role. The opening wizard page displays a checklist of preliminary tasks (see Figure 3-2), most of which you probably completed automatically during installation of the operating system.

When you click Next, the wizard checks the NIC to make sure the computer can communicate with the network, and then displays the list of roles you can assign to the server. I'll go over the basic information for each server role in the following sections.

File Server

Most administrators set up file servers to hold user data files, because this paradigm provides many advantages to both the users and the administrators. The biggest advantage is that backing up a file server ensures that all user data is backed up.

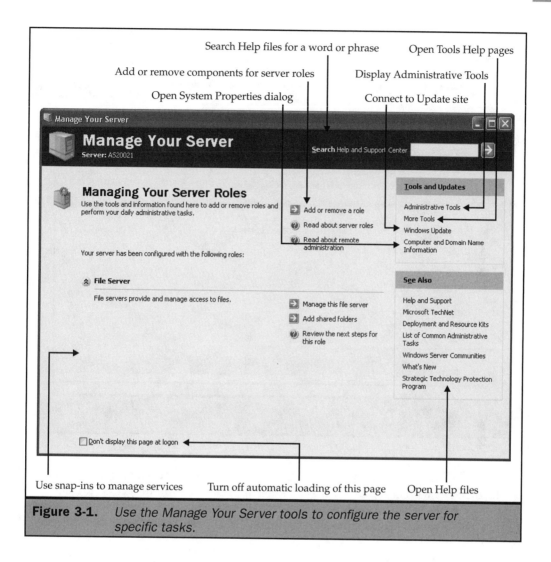

Search Help files for a word or phrase

Open Tools Help pages

Add or remove components for server roles

Display Administrative Tools

Open System Properties dialog

Connect to Update site

Figure 3-1. *Use the Manage Your Server tools to configure the server for specific tasks.*

I've never met an administrator who managed to enforce rules about backing up when users are permitted to save data on their local computers. We've all received anguished calls from users with dead or corrupted drives, and questioning the users always produces an admission that no recent backups exist (or, no backups ever existed). Additionally, saving data to file servers is the only way to go if you have roaming users.

For file servers, use computers that have large-capacity drives. In fact, installing multiple large drives is a good idea. Since I/O is the biggest consideration for file servers, be sure you buy the fastest drives you can afford.

When you set up file servers, you should make sure that your users' application configuration options point to the file server as the default location for data files.

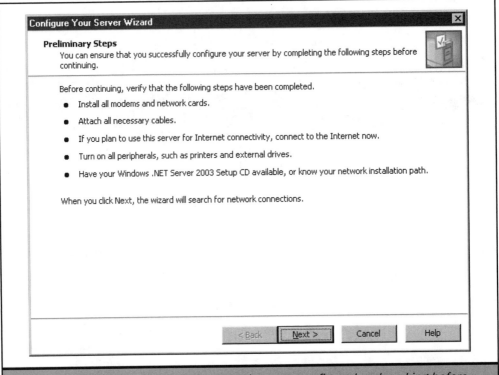

Figure 3-2.   *Be sure all physical connections are configured and working before installing server components.*

Depending on the application, you may be able to do this by setting options during deployment, or with group policies. (For some applications, you may need to map a drive to the users' sharepoints.)

For a file server, the Configure Your Server Wizard offers the following configuration options:

■ Disk quotas (assuming the computer is formatted for NTFS); see Chapter 16 to learn more about disk quotas

■ Indexing services

The wizard also launches the Share a Folder Wizard, which lets you share existing folders, or create new shared folders.

Print Server

When you set up a server as a print server, the wizard walks you through the steps that provide printer drivers for client computers. You can even load drivers for downlevel (earlier than Windows 2000) clients to make it easier for downlevel users to install printers.

You must have the printer drivers available, and many times you can access those drivers from the appropriate operating system CD. Or, you can copy the downlevel drivers to the server or to a floppy disk before you launch the wizard.

Tip   *It's a good idea to go to the manufacturer's web site to see if newer drivers are available.*

If you're installing drivers for Windows Server 2003/Windows 2000/Windows XP, clicking Next starts the Add Printer Wizard. If you're also installing drivers for downlevel clients, the Add Printer Drivers Wizard runs in addition to the Add Printer Wizard.

Network printing is I/O intensive, so it's best to put a fast drive in the file server. Also, I add a second parallel port (which costs less than $10) to my file servers in order to support more than one printer. You can also support multiple printers by way of a USB port, since most new printers offer USB connections. In fact, one nifty device I found is a USB port extender, which turns a single USB port into a four-port connection. Mine is a Linksys, but other manufacturers are probably offering a similar device now that USB connections are becoming so popular. Your Windows Server 2003 server can comfortably support multiple printers without any degradation in performance.

Note   *To learn more about managing network printing services, see Chapter 9.*

Application Server

The server role "application server" really means "web application server." If you're only interested in letting network users access applications such as Word or Excel, you can install Terminal Server.

This doesn't mean you're setting up an application server to provide services to the world (although you could). Most administrators who establish application servers want to let their users access the server over the Internet, or want users to be able to access web technologies (such as ftp transfers or HTML-based documents).

When you use the Configure Your Server Wizard to create an application server, the following Windows components are automatically installed:

- **Internet Information Services (IIS)**   Provides the infrastructure for web applications and web services.

- **Application Server console**   Provides administrative tools for managing web applications.

- **COM+**   An extension to the Component Object Model (COM) that adds developer features to the built-in integrated COM functions.

- **Distributed Transaction Coordinator (DTC)**   Coordinates COM+ transactions

In addition, you can optionally choose the following features:

- **Install FrontPage Server Extensions**   Enable users to administer and publish a web site remotely.
- **Enable ASP.NET**   A web application platform for deploying enterprise-class web-based applications.

Mail Server

A mail server collects e-mail from an ISP-based mail server and distributes the e-mail to users. This is a way to centralize mail services, instead of having each user independently go out to the ISP and collect mail. In addition, when you configure a Windows Server 2003 server for this role, the server acts as an SMTP server.

Before you can configure a mail server, you must contact your ISP to get a static IP address for the computer, and you also must make sure your ISP has a Mail eXchanger (MX) record that matches the mail server's name for your e-mail domain name.

The wizard walks you through the configuration steps (which include settings for authentication), and when you finish, you can use the POP3 Service snap-in to manage your mail server.

Terminal Server

A terminal server gives users access to Windows-based applications. You can install a terminal server on any version of Windows Server 2003 except Web Edition.

With a terminal server, you install one copy of an application and then let users access the application on the server. Users can save data files, maintain their own settings, and generally work with software as if that software had been installed on their own computers.

   Appendix A contains an overview of the way a terminal server works in Windows Server 2003.

Remote Access/VPN Server

This server role is designed to let remote users access the LAN to which the server is attached. Users can use dial-up connections, or connect from their browsers. In addition to providing this access point, or gateway, a remote access/ VPN server can provide Network Address Translation (NAT). With VPN and NAT, your client users can determine the IP addresses of the computers on your private network, but other Internet users cannot.

While old-fashioned dial-up connections continue to exist (often used by employees who dial in from home), VPNs are growing in popularity. The availability of broadband connections has made a VPN a useful tool, providing a way for mobile users, and branch office users, to have access to network services.

If you want to use your Windows Server 2003 computer for this role, the machine should be multihomed, so the LAN and the broadband connection exist separately (and apart).

The wizard walks you through all the steps, offering configuration options that depend on the way your remote users join your network. Generally, you should be prepared to make the following configuration decisions:

- **Assign NICs** Tell the wizard which NIC is dedicated to the broadband connection, and which NIC is attached to the LAN.

- **Assign IP addresses to incoming clients** If your LAN has a DHCP server, your remote access/VPN server can lease ten addresses at a time and assign those addresses to remote clients. If you lack a DHCP server, you can configure your remote access/VPN server to generate and assign IP addresses to remote clients. You must configure the range of IP addresses you're using for this purpose.

- **Configure RAS/RRAS services if you're allowing dial-up connections** Note that RAS is built into Windows Server 2003, and doesn't have to be installed as a Windows component.

Domain Controller

A domain controller (DC) contains the Active Directory and manages logons. You can use the wizard to install the first DC, or, if you've already installed a DC, the wizard walks you through the steps to install additional DCs, as follows:

- An additional domain controller for an existing domain
- A domain controller for a new forest
- A domain controller for a new child domain
- A domain controller for a new domain tree

See Chapter 18 to learn about installing and configuring domain controllers.

DNS Server

A DNS server provides the name resolution service required by Active Directory. See Chapter 12 to learn about DNS.

DHCP Server

DHCP servers provide IP addresses for the computers on your network. See Chapter 11 for detailed information on DHCP.

Streaming Media Server

If you need to deliver Windows Media content (streaming audio and video), you can configure a Windows Server 2003 computer as a streaming media server. The wizard installs Windows Media Services, which permit you to deliver digital media, in real time, to LAN, dial-up, and VPN clients.

WINS Server

When Microsoft released Windows 2000, its marketing strategy included a lot of hoopla about the demise of the need for WINS. It's a rumor you shouldn't rely on. I know of no administrators who deployed Windows 2000 who were able to walk away from the need to configure and maintain WINS services, and the release of Windows Server 2003 doesn't change that statement.

Even after you deploy a Windows Server 2003 domain, it's likely you'll continue to need WINS for some time. This is not only an issue of downlevel clients that require NetBIOS name resolution, it's probably also the fact that you're running applications that make WINS calls. (Microsoft Office springs to mind; I love irony.)

Setting up a WINS server and maintaining WINS services is easy, because Windows Server 2003 works efficiently, and on automatic pilot, for these tasks. Read Chapter 12 to learn more about running WINS.

Removing Server Roles

As you tune, tweak, and optimize your enterprise, it's common to reshuffle the way servers provide network services to users. You may have some servers that are performing multiple roles, and when you purchase new hardware, you can move roles to new computers. Or, you may find that some dual-role servers are experiencing heavy user demand and your system is bogging down.

The Manage Your Server feature can remove roles as quickly and efficiently as it adds them. To start, click Add Or Remove A Role, which launches the Configure Your Server Wizard you saw when you created a role. Click Next in the first window (the preliminary information), and after Windows checks your network connectivity, you'll see the list of server roles. The roles you've assigned this computer are indicated by a Yes in the Configured column. If you manually assigned a role by installing a Windows component instead of using the Configure Your Server Wizard, you'll see that role listed with a Yes (see the section "Set Up Server Roles Manually").

Select the listing for the role you want to remove, and click Next to display the Role Removal Confirmation wizard window, shown in Figure 3-3.

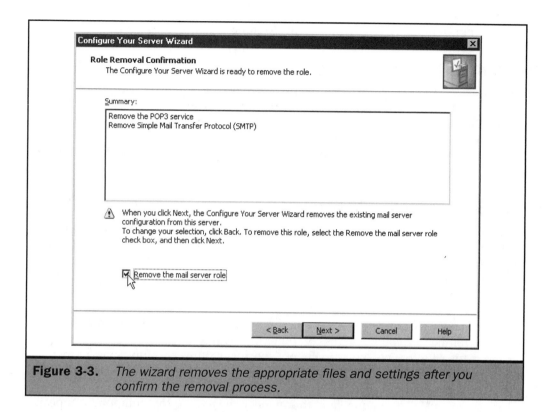

Figure 3-3. *The wizard removes the appropriate files and settings after you confirm the removal process.*

Click the confirmation check box to place a check mark in the box, and then click Next. The wizard removes files and changes configuration settings as necessary.

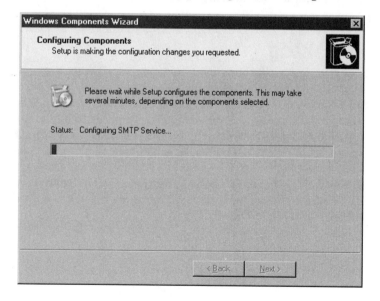

Click Finish in the final wizard window to complete the process.

Configure Your Server Log

Windows Server 2003 keeps a log of the processes performed by the Configure Your Server Wizard. To view the log, click Add Or Remove A Role in the Manage Your Server window, and click Next until you get to the Server Role listing in the Configure Your Server Wizard. Then click View Your Server Log.

Alternatively, travel to %SystemRoot%\debug and open the text file named Configure Your Server.log.

Set Up Server Roles Manually

If you're predisposed to do it yourself, and generally eschew wizards, you can manually set up any Windows Server 2003 server for any role. Most of the available server roles require installation of one or more Windows components. The exceptions are the roles of file server (which only requires you to share folders) and print server (which requires that you share attached printers).

Open the Add or Remove Programs applet in Control Panel and click Add/Remove Windows Components. Then scroll through the list to find the component you need for the role you want this computer to play in your network.

For many components, you can choose specific features and functions, or install all the features available for the component. Select a component and click the Details button to see the individual components.

When you install a component in this manner, the role for that component appears in the list of roles that are marked Yes under the configured column in the Configure Your Server Wizard. You can remove the component (and the role) manually in the Add or Remove Programs applet, or with the wizard.

Remote Desktop

The remote desktop feature is nifty and, if you try it, you won't want to live without it. The remote desktop feature was originally introduced in Windows 2000, as part of Terminal Services Administrative Mode. You could install Terminal Services on a Windows 2000 server in either of two modes: Administrative mode or Application mode. Administrative mode provided two free licenses for accessing the server in order to perform administrative tasks. Administrators didn't have to travel to the server to perform those tasks—they could work at their own computers.

In Windows Server 2003, the remote desktop feature is built in to the server operating system. Its actual name is Remote Desktop for Administration, but it is universally referred to as *Remote Desktop*.

The client-side software (called Remote Desktop Connection) is built in to Windows XP (the client member of the Windows Server 2003 family). For versions of Windows earlier than XP, you can install the client-side software (see the section "Client Remote Connection Software").

Remote desktop uses the Terminal Services Remote Desktop Protocol (RDP) on port 3389. RDP brings the interface from the server to the client, and sends keyboard and mouse clicks from the client to the server. You're logged on to the server remotely as if you were working locally. Windows Server 2003 can support two simultaneous remote connections, as well as a console session, and each session operates independently of the others.

To use remote desktop to administer servers, you must first complete two tasks:

- Enable the feature on the server and give access to appropriate users.
- Set up the client-side software on your own computer.

Enable Remote Desktop on the Server

To enable remote desktop access on your Windows Server 2003 computer, open the System Properties dialog by right-clicking My Computer and choosing Properties from the shortcut menu. Move to the Remote tab (see Figure 3-4) and select the option to accept remote desktop access.

Once the feature is enabled, you need to establish a list of users who can access the server remotely. Members of the Administrators group are automatically permitted access to the server, but you may want to add additional users. You can do so one user at a time, or you can populate the remote desktop group with appropriate users. To begin, click Select Remote Users to open the Remote Desktop Users dialog.

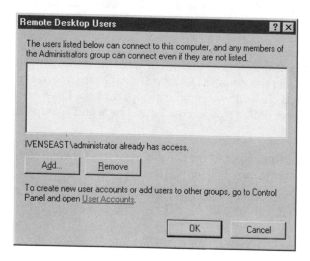

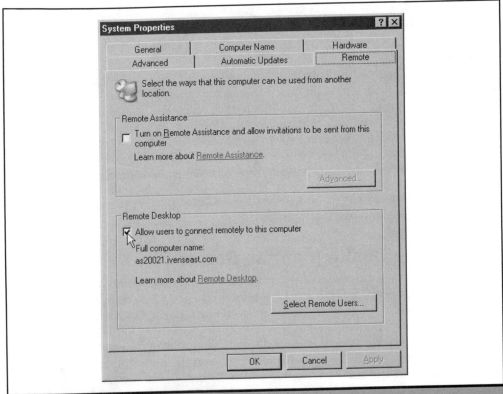

Figure 3-4. *The first step is to make sure the computer accepts remote connections.*

To add users and/or groups manually, click Add and use the tools in the Select Users dialog to choose appropriate users. The most efficient way to give users remote access rights is to select the Remote Desktop Users Group. However, by default, that group is unpopulated. To add users to the group, click the User Accounts link in the Remote Desktop Users dialog to open the Local Users and Groups snap-in. Then take the following steps:

1. Select the Groups object in the console pane, and then double-click the Remote Desktop Users Group object in the details pane.

2. In the group's Properties dialog, click Add to open the Select Users, Computers, or Groups dialog.

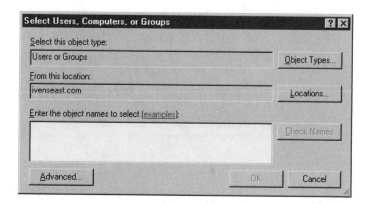

3. If the From This Location field is displaying the local computer, click Locations and select the domain or the entire directory (if you have multiple domains from which you want to select users).

4. Enter the names of the users you want to add to the group, or click Advanced to use the search features of this dialog to find those users. If you enter logon names, click Check Names to make sure the name exists and to expand the name to its fully qualified domain name.

5. When you have finished adding users to the group, click OK to return to the group's Properties dialog, where all the members are listed (see Figure 3-5).

6. Click OK to return to the Local Users and Groups snap-in, and then close the MMC to return to the Remote Desktop Users dialog.

7. Close the Remote Desktop Users dialog, even though it doesn't list any names. The Remote Desktop Users group is automatically given remote access to the computer (the next time you open the Remote Desktop Users dialog, you'll see a list of all users in the group).

Note *The users you add to the Remote Desktop Users group don't have to have elevated privileges; you can select ordinary domain users. This lets those users administer the server without having to log on as Administrator.*

Caution *To protect the server, you should make sure the users in the Remote Desktop Users group are using complicated passwords.*

After the server is configured for remote desktop access, users can administer the server over any of the following connection types:

- Network (LAN)
- Dial-up
- Virtual private networking

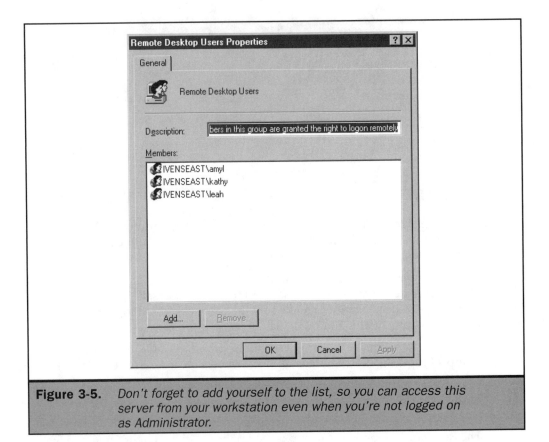

Figure 3-5. *Don't forget to add yourself to the list, so you can access this server from your workstation even when you're not logged on as Administrator.*

Now it's time to set up your workstation, and the workstations of any other users who will be administering the server remotely.

Client Remote Connection Software

Windows XP has the client side of remote desktop built in, so connecting to your Windows Server 2003 computer from Windows XP is a matter of point, click, and voila! Simply choose Start | All Programs | Accessories | Communications | Remote Desktop Connection to open the Remote Desktop Connection dialog.

Right-click the Remote Desktop Connection listing and choose Pin To Start Menu to avoid navigating through the menus in the future, or create a shortcut on the Quick Launch toolbar.

Install Remote Connection Client on Downlevel Computers

You can install the Remote Desktop Connection client software on other versions of Windows with the Windows Server 2003 CD, or from a network sharepoint that contains the Windows Server 2003 installation files:

1. Run Setup (which may run automatically when you insert the Windows Server 2003 CD in the drive).

2. Choose Perform Additional Tasks.

3. Choose Set Up Remote Desktop Connection.

4. Follow the wizard's prompts to accept the license agreement, and to install the software for all users of the computer, or only for the current user.

5. When the wizard finishes installing files, the program listing appears on the Programs menu.

The remote connection software on the Windows Server 2003 CD is version 5.2, which is a later version of the application than version 5.1, which shipped with Windows XP and Windows XP Service Pack 1. Version 5.2 has an additional feature for accessing the server's console session (without this version, you can only access the console session via the command line). See the section "Joining the Console Session" for more information. You may want to update your Windows XP remote connection software.

Configure Advanced Connection Options

You can configure the connection to meet your own specifications by clicking the Options button to expose the full range of options, as shown in Figure 3-6.

General Tab of the Remote Desktop Connection   On the General tab, you have two extremely useful options:

- You can save the password.
- You can save the connection, along with the configuration options you establish.

After you've configured all the options for a connection, click Save As to save the connection file, which is a remote desktop protocol (.rdp) file. Name the .rdp file appropriately to remind yourself of the remote server and the settings. To change any of the settings in a saved connection, right-click the file and choose Edit from the shortcut menu.

You can create, customize, and save multiple .rdp files, including files for connecting to the same server with different settings. The connection files you save are stored in your My Documents folder. You can move a shortcut to a connection file to the desktop or the Quick Launch toolbar. When you open a saved .rdp file, any changes you make to the configuration options are written back to your saved file.

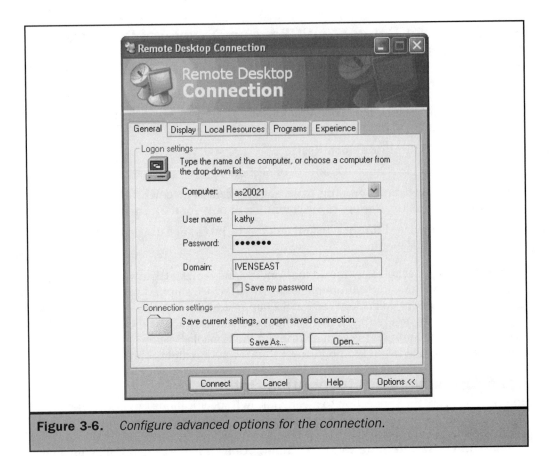

Figure 3-6. *Configure advanced options for the connection.*

A default connection file, containing all the default settings, exists in your My Documents folder. It's hidden, and its name is default.rdp. If you're not working with a saved .rdp file, each time you change the configuration options in any of the tabs of the Remote Desktop Connection dialog, those changes are written back to the default connection file.

Display Tab of the Remote Desktop Connection   The Display tab offers options for configuring the appearance of the remote desktop window. Remember that the settings on the server may interfere with your choices (depending on the hardware and drivers installed on the server).

Local Resources Tab of the Remote Desktop Connection   The Local Resources tab has some interesting options, as shown in Figure 3-7. You can configure resources as follows:

- Sounds can play locally, at the remote computer, or not at all.

- Windows key combinations can work locally, at the remote computer, or only in full-screen mode.

- You can make the local disk drives, printers, and serial ports available for the session.

By default, the local printer is available, but if you want to move files, or cut and paste between applications running on both computers, you should enable the option to make local drives available. All local drives, including mapped drives, are available (see the section "Moving Data Between Computers").

Programs Tab   The Programs tab offers a way to configure the remote connection to start a program as soon as you begin a remote session. However, this feature isn't really available unless you're connecting to a Terminal Server computer.

Experience Tab   Use the Experience tab to configure connection speed and Windows elements, as shown in Figure 3-8.

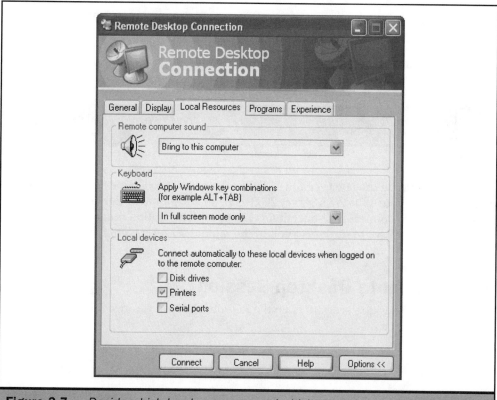

Figure 3-7.   *Decide which local resources and which remote resources you want to access.*

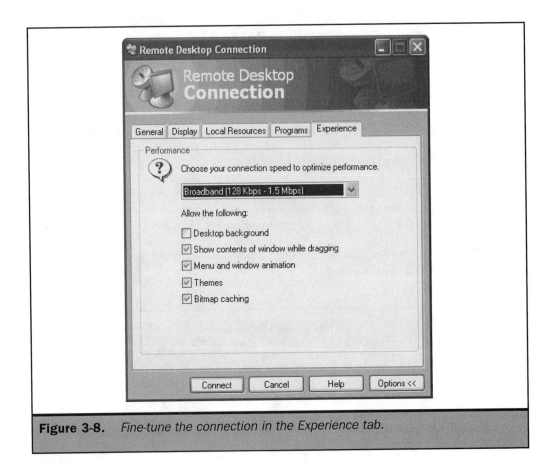

Figure 3-8.   *Fine-tune the connection in the Experience tab.*

If you're running the later version of the Remote Desktop Connection (the version that comes with your Windows Server 2003 CD), an additional option exists on the Experience tab: Reconnect If Connection Is Dropped. This option is enabled by default, and the system will try to reconnect you to the remote server if something interrupts the connection.

Starting a Remote Desktop Session

To start a remote desktop session, open the Remote Desktop Connection program.

In the Computer field, enter the target server as follows:

■ For a LAN or VPN connection, enter the server name.

■ For an Internet connection, enter the server's IP address.

Note   *The drop-down list on the Remote Desktop Connection dialog also contains the command Browse For More, but it doesn't work for remote desktop. The browser searches the domain for servers that have Terminal Server installed, and won't expand the object for the domain, except to display those servers. During the beta test period for Windows Server 2003, I submitted an enhancement request to include browsing for servers enabled for remote desktop. I was told that although remote desktop uses the same functions as Terminal Server (RDP on port 3389), the programming code is different. I'm not sure whether that means the enhancement is being considered or not.*

Click Connect to open the Log On to Windows dialog for the remote server (see Figure 3-9). Enter your password and click OK.

You can connect to the Windows Server 2003 computer as long as it's running; an interactive user does not have to log on for you to have access to the computer.

On the server, your remote connection launches a new session. Any programs that are configured to launch at startup do so (for example, antivirus software). The Start menu, taskbar, and other elements you see on the screen are from the server.

If two remote users are already accessing the server (that's the limit), the system issues an error message.

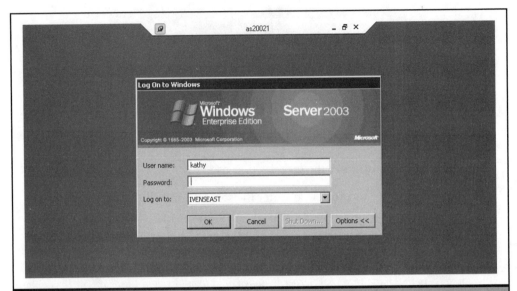

Figure 3-9.   *The push-pin on the left side of the connection bar controls whether the connection bar is always displayed (pin in), or only when the mouse is over its area (pin out).*

Running a Remote Desktop Session

Once you're connected, you can administer the remote server. You can open and manipulate Control Panel applet settings, configure the server (including promoting it to a domain controller if it isn't a DC), run system tools, and generally work as if you were sitting in front of the server. If the server is a DC, you can run administrative tasks such as adding users and computers and setting domain-wide group policies.

You can also run applications and save the data. The My Documents folder you see in the Save As dialog is a folder that is created for you the first time you log on to the Windows Server 2003 computer with remote desktop. In fact, you have a subfolder hierarchy on the computer, just as you would if you'd logged on interactively.

You can even perform tasks that require a reboot, or shut down the server using Start | Shut Down. You're warned that you'll be affecting any other users working at the computer, and then you're automatically disconnected from the remote session.

However, my experience has been that reboots are dangerous unless someone is available at the server site to intervene in case there's a problem restarting. For example, I once restarted a remote server that had a floppy disk in drive A. I stared at the message about a non-system disk with a feeling of complete helplessness. Luckily, the server wasn't critical to the LAN, so the downtime that elapsed until I reached someone by telephone didn't cause users a major problem.

Printing

The default setting for remote connections is to enable the local (client-side) printer, which makes sense (you'd have little reason to print a document you couldn't see). When you connect to the remote server, your local printers are detected by the server, and if a driver for your printer exists on the server, a server-based print queue is established. If no driver for your printer exists on the server, you must install one before you can print to your local printer during the session.

The server queue sends jobs to a printer queue that's established on the local computer the first time you print from a remote session. Thereafter, whenever you connect, the server searches the local computer for the remote desktop print queue, and when it finds one, it automatically creates the server queue (instead of waiting for you to initiate a print job to create the server queue).

 Unlike the usual Windows print queue, the server queue doesn't keep print jobs when you disconnect in order to print when you reconnect. Instead, the jobs are deleted upon disconnection.

Moving Data Between Computers

You can cut or copy information from one computer to another, as long as you configured your connection to make local drives available. The data can be selections from documents that are pasted between applications running on each computer, or files that are copied or moved between computers.

Open My Computer or Windows Explorer to see the server's drives (called local drives because you're working on the server), and the drives for the client-side computer (your local computer). As you can see in Figure 3-10, your local drives, including any mapped drives, are available.

Leaving a Remote Desktop Session

You have two ways to disengage from the remote server:

- Disconnect from the session.
- Log off.

Disconnecting from the session returns you to your local computer, while any processes you initiated on the server continue to run. If you were performing a backup, you can reconnect (connect using the same username) to check on progress, or to close

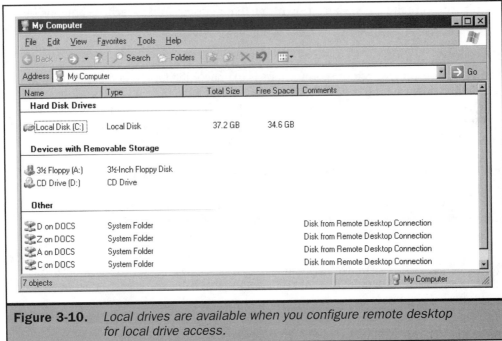

Figure 3-10.   *Local drives are available when you configure remote desktop for local drive access.*

applications. To disconnect, click the X on the right side of the connection bar. Then click OK in the Disconnect Windows Session dialog.

Logging off has the same effect as logging off from the server when you're working right at the server. To log off, choose Start | Log Off, which opens the same dialog you'd see if you were logging off the Windows Server 2003 server interactively.

However, unlike logging off interactively, remote desktop doesn't display the Welcome to Windows dialog that asks you to press CTRL-ALT-DEL to log on again. The remote session is closed, and you're returned to your local computer's desktop.

Managing the Connections from the Server

If you're working at the Windows Server 2003 console while remote users are logged in, you don't see any evidence of the other users' actions. They can open software, copy data, and perform other tasks without your screen changing. However, you can see who's logged in by opening Task Manager and going to the Users tab.

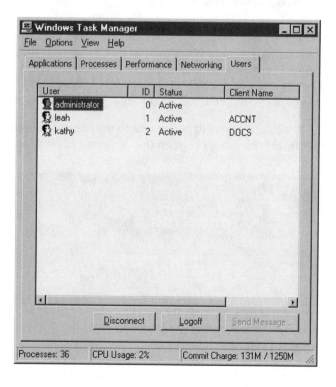

To send a message, select the username and click Send Message.

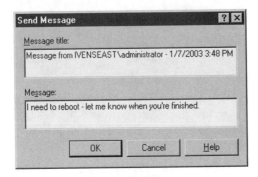

To disconnect or log off a user, select the username and click the appropriate button. The user is notified that the connection was disconnected/logged off by the server.

Joining the Console Session

A server that's enabled for remote desktop can support two remote sessions in addition to the regular (interactive) console session. You can also take over the console session remotely if you have some reason to work exactly as if you were sitting in front of the computer. If you do so, you bump the current interactive user, if one is logged on.

If you're running remote desktop 5.2 (or higher), you can perform this action in the GUI, but if you're working with version 5.1, you must use the command line.

■ In version 5.2, just add the switch **/console** to the name or IP address of the server (don't forget the space between the server name and the switch).

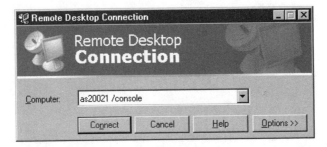

■ In version 5.1, open a command window and enter the following command: **mstsc -v:***servername* **/F -console.**

If a user is logged on to the computer, the system warns you that you'll be logging that user off.

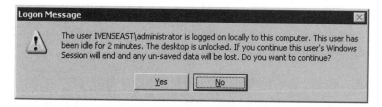

When you take the console session, if an administrator attempts to log on interactively, a message appears to explain that the computer is locked and only the remote user or an administrator can unlock the computer. If the administrator opts to unlock the computer and take the console session, you, as the remote user, are logged off. You can use the same steps to log on to the console session again, thus initiating a tug of war between you and the interactive user. Try to come up with a diplomatic way to handle this.

Using a Snap-in for Remote Desktop

You can use a snap-in to manage your remote desktop activities from your Windows XP workstation, if you prefer the MMC to the remote desktop dialog. The snap-in doesn't exist on Windows XP computers by default, but you can add it.

The file, adminpak.msi, is in the i386 folder on the Windows Server 2003 CD. You can copy the file to any computer, or to a network share. Right-click the file listing and choose Install from the shortcut menu.

Adminpak.msi is a collection of many snap-ins, not just the remote desktop tool. You can use these tools to perform remote administration tasks on your Windows Server 2003 computer from your own Windows XP workstation.

Note   *Adminpak.msi does not install on Windows 2000 computers unless you update the Microsoft Installer for those computers.*

The new snap-ins are installed to your Administrative Tools submenu. Choose Remote Desktops to open the snap-in.

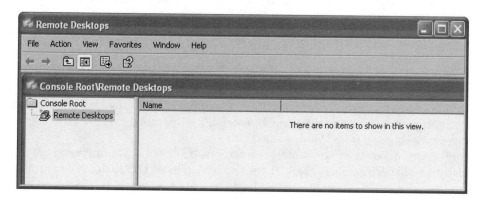

To create and configure a connection, right-click the Remote Desktops object in the console pane, and choose Add New Connection from the shortcut menu. Then, fill in the data fields in the Add New Connection dialog.

Notice that the option to take the console session is selected by default, and you probably want to deselect it. When you connect to the Windows Server 2003 computer, the Log On to Windows dialog opens in the details pane of the MMC.

You can set up as many connections as you need, and don't forget to save the console when you close the MMC. Thereafter, when you open the snap-in, all your connections appear in the console pane. Double-click the appropriate icon to connect to that server. You can connect to multiple servers and switch among them by selecting each server in the console pane.

Don't forget to log off before you close the MMC.

Changes in IIS

The good news is that Windows Server 2003 does not automatically install the Internet Information Services component when you install the operating system. This is a major (and welcome) change from Windows 2000.

For the vast majority of your enterprise servers, IIS not only is unnecessary, it can be a detriment to performance levels. There's no reason to add IIS to domain controllers, file servers, print servers, Terminal Server hosts, or any other server you install on your network to provide services to your users.

In addition, a host of security problems that have been "patched" by Microsoft had their genesis in the IIS component that was automatically added to Windows server editions. Skipping IIS enhances security without the need to go through all your Windows servers and either remove the IIS component or apply security patches.

Use Web Edition for IIS

New to the Windows server family, Windows Server 2003 Web Edition is designed from the ground up to run your web sites. It's easy to deploy, easy to manage, and is preconfigured to install and enable all the features you need for web hosting.

Web Edition is the only version of Windows Server 2003 that automatically installs IIS components during the installation of the operating system. In addition, Web Edition automatically installs other components you need for your web services, including the following:

■ Remote administration tools

■ Web Distributed Authoring and Versioning (WebDAV)

■ Network Load Balancing

■ SSL configuration via wizards

Because it's specifically designed for web site hosting, Windows Server 2003 Web Edition does not support the following features:

■ Domain controller (Active Directory will not install)

■ Printer sharing

■ IAS

■ Clusters

■ Windows Media Services

Installing IIS

If you want to use a Windows Server 2003 computer for your web site, and you need any of the services that won't run on Web Edition, you can install IIS and other web site components on a computer running Windows Server 2003 Standard or Enterprise Edition. You have two methods for installing IIS:

■ Use Manage Your Server, and select the Application Server role.

■ Use Add/Remove Windows Components in the Add or Remove Programs applet in Control Panel (see the instructions on the following page).

The individual components you include depend on the reason you're installing IIS. For example, you'd use different (and fewer) components to set up an enterprise-wide application server than you'd use to set up a web server.

The Add/Remove Windows Components feature offers more subcomponents than does the wizard that walks you through installing the Application Server role when you use Manage Your Server. Use the following steps to install IIS via Control Panel:

1. Open Add or Remove Programs in Control Panel, and click Add/Remove Windows Components.

2. Select the listing for Application Server, and click Details.

3. In the Application Server dialog box, under Subcomponents of Application Server, select Internet Information Services (IIS), and click Details.

4. In the Internet Information Services (IIS) dialog box, under Subcomponents of Internet Information Services (IIS), do either of the following:

   ■ To add optional components, select the check box next to the component that you want to install.

   ■ To remove optional components, clear the check box next to the component that you want to remove.

5. Click OK until you return to the Windows Component Wizard.

6. Click Next, and then click Finish.

Preventing IIS Installation

You can prevent the installation of IIS on any Windows Server 2003 computer by means of a new group policy. You can apply the policy locally or across the domain.

To apply the policy locally, choose Start | Run, type **gpedit.msc**, and click OK. In the Group Policy Object Editor, expand the Computer Configuration object in the console pane to \Administrative Templates\Windows Components\Internet Information Services (see Figure 3-11).

The only policy in the details pane is Prevent IIS Installation. Double-click the policy listing and select Enabled.

To apply the policy to a domain or OU, follow these steps:

1. Open Active Directory Users and Computers.

2. Right-click the object for the domain or OU for which you want to apply the policy, and choose Properties from the shortcut menu.

3. Move to the Group Policy tab and select the Group Policy Object.

4. Click Edit to open the GP Editor.

5. In the console pane, expand the Computer Configuration object to \Administrative Templates\Windows Components\Internet Information Services.

6. Double-click the Prevent IIS Installation policy in the details pane, and select Enabled.

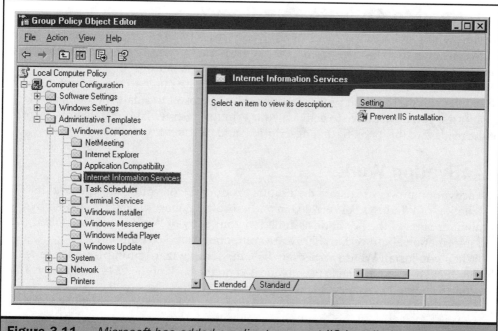

Figure 3-11. *Microsoft has added a policy to prevent IIS installation to Windows Server 2003.*

Activation

Activation ranks way up there as one of the most misunderstood functions ever introduced. Many experienced, well-known, technology journalists covered this subject without bothering to check the facts. *Activation* is nothing more than creating a relationship between the installed copy of Windows Server 2003 and a computer, identifying the computer by means of certain hardware components. The motivation for this function is, of course, to enforce the terms of the End User License Agreement (EULA), which makes it illegal to buy a copy of the operating system and install it on multiple computers, instead of buying a copy (and a license) for each computer. The operative word is *piracy*, which is a euphemism for stealing.

Activation is not the same as registration. With activation, no personal information (not even your name, even if you entered your name in any of the setup wizard windows) is sent to Microsoft. You can, if you wish, register your copy of Windows Server 2003, but it's not a required step. Registration, which provides Microsoft with your name and address, results in mail from Microsoft to tell you about new updates, new products, and security warnings.

Do You Need to Activate Your Copy?

Anyone who purchases a copy of Windows Server 2003 from a retailer must activate. OEM consumer (not business) computer preloads are frequently activated by the OEM before delivery, but if not, you have to activate your installation.

If you buy Windows Server 2003 through a corporate purchasing program, using any of the volume discount programs offered by Microsoft to small, medium, and large businesses, you do *not* have to activate your Windows Server 2003 installations. Most of the readers of this book fit that description, and can skip this section.

How Activation Works

The activation process registers the unique Product ID for your computer and its installation of Windows Server 2003 in a Microsoft database. The ID is created by combining parts of the key code assigned to your copy of Windows Server 2003 and information about certain hardware components in the computer.

When you install Windows Server 2003, the setup wizard prompts you to enter the product key code, which is usually located on the back of the CD-ROM folder. The key code contains 25 characters in five groups of five characters each.

The setup program also scans system hardware components (all of which contain readable identifiers), reads information about the hardware, and creates an alphanumeric string that uses some of that information.

Using an algorithm that combines parts of the key code and the alphanumeric string created from the hardware scan, your installation of Windows Server 2003 is assigned a unique 20-character Product ID. You can see your ID number on the General tab of the System Properties dialog. This is the number that is registered with Microsoft.

If you reinstall Windows Server 2003 on the same computer, even if you've changed one of the hardware components, you shouldn't have to reactivate your copy. If you reinstall your copy on a new computer, because you got rid of the old computer, your activation won't take, and you'll have to call Microsoft and explain the situation. If you reinstall your copy on the same computer, but you've changed a number of hardware components (perhaps the hard drive controller, the hard drive, and a NIC), you may have to reactivate your copy. My own experience when this occurred was positive, and I was given an activation code immediately.

Activating Your Installation

An Activate icon appears in the notification area of the taskbar until you complete the activation process. Click the icon to launch the activation process. The window that opens offers activation through the Internet or by telephone.

If you start to activate, and then cancel, the icon may disappear. In that case, choose Start | Programs | Activate Windows (the program listing remains until activation is complete).

Activating over the Internet

If you have a modem (telephone, cable, or DSL), select the option to activate over the Internet. You don't need to have set up your connection to an ISP, because you'll connect directly to a Microsoft server. Click Next, and then specify whether you want to register your product in addition to activating it. If you opt to register, you'll need to provide personal information (name, address, e-mail address).

Click Next and wait a few seconds. When the process is complete, Windows displays the message "You have successfully activated your copy of Windows."

Activating by Telephone

If you opt to activate your installation by telephone, click Next and follow these steps:

1. Select a location (country) to display the appropriate telephone numbers.

2. Call the number, and give the customer service representative the Installation ID Number displayed on the window.

3. Type the confirmation ID number that the service representative gives you in the appropriate boxes.

4. Click Next to see a success message for activation.

Activating after the Grace Period

If you don't activate Windows within the grace period, the operating system won't let you log on to the computer. However, Windows won't shut down a running computer, so you'll encounter the problem when you restart the computer.

If you restart the computer after the grace period and can't log on, you'll have to restart your computer and boot into Safe Mode Minimum (not Safe Mode with Networking). Then, choose Start | Programs | Activate Windows. If your Internet connection is over your LAN, you'll have to use telephone activation.

Once your installation is activated, choose Start | Shutdown | Restart to boot normally into Windows and log on to the computer.

Software Compatibility Tools

Most, if not all, the software you've been running should run perfectly well on Windows Server 2003. The exceptions are usually programs that are coded to query the operating system version, and accept only certain responses. It's been my experience that such coding usually exists in vertical applications (usually databases), and custom applications that were created by in-house or subcontracted programmers.

> **Note** *I'm totally ignoring games in my discussion of compatibility.*

You may not be quite as lucky. You may face an error message that says "This program cannot run because you're not running Windows NT" (substitute any prior version of Windows). Or, the program may not run at all when you launch it. Don't panic yet, because Windows Server 2003 has compatibility functions that may let you run that software as if it were running under the Windows version it's looking for. The semi-technical jargon for this situation is "faking it out."

You can use the Windows Server 2003 compatibility tools in two ways: test your software with the compatibility wizard, and manually set an application to run under compatibility mode.

In addition, the Windows Server 2003 compatibility features can help you overcome incompatibility issues apart from version problems:

- Display issues (including working with themes) that older software applications can't manage (or get confused by).

- Permissions settings, and you can use the wizard to give wholesale permissions for the program to all your users.

> **Note** *The compatibility tools in Windows Server 2003 are only for Windows software, not for DOS applications.*

Test Compatibility with the Wizard

You can test a program for compatibility with the Program Compatibility Wizard, which is on the Accessories menu. The wizard never gets bored testing various versions of Windows over and over, until it finds the version that runs your program perfectly.

The wizard opens with a welcoming message that includes a warning that you shouldn't use this wizard to test antivirus, backup, or system programs. Assuming the software you want to test doesn't fall into any of those categories, click Next to get started.

The next wizard window asks you how to find the program you want to test, offering the following options:

- **I want to choose from a list of programs** Select this option if the program has been installed on your Windows Server 2003 computer. Click Next to see a list of programs that were installed using Windows installer functions.

- **I want to use the program in the CD-ROM drive** Choose this option if you want to check a program on CD before you install it. The wizard locates the installation file on the CD (usually setup.exe or install.exe) and automatically selects it as the file to be tested.

■ **I want to locate the program manually**   Select this option to check a program that exists on your drive but isn't listed in the installed programs list that appears with the first option. Click Next and enter the path to the program's file, or click Browse to locate it.

Here are some guidelines to follow when deciding which of the preceding options to choose:

■ If you're testing a program on a CD, Windows Server 2003 won't be able to write the needed information after you determine the proper compatibility mode. This is an investigative task. When you learn what works, install the program, and then use the manual compatibility features (discussed next) to apply the compatibility settings.

■ The wizard's definition of a program file includes any filename with the following extensions: .exe, .com, .cmd, .bat., .pif, and .lnk. If you're selecting the program manually, when you get to the program's folder, you may see more than one filename (perhaps a .bat file that launches an .exe file). You must select the file that is the program's real executable (usually the .exe file).

Version Compatibility

After you've selected the program file, click Next and select a compatibility mode. As you can see in Figure 3-12, you can ask the wizard to test any previous version of Windows.

■ If the program was running properly in the Windows version you used before you upgraded to Windows Server 2003, select that version.

■ If you haven't yet run this program, contact the manufacturer (or programmer), and ascertain the appropriate Windows version.

■ If your compatibility problems (discovered or expected) aren't based on version, but are instead display or permissions issues, select the option Do Not Apply A Compatibility Mode.

Click Next after you make your selection.

Display Compatibility

Select the display options this program supports, and click Next. If you don't expect the program to have any problems with the display features in Windows Server 2003, just click Next. If, during the test, you find that some of the program's icons or dialogs are difficult to read, you can rerun the wizard and make changes in this window.

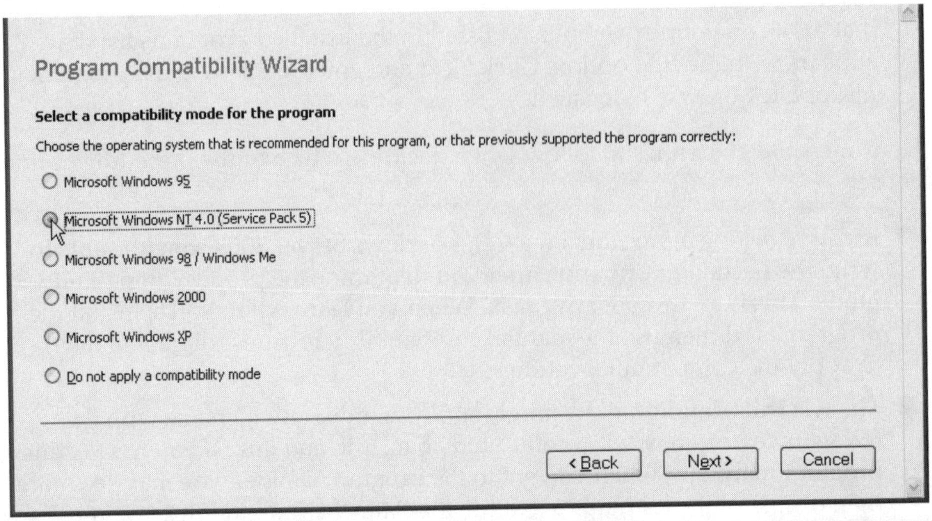

Figure 3-12.   *Select your best guess–you can always try another version.*

Permissions

If the program produced access errors for users, or if nothing happened when users selected the program (frequently a result of access permissions), you can configure the application for looser permissions. This is much easier than changing folder permissions, especially for software that accesses multiple folders.

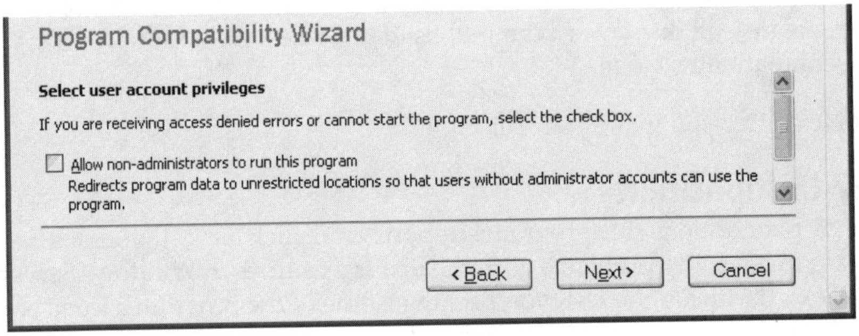

Test Your Compatibility Settings

The next wizard window displays a summary of your compatibility settings. If you want to change anything, use the Back button to return to previous windows. Otherwise, click Next to test-run the application. Put the program through its paces.

If you're testing a setup/installation file on a CD, and the program opens properly and seems to work, cancel the installation. Copy the contents of the CD to the hard drive and either run the wizard again (so the wizard can write the necessary changes) or apply the compatibility settings manually. It's also a good idea to test the software itself after it's installed. Use the resulting compatibility settings by sharing the folder and installing the software on user computers from that sharepoint.

When you close the program, you're returned to a wizard window that wants to know how the program worked. Select one of the following options:

- **Yes, set the program to always use these compatibility settings**   Select this option if the program worked properly using the options you selected.

- **No, try different compatibility settings**   Select this option to rerun the wizard (be sure to keep track of the settings you select so you know what didn't work).

- **No, I am finished trying compatibility settings**   The results were so awful you believe that different settings wouldn't work, and you plan to contact the software company or programmer.

Click Next. If you selected the option to try different settings, the wizard returns to the first settings page (selecting the operating system version). If you selected either of the other two options, the wizard offers to send the temporary files it created to Microsoft (perhaps your solution, or lack of solution, will end up in a Knowledge Base article). Select Yes or No, and click Next.

If you click the link to the temporary files that were created, you can view the file names. If you wish to see the contents, open Windows Explorer or My Computer, travel to the container folder (\Documents and Settings\<UserName>\Local Settings\ Temp), and open the files in Notepad.

Click Next, then click Finish in the final wizard window.

Set Compatibility Options Manually

If you know what changes you must make to run the program in Windows Server 2003, you can set the compatibility options manually. This works only for installed software, not on CD installation disks (because Windows must write the changes you make).

Right-click the software's program file and choose Properties from the shortcut menu. Move to the Compatibility tab, which looks like Figure 3-13. Select the options you need to change, and then click OK.

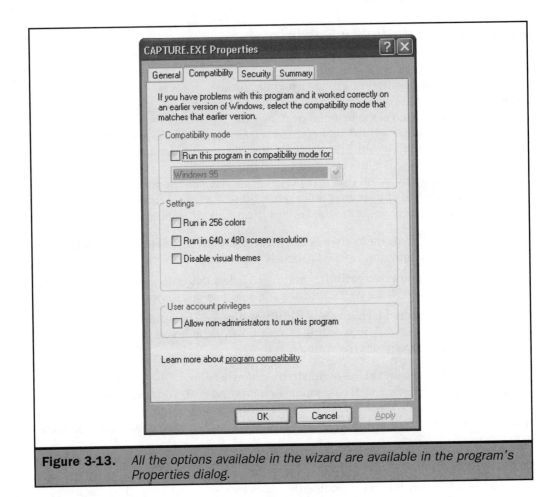

Figure 3-13. *All the options available in the wizard are available in the program's Properties dialog.*

If you can't solve your application problems with the Windows Server 2003 compatibility features, you need to contact the software company. You'll probably learn the company is updating its software for later versions of Windows (if not, it's probably planning to go out of business).

Chapter 4

The Windows Server 2003 Registry

Starting with Windows 95, Microsoft designed a single repository, called the *registry*, to hold information about the operating system and installed applications. The registry is a database, and it's involved in almost everything you do. It contains information about the computer, its hardware, the peripherals attached to the computer, installed software, and the users who log on to the computer.

Software applications use the registry all the time, employing standard Win32 APIs to get the data they need. Software installation programs use standard APIs to add, modify, or remove registry data. In fact, the registry really belongs to software (including the operating system), and the purpose of the registry is to provide information to software, not to users. Users are expected to stay out.

Most of the data in the registry that results from user action is placed there as a result of the user's work with a dialog (for example, the applets in the Control Panel), or as a result of group policies. You're supposed to make registry changes for configuration items through the use of GUI-based windows and dialog boxes.

However, the reality is that many of us find that working directly in the registry is faster and easier than drilling down through layers of dialog. Additionally, some problems can only be resolved by direct registry changes.

Overview of the Registry

The registry grew out of a number of control files and databases that existed in previous versions of Windows, traveling a logical road to today's incarnation of the way Windows Server 2003 stores settings.

Microsoft Windows 3.1, which was the first widely used version of Windows (especially in business), used three file types to define a computer's hardware and application software for the operating system. Two of the file types were initialization files, which have the extension .ini, and the third file type was a registration database. Among the initialization files (.ini files) were files included in Windows, and a bunch of private .ini files from application software.

Windows 3.1x used six .ini files to load and control the Windows environment (control.ini, progman.ini, protocol.ini, system.ini, win.ini, and winfile.ini).

The win.ini file was the primary location for information pertaining to the software configuration of the operating system, along with any specific system-wide information added by application software. Because every application made changes to win.ini (usually with the attitude that it was the only application installed on the computer), this .ini file usually grew very large, very fast. The size caused problems when it exceeded 64KB. The operating system permitted win.ini to grow beyond 64KB (and didn't bother to inform the user that this limit had been reached) even though any entry beyond that 64KB boundary was ignored. When applications added entries to the top sections of the win.ini file, information at the bottom of the file was pushed beyond the initialization boundary, and that information wasn't implemented. Applications that expected these lost entries to be initialized failed, either totally or by losing functionality. In an attempt to prevent this problem, Microsoft recommended that application developers store application-specific information in private .ini files that pertained only to their application. While this helped, many application developers continued to put large amounts of information in the win.ini file.

The system.ini file served as the primary repository for system information about the hardware installed in the computer, pointing the operating system to hardware and related software components (device drivers, shells, and so forth).

The progman.ini file contained the initialization settings for the Windows Program Manager, and winfile.ini contained the settings for the Windows File Manager. The absence of these files wouldn't prevent Windows from running (which is not the case with system.ini or win.ini), but the default configuration for the applications they control were loaded, absent any customizations made by the user.

The protocol.ini file, which first appeared with the Windows for Workgroups version of Windows 3.1x, held initialization information for Windows networking.

Private initialization files were the .ini files added to the Windows directory by third-party applications installed on the system. These files contained specific information about the state of the application, including items such as screen position, the most recently used file list, and so on.

A win.ini file exists on most Windows NT/ 2000/Server 2003 systems, and its role is to support 16-bit applications.

The last file that Windows 3.1x used for system configuration was reg.dat. This was the Windows 3.1 Registration Database and is the direct predecessor of the registry. (It didn't take long for users to shorten the name *Registration Database* to *registry*.) This database, which contained nested structures from a single root (HKEY_CLASSES_ROOT), held the information needed to maintain file extension associations and Object Linking and Embedding (OLE) drag-and-drop support. Unlike .ini files, which are simple ASCII text files that you can edit in any text editor, the reg.dat file was a binary file and came with its own editing application, the Registration Information Editor (Regedit.exe). This first registry had some serious limitations, in the form of a single hierarchy and a size limit of 64KB for the reg.dat file.

A large problem with the Windows 3.1 registry was the manner in which the operating system used it, or rather, didn't use it. There was no particular sense of urgency about keeping the registration database up-to-date and accurate. Applications could write to it, or not. No "oversight committee" standards were built into the operating system to ensure that a software application told the registry the same thing it told its own .ini files, or the system .ini files. If software configuration, .ini files, and the registration database had matching information, it was frequently a coincidence. In addition, the communication methods to query and write to the registry were cumbersome and required quite a bit of overhead, frequently slowing down the system. Lastly, user settings didn't exist, so multiple users on the same computer lived with the settings left behind by the last user.

When Microsoft released the first incarnation of Windows NT (NT 3.1), the registry had been made more flexible and more powerful. The 64KB limit was removed. The hierarchical structure was expanded to include multiple nested containers, and the

---

The .ini File Lives!

The fact is, .ini files continue to play a role in the newer versions of Windows. Do a search on your Windows Server 2003 computer for .ini files, and you'll be surprised at the number of files you'll find. After I configured computer roles, but before I installed any applications, searching for *.ini on my Windows Server 2003 computer resulted in 228 .ini files.

Microsoft's rules for developers include the guideline that a program should write its installation settings in HKEY_LOCAL_MACHINE\Software*VendorName* and write all user-specific settings in HKEY_CURRENT_USER\Software\VendorName. Too many software companies ignore this rule, or don't fulfill it properly. Some applications create the subkeys but don't populate them with data. Some applications write registry data that clearly obstructs the rule, for instance registering command-line information that points to an .ini file instead of the program's executable file.

---

registry-handling code was reworked to keep performance at a high level. Remote administration was enabled, making the life of a network administrator easier. Microsoft pushed developers to use the registry for variables and settings, and even made its own programs registry-friendly.

Another significant change with the release of Windows NT 3.1 was the introduction of Regedt32. This new 32-bit registry editor displayed each subtree in its own window and provided powerful new commands such as the ability to connect to the registries of remote computers and the important ability to secure registry keys.

Windows NT 4 and Windows 95 (and later Windows 98) were released with remarkably similar registries. Both added new subtrees: HKEY_CURRENT_CONFIG and HKEY_DYN_DATA.

All of these changes and improvements brought us to the registry for Windows Server 2003 (as well as Windows 2000)—the subject of this chapter.

Registry Structure

The registry is a hierarchical database consisting of nested containers and data, as follows:

- **Subtrees**   The roots or primary divisions of the hierarchy.
- **Keys**   The primary subcontainers under the subtrees. Keys can contain subkeys or entries.
- **Subkeys**   Child keys. Subkeys can contain additional subkeys or entries.
- **Entries**   The actual data that affects the system. Entries appear in the right pane of the registry editor.

The notation HKEY *for the subtree derives from the fact that the designers of the registry consider the root a handle to that key.* HKEY *is easier to type than* HandleToKEY.

Hives and Hive Files

Physically, the registry is a set of files, which are called *hives*. A hive is a portion of the registry (a specific section of keys, subkeys, and values) that appears as a file on your computer. Hive files can only be viewed or edited with a registry editor. However, they can be copied anywhere, which is one way to back them up manually. (Most backup software, including the built-in backup application in Windows Server 2003, has an option for backing up the registry.)

Registry hive files are saved as .dat files, and each of those files has a corresponding .log file, which acts as a transaction log for the main .dat file. Each .dat file has a partner file with the extension .log, and the partnership creates a form of fault tolerance. When changes are made and the hive file needs to be updated, changes are written first to the .log file, which acts like a transaction file. (If you're familiar with Microsoft Exchange Server, or the general approach of the Jet database/transaction file, this is the same paradigm.)

When the .log file has been updated, the transactions are written to disk, and then the hive file is updated from the disk write. The disk write is forced; this is not one of those "put it in the cache and write when you have time" procedures. If the system crashes before the hive file is updated, the transactions in the .log file can be rolled back to put the previous settings into effect.

The registry itself keeps a record of the hive files at HKEY_LOCAL_MACHINE\ System\CurrentControlSet\Control\Hive list. When you view the list, you find a couple of interesting items.

First, there's a listing for the Hardware key, but no hive file is named in the data pane. This is because the Hardware key is built from scratch during bootup. The ntdetect.com file gathers the information needed to populate the key—the operating system does not fetch the information from a hive file.

The second point of interest is the format of the path to the file, which is \Device\ HarddiskVolume1\Windows\System32\Config\<*filename*> (except for the logged-on user setting files that are in subdirectories of \Device\HarddiskVolume1\Documents and Settings). If you didn't use Windows as the target for your Windows Server 2003 installation, the directory name you used is substituted (throughout this book I use %SystemRoot% to mean that directory). This format gives a clue to the point at which this information is accessed by Windows during operating system startup. The operating system doesn't read or assign drive letters until well into the startup process, so this is the only way Windows can find the location.

Table 4-1 shows the location of the hive files (and their contents) on your Windows Server 2003 computer.

Registry Hive	Disk File
HKEY_LOCAL_MACHINE\SAM	%SystemRoot%\System32\Config\Sam
HKEY_LOCAL_MACHINE\Security	%SystemRoot%\System32\Config\Security
HKEY_LOCAL_MACHINE\Software	%SystemRoot%\System32\Config\Software
HKEY_LOCAL_MACHINE\System	%SystemRoot%\System32\Config\System
HKEY_CURRENT_CONFIG	%SystemRoot%\System32\Config\System
HKEY_CURRENT_USER	%SystemDrive%\Documents and Settings\<*username*>\Ntuser.dat
HKEY_USERS\.Default	%SystemDrive%\Documents and Settings\Default User\Ntuser.dat

Table 4-1.   *Location and Contents of Hive Files on a Windows Server 2003 Computer*

Registry Data Items

Data entry items are the bottom of the registry hierarchy. They hold the data that determines the behavior of the keys and subkeys (although not all keys and subkeys contain data entries). Entries appear in the right pane of the registry editor.

An entry has three elements:

- Name
- Data type
- Data value

Entry Name

The name of an entry is almost always (but not always) one word, even if it's really a multiword name. For example, AutoRepeatRate is an entry name in the Keyboard Response subkey. When you edit the registry, you can add new entries and give them a name, but not from your imagination. Names must be recognized by the operating system or the application that uses the entry, and you need to know what the name is before adding an entry.

Entry Data Types

Every entry has a *data type,* which is the specific kind of data that entry can store. Ten data types are available, but some aren't used by Windows Server 2003. The following sections describe the data types you'll run into.

REG_DWORD   The REG_DWORD data type is a double word—two 16-bit words, making the value 32 bits. This is the most common data type in the registry, and it's used for a variety of entries. You'll find entries with device driver information, Boolean values, quantities such as the number of seconds that can elapse before something happens or doesn't happen, and other assorted information.

In Regedit, REG_DWORD entries are displayed in hex (hexadecimal format), but you can switch to decimal or binary format (depending on the entry) if you need to perform an edit. I can't convert hex to anything in my head, so when I want to change a figure such as a timeout interval, I have to change the format in order to accomplish my task. If you have the ability to covert hex in your head, you'll work faster.

REG_BINARY   Entries that use a REG_BINARY data type are entries in which the data is raw binary data. "Raw" means there are no terminators, nothing except the raw data that's placed there. This data type is used mostly for hardware component information. The data can be displayed and edited in either binary or hexadecimal format in Regedit.

REG_SZ   Entries of type REG_SZ are fixed-length text strings. Most of the entries that use this type are either Boolean or have short text string values. This is a very common data type, probably arising almost as frequently as the REG_DWORD type.

The notation *SZ* means String/Zero byte termination, because the entries are terminated with a zero byte at the end (a zero is added to the end of the string). Regedit hides the terminating zero, so you don't have to think about it (unless you're writing a software application that manipulates the registry, in which case you must remember to pay attention to the terminating byte).

When you view or edit an entry of this type in Regedit, the window that opens is titled "String Editor."

REG_MULTI_SZ   This entry type is used by data entries that comprise multiple text strings. The strings are separated by commas or spaces, and the entry is terminated by two null characters (unseen in the registry editor). In Regedit, the edit window displays binary data (although you can see the text on the right side of the window).

When applications do a lookup on any REG_MULTI_SZ entry, they're sent the entire entry; they cannot ask for a specific string (which is important to know if you're a programmer).

REG_EXPAND_SZ   This entry type is used when an entry includes one or more variables that have to be resolved by an operating system service or an application. The variables are the same variables you use in batch files and scripts (for example, %SystemRoot% or %UserName%). I've never figured out why the registry itself doesn't resolve the variable and pass it to the requesting service or program—after all, it knows where to find the information.

REG_FULL_RESOURCE_DESCRIPTOR   This entry type is used to store a resource list for hardware components. The contents are a nested array, consolidating the resources for a component (or a driver). Regedit displays this information in binary format.

REG_LINK   This entry type contains a symbolic link between data and a registry value. For example, an application that needs to know the unique ID of a user (perhaps for settings information) can look up the security ID of the current user (HKEY_ CURRENT_USER).

REG_DWORD_LITTLE_ENDIAN   This is an entry type that's a sibling of the REG_ DWORD entry type. It is most commonly used for storing numbers. The data value is a 32-bit number in which the most important byte is displayed as a high-order (leftmost) byte. This entry type only exists in Windows Server 2003, Windows 2000, and Windows 98. Technically, it exists in Windows NT, but the registry in Windows NT automatically converts data written as REG_DWORD_LITTLE_ENDIAN to standard REG_DWORD.

REG_DWORD_BIG_ENDIAN   This entry type is the opposite of REG_DWORD_ LITTLE_ENDIAN. The most significant byte is displayed as the low-order (rightmost) byte, and it's used by machine platforms that place bytes in that order (PowerPC and Alpha). Because Windows Server 2003 doesn't support those platforms, any leftover registry items of this type are ignored.

HKEY_CLASSES_ROOT

HKEY_CLASSES_ROOT is filled with all sorts of basic information. You rarely have a reason to work interactively in this subtree; it's a collection of the building blocks that make the operating system and applications run. Two types of data exist in this subtree:

- File association information
- Configuration data for COM objects

Per-User Class Registration

The most interesting thing about this subtree is the way it changed with the introduction of Windows 2000. The subtree is an alias, and in Windows NT its source was HKEY_ LOCAL_MACHINE\Software\Classes. In Windows Server 2003/2000, the subtree is still an alias, but it derives its data from two sources:

- HKEY_LOCAL_MACHINE\Software\Classes
- HKEY_CURRENT_USER\Software\Classes

The latter registry key didn't exist in its present configuration before Windows 2000. (Although the key exists in Windows 98, its contents aren't what they are in Windows Server 2003/2000. In Windows 98, the key contains CLSIDs for the default OS desktop icons.)

Microsoft names this new user-based source for HKEY_CLASSES_ROOT *per-user class registration*. This feature means that computers with multiple users can have different class information registered when any specific user installs software. The per-user information can involve any number of class-registration changes, creating multiple sets of unique entries for software that's installed on the computer.

An important benefit of per-user class registration accrues to roaming users (sharing computers is a less frequent occurrence than roaming users in many enterprises). No matter where a user is when she logs on, all the class IDs, file associations, and other software registry associations are intact, because the class registration information travels with the user. However, this feature only works if you use IntelliMirror features to establish roaming user profiles, because the operating system loads the class registration information after the basic user profile loads, using IntelliMirror extensions (the class registration information is written to the local portion of the profile during the logon process).

You can't write to the registry to use per-user class registration; it's a programming task. The instructions and tools for writing to the user-based keys are in the programmer development kits.

HKEY_CLASSES_ROOT Data

The data items in the HKEY_CLASSES_ROOT subtree provide the operating system with information about the objects that are installed. Scrolling through the subtree, you see two sets of keys arranged alphabetically:

- The first alphabetic set of keys contains all possible file extensions, from * to .z*
- The second set of keys are program and object IDs

File Associations   While the notion of "file association" started way back in Windows 3.1, the current incarnation of the HKEY_CLASSES_ROOT subtree has certainly grown in size and function.

Subkeys that exist for any specific extension contain information that's used for COM, VB, automation, and scripting processes. The data pane for an extension key usually identifies the file type of the extension. For example, the .avi key contains a REG_SZ data item named Content Type with the value video/avi.

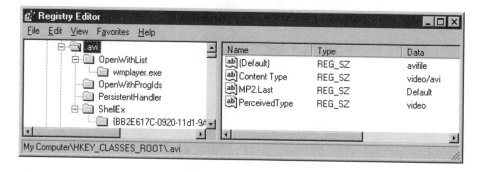

Registered file types have subkeys that hold information the system uses when working with those file types. For instance, the subkey named ShellNew tells the operating system how to create a new instance of that file type. Some extension keys have subkeys that associate the extension to one or more programs (and each of those subkeys has a ShellNew subkey).

For example, when you install the operating system, the file extension .doc is automatically registered to WordPad.exe. Selecting the .doc key in HKEY_CLASSES_ROOT displays the Default data item with a value Wordpad.Document.1. If you install Microsoft Word, a second data item named Content Type is added to the right pane, and its value is application/msword. That's because Microsoft's installation process for Word doesn't overwrite the association to WordPad; it adds itself as a second association. Not all software works like this, and you may find that installing some software applications overwrites previous file extension associations.

If you need to change file associations, don't use the registry. Instead, use the File Types tab in the Folder Options dialog (which you can find in Control Panel, or on the Tools menu of system folders). You can add associations if you want to have more than one program associated with an extension, or you can change the association from one program to another.

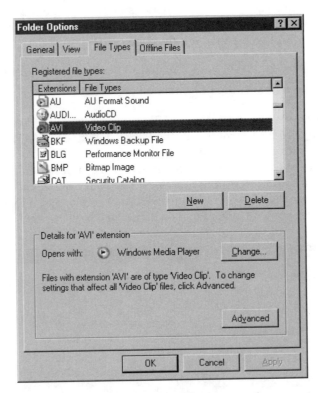

Object IDs The second set of keys in HKEY_CLASSES_ROOT are mostly program and object IDs, along with some parent keys that maintain other classes of information (for example, CLSID). Almost all of these keys have subkeys, and the number and type of subkeys depend on the object and the type of information the operating system needs about that object. One or more of the following subkeys frequently exist for file types that have been registered:

- **CLSID**   Specifies the unique class ID of this object type.
- **DefaultIcon**   Points to the file that holds the icon for this file type. Usually, the file is an .exe or a .dll file. The format of the data is Path,x (where x is the integer ID of the icon that's contained in the file). Most files that have icons have multiple icons, and the integer IDs start with 0.
- **Protocol**   Holds information that the system needs to support linking, embedding, and editing of the file type.
- **Shell**   Has subkeys that contain information about the types of operations you can perform on the file type.

You can see the way the Shell subkey data works in Windows Explorer or My Computer. When you right-click a file with a registered extension and choose Open, the system checks the \Shell\Open\Command subkey and executes the command it finds in the data item. If you choose Print, the system uses the command it finds in the \Shell\Print\Command subkey.

HKEY_CURRENT_USER

HKEY_CURRENT_USER holds the profile for the currently logged-on user. It's an alias for HKEY_USERS*<SecurityID of the logged on user>*. This subtree actually contains no data; it stores only a pointer to the contents of its real subtree and displays that information. However, it's important to know that making changes to the contents of either subtree changes both.

This is a time-saving device for both the operating system and applications, as they look up user settings before performing tasks. Without the HKEY_CURRENT_USER alias subtree, the lookups would have to be directed to the correct SID keys in HKEY_USERS to make sure the right settings are used. That would require a preliminary lookup to determine the current user's SID.

When a user logs on, HKEY_CURRENT_USER is created anew, using the data that makes up the profile of the logging-on user. If this is the first time the user logged on, no profile exists, so the operating system loads the settings of Default User. When the new user logs off, the profile is saved under the user's name. Any configuration changes the user made are saved.

User Profiles

User profiles hold settings for each user, including operating system settings, application settings, and policies. The settings are contained in the file NTUSER.DAT, which exists in each user's subfolder (%SystemDrive%\Documents and Settings*<CurrentUserName>*).

The process of creating a profile for each user begins by loading a copy of the Default User profile. The NTUSER.DAT file in %SystemDrive%\Documents and Settings\Default User contains the configuration settings for the default user, which is stored in the registry under HKEY_USERS\.DEFAULT. Every user profile also uses the common program groups that are located in %SystemDrive%\Documents and Settings\All Users.

The convention for establishing user profile folders (including the Default User profile and the All Users profile) in Windows Server 2003 differs from the convention used in Windows NT 4.0:

- For a fresh install of Windows Server 2003, or for an upgrade over Windows 2000/9x, a folder for user profiles is created on the same drive as the Windows 2000 installation, to wit: %SystemDrive%:\Documents and Settings.

- For a Windows Server 2003 upgrade over Windows NT, user profile folders are kept in the same location as they were in Windows NT, to wit: %SystemRoot%\Profiles.

Note *The path to a user's profile is usually represented by the variable %ProfilePath%, and the user's folder name is created by using the user ID.*

The NTUSER.DAT file is the registry portion of the logged-on user's profile (essentially HKEY_CURRENT_USER), and it's loaded into the registry during logon. The profile subfolder also contains subfolders that hold additional settings.

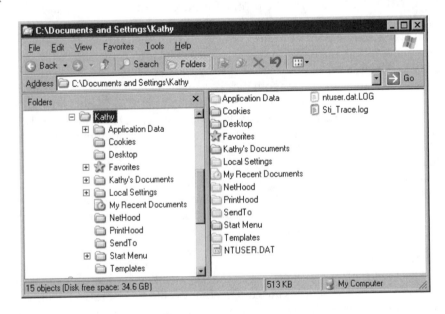

In addition to local profiles, Windows Server 2003, like Windows 2000/NT, supports two additional types of profiles: roaming and mandatory. See Chapter 21 for more information about user profiles.

HKEY_CURRENT_USER Data

A nested hierarchy of subkeys contains the settings for the environment of the current logged-on user. Almost all of the configuration settings that are recorded here are changed via the GUI, not interactively in the registry.

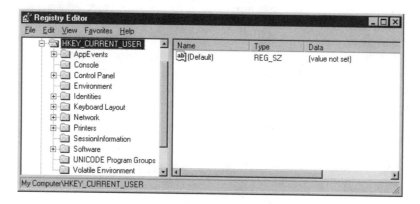

AppEvents   Continuing the tradition that started with Windows 9*x*, Microsoft dedicates an entire registry key to linking sounds to events. The key has two subkeys:

- **EventLabels**   A group of subkeys with names that are really labels for types of events. The data item in each key is a description of the label (and frequently the description matches the label exactly).
- **Schemes**   Contains additional subkeys that hold a variety of settings, including the actual names of the sound files that are linked to events.

Users link sound files to events in the Sounds and Audio Devices applet in Control Panel. In addition, some applications add schemes, sound files, and event descriptions (for example, AOL's "You've Got Mail," which comes to you from a company badly in need of grammar lessons, or the little tune that announces new mail in Eudora).

Console   The Console key stores settings for the Windows Server 2003 console subsystem, which runs all character-based applications (including the Command Processor, which you use for command-line work). See Chapter 7 for information about setting configuration options for the command window.

Control Panel   This key and its subkeys contain settings that control the appearance of the desktop, along with user-defined options for many of the Control Panel applets.

When you expand the key, you see subkey names that obviously match some of the applets, along with a number of other settings categories. The values of the data items change when users make changes to options in the Control Panel applets. Most of the options take effect immediately, without any need to restart the operating system.

Don't be deceived by the notion that because these settings generally affect only the user interface, they're harmless. Administrators who fall for that belief, and give users total freedom to alter default settings, are frequently sorry. Some of the settings in the Control Panel key and its subkeys are more powerful than they seem. For example, an inexperienced user who messes around with video settings can create enough damage to keep the computer from booting normally. A password-protected screen saver is important for a client machine that could have sensitive data on the screen, and a user who finds that feature annoying might disable it and then head for the coffee shop with your payroll records displayed on the monitor. And, of course, stories abound in the help desk community about users who enable the password-protected screen saver feature without bothering to write down or remember the password, and every time they leave their desks, the help desk can expect a call.

Windows Server 2003 provides a full range of group policies to control access to the Control Panel applets (see Chapter 22 for specifics).

Environment   This key contains data entries that represent environment variables settings for the logged-on user.

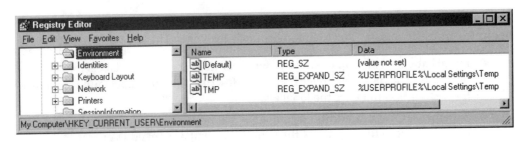

Both the Temp and Tmp environment variables are included because applications might use either terminology.

In addition to (or, even better, instead of) using the registry to work with these settings, you can view and modify the settings in the System Properties dialog (right-click My Computer and choose Properties). On the Advanced tab, click Environment Variables to see information similar to that shown in Figure 4-1.

If you make changes to the environment settings, via either the registry or the System Properties dialog, the new settings don't take effect until the next time the user logs on.

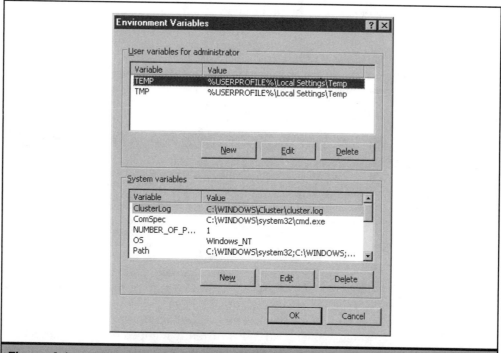

Figure 4-1.   *Add user environment settings in the System Properties dialog.*

Caution   *The data items in the Environment key must be REG_EXPAND_SZ data types. If you enter an item of a different type, or you change the existing data type, the system will not replace the variable with its value.*

Identities   This key, which doesn't exist in previous versions of Windows, is undocumented by Microsoft. It seems to be an ID for the current user, but not the primary ID. In HKEY_USERS, each user has a unique ID. The current user's unique ID key has a subkey that matches the value of this data item.

Keyboard Layout   This subkey stores information about the installed keyboard layouts, including hardware and driver settings. In addition, if the user adds more keyboards (keyboard language files), information about those keyboards is maintained in the subkeys.

Hardware and driver changes should be effected in the Keyboard applet in Control Panel. Additional keyboards are added in the Regional and Language Options applet.

Network   This key only exists if the current user has mapped network drives. The key itself is a parent key and holds no important data. A child subkey exists for each persistent mapped drive, and the subkey is named for the drive letter to which the share is mapped.

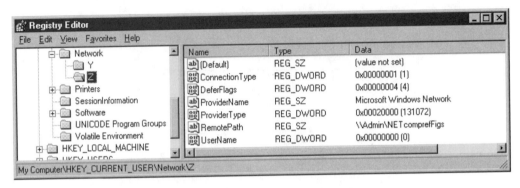

If a user maps a drive and does not select the option Reconnect At Logon, the mapped drive is not written to the registry. (All currently mapped drives, regardless of the persistent state, have icons in My Computer.)

 The default condition of the Reconnect At Logon option is whatever was selected the last time the user mapped a drive.

Each subkey holds information about its connection:

- **ConnectionType**   Specifies the type of connection for this mapping. A value of 1 means drive redirection; a value of 2 means printer redirection.

- **DeferFlags**   This key isn't documented by Microsoft (although the documentation team tells me they hope to add information some time in the future). In my registry, all mapped drives have a value of 4. A value of 4 usually indicates a dependency on a specific set of circumstances, where 1 = one thing, 2 = something else, and so on. (If I ever figure it out, I'll post the information at www.admin911.com.)

- **ProviderName**   Specifies the network provider that makes the connection. By default, Microsoft Windows Network is the value (which you can mentally translate as Microsoft LanMan).

- **ProviderType**   Identifies the provider used for the connection. The value is a constant assigned by Microsoft. For Microsoft LanMan, the constant is 0x20000 (open the data item to see the hex data). For third-party providers, the value is a constant assigned to the provider.

- **RemotePath**   The UNC to the mapped share.
- **UserName**   Specifies a username to be used for the connection. By default, this data item has no value, because most of the time, the user is the logged-on user. However, if the mapping configuration specifies a different username for connecting to this mapped drive, that username appears as the value for this data item. (The Map Network Drive Wizard has an option named Connect Using a Different User Name, which accepts a username and password for the connection that's being configured.)

Printers   This subkey contains information about the printers installed on the computer, including user-set configuration options.

Session Information   This subkey seems to contain information about the applications in use in the current session (the only data item in my registry is ProgramCount, which has a value equal to the number of programs that are currently open). I use the word "seems" because it's undocumented. Microsoft's registry documentation team told me they hadn't documented this key, but plan to in a future version of Windows.

Software   This key stores application user settings and program variables that are specific to the logged-on user. The data items change as users make configuration changes. The subkeys under this key are not just created by software installation programs—the operating system keeps all sorts of important settings here. It's beyond the scope of this book to engage in a detailed discussion of user settings.

UNICODE Program Groups   This key exists for downlevel compatibility, for users who run Program Manager. The data items, if any exist, define the contents of all personal program groups in Program Manager.

Volatile Environment   This key contains the settings for the current user's session.

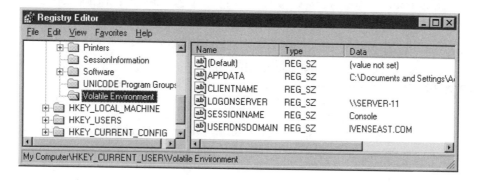

HKEY_LOCAL_MACHINE

This subtree holds information about the computer, its hardware, installed device drivers, and configuration options (for both security and software settings) that affect all users of the computer. It contains five keys: Hardware, SAM, Security, Software, and System. All of the keys, save Hardware, exist on disk as hive files.

HKLM\Hardware

Ntdetect.com (the Windows Server 2003 "hardware recognizer") builds the contents of this key from scratch during startup. The information is held in RAM (you can think of it as a RAM-based hive file) so that Windows can find information about the machine as the operating system continues loading. The hierarchy of subkeys holds information about all the hardware components of the computer.

HKLM\SAM

This data for the Security Accounts Manager (SAM) isn't accessible via the registry editors. The SAM hive, located by default in %SystemRoot%\System32\Config, is the repository of this user and group data. The SAM data consists of all local users and groups, including user access permissions for folders, files, and peripherals. A lot of the information about domain groups and users that was in the SAM hive in Windows NT 4 is in Active Directory in Windows Server 2003 (and Windows 2000).

HKLM\Security

Like the SAM subkey, the Security subkey keeps its data in its hive and prevents users from viewing or altering it interactively in the registry editor. The Security hive is in the same location on your hard drive as the SAM hive.

The contents of the Security hive are related to security issues (not a surprise), and the data differs depending on whether or not you have a mixed-mode network. If Windows NT servers are still playing a role in authentication, the Security hive holds configuration settings for NT 4 user and group policies in addition to Windows Server 2003/Windows 2000 security policies.

HKLM\Software

This is an extensive and crowded key, holding multiple layers of subkeys in its hierarchy. Software companies generally add a key to this subtree (and usually add the same key to HKEY_CURRENT_USER\Software), with subkeys for the product name, version, or other components.

The operating system keeps computer settings here, including settings that are put into effect by group policies.

HKLM\System

This key is enormous! Many of its subkeys and data items control the operating system startup (covered in Chapter 5); other subkeys and data items control almost everything the operating system does (especially kernel services). This is the definitive resource for computer configuration settings, but it's beyond the scope of this book to cover them in detail.

HKEY_USERS

This subtree contains subkeys for the Default User profile and all known user profiles for the computer. Each individual user profile subkey is identified by a Security ID, and expands to a full complement of settings subkeys (which become HKEY_CURRENT_USER as each individual user logs on).

HKEY_CURRENT_CONFIG

This subtree holds information about the hardware profile used by this computer at startup. It's an alias for HKEY_LOCAL_MACHINE\System\CurrentControlSet\Hardware Profiles\Current.

Regedit.exe

The only registry editor in Windows Server 2003 is Regedit.exe; regedt32 is gone. (If you open Start | Run and enter **regedt32**, Regedit.exe opens). Most of us who work in the registry frequently have always preferred the interface of Regedit.exe, and only used regedt32 to set security settings. Now, the security settings are available in Regedit.exe, so we won't miss regedt32.

Prevent Regedit from Displaying the Last Accessed Key

One thing I dislike about Regedit in Windows Server 2003 (and in Windows 2000) is the fact that when you open the editor, it displays the last key you accessed. Sometimes that's a key way down the tree, and it's a lot of work to scroll, unexpand, and otherwise wend your way through the left pane in order to get to the key you want to use this time. To change the behavior, you have to perform two steps:

- Delete the information about the last key you accessed.
- Stop the system from writing that information the next time you access a key.

To perform these tasks, follow these steps:

1. Go to HKEY_CURRENT_USER\Software\Microsoft\Windows\CurrentVersion\Applets\Regedit.
2. Double-click the LastKey data item in the right pane, and delete the value, creating an empty string.
3. Click OK to close the String Editor.
4. Right-click the Regedit key in the left pane again, and choose Permissions from the shortcut menu.

5. Click Advanced to open the Advanced Security Settings dialog.

6. Select your username, and click Edit to open the Permission Entry dialog.

7. Select Deny for the Set Value permission. A new item of the type Deny now exists for your user account.

8. Select that new Deny <your user account> item and click Edit. Then choose This Key Only from the drop-down list in the Apply Onto field. (This limits the Set Value denial to the Regedit subkey, and prevents it from affecting the Favorites subkey.)

9. Click OK three times to close the Permissions dialog (when you click OK the second time, you're asked to confirm the fact that you made these changes).

The Regedit key does not exist if you haven't yet run Regedit on the computer. If the key isn't there, don't add it to the registry manually—instead, open and close Regedit to create the key, then open Regedit again to perform these steps.

If you don't want to go through these steps, you can close all the keys manually by holding down the SHIFT key and continuously pressing the LEFTARROW key until all of the hierarchy is collapsed. Personally, I find this a real pain.

Accessing Remote Registries

You can use Regedit to search or manipulate the registry of another computer on your network. Choose File | Connect Network Registry to open the Select Computer dialog. Enter the name of the computer you want to connect to, or click Advanced to search for the computer.

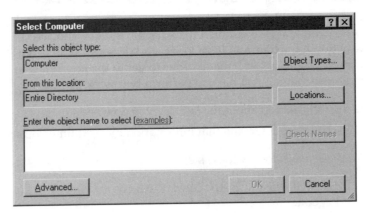

The subtrees of the remote registry are displayed below the subtrees of your local registry. Note that only the two real subtrees are listed for the remote computer (remember, all the other subtrees are derived from these two subtrees).

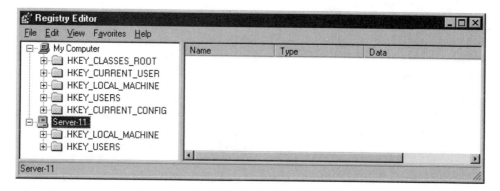

You can connect to more than one remote registry simultaneously, and each set of subtrees is identified by the computer name.

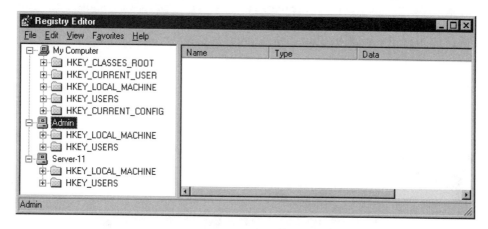

To disconnect from a remote computer's registry, choose File | Disconnect Network Registry. In the Disconnect Network Registry dialog box, click the name of the appropriate computer, and click OK.

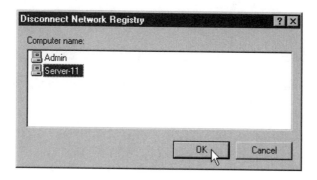

If you don't remember to disconnect, closing Regedit automatically disconnects any remote registries.

Searching the Registry

Regedit provides a robust and efficient search feature for finding registry data. My most frequent reason for opening Regedit is to search for data after I uninstall an application. I've found that very few uninstall programs clean out the registry properly. In addition, sometimes a registry search is the only way to find the cause of an error message about a missing executable file during startup.

Registry searches are "top down," which means the search starts at the point you select before starting the search. If you start at the top (My Computer), the search encompasses all the subtrees. Unless you have some reason to search for class information, it's best to start at HKEY_CURRENT_USER or HKEY_LOCAL_MACHINE. If you're reasonably sure the data is in some specific section of the registry, expand the appropriate subtree and start your search at the logical key or subkey.

You can open the Regedit Find dialog using any of the following actions:

- Choose Edit | Find
- Press F3
- Press CTRL-F

After you begin a search, F3 doesn't open the Find dialog box; instead, it searches for the next occurrence of the string you're searching for.

In the Find dialog, enter the string you're looking for and, if appropriate, select a specific type of data. Then click Find Next.

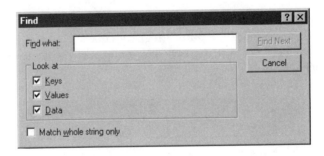

When your search string is found, if it's not the item you need, press F3 to find the next occurrence.

It's often difficult to figure out whether the string you're searching for is a key, a data item, or a value. Applications may add subkeys that have names you'd logically assume would be the name of data items.

Creating Favorites

If there are registry keys you visit often to examine or manipulate data, you can store those keys in a Favorites list for quick access. To add a key to your list, select the key and choose Favorites | Add To Favorites. The Add to Favorites dialog opens so that you can name the item. By default, the name of the key is displayed, but you may want to change the terminology for clarity. For example, I added the subkey HKCU\Software\Microsoft\Windows\CurrentVersion\Policies to my Favorites list. The dialog displayed the name Policies, but since there are multiple subkeys with that name, I changed the listing to make it clear it was the key that held user-based policies.

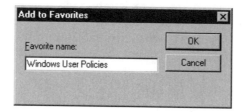

Your list of favorite keys appears on the Favorites menu. Click a listing to move immediately to that subkey.

To remove a listing from your Favorites list, choose Favorites | Remove Favorites. In the Remove Favorites dialog, select the listing you want to get rid of, and click OK.

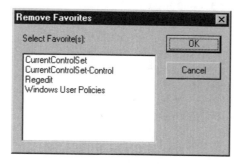

Unlike the Favorites list in Internet Explorer, you can't rename a listing. Instead, you must remove the listing and add it again. The quickest way to do this is to click the listing to travel to its key, remove the listing, and then choose Add To Favorites (you're at the key) to re-create the listing (this time, using a better, more descriptive name).

Tweak and Troubleshoot with the Registry

Sometimes the only way to fix a problem is to manipulate the registry. Many times this is the result of a conversation with support personnel at Microsoft or a software company, or as a result of instructions you find in a Microsoft Knowledge Base article. You can add, remove, or change registry subkeys and data items.

Exporting Keys

Before you manipulate registry data, always back up the subkey you're working in so you can restore the original data if your changes backfire. To accomplish this, select the subkey you're planning to work with and choose File | Export. In the Export Registry File dialog, name the file, and choose Registration File (*.reg) as the file type. By default, Windows Server 2003 chooses your My Documents folder as the location, but you can save the file anywhere.

The default file type for exports is a registration file, which has the extension .reg. Registration files contain all the data in the selected key and any subkeys. For example, exporting the key HKCU\Network (which has subkeys for the two mapped drives on my computer) results in the following text:

```
Windows Registry Editor Version 5.00

[HKEY_CURRENT_USER\Network]
[HKEY_CURRENT_USER\Network\Y]
"RemotePath"="\\\\Admin\\NET Server CR"
"UserName"=dword:00000000
"ProviderName"="Microsoft Windows Network"
"ProviderType"=dword:00020000
"ConnectionType"=dword:00000001
"DeferFlags"=dword:00000004
[HKEY_CURRENT_USER\Network\Z]
"RemotePath"="\\\\Admin\\NETcomprefFigs"
"UserName"=dword:00000000
"ProviderName"="Microsoft Windows Network"
"ProviderType"=dword:00020000
"ConnectionType"=dword:00000001
"DeferFlags"=dword:00000004
```

The default action for a .reg file (the result of double-clicking the file listing) is merge, which means to write the contents of the file to the registry (the same as choosing File | Import from the Regedit menu bar). In fact, distributing .reg files is a nifty way to make needed registry changes to multiple computers (see the section "Using Registration Files," later in this chapter).

However, if you only want to view the contents of a .reg file, right-click its listing and choose Edit, which opens the file in Notepad.

Note | *Registration files are Unicode text files.*

If you make changes to a key, and then change your mind, you can double-click the .reg file you created to restore the original data to the key and its subkeys. Windows asks you to confirm your action.

When a .reg file merges into the registry, all the data in the file is written to the registry. However, if you added a new subkey, or a new data item to an existing subkey, the new element isn't removed when you merge the original data back. Windows doesn't delete the current contents of the key you're manipulating before merging the data in the .reg file. If you add something to the registry, and then decide to restore the original data, you must manually remove any new objects.

Note | *You can also save registry files as other file types: for Windows 9x/NT registries, as binary hive files, or as text files. In addition, you can load and unload hive files. It's beyond the scope of this book to delve into these details, but you can learn more about the registry in my book* Admin911: Windows 2000 Registry, *published by McGraw-Hill/Osborne (2000). Almost all of the discussions apply to Windows Server 2003.*

Adding Items to the Registry

You can add keys or data items to the registry from within Regedit. Most of the time, user-added items are data items within a subkey, but occasionally you need to add a new subkey, and then populate it with data items.

To add a subkey:

1. Right-click the parent key, and choose New | Key.

2. Name the new key (using the instructions from documentation or support personnel).

To add a data item:

1. Right-click its container key, and choose New | *<ValueType>* (you must know the correct value type of a data item you're adding to the registry).

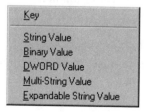

2. Name the data item (using the instructions from documentation or support personnel).

3. Double-click the data item and the appropriate value.

Deleting Registry Items

You can delete any key or data item from the registry except the subtrees. Right-click the item you want to get rid of and choose Delete from the shortcut menu. Windows asks you to confirm your action. Deleting a registry item can be dangerous, so be sure you've been given the proper instructions, and follow them carefully.

Changing Registry Item Values

Registry values come in a variety of flavors: text, hex, decimal, and binary. The value type is generally, but not always, connected to the data item type. You can change the value of an existing data item by double-clicking the item in the right pane to open its edit dialog.

Using Registration Files

Probably the most common use of .reg files is to restore a key you exported as a backup measure before hacking a registry key. This is an almost painless way to repair user-inflicted damage on the registry.

Software applications frequently have .reg files in their installation files group, and use them to register configuration information. Anyone can write a .reg file (the writing part is easy; it's the result of sending the file to the registry that's the dangerous part).

You can make use of .reg files to empower your administration of the registries on your system. Once you understand how they work and what they do, you can use them to control users, software settings, computer settings, or anything else that's stored in the registry.

Writing and using .reg files is a way to send registry changes to one or more computers on your system instead of opening the registry on each computer and making each change interactively. Such registry changes are extremely effective and are commonly used in the following circumstances:

- You want to exempt certain computers and users from domain-wide policies that have been imposed.

- You want to restrict certain users from being able to use specific features.

- You want to offer users the opportunity to tweak their systems.

While you have the power of group policies for your Windows Server 2003/XP/2000 computers, you can use .reg files to make registry changes to control user access and behavior on downlevel computers.

If you write applications, even if the code you write is for internal use only (as opposed to programming for a major software company), you can use .reg files to configure the registry for your program.

Architecture of a .reg File

Registration files are text files with a .reg extension, using the following format:

```
NameOfTool
blank line
[Registry path]
"DataItemName"=DataType:value
"DataItemName"=DataType:value
"DataItemName"=DataType:value
```

Name of Tool   The first line identifies the tool that's being used to carry out this procedure:

- For Windows Server 2003/2000/XP: Windows Registry Editor Version 5.00
- For all versions of Windows 9x/NT: REGEDIT4

A blank line follows the tool name line.

Registry Path   The registry path to the key that holds the values you're importing is enclosed in square brackets, with each level of the hierarchy separated by a backslash—for example, [HKEY_LOCAL_MACHINE\SOFTWARE\Policies\Microsoft\Windows\System]. You can have multiple registry paths in a registration file.

Note   *If the bottom of the hierarchy you enter in the .reg file doesn't exist in the current registry, you're creating a new subkey. The contents of registry files are sent to the registry in the order in which you entered them—if you're creating a new key and a subkey below that key, enter the lines in the right order.*

Data   The data you're sending to the registry is entered in the following manner:

```
"DataItemName"=DataItemType:DataItemValue
```

- The name of the data item is enclosed in quotation marks.
- An equal sign (=) immediately follows the name of the data item.
- The data item type immediately follows the equal sign and is followed by a colon (:).
- The data item value must be entered in the appropriate format (string, hex, decimal, or binary).

You can enter multiple data item lines for the same registry path; for example:

```
"GroupPolicyRefreshTime"=dword:00000014
"GroupPolicyRefreshTimeOffset"=dword:0000000f
```

The preceding two lines reflect hex entries for the data values: 00000014 is the hex equivalent of 20, and 0000000f is the hex equivalent of 15. If you're not comfortable with hex or other nonreadable data, restrict your .reg file creation efforts to registry data items that contain strings, or data items that use 0 and 1 to turn a policy/restriction off and on. The registry does not have a Boolean data type (it should). You'll be relieved to know that you can send that Boolean data to the registry via a DWORD (4 byte) or String (2 byte) item type in a .reg file, without worrying about entering the full string in your file. Just enter **1**, and when you look at the registry, you see 0x00000001(1).

Merging a Registration File

Registration files work by merging the contents of the .reg file with the registry, via Regedit.exe. There are three ways to send the contents of the file to the registry:

- Double-click the file (the default associated action for a .reg file is merge).
- Enter **Regedit filename.reg** at the command line.
- Choose File | Import from the Regedit menu bar.

 *If you want to run .reg files from the command line in quiet mode, or write batch files that merge .reg files without user intervention, use the Regedit command with the following syntax: **Regedit /s filename.reg**.*

The following actions occur when you send a .reg file to the registry:

- If the path in the file does not currently exist, it's added.
- If a data item does not currently exist, it's added (along with its value).
- If a data item does exist, its value is overwritten with the value in the .reg file.

Registration files work even if you've applied a group policy to disable registry editing tools (otherwise, software and the system couldn't manipulate the registry as needed).

You can distribute a .reg file via e-mail or have users copy it from a network sharepoint during logon (via a command in a logon script). Then you can give each user the option to use it.

Sample Registration File

As an example, here's the text of a .reg file that I merge into all the computers on my network. It adds the option to open a command window to the shortcut menu for folders. I prefer to open a Command Prompt window in a specific location instead of using the **CD** command to navigate through folders.

```
Windows Registry Editor Version 5.00

[HKEY_CLASSES_ROOT\Directory\shell\OpenNew]
@="Command Window Here"
[HKEY_CLASSES_ROOT\Directory\shell\OpenNew\Command]
@="cmd.exe /k cd %1"
```

To create the .reg file by changing a registry and exporting the key, perform the following actions in Regedit:

1. Select the HKEY_CLASSES_ROOT\Directory\shell key.

2. Create a new subkey named **OpenNew**.

3. Open the Default data item in the right pane, and make its value Command Window Here. (This Registry value represents the phrase that appears on the shortcut menu, so you can substitute a phrase of your own.)

4. Create a new subkey named Command under the new OpenNew subkey.

5. Open the Default item in the Command subkey and enter the value **cmd.exe /k cd %1**.

6. Select the OpenNew subkey and choose File | Export to create a .reg file that contains the new subkeys and their data.

If you have multiple drives on your computer, you can add a similar command for the shortcut menu that appears when you right-click a drive object in Windows Explorer or My Computer. The instructions are the same as those for creating the command for folders, with the following changes:

■ Use the HKEY_CLASSES_ROOT\Drive\shell key as the starting point.

■ Enter **cmd.exe /k** as the value of the Default item in the HKEY_CLASSES_ROOT\Drive\shell\OpenNew\Command subkey.

Export the HKEY_CLASSES_ROOT\Drive\shell key and distribute the .reg file to all users who would like this nifty tweak.

Deleting Registry Items with a .reg File

You can also use a .reg file to remove subkeys and data items. In fact, it's dangerously easy to do so.

■ To delete a subkey, enter a hyphen (minus sign) at the beginning of the key name.

■ To delete an individual data item, enter a hyphen instead of a value ("DataItemName"=-).

Registry Security

Working with security for registry keys is very similar to the security paradigm you have at your disposal with the NTFS file system. You can apply permissions to keys and subkeys by group or user, determine whether you want permissions to be inheritable, and make the whole hierarchy of permissions as granular as you wish. In other words, just like NTFS, every registry key has an Access Control List (ACL).

The default security levels for the registry are rather tight. Administrators have full access to the entire registry, but other users have full access only to the keys related to their own user accounts (which include HKEY_CURRENT_USER), as well as read-only access to the keys related to the computer and its installed software. Nevertheless, you may want to tinker with registry security in order to give or retract permissions on a user or group basis. This section covers the tasks related to setting permissions.

Understanding Permissions

The permissions you can apply to a registry key are available on two levels:

- Basic permissions, which are composites of specific permissions
- Specific permissions

The basic permissions are broad definitions, and they represent groupings of specific (more granular) permissions. For most keys, the basic permissions are Full Control and Read.

The specific permissions are described in Table 4-2. All the permissions in Table 4-2 are granted to users and groups who are given Full Control. Permissions that don't fall under the permissions for Read (marked with Yes in Table 4-2) are referred to as *special permissions*.

Permission	Description	Included in Read Permission?
Query Value	View the value of a data item	Yes
Set Value	Change the value of a data item	No
Create Subkey	Create a subkey	No
Enumerate Subkeys	View all subkeys	Yes
Notify	Receive or set audit notices	Yes
Create Link	Create a link to another key	No

Table 4-2. *Permissions Applied to Registry Keys*

Permission	Description	Included in Read Permission?
Delete	Remove the key (and subkeys)	No
Write DAC	Change the DAC permissions	No
Write Owner	Change the owner	No
Read Control	Read the ACL	Yes

Table 4-2.   _Permissions Applied to Registry Keys_ (continued)

Working with Permissions

To view or set permissions on a registry key (including the top-level subtrees), right-click the key and choose Permissions from the shortcut menu. The Permissions dialog for the key opens, resembling Figure 4-2.

As you select each user or group, you can see the permissions. Permissions that are grayed out are inherited from parent keys and can't be changed in this dialog.

Add Users or Groups to the Permissions List

You can add users or groups to the key's permissions list with the following steps:

1. Click Add to open the Select Users, Computers, or Groups dialog.

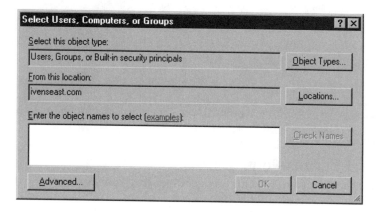

2. Click Locations, and select the computer or domain you want to use.

3. If you know the names, enter the users and/or groups you want to add, separating each name with a semicolon. If you don't know the names, click Advanced to set up search criteria and select names that match your search. When you are finished entering names, click OK.

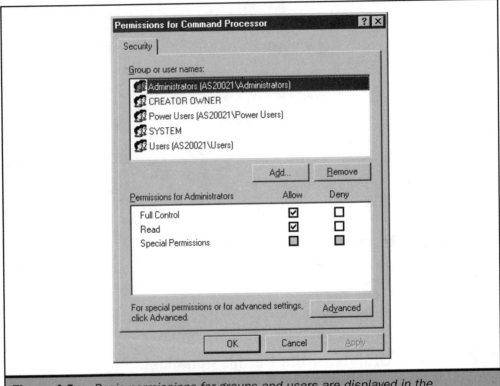

Figure 4-2.   *Basic permissions for groups and users are displayed in the Permissions dialog.*

4. Back in the Permissions dialog, select each new listing and assign Read or Full Control permission. (See the next section, "Set Special Permissions," if you don't want to use either of the two basic permissions.)

5. Click OK when you're finished setting permissions.

You can also remove a user or group in this dialog, by selecting the appropriate listing and clicking Remove.

Set Special Permissions

If you want to make permissions for any group or user more granular, you can set special permissions, using the following steps:

1. In the Permissions dialog, click Advanced to open the Advanced Security Settings dialog for the key.

2. Double-click the user or group for whom you want to set up special permissions (see Figure 4-3).

3. Under Permissions, select the Allow or Deny check box for each permission you want to allow or deny.

4. Set the inheritance by selecting one of the following options from the drop-down list in the Apply Onto field:

■ This key only

■ This key and subkeys

■ Subkeys only

5. Click OK to return to the Advanced Security Settings dialog. Configure permissions for another user/group, or click OK twice to close all dialogs.

Caution *Don't change any permissions for System, because you could cause problems for the operating system and installed applications.*

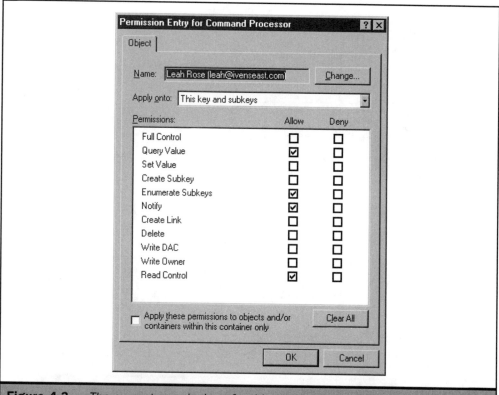

Figure 4-3. *The current permissions for this user were set by originally selecting the basic Read permissions.*

Change Ownership of a Key

The owner of a registry key can specify the users and groups that can manipulate that key, which gives an individual complete power. Taking ownership of a registry key is not a common task, and should only be performed by an administrator who is having a problem gaining access to the key (usually as a result of previously changing ACLs inappropriately). By default, for Windows Server 2003 computers, ownership is set as follows:

- For computers running as member servers, members of the local Administrators group.

- For computers acting as DCs, members of the Domain Administrators group.

To view or change ownership, right-click the key and choose Permissions from the shortcut menu. Click Advanced, and then click the Owner tab. As you can see in Figure 4-4,

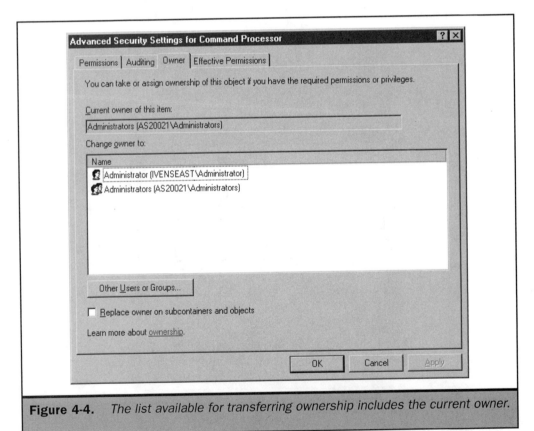

Figure 4-4. The list available for transferring ownership includes the current owner.

the Owner tab displays the current owner at the top of the dialog, and lists all the eligible users who could become owners.

You can transfer ownership to any name in the list. If you want to pick an owner other than the currently available Administrator groups, click Other Users Or Groups to open the Select User, Computer, or Group dialog. Choose the name you want to add to the list, and then return to the Owner tab and select that name. However, before giving ownership to a user or group, you must change the permissions so that the permission to Write Owner is allowed (giving the new owner the right to manipulate ownership).

Auditing the Registry

You may find a need to audit certain activities on the registry in an effort to troubleshoot a problem. Or, you may just suffer from terminal curiosity (that's not a pun) and have plenty of disk space available to record information to satisfy your curiosity.

You have a great deal of power and flexibility available when you audit registry activity; you can audit keys, users, groups, or any combination. Auditing registry activities involves three steps:

1. Enable auditing as a group policy.
2. Set auditing configuration options on the registry.
3. Check the audit log in the Event Viewer's Security log.

Enable Auditing

Before you can audit registry activity, you must enable auditing, which is disabled by default in Windows Server 2003. Auditing is enabled/disabled by group policy, and you can use a domain-based policy or a local policy to turn on the auditing feature, depending on the registry activity you want to audit.

Enable Auditing for the Domain   To enable registry auditing across the domain, open the Active Directory Users and Computers snap-in, and then take the following actions:

1. Open the Properties dialog for the domain.
2. Click the Group Policy tab.
3. Select the Default Domain Policy object and click Edit.
4. In the Group Policy console that opens, travel to Computer Configuration\ Windows Settings\Security Settings\Local Policies\Audit Policy.

5. Double-click the Audit object access listing in the details pane to open its Properties dialog.

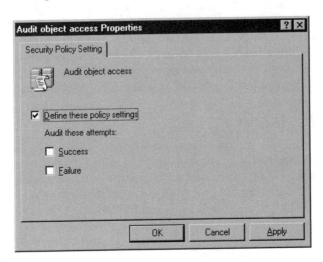

6. Enable the policy by selecting the Define These Policy Settings check box and opt to audit success, failure, or both.

 The registry audit policies also let you select success or failure for each type of registry access. This permits very selective filtering, avoiding the risk that the log file will grow to an enormous size.

Enable Auditing on a Local Computer   To enable registry auditing on a computer, follow these steps:

1. Open the Local Security Settings administrative tool.

2. In the console pane, expand Local Policies and select Audit Policy.

3. Double-click the Audit object access listing in the details pane, and select the actions you want to audit.

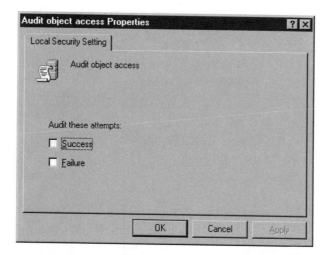

Set Audit Options in the Registry

After you've enabled auditing, you can specify the actions you want to audit. Open Regedit, right-click the parent key you want to use as the top of the auditing process (by default, auditing is inherited by subkeys), and choose Permissions from the shortcut menu. Click Advanced and move to the Auditing tab. Click Add to begin adding the users and groups you want to audit, using the following guidelines:

- If you're auditing in order to watch a particular person's activities, select that person.

- If you're auditing in order to see who's doing what on the registry, it's best to select the Everyone group.

- If you have a mixed agenda, select the appropriate groups and users.

As you select each user/group, select the actions you want to audit, as shown in Figure 4-5.

By default, auditing is performed on the current key and inherited by subkeys. You can alter the default behavior by selecting a different option from the Apply Onto drop-down list. The available options are: This Key Only, This Key And Subkeys, Subkeys Only.

Here are some tips for configuring your audit trail:

- Turning on auditing causes a performance hit. The more groups and users you add, and the more tasks you include in the audit, the more you affect performance.

- There's rarely a good reason to audit individuals for failures, because most of the time, a failure is due to a user's lack of permissions. If the user can't perform a task, there's no point in reporting it as an audited event (unless you have some compelling reason to prove that a user is trying to accomplish tasks in vain). If software applications are producing errors, and support personnel have suggested a problem with accessing registry data, audit SYSTEM for failures.

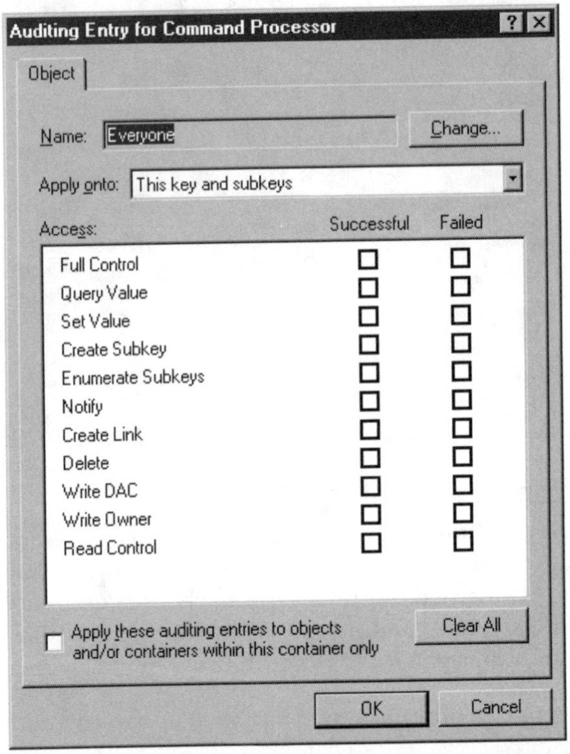

Figure 4-5.   *Select the action and result for each registry task you want to audit.*

■ Don't audit for success for common tasks that do no harm, such as querying a value. There's no particular reason to care, and the log becomes enormous.

Examine the Audit Log

Auditing is a security event, so the results of auditing are in the Security log of the Event Viewer. Open the Event Viewer and select the Security log to inspect the audited events.

Reg.exe

Reg.exe is a robust and multifaceted command-line tool that you can use to manipulate registry entries. Like the **net** command, reg.exe requires a second command, for instance **reg add**. The program works for local and remote registries. However, when you use this tool against a remote registry, you can only work with HKEY_LOCAL_MACHINE and HKEY_CURRENT_USER.

General Guidelines for Reg.exe

Some general rules and guidelines apply for the **reg** commands, and I'll describe them here rather than repeat them for each command.

When you enter a key or subkey name, you must enter the complete key path, starting with the subtree. However, you can abbreviate the subtree names as follows:

Abbreviation	Subtree
HKCR	HKEY_CLASSES_ROOT
HKLM	HKEY_LOCAL_MACHINE
HKCU	HKEY_CURRENT_USER
HKCC	HKEY_CURRENT_CONFIGURATION

In addition, the following tips should be helpful:

- Case is irrelevant for existing keys in the path.
- The name of a new key is case sensitive.
- Key names that contain spaces must be enclosed in quotation marks.
- Case is irrelevant for existing data items.
- The name of a new data item is case sensitive, as is its value.

"Case sensitive" means the data is written to the registry as you enter it, using the capitalization scheme you prefer. The registry itself usually doesn't care, because with few exceptions, registry lookups are not case sensitive for keys, data items, or values. However, you may prefer to enter NewFeatureName instead of newfeaturename because the capitalization makes it easier to read the entry.

Reg Add

Use the **reg add** command to add a key or a data item to the registry (or both at once). The syntax is:

reg add [*Machine*\]*KeyName* [**/v** *ValueName* | **/ve**] [**/t** *Type*] [**/s** *Separator*] [**/d** *Data*] [**/f**]

where:

Machine is the name of a remote computer. Omit this parameter if you're working on the local machine. *KeyName* is the name of the key where the new entry is located, or the name of a new key you're adding to the registry. If you're adding a key, you can omit all other parameters (covered next). For example, if you have an existing key named HKEY_CURRENT_USER\Software\CompanyDatabase and you want to add a subkey named ColorScheme, enter the following command:

```
reg add HKCU\Software\ CompanyDatabase\ColorScheme
```

The system returns the message "The operation completed successfully."

 Note   *If you use a space in a name without using quotation marks, the system assumes that anything after the first word is a parameter and issues an error message. The error message says: "To [sic] many command-line parameters."*

The following parameters are used if you're entering a new data item. To enter both a new key and a new data item at the same time, merely enter the name of the new key at the end of the registry path.

/v *ValueName* is the name of the new data item. If the name contains spaces, use quotation marks around the string.

/ve specifies a null value.

/t *Type* specifies the data type for the new value. If you omit this parameter, the data type is assumed to be REG_SZ.

/s *Separator* specifies the character you want to use as the separator for multiple data strings (for REG_MULTI_SZ data types).

/d *Data* is the data you want to assign to the data item you're adding.

/f forces an overwrite of the value of an existing entry.

Reg Delete

Use the **reg delete** command to remove subkeys or data items (or both) from the registry. The syntax is:

reg delete [*Machine*\]*KeyName* [**/v** *ValueName* [**/va**] [**/f**]

where:

Machine is the name of a remote computer. Omit the parameter if you're working on the local registry.

KeyName is the target subkey for the entry (or the subkey you want to delete). Use the complete path.

/v *ValueName* deletes the data item named in the *ValueName* variable. Use quotation marks around names with spaces.

/va deletes all the data items in the target subkey.

/ve deletes a null data item.

/f forces the delete action without confirmation.

Reg Copy

Use the **reg copy** command to copy a registry entry to a new location in the local or remote registry. The syntax is:

reg copy [*Machine*\]*SourceKey* [*Machine*\]*DestinationKey* [**/s**] [**/f**]

where:

Machine\]*SourceKey* is the computer name and registry path for the source computer. Omit the machine parameter if the source is the local computer.

Machine\]*DestinationKey* is the computer name and registry path for the target computer. Omit the machine parameter if the target is the local computer.

/s copies all subkeys beneath the last key in the path, along with the data items contained in those subkeys.

/f forces the copy without prompting the user for confirmation.

Reg Compare

Use the **reg compare** command to compare a registry entry with another registry entry on the local or remote computer. The syntax is:

reg compare [*Machine*\]*KeyName1* [*Machine*\]*KeyName2* [**/v** *ValueName*] [**/s**] [Output]

where:

Machine is the name of the computer. Skip this parameter for a local computer.

KeyName1, KeyName2 specifies the complete registry path for both the first and second subkeys.

/v *ValueName* compares the value of the data item specified by *ValueName* (use quotation marks around data items with spaces).

/s compares all subkeys and their data items.

Output takes one of the following arguments:

- **/oa** outputs all differences and matches.
- **/od** outputs only differences.
- **/os** outputs only matches.
- **/on** specifies no output.

The system responds with one of the following return codes:

- **0**   The compare was successful, and the result compared is identical.
- **1**   The compare failed.
- **2**   The compare was successful, and the result compared is different.

Reg Export

Use the **reg export** command to export a registry entry to a file. The command matches the action of choosing Registry | Export Registry File while working in Regedit. This command only works against the local registry. The syntax is:

reg export *KeyName FileName* [**/y**]

where:

KeyName is the full path to the key you want to export.

FileName is the name of the .reg file to which you're exporting the key.

/y overwrites an existing file with the name *FileName* without asking you to confirm.

Reg Import

Use the **reg import** command to import a registry entry from a registry file. The syntax is:

reg import *FileName*

where

FileName is the name of the .reg file you're importing.

This command-line tool provides the same function as choosing Registry | Import File from Regedit, or double-clicking a .reg file.

Reg Save

Use the **reg save** command to save a key to a hive file. The syntax is:

reg save *Machine KeyName FileName* [**/y**]

where:

Machine is the name of the remote computer (omit the parameter for the local computer).

KeyName is the full path to the key.

FileName is the target file (with an .hiv extension).

/y overwrites an existing file with the same filename, without asking you to confirm the overwrite.

Reg Restore

Use the **reg restore** command to restore a key from an HIV file created by the **reg save** command. The syntax is:

reg restore [*Machine*\] *KeyName FileName*

where:

Machine is the name of the remote computer (omit the parameter for the local computer).

KeyName is the full path to the target key.

FileName is the name of the file you saved and now want to restore.

Reg Load

Use the **reg load** command to load a hive file (created with the **reg save** command) into a different part of the registry. This is useful if you're troubleshooting registry entries. The syntax is:

reg load [*Machine*\] *KeyName FileName*

where:

Machine is the name of the remote computer (omit this parameter for the local computer).

KeyName is the full path to the registry location you want to use to hold the hive.

FileName is the name of the hive.

 Note   *The key is not persistent, and it disappears when you reboot the computer.*

Reg Unload

Use the **reg unload** command to remove the hive you loaded with the **reg load** command. The syntax is:

Reg unload *Machine KeyName*

where:

Machine is the name of the remote computer (omit this parameter for the local computer).

KeyName is the full path to the registry location that is holding the file you loaded.

Reg Query

Use the **reg query** command to gain information about an entry or multiple entries in a key or subkey. The syntax is:

reg query *Machine KeyName* [{**/v** *ValueName* | **/ve**}] [**/s**][**/se** *Separator*] [**/f** *Data*] [{**/k** | **/d**}] [**/c**] [**/e**] [**/t** *Type*] [**/z**]

where:

Machine is the name of the remote computer (omit this parameter for the local computer).

KeyName is the full path to the key you're querying.

/v *ValueName* is the registry value being queried. If omitted, all the values in *KeyName* are returned. *ValueName* is optional if the **/f** option is used.

/ve queries for value names that are empty.

/s queries all subkeys and value names.

/se *Separator* specifies the value separator you want to look for in values of type REG_MULTI_SZ. If *Separator* is not specified, the system uses \0.

Regmon

A colleague on one of the magazines I write for (*Windows & .NET Magazine*) is a brilliant operating system expert. For years (since Windows NT), I've been using a utility he wrote called Regmon, which lets me spy on registry access by applications in real time.

You can set filters to limit the type of information the program reports, and you can select a listing and jump right to the registry subkey referenced in that listing. This is a cool way to track the registry items that are added during installation of software. Start regmon.exe before the install program begins copying files and writing registry keys, and you'll know everything that happened to the registry. Save the results, and then examine those entries after you've uninstalled the software. Since most uninstall procedures fail to get rid of all the registry information that was written, you can clean up your registry manually.

Regmon is free, and you can download it from www.sysinternals.com. You'll find all sorts of nifty utilities on the web site in addition to this one. This site is an administrator's toy store.

The Complete Reference

Chapter 5

Booting

The most frustrating call for help an IT professional receives is the one from a user who starts the conversation with the words "my computer won't start." Sometimes the words should be taken literally, because nothing happens when the user presses the power button (and how many times have you investigated that problem to find the plug on the floor instead of in the wall?). Most of the time, however, something untoward happened during the startup process, either during the computer's POST or during the startup procedures for the operating system.

It's much easier to diagnose and cure the problem (if it's curable) if you understand the boot process, and that's what this chapter is about.

The phrase "boot failure" is used to describe both machine and operating system problems. Back in the "old days," when we were booting into MS-DOS, the boot process was almost entirely comprised of hardware issues. The POST took a lot longer than the operating system startup, and the hardware was the source of most boot failure problems. After the POST, DOS just showed up, announcing its arrival with a blinking cursor at a command prompt. The only moment of panic we had was caused by the display of the message "non-system disk or disk error," which more often than not was caused by the presence of a floppy disk.

That's an exaggeration of course, because DOS didn't just accidentally or magically show up—we formatted the drive to place system files (the most important was io.sys) on the boot sector. One of the innovations that appeared with DOS version 5 was the fact that only a pointer to io.sys was put on the master boot sector, while the file itself was located on the boot partition (outside of the master boot sector). This new paradigm made it possible for other operating systems to modify the master boot sector by installing their own pointers to their own system startup files. Windows Server 2003 (and Windows 2000/Windows NT) use that pattern.

Hardware Bootup

This book is about Windows Server 2003, so I'm not going to spend a lot of time discussing the hardware side of the boot process. However, the interdependency between today's versions of Windows and the system's hardware has blurred some of the previous distinctions between hardware boot and operating system boot, so it's worth a moment of time to explain the hardware, because of the reliance of Windows on hardware.

Computer hardware has become more reliable over the years, and the BIOS features have become much more robust. This means, of course, that you stand a much better chance of facing an operating system problem than a hardware component problem when a system fails to boot.

The one piece of computer hardware that seems to be lacking in the category of "better and more robust design" is the power supply. In the decades I've been building, maintaining, and supporting computers, I have to say that I've encountered more hardware problems that were due to power supply problems than from any other component. When a power supply starts to die, it can take a lot of other components with it. Because the power supply is actually a converter, when it doesn't do its job properly it can damage other components. Some years ago, at a seminar given by a major manufacturer on the subject of "hot swapping" (it was a futuristic concept at the time), I remember long discussions among the attending consultants about the failure of any manufacturer to produce a power supply that would be trouble-free. The host company told us "nobody wants to pay for it."

I'm not the only consultant/administrator who has learned to keep an eye and ear tuned for power supply problems. Focus your eye on the back fan, and make sure you clean off the dust and grease. In fact, periodically open the box and vacuum the interior. Dust causes a reduction in air flow, and a reduction in air flow causes power supply failures.

Focus your ear on the sound of the power supply when a computer is turned on— if you hear a continuous sound that reminds you of a jet engine, the power supply is in trouble. Replace it before its problems damage other components.

POST

Immediately after you turn on a computer, the processor handles the BIOS control of the system. The BIOS starts with POST, checking video first, followed by memory. Then it loads the information it has about the drives and checks them. Following that is a date and time check, and then a port check. All the information the BIOS uses is in the computer's CMOS (Complementary Metal Oxide Semiconductor), which is powered by its own battery.

The POST covers more than a check for the existence of hardware; it also checks the hardware settings. Today, hard drive settings are written automatically when you install the drive, and those of you who never had to enter settings for cylinders, heads, landing zones, and bad sectors probably don't realize why those of us who are old-timers consider that fact a miracle.

When the BIOS checks drive settings, if it finds a SCSI controller, it launches the controller's own configuration checkup. SCSI controller settings are not configured or kept in the CMOS settings. If the SCSI controller has a problem, it reports it independently of any problems found and reported by the BIOS.

BIOS errors are reported to the screen, along with beeps to get your attention. Some BIOS errors are displayed as numbers, and at one time all BIOS manufacturers used the same numbers (those used by IBM), but that's no longer true, so you need the documentation that came with your computer to interpret them. Luckily, today you're far more likely to see text instead of numbers, such as "hard drive controller failure," or the amusing "Keyboard error, press F1 to continue."

Memory Errors

In the old days, memory components had an extra chip called a "parity chip," and part of the BIOS test was a parity test. Memory components no longer include parity checking, because it's not really necessary any more—memory manufacturing has advanced to the point where it's highly unusual to see failure.

However, after you add memory to a machine, it's common to see a memory error message during the next boot. The message may use terms such as "mismatched memory information," which means the amount of memory recorded in CMOS doesn't match the amount of memory found during bootup.

Resolve this problem by restarting the computer and entering the BIOS setup program. It's been my experience that doing this jump-starts the solution, because the correct memory count automatically appears in the BIOS setup screen. Just exit the BIOS setup program. The error message you saw is actually a confirmation that the system sees the memory you installed, but it didn't match the total recorded in CMOS. Entering the setup program caused the system to check the memory count and adjust it, matching the physical memory total.

If you add memory to a computer, and the RAM count during bootup doesn't match the new total, and you don't see an error message about a mismatched memory count, you have a more serious problem: the system didn't find the new memory. This is almost always caused by an error in physically inserting the memory, such as using the wrong slot, or not inserting the teeth properly. However, I've also seen this occur when the wrong memory type was inserted (somebody inserted DRAM in an older computer with EDO), or the motherboard doesn't like mixing SIMMs and DIMMs, or doesn't like mixed memory speeds. Some motherboards require a change in dip switches or jumper configuration (although that's disappearing). You must check the documentation for the motherboard before adding memory to a computer.

Drive Errors

If you see a hard drive error during POST, you have a serious problem. Of course, you don't panic, because you back up every night, right? Actually, I've found that at least half the time the problem is the controller, not the drive, and replacing the controller lets the drive boot normally, with all data intact. If an embedded controller dies, you don't have to buy a new motherboard, because you can buy a controller card. Check the documentation for the motherboard to see the tasks required to make the BIOS see the card instead of looking for the embedded chip.

If the problem is indeed the drive, you have more work to do than merely replacing a controller. In addition to replacing the hardware, you have to reinstall the operating system and applications, and restore the last backup.

Sometimes it's a bit difficult to tell whether the hard drive problem is a hardware problem or an operating system problem, because the point at which the BIOS turns the boot process over to the hard drive is also the point at which the operating system is beginning its own boot process. If the operating system boot files can't be opened, the problem could be a corrupt file (an operating system problem), or a missing file (which could be a hardware problem if the drive is corrupt). To identify the source of the problem, use a bootable floppy to see whether you can access the hard drive.

SCSI Errors

To gain all the advantages of SCSI, you have to put up with some of the annoyances (although it's my opinion that the scales definitely tip in favor of using SCSI, especially on servers). SCSI carries some additional overhead, including the use of independent BIOS programs, which means you have to worry about additional BIOS settings. In this section I'll discuss some of the SCSI boot problems I've encountered over the years.

One common problem is improper termination when an administrator adds additional SCSI devices to a machine. Also, remember that every device in a SCSI chain has to have its own unique SCSI address. If you add a second SCSI controller, avoid conflicts by checking the IRQ, I/O, and DMA settings.

Many SCSI controllers send a message to the screen at the end of the BIOS boot, using text that indicates that the BIOS has been installed successfully. It's important to realize that the message refers to the controller, not to the attached devices. If the system hangs after the SCSI BIOS loads, it means the controller is fine, but the drive isn't. Don't panic, especially if you've just installed the drive, because the drive may be fine. Check the following:

- Make sure the SCSI chain is terminated properly.

- Make sure you configured the SCSI drive to "spin up" on power-up, not on detection. Drives that are configured to spin up on detection often time out and then won't respond when the power arrives. Check your SCSI documentation to see whether this is a BIOS setting or a jumper change.

- Make sure the boot drive is set to drive 0.

I've seen some SCSI boot problems that were related to the relationship between the hardware and the operating system. For example, when you install the operating system, it expects to find the SCSI settings that existed at that time whenever you start the OS. If you make a change in SCSI settings, the operating system may not boot. One common cause of this is the enabled/disabled setting for the SCSI BIOS. Windows can co-exist with SCSI controllers either way: with the SCSI BIOS enabled or disabled. Windows is capable of managing all the interaction between the controller and the operating system, but when you tell Windows which way to behave during installation, you can't change your mind later (unless you want to reinstall the operating system).

Operating System Boot

During installation, the Windows Server 2003 Setup program placed data on the first sector of your computer's primary partition (the boot sector). The data is the Master Boot Record (MBR), and it holds executable instructions on an *x*86 computer. In addition to the executable instructions, the MBR has a table with up to four entries, defining the locations of the primary partitions on the disk. The installation program also copied the two files that initiate the Windows Server 2003 boot sequence (Ntldr and Ntdetect.com)

Understanding Partition Tables

The reason the MBR has a partition table that has a maximum of four entries is that a hard drive can only contain four primary partitions. However, to provide more logical drives, you can use extended partitions. Extended partitions can be nested, so in theory the number of logical drives you can have on a computer is unlimited.

Every partition has a partition table, containing the following fields:

- Boot flag (which contains a logical value indicating bootable/not bootable)
- Starting side
- Starting cylinder
- Starting sector
- System indicator (specifies the type of file system)
- Ending side
- Ending cylinder
- Ending sector
- Relative sectors
- Number of sectors

to the root directory of the boot drive, and placed Boot.ini, the file that contains startup options, on the root directory of the boot drive. (See the section "About Boot.ini" later in this chapter.)

Note *If the boot sector that's targeted by Windows Server 2003 was previously formatted for DOS (Windows 9x qualifies as DOS), Setup copies the existing contents of the boot sector to a file named bootsect.dos, and places it in the root directory of the boot drive. This permits dual-boots with Windows 9x.*

MBR Code Executes

As the last step of the BIOS boot process, your computer reads the MBR into memory and then transfers control to that MBR code. The executable code searches the primary partition table for a flag on a partition that indicates that the partition is bootable. When the MBR finds the first bootable partition, it reads the first sector of the partition, which is the boot sector.

The Windows Server 2003 startup files are on the system partition, and the operating system files are on the boot partition, with the following details:

- The system partition holds hardware-specific files that are needed to boot Windows Server 2003, including the MBR. On *x86* machines this must be a primary partition that's marked active. It's always drive 0, because that's the drive the BIOS accesses to turn the boot process over to the MBR.

■ The boot partition holds the operating system files, the %SystemRoot% directory. The support files (\%SystemRoot%\System) must also be on the boot partition.

It's not necessary to make the system partition and the boot partition the same partition, although that's the common approach.

Windows Server 2003 Startup Files Execute

The boot-sector code reads Ntldr into memory to start the operating system boot process. Ntldr contains read-only NTFS and FAT code. It starts running in real mode, and its first job is to switch the system to a form of protected mode. This first instance of protected mode cannot perform physical-to-virtual translations for hardware protection—that feature becomes available when the operating system has finished booting.

All the physical memory is available to the operating system, and the computer is operating as a 32-bit machine. Ntldr enables paging and creates the page tables. Next, it reads Boot.ini from the root directory and, if called for, displays the boot selection menu on the monitor. If Ntldr is either missing or corrupt, you'll see this error message:

```
Ntldr is missing.
Press CTRL-ALT-DEL to restart.
```

Don't bother using the suggested sequence; it just restarts the cycle that results in the same error message. You must replace Ntldr. Boot with your bootable floppy (see "Creating a Bootable Floppy Disk" later in this chapter).

■ If Ntldr is missing, copy it from the floppy disk to the root directory of the boot drive (usually C:).

■ If Ntldr exists on the hard drive, it's probably corrupted. To replace it, you must first change the read-only attribute.

If you don't have a bootable floppy, you'll have to start the Windows Server 2003 Setup program from the CD, and then choose Repair. See Chapter 26 for information about recovering a failed operating system.

Boot Selection Menu Displays

If the computer is dual-booting, the boot selection menu appears, displaying the operating system choices available on the computer. If the user doesn't make a selection before the specified time for choosing an operating system elapses, the default operating system (which is usually Windows Server 2003) starts.

Using an arrow key to move through the selections stops the countdown clock, giving users plenty of time to make a decision.

Ntdetect Launches

Ntldr launches Ntdetect.com. Ntdetect queries the system's BIOS for device and configuration information. The information Ntdetect gathers is sent to the registry and placed in the subkeys under HKEY_LOCAL_MACHINE\Hardware\Description.

If there's a problem with Ntdetect (it's either missing or corrupt), you probably won't see an error message. Instead, the boot process may just stop. The cure for a missing or corrupt Ntdetect.com is to replace it. Use a bootable floppy disk to boot your computer, and copy Ntdetect from that floppy disk to the root directory of your hard drive.

Ntoskrnl Runs and HAL Is Loaded

After Ntdetect finishes its hardware-checking routines, it turns the operating system boot process back to Ntldr, which launches Ntoskrnl.exe and loads Hal.dll (both files are in the \%SystemRoot%\system32 directory).

Ntoskrnl.exe contains the kernel and executive subsystems. This is the core file for the kernel-mode component of Windows Server 2003. It contains the Executive, the Kernel, the Cache Manager, the Memory Manager, the Scheduler, the Security Reference Monitor, and more. Ntoskrnl.exe is the file that really gets Windows Server 2003 running.

In order for hardware to interact with the operating system, Ntoskrnl.exe needs the Hal.dll, which has the code that permits that interaction (the filename stands for Hardware Abstraction Layer).

Sometimes you may see an error that indicates a problem with Ntoskrnl.exe, but the error is frequently spurious, and is caused by the fact that the directory referenced in Boot.ini doesn't match the name of the directory into which the Windows Server 2003 system files were installed. This generally means that someone renamed the %SystemRoot% directory, or created a new directory and moved the Windows Server 2003 files into it. Move the files back to the location specified in Boot.ini. (On the other hand, it could mean that someone edited Boot.ini, in which case you need to correct that error.)

Drivers and Services Load

Ntldr now loads the low-level system services and device drivers, but the services are not initialized—that occurs later. This is the end of the boot sequence, and the process that starts at this point is called the *load sequence,* or the *kernel phase.*

Ntldr has a pecking order for loading system services and devices drivers. When you install Windows Server 2003, the drivers that match your equipment aren't the only drivers copied to your computer. Every driver known to any Microsoft programmer has an entry in the registry. Open the registry and go to HKEY_LOCAL_MACHINE\System\CurrentControlSet\Services to see a very long list of services and device drivers. Select any subkey and look at the REG_DWORD data item named Start. The data is a hex entry and it ends with a number in parentheses. That number gives Ntldr its pecking order:

- The data value (0) means the service is loaded during the kernel load phase.
- The data value (1) means the service is loaded during the kernel initialization phase (the next phase).
- The data value (2) means the service is loaded during the services load phase.
- The data value (3) means the service is enabled, but not initialized (the service requires a manual startup, which you perform in the Services snap-in).
- The data value (4) means the service is not enabled.

Operating System Loads

Ntoskrnl.exe begins to load the operating system. The Windows Server 2003 kernel is initialized and subsystems are loaded and initialized, providing the basic systems that are needed to complete the task of loading the operating system. The boot drivers that were loaded earlier by Ntldr are now initialized, followed by initialization of the rest of the drivers and services.

When the first-level drivers are initialized, you may encounter a problem, usually in the form of a STOP on a Blue Screen of Death. This almost always occurs during the first boot after you've updated a driver. Ntoskrnl initializes the driver, and the operating system balks.

Use the Advanced Menu options to load the Last Known Good Configuration (see the section "The Advanced Options Menu" later in this chapter). Then either obtain a better driver from the manufacturer or stick with the previous driver.

Sans a driver error, the Windows Server 2003 kernel and executive systems are now operational. The Session Manager Subsystem (Smss.exe) sets up the user environment. Information in the registry is checked, and the remaining drivers and software that require loading are loaded. The kernel loads Kernel32.dll, Gdi32.dll, and User32.dll, which provide the Win32 API services that client programs require.

The Computer Logs On

While the kernel is loading and initializing drivers, the computer logs on to the domain. Using its machine account (a unique name, and its own password), the computer opens a secure channel (sometimes called a *clear channel*) to a domain controller. This all occurs before the user logon features are available.

Machine accounts are used between client computers, member servers, and domain controllers. Within each domain, the same thing occurs among multiple domain controllers. Computers use the secure channel to exchange the information necessary for authentication and authorization functions. Machine accounts enhance the security of your network, making sure that a computer attempting to send sensitive information is really a member of the domain.

As an additional security feature, computers (like users in a security-conscious network configuration) have to change their passwords periodically. By default, in Windows Server 2003, the password change interval is set for 30 days. When it's time to change the password, the computer generates a new password and sends it through the secure channel (which it accessed using its previous password) to the nearest DC. Thereafter, the computer must use the new password to access a secure channel.

The DC updates its database and immediately replicates the computer password change to the other DCs in the domain. Computer account passwords are flagged as *Announce Immediately* events, meaning they don't wait for the next scheduled DC replication.

Sometimes this causes some serious performance hits. If many (or all) of the computers in your domain have passwords that elapse on the same day, the work the DCs have to do immediately can slow down other important DC tasks (such as authenticating users, or running scheduled replications). It's even worse if you have a DC that's providing other services (such as acting as a DNS server).

> **Note** *If you're upgrading to Windows Server 2003 from Windows NT, one thing to be grateful for is that the default password time-to-live of 30 days is a lot less onerous for the DCs than is the Windows NT default of 7 days. It wasn't until Service Pack 4 for NT that Microsoft even provided tools and registry keys to let you manage computer password changes.*

On the other hand, you may feel the default settings for secure channel communications aren't as strong as they could be—you can enhance security for this communication function if you need to (although there's a trade-off in terms of performance).

Windows Server 2003 provides a way for you to change security policy settings to manage computer passwords. You can change the way machine passwords are managed for the domain, for an OU, or for an individual computer (although that would be uncommon, because it's not efficient to try to improve performance by configuring one computer at a time).

Change Machine Password Settings for Domains and OUs

To change the way machine accounts manage passwords on a domain or in an OU, follow these steps:

1. On a DC, open Active Directory Users and Computers, and right-click the domain object or the OU object.

2. Choose Properties from the shortcut menu, and move to the Group Policy tab.

3. For a domain, select Default Domain Policy and click Edit.

4. For an OU, click New, then click Edit (unless you've already added a Group Policy, in which case, select it and click Edit).

5. Expand the console tree to Computer Configuration\Windows Settings\ Security Settings\Local Policies\Security Options.

Dual-boot Computers and Computer Passwords

If you're dual-booting a computer, you should be aware that Windows sees each installation as a separate computer, and a separate machine account. Each installation generates its own unique password.

You must create a unique computer name for each version of Windows in a dual-booting computer; otherwise, the name/password combination fails when the computer attempts to create a secure channel for logging on to the domain.

In the details pane, select the policy you want to use to change the configuration for machine accounts. For computers that are not domain controllers, the configuration options are those that are labeled Domain Member; for computers that are DCs, the options are those labeled Domain Controller (see Figure 5-1).

Member Computer Policies

Several group policies are available for changing the way member computers manage their machine accounts, and their communications with the DC.

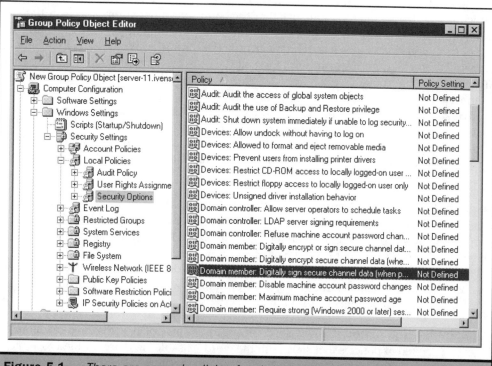

Figure 5-1. *There are several policies for changing the way machine accounts manage passwords and secure communications.*

Digitally Encrypt or Sign Secure Channel Data (Always)   This policy is not enabled by default, but if you have computers in an OU, or an individual computer, for which you want to enable this policy, double-click the listing and select the Enable radio button. It's almost never necessary to enable this policy, because the policy Digitally encrypt or sign secure channel data (when possible) is enabled by default (that policy is discussed next). If digitally encrypted or signed channel data is always possible, then data will always be encrypted. You should take the following facts into consideration before deciding to enable this policy:

- Logon information that's transmitted over the secure channel is always encrypted, even if all other traffic across the secure channel isn't.

- The secure channel traffic managed by this policy is only the traffic initiated by the domain member computer.

- You cannot enable this policy unless all the domain controllers on the domain are running Windows NT 4 Service Pack 6 or higher.

- If you enable this policy, the policy Digitally sign secure channel data (when possible) is also assumed to be enabled (irrespective of its setting).

Digitally Encrypt or Sign Secure Channel Data (When Possible)   This setting, which is enabled by default, specifies that the computer must attempt to negotiate encryption for all the traffic it initiates over the secure channel. If the domain controller supports encryption of all secure channel traffic (DCs running Windows NT 4.0 Service Pack 6 or higher support encryption), then all the traffic is encrypted. If the DC doesn't support encryption of all traffic, only logon information that's sent over the secure channel is encrypted.

I cannot think of a single reason (or excuse) for disabling this policy. Not only would that action substantially lower the security of your network, but it may interfere with applications that use the secure channel, because many API calls in applications written for Windows Server 2003/Windows 2000 require that the secure channel be encrypted or signed.

Digitally Sign Secure Channel Data (When Possible)   This policy, which is enabled by default, specifies that the computer attempts to negotiate signing for all the traffic it initiates over the secure channel. As long as the DC supports signing of secure channel traffic (DCs running NT4 SP6 or higher do), all secure channel traffic is signed.

Signing differs from encryption in that encryption is designed to stop outsiders from reading data that's passed through the secure channel, whereas signing is designed to stop outsiders from tampering with the data.

Disable Machine Account Password Changes   This policy is disabled by default (I get so annoyed at policies that start with the word "disable" and are enabled to avoid disabling something). If you enable the policy, you're disabling the security inherent in password changes, because you're telling the computers to stop changing their passwords. This means a hacker who found some way to break the password has permanent access to the secure channel data initiated by the computer.

Some administrators enable this policy because a computer is denied access to the domain. In every case, the computer was dual-booting and the administrator didn't realize that each Windows installation requires a discrete computer name in order to create a machine account (discussed earlier in this chapter).

Maximum Machine Account Password Age   Double-click this policy to change the default setting for the interval set for creating a new password. The policy is labeled "not defined" but the truth is that it's defined as 30 days. To change the interval between password changes, select Define the Policy Setting, and specify the new interval, in days.

You can use this policy to reduce the strain on the DCs. Most of the time, this isn't necessary (or advisable), but if you rolled out a new Windows Server 2003 domain, it's possible that all the computers that log on to the domain now have the same password expiration date. For most of my clients, that means hundreds of computers trying to notify the DCs of a new password, followed by instant replication of each password to the other DCs. For many of you, the numbers are in the thousands.

 To stagger the workload for the DC, it's a good idea to make this change on an OU basis, setting a different interval for each OU.

Require Strong (Windows 2000 or Later) Session Key   This setting, disabled by default, specifies whether 128-bit key strength is required for encrypted secure channel data. You cannot enable this setting unless all the domain controllers are running Windows 2000 or Windows Server 2003.

Domain Controller Policy

For domain controllers, only one policy is available for configuring the traffic across the secure channel: Refuse machine account password changes. The policy is disabled by default, and if you enable it, the DCs will refuse to accept machine account password changes. I cannot think of a single reason to enable this policy (and, in fact, I can't think of a reason to include the policy in the GPE, but probably some administrator had some weird problem and the result was to include this policy).

Set Individual Computer Password Policies

You can make any of the member computer policy changes on a single Windows Server 2003 computer, using the following steps:

1. Open Local Security Policy from the Administrative Tools menu.
2. Expand the console tree to Local Policies\Security Options.

3. In the details pane, select the domain member policy you want to change for this computer.

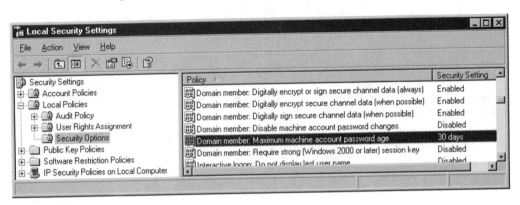

Logon Services Load

The next step in operating system startup is that the Win32 subsystem launches Winlogon.exe, which sends the logon dialog box to the screen, and loads the Local Security Authority (Lsass.exe).

The logon process begins, so enter a username and password in the Log On To Windows dialog. If no error occurs, the system logs you on and you can go to work. At this point you've completed a Windows Server 2003 startup.

About Boot.ini

The contents of the onscreen menu, if one appears, are determined by Boot.ini. However, the role of Boot.ini extends beyond presenting a menu of choices for users. This file is an important element in the machinery that controls the operating system boot process.

Boot.ini Contents

Boot.ini is a text file that holds the information needed to complete the boot process. You can edit the file in any text editor (the file is read-only and hidden, so you must change the attributes before you can save your edits—don't forget to change the attributes back when you've finished editing).

Like any .ini file, each section of the file is headed by a section title enclosed in brackets. The information in the file is created during installation of the operating system, so it's specific to the computer. The file has two sections:

- [boot loader]
- [operating systems]

The [boot loader] section contains the timeout specification along with the path to the default operating system. The timeout specification is the amount of time, in seconds, during which the user can make a selection from the onscreen menu. By default, the timeout duration is 30 seconds, and the user sees a countdown to 0 on the screen. The default operating system loads if the user fails to make a choice within that time.

You can change the default operating system and the length of the countdown without editing Boot.ini:

1. Open the System applet in Control Panel (the quick method is to right-click My Computer and choose Properties).

2. Move to the Advanced tab.

3. In the Startup and Recovery section, click Settings to access the fields for changing the default OS or the time specification for the display of the onscreen menu (see Figure 5-2).

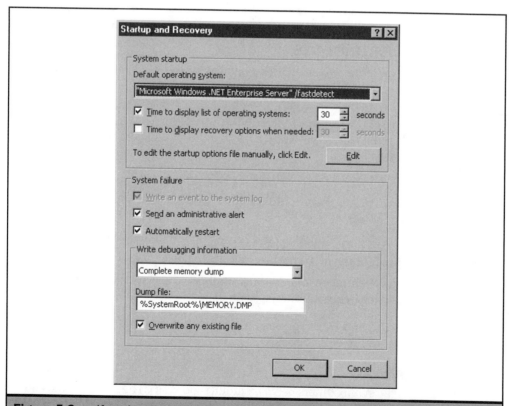

Figure 5-2.   *If you're dual-booting, you can change the way the boot menu works.*

If there aren't any choices because only one operating system exists, and you haven't preloaded the Recovery Console, Windows Server 2003 doesn't bother to display the menu.

The [operating systems] section contains the path(s) to the operating system(s) installed on the computer. In *x86*-based computers, each path is entered on its own line. The format of the information is based on the conventions in the Advanced RISC Computing (ARC) specifications.

Text strings enclosed by quotation marks indicate the text that displays in the onscreen menu. For example, here's the Boot.ini file that was automatically placed on the root of the boot drive during installation of Windows Server 2003 on a new drive:

```
[boot loader]
timeout=30
default=multi(0)disk(0)rdisk(0)partition(1)\WINDOWS
[operating systems]
multi(0)disk(0)rdisk(0)partition(1)\WINDOWS="Windows Server 2003" /fastdetect
```

x86 ARC Path Statements

On *x86* computers, there are two structures available for the ARC path—a line that begins with multi() or a line that begins with scsi():

```
multi(A)disk(B)rdisk(C)partition(D)\<%SystemRoot%>
scsi(A)disk(B)rdisk(C)partition(D)\<%SystemRoot%>
```

where:

- **A** is the ordinal number for the adapter (the first adapter is 0, which should be the boot adapter).
- **B** is disk parameter information, and is used only with the scsi() syntax.
- **C** is the ordinal for the disk attached to the adapter.
- **D** is the partition number, and the first number is 1 (as opposed to adapters and drives, which begin numbering with 0).

The way the A, B, C, and D parameters are used differs between the multi() syntax and the scsi() syntax, and is explained next.

The multi() Syntax

For *x86* computers, the syntax differs between multi() and scsi(). The multi() syntax tells Windows to depend on the computer BIOS to load the system files. This means that the operating system uses INT 13 BIOS calls to find and load Ntoskrnl.exe and any other files needed to boot the operating system. In early versions of Windows NT, the multi() syntax was valid only for IDE and ESDI drives, but for Windows NT 3.5 and higher, the syntax can be used for SCSI drives also, as long as the SCSI device is configured to use INT 13 BIOS calls.

You can invoke the multi() syntax to start Windows on any drive, as long as those drives are identified through the standard INT 13 interface. Because support for INT 13 calls varies among disk controllers, and also because most system BIOS can identify only one disk controller through INT 13, the reality is that it's only possible to use the multi() syntax to launch Windows from the first two drives attached to the primary disk controller (or the first four drives if you have a dual-channel EIDE controller).

- In an IDE system, the multi() syntax works for up to four drives (the maximum number of drives permitted on the primary and secondary channels of a dual-channel controller).

- In a SCSI-only system, the multi() syntax works for the first two drives on the SCSI controller that loads first during bootup.

- In a mixed system (SCSI and IDE), the multi() syntax works only for the IDE drives attached to the first IDE controller.

Using the explanations for the parameters given earlier in this chapter, the specifics for the ARC path statement using the multi() syntax are as follows:

- **A** is the ordinal number for the adapter (the first adapter is 0, which should be the boot adapter).

- **B** is always 0 because the multi() syntax invokes the INT 13 call and does not use the disk() parameter information.

- **C** is the ordinal for the disk attached to the adapter (a number between 0 and 3, depending on the number of drives on the adapter).

- **D** is the partition number, and the first number is 1 (as opposed to adapters and drives, which begin numbering with 0).

The scsi() Syntax

For *x*86-based computers, it's common to use the scsi() syntax if you boot Windows Server 2003 from a SCSI device. The scsi() syntax tells Windows Server 2003 to load and use a device driver to access the boot partition. For an *x*86-based computer, that driver is Ntbootdd.sys, placed on the root of the system partition during installation (it's a renamed copy of the device driver for the specific adapter).

Note *For a RISC-based computer, the driver is built into the firmware. I mention that as an interesting technical fact, but it won't affect you because Windows Server 2003 runs only on x86-based computers.*

Here are the specifics for the parameters in the ARC path when you use the scsi() syntax on an *x86* computer:

- **A** is the ordinal number for the adapter linked to the Ntbootdd.sys driver.
- **B** is the SCSI ID for the target disk.
- **C** is the SCSI logical unit (LUN). While this could be a separate disk, most SCSI setups have only one LUN per SCSI ID.
- **D** is the partition.

If you have multiple SCSI controllers, each of which uses a different device driver, the value of A is the controller linked to Ntbootdd.sys. During installation of Windows Server 2003, the drive attached to one of the controllers is determined to be the boot drive. Setup copies the driver for that controller to the root directory of the system partition, changing the driver filename to Ntbootdd.sys.

Technically, you don't have to use the scsi() syntax for SCSI drives, unless either one of the following conditions exists (both of these prevent INT 13 BIOS calls from working):

- The BIOS is disabled on the controller that has the disk on which Windows Server 2003 is installed.
- The boot partition starts or extends beyond the 1024th cylinder of the drive.

However, even if your SCSI drive is able to work with INT 13 BIOS calls, it's preferable to use the scsi() syntax, which forces the use of Ntbootdd.sys to continue the operating system startup.

The signature( ) Syntax

In Windows Server 2003, the signature() syntax is supported in the ARC path entry in Boot.ini. This syntax may be used if either one of the following conditions exists:

- The partition on which Windows Server 2003 is installed is larger than 7.8GB, or the ending cylinder number is greater than 1024 for the partition.
- The drive on which you installed Windows Server 2003 is connected to a SCSI controller in which the BIOS is disabled (INT 13 BIOS calls cannot be used during bootup).

The signature() syntax is technically the same as the scsi() syntax, but is used to support the Plug and Play architecture available in Windows Server 2003. Using the signature() syntax forces Ntldr to locate the drive whose disk signature matches the value in the parentheses, even if the drive is connected to a different SCSI controller number. This is important if you add SCSI controllers.

The value that's placed in the parentheses is derived from the physical disk's MBR, and is a unique hexadecimal number. The value is written to the MBR during the text-mode portion of Setup. As with the scsi() syntax, the signature() syntax requires the specific SCSI driver, renamed to Ntbootdd.sys, on the root of your drive.

Tweaking Boot.ini

You can enhance the operating system boot process by tweaking the entries in the Boot.ini file.

Change the Timeout Duration

The most common alteration made to Boot.ini is to change the timeout duration from 30 seconds to some smaller number. (You can also make this change in the System applet in the Control Panel, as explained earlier in this chapter in the section "Boot.ini Contents.")

 Sometimes users set the timeout duration to 0, so the computer automatically boots into the default operating system. This is not recommended, not just because it eliminates the opportunity to load the previous operating system (if one exists), but because it inhibits the ability to press F8 to display the troubleshooting menu.

Unlike in Windows NT, you cannot eliminate the timeout duration and leave the onscreen menu up until the user makes a choice (even if it takes forever). If you edit Boot.ini and change the timeout duration to –1, it's ignored. During the next boot, the duration is reset to its previous state.

However, you can force the menu to stay on the screen until you're ready to make a decision by pressing any key except the ENTER key, or by using an arrow to highlight a different choice. Because it requires user intervention, this does not help if your goal is to have the menu remain on the screen until the user is available (perhaps he or she is at the coffee machine).

Force a Menu to Display

If you're not dual-booting, or you haven't installed the recovery console on your computer, you never see a menu—Windows Server 2003 just boots automatically. If you need to access the Advanced Options menu, you must press F8 between the time the POST finishes and Windows Server 2003 boots. That interval is a very small window, and it's frequently difficult to use the F8 key to invoke the Advanced Options menu. I've seen users lean on the key so long they cause a keyboard buffer problem, and I've seen users "miss" the interval several times, constantly shutting down the computer to try again.

For users (including yourself) who should have easy access to the Advanced Options menu, you can force Windows Server 2003 to display a startup menu, along with its message to press F8 if you need to enter the Advanced Options menu. To accomplish this, you just need to fake a choice; create a second entry so Windows Server 2003 thinks the user has the ability to make a choice.

For a computer that only boots Windows Server 2003, the Boot.ini file probably looks something like this:

```
[boot loader]
timeout=30
default=multi(0)disk(0)rdisk(0)partition(1)\WINDOWS
[operating systems]
multi(0)disk(0)rdisk(0)partition(1)\WINDOWS="Windows Server 2003" /fastdetect
```

Use these steps to change the contents of Boot.ini to force the menu to appear:

1. Change the attributes of Boot.ini to remove the read-only attribute, so you can save your changes (change back after you're finished).

2. Select and copy the last line, and paste it under the existing last line.

3. Remove any switches (in this case /fastdetect).

4. Change the text within the quotation marks (the text that actually appears on the screen) to avoid confusing the user. For example, "Ignore this entry, choose Windows .NET to boot the OS."

5. If you wish, change the timeout value at the top of the file to lengthen or shorten the elapsed time before Windows Server 2003 starts automatically.

6. Save the changes.

Hereafter, every time you start the computer, a startup menu appears, to make it easier to invoke the Advanced Options menu when needed.

Boot.ini Parameters

You can add switches to the lines in Boot.ini, and some of the commonly used parameters include the following:

- **/BASEVIDEO** Forces the system into 640×480, 16-color VGA mode.

- **/BAUDRATE=NNNN** Sets the baud rate of the debug port. The default baud rate for the port is 19,200, but 9,600 is the preferable rate for remote debugging via modem. Using the /BAUDRATE switch automatically uses the /DEBUG switch.

- **/BOOTLOG** Writes a log of the boot process to %SystemRoot%\Ntbtlog.txt. The log file contains a list of drivers that load or do not load during boot.

- **/CRASHDEBUG** Enables the debug COM port for debugging if Windows Server 2003 crashes (has a STOP error), but allows you to continue to use the COM port for regular modem operations.

- **/DEBUG** Enables the kernel debugger to perform live remote debugging through the COM port.

- **/DEBUGPORT=COMX**   Chooses a COM port for the debug port. By default, the debug port is COM2 if it exists. If COM2 doesn't exist, the default changes to COM1.

- **/FASTDETECT**   Tells Ntdetect not to check parallel and serial ports, instead letting the Plug and Play drivers perform that task. Microsoft says that the switch is added automatically to the Boot.ini line that references Windows Server 2003 if you are dual-booting with a previous version of Windows. However, the switch is usually added to computers that did not contain a previous version of any operating system and do not dual-boot.

- **/INTAFFINITY**   Forces the multiprocessor HAL (Halmps.dll) to set interrupt affinities so that only the highest numbered processor in an SMP receives interrupts. By default, the multiprocessor HAL permits all processors to receive interrupts.

- **/NODEBUG**   Disables the kernel debugger. This speeds up the boot process, but if you run code that has a hard-coded debug breakpoint, a blue screen results.

- **/NOGUIBOOT**   Stops initialization of the VGA video driver that's responsible for presenting bitmapped graphics during the boot process. The driver is used to display progress information during bootup, and, more importantly, displays the Blue Screen of Death, so disabling it will disable Win2K's ability to do those things as well.

- **/NOSERIALMICE:COMX**   Disables the mouse port check for the specified COM port. This is useful if you have a UPS on COM1 and don't want the operating system to check the port for a mouse (see the sidebar "When to Block Serial Port Checks").

- **/PAE**   Has NTLDR load ntkrnlpa.exe. This program supports the version of the *x*86 kernel that is able to take advantage of Intel Physical Address Extensions (PAE) even when a system doesn't have more than 4GB of physical memory. (PAE permits an *x*86 system to have up to 64GB of physical memory, but the operating system must be specially coded to use memory beyond 4GB, which is the standard *x*86 limit.) The PAE version of the Windows Server 2003 kernel presents 64-bit physical addresses to device drivers, so this switch is useful for testing device driver support for large-memory systems.

- **/NOPAE**   Forces NTLDR to load the non-PAE version of the kernel, even if the system contains more than 4GB of RAM and can support PAE.

- **/NOLOWMEM**   Works only if the /PAE switch is used and the system has more than 4GB of physical memory. Using the /NOLOWMEM switch tells the PAE-enabled version of the Win2K kernel, ntkrnlpa.exe, not to use the first 4GB of physical memory. Instead, it will load all applications and device drivers and allocate all memory pools from above that boundary. Use this switch only when you are testing device driver compatibility with large-memory systems.

- **/SOS**   Forces the loader to display the names of modules that are being loaded.

When to Block Serial Port Checks

Ntdetect.com searches for a pointing device (usually a mouse) during startup. This is why you can switch mouse ports (if you use a serial mouse) before turning on the computer, and trust Windows to find it, eliminating the need to go into Control Panel to reconfigure the mouse connection. To accomplish this, Ntdetect.com sends data to the serial ports. If a serial mouse is located, Windows disables the port in order to load and use a device driver for the mouse (remember, no application can use the port to gain direct access to hardware in a multitasking operating system).

Sometimes a modem responds to the query, and Ntdetect thinks it's a mouse, disables the port, and loads a mouse driver. This doesn't do you any good when you want to use the modem.

Sometimes a UPS with a serial port connection (for a shutdown program) responds to the data, which can cause several problems: the UPS thinks the ensuing port shutdown is a signal of impending power loss and starts its shutdown procedures; or the port shutdown disables the UPS automatic shutdown feature.

If you don't use a serial mouse, and you've encountered any problems with devices attached to serial ports, use the /NOSERIALMICE switch in your boot.ini file.

Hide Menu Choices

You can hide items on the onscreen menu. For example, if a computer is dual-booting, but you only want users (except for yourself) to have one option, you can hide the other option.

To make menu items inaccessible, add the entry [any text] to the Boot.ini file at the point where you want the onscreen menu to end. Everything below that entry is invisible and inaccessible. For example, here's a Boot.ini file that prevents users from accessing Windows 2000 Server on a system that's dual-booting Windows Server 2003 and Windows 2000:

```
[boot loader]
timeout=30
default=multi(0)disk(0)rdisk(0)partition(1)\WINDOWS
[operating systems]
multi(0)disk(0)rdisk(0)partition(1)\WINDOWS="Windows Server 2003" /fastdetect
[any text]
multi(0)disk(0)rdisk(1)partition(1)\WINNT="Windows 2000 Server"
```

If you want to permit access to the lines below the [any text] entry, just remove the entry. Don't forget to change the attributes of boot.ini, removing the read-only attribute before saving the file.

The Advanced Options Menu

If there's a problem booting the operating system, start your computer again, and this time use the Advanced Options menu, which is invoked by pressing F8.

- If a menu appears, notice the line at the bottom of your screen: For troubleshooting and advanced startup options for Windows 2000, press F8.
- If no menu appears because the system automatically boots into Windows Server 2003, you can press F8 after the POST is over.

Pressing F8 brings up a menu with these choices that are designed to help you repair the problem that prevented a good boot:

- Safe Mode
- Safe Mode with Networking
- Safe Mode with Command Prompt
- Enable Boot Logging
- Enable VGA Mode
- Last Known Good Configuration
- Directory Services Restore Mode (domain controllers only)
- Debugging Mode
- Start Windows Normally
- Reboot
- Return to OS Choices Menu

Note *If you used Remote Install Services to install Windows Server 2003, the advanced startup options may include additional options related to RIS.*

Use the arrow keys to select the advanced startup option you want to use, and press ENTER.

Safe Mode

The best part of Safe Mode is that it allows access to all your drives, regardless of the file system. If it works, you can make configuration changes to correct the problem. For instance, it's common to need Safe Mode to remove a newly installed driver that doesn't work properly, or to undo some configuration scheme you've experimented with that prevented a good boot. The following three Safe Mode options are available:

- **Safe Mode**   Loads only the basic files and drivers needed to get the operating system up and running: mouse, monitor, keyboard, storage, base video, and default system services.

■ **Safe Mode with Networking**   Adds network support (NIC drivers), although this won't work with PCMCIA NICs.

■ **Safe Mode with Command Prompt**   Brings the system up in text mode, instead of the usual GUI. Use this option if you had a problem with explorer.exe (not Windows Explorer, the GUI shell, which is launched by explorer.exe). You can perform all sorts of tasks in command mode, including opening GUI windows (if you know the name of the file that opens each window). If the explorer.exe shell is working properly (or you replace it while working in text mode), you can open it and use the Start | Shut Down sequence to restart the computer. Otherwise, to shut down the computer so you can restart, enter the command **shutdown**, or press CTRL-ALT-DEL to open the Windows Security dialog, and choose Shut Down.

    Using any of the Safe Mode options causes a log file to be written to %SystemRoot%\ Ntbtlog.txt. See "Enable Boot Logging" in this section.

Enable Boot Logging

This option instructs Windows Server 2003 to create a log file (%SystemRoot%\ Ntbtlog.txt). The file displays a list of all the drivers that are loaded, or not loaded. Here's a small section of a typical Ntbtlog.txt file (this is a Unicode file, by the way):

```
Loaded driver \WINDOWS\system32\ntoskrnl.exe
Loaded driver \WINDOWS\system32\hal.dll
Loaded driver \WINDOWS\system32\KDCOM.DLL
Loaded driver \WINDOWS\system32\BOOTVID.dll
Loaded driver ACPI.sys
Loaded driver \WINDOWS\system32\DRIVERS\WMILIB.SYS
Loaded driver pci.sys
Loaded driver isapnp.sys
Loaded driver viaide.sys
Loaded driver \WINDOWS\system32\DRIVERS\PCIIDEX.SYS
Loaded driver MountMgr.sys
Loaded driver ftdisk.sys
Loaded driver dmload.sys
Loaded driver dmio.sys
Loaded driver PartMgr.sys
Loaded driver VolSnap.sys
Loaded driver atapi.sys
Loaded driver disk.sys
Loaded driver Ntfs.sys
Did not load driver \SystemRoot\System32\Drivers\Changer.SYS
```

Enable VGA Mode

Familiar to Windows NT 4 users, this option starts Windows Server 2003 using the basic VGA driver. Use this choice after you install a new video driver for your video card that doesn't work (which is quite apparent when the operating system GUI mounts the next time you try to boot). The basic video driver is the same driver used when you start Windows Server 2003 with any of the Safe Mode choices. Change the driver and then restart the computer.

Last Known Good Configuration

Use this option to start Windows Server 2003 with the registry settings that were saved at the last normal shutdown. This option doesn't solve problems caused by missing or corrupt drivers, but it's useful in overcoming problems caused by configuration changes you made in your last session. Those changes are lost, which is usually a good thing.

Windows uses the registry to determine, and load, the last known good configuration, which is the configuration that was written to the registry after a good (successful) startup. Incidentally, the definition of "good" means all systems worked, and a user successfully logged on.

The registry entries that the operating system uses to start up are contained in a series of registry keys with the words *ControlSet* in the key names. During startup, Windows Server 2003 reads the CurrentControlSet key to gain information about the hardware installed on the computer as well as the system services required to boot the operating system.

The System subkey of HKEY_LOCAL_MACHINE holds the three control sets available to Windows Server 2003 during bootup: ControlSet001, ControlSet002, and CurrentControlSet. Each key has identical subkey structures.

The registry even has a discrete key to help you figure out which control set is which, and what each is used for: HKEY_LOCAL_MACHINE\System\Select.

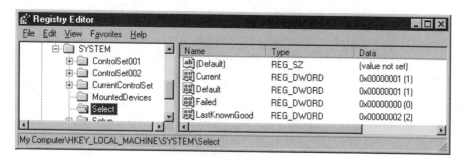

The information in the Select subkey reveals that ControlSet001 and CurrentControlSet are identical; all the values are the same. Windows Server 2003 provides the duplicate of ControlSet001 named CurrentControlSet so that applications don't have to worry about which numbered set is used for booting.

- The Current data item represents the control set Windows Server 2003 used during the startup for the current session.

- The Default data item represents the control set Windows Server 2003 will use the next time it boots, which is the same control set used this time.

- The LastKnownGood data item represents the control set Windows Server 2003 will use if you select Last Known Good during bootup.

- The Failed data item refers to the control set in which Windows Server 2003 saves the data from a failed boot. This control set doesn't actually exist until the first time a user invokes the Last Known Good option.

Each time the operating system boots successfully, it copies the data in CurrentControlSet and ControlSet001 to ControlSet002. Then, as you make configuration changes, they're written to the CurrentControlSet and ControlSet001. If the next startup is flawed, choosing Last Known Good instructs Windows Server 2003 to use the data in ControlSet002, which represents the state of your system the last time it booted properly.

Registry Changes after Using Last Known Good

If you check the System subkeys after you use the Last Known Good boot option, you can see the way Windows Server 2003 handles the changed control sets.

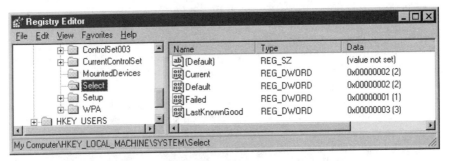

A new control set subkey, ControlSet003, exists in case you must use Last Known Good again. Windows Server 2003 has moved that stable, working control set that was the previously "last successful startup" back one rung on the ladder. If you make configuration changes at this point, hoping to install the right stuff this time (having failed the last time), and the new changes are also failures, the stable startup control set is still available. If you continue to use the Last Known Good boot option, and you also continue to make configuration changes that don't work, Windows Server 2003 will create as many control sets as it needs to keep that last good set available for you.

Directory Services Restore Mode

This option is only available for domain controllers, and it restores the system state of a DC, which includes %SystemRoot%\Sysvol (where the domain's public files that are replicated among the domain controllers are stored), and Active Directory.

Debugging Mode

Use this option to start Windows Server 2003 and send debugging information to another computer through a serial cable. This is helpful if you need to monitor the startup process from another computer.

Creating a Bootable Floppy Disk

If one of the files that load early in the operating system boot process (Ntldr, Ntdetect.com, or Boot.ini) is missing or corrupted, you can't get to the Advanced Options menu to repair your system. You can remedy this by using a boot disk that's created specifically for your Windows Server 2003 installation.

Creating a Bootable Floppy Disk from Your Own System

If you're smart, you'll create a bootable floppy disk as soon as your Windows Server 2003 installation is up and running (without error). Unfortunately, users rarely heed this advice and don't think about the need for a bootable floppy disk until there's a problem booting. However, if you're a resourceful person who plans ahead, here's how to accomplish this task:

1. Put a floppy disk in the drive.
2. Open My Computer or Windows Explorer and right-click on the floppy drive object.
3. Choose Format from the shortcut menu and format the disk using the default options.
4. Copy the following files from the root directory of your hard drive to the floppy disk:
   - Ntdetect.com
   - Ntldr
   - Boot.ini
   - Ntbootdd.sys (if it exists)

Test the disk by restarting the operating system.

Ntbootdds.sys only exists if you have a SCSI system. It's your SCSI driver, renamed.

Creating a Bootable Floppy Disk on Another Windows Server 2003 Computer

If it's too late, and you need a bootable floppy disk to start a broken system, you can create one from another computer that's running Windows Server 2003 and the same file system (NTFS, FAT, or FAT32):

1. Follow the steps described for creating a boot floppy from your own computer.

2. Open Boot.ini and examine it to make sure it matches your own configuration. If it doesn't, use the information in the earlier section "About Boot.ini" to adjust the settings.

3. If you have a different SCSI controller, find the correct driver file and copy it to the floppy disk. Delete the Ntbootdd.sys file you copied from the computer you used to create the disk, and then rename your SCSI driver to Ntbootdd.sys.

4. If the source computer uses an IDE controller, and your system has a SCSI controller, use Notepad to adjust the setting in Boot.ini and then copy the correct SCSI driver to the floppy disk and rename it Ntbootdd.sys.

5. If the source computer uses a SCSI controller, and your system has an IDE controller, use Notepad to adjust the setting in Boot.ini and delete Ntbootdd.sys if you copied it from the source computer.

Test the bootable floppy disk on your computer.

Creating a Bootable Floppy Disk on a Computer Running a Different Version of Windows

If you cannot find another computer that's running the same version of Windows Server 2003, you can create a bootable floppy from any computer running Windows NT 4 or later (including client versions of Windows). You'll need the Windows Server 2003 CD, or access to the network sharepoint that has the installation files for Windows Server 2003. Then follow these steps:

1. Format a floppy disk using the default settings.

2. On the CD or the shared network folder, select Ntldr and Ntdetect.com.

3. Right-click and choose Send To I 3 1/2 Floppy (A).

4. If your computer has a SCSI controller, copy the driver to the floppy disk and rename the file Ntbootdd.sys.

5. Use the boot.ini file as a model, and change the contents to match the setup of your computer. Remember that you'll have to change the reference WINNT to Windows, since Windows Server 2003 uses Windows as the folder name for system files.

Creating a Quick Boot.ini File

Your emergency Boot.ini file only has to load Windows Server 2003, so there's no need to worry about any lines in the boot.ini file that refer to another operating system, even if your computer is configured for dual-booting. Here's an example:

```
[boot loader]
timeout=30
Default= scsi(0)disk(0)rdisk(0)partition(1)\Windows
[operating systems]
scsi(0)disk(0)rdisk(0)partition(1)\Windows=" Windows Server 2003"
```

If your computer boots from an IDE hard drive, replace scsi(0) with multi(0).

Tip *The text you place within the quotation marks doesn't have to match the original text of your computer's boot.ini file; it's the text that displays on the menu. It has no effect on the way Windows finds the boot files.*

The
Complete
Reference

Chapter 6

Windows Server 2003
User Interface

The user interface you encounter when you run Windows Server 2003 for the first time is a cross between Windows 2000 and Windows XP, although it's cleaner and a bit more efficient than either. If you're coming to Windows Server 2003 from Windows NT, the interface looks and behaves in a new and different way. In this chapter, I'll discuss the Windows Server 2003 interface and its eminently configurable characteristics.

First Boot

The first time you boot Windows Server 2003 regularly (as opposed to any reboots that take place during installation), you'll notice three things: an incomplete logon dialog, a full-screen Manage Your Server window, and video settings that seem primitive.

First Logon

The first time you log on, the Welcome to Windows dialog appears, instructing you to use SAS, the security attention sequence (CTRL-ALT-DELETE), to begin. The ensuing Log on to Windows dialog only has fields for your logon name and your password. The field that provides an option to choose between logging on to the local computer or a domain is missing.

If you configured your network settings during installation, click the Options button on the dialog to display the third field (Log On To), and then use the drop-down list to choose the domain you want to log on to. If you didn't configure network settings during installation, no domain logon choices are available; you can only log on to the local computer (see the next section, "Joining a Domain").

Joining a Domain

To log on to a domain, a computer must have an account on that domain. Like user accounts, computer accounts are a way to authenticate computer access to the network and to the resources on the domain. Also like user accounts, every computer account must be unique. Computer accounts can be created on a domain in two ways:

- An administrator adds the computer account to the domain using Active Directory Users and Computers.

- A user with rights to join a computer to a domain logs on to the domain from a computer, and creates the computer account during the logon process.

To join a computer to a domain, follow these steps:

1. Right-click My Computer and choose Properties from the shortcut menu.

2. Move to the Computer Name tab.

3. Click Change to open the Computer Name Changes dialog.

4. Select Domain, and enter the name of the domain. (You can type either the NetBIOS name or the FQDN.)

5. Click OK.

A dialog appears asking for your logon name and password. The logon name must exist on the domain. If the computer name already exists on the domain, your domain logon name must have sufficient rights to join a pre-created computer account to the domain. If the computer name doesn't exist on the domain, your domain logon name must have sufficient rights to create a computer account. Membership in the Administrators group for the local computer, and in the Domain Admins group on the domain, provides all the necessary rights. After a few seconds (or, sometimes, after many seconds), you see a Welcome to *DomainName* dialog.

Local vs. Domain Logon Names and the Interface

The process described in the previous paragraphs has an effect on the interface you work with in Windows Server 2003. Even if you log on to the local computer and to the domain with the same logon name, you're not really using the same account. Windows differentiates between local accounts and computer accounts. For example, many administrators log on to Windows Server 2003 the first time using the Administrator account. Then, when they join the computer to the domain, they use the Administrator account again (usually with a different password) in order to make sure they can successfully join the computer to the domain.

Windows Server 2003 creates two separate accounts in this scenario: one for the local name and one for the domain name. When the interface is customized, the settings are saved in the profile of the logged-on account. As a result, the following two rules apply:

- When you're logged on to the local computer and make changes to configuration settings, you won't see the changes when you log on to the domain using the same name (and vice versa).

- The Documents and Settings folder has a separate subfolder for each instance of the logon name (one for the local name and one for the domain name).

Manage Your Server

The Manage Your Server window opens in full screen mode every time you boot the computer, until you check the option Don't Display This Page at Logon (the check box is in the lower-left corner). You can use this window to select a role for the computer and to remove a role from a computer. Wizards walk you through the steps, and specific configuration information about various roles is found throughout this book.

Video Settings

After the first boot, your video settings seem primitive—icons are larger and fuzzier than you'd expect. Even though Windows Server 2003 found your video controller and its driver, it's loading the same (low) video settings it used during installation. However, the system is smart enough to know this. Within seconds of your first boot, you see the following message: "Your computer screen resolution and color depth are currently set to a very low level. You can get a better picture by increasing these settings. To do this, click this balloon."

Clicking the balloon opens the Display Settings dialog, with a message asking if you want Windows to automatically correct your screen resolution and color depth settings. Click Yes to increase the resolution and colors. Most of the time, Windows resets your video to less than the highest resolution your controller can manage, but does set the highest supported color settings. You're free to tinker with the video configuration after Windows Server 2003 resets your video. To do so, right-click a blank spot on the desktop and choose Properties. Then use the Settings tab in the Display Properties dialog to make changes.

The Desktop

The default desktop is sparse, almost naked, containing only the Recycle Bin and the taskbar. The background is a soft blue, lacking the landscape motif of the other operating system in the Windows Server 2003 family, Windows XP.

Windows Server 2003, like its client-side family member Windows XP, offers themes for configuring the interface. A theme (the official terminology is *desktop theme*) is a set of predefined interface components, including:

- Icons
- Fonts
- Colors
- Sounds
- Mouse pointers
- Screen saver
- Window elements (title bars, fonts, and so on)

You can change existing themes, or create your own themes. If you're the administrator (or have some measure of clout), you can design a theme and make it the company theme for all Windows Server 2003 computers in your enterprise. This is easy, because themes are files that can be copied or even e-mailed, and then installed. In fact, themes designed in Windows Server 2003 can be used on Windows XP computers (and vice versa).

Enabling the Themes Service

Before you can work with themes, you must enable the Themes service, which is disabled by default in Windows Server 2003. To accomplish this, follow these steps:

1. Open the Services snap-in from the Administrative Tools menu.
2. Double-click the Themes listing.
3. Select Automatic as the Startup type, and click Apply (which activates the Start button).
4. Click Start to start the service.
5. After the service is running, click OK.

You could also select Manual for the service startup type, and start the service, but every time you boot the computer, you'd have to start the service manually if you wanted to work with themes.

Switching Themes

The default theme for Windows Server 2003 is Windows Classic, and unlike other versions of Windows, you don't have a lot of installed themes to choose from. However, you can switch to another theme in the Themes tab of the Display Properties dialog by selecting one of the following choices from the drop-down list:

- *ThemeName*   A theme that's available.
- **Browse**   Opens the Open Theme dialog. By default, the dialog opens in the Program Files folder, but you can navigate through your computer to locate a theme file (*.theme) you've transferred from another computer on the network, or from the Internet.
- **More themes online**   Opens Internet Explorer and travels to a Microsoft site where you can purchase a Windows add-on that includes graphical files. Click the Themes link on the left side of the window to see if you like the themes enough to buy them.

Modifying Themes

You can change any component in a theme to suit your own tastes. When you modify a theme, you should save the new theme with a unique name. If you don't, your changes are saved automatically with the name Modified Theme. However, if you ever select a different theme, the Modified Theme name disappears, and you can't reload it.

Not all changes in a theme create a new Modified Theme, because some components operate independently of a theme, to wit:

- Screen saver choices (including None)
- All options on the Settings tab
- Adding, removing, or changing desktop icons (click the Customize Desktop button on the Desktop tab of the Display Properties dialog)
- Changes you make in the Mouse or Sounds and Audio Devices applets

Use the tabs in the Display Properties dialog to make changes to components. When you finish modifying components, click the Save As button on the Themes tab to save the new configuration settings as a theme. By default, Windows Server 2003 saves themes in My Documents.

Deleting Themes

You can delete any theme except the built-in system themes. To delete a theme you saved after modifications, or a theme you acquired, select the theme from the drop-down list on the Themes tab and then click Delete.

Start Menu

The interface for the Start menu is also new for Windows server products. It's a two-pane interface, similar to the Windows XP Start menu, but it's more efficient because it's designed for managing a server and a network. As you can see in Figure 6-1, this is an administrator's menu! The Administrative Tools menu and a command window are available at the top level of the Start menu hierarchy, so you don't have to navigate through submenus.

If you prefer, you can switch back to the Classic Start menu, which is discussed later in this chapter in the section "Enabling the Classic Start Menu."

Start Menu Left Pane

The left pane of the Start menu is divided by two horizontal separators, which work as follows:

- Program listings above the top separator are *pinned* to the menu, and you can pin any applications you wish. Microsoft has "prepinned" Manage Your Server and Windows Explorer.
- Program listings below the top separator are recently accessed programs (for convenience, Windows prepopulates the list with Command Prompt and Notepad).

■ Below the bottom separator is the All Programs listing, which works the same way the Programs listing works in previous versions of Windows.

Pinning Program Listings to the Start Menu

For one-click access to your oft-used applications, you can pin shortcuts to the top of the Start menu. To make this task super easy, Windows Server 2003 has a new command on the shortcut menu that appears when you right-click an executable file: Pin to Start Menu.

You can remove program listings from the pinned items list by right-clicking the listing and choosing Unpin from Start menu. To change the order of the programs on the pinned items list, drag a listing to a new position.

You can also put listings for Internet Explorer and Outlook Express on the top of the Start menu. To do so, follow these steps:

1. Right-click the Start button and choose Properties to open the Start Menu tab of the Taskbar and Start Menu Properties dialog.

2. Click Customize to open the Customize Start Menu dialog.

3. In the Show on Start Menu section of the dialog, select Internet, or E-mail, or both, to put shortcuts to IE and Outlook Express on the Start menu.

4. Click OK twice.

Figure 6-1. *Important administrator tools are one click away.*

These are not pinned, at least technically, because no Unpin from Start Menu command appears on their shortcut menus. You can clear these listings in either of the following ways:

- Use the preceding steps, and deselect the item(s).
- Right-click the listing and choose Remove From This List.

Frequently Used Programs List

As you open applications, Windows puts their listings on the bottom section of the left pane. (Technically, this list is called the frequently used programs list, but most of us refer to it as the *programs list*.) For convenience, Windows prepopulates the list with Command Prompt and Notepad. You can delete any listing by right-clicking its icon and choosing Remove From This List.

Changing the Number of Listed Programs   By default, Windows Server 2003 displays six programs on the list, and replaces existing application listings with newer ones. The prepopulated listings aren't shoved out to make room for new listings, so you have an effective limit of four listings. You can modify the maximum number with the following steps:

1. Right-click the Start button and choose Properties to open the Start Menu tab of the Taskbar and Start Menu Properties dialog.

2. Click Customize to open the Customize Start Menu dialog.

3. Specify a maximum number of programs on the Start menu.

4. Click OK twice.

Clearing the Programs List   The Customize Start Menu dialog also has a button labeled Clear List. Click the button to clear all programs from the list, including the programs Windows Server 2003 initially placed on the list.

Using the Shortcuts on the Programs List   There are a couple of things to notice about the shortcuts that appear on the programs list. First, the objects that are displayed are literal—if you open an application from a desktop shortcut, the listing appears as Shortcut to *ProgramName*, instead of *ProgramName*. Second, among the commands on the right-click menus for the objects are a couple of truly useful commands: Pin to Start Menu, and Run As.

If you want a cleaner Start menu, right-click the listings of programs you use often, and choose Pin to Start Menu, to make them permanent residents at the top of the left pane. Then set a maximum of zero for the number of programs on the list. For an even cleaner Start menu, move your oft-used program listings to the QuickLaunch toolbar.

The Run As command is tremendously useful for administrative tools, because so many of the tasks you perform on a server require administrator rights. It's not a good idea to log on to a server (or any other computer, for that matter) with the Administrator account, so Run As lets you get your administrative work done without having to log off and log on again.

Right Pane of the Start Menu

The right pane of the Start menu contains links, commands, and menus—and it's highly customizable. To make the menu convenient, the important programs and system tools are listed in the right pane, and display their contents when you point to them. This makes it extremely easy to work with a Control Panel applet, or to open an Administrative snap-in. To modify the contents of the right pane, follow these steps:

1. Right-click the Start button and choose Properties to open the Start Menu tab of the Taskbar and Start Menu Properties dialog.
2. Click Customize to open the Customize Start Menu dialog.
3. Move to the Advanced tab and select or deselect options as you wish.
4. Click OK twice.

Enabling the Classic Start Menu

If you're having trouble getting used to the new paradigm for the Start menu, you can switch to the more familiar interface of the Classic Start menu. To do so, right-click the Start button and choose Properties. In the Taskbar and Start Menu Properties dialog, select Classic Menu.

When you click OK, the next time you click the Start button, you'll see that the Start menu has changed to the one-pane version you're used to from previous versions of Windows. But that's not all—to make your interface a complete trip down this nostalgic road, the following icons are added to the desktop:

- My Documents
- My Computer
- My Network Places
- Internet Explorer

In addition, the Customize button for this Classic Start menu is activated. Click it to open the Customize Classic Start Menu dialog, where you can add, remove, and modify the objects on the menu.

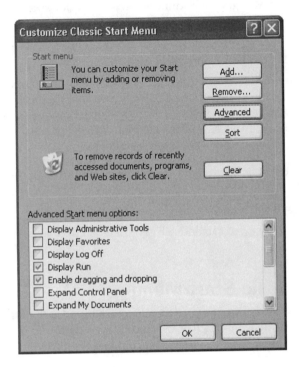

Taskbar

The Windows Server 2003 taskbar has the same interface as in previous versions of Windows, but contains a few new features, which I'll discuss in this section. The taskbar is divided into three basic sections—from left to right:

- Start button
- Taskbar area, which holds any toolbars you choose to display, and also contains buttons for each open application
- Notification area (called the *taskbar tray* in previous versions of Windows)

Notification Area

Windows Server 2003 manages the notification area in a new way, limiting the number of visible icons in order to make the taskbar less crowded. You can, however, customize the behavior of the notification area (see "Managing the Notification Area").

By default, the icons that appear in the notification area are an icon for the time, an icon you can click to check the Microsoft web site for updates to Windows Server 2003, and an icon for adjusting speaker volume (if the computer contains a sound controller).

Note   *Until you activate Windows, an activation icon appears in the notification area.*

Some applications, especially those that load at bootup, also place icons in the notification area. In addition, an icon appears when your e-mail client receives new messages or when you open Task Manager.

Add an Icon for the NIC

It's a good idea to display an icon for your NIC in the notification area, because you can keep an eye on connectivity. If there's a problem with the cable, a red X appears on the icon, and when the computer is exchanging data with another device, the icon flashes. To put an icon for your NIC in the notification area, select the Network Connections object in Control Panel, and then select the Local Area Connection object. Click Properties, and select the option Show icon in notification area when connected.

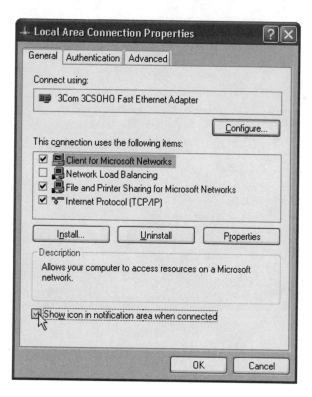

Managing the Notification Area

As the number of icons in the notification area increases, Windows Server 2003 doesn't necessarily expand the space required to hold them. Instead, using a "last accessed" approach, the system hides icons. When hidden icons exist, a left-facing arrow is displayed on the left edge of the notification area. Click the arrow to see all the icons—the arrow changes direction so that you can click it again to hide the inactive icons. You can enable or disable this feature, and even specify the hide/show behavior for specific icons by taking the following steps:

1. Right-click a blank spot on the taskbar and choose Properties.

2. Select or deselect the option Hide inactive icons.

3. Selecting the option in Step 2 activates the Customize button, which you can click to specify the hide/show default for specific icons.

4. Click the icon of interest, and select the default behavior from the drop-down list.

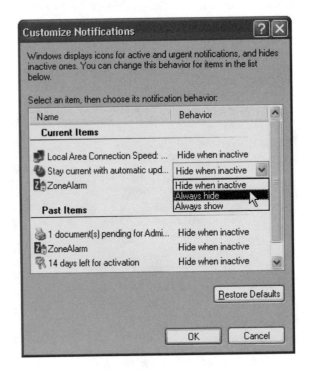

Grouping Taskbar Buttons

The taskbar gets crowded with buttons when you're working with multiple applications, or with multiple documents in an application. Windows Server 2003 offers a new feature, *button grouping,* that makes it easier to see and use taskbar buttons. As the taskbar becomes more crowded, the button grouping feature changes to accommodate the increased number of buttons.

To start, Windows Server 2003 displays adjacent buttons for documents opened by the same application, so you can find (and switch among) documents easily.

 If a document name is too long for its button, Windows fades the last letters on the right side of the button to indicate additional text. Point to the button to see the full name of the document, as well as the name of its application.

As the taskbar becomes more crowded, Windows Server 2003 combines all the documents for each application into a single taskbar button that's labeled with the name of the application. A triangle appears on the right side of the button to indicate that multiple documents are open in this application.

Clicking the triangle displays a list of all the documents for the application, and you can select the document you want. Then you can switch to that document, or close it.

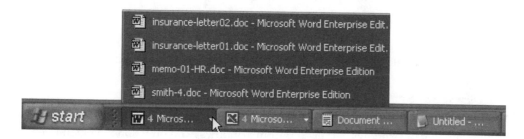

Right-clicking the triangle displays a list of commands you can apply to all the documents.

Note   *If you don't like the button grouping feature, you can disable it by deselecting the option Group similar taskbar buttons on the Taskbar and Start Menu Properties dialog.*

Locking the Taskbar

One new feature is the ability to lock the taskbar. This means you won't inadvertently move it, which, for many users, is a welcome curb on their reckless mouse actions. If you have a problem adding toolbars or adjusting the size of taskbar elements, right-click a blank spot on the taskbar to display the shortcut menu. If a check mark appears next to the command Lock the Taskbar, click the command to unlock the taskbar, then try your taskbar adjustment again.

Taskbar Toolbars

You can add toolbars to the taskbar by right-clicking a blank spot on the taskbar, pointing to Toolbars, and then selecting a toolbar from the following list:

- The Quick Launch toolbar holds icons you can click to open programs. By default, the Quick Launch toolbar has icons for Internet Explorer and the desktop.
- The Address toolbar lets you quickly go to any web page you specify.
- The Links bar holds links to web addresses.
- The Desktop toolbar holds copies of your desktop icons.
- The New toolbar lets you place a shortcut to a folder on the taskbar.

Folder Behavior and Views

If you're moving to Windows Server 2003 from Windows NT, you'll notice a big difference in the way you view folders and their contents. In addition, you'll see some new options for customizing the way folders work, and you'll find that some of the options you previously used have moved to different menus.

Probably the most-used folder customization is changing the view options. If you've been using Windows NT, note that to get to the view options in system windows, you choose Tools | Folder Options.

Folder Opening Behavior

The General tab of the Folder Options dialog (see Figure 6-2) contains the options that determine the look and behavior of folders when you first open them.

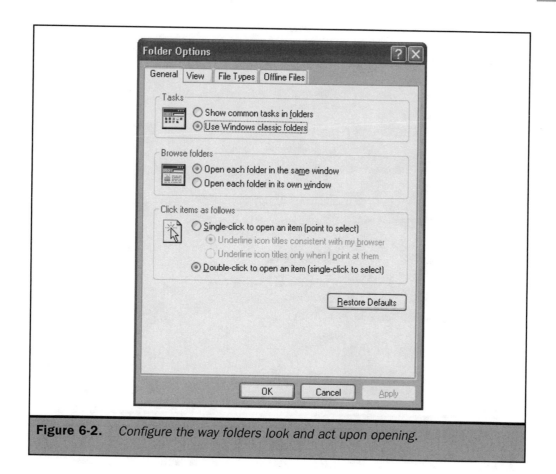

Figure 6-2.   *Configure the way folders look and act upon opening.*

If you want to see links to related folders in the left pane of a window, select the option Show common tasks in folders. The links differ, depending on the system window you've opened. For example, as you can see in Figure 6-3, opening My Computer results in a display of links to other related system windows.

You can specify the way folder windows open as you navigate through subfolders. You can opt to open each folder in the same window, or open a new window for each folder you select.

You might want to change the way you select and open objects in folders. By default, the system selects an object when you click its listing, and opens the object when you double-click its listing. You can change that behavior if you prefer to open an object with a single click, and select an object by pointing at it. If you choose this behavior, you can specify when object titles are underlined.

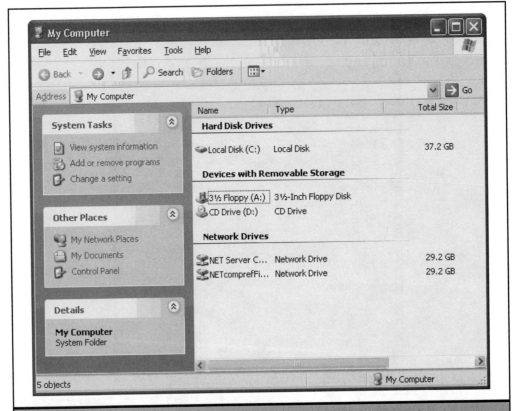

Figure 6-3.   *From My Computer, you have one-click access to related system windows.*

Viewing Folders and Files

The View tab of the Folder Options dialog, shown in Figure 6-4, offers a host of options for viewing the contents of folders. Most administrators change the following options to avoid the annoyances of the built-in restrictions:

- Select the option to display the contents of system folders.
- Change the option for hidden files and folders to show those objects.
- Deselect the option to hide protected operating system files (Windows issues a warning and makes you confirm this decision).

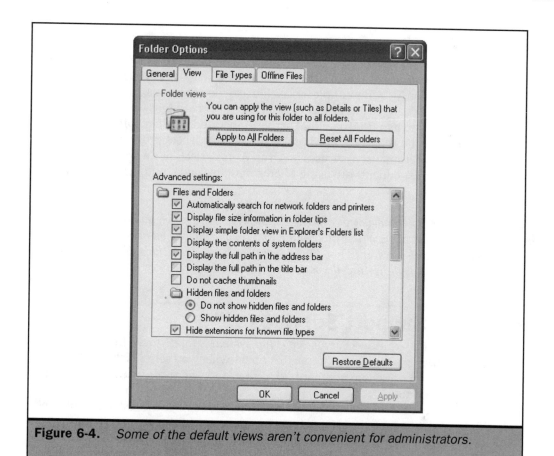

Figure 6-4.   *Some of the default views aren't convenient for administrators.*

Show File Extensions to Avoid Danger

There is one change in the View options you should make for all users and all computers on your network. Deselect the option Hide extensions for known file types. This is a dangerous setting and I've never understood why Microsoft makes it the default setting. This setting probably launches more viruses than we'll ever know about. Even with diligent attention to keeping your antivirus software up to date, you can get a new virus before a detection method is available from your antivirus software vendor. When you receive an e-mail attachment named filename.txt, you know that it's highly improbable the file contains a virus. However, without the ability to see file extensions, you won't know that the real name is filename.txt.exe. The executable extension is at least a clue that the file could be dangerous. Make this change on your home computers, and advise your users to do the same on their own home systems.

File Associations

In the File Types tab, you make changes to the association of file extensions to applications. Applications usually create file associations during installation, but you may want to change an association, or add multiple associations to file extensions.

One important change I suggest is to associate the .vbs extension with Notepad. This is a good way to avoid viruses that arrive embedded in Microsoft Office macros. Even if your company is using a word processor or spreadsheet program that doesn't present any danger from macro viruses (such as WordPerfect), it's a sure bet that some of your e-mail correspondents are using Microsoft Office and could inadvertently send you a macro virus.

Note *The Folder Options dialog also has an Offline Files tab to enable and configure that feature. However, the offline files feature isn't commonly used on network servers (it's usually an end-user feature), so I'm not going to discuss the details. If you have some reason to enable the feature, the options are self-explanatory.*

Help and Support Services

The interface for the Windows Server 2003 help system is totally new. In fact, even the name is new. The title bar on the window that opens when you select Help and Support from the Start menu says Help and Support Center, and Microsoft frequently refers to the help system as HSC.

The help system is designed like a web page, and if you're connected to the Internet, it uses web pages as part of the help system. The majority of the real estate in the opening window is taken up by two columns of links: titles of help content files on the left, and titles of help pages for specific tasks on the right. The toolbar is similar to the toolbar for Internet Explorer, containing familiar icons such as Back, Forward, Home, History, Favorites, and so on.

Using the Index

Click the Index icon on the toolbar to open the help index. As you type characters, the index listing moves to the section that matches your characters.

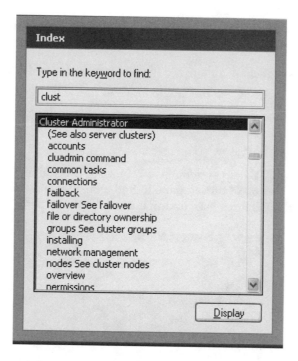

Double-click a topic listing (or select the listing and click Display) to see the help page for that topic. If the topic is covered in multiple help pages, a list of pages is displayed so you can select the specific topic.

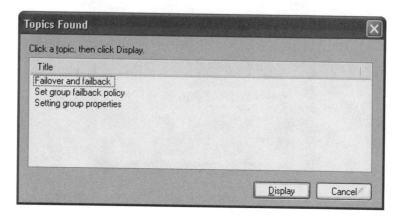

The help page is displayed in the right pane. Within the text, you may see color text that's underlined, indicating one of the following types of links:

■ **Definitions**   Click the link to see the glossary entry for the term.

■ **Other help pages**   Click the link to move to the help page for the topic.

■ **Tools**   Click the link to open the tool or snap-in window referenced by the link.

Searching for Topics

The Windows Server 2003 help system has a robust search engine. Enter a word in the Search box at the top of the left pane to find all help pages that contain that word. The system returns three lists, noting the number of help pages for each list:

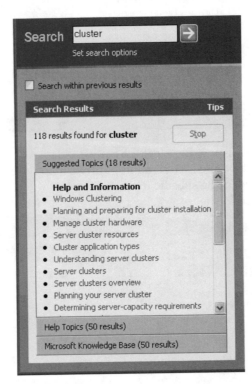

■ **Suggested Topics**   The system's "best guess" for relevant information on your search term.

■ **Help Topics**   All help pages containing the search term.

■ **Microsoft Knowledge Base**   Knowledge Base articles on Microsoft's web site that contain your search term.

To fine-tune your search, enter a new term in the Search box and select the option Search Within Previous Results. The system searches the currently found help pages, and returns the help pages that contain both the original search word and the new search word. For searches that produce large numbers of returns, you can repeat this process until you're working with a manageable number of pages. Then select a specific listing to see its associated help page in the right pane.

When you use the search feature to locate a help page, the text that matches the search is highlighted in the help page, which can be both helpful (especially in a large help page) and annoying.

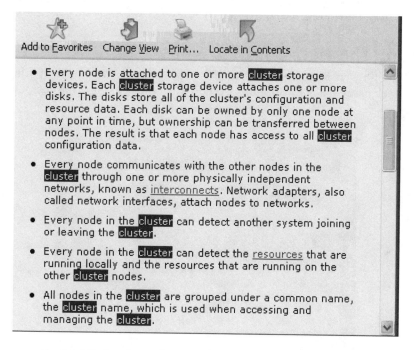

To remove the highlights from the matching text, right-click anywhere in the help page and choose Refresh from the shortcut menu. You can also turn off this feature, which is covered in the section "Customize the Search Function," later in this chapter.

Working with Help Pages

You can do more with the help pages that appear in the right pane than simply read them. For example, it's frequently convenient to have a printed copy of instructions, and you can click the Print icon on the toolbar above the help page to send a copy of the page to the printer.

If you want to copy text from the help page to another application, you can copy all or selected text, as follows:

- To select all the text, right-click anywhere in the help page and choose Select All. Then right-click again and choose Copy.

- To copy some of the text, drag your mouse to select the text you need. Then position your mouse pointer anywhere in the selected text, right-click, and choose Copy.

If you click a link in a help page to travel to another help page, use the Back button on the HSC window to return to the original page.

Customizing the Help System

The HSC is highly customizable, and includes the ability to share the help files with other network users. Click the Options icon on the toolbar to view the customization categories.

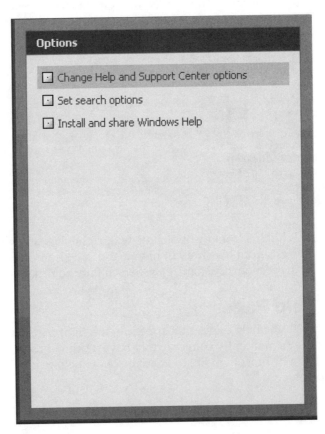

Changing the HSC Options

In the left pane of the HSC window, select Change Help and Support Center Options to display the list of options in the right pane. Then select or deselect options to suit your own needs.

Customize the Search Function

You can customize all the facets of the HSC search feature by selecting Set Search Options in the left pane. The right pane displays the available options, all of which are self-explanatory.

Install and Share Help Files

You can install and share help files for Windows Server 2003 and Windows XP, which means you have access to help when you're administering servers or workstations from your own desktop (assuming your own workstation is running either Windows Server 2003 or Windows XP). To accomplish this, select Install and Share Windows Help in the left pane and then select the appropriate task in the right pane. Each selection presents an easy-to-use dialog that completes the selected task.

> Switch from one operating system's Help content to another
>
> Install Help content from another Windows computer
>
> Install Help content from a CD or disk image
>
> Share your Help content with others on your network
>
> Uninstall Help that you have installed from another Windows operating system

Chapter 7

The Command Prompt

Command processors are applications that let you interact directly with the operating system, instead of using a graphical interface to send instructions and commands to the operating system. Bypassing the GUI makes everything faster. You can use a command processor to issue commands, or to run command-based applications (also called text-based applications).

If you previously used Windows NT, you'll find that Windows Server 2003 includes some changes (and they're all improvements) to the command-line interface and also to some commands. Most of these changes originally appeared in Windows 2000, so if you're migrating to Windows Server 2003 from Windows 2000, you should be comfortable using the new features in the command prompt.

Tricks and Tips for the Command Prompt

Before I get into all the technical function of the Windows Server 2003 command processor, I'll use the next few sections to share some fast facts and tips.

Finding the Command Prompt Menu Item

If you're migrating to Windows Server 2003 from Windows NT, it's important to know that the Command Prompt menu item has moved to the Accessories submenu. (It actually took up this new residence in Windows 2000, so if you're upgrading from that OS, you won't go crazy trying to find it.)

However, Windows Server 2003 also puts a shortcut to the Command Prompt at the top of the Start menu, above the horizontal line. For command-line junkies like me, this is a real convenience.

Quick Access to a Command Prompt from the GUI

As a command-line fan, I need a quick way to get to the command window. In addition, I want to open a command window in a specific location (a folder) instead of using the **cd** command to navigate through my computer's hierarchy. The solution is to add a command to open a command window on shortcut menus in Windows Explorer or My Computer. To accomplish this, follow these steps:

1. Open Regedit, and go to the HKEY_CLASSES_ROOT\Directory\shell key.

2. Create a new subkey under the Directory\shell key, by selecting New | Key from the Edit menu, and name the new subkey OpenNew.

3. Open the Default data item in the right pane, and change its value to Open A Command Window. The value you enter is the phrase that appears on the shortcut menu, so you can substitute any wording you prefer.

4. Select the OpenNew subkey, and create a new subkey beneath it, named Command.

5. Open the Default data item in the Command subkey, and enter **cmd.exe /k cd %1** as the value.

You can add a similar command for the shortcut menu that appears when you right-click a drive object in Windows Explorer or My Computer. The instructions are the same as those for creating the command for folders, except for these two differences:

- Use the subkey HKEY_CLASSES_ROOT\Drive\shell as the starting point.
- Enter **cmd.exe /k** as the value of the Default item in the new subkey HKEY_CLASSES_ROOT\Drive\shell\OpenNew\Command.

Quick Tricks for Keystrokes

Way back in the stone age of computing (the 1980s), when the command line was all we had, we learned how to apply shortcuts to avoid all that typing. The first trick was to be very careful about entering commands, because if you made a mistake, you had to start all over. Back then, the LEFTARROW key deleted the characters it met, just as if it were the BACKSPACE key. Some of the shortcut tricks we learned still work:

- Use F3 to re-enter the previous command.
- Use F2, followed by the first letter that was wrong in your last entry, to re-enter the previous command up to that letter. Then correct the character and use F3 to enter the rest of the command automatically. (This was an undocumented trick in early versions of DOS—but it's taken for granted now, and in Windows Server 2003, when you press F2, a little box opens that says "Enter char to copy up to:.")

Note *F3 and F2 are part of the doskey.exe feature set, which is covered in the next section.*

- Enter **dir *.** to see a listing of all items that lack file extensions. This is useful for seeing a list of directories, although the display also includes any files that don't have extensions.
- Enter **cd ..** to move up one directory.
- Enter **cd** to jump to the root directory.

Use Doskey to Recall and Edit Commands

Windows Server 2003 launches doskey.exe by default, which causes the commands you enter in a command session to be put into memory so you can recall them. The command buffer doesn't survive the session. Table 7-1 describes some of the commonly used keystrokes that take advantage of the doskey recall and editing features.

Keystroke	Action
UPARROW	Recalls the previous command.
DOWNARROW	Recalls the command you used after the command you recalled.
PAGEUP	Recalls the oldest command in the session.
PAGEDOWN	Recalls the most recent command.
LEFTARROW	Moves the cursor back one character.
RIGHTARROW	Moves the cursor forward one character.
CTRL-LEFTARROW	Moves the cursor back one word.
CTRL-RIGHTARROW	Moves the cursor forward one word.
HOME	Moves the cursor to the beginning of the line.
END	Moves the cursor to the end of the line.
ESC	Clears the command.
F4	Deletes characters from the current cursor position up to a character you specify. Press F4 and type a character to have doskey delete all the characters from the current cursor position to the first instance of the character you specified.
F7	Displays all commands stored in memory for this session in a pop-up box. Use the ARROW keys to choose the command you need, and then press ENTER to run that command. Or, press F9, enter the command's list number, and then press ENTER.
ALT-F7	Deletes all commands stored in memory for the current session.
F8	Displays all commands in memory that start with the characters you type before pressing F8.
F9	Allows you to re-enter a command by specifying its number (see the instructions for F7).

Table 7-1.   *Commonly Used Doskey Keystrokes*

The Command Prompt Window

When you need to execute commands, Windows Server 2003 presents a Command Prompt window. You have several windows to choose from, as follows:

- If you open %SystemRoot%\System32\Command.com, the window's title bar displays the path to command.com. The prompt is %SystemRoot%\System32. This window is running the MS-DOS application Command.com.

- If you choose the menu item Command Prompt (from the Accessories submenu), the window's title bar says Command Prompt. The prompt is C:\Documents and Settings*UserName*. This window is running Cmd.exe.

- If you open the Start menu, choose Run, and then enter **cmd** (or **cmd.exe**), the window's title bar displays the path to cmd.exe. The prompt is C:\Documents and Settings\<*UserName*>C:\>. This window is running Cmd.exe.

Change the Properties of the Command Prompt Window

The Console applet that was available in the Control Panel in Windows NT 4 is gone, and customization of the Command Prompt window is accomplished from the window itself. Right-click the title bar of the window to display the menu shown here.

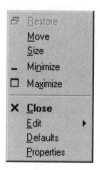

You can use either the Defaults command or the Properties command to customize the Command Prompt window—the same choices appear in the resulting dialog. There is a difference, however, in the way each command affects your system:

- The Defaults command permanently changes the settings for all Command Prompt windows. The changes you make are not put into effect in the current window, but you'll see them in the Command Prompt windows you open hereafter.

■ The Properties command changes the settings for the current Command Prompt window. The changes take effect immediately. However, when you click OK, you have the opportunity to make the changes permanent, affecting all future sessions in this command processor (launched from the shortcut you used to open the command session).

If you apply the changes only to the current session, the next time you use the same shortcut to open a command window, you won't see the configuration changes. If you opt to modify the shortcut, the changes are applied and saved only to the command window that appears when you use the same shortcut you used to open the window for which you made configuration changes. If you made changes in the window that opened as a result of choosing the Command Prompt listing on the Accessories menu, you won't see your changes if you open a window via a shortcut on your Quick Launch toolbar (even if you copied the Accessories menu listing to the toolbar).

Options Tab

The choices available in the Options tab (see Figure 7-1) cover a variety of configuration options:

■ **Cursor Size**   Change the size of the blinking cursor. Small is an underline, Medium is a small square, and Large is a square the same size as the font.

■ **Command History**   The Buffer Size is the number of commands stored in the buffer. The Number of Buffers is really the number of processes that can maintain history buffers. Increasing either one of these options uses more memory. Enable the Discard Old Duplicates check box to have the system eliminate duplicate commands in the buffer history.

■ **Display Options**   You can change the size of the window from Window (the default) to Full Screen. To toggle between Window and Full Screen while you're working in the Command Prompt window, press ALT-ENTER.

■ **Edit Options**   Select Quick Edit Mode to drag the mouse for cutting, copying, and pasting text, instead of using the Edit menu. Select Insert Mode to insert text in the Command Prompt window instead of overwriting existing text.

Tip   *Insert Mode is handy if you're not a terrific typist; it lets you back up through a command and parameters and correct typing errors.*

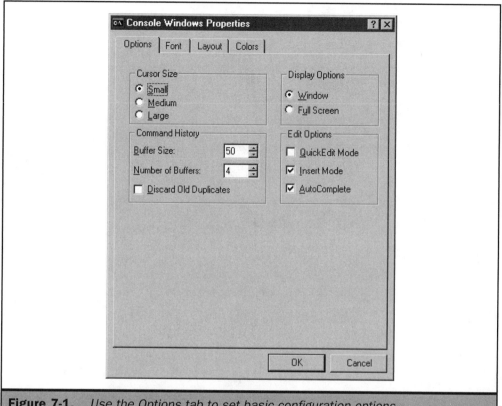

Figure 7-1.   *Use the Options tab to set basic configuration options.*

Font Tab

Use the Font tab (see Figure 7-2) to change the appearance of the contents of the command window.

You can opt to use Raster Fonts (the default) or a TrueType font (Lucinda Console). The Size section of the dialog changes its options, depending on the type of font you selected:

■ Change the size of the Raster font by selecting a different pixel measurement.

■ Change the size of the TrueType font by selecting a different point size, or enter a point size directly in the text box at the top of the list. (Click the Bold Fonts check box to use bold TrueType fonts in the command window.)

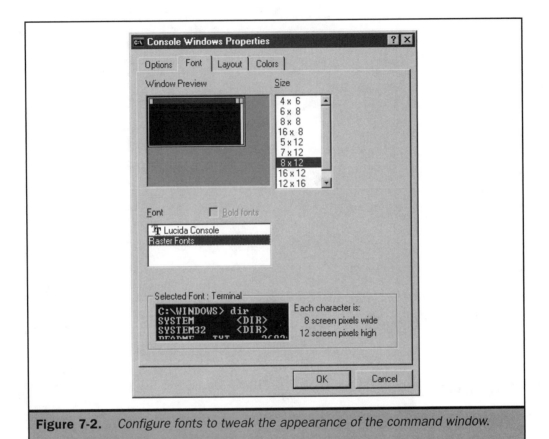

Figure 7-2.   *Configure fonts to tweak the appearance of the command window.*

As you make changes, you can see the effects in the Window Preview section at the top of the dialog, and in the Selected Font section at the bottom of the dialog.

Layout Tab

Use the Layout tab (see Figure 7-3) to size and position the Command Prompt window with the following options:

- **Screen Buffer Size**   Specify the width and height of the screen buffer. The width is the number of characters that display on a line. The height is the number of lines that display for text that's in the buffer. If the size of the window is smaller than the size of the buffer, scroll bars appear, enabling you to view the contents of the entire buffer.

- **Window Size**   Specify the width (number of characters) and height (number of lines) for the window.

■ **Window Position**   By default, the system positions the window, but you can deselect that option and specify the left and top settings for the window's position on your monitor. This is useful if you keep a command window open most of the time, and you want to position it for easy access when application windows are also open on your screen.

Window Colors Tab

Use the Colors tab to set the color for each of the following elements:

■ Screen Text

■ Screen Background

■ Popup Text

■ Popup Background

Note   *Pop-up command windows are those windows that open automatically as a result of some user action.*

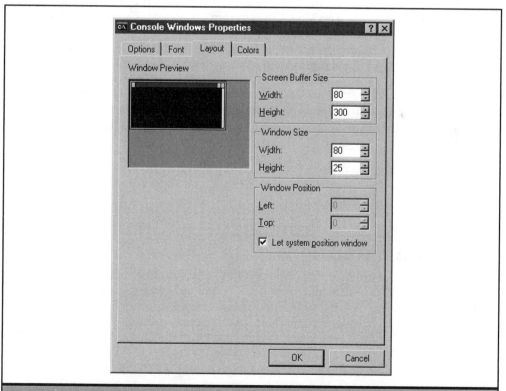

Figure 7-3.   *Use the Layout tab to redesign the Command Prompt window.*

Copy and Paste in the Command Prompt Window

To copy text from a Command Prompt window, select the text using one of these methods:

- If you've configured the Command Prompt window for Quick Edit Mode, drag your mouse across the text you want to copy and press ENTER to place it on the clipboard.

- If you haven't configured the Command Prompt window for Quick Edit Mode, right-click the title bar and choose Edit | Mark. Then position your cursor at the beginning of the text you want to copy. Hold down the SHIFT key and click the end of the text you want to copy. Alternatively, drag your mouse to select the text after you choose Edit | Mark. With the text highlighted, press ENTER to place the text on the clipboard.

Note   *You cannot cut text from a Command Prompt window, you can only copy.*

To paste the text into a Windows application window, choose Edit | Paste or press CTRL-V. To paste the text into an MS-DOS program (or another Command Prompt window), right-click the title bar and choose Edit | Paste.

To Paste text from another application into a Command Prompt window, position your cursor at the point of insertion. Then use one of these methods to paste the text:

- If you have configured the Command Prompt window for Quick Edit Mode, right-click to paste the text automatically.

- If you haven't configured the Command Prompt window for Quick Edit Mode, right-click and choose Paste from the menu that appears.

- If you're truly a command-line freak and prefer to do everything at the keyboard instead of using a mouse, press ALT-SPACE and then enter **e, p** (stands for edit, paste).

Command Extensions

The power of the Windows Server 2003 command line is augmented by command extensions, which add functionality to specific commands. Extensions are enabled by default (see the section "Disabling Command Extensions" to learn how to turn off extensions).

Commands with Extensions

The following is a list of commands that support extensions. The extensions are particular to each command, and you can get specific information by entering *command /?* at the command line.

- Assoc
- Call
- Cd or Chdir
- Del or Erase
- Endlocal
- For
- Ftype
- Goto
- If
- Md or Mkdir
- Popd
- Prompt
- Pushd
- Set
- Setlocal
- Shift
- Start

Disabling Command Extensions

Extensions are enabled by default, but you can disable them for a single session in the command processor, or disable them permanently.

Disabling Command Extensions for a Single Command Session

To disable and re-enable command extensions during a single command processor session, enter **cmd /e:on** or **cmd /e:off** at the command line. For example, you may want to disable command extensions when you're using the cd command, and then re-enable command extensions for the rest of the tasks you're performing in that session.

Permanently Disabling Command Extensions

If you want to turn extensions off or on for all command sessions, you must change the registry. You can apply the setting to the computer (affecting every user) or to the current user. Open Regedit and travel to either of the following subkeys:

- To enable or disable extensions for the computer, go to HKEY_LOCAL_MACHINE\ Software\Microsoft\Command Processor.

- To enable or disable extensions for the current user on a computer, go to HKEY_CURRENT_USER\Software\Microsoft\Command Processor.

Open the REG_DWORD data item named EnableExtensions, and enter **1** (on) or **0** (off). By default, this data type is hex, so your entry is translated to 0x1 or 0x0.

Managing Conflicts in Command Extensions Configuration

If the enabling configuration differs among the setting locations, there's a pecking order for extensions enabling:

1. Command-line entry (**cmd /e:X** where *X* is on or off).

2. Current User registry setting.

3. Local Computer registry setting.

Folder and Filename Completion

Folder and filename completion is a feature that lets you type a partial directory name or filename against a command, and then let the system autocomplete the full file or directory name. The feature works by means of a control character you enter that invokes the function. For example, you can enter **cd \pro** *control character* to get to the Programs Files directory, or enter **type myf** *control character* to display the contents of myfile.txt on the screen. If multiple directories or files match the characters you enter, pressing the control character again moves you to the next instance. When you get to the correct target, press ENTER to complete the command. If no target matches your string, the system beeps.

Name completion is not turned on by default, but you can invoke it for a single command session, or make it a permanent feature.

Enable Folder and Filename Completion for a Command Session

If you want to enable folder and filename completion for the command session you're currently working in, you can perform that task right at the command line. Enter **cmd /f:on** to turn on the feature; enter **cmd /f:off** to turn off the feature. Then use CTRL-D to complete a directory entry, and use CTRL-F to complete a filename entry.

Enable Folder and Filename Completion Permanently

If you want to make the feature permanent, a registry entry accomplishes that task. You can enable autocompletion either for the computer or for the current user. Most of the time, it's easiest to enable this feature for the computer, so that it's available to all users. However, you can turn the feature off for any individual user, or you can use different control characters for the user than you applied to the computer. Whenever there's a conflict between the computer settings and the user settings, the user settings win.

Enable Folder and Filename Completion for a Computer

To enable name completion for the computer, open Regedit and go to HKEY_LOCAL_MACHINE\Software\Microsoft\Command Processor.

- For directory name completion, open the value item CompletionChar and enter the control character you want to use, in hex.
- For filename completion, open the value item PathCompletionChar and enter the control character you want to use, in hex.

Enable Folder and Filename Completion for the Current User

To enable name completion for the current user, open Regedit, go to HKEY_CURRENT_USER\Software\Microsoft\Command Processor, and perform the same steps described for entering the settings for the computer.

Choose the Control Character

The control characters are entered in the registry as hex. For example, if you want to use the TAB key as the control character, the control character is 0×9 (you can enter **9** as the value and the system will convert it to hex). If you want to use the same characters you enter when you're enabling the feature for a single command session, use 0×4 for CTRL-D and 0×6 for CTRL-F.

Filename Completion vs. Folder Completion

Here's a quick explanation of the differences between the filename and directory name completion functions:

- The filename completion feature works on directories, too, because it's actually searching for a complete path, matching against both file and directory names.
- If the file completion control character is used on a command that works only against directories (for example, cd or rd), only directory names are searched.
- The directory completion function matches only against directory names, which makes it faster for directory searching than the filename completion function when there are both files and directories with matching strings.
- You can use the same control character for both the directory name and filename autocompletion feature.

If the control characters you use to enable this feature for the computer are different from the control characters you use to enable the feature for the current user, the current user settings have precedence.

If you spend a lot of time at the command line (some of us are really command-line freaks and are comfortable and happy entering text), this function is extremely useful. Not only does it save typing, it also eliminates those frustrating moments when you either make a typo or forget the exact spelling of a directory or filename. To make all of this even easier, here are some tips on using the name completion feature:

- You must enter a space between directory commands, such as **cd** or **rd**, and the backslash.

- The completion function automatically places quotation marks around names that contain spaces, so you don't have to enter the quotation marks.

- You can use the LEFTARROW key to back up and then enter the control character again. All text to the right of the cursor is discarded. This is handy if you want to widen the search by shortening the string.

- After searching, if you edit the string and press the control character again, the existing list of matches is ignored and a new list is generated.

Wildcard Shortcuts

Windows Server 2003 has a command-line wildcard shortcut feature. You can enter a command and a string representing a partial name (of a directory or a file, depending on the command) and end the string with a wildcard. Windows executes the command against every matching directory or folder. Most of us are aware of this feature and use it constantly, as in the command **dir *.txt** or **dir tr***.

However, the wildcard also works with other commands, such as **cd**. If you enter the command **cd \wi*** on a computer that has a directory named Windows, the command executes properly. If you enter the same command on a computer that has a directory named Windows and a directory named Wizards, the command executes against the first match (Windows).

This feature does not offer the flexibility and user-control of the name completion feature, which displays each match as you continue to press the control character, and leaves it to the user to press the ENTER key when the appropriate command appears.

Windows Server 2003 Commands

The command line is a favored tool for many administrators and power users, especially those of us whose computing roots go back to the DOS-only world. This section discusses commands that have disappeared or changed from Windows NT/9x. The information presented here also applies to Windows 2000/XP.

Commands Not Supported in Windows Server 2003

A number of MS-DOS commands (16-bit commands) have disappeared from Windows Server 2003. In fact, some of them had already disappeared in Windows NT 4 and Windows 2000, but they're covered here in case you hadn't noticed, or you're migrating from Windows NT 3.*x* or a non-Windows environment. Table 7-2 describes the obsolete 16-bit commands.

Unsupported Command	Explanation
Assign	No longer supported.
Backup	No longer supported.
Choice	No longer supported.
Ctty	No longer supported.
Dblspace	No longer supported.
Deltree	Replaced by rmdir /s, which removes directories that contain files and subdirectories.
Dosshell	Not needed.
Drvspace	No longer supported.
Emm386	Not needed.
Fasthelp	Not needed; use the help command instead.
Fdisk	Replaced by Disk Management.
Include	Multiple configurations of the MS-DOS subsystem are not supported.
Interlnk	No longer supported.
Intersrv	No longer supported.
Join	Not needed with the support for larger partitions.
Memmaker	Not needed; the operating system automatically optimizes the way the MS-DOS subsystem uses memory.
Menucolor	Multiple configurations of the MS-DOS subsystem are not supported.

Table 7-2.   *MS-DOS Commands That Are Not Available in Windows Server 2003*

Unsupported Command	Explanation
Menudefault	Multiple configurations of the MS-DOS subsystem are not supported.
Menuitem	Multiple configurations of the MS-DOS subsystem are not supported.
Mirror	No longer supported.
Msav	No longer supported.
Msbackup	Not needed; use ntbackup for tape drive targets, or use xcopy for hard drive targets.
Mscdex	Not needed; Windows Server 2003 provides CD-ROM access for the MS-DOS subsystem.
Msd	Not needed; use the System Information snap-in.
Numlock	No longer supported.
Power	No longer supported.
Restore	No longer supported.
Scandisk	No longer supported; use chkdsk.
Smartdrv	Not needed; Windows Server 2003 provides caching for the MS-DOS subsystem automatically.
Submenu	Multiple configurations of the MS-DOS subsystem are not supported.
Sys	Windows Server 2003 system files will not fit on a floppy disk.
Undelete	No longer supported.
Unformat	No longer supported.
Vsafe	No longer supported.

Table 7-2.   *MS-DOS Commands That Are Not Available in Windows Server 2003 (continued)*

Notice that the list in Table 7-2 omits some 16-bit commands that you may still be using (especially in legacy batch files). When you invoke these commands, the command session behaves like a 16-bit session. This means the display of directory names changes to the 8.3 format. In fact, the prompt changes to the 8.3 format. To return to the standard

Windows Server 2003 display, enter **cd*original directory*—**for example, cd\documents and settings*username*.

Commands Not Supported in Enterprise or DataCenter Server

If you're running Windows Server 2003 Enterprise Server or DataCenter Server, or any 64-bit version of any Windows OS, the following 16-bit commands are not available:

- Append
- Debug
- Edit
- Edlin
- Exe2bin
- Expand
- Graphics
- Loadfix
- Loadhigh (lh)
- Mem
- Setver
- Share

The following commands are not used by Windows Server 2003, but are accepted for compatibility with MS-DOS files and programs:

- Fastopen
- Forcedos
- Nlsfunc

Commands That Have Changed

Some of the commands that are available in Windows Server 2003 have changed since Windows *9x*, and for the most part the changes bring additional power.

Chcp

This command displays or configures the active code page number. It has changed in that it now changes code pages for all command windows.

- Use the command without parameters to display the active code page number.
- Use the syntax **chcp** *nnn* to specify the code page number *nnn*.

Del or Erase

This command supports the following switches (not all are new):

- **file or directory** (including wildcards) targets the named file or directory.
- **/P** prompts for confirmation before deleting each file (available in earlier versions of Windows).
- **/F** forces deletion of read-only files.
- **/S** deletes specified files from all subdirectories in which they exist; displays the files that are being deleted with command extensions enabled (the default); displays the files it could not find if command extensions are disabled.
- **/Q** indicates quiet mode (do not ask for confirmation on global wildcard).
- **/A** selects files based on attributes. Use the standard attribute abbreviations when selecting by attribute: R S H A (use the minus sign to indicate "not").

Dir

The following parameters are available for Dir (not all are new):

- **[drive:][path][filename]** specifies the drive, directory, and/or files to list.
- **/A** displays files with specified attributes, as follows:
  - **D** Directories
  - **R** Read-only files
  - **H** Hidden files
  - **A** Files ready for archiving
  - **S** System files
- **/B** uses bare format (no heading information or summary).
- **/C** displays the thousand separator in file sizes (the default); use –C to disable.
- **/D** displays the same as /W (wide), but files are listed sorted by column.
- **/L** displays in lowercase.
- **/N** displays filenames on the far right.
- **/O** lists in sorted order as follows:
  - **N** By name (alphabetic)
  - **S** By size (smallest first)
  - **E** By extension (alphabetic)
  - **D** By date/time (oldest first)
  - **G** Group directories first

- **/P** pauses after each screenful of information.

- **/Q** displays the file owner.

- **/S** displays the files in the specified directory and all subdirectories.

- **/T** controls which time field is displayed or used for sorting, as follows:

  - **C**   Creation

  - **A**   Last access (earliest first)

  - **W**   Last written

- **/W** displays in wide list format.

- **/X** displays the short names generated for non-8.3 filenames (like **/N** with the short name inserted before the long name, but if no short name is present, blanks are displayed).

- **/4** displays four-digit years.

Diskcopy

Diskcopy no longer supports the /1 parameter, which copied only the first side of the disk.

Format

The Format command takes any of the following syntax forms:

- **Format** *volume* [/FS:*file-system*] [/V:*label*] [/Q] [/A:*size*] [/C] [/X]

- **Format** *volume* [/V:*label*] [/Q] [/F:*size*]

- **Format** *volume* [/V:*label*] [/Q] [/T:*tracks* /N:*sectors*]

- **Format** *volume* [/V:*label*] [/Q] [/1] [/4]

- **Format** *volume* [/Q] [/1] [/4] [/8]

where:

- *volume* is the drive letter (must be followed by a colon), mount point, or volume name

- /FS:*file-system* is the type of file system.

- /V:*label* is the volume label (the symbols ^ and & are permitted in the volume label).

- /Q specifies quick format.

- /C specifies that files created on the volume will be compressed by default.

- /X forces the volume to dismount first if necessary (closes all open handles).

- **/A:***size* forces an override of the default allocation unit size:
  - NTFS supports 512, 1024, 2048, 4096, 8192, 16K, 32K, 64K
  - FAT supports 512, 1024, 2048, 4096, 8192, 16K, 32K, 64K (128K, 256K for sector size > 512 bytes)
  - FAT32 supports 512, 1024, 2048, 4096, 8192, 16K, 32K, 64K (128K, 256K for sector size > 512 bytes)
- **/F:***size* specifies the size of the floppy disk to format (160, 180, 320, 360, 640, 720, 1.2, 1.23, 1.44, 2.88, or 20.8) (available in Windows 9*x*).
- **/T:***tracks* specifies the number of tracks per disk side.
- **/N:***sectors* specifies the number of sectors per track.

Label

You can now use the caret (^) and ampersand (&) symbols in a volume label.

More

Unlike its counterpart in legacy versions of Windows, the Windows Server 2003 More command has parameters:

- **/E** enables extended features.
- **/C** clears screen before displaying page.
- **/P** expands FormFeed characters.
- **/S** squeezes multiple blank lines into a single line.
- **/T***n* expands tabs to *n* spaces (default is 8).

The following switches can be present in the More environment variable:

- **+***n* starts displaying the first file at line *n*.
- **files** specifies a list of files to display (separate filenames with blanks).

If extended features are enabled, the following commands can be used at the "More" prompt:

- **P** *n* displays next *n* lines.
- **S** *n* skips next *n* lines.
- **F** displays next file.
- **Q** quits.
- **=** shows the line number.
- **?** shows help line.
- **<space>** displays next page.
- **<ret>** displays next line.

Prompt

Windows Server 2003, like Windows 2000, supports the following new additions to your command prompt:

- **$A**   Ampersand
- **$C**   Open parentheses
- **$F**   Close parentheses
- **$S**   Space

Xcopy

A new /g switch lets you keep file encryption when you copy encrypted files to a volume that doesn't support file encryption.

Using UNCs on the Command Line

You can use the Windows Server 2003 command line to reach across the network and manipulate directories and files on other computers. (Of course, your ability to do this is dependent on your permissions.)

Viewing and Manipulating Files via UNCs

The following command-line examples display some of the ways you can use UNCs on the command line:

- dir \\ComputerName\ShareName
- dir \\ComputerName\ShareName\Subdirectory_of_ShareName
- copy \\ComputerName\ShareName\Filename c:\my documents
- del \\ComputerName\ShareName\Filename(s)

Using Pushd and Popd to Access Remote Computers

The **cd** command doesn't work with a UNC address, so you can't move to a remote share as easily as you can on your local computer. However, you can use pushd to automatically assign a temporary drive letter to a remote share, and move to that share automatically. Then, you can use popd to remove the temporary drive letter. The following sections on pushd and popd assume that command extensions are enabled for the command processor (the default state of Windows Server 2003). If you disable command extensions, pushd won't work with UNC paths.

To use pushd, enter the following command:

pushd *ComputerName******ShareName*

where *ShareName* is a shared drive or a directory.

When you press ENTER, the command launches the following three actions:

- Stores the path of the current directory in memory so that it's available to popd later (popd returns you to this drive when you use it to remove the drive assignment you're making with pushd).

- Assigns a drive letter to the UNC path you entered. Drive letters are automatically assigned starting with z: and working backwards.

- Moves you to the target share, displaying a prompt for the automatically assigned drive letter.

Once your prompt changes to the assigned drive letter, you are working in the remote share and you can manipulate directories and files at will, just as if you were working locally. All the commands available locally are available to you in this remote share.

You can use pushd as often as you wish, and Windows Server 2003 will keep the path of each drive letter/share assignment until you've worked your way so far down the alphabet that you've bumped into local drive letters (at which point pushd refuses to cooperate). To move among multiple remote shares, just enter the appropriate drive letter at the command prompt.

The assignments made by pushd don't survive the current command session, so if you're planning to move back and forth between your local computer and remote shares, keep the command window open (you can, of course, minimize it).

To release the drive letter, enter **popd** at the command line, which removes the last assigned drive letter. If you only assigned one drive letter with pushd, popd returns you to the local directory you were on when you issued the pushd command. If you assigned multiple drive letters, popd removes the last assigned drive letter and moves you to the next-to-last drive letter you assigned. Continue to enter popd at the command line to remove additional drive letters, until you're returned to the original local drive. If you want to remove all the assigned drive letters, just close the command session.

PUSHD is very convenient if you use batch files for remote systems management. You could use a batch file to remove certain files from multiple machines with the following line in your batch file:

- pushd \\servername\share
- del filename.ext

Pushd and Net Use

You can, of course, avail yourself of the net use command to map drives to remote shares. Here are some useful comparative facts about pushd and net use:

- Drives created by net use survive the command session. They also survive a reboot if you use the /persistent:yes switch. Note that the /persistent:yes switch may be the default, because the default state of this parameter is whatever you last used either in the GUI or the command line. If you've never mapped a drive, Windows Server 2003 has set the default to yes.

- You can enter **net use** at the command line to see all the mapped drives you've created with net use and/or with pushd.

- If you create a drive with net use that assigns a drive letter already assigned by pushd, net use issues an error to tell you the drive letter is in use.

- If you create a drive with net use, using z:, and then use pushd, pushd will return y: as the assigned drive (it checks the drive letters in use, whether they were mapped by net use or by pushd).

- You can delete a drive mapping created by either pushd or net use by entering **net use** *DriveLetter*: **/del** at the command line.

Use Subst for Local Virtual Drives

You can use the virtual drive paradigm that pushd provides for remote shares to navigate through your local computer. This is easier than entering **cd***DirectoryName* for all those directories with long names (like \documents and settings, or \program files\internet explorer).

Use Pushd in Batch Files

I'm a command-line junkie, and I use a lot of command-line tools to accomplish tasks. I therefore use a batch file to pre-assign all the remote directories I commonly visit. Here's my batch file:

```
pushd \\western\western-c
pushd \\wks12\wks12-c\windows\profiles\kathy\my documents
pushd \\docs\newsletters
```

- The first line points to the shared hard drive of a computer named western (giving me full access to all directories on the drive).

- The second line points to the My Documents folder for me on a Windows 98 SE computer named wks12 (in Windows 98 SE, profiles are stored under \Windows\Profiles*UserName*). The My Documents folder isn't shared, but drive C: is, and this line illustrates that you can travel through the unshared subdirectories of a share to assign a drive letter.

- The third line points to a share named newsletters on a computer named docs.

Notice this batch file does not end with the **exit** command. That would close the command window, removing all the drive assignments, because they don't survive the command session. For this reason, I run the batch file from the command line. If I were to open the batch file from Windows Explorer, My Computer, or an entry in the Startup folder of the Programs menu, the command window would close, ending the session, when the batch file finished its commands.

You can use the subst command (**subst** *DriveLetter: Path*) to assign a drive letter to a local path. Unlike pushd, the drive letter is not assigned automatically; you must specify it manually. This means you must know what drives are available for the subst command. You can't use a drive letter that's already in use, so to help you remember what you've done, check for drive letters that may be in use via net use or pushd by entering **net use** at the command line.

Enter **subst** without parameters at the command line, and the system returns the mappings created by subst. (Virtual drives that are created by the subst command aren't displayed when you enter **net use**.) To remove a local virtual drive, enter **subst** *DriveLetter:* **/d**. Unlike pushd, virtual drives created by subst survive a command session. They don't survive a reboot.

Help for Commands

The Windows Server 2003 Help and Support system contains an alphabetical listing of every available command, along with syntax information. In the Help and Support Services window, enter **command-line reference a-z** in the Search field. Select that page from the Results pane and choose Add to Favorites. Then you just have to click the Favorites tool on the Help and Support Services window for easy access to command information.

You can also get help on any command by entering *CommandName* **/?** at a command prompt.

The
Complete
Reference

Chapter 8

System Maintenance Tools

Windows Server 2003 provides housekeeping tools you can use to make sure your server purrs along. Consistent periodic maintenance is important, and those who fail to perform maintenance tasks usually regret the omission. This chapter covers the basic system maintenance tools for Windows Server 2003 versions.

Defragmentation

When you open a data file in a software application, make changes to the file, and save it again, the file's original location on the drive may not have room for the new, larger document. The operating system splits the document, using one part of the drive for some of the file and another part for the rest. As you continue to expand the size of the file, it may be saved to multiple locations on the drive. Now the file is said to be *fragmented*. Every time you open a file that's fragmented, the system must search the drive to find all its parts. This searching procedure slows down your work because it takes multiple disk reads to load the file.

When you delete files and folders, especially if you delete groups of files and folders, you create small locations of available space, and as you continue to work, creating and saving files, it's less likely that the files will nestle neatly into one contiguous space. Eventually, every time you create a file or a folder, or save a changed file, it requires more time to complete the write to the drive, because the system must make multiple writes to multiple locations to hold the new object. Your drive is fragmented. Windows Server 2003 provides two built-in programs to defragment your drives:

- Disk Defragmenter, on the System Tools submenu of the Accessories menu. Selecting this menu option opens an MMC snap-in, dfrg.msc.

- Defrag.exe, which works from the command line.

You can use either utility to optimize your drive by defragmenting the files (commonly called *defragging*). A defragmenter works by gathering all the pieces of a file and writing them back to the drive in one contiguous location. The program makes room for each file by moving other files (which may also be fragmented) out of the way, placing them in a temporary location until it's their turn to be defragmented.

Disk Defragmenter Snap-in

Launch the GUI version of the built-in defragger by opening the Accessories submenu, pointing to the System Tools submenu, and choosing Disk Defragmenter. You must have administrator rights to use this snap-in.

You can create a desktop shortcut to the Disk Defragmenter. Right-drag the program file (%SystemRoot%\System32\dfrg.msc) to the desktop, and choose Create Shortcut(s) Here from the shortcut menu. You can move the shortcut to your Quick Launch toolbar if you wish.

Analyze the Drive

The Disk Defragmenter window, shown in Figure 8-1, lists the local drives, along with information about the installed file system, capacity, and disk space usage. It's a good idea to have Disk Defragmenter analyze the disk before running a defragmentation procedure. In fact, it's foolish not to analyze first, because defragging is an intensive, lengthy procedure, and an analysis could show there's no need to defrag the drive.

Starting an analysis is easy—there is no shortage of methods for launching the Analyze process:

- Right-click a drive and choose Analyze from the shortcut menu.
- Select a drive and click the Analyze button.
- Select a drive and choose Analyze from the Action menu.

Caution *Open files cannot be analyzed (or defragged), so close all applications and utilities before beginning this process.*

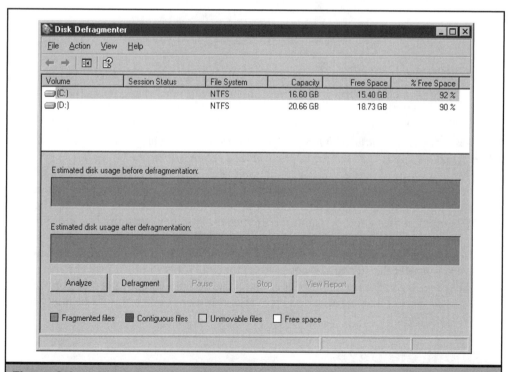

Figure 8-1. *All local drives are displayed in the Disk Defragmenter window.*

The Analyze function inspects the drive, and you can watch the progress in the Analysis Display bar. The display is color-coded:

- Blue = contiguous files
- Red = fragged files
- White = free space
- Green = system files (cannot be moved).

You can click the Pause button to halt the process if you need to retrieve a file or perform some other task on the computer. The button title changes to Resume so you can start the analysis again. Use the Stop button to halt the entire process. When the analysis is complete, a message box displays to advise you whether your drive needs to be defragmented.

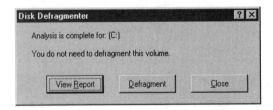

For detailed information about the state of the drive, click View Report to see which files and folders are fragmented and the number of fragmented segments that exist for each (see Figure 8-2).

You can use the buttons on the Analysis Report window to print the report, or save it as a text file, if you have some reason to require a permanent record.

Scroll through the list of folders and files on the report, and if files you use frequently are highly fragmented, that's probably why your system has seemed sluggish. The more fragmented files you open, and the greater the number of fragments, the slower your system performs.

After viewing the report, if you decide you want to defrag the drive even though Disk Defragmenter doesn't find it necessary, you can. You should run the Analyze procedure regularly; the frequency depends on the activity level of the computer. For instance, file servers that are accessed by a large number of users should be analyzed at least weekly.

Defragment the Drive

You can defrag a drive immediately after running the Analyze procedure (a Defragment button appears on both the Analysis Complete message box and the Analysis Report window), or wait until later. Open files cannot be defragged, so be sure to close all applications. If you're defragging a file server, perform the task during non-business hours. Start the defragmentation procedure by selecting the appropriate drive and using one of these methods:

- Click the Defragment button.
- Choose Defragment from the Action menu.
- Right-click the drive's listing and choose Defragment from the shortcut menu.

Before the defragging starts, the drive is re-analyzed (even if you just finished running the Analyze procedure); then the defragmentation procedure begins. The Analyze display bar shows the graphical representation of your drive as analyzed, and the Defragmentation display bar shows the condition of your drive as defragging proceeds. You can track the progress in the Defragmentation display bar, but it's probably better to find something else to do, because this process takes quite a bit of time. When defragmentation is complete, a message announces that fact. Use the View Report button in the message box to see a detailed report on the drive's new fragmentation state.

Limitations of the Disk Defragmenter

The Disk Defragmenter application that is included with Windows Server 2003 has some serious limitations. Microsoft programmers didn't write this software; it's obtained from

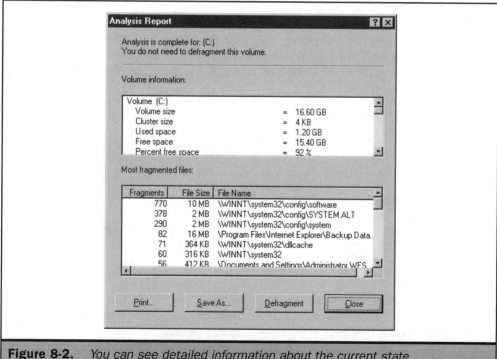

Figure 8-2. *You can see detailed information about the current state of fragmentation.*

Executive Software, who provided a limited version of its full retail product. Here are the limitations:

- You cannot schedule the Disk Defragmenter.
- You can only defrag local volumes; this version has no capacity for remote procedures.
- You can defrag only one volume at a time.
- The program cannot be scripted.

The real retail copy of Diskeeper isn't limited, and you can purchase a full retail copy of the program from Executive Software (www.execsoft.com).

   Because file servers are the most common victims of fragmentation, and at the same time cannot be defragmented during normal business hours, the lack of scheduling is bothersome (unless you like coming to the office at 2 o'clock in the morning). For that reason alone, it's worth investigating the cost of purchasing the full product.

Defrag.exe

New to Windows Server 2003 is defrag.exe, a command-line program that you can use instead of the snap-in. This executable calls the same code the snap-in calls (the Executive Software Disk Defragmenter).

Using defrag.exe has several advantages, and the biggest benefit is that you can schedule it, using the Windows Server 2003 Task Scheduler, which isn't possible with the snap-in. The other advantage, which is probably only considered an advantage to command-line junkies, is that it has the speed and efficiency of a command-line application.

The syntax for defrag.exe is

defrag *volume:* {/**a**] [/**f**] [/**v**]

where:

volume: is the drive letter of the volume you want to defrag.

/**a** only runs the analyze process.

/**f** forces defragmentation of the volume even if an analysis shows it doesn't need to be defragmented.

/**v** displays verbose output while the program is running.

If you enter **defrag** *volume letter:* at the command line, without any switches, the program performs an analysis, then defrags the drive. In fact, the program always performs an analysis first, even if you specify the /**f** switch.

If you don't opt to display verbose output, the program displays a summary of the analysis, and then you see a blinking cursor. When defragging is complete, you're returned to the command prompt. If you choose the **/v** switch, the program displays information about the defragmentation state of the folders and files from the analysis process (the Analysis Report), and then displays the same report, hopefully with better statistics (called the Defragmentation Report), after the defragging process.

The two reports are difficult to compare in the command window, because you have to keep scrolling up to see the analysis numbers, to compare them to the defragged numbers that are displayed further down. I find it easier to redirect the output of the reports, and then open the resulting data file in a word processor so that I can manipulate the display for easier interpretation. To redirect an onscreen report, add the following to the end of the command:

> *filename.ext* (use the filename and extension you prefer)

Press CTRL-C to stop the program. Unlike the built-in Disk Defragmenter, you can't pause defrag.exe.

 You cannot run defrag.exe and the built-in Disk Defragmenter simultaneously. Whichever program starts first wins, and the second program fails.

Troubleshooting Defragmentation

Don't be surprised if, after the defragging process is complete, your drive is still somewhat fragmented. There are a number of scenarios that can cause this, and some of them can be corrected.

Some System Files are Never Defragged

The disk defragger is hard-coded to omit certain system files. Microsoft and Executive Software have documented the following omitted files:

- Bootsect.dos
- Safeboot.fs
- Safeboot.csv
- Safeboot.rsv
- Hiberfil.sys
- Memory.dmp (if it exists)
- Paging file (see the next section for a possible workaround)

 In Windows Server 2003, the ShellIconCache file is no longer excluded (it was excluded in Windows 2000).

Memory.dmp is a file that exists if you've configured your system to write the file when the system encounters a STOP error (Blue Screen of Death). The file is on the exclusion list in Windows Server 2003 because the disk locations where this file is stored are loaded by the kernel when the system boots, and stored in memory. These disk locations are then used to write the dump file, should it be needed. Because the location is in memory, the defragger cannot move it.

Defragmenting the System Paging File

The *system paging file* (sometimes called the *swap file*) is always held open for exclusive use by the operating system, and therefore cannot be defragmented. However, if the paging file becomes fragmented, performance suffers quite noticeably. You can remedy the problem if you have a second drive or partition on your computer. Here's how:

1. Open the System applet in Control Panel, or right-click My Computer and choose Properties from the shortcut menu.

2. In the System Properties dialog, move to the Advanced tab and click the Settings button in the Performance section of the dialog.

3. In the Performance Options dialog, move to the Advanced tab.

4. Click the Change button in the Virtual Memory section of the dialog to open the Virtual Memory dialog shown in Figure 8-3.

5. Select another drive and configure a paging file with the same size specifications as the original paging file.

6. Select the original drive and then select No Paging File.

7. Reboot to force the system to use the new paging file.

8. Run Disk Defragmenter on the drive that originally held the paging file. You're not defragging the paging file, of course, because it's no longer there. Defragging the drive should create enough contiguous space to hold the paging file when you return it.

9. Move the paging file back to its original drive, using these same steps.

After you reboot, the paging file is created anew, as a contiguous file, on the original drive.

Insufficient Free Space Impairs Defragmentation

If you defrag a drive and the report that displays afterwards shows that many files are still fragmented, you may not have had enough free space on the disk to permit the software to temporarily "park" file fragments. Run the Analyze procedure again to see if the software still recommends defragmenting the drive (this frequently occurs). In fact, even if the analysis reports back that the drive doesn't need to be defragged, you still may want to run the defragmentation process to optimize the drive a bit more.

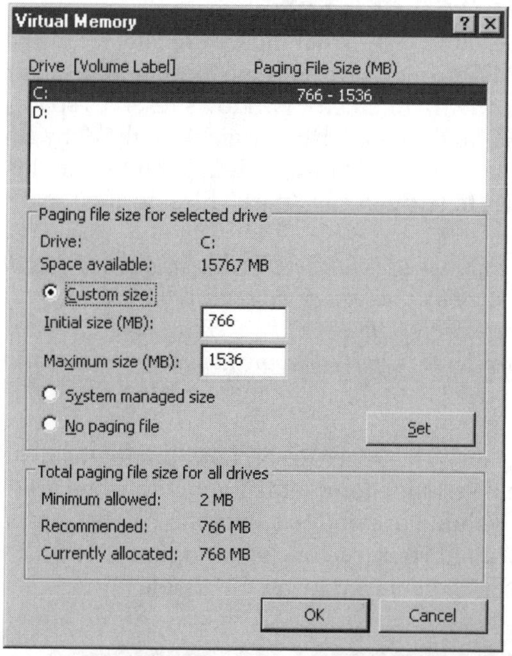

Virtual Memory   ? ✕

Drive [Volume Label]   Paging File Size (MB)

C: 766 - 1536
D:

Paging file size for selected drive

Drive: C:
Space available: 15767 MB

○ Custom size:

Initial size (MB):   766

Maximum size (MB):   1536

○ System managed size

○ No paging file   Set

Total paging file size for all drives

Minimum allowed: 2 MB
Recommended: 766 MB
Currently allocated: 768 MB

OK   Cancel

Figure 8-3.   *If you have two drives, you can temporarily move the paging file.*

As drives get crowded and free space shrinks, it's not uncommon to have to run the defragmentation utility several times in a row in order to get a drive defragged enough to improve productivity. Each time the process runs, Disk Defragmenter does as much as possible, given the constraints of inadequate disk space.

Tip   *The defragger requires at least 15 percent of your disk to be free, but 25 percent is a better goal.*

The optimal solution is to move a substantial number of files off the drive, by copying the files to another drive or another computer on the network. That solution works best after you've defragged the drive once or twice in a single session. Look at the report and note the names of the files that have been successfully defragged (find the largest contiguous files in the list). Copy those files to another drive or computer to give Disk Defragmenter chunks of contiguous space to work with. During the defragging process, the software also tries to put all the free space in contiguous blocks, which enhances the probability that the files you removed can be put into contiguous locations when you copy them back.

Disk Space Reserved in NTFS

NTFS has a Master File Table (MFT) that must be located at the beginning of the volume. The MFT holds information about the location of files (or multiple locations of files for those files that are fragmented). Windows reserves space at the beginning of the volume for the MFT, so that space isn't available to the defragmentation application. Not only must the defragger avoid locating defragged files in this reserved space, it can't even use the space to temporarily "park" files during the defragging process.

If you dig deeper into the use of this reserved space, you'll find that Windows does occasionally use it for storage of data other than the MFT. This isn't great, but if you lack enough free space on your drive, the operating system doesn't have much choice. This is another reason to perform ongoing housekeeping to make sure your drive has sufficient free space.

When you're calculating free space for NTFS volumes, the math isn't straightforward. One-eighth of a drive is set aside for the MFT zone, so when you view the used/free statistics for an NTFS volume in Windows Explorer or My Computer, you must account for this to calculate your true free space figure. Deduct about 12 percent from the free space figure that's displayed to get the usable figure.

Optimize Disk Defragmenter Performance

You can make the defragger more efficient by following some rules and procedures. Running the application after certain events lets you keep the workload level down, making the defragging process more efficient (and faster). Here are some rules to follow in order to accomplish this:

- Defrag after you uninstall an application.
- Defrag every time you delete a large number of files (or a smaller number of very large files).
- Defrag before installing an application, especially before installing any back office type of application (such as Exchange Server, Oracle, or SQL Server) on a server.
- Defrag after you update the operating system (for example, install a service pack, or reinstall OS files to repair a damaged system).

Scheduled Tasks

Scheduled Tasks is a task scheduler that's installed with Windows Server 2003, and you can use it to launch applications and utilities on a schedule you devise. The best use of Scheduled Tasks is to make sure maintenance tools run regularly. The tasks you create are files (with the extension .job) that can be exchanged via e-mail, or copied to remote computers, permitting you to create and run scheduled tasks on other computers. The .job task files are located in %SystemRoot%\Tasks.

You can launch this utility from Control Panel, or from the Start menu (in the System Tools submenu under Accessories). The Scheduled Tasks window opens to display an icon named Add Scheduled Task, along with icons for any existing tasks.

 Be sure the date and time of the computer are correct when you're running scheduled tasks.

Scheduled Tasks Execution File

If you're fascinated by the behind-the-scenes stuff, you may be interested to know that Scheduled Tasks isn't an application, or at least it has no executable. The utility runs as a DLL launched by explorer.exe, with the path statement:

```
%SystemRoot%\explorer.exe
::{20D04FE0-3AEA-1069-A2D8-08002B30309D}\::{21EC2020-3AEA-1069-A2DD-08002B30
309D}\::{D6277990-4C6A-11CF-8D87-00AA0060F5BF}
```

where:

```
{20D04FE0-3AEA-1069-A2D8-08002B30309D} is a CLSID for My Computer objects.

{21EC2020-3AEA-1069-A2DD-08002B30309D} is a CLSID for Control Panel objects.

{D6277990-4C6A-11CF-8D87-00AA0060F5BF} is a CLSID for a variety of icons and
objects referencing mstask.dll.
```

Use the Scheduled Task Wizard

Open the Add Scheduled Task icon to launch the wizard, and click Next to move past the welcome window. The wizard presents a list of the application files on your computer.

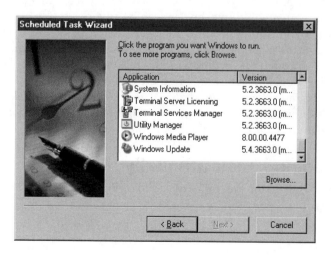

The list of applications displayed in the wizard window includes the components you installed with the operating system, and any third-party software you installed that appears in the list of applications in the Add or Remove Programs applet.

 Don't configure Windows Backup from the Scheduled Tasks window; it works in the other direction. The backup program has its own scheduling function, which automatically transfers the scheduled backup job to the Scheduled Tasks list.

If the application you want to schedule isn't in the list (usually this means a command-line program), click Browse to open the Select Program To Schedule window. This window is similar to any Open window, and you can select a local application, script, or document, or you can troll the network to select an object on a remote computer. In the next wizard window, you begin to configure the task.

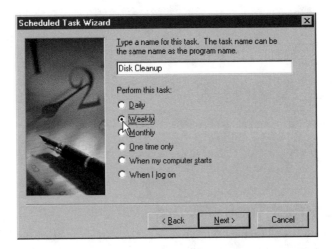

If you select the option When I log on, the task is connected to a username, which you enter in a subsequent window. The user can be anyone; you're not limited to doing this for your own logon. You must know the user's logon password to configure this option, and the user must have sufficient rights to launch the program.

Continue to go through the wizard window to configure this task. The last wizard window offers the usual Finish button, but there's also an option to let the Finish button open the Advanced Properties dialog that is created for the task. The task's Properties dialog offers additional configuration options (see the next section on creating a task manually for information about all the options).

Create a Scheduled Task Manually

If you want to leap right to the Properties dialog to configure your task, instead of stepping through the wizard, use one of these methods to create a new task:

- Choose File | New | Scheduled Task in the Scheduled Tasks window.
- Right-click a blank spot in the Scheduled Tasks window and choose New | Scheduled Task from the shortcut menu.

A new icon appears in the window, titled New Task. The title is in Edit mode so that you can enter a name for the new task. After you name the task, right-click its icon and choose Properties from the shortcut menu to open the task's Properties dialog (see Figure 8-4).

The following sections provide guidelines for using the Properties dialog to configure a task.

Task Tab

The options on the Task tab are pretty much self-explanatory, but there are a couple of guidelines you should be aware of.

If the task launches a program, you can add parameters to the executable file. Be sure the parameters are complete and accurate, and don't include any functions that require interactive actions. If you're using a switch that requires you to name an input

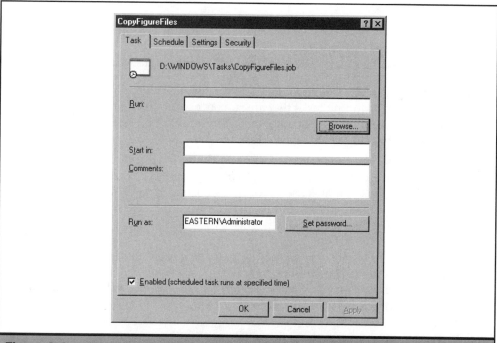

Figure 8-4.   *Configure a new task manually using its Properties dialog.*

file, be sure the file exists and you have typed its path correctly. Don't use a parameter that calls for confirmation, unless there's a way to use a parameter to send a Y/N response.

You can use the Run As field to enter the username and password under which this task runs. Be sure the user you enter has sufficient permissions to run the executable file.

Schedule Tab

The Schedule tab is the place to specify the frequency for the schedule, but there's a difference between the options presented in the wizard and those presented in the Properties dialog. The difference is a missing ingredient. The wizard offers a Weekdays option when you select Daily; the Properties dialog doesn't. If you want to run this task only on weekdays, you must select Weekly and then click the five business days of the week to create your workweek.

You can narrow or broaden the schedule configuration by clicking Advanced, and choosing the appropriate options (the options that are offered differ depending on the schedule category you chose).

> **Note**   *There are no advanced options for the following choices: System Startup, Logon, or When Idle.*

Settings Tab

The Settings tab offers options that let you control the way the task operates under certain system conditions (see Figure 8-5).

In the Scheduled Task Completed section of the Settings tab, you have two options:

- **Delete the task if it is not scheduled to run again.** This applies to tasks that have an end date (including tasks that are run once, of course). The job, along with its file, is removed after the last automatic occurrence. Don't select this option if this task might be reincarnated periodically.

- **Stop the task if it runs for:** *specified time.* Enter the duration of time you'll permit for this task to complete its job (the default is 72 hours, which is ridiculous). This option is useful for time-consuming tasks that you configure for middle-of-the-night operations and you want to make sure they're not running when the business day begins.

> **Tip**   *Don't specify a duration limit for backing up (or for any other critical task), because you want that task to run to completion regardless of the amount of time it requires. Instead, if the task runs for a long time, move the start time to an earlier setting to ensure the task is finished before the workday begins.*

In the Idle Time section of the Settings tab, specify the options for a task that you configured for execution during idle time.

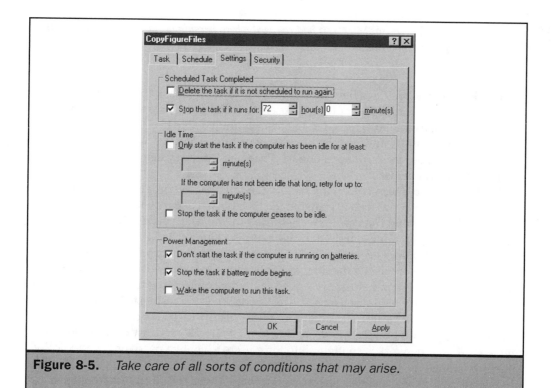

Figure 8-5.   *Take care of all sorts of conditions that may arise.*

The definition of *idle time* is "no mouse or keyboard activity." That, of course, doesn't mean a computer is idle, because all sorts of stuff could be going on, including downloads, database searches, replication, or other automated tasks. The Idle Time options don't help you make scheduled tasks run more efficiently, and you shouldn't schedule two processor-intensive or I/O-intensive tasks at the same time unless you're prepared to let them run for longer than they would if they were running alone.

In the Power Management section of the Settings tab, specify the behavior you desire if battery power issues arise when the task is scheduled (or already running). This option applies to laptops—it has nothing to do with computers that are switched over to UPS power devices when electrical power is lost. (In fact, if you're running UPS software such as PowerChute, your computer is probably configured for automatic shutdown.) An option to wake the computer to run this task appears for computers that support that feature.

Security Tab

The Security tab for scheduled tasks is back! If you're moving to Windows Server 2003 from Windows NT 4, you didn't know that it went missing, but Windows 2000 eliminated this feature. Many of us submitted bug reports over this issue during the beta test of Windows 2000, and during the first few beta releases of 2003 Server (it was still missing). Now it's back.

At the time of writing, Microsoft had released a beta version of the .dll that returns the Security tab to the Windows XP Task Scheduler (missing in Windows 2000 Professional). Look for the feature in a future Windows XP service pack.

The Security tab provides permissions and rights for this task file. Set the security options you need to allow the appropriate users to make changes to the task's properties. For example, the user who is linked to the task should be able to change the schedule, as should all the administrators who have responsibility for tasks. On the other hand, you don't want other users, or someone who has hacked the system, to be able to run, delete, or modify any tasks.

The Security tab doesn't affect the security settings for the program that's running under the task—the program's executable file has its own Security tab. When the task runs, its linked program runs as if it were started by the user you specified, with that user's security context. For example, if the user specified for a scheduled task is a member of the Backup Operators group on the local computer, the program specified in the scheduled task file runs as if a member of the Backup Operators group is logged on to the local computer. If another user is logged on to the computer at the time a scheduled task specified for a different user runs, the task runs but is not visible to the current user.

If a logged-on user creates a task that runs under her own account, or if an administrator creates a task that runs under a specific user account, that task's security context can cause problems. If your network is configured to force users to change passwords periodically, you must change the password attached to the scheduled tasks for each user. Changing one task password also changes the password for all other tasks linked to that user.

However, changing passwords for tasks is just too much trouble (mainly because the odds that you'll remember to do this are daunting). In addition, users change departments and computers, or leave the company. Because the Administrator's password never expires, it's best to use the Administrator account for tasks. Even better, create a user with administrative privileges for tasks, and change the configuration for that user so that passwords never expire.

Modify or Delete Scheduled Tasks

To change the properties of any task, open the Scheduled Tasks window and then open the task. Move to the appropriate tab of the Properties dialog and make the needed changes.

To delete a scheduled task, select it and choose your favorite method for deleting:

- Press the DEL key.
- Click the Delete icon on the toolbar.
- Right-click the task and choose Delete from the shortcut menu.
- Choose Delete from the File menu.

Deleted tasks are sent to the Recycle Bin. If you don't want a task to run, but you think you might need it in the future, instead of deleting it, disable it. To do that, clear the Enabled check box on the Task tab of the task's Properties dialog.

Run and Stop Scheduled Tasks

You can run any task at any time if you don't want to wait for the next scheduled occurrence. In the Scheduled Tasks window, select the task and choose File | Run, or right-click the task and choose Run from the shortcut menu.

If a task is running and you want to stop it, open the Scheduled Tasks window, right-click the task's object, and choose End Task from the shortcut menu. It may take a moment or two for the message to reach the task.

Check the Status of Scheduled Tasks

You can gain information about the status of a task by changing the view of the Scheduled Tasks window to the Details view. The columns provide information about each task.

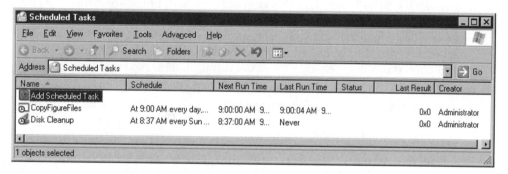

 Click on a column to sort the list by that column—click the same column again to reverse the sort order.

The Status column can have any of the following notations:

Notation	Meaning
Empty	The task is not running
Running	The task is currently running
Missed	The system missed the opportunity to run the task (usually means the computer wasn't running at the scheduled time)
Could not start	The last attempt to run the task failed

 When you boot the computer that was not running at the scheduled time, and therefore missed a task, you see a message dialog during Windows startup that informs you that a scheduled event may have been missed.

Check the log file to see detailed information about the performance of tasks. You can access the log file by choosing Advanced | View Log on the Scheduled Tasks folder menu bar, or by opening the log in Notepad. The log file is SystemRoot%\SchedLgU.Txt.

Set Global Options for Scheduled Tasks

The Advanced menu in the Scheduled Tasks window offers options for manipulating the way scheduled tasks operate:

- **Stop Using Task Scheduler**   Selecting this command disables any scheduled tasks until you return to the Advanced menu and select Start Using Task Scheduler. In addition, the Task Scheduler will not automatically run the next time you start Windows Server 2003 unless you've restarted it before rebooting.

- **Pause Task Scheduler**   Use this command to temporarily halt running tasks and prevent scheduled tasks from starting. This command is useful for stopping tasks while you install software. To resume scheduled tasks, select Continue Task Scheduler from the Advanced menu. Any tasks scheduled to run during the time you paused the Task Scheduler will not run until their next scheduled times.

- **Notify Me of Missed Tasks**   This command does not mean what it says. It does not notify you of missed tasks; it only notifies you about a failure of the Schedule Task service itself. Tasks that fail to run due to corrupt or missing executables don't kick off a notification.

- **AT Service Account**   Use this command to change the user account that runs tasks that are scheduled with the AT command (the default account is System). Selecting the command opens the AT Service Account Configuration dialog, where you can select a user account (and enter and confirm the password for that account). This is almost never a good idea; you should usually let the System account run tasks.

- **View Log**   Select this command to open the task log in Notepad, where you can track the success or failure of your scheduled tasks.

 Note   *The log file is %SystemRoot%\SchedLgU.Txt.*

Work with Tasks on Remote Computers

You can view, add, or modify the scheduled tasks on a remote computer, depending on the permissions you have for manipulating that computer. Even without the ability to access the tasks on another computer, you can send tasks to users on other computers in the form of .job files.

Scheduled Tasks Folder vs. Tasks Folder

When you are working with tasks on remote computers, it's important to understand that the Scheduled Tasks folder, which you can find in Control Panel, and the %SystemRoot%\Tasks folder are not the same when you are looking at a remote computer.

If you open each folder on your local computer, the contents are identical. Most people assume the same is true if they access a remote computer. They're wrong.

If you open the %SystemRoot%\Tasks folder on a remote computer, it's going to look extremely familiar, because you're looking at the contents of your own %SystemRoot%\ Tasks folder (it's a mirror image—the Recycle Bin works the same way). Here are the rules:

- If you delete a job from what seems to be the remote Tasks folder, you're deleting it from your own folder.

- The system will not permit you to drag a job between Tasks folders, because you're really trying to drag a job to itself.

View Tasks on a Remote Computer

To view the Scheduled Tasks folder on another computer, you have to locate the Scheduled Tasks folder. Open My Network Places and expand the remote computer listing to locate the Scheduled Tasks folder. It's easy to spot, because there's a clock on the folder icon. Select the folder to see its contents (use the Details view to gain the most information). Here are the rules:

- The drive containing the Scheduled Tasks folder must be shared to provide access to the folder.

- You cannot map a drive to the Scheduled Tasks folder.

If you have the appropriate level of permissions, you can delete or modify the jobs on the target computer.

Send Tasks to Remote Computers

You can drag or copy a task between your computer and a remote computer, with these caveats:

- The file on which the job depends (usually an executable) must exist on the target computer.

- The properties of the job may need to be adjusted to reflect the path to the file on the target computer.

- The properties of the job may need to be adjusted to reflect a different username.

If you have access to the Scheduled Tasks folder on the target computer, the best way to accomplish this is to right-drag the task between the local Scheduled Tasks folder and the remote Scheduled Tasks folder. Choose Copy Here from the menu that appears when you release the right mouse button (left-dragging moves the job instead of copying it). Alternatively, you can copy and paste the job between the Scheduled Tasks folders, using the commands available on the right-click shortcut menus.

If you don't have access to the remote computer's Scheduled Tasks folder, copy and paste the job anywhere on the target computer and let the user move the file into his or her Scheduled Tasks folder.

Caution *Don't use the %SystemRoot%\Tasks folder as the source or target of a copy/paste procedure.*

Send and Receive Tasks via E-mail

You can e-mail a task file (*taskname*.job) to another user, using the standard method for attaching a file to a message. However, if your e-mail software doesn't let you enter Control Panel to open the Scheduled Tasks folder, you won't be able to access the .job file when you click the Attach icon. The solution is to open Control Panel, open the Scheduled Tasks folder, and copy the job listing to a folder you can access from your e-mail software (I use the root of drive C). Then attach that copy to your e-mail.

The recipient merely needs to drag or copy/cut/paste the file to the Scheduled Tasks folder.

AT.exe

If you used the AT command in Windows NT and/or Windows 2000, you're familiar with the concept of scheduling programs. The AT command is still available in Windows Server 2003, and you can use it to schedule tasks.

Task Scheduler and the AT command work together. When you schedule a task via the AT command, that task appears in the Scheduled Tasks window. You can reconfigure the task using the switches available in the AT command, or use the features in Scheduled Tasks to modify the configuration of a task you scheduled with the AT command.

However, once you use Scheduled Tasks to change the configuration, the AT modifiers no longer work on that task—you've committed your modification efforts to Scheduled Tasks.

The syntax for AT.exe is

at [*ComputerName*] [{[*ID*] [/delete] | /delete [/yes]}]

at [[*ComputerName*] *hours:minutes* [/interactive] [{/every:*date*[,...] | /next:*date*[,...]}] *command*]

where:

ComputerName specifies a remote computer (if omitted, the local computer is used).

ID is the identification number assigned to an existing scheduled command.

/delete cancels a scheduled command. If you omit the command's *ID*, all scheduled commands on the computer are canceled.

/yes provides the answer Yes to confirmation queries when you delete scheduled events.

hours:minutes is the time at which you want to run the command, using 24-hour notation.

/interactive permits *command* to interact with the desktop of the user who is logged on when *command* runs.

/every: runs *command* on every specified day or days of the week or month.

date specifies the date that you want to run the command. Specify one or more days of the week (**M,T,W,Th,F,S,Su**) or one or more days of the month (1 through 31). Separate multiple date entries with commas. If you omit *date*, the program uses the current day of the month.

/next: runs *command* on the next occurrence of the day.

command is the program or batch program you want to run. If the command requires a path as an argument, use the absolute path. If the command is on a remote computer, use a UNC rather than a mapped drive letter.

You can enter **at** without parameters to get information about the commands you've scheduled with the AT.exe program. The display does not include scheduled tasks that were created in the Scheduled Tasks GUI, nor does it include scheduled tasks that were created with AT.exe but later modified in the Scheduled Tasks GUI. Entering **at** *ComputerName* performs the same action on a remote computer.

Schtasks.exe

New to Windows Server 2003 (and Windows XP), schtasks.exe is like having AT.exe wake up one morning full of steroids, and equipped with a logical brain. This is a great alternative to AT.exe, and the only reason I can think of to continue to have AT.exe on your drive is to take care of the legacy scheduled commands you haven't gotten around to redoing with schtasks.exe.

Schtasks.exe is a command-line version of the Scheduled Tasks utility, so whatever you do in one place is reflected in the other. Unlike AT.exe, you don't have to worry that if you make a change in the GUI after creating a scheduled task with schtasks.exe, you'll never be able to use schtasks.exe on the task again.

In this section, I'll describe two sets of syntax information:

- Syntax and parameters for creating tasks
- Syntax and parameters for working with existing tasks

Create Tasks with Schtasks.exe.

You can create tasks at the command line with an amazing degree of configuration detail. The syntax for creating tasks with schtasks.exe is

schtasks /create /tn *taskname* **/tr** *taskrun* **/sc** *schedule* [**/mo** *modifier*] [**/d** *day*] [**/i** *idletime*] [**/st** *starttime*] [**/sd** *startdate*] [**/ed** *enddate*] [**/s** *computer*] [**/ru** *user* [**/rp** *password*]]

where:

/create is required as the first parameter.
/tn *taskname* is the name for the task.
/tr *taskrun* specifies the path and filename of the program or command that runs.
/sc *schedule* specifies the schedule type, using the following schedule type options:

Minute, Hourly, Daily, Weekly, Monthly	Specifies the time unit
Once	The task runs only once, at the specified date and time
Onstart	The task runs at startup (either on a specified date or the next time the system starts)
Onlogon	The task runs when the user logs on (either on a specified date or the next time the user logs on)
Onidle	The tasks runs whenever the system is idle for a specified period of time (either on a specified date or the next time the system is idle)

/mo *modifier* specifies how often the task runs within its schedule type. This parameter is used as follows:

- Required for a monthly schedule type
- Optional for a minute, hourly, daily, or weekly schedule type
- begin text inlin

/d *day* specifies a day of the week. This parameter is used as follows:

- Valid values are mon, tue, wed, thu, fri, sat, and sun
- Required for a monthly schedule with a first, second, third, fourth, or last modifier
- Optional for a weekly schedule

/i *idletime* specifies how many minutes the computer must be idle before the task starts. Valid entries are whole numbers between 1 and 999.

/st *starttime* specifies the time of day that the task starts in hh:mm:ss format, used as follows:

- Required with a once schedule type
- Optional with minute, hourly, daily, weekly, and monthly schedule types

/sd *startdate* specifies the start date for the task in mm/dd/yyyy format, used as follows:

- Required for a once schedule type
- Optional with all other schedule types

/ed *enddate* specifies the date that the task stops running.

/s *computer* specifies the name or IP address of a remote computer (with or without backslashes), and omitting the parameter targets the local computer.

/ru *user* runs the tasks with the permission level of the *user* account. If omitted, the task runs with the permissions of the user logged on at the time the task runs.

/rp *password* specifies the password of the user account that is specified in the **/ru** *user* parameter. If omitted, the user is prompted for the password when the task runs.

Manage Existing Tasks with Schtasks.exe

Schtasks.exe provides quite a few syntax options and parameters for managing existing tasks.

Query for Task Information

You can view a list of tasks by entering **schtasks /query** at the command line. The resulting display includes all tasks, including those created in the Task Scheduler GUI and by using schtasks.exe at the command line. This is an important difference between the capabilities of schtasks.exe and AT.exe.

Increase the power of the /query parameter by using the following syntax:

schtasks /query [/s *ServerName***] [/fo** *format***] [/nh] [/v]**

where:

/s *ServerName* specifies a remote computer as the target for the command.
/fo *format* specifies the format for the display, using any of the following values:

- table (this is the default display)
- list
- csv

/nh eliminates the display of column headers in table and csv formats.

The /nh switch is useful when redirecting output to a file, especially with the csv format. The resulting file can be loaded into a database or spreadsheet.

/v specifies verbose mode, which displays all the known information about each task.

Verbose mode produces an unformatted display with lots of information. It's difficult to read. And, it's probably more than you needed to know. If you need this information, it's easier to open the Schedule Tasks program and check the task's properties.

Delete Tasks

When you delete tasks with schtasks.exe, the system first asks for a confirmation of the deletion (unless you use the /f switch), then returns a success message. To delete tasks with schtasks.exe, use the following syntax:

schtasks /delete /tn *taskname* **[/s** *ServerName***] [/f]**

where:

/delete is the command and is required.

/tn *taskname* specifies the task (use **/tn** * to indicate all tasks).

/s *ServerName* specifies a remote computer as the target system (omit for local computer).

/f forces deletion even if the task is currently running and also runs in quiet mode (no confirmation required).

The /f parameter has a "take no prisoners" attitude, so use it judiciously.

If you use schtasks.exe with a task filename as the target, and you see an error message telling you the data is invalid, the task file is corrupted. You can't fix or recover a corrupted task; you must delete the task and rebuild it.

Disk Cleanup

Disk Cleanup is like a trash hauling service that gets rid of all the stuff that's hanging around that you don't need and won't ever use again. Unlike the junk in your house, you can't hold a lawn sale to entice other junk-collectors to buy your outdated, unwanted computer files. Disk Cleanup works only on local drives, and only on one drive at a time.

Run Disk Cleanup

To run Disk Cleanup, use either of these methods:

- Choose Start | Run and enter **cleanmgr**, and then click OK.
- Choose Disk Cleanup from the System Tools submenu of the Accessories menu.

If you have multiple drives, you must first select the drive to clean up. The program scans your drive to see how many, and which, files can be removed.

Decide What to Delete

After the analysis is complete (which could take a long time on a large drive, if you haven't used this program in a while), the Disk Cleanup dialog displays check marks next to the categories of file types that can be safely deleted (see Figure 8-6).

You can select additional file categories, and deselect some of the categories that were preselected for you, by adding or removing check marks. As you change the settings, the total amount of disk space you'll regain is displayed. Select and deselect categories; then click OK to clean up your drive. The system displays a confirmation dialog; click Yes to confirm that you want to delete the selected files.

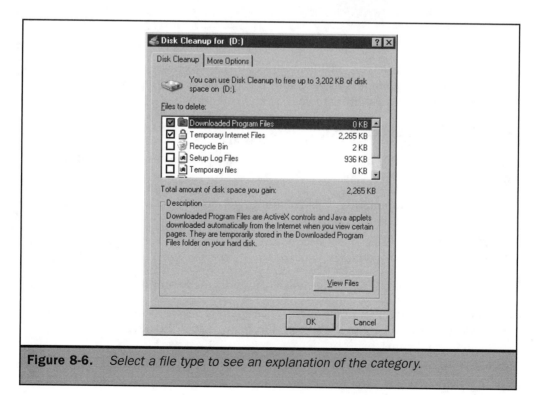

Figure 8-6.   *Select a file type to see an explanation of the category.*

If you have multiple drives, only the drive that holds the SystemRoot folder displays all file type categories. If you select any other drive, only the Recycle Bin, the option to compress old files (discussed next), and the Catalog files (from previous indexing processes) are available for cleanup.

Compress Old Files

Scroll through the display to find the listing named Compress old files. Disk Cleanup is not offering to remove compressed files; instead, this is an offer to keep older files in a compressed format. Compressing the files uses less disk space.

Select the Compress old files listing and click the Options button to specify how many days must have elapsed since the last time you accessed a file in order to qualify the file for compression.

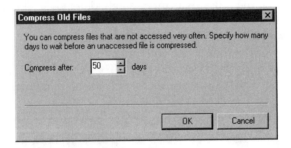

File compression is only available for drives that are formatted for the NTFS file system. If you opt to compress files, be sure to configure Folder Options to display compressed files with an alternate color.

Additional Options for Disk Cleanup

The Disk Cleanup dialog has a More Options tab that presents two additional clean-up alternatives:

- **Windows components** Lets you remove optional Windows components that you installed but don't use.
- **Installed programs** Lets you remove programs you've installed but aren't planning to use anymore.

Selecting either of the following choices produces the appropriate Windows dialog:

- **Optional Windows Components** Displays the Add or Remove Windows Components dialog that is accessed from the Add or Remove Programs applet in Control Panel.

- **Installed Programs**   Displays the Add or Remove Programs dialog that lists installed software.

Using Cleanmgr.exe

The command-line version of the disk cleanup tool, cleanmgr.exe, offers a number of switches you can use to automate the cleanup process and make it more efficient. (Incidentally, cleanmgr.exe doesn't appear in the command-line reference section of the Windows Server 2003 help files, so you might want to put a bookmark in this page.) Cleanmgr.exe supports the following command-line switches:

- **/d** *driveletter*   Selects the drive you want to clean.

- **/sageset:** *n*   Displays the Disk Cleanup Settings dialog so that you can select the settings you want for cleanup, and assign those settings to a number (*n*). The system then creates a registry key to store those settings, linking them to the value *n*. The *n* value can be any integer value from 0 to 65535, and it is merely a number you've assigned to this particular set of options; in effect, you're creating a version number for the disk cleanup feature that uses these settings. For example, you could specify a cleanup of the Recycle Bin and Temporary Internet Files and give that configuration an *n* value of 1. You could create another configuration set, using different file types or specifying that old files be compressed, and give that configuration an *n* value of 2.

- **/sagerun:** *n*   Runs the specified tasks that you assigned to the *n* value with the \sageset switch.

One advantage of this method for designing multiple configuration options for Disk Cleanup is that you can use cleanmgr.exe with the appropriate switches in the Task Scheduler. Once you've created all your sageset values at the command line, add the **sagerun:** *n* switch to the command in Task Scheduler (substituting your own number for *n*). You can schedule the configuration that cleans up the Recycle Bin, Temporary Internet Files, and other common file types daily, and run the configuration that compresses files or removes old index entries weekly.

System Information

The Windows Server 2003 System Information tool displays configuration information about the local system, or a remote computer. You can open the tool in several ways:

- Choose Start | All Programs | Accessories | System Tools | System Information.
- Choose Start | Run and enter **msinfo32**.

The System Information window offers numerous categories in the left pane, and opens with the System Summary item selected, which displays basic information about the computer in the right pane.

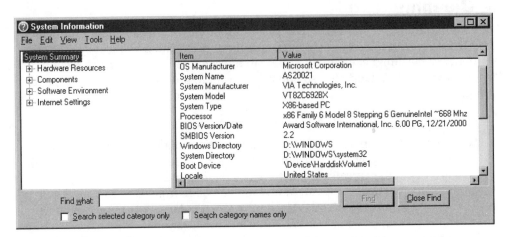

It's unusual for an administrator to have to spend much time using this tool for day-to-day administrative tasks. However, it's not unusual for support desk personnel (Microsoft or third-party hardware/software vendors) to ask callers to open System Information to look for specific data.

If you need to find information about a specific item, you can navigate through the left pane, or use the command-line version of the tool with parameters that limit the display to the type of information you're looking for. I'll cover both methods in the following sections.

Navigating the System Information Window

Expanding the categories in the left pane exposes subcategories (and some subcategories have additional subcategories). The list seems almost interminable. However, the program offers a Find feature that makes it easier to locate the information you need. Enter a word or phrase to search for in the Find what box, then take the appropriate action:

- To search all categories and all items in the details pane, click Find after you enter the text you're searching for.

- To limit the search to a specific category, including data in the details pane, select the category and then click the check box Search Selected Category Only. If the category has subcategories, they're automatically included in the search effort.

- To search for a match only in the console pane, ignoring the items in the details pane, click the check box Search Category Names Only.

Tip *If you don't see the Find what box on the bottom of the console, press CTRL-F to toggle the feature on, or choose Edit | Hide Find to remove the check mark.*

Save System Data to a File

You may be asked to save the system information in a file, and then e-mail the file to a support technician (or upload the file to a web site). To accomplish this, choose File | Save and enter a location and filename in the Save As dialog.

System information files are saved with the extension .nfo. By default, Windows Server 2003 .nfo files are saved for version 7.0 of System Information. The Save As dialog offers a second file type for version 5.0/6.0 .nfo files. Use this file type if you're connected to a remote computer that's running a Windows version earlier than Windows Server 2003. Opening a saved .nfo file opens the System Information window with the saved data displayed.

Export System Data

You can export system data to a text file, which you can examine in a word processor or text editor. You can use this file on any computer, regardless of the operating system, because it doesn't open the System Information program from which it was derived.

Choose File | Export and enter a location and filename for your data file (the system automatically adds the .txt file extension). The resulting file resembles an .ini file—it has [sections] followed by data for each section.

You can export specific data by selecting a category or subcategory in the left pane before you export data. Only the data attached to your selection is exported.

You can also get a text report by printing the system information (using File | Print). This is an enormous file, and could require more paper than your printer tray holds. While you have the ability to limit the amount of data that prints by choosing a specific category, it's almost always better to export the file. Then you can print the specific sections for which you need a hard copy.

Run a System Tool from the System Information Window

The Tools menu offers a number of the built-in Windows Server 2003 configuration and analysis tools you can use to troubleshoot your system. Many times, support technicians ask users to run one of these tools to assist them as they attempt to resolve problems.

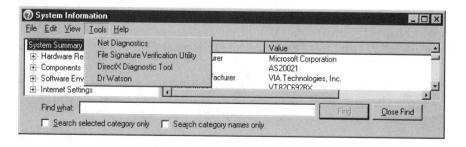

Connect to a Remote Computer

You can run System Information against a remote computer, as long as you have the appropriate rights on that computer. To connect, use one of these actions:

- Press CTRL-R.
- Choose View | Remote Computer from the menu bar.

In the Remote Computer dialog, enter the name of the target computer. You don't have to use a UNC format, just enter the machine name. When you're connected, the System Summary category displays the name of the remote computer—otherwise, everything else is the same and all functions work as if you were working locally.

To return to your local computer, press CTRL-R and select My Computer. Exiting the program also disconnects you from a remote computer.

Use Msinfo32.exe

You can use the System Information tool from the command line to launch the System Information window. Because of the robust controls you gain via command-line parameters, using the command-line version of msinfo32 is a good way to control the amount of information System Information displays. You can be very precise about what you want to see.

However, accomplishing this is a bit complicated. If you open a command session and enter **msinfo32.exe**, the system returns an error.

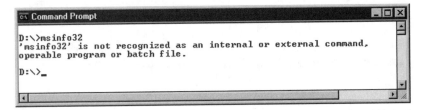

The program msinfo32.exe is located in the Program Files\Common Files\ Microsoft Shared\MSInfo folder, which, by default, is not in your path. However, you don't have to wend your way through that path to open the program—you can overcome the problem in either of two ways:

- Enter **winmsd** at the command prompt. (Winmsd.exe, which appeared in Windows NT, launched the Windows NT diagnostics application. In Windows Server 2003/Windows 2000, winmsd.exe is an application stub that launches msinfo32.exe.)
- Enter **start msinfo32** at the command prompt. (The Start command launches a second instance of the command processor and completes the entered command, which in this case is msinfo32.)

The following parameters are available for msinfo32.exe:

/categories (+ | -)(all | *categoryname*) + | -(*categoryname*)... displays or outputs specified categories.

/category *categoryname* specifies a specific category at startup.

/msinfo_file=*filename* opens a saved .nfo file.

/nfo or /s *filename* outputs an .nfo file to the specified filename.

/report *filename* outputs a text-format file to the specified filename.

/computer *computername* connects to the named computer.

To select or deselect a major category, use the following rules:

To See This Category	Enter This Text
System Summary	SystemSummary
Hardware Resources	Resources
Components	Components
Software Environment	SWEnv
Internet Explorer	InternetExplorer
Applications	Apps

In the following sections, you'll find the command-line text required to specify subcategories.

Subcategories for Hardware Resources

To See This Subcategory	Enter This Text
Conflict/Sharing	ResourcesConflicts
DMA	ResourcesDMA
Forced Hardware	ResourcesForcedHardware
I/O	ResourcesIO
IRQs	ResourcesIRQS
Memory	ResourcesMemory

Subcategories for Components

To See This Subcategory	Enter This Text
Multimedia	ComponentsMultimedia
Display	ComponentsDisplay
Infrared	ComponentsInfrared
Input	ComponentsInput
Modem	ComponentsModem
Network	ComponentsNetwork
Ports	ComponentsPorts
Storage	ComponentsStorage
Printing	ComponentsPrinting
Problem Devices	ComponentsProblemDevices
USB	ComponentsUSB

Subcategories for Software Environment

To See This Subcategory	Enter This Text
Drivers	SWEnvDrivers
Environment Variables	SWEnvEnvVars
Jobs	SWEnvJobs
Network Connections	SWEnvNetConn
Running Tasks	SWEnvRunningTasks
Loaded Modules	SWEnvLoadedModules
Services	SWEnvServices
Program Groups	SWEnvProgramGroup
Startup Programs	SWEnvStartupPrograms
OLE Registration	SWEnvOLEReg

Start /wait msinfo32.exe

Entering the command **start /wait msinfo32.exe [parameters as needed]** tells the system not to process the next item until the current item completes. This ensures that the computer is not overloaded because of the large amount of CPU time some of the categories require. This is especially important if you use msinfo32.exe in a batch file.

Local Computer Management Snap-in

Windows Server 2003 provides an MMC snap-in for managing almost everything on your computer (or on a remote computer, if you have the permissions to do so). Most of the tools available in the Local Computer Management snap-in can be accessed from the menu system or the command line. However, opening one MMC console to gain access to multiple tools is certainly easier.

To open the Local Computer Management snap-in, right-click My Computer and choose Manage from the shortcut menu to see the MMC console shown in Figure 8-7.

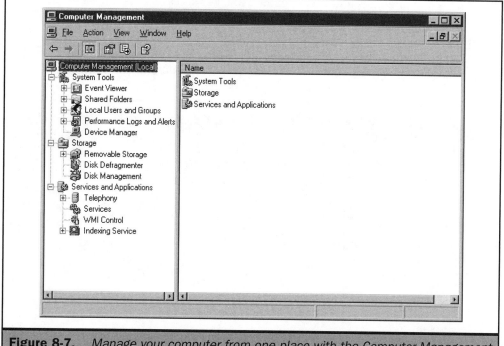

Figure 8-7.   *Manage your computer from one place with the Computer Management snap-in.*

System Tools Tree

Expanding all the objects under the System Tools item in the console pane displays a large number of snap-ins, system tools, and configuration items (see Figure 8-8).

Event Viewer

Use Event Viewer to gather information about events that occurred on your system. You can access Event Viewer through this Computer Management snap-in or from the Administrative Tools folder in Control Panel. (If you're migrating to Windows Server 2003 from Windows NT, it's important to know this in order to save your sanity.)

Event Viewer Logs   Information about the activity, behavior, and problems your system is experiencing is kept in logs. By default, the Windows Server 2003 Event Viewer has three logs:

- **Application log**   Holds events logged by applications. Application developers decide which events to monitor.

- **Security log**   Records events that have been configured for auditing, such as logon attempts, and events related to users accessing resources. As an administrator, you can decide which events are recorded in the security log.

- **System log**   Contains events logged by the Windows Server 2003 system components. This usually turns out to be reports of failures in drivers or system services. The types of events that are recorded are built into Windows Server 2003.

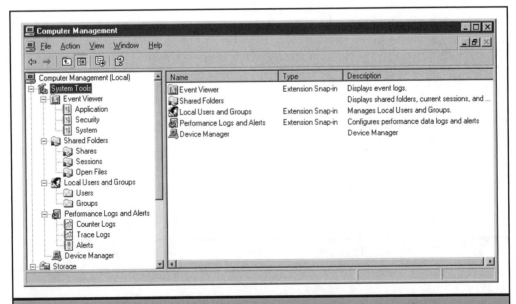

Figure 8-8.   *Manage system configuration options, events, and performance via the System Tools objects.*

If Windows Server 2003 is acting as a domain controller or a DNS server, additional logs are placed into Event Viewer to track those services.

Events Event Viewer displays a variety of event types, each of which has its own level of significance, and its own icon type in the event logs. To see event details, double-click the event's listing in Event Viewer.

- **Error** Indicates a significant problem that could involve a loss of functionality, such as drivers and services that fail to start properly

- **Warning** Indicates a problem that might become serious if you don't attend to it

- **Information** Strictly informational, and not an indication of a future or present problem

- **Success Audit** A security event that succeeded, and is reported because the system or an administrator opted to audit that event

- **Failure Audit** A security event that failed, and is reported because the system or an administrator opted to audit that event

Configure Event Viewer The event logs you're using start automatically, when you start the operating system. The log files have a finite size and overwrite events in a manner determined by the log's configuration options. To see or change the configuration options, right-click a log's listing in Event Viewer and choose Properties from the shortcut menu.

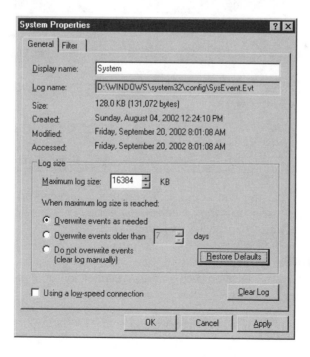

Changes you make to the configuration settings are dependent on your situation. For example, you can configure the log to automatically overwrite events after a given number of days (the default setting is 7 days), in order to keep the log file from growing extremely large. Then, every seven days, you can archive the log and clear the current entries. However, if you make a major change in the system, or you configure an aggressive auditing plan, a log may record many events. If the log becomes filled, and there are no events older than seven days, Event Viewer has nothing to discard to make room for more events.

Filter Event Types   Each log's Properties dialog has a Filter tab, which you can use to configure the types of events you want to see. You can use the options on the dialog to make your selections as narrow as you wish.

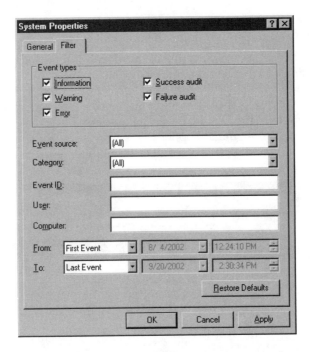

For example, you may not care about seeing Information events on certain computers, or only want to see those events for a week or so after a major change in the system's configuration. Merely select and deselect filters as needed.

Shared Folders

The Shared Folders snap-in lets you keep an eye on connections and resource use, offering information via three subfolders in the console pane.

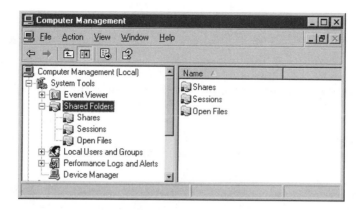

Shares   Open the Shares object to see the shared resources on the computer. The columns in the details pane offer information about each share.

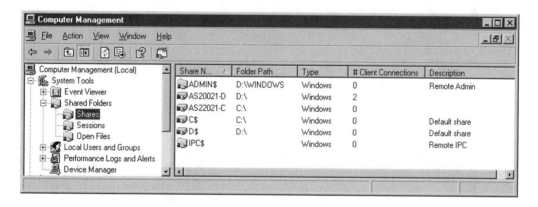

Column	Information
Share Name	The shared resource: a shared directory, named pipe, shared printer, and so forth
Folder Path	The path to the shared resource
Type	The type of network connection: Windows, NetWare, Macintosh
# Client Connections	The number of users currently connected to the shared resource
Description	The description text for the shared resource

Press F5 to refresh the display, which ensures you're looking at the accurate number of current users.

Create a new share by right-clicking the Share object in the console pane and choosing New File Share from the shortcut menu. Configure existing shares by right-clicking the appropriate listing in the details pane and choosing Properties from the shortcut menu.

Send a message to any or all computers used by connected users by right-clicking the Shares object in the console pane and choosing All Tasks | Send Console Message. Enter a message and select or remove the receiving computers as desired.

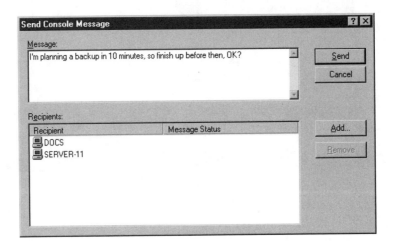

Click Add to select other computers on the network (those that aren't presently connected to this computer) to receive the message.

If any connected users are working from computers running Windows 9x, the message won't be received unless the computer has WinPopup installed. Windows NT/2000/XP/2003 have Messenger Service capabilities built in to the operating system, and users receive your message in a Messenger Service window.

 At the time of writing, console messages that are sent to connected domain controllers fail. I'm attempting to track down the problem with Microsoft. Information that becomes available on this subject will be available at www.admin911.com.

Sessions   A session exists when a remote user accesses a shared resource. The Sessions object displays the following information:

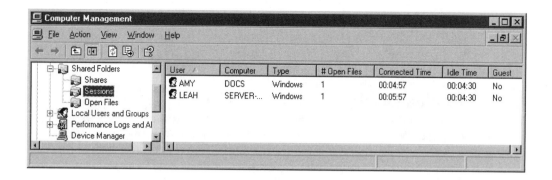

Column	Information
User	Users currently connected to the computer
Computer	Name of the connected user's computer
Type	Type of network connection: Windows, NetWare, or Macintosh
# Open Files	Number of resources opened on this computer by this user
Connected Time	Elapsed time for the session
Idle Time	Elapsed time since this user performed an action
Guest	Specifies whether this user is connected as a guest

You can disconnect all the users who are attached to the computer by right-clicking the Sessions object in the console pane and choosing Disconnect All Sessions from the shortcut menu. You can disconnect an individual user by right-clicking the user's session listing in the details pane and choosing Close Session from the shortcut menu.

    It's a nice gesture to send a console message before abruptly ending a user's session.

Open Files   The Open Files object holds information about which files have been opened, by whom, and what those people are doing.

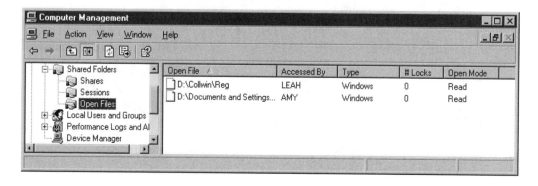

You can close all the open files by right-clicking the Open Files object and selecting Disconnect All Open Files from the shortcut menu. You can close a specific open file by right-clicking its listing in the details pane and selecting Close Open File from the shortcut menu.

Local Users and Groups

The Local Users and Groups tool is for managing users and groups that log on to this computer, as opposed to logging on to a domain. If your Windows Server 2003 computer is a domain controller, this tool isn't available. Domain controllers are restricted to managing domain users and groups.

Manage Local Users   Select the User object in the console pane to see the list of users in the display pane. By default, Windows Server 2003 creates an Administrator account and a Guest account (other accounts may exist depending on the installed components).

> **Note**   *When a computer is part of a domain, it's perfectly possible that multiple users who don't exist in the local User list have logged on to the domain using this computer. Local computers only authenticate users who select a local computer logon instead of a domain logon in the Windows Logon dialog.*

The Administrator account is the local account that is created by Windows Server 2003 to install the operating system. You use this account during installation and configuration of the OS, and the final use of this account should be to create an account for yourself (make yourself a member of the Administrators group).

The Administrator account can't be deleted, disabled, or removed from the Administrators local group, ensuring that you never lock yourself out of the computer (unless you forget the password).

The Administrator account has its own set of subfolders under %SystemDrive%\ Documents and Settings. If you log on to the domain with this account (which you can do if you know the password for the Administrator account on the DC), Windows Server 2003 will create a second Administrator account locally, named Administrator .DOMAIN_NAME. This account also has a set of subfolders under %SystemDrive%\ Documents and Settings.

By default, Windows Server 2003 disables the Guest account, which is a safe approach, and usually doesn't require a change. If the Guest account is enabled, users can log in as Guest without a password. However, the Guest account is a member of the Guest group, where permissions and rights are severely limited.

Add Local Users   To add users to the local computer, right-click the Users object in the console pane and choose New User from the shortcut menu. The New User dialog appears (see Figure 8-9), where you enter basic information about this user.

Following are some guidelines for entering data in this dialog:

- The User Name field is the logon name, such as kathyi, kathy, kivens, or whatever format you usually encourage.

- The User Name must be unique on the computer and can contain up to 20 uppercase or lowercase characters except for the following: " / \ [ ] : ; | = , + * ? < >.

- The Full Name and Description fields are optional, but useful for searching if you create a lot of local users.

- You can enter a password (don't forget to tell the new user what it is), or omit the password if you know the user is going to log on immediately to create a new, private password.

- If you're creating the real, permanent password, deselect the option to change the password at the next logon. You can also select one of the other password options.

Configure Local Users   After you've created a new user, double-click the user's name in the details pane of the console to open the user's Properties dialog. Here, you can manage the user's rights and permissions:

- Set Group membership in the Member Of tab. The user is automatically a member of the Users group, which has limited rights and permissions (the same as the Guest group). Click Add to add the user to additional groups as required.

Note   *The Add dialog for adding groups has changed from Windows 2000. The list of existing groups doesn't appear, and you must click the Advanced button and initiate a search.*

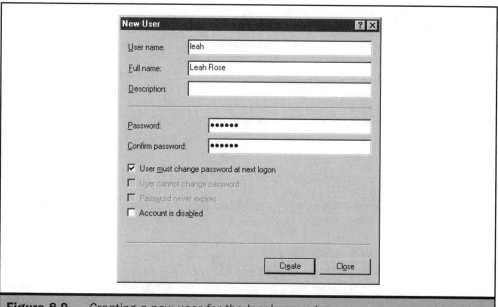

Figure 8-9.   *Creating a new user for the local computer*

- The Profile tab is for configuring roaming and mandatory profiles, and setting a home folder (usually on the network). Because this is a local user, who probably also logs on to the domain with a domain-based username (which can be the same username), it's uncommon to dabble with these settings on the local computer. Use the tools on the DC to set domain configuration options for the user.

- All the other tabs are for configuration of Terminal Server and Dial-in user properties, and are covered in the appropriate chapters in this book.

Manage Local Groups   Windows Server 2003 creates a number of built-in groups during installation of the operating system. Except for the Replicator group (which has a specific role and should not have ordinary users as members), you can add local users to groups if you want to increase their permissions on the computer. Making a user a member of a group is the efficient way to control permissions and rights (otherwise you have to apply rights and permissions one person at a time).

Create Local Groups   You can create local groups to establish a specific group of permissions that might be needed for the local computer. In a network environment, it's unusual for a computer to behave in a stand-alone fashion, so most of this work is performed on the domain level.

However, if you want to add a local group, right-click the Groups object in the console pane and select New Group from the shortcut menu. In the New Group dialog (see Figure 8-10), name the group and, optionally, provide a description.

Add Members to Local Groups   You can click the Add button in the New Group dialog to begin adding members to the group, or close the dialog and add members later by double-clicking the group's listing in the details pane. If the computer participates in a domain, members of the group can be local users, domain users, or domain global groups.

In the Select Users or Groups dialog, choose the object you want to add to the group, using the following guidelines:

- Click Object Types to select User or Group or both.
- Click Locations to choose the local computer, the domain, or one of the domain's global groups.
- Click Advanced to open a Search dialog where you can further refine your criteria.

After you've selected your criteria, click Find Now to display the list of objects available to you, and begin adding members to your group.

Performance Logs and Alerts

You can keep an eye on the health of the computer, and troubleshoot impending or actual problems, by using the performance monitors built into the operating system. See Chapter 26 for information on these topics.

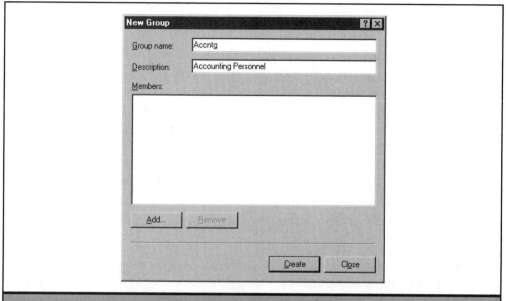

Figure 8-10.   *Creating a new group starts with the basic information.*

Device Manager

Device Manager is an indispensable tool for troubleshooting hardware problems, updating drivers, and changing the configuration of installed hardware devices. Here are some guidelines to keep in mind when using Device Manager:

- You must have administrative privileges on the computer.
- You can only manage local devices.
- Network policy settings may prevent you from making changes to devices.

The Device Manager snap-in is available as a stand-alone snap-in, in addition to being part of the Computer Management snap-in. To open the stand-alone version, right-click My Computer and choose Properties from the shortcut menu. Select the Hardware tab and click Device Manager.

View System Devices   The first and most obvious service Device Manager provides is a quick view of your system and all the hardware devices installed. It lets you know, at a glance, if there are any immediate hardware problems or conflicts by flagging those devices that are not working properly (yellow exclamation point) or that it does not recognize (yellow question mark). In addition to providing an overview of your system hardware, Device Manager also offers a variety of ways to view the information. The View menu offers the following views:

- **Devices by type**   The default view, which lists the installed devices alphabetically by type.

- **Devices by connection**   Lists the connection types, with all devices on the connection appearing as a subset of the connection type.

- **Resources by type**   Displays devices as subsets of the resources they are using. Resources include DMA, I/O, IRQ, and memory address.

- **Resources by connection**   Similar to the Resources by type view, this view displays the resource list with connection types as the subset.

- **Show hidden devices**   Handy for locating devices that have been disconnected but not uninstalled from the computer. It also displays non–Plug and Play devices that are installed.

Print Reports on System Devices   In addition to viewing the device information, you can print reports by selecting Print from the Action menu. There are three reports available:

- **System summary**   Contains basic system information such as operating system, processor, and installed memory. In addition, the report contains summaries of disk drive information, IRQ usage, DMA usage, memory usage, and I/O ports usage.

- **Selected class or device**   Contains details about a device you selected before invoking the Print command. Included in the report are the device's class, its description or name, the resources it's using, and information about device drivers.

- **All devices and system summary**   Prints the same information as the System summary report, then the information in the selected class or device report for every installed device.

It's a good idea to print the All devices and system summary report for each computer and keep the printout either in the desk on which the computer sits or in an accessible file folder. Alternatively, you can print all the reports to a file and amass the information in one large "our network computers" document.

Manipulate Devices   You can also manage devices in Device Manager. You can modify settings, change drivers, enable and disable devices, and uninstall devices. To access the properties of a device, double-click its listing, or right-click the listing and choose Properties from the shortcut menu. Because every device requires a device driver, each Properties dialog contains at least the following two tabs:

- **General**   Provides basic information, such as device name, type, and manufacturer, as well as its current status (working or not), a troubleshooter in case the device isn't working, and a Device Usage option to enable or disable the device.

- **Driver** Provides information about the driver currently installed for the device. This includes the driver name, provider, date, version, and digital signature, if any.

Click Driver Details to open the Driver File Details dialog, which displays the path and name(s) of installed driver(s). You can use the buttons in the dialog to uninstall the current driver, or update it.

If the device uses system resources, there's a Resources tab that lists the resources being used, and provides an option for manually changing them. Don't perform this action unless you're very comfortable with hardware issues. The Resources tab also contains a conflicting device list that alerts you to any resource conflicts between the selected device and any other installed devices.

An Advanced tab appears for devices that have additional options that can be set by the user. You may find other devices with special tabs of their own. For example, installed ports contain a Port Settings tab, modems have Modem and Diagnostics tabs, and the USB Root Hub contains a Power tab.

Remove Devices In addition to viewing installed devices and modifying their properties, you can also use Device Manager to remove devices. To remove a device, right-click its listing and select Uninstall from the shortcut menu. You can also remove a device by opening its Properties dialog, selecting the Driver tab, and clicking the Uninstall button.

Storage

Storage is the second category item in the Computer Management console pane. Its subcategories include tools for managing removable storage, defragmenting disks, and managing disks. Defragmenting disks is covered at the beginning of this chapter, and I'll cover the other two tools in this section.

Removable Storage

Removable Storage Management (RSM) tracks and manages removable media (tapes and discs) and hardware (drives, changers, and jukeboxes). To manage the media, RSM labels and catalogs the tapes and discs. Managing the hardware involves controlling the slots and doors in order to access and remove the media. RSM doesn't work alone; it is the media management arm for applications and features that interact with removable media, such as Backup and Remote Storage.

> **Note** *To use CDs with RSM, the discs must be rewritable and must be formatted with the CDFS file system. Optical media can be formatted with FAT, FAT32, or NTFS.*

RSM cannot support more than one computer-removable media connection. All applications that use removable media must run on the same computer that connects to a specific media library. Within the context of RSM, the word "library" means a data storage system that consists of removable media and the hardware that reads and writes to that media. There are two library types: robotic libraries, which are automated, multiple-drive devices; and stand-alone libraries, which are manually loaded, single-drive devices.

 In Windows Server 2003, your ATAPI CD-ROM changer has only a single drive letter assigned. RSM mounts, dismounts, and manages all the removable media.

In addition to the RSM tool you see in the Computer Management snap-in, Windows Server 2003 provides a preconfigured console for RSM, named ntmsmgr.msc (it's located in %SystemRoot%\System32). Use the Run command to launch this stand-alone snap-in. If you work with RSM a lot, create a desktop or taskbar shortcut to this MMC file.

You can view or set the configuration properties for the RSM components by selecting the appropriate object in the console pane. You'll probably find you spend most of your time working with media (moving media in and out of media pools or ascertaining the state of media) or library management. In the following sections, I'll define and discuss the library and media elements in RSM.

Libraries   As I mentioned earlier in this section, a *library* is the combination of media and the device used to read and write to that media. There are two types of libraries: automated, and stand-alone.

Technically, you could say there's a third library, the offline library. RSM tracks offline media when the media is not contained in a library. The media could be anywhere—in your desk, on a shelf, or in your lunch box. Because RSM tracks offline media, we can say that all media that's currently offline is part of the offline library.

Automated Libraries   *Automated libraries* are automated drives that can hold multiple physical media (tapes or discs). Sometimes these devices are called *changers* or *jukeboxes*. There's usually a robotic subsystem (sometimes called *drive bays*) that moves the media in and out of slots. The slots can be storage slots (the media is parked when not being accessed) or drive slots (the media is the active target). Some automated libraries have additional hardware components such as doors, cleaning cartridges, bar-code readers, and inject/eject ports. Those additional components are also managed by RSM.

Stand-Alone Libraries   *Stand-alone libraries* are single-drive units that are not automated. The drive holds a single tape or a single CD, and the media must be inserted manually.

Library Inventories   On an automated library, you can perform an inventory to ensure that all media in the library is accounted for. There are two inventory types:

- **Fast inventory**   Checks for changes in the state of each slot (from full to empty and vice versa), and if media is in the slot, reads the on-media identifier.
- **Full inventory**   Identifies each piece of media. If the media is bar-coded, the inventory reads the bar codes. If the media is not bar-coded, the inventory process reads the on-media identifier (which can take a long time).

To set the default inventory type, expand the Libraries object in the console pane and right-click the library object you want to configure. Choose Properties and set the Inventory type in the General tab (the choices are Fast, Full, and None).

To perform the inventory, right-click the library object and select Inventory from the shortcut menu. The inventory results are displayed in the right pane.

Media Pools   All media belongs to a *media pool*, a collection of media that shares certain attributes, including media type and management policies. Media pools have a hierarchical structure that starts with the media pool class. There are two classes:

- **Application media pools**   Created by software applications for the purpose of grouping and tracking media. In Windows 2000, Backup and Remote Storage each maintains an application media pool.

- **System media pools**   Created and managed by RSM, and include the following pools:

  - Unrecognized

  - Free

  - Import

> **Note**   *Media can be moved from one media pool to another, and that job is always managed by RSM.*

Unrecognized media pools hold media that RSM doesn't recognize. This is usually because the media is totally blank and has not yet received an ID from RSM (which occurs when you insert the media in the library). However, media that has an ID that RSM is unable to read or understand also becomes part of the Unrecognized media pool. Media in the Unrecognized pools is not listed in the RSM database and is therefore not available to applications.

Free media pools hold media that is not currently being used by applications. The media is available for use by any application that needs it. It's assumed that any data on the media is not needed, and this is usually accurate, because the data is an old backup that would not be useful for a restore procedure. You can configure RSM to have applications draw media from the Free media pool automatically, whenever an application runs out of media in its own pool. If you don't configure automatic draws from the Free pool, you must move media manually into the application pool when it's needed.

Import media pools contain media that is recognized as a valid media type, but has not been used by RSM. Typically, media lands in the Import pool when it is brought to an RSM system from a different RSM system within the organization. You can move media from an Import pool into a Free pool or an Application pool.

A media pool can contain media, or other media pools. A media pool cannot contain both media and other pools; it is either a single structure or a hierarchical structure. For example, the Free pool could contain media pools for each type of media.

A library can include media from various media pools, and a single media pool can work with multiple libraries.

Media Identification   In order to track media and keep its inventory records, RSM identifies each unit of media. There are two identification methods: on-media identifiers and bar codes.

On-media identifiers are recorded electronically the first time the media is inserted into a library. The identifier has two parts:

- **Label type**   Identifies the format used to record data. The format is dependent on the type of media.

- **Label ID**   A unique identifier for the specific disc or tape.

Bar-code identifiers are available if your library supports bar codes. RSM can identify media from the bar codes you supply. Media that use bar codes also receive on-media IDs, and RSM can use either method to identify the tape or disc. Bar codes are easier because you don't have to mount the media in the drive in order to identify it.

Media Formats   RSM uses a Media Label Library (MLL) to manage on-media identifiers. An MLL is a DLL that's used to interpret the format of a media label that was written by an application. RSM supports FAT, NTFS, and CDFS for disk media, and MTF (Microsoft Tape Format) for tape media. RSM can discern which application wrote the media label by checking the registered MLLs. Developers who distribute applications that use another media format must provide MLLs.

Media States   The media state is the current operational status of a tape or disc. RSM uses the on-media identifier or the bar code to ascertain the current state. Media states are determined on two levels: physical state and side state.

The *physical* state identifies the current status regarding the media's location and physical use. There are five possible physical states, described in Table 8-1.

The *side* state is the status of the side(s) where data is stored. Every type of media has either one or two sides. For example, magnetic-optical disks have two sides, while tape has a single side. RSM tracks the sides of media, as described in Table 8-2.

 An allocation maximum is set by an administrator to control the number of times an application can allocate and deallocate the media. RSM checks the count each time a side is deallocated, and when the maximum is reached, the side is decommissioned. This feature lets administrators prevent media from being used beyond its normal useful life (especially important with tape).

Managing Media Pools   Use the Removable Storage tool to manage media pools. You can create a pool, delete a pool, and move media between pools.

Physical State	Description
Idle	The media is offline, either in a storage slot (in a robotic device) or physically absent (stored).
In Use	RSM is currently moving the media.
Loaded	The media is mounted in a drive and is available for reading or writing data.
Mounted	The media is in a drive but not yet available for reading or writing data.
Unloaded	The media has been dismounted and is waiting for someone to physically remove it.

Table 8-1.   *Descriptions for Media Physical States*

Side State	Description
Allocated	The side is reserved by an application and is not available to any other application.
Available	The side is available for use by an application.
Completed	The side is full.
Decommissioned	The side is not available because it has reached its allocation maximum (see Note on allocation maximum).
Imported	The side's label type is recognized. The label ID is not recognized.
Incompatible	The media type is not compatible with the library and should be removed.
Reserved	The side is only available to a specific application. This state applies to two-sided media where one side is allocated.
Unprepared	The side is in a Free media pool and has not yet received a free media label.
Unrecognized	RSM does not recognize the side's label type and ID.

Table 8-2.   *Descriptions of Side States for Removable Media*

You can create a media pool for an application, either as a new top-level pool or within an existing application pool (but not within the system pools, Free, Import, or Unrecognized):

- To create a top-level media pool, right-click the Media Pools object in the console tree and select Create Media Pool from the shortcut menu.

- To create a media pool within an existing pool, right-click the existing pool and select Create Media Pool from the shortcut menu.

Configure the new media pool in the Create a New Media Pool Properties dialog, using the following guidelines:

- Enter a name for the new media pool.

- Enter a description (optional).

- In the Media information section, configure the media pool to hold other media pools, or to hold media.

- Enter the media type if the pool contains media.

- Select allocation/deallocation/reallocation options as follows:

  - Automatically draw media from a Free pool when this media pool runs out of media. Don't select this option if you prefer to move media from a Free pool to this pool manually (using the RSM console).

  - Automatically return media to a Free pool when the media is no longer needed by an application. Don't select this option if you prefer to move the media to the Free pool manually.

  - Limit the number of times the media can be allocated by other media pools.

- Use the Security tab to give permissions to users and groups to manipulate this media pool.

To delete an application media pool from the Removable Storage console, expand the Media Pools object in the console pane. Right-click the media pool you want to remove and choose Delete from the shortcut menu. You're asked to confirm your action.

Move Media to Another Pool   To move media from one media pool to another, drag the tape or disk from the details pane to the applicable media pool in the console pane. Expand the object first if either the source or target media pool is in a hierarchy

Eject Media   Always eject media from the RSM console so the RSM program knows that the media is removed from the library. The method you use differs between stand-alone libraries and automated libraries:

- If the media is in a stand-alone library, right-click the appropriate library object and choose Eject from the shortcut menu.

■ If the media is in an automated library, right-click the library's media object and choose Eject from the shortcut menu. Then follow the steps in the Media Eject Wizard.

Cleaning Media   RSM keeps records on media-cleaning procedures, so you should use the RSM console when you perform a cleaning operation. The steps you use in the console differ between a stand-alone library and a robotic library.

To clean media in a stand-alone library, manually insert the cleaning cartridge. Then, to notify RSM, open the console, right-click the drive, and choose Mark As Clean from the shortcut menu.

To clean media in a robotic library, right-click the appropriate library and choose Cleaner Management from the shortcut menu. The Cleaner Management Wizard walks you through the steps (including instructions for inserting a cleaning cartridge).

RSM Tricks and Tips   RSM is quite powerful, but at the same time it requires a commitment to keep on top of it or it won't work properly for you. If you use a tape backup device, RSM is going to become an important part of your professional life.

The trick is to remember that whatever you do with removable media, do it through the RSM console. Don't move a tape, clean a tape, throw a tape away, or introduce new tapes without telling RSM.

If you have to restore files from a tape backup, you may encounter a problem with the tape—not a physical problem, but a problem with mounting the tape so its contents or catalog can be read. Sometimes, the backup application may show a cycle of mounting, cataloging, and dismounting the tape, over and over. This is almost always caused by the fact that the on-media label does not match the RSM database information for the tape that was mounted. The media in the tape library may have been switched with another tape, or placed in the wrong slot. Use the RSM Eject Media and Inject Media Wizards instead of manually removing and replacing media. This permits RSM to keep track of the media.

If it's too late to heed my advice, and the tape you need for a restore is endlessly cycling, here's the fix: cancel the restore and perform a full inventory of the library.

Understanding the Work Queue   RSM can't multitask; it works sequentially, plugging away at one task at a time. If your tape unit has multiple drives and you want RSM to prepare two tapes, it will finish the first tape before beginning the second, even though both tapes are equally accessible.

You can keep an eye on the progress of multiple jobs by viewing the RSM Work Queue. To get there, select the Work Queue object in the console pane. The details pane displays the tasks and their status.

Disk Management

The disk management tool is the place to perform disk-related tasks, such as managing partitions and volumes, assigning drive letters, and, for Windows Server 2003 versions, creating and repairing fault-tolerant volumes.

Fault-tolerant volumes are part of a very large and complicated hardware issue, and a discussion is beyond the scope of this book.

 Disk management has changed substantially in Windows 2003, compared to Windows NT. If you're moving to Windows 2003 from Windows 2000, you're already familiar with the tools and procedures.

When you select the Disk Management object in the console pane, the display pane shows you information about the disks on the computer (see Figure 8-11). Incidentally, this is the way to find out whether the multiple drives that appear in My Computer are partitions of a single disk, or separate disks.

Manage Drives   You can manipulate the drives on your system with the Disk Management snap-in. Most of the tasks are rather dangerous if you don't take the time to read the documentation thoroughly. Listing all the tasks here would be overwhelming, because the permutations and combinations of possibilities are enormous.

Manage Drive Letters   Drive letter assignments are handled differently in Windows Server 2003 than they were in Windows NT (and earlier). For instance, if you have an ATAPI CD-ROM changer, it is assigned a single drive letter. Removable Storage Manager mounts, dismounts, and manages all its media. In Windows NT 4, such a device has a separate drive letter for each piece of media the device is capable of managing, and as you call for each drive letter, the media is swapped automatically.

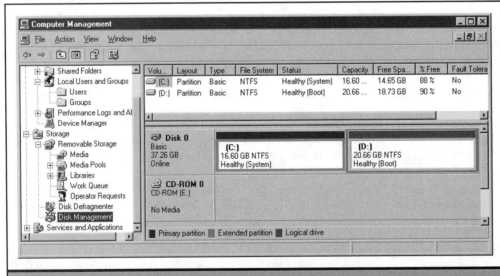

Figure 8-11.   Get a quick view of the disks on your system in the Disk Management snap-in.

In Windows Server 2003, drive letters are assigned to volumes by the Mount Manager (MountMgr) program. When a drive letter is assigned to a volume, that drive letter is reserved for that volume in the MountMgr database (which is in the registry).

When you perform a Windows Server 2003 upgrade from Windows NT, the existing drive letter assignments are exported to the Win_nt.~bt\Migrate.inf file so that the text-mode setup process can read and import the information into the MountMgr database.

When you perform a Windows Server 2003 upgrade from Windows 2000, the system maintains the existing drive letter information (Windows 2000 handles these functions the same way Windows Server 2003 does).

During a fresh Windows Server 2003 installation, MountMgr follows a procedure for assigning letters and then continues to use that procedure for volumes or drives that are added to the system.

Here are the steps, in order, that Setup performs to determine drive letter assignments:

1. Scan all fixed disks as they are enumerated. Start with active primary partitions (if there are any marked active). Then move to the first primary partition on each drive. The drive letters are assigned in order, using the next available letter (no letters before C are used).

2. Scan all fixed hard disks and assign drive letters to all logical drives in an extended partition. Scan removable disks (Zip, magnetic-optical, and so on) as enumerated. Assign each the next available letter (no letters before C).

3. Assign letters to floppy drives, starting with A.

4. Assign letters to CD-ROM drives, using the next available letter (no letters before D).

There is an exception to this scheme. Legacy Fault Tolerant sets on basic disks record their last-used drive letter in a private region on the physical disk. During installation of Windows Server 2003, these drive letters are noted and given priority during the drive assignment process. Therefore, legacy FT-sets are assigned drive letters before any other drive letters are assigned to other basic disk partitions.

Assigned drive letters are persistent, and should remain as is unless a volume is deleted or manually changed using Disk Management. An exception occurs if a volume (removable disk) is offline, and a new volume is brought online. The new volume may receive the offline volume's drive letter. To keep your drive letter assignments intact, keep existing volumes online when you introduce new volumes.

Logical Disk Manager (LDM) tracks the last drive letter assigned to a dynamic volume in its configuration database. This database is located in a 1MB private region at the end of each dynamic disk. When MountMgr is assigning letters to dynamic volumes, LDM is queried to see if it has a "suggested drive letter," based on the information in its configuration database.

MountMgr assigns drive letters to dynamic volumes using the following guidelines:

■ If the MountMgr database in the registry already has a drive letter recorded for the volume, the volume gets that drive letter.

- If the MountMgr database does not contain a drive letter for the volume, MountMgr asks LDM for a "suggested" drive letter. LDM checks its configuration database, and if a recorded drive letter is found, that letter is suggested to MountMgr.

- If this suggested drive letter is available, it is assigned to the volume and recorded in the MountMgr database so it can be used during the next mount.

- If the suggested drive letter is already used, the volume is assigned the next available drive letter.

- If LDM does not have a suggested drive letter, the volume is assigned the next available letter.

To manipulate drive letter assignments manually, right-click the target drive and choose Change Drive Letter and Paths from the shortcut menu.

Services and Applications

The last snap-in in the console pane of the Computer Management console is Services and Applications. Selecting the Services object in the console pane displays information about the installed services. Information about manipulating services can be found throughout this book, so I won't go into a long discussion here.

You can use the Properties dialog for any service to change its configuration, but step carefully—this can be dangerous territory.

- **On the General tab** you can change the method of startup for the service. You can also start, stop, pause, and resume the service.

- **On the Logon tab** you can change the account attached to this service.

- **On the Recovery tab** you can select actions if the service fails. Possible actions include restarting the service, restarting the computer, or launching a file (usually a notification program to let an administrator know what's happening).

- **On the Dependencies tab** you can view the names of services that are dependent on this service, and the names of services this service depends on. This is an important set of guidelines when you're making changes to the service's behavior.

The
Complete
Reference

Chapter 9

Printing

The installation and configuration of printers and printing services in Windows Server 2003 is easy compared to what you have to go through to install and configure other NOS print services and print servers. Of course, achieving all this simplicity takes a great deal of complicated work, most of which is performed by the operating system kernel, working in the background.

In this chapter, I'll discuss the way Windows Server 2003 accomplishes printing, and the components involved in the printing processes. I'll also cover the basic setup and configuration choices you have as you set up printing services for your network.

New Printing Features

If you're migrating to Windows Server 2003 from Windows NT, you'll find a number of major enhancements and improvements to printing in Windows Server 2003. If you've been running Windows 2000, you've already encountered most of these changes, but Windows Server 2003 introduces a few more innovations.

Of course, all the Windows Server 2003 printing features are covered in detail in this chapter. However, for the impatiently curious, here's a brief summary of the important modifications:

- **Remote port administration** Remote administration of printers has been extended to include the ability to perform remote printer port administration. (Introduced in Windows 2000.)

- **Standard port for TCP/IP** A new port, called the *standard* port, is available for easy installation of most TCP/IP printers on your network. If you ever set up TCP/IP printing in Windows NT 4, you'll appreciate the fact that you don't have to go through all those steps in all those dialogs. (Introduced in Windows 2000.)

- **Internet printing** Printing is integrated with the Internet, and users can access print servers on an intranet or on the Internet via a URL. (Introduced in Windows 2000.)

- **Print queue monitors** You can monitor the performance of a local or a remote printer with the System Monitor's Print Queue object. Counters are available for numerous performance criteria. (Introduced in Windows 2000.)

- **Users can change settings** Users running Windows XP Professional and Windows Server 2003 can alter personal settings for document defaults. This ability has not been available to users running NT or Windows 2000 (although it was available to users running Windows 9x).

- **New Print dialog** The standard Print dialog that appears when you're printing from an application has changed. You can now install a printer directly from the Print dialog.

- **Printers folder name change** The Printers folder is now called Printers and Faxes.

- **Automatic installation of printer drivers on all nodes in a cluster** When you install a printer driver on one node of a cluster, the driver is automatically installed on all the other nodes.
- **Kernel-mode printer driver blocking** An administrator can prevent the installation of kernel-mode printer drivers by users through a group policy.

Printing Basics

Windows Server 2003 is a protected-mode operating system with no direct access to hardware. Therefore, virtual printers (sometimes called *logical* printers) are used to control the printing features and to interact with the physical printing devices. Sending a print job to the printer means sending the job to the virtual device. The important things to keep in mind are the following:

- The icons that are displayed in printer listings represent virtual printers.
- Users send a print job to a virtual printer, not a physical printer.
- Installed printer drivers are loaded at print time and sent to the virtual printer.
- Configuration changes to a printer's properties are made to the virtual printer, but the options must match the capabilities of the physical printer.

Printing Processes

Before a print job is actually sent to the printer, the operating system performs a number of processes. What follows is a brief overview of those processes, starting at the point a user sends a document to a printer. (I'm assuming the software is a Windows application.) I'll discuss the printing components that operate in these processes in the section, "Printing Components," later in this chapter.

Create the Output File

The Windows application calls the Graphical Device Interface (GDI), which in turn calls the printer driver associated with the target printer. Using the document information provided by the application, the GDI and the driver contribute data to create an enhanced metafile (EMF) containing the GDI calls and the printer driver information. The Windows application then calls the client side of the spooler (Winspool.drv).

Once the printer driver is loaded into memory, all of the printer-specific codes and instruction sets are available to the processes that follow.

Note *Non-Windows OS and application printing processes don't use the GDI. A component similar to the Windows GDI performs the same task.*

The output file contains instructions, called *Device Driver Interface (DDI) calls,* which are sent to the printer driver. The output file is called a *DDI Journal file.* The graphics engine (%SystemRoot%\System32\gdi32.dll) translates the GDI commands into the DDI commands that can be read by the operating system's print processors and by the printer driver.

Process the Output File

The output file is passed to the local spooler, which examines the data type and then passes the print job to the print processor. It also sends information about the data type. The print processor creates the print data format that the physical printer expects. See the sections on print processors later in this chapter for information about data types and data formats.

 Regardless of whether the file is being sent to a local or network physical printer, the output file is always passed to the local spooler.

Route the Print Job

The client computer uses a Remote Procedure Call (RPC) to send the print job to the Windows router on the print server. The router accepts the job from the client computer, and checks the location of the physical printer. Then the router sends the processed job to the spooler for the physical printer. If the printer is local, that just means the processed job is sent back to the client spooler and the local computer is considered to be the print server.

Send the Print Job

The spooler on the print server hands the print job off to the operating system's print monitor. The print monitor checks the destination port, and if it is free, it sends the print job. If the port is not free, the print monitor holds the print job in the queue in the spooler until the port is free. The print monitor also manages communication between the printer and the sending user, if the printer/cable supports bidirectional communication.

Printing Components

All the steps the operating system performs to move a print job from an application to a physical printer require the use of a number of components and processes provided by the operating system.

Spooler

The *spooler* is software—a group of DLLs that take care of the chores that must be accomplished when a document is sent to the printer. Those chores include:

- Tracking the printer ports associated with each printer.
- Tracking the configuration of the physical printer, such as memory, trays, and so on.
- Assigning priorities to the print jobs in the queue.
- Sending the print job through a series of software processes that depend on the type of job, the type of data, and the location of the physical printer.
- Sending the job to the physical printer.

The spooler receives the print job, stores the job on disk, and then passes the job through the print processes and on to the physical printer. As soon as the print job is stored on disk, the user can go back to work in the sending application. All of the print processing is performed in the background.

By default, the directory used for spooling is %SystemRoot%\System32\Spool\ Printers. You can change the location of the spooler, and it's frequently a good idea to do so if you have another drive (with more free space) on the computer. The spool files on a print server can take up quite a bit of disk space.

If the print server has a second drive that's attached to a separate controller, you can also improve I/O performance on the default spooler drive by moving the spooler to a drive on the other, separate controller.

To move the spooler, open the Printers and Faxes folder and choose Server Properties from the File menu ("Server" means print server, so this menu item is also present on workstations that provide shared printers). In the Print Server Properties dialog, move to the Advanced tab, which displays the location of the spool folder. Enter a new location, with these guidelines in mind:

- Don't put the spool folder on the root. Windows Server 2003 doesn't accept this configuration and will revert the spool folder to its original location (I used D:\Printing\Spool\Printers).
- Don't perform this action while print jobs are active; those jobs will never print.
- If the directory you specify doesn't exist, it's created for you, but if the directory is a subdirectory, the parent directory must already exist. In other words, the system is willing to create only the bottom level of the path automatically, so it's best to create the full path manually before moving the spooler.
- If the spooler is on an NTFS partition, be sure that Everyone has write permissions for the spool directory.

The new location is written back to the registry immediately and is effective immediately. The registry key is HKEY_LOCAL_MACHINE\Software\Microsoft\ Windows NT\CurrentVersion\Print\Printers. The data item is DefaultSpoolDirectory (a REG_SZ data type).

If the new location doesn't take effect, you need to stop and restart the Print Spooler service, using these steps:

1. In Control Panel, open the Administrative Tools applet.

2. Open the Services console.

3. Select Print Spooler.

4. If you're using Extended view, click Stop, then click Restart in the console pane.

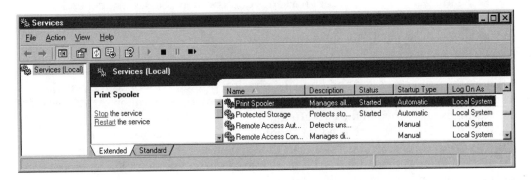

5. If you're using Standard view in the console, right-click the listing and choose Stop from the shortcut menu. Then right-click again, and choose Restart.

You can also stop and start the Print Spooler service from the command line with the commands **net stop spooler** and **net start spooler**.

Spool Files

The spooler directory holds the spool files (the list of spool files is called the *queue*). For each spooled print job, there are two files written to the spooler directory:

- **The spool file** This file is actually the print job. It has an .spl extension.
- **The shadow file** This file contains the administrative information needed to print the job (the target printer, the job's priority, the name of the sending user, and so on). The file has an extension of .shd.

If the print server is shut down before all the spooled jobs are printed, when the print server is restarted, printing restarts, because the presence of spool and shadow files starts the printing process.

Printer Drivers

Printer drivers translate the data and codes in the print job document into the form needed by the printer. The operating system uses the printer driver for three specific tasks, and breaks down the functions of the printer driver into those distinct parts. The three individual parts, each of which is a set of files, are the following:

- Graphics drivers

- Printer interface drivers
- Characterization data files

Each of these components plays a specific role in print processing.

Graphics Drivers

The imaging functions (rendering of graphic images) are implemented by Windows Server 2003 as a DLL. The Print Graphics Driver DLL provides the API calls that are used as a graphics device interface during the building of the DDI Journal file. The graphics driver also converts the DDI commands into commands that printers can accept. These files are stored in subdirectories under %SystemRoot%\System32\ Spool\Drivers\w32x86.

Printer Interface Drivers

The printer interface files (which are .dll files) provide the options a user can choose when configuring a printer. Specifically, they display the Properties and Printing Preferences dialogs.

Characterization Data Files

These files contain the information provided by printer manufacturers about the printer's capabilities and configuration options, such as whether it prints on both sides of the paper, the maximum paper size it accepts, and so on.

Print Queue

The lineup of print job files in the spool directory waiting to be sent to the physical printer is called the queue.

If you have Novell NetWare or OS/2 in your professional history, you have to redefine your definition of the word "queue." The queue used by those other network operating systems is the primary software interface between the applications and the physical printer. The queue's relationship to the printer is a one-to-one concept.

In OS/2, for example, when a user sends a print job to a printer, the job is intercepted by the OS/2 spooler, which holds the job in a queue that is really a virtual alias to a specific physical printer. The print job is submitted to the queue for handling; the queue is not a collection of print files that have already been "handled" by the operating system. The spooler and the queue are a merged concept. The printer driver, the spooler, and the queue do not individually manipulate the print job; the job is grabbed, held, and shipped to the physical printer by one entity, the queue.

NetWare 3.*x* (and NetWare 4.*x* if you opt to use a queue instead of a virtual printer) operates in much the same manner as OS/2, except setting up the queue and the printer server requires much more work.

For raster printers, these files are called *minidrivers* and are usually implemented as DLLs (although you may see other extensions such as .gpd or .pcd). They are source-code compatible across platforms and processors.

For PostScript printers, these are *PostScript Printer Description (PPD) files,* which are text files provided by the manufacturer. They are binary compatible across platforms and processors.

Windows Server 2003 Print Processor

The print processor does the rendering of the print job after it receives the file from the spooler. *Rendering* means translating all the data in the print job into data that is understood and accepted by the printer.

Before passing the job, the spooler checks for the data type. If rendering is necessary, it passes along rendering information to the print processor in addition to the print job. The question of whether or not the job needs processing is dependent upon the data type sent by the client application.

Windows NT/2000/XP/2003 Server use EMF as the default data type, and the print processor can pass the job to the printer with full confidence that the printer can understand and handle the print job.

You can find the print processor and configuration for data type in the printer's Properties dialog by clicking the Print Processor button on the Advanced tab.

The various data types are as follows:

- **RAW**   This data type indicates that the job has been rendered and is ready for the printer. The print processor takes no action. RAW is used by non-Windows NT4/2000/XP/2003 Server clients, and is the default data type for all PostScript printers.

- **RAW [FF appended]**   This data type indicates that the client has sent a document with no form feed at the end of the job (needed to make the last page eject). The print processor adds a form feed and takes no other action.

- **RAW [FF auto]**   This data type works the same as RAW [FF appended], but the print process checks for the presence of a form feed at the end of the job, and adds one if it's missing.

- **TEXT**   This data type indicates that the job is simple text, and is usually applied to print jobs that are being sent to PostScript printers or plotters (which don't accept text as a valid data type). The print processor uses the printer driver to render the job into printer commands that are acceptable to the target printer.

- **EMF**   The Enhanced Metafiles (EMF) data type is the default, used by most applications that are written for Windows NT 4, Windows 2000, Windows XP, and Windows Server 2003. EMF information is generated by the GDI before spooling; then the spooler delivers the print job to the queue in the background. EMF files are typically smaller than RAW data type files. More important, they are portable and can be translated to meet the expectations of almost any printer.

Other Print Processors

In addition to the print processor that is built into Windows Server 2003, you can add additional print processors to your system. Some print processors are available as optional components in Windows Server 2003, as described in Table 9-1.

Additional print processors are available from third-party sources. For example, software applications that produce data requiring special handling in order to be understood by the printer usually provide a print processor.

Print Router

The *print router* accepts requests to print from clients, and determines the spooler component that should be used to fulfill the request. It works between the client and the print server (which may be the same computer, of course). The print router is implemented with Winspool.drv in %SystemRoot%\System32, and the communication between the client and the print router is accomplished with RPCs.

The first task of the print router is to find the physical printer to which the print job is to be delivered. When the printer is found, the router looks at its printer driver and compares that to the printer driver on the client computer (if there is one). If there is no

Component	Service	Availability
Print Services for UNIX	Printing that uses TCP/IP protocol	Optional component in Windows Server 2003
Peer Web Services	Printing to the Internet from Windows XP Professional	Windows XP Professional Resource Kit
File and Print Services for NetWare	Printing to Windows Server 2003 from computers running NetWare	Microsoft Services for NetWare (sold separately)
Client Service for NetWare	Printing to NetWare servers from Windows XP Professional	Optional component in Windows XP Professional
Gateway Service for NetWare	Printing to and from NetWare print queues by using Windows Server 2003 (also provides a gateway for SMB clients to print to NetWare print queues)	Optional component in Windows Server 2003
Print Services for Macintosh	Printing to Windows Server 2003 from Macintosh computers	Optional component in Windows Server 2003

Table 9-1. *Optional Print Processors for Windows Server 2003*

printer driver on the client, or if the date of the client's printer driver is earlier than the date of the driver on the print server, the driver on the print server is loaded for the client.

If the client receives no error message ("printer not found") from the print router, the job is processed by the client (now assured of having the correct driver), which means the job is placed in the local spooler. If the print server is not the client computer, the print router copies the job from the client spooler to the print server spooler.

Print Monitors

The *print monitor* is the component that controls the port as well as the communication between the port and the spooler. It sends the print jobs to the port by performing the following tasks:

- Accesses the port (sends the print job)
- Releases access to the port at the end of a print job
- Sends notification to the spooler when a print job has finished printing (the spooler then deletes the job from the queue)
- Monitors the printer for error messages

A print monitor that performs the tasks described here is sometimes called a *port monitor*. If the printer supports bidirectional printing, a print monitor also acts as a *language monitor*, facilitating the two-way communication between the printer and the print server's spooler. This gives the spooler configuration and status information about the printer.

However, the most important job of a print monitor is to control port I/O, and there are print monitors for any type of port you use or install in your Windows Server 2003 system. Table 9-2 presents a summary of Windows Server 2003 print monitor support.

Note *IR ports aren't listed in the Ports tab of a printer's Properties dialog unless the computer contains an IR device. USB and IEEE 1394 ports never appear as choices in the Ports tab of a printer's Properties dialog, because you can select them manually. If you connect a printer to either a USB or IEEE 1394 port, Windows Server 2003 autodetects the connection and installs the port and port monitor automatically.*

Local Print Monitor

The local print monitor (%SystemRoot%\System32\Localmon.dll) controls the local ports. The following port assignments for printers are considered local (any printer can be configured to print to any port in this list):

- Parallel
- Serial

- File (the print monitor prompts for a filename when you use this port)
- Explicit filenames (each job sent to a specific filename overwrites the last job sent to that filename)
- UNC designations for a shared remote printer
- NUL
- IR
- USB
- IEEE 1394

Standard Port Monitor

The preferred port monitor for network printers in Windows Server 2003 is the standard TCP/IP port monitor. *Network printers* means network-ready printers that contain NICs (such as the HP JetDirect), and external network boxes (such as the Intel NetPort). The standard port monitor can support many printers on one server, and uses Simple Network Management Protocol (SNMP) to configure and monitor printers.

Because a standard port monitor is compatible with RFC 1759, which is the standard for the Management Information Base, the monitor provides more detailed information about printer status than a LPR port monitor.

Port	Target Printer(s)	Availability in Windows Server 2003
Local port (parallel, serial, USB, 1394, IR)	Printers connected to the computer	Built in
Standard TCP/IP port	TCP/IP network-ready printer devices	Built in
AppleTalk printing devices	AppleTalk printers	After installing the AppleTalk protocol
LPR port	TCP/IP printers connected to a UNIX (or VAX) server	After installing Print Services for UNIX
HTTP	Internet printing	After installing IIS
Port for NetWare-based printers	NetWare printing resources	After installing NW Link protocol and Client Services for NetWare

Table 9-2.   *Print Monitor Support in Windows Server 2003*

Use the NUL Port for Testing

The NUL port is generally used for testing network printing. Set a printer to use the NUL port and pause it (so you can see jobs waiting; otherwise the jobs pass through the port too fast to watch them). Then send a job to that printer from a connected client. You should be able to see the job when you open the printer object. If you don't see the job, check the setup to make sure the printer is configured for the NUL port. If you do see the job, your test is successful. Resume printing, which really does nothing because jobs sent to a NUL port just disappear. Instead of paper, documents print to thin air as they travel to lost document la-la land.

To use the standard port monitor, the print server must be running the TCP/IP protocol (since this is the default networking protocol for Windows Server 2003, this shouldn't be a problem).

Note   *Although clients are usually running TCP/IP in a Windows 2000 or Windows Server 2003 domain, it's not necessary for clients to run TCP/IP in order to print to a network printer via a print server that's using the standard print monitor. After all, only the print server needs to communicate with the printer. Clients can run any common transport protocol to communicate with the print server.*

The standard port monitor sends documents to printers via one of two print server protocols: RAW or LPR. Between them, those protocols cover the communication requirements for almost all TCP/IP network printers.

For most network printers, the RAW print server protocol is the default communication type. The print server opens a TCP stream to one of the printer's ports (usually 9101 for LPT1, 9102 for LPT2, and so on). The print server disconnects from the port when it has finished sending the data. However, if necessary (meaning, if the printer requires it), you can configure the standard port monitor to use LPR.

Note   *The standard port monitor does not conform to the RFC 1179 requirement that the source TCP port lie between port 721 and port 731, because that limits the print server to managing 11 printers. Therefore, the Windows Server 2003 standard port monitor uses ports from the unreserved pool of ports (which are ports 1024 and above).*

To add a port that uses the standard port monitor, follow these steps:

1. Open Printers and Faxes.
2. Right-click the network printer you want to configure, and choose Properties from the shortcut menu.
3. Go to the Ports tab.
4. Click the Add Port button and select Standard TCP/IP Port from the list of available port types.

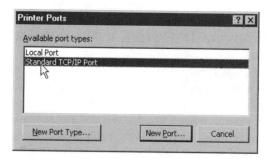

5. Click New Port to launch the Add Standard TCP/IP Port Wizard, and then click Next.

6. In the Printer Name or IP Address box, enter the name or IP address of a network printer.

7. In the Port Name box, the wizard uses the printer's identification you entered in the Printer Name box, which is usually appropriate. You can, if you wish, enter a different name for the port.

8. Click Next.

Windows Server 2003 queries the device via SNMP. Using the values that are returned, the appropriate device options are displayed. You may have to make some additional configuration selections, depending on the features of the printer.

If the wizard presents the window named Additional Port Information Required, do one of the following:

■ Click Standard, and then select one of the devices that's listed. If you don't know the details about the port, use the Generic Network Card selection.

■ Click Custom, and configure the port yourself in the Configure Standard TCP/IP Port Monitor window.

 If the wizard doesn't know the printer protocol, it asks you for that information. You'll need the printer vendor's documentation to know whether to select RAW or LPR.

Click Finish, and the new port is listed on the Ports tab of the network printer's Properties dialog.

Macintosh Print Monitor

The Macintosh print monitor (Sfmmon.dll) controls printing over AppleTalk protocols. Only print servers running Windows Server 2003 can receive Macintosh AppleTalk print jobs; a Windows XP Professional computer that's acting as a print server is unable to print jobs from Macintosh clients.

HP Print Monitor and DLC No Longer Supported

Windows Server 2003 does not support the Data Link Control (DLC) printing protocol. DLC is the default protocol for using hpmon from Hewlett-Packard. To support a printer that currently uses hpmon on a Windows Server 2003 print server, you must upgrade the current HP JetDirect network adapter in favor of one that supports IP. Then, you can use the standard port monitor.

Alternatively, you can use a print server running Windows 2000 or Windows NT 4 to provide printing services. For those of you who don't want to upgrade the hardware, and will instead use an older version of Windows for these printers, directions for installing and configuring DLC and hpmon can be found in *Windows 2000: The Complete Reference* (Osborne/McGraw-Hill).

To support Macintosh printing, you must have the following components:

- The AppleTalk protocol, to communicate between the client and the print server
- Print Services for Macintosh, which supplies the Macintosh print monitor
- An AppleTalk port

Install AppleTalk   To install the AppleTalk protocol, follow these steps:

1. Open the Network and Internet Connections applet in Control Panel.
2. Open the Network Connections applet.
3. Right-click Local Area Connection and select Properties.
4. In the Local Area Connection Properties dialog, click the Install button.
5. Select Protocol and click Add.
6. Select AppleTalk Protocol and click OK.

The files are transferred from the Windows Server 2003 CD-ROM. To your Macintosh clients, the Windows Server 2003 print server looks like an AppleTalk device.

Install Print Services for Macintosh   To add Print Services for Macintosh to the appropriate print server, use these steps:

1. Open the Add or Remove Programs applet in Control Panel.
2. Click the Add/Remove Windows Components icon to open the Windows Components Wizard.
3. In the Windows Components list, locate Other Network File And Print Services. Select that listing, but don't click the check box (you don't want to select the entire installation option).
4. Click Details to display the available services, which are File Services For Macintosh, Print Services For Macintosh, and Print Services For UNIX.

5. Select Print Services For Macintosh and click OK.

6. Follow any additional prompts to install the services from the Windows Server 2003 CD-ROM.

 If you perform this task on Windows XP Professional, you see only Print Services For UNIX, because Windows XP Professional does not support Macintosh File And Print services.

Install an AppleTalk Port   To install an AppleTalk port and the attendant printer, follow these steps:

1. Open the Printers and Faxes folder.

2. Open the Add Printer object to start the Add Printer Wizard and click Next.

3. Select Local Printer, and make sure the automatic detection check box is deselected; then click Next.

4. Select the Create A New Port option to activate the Type text box.

5. Click the arrow to the right of the Type text box and select AppleTalk Printing Devices; then click Next.

6. From the AppleTalk Printing Devices list, click the AppleTalk printer you want to add, and then click OK.

7. Click Yes to capture this AppleTalk device.

8. Follow the onscreen instructions to complete the installation for this printer.

What You Need Depends on What You're Doing   Here are the guidelines for supporting Macintosh printing on your network:

- To print from Windows Server 2003 to an AppleTalk printer, you only need to install the AppleTalk protocol, which lets you add an AppleTalk port (available for both Windows Server 2003 and Windows XP Professional).

- If you want to have Macintosh clients print to shared printers, you must have both the AppleTalk protocol and Services For Macintosh installed on the Windows Server 2003 that's acting as the print server (Windows XP Professional cannot support this).

LPR Print Monitors

In the UNIX environment, an application can use a *line printer remote (LPR)* service to send a document to a print spooler service on another computer. LPR is a part of the protocols developed with and for TCP/IP to provide printing services for UNIX (actually, it started with Berkeley UNIX, which only some of us who are quite old can remember). Today, LRP still works for many UNIX clients.

In Windows NT 4, LPR was needed for printing across TCP/IP (even if there were no UNIX computers in sight), but that changed with Windows 2000, which treated

TCP/IP as a standard port. Windows Server 2003 offers the same LPR functionality as Windows 2000.

That doesn't mean you won't need LPR; it just means you won't need it for printing over TCP/IP within the Windows Server 2003 environment. However, you will need LRP to provide printing services in an environment that includes UNIX.

LPR protocols permit client applications to send print jobs directly to a print spooler on a print server. The client side of this is called LPR, and the host side is called *line printer daemon (LPD)*. Microsoft Print Services For UNIX provides both the LPR and LPD services.

On the client side, Windows Server 2003 supports LPR with an executable file named Lpr.exe (in %SystemRoot%\System32). This executable, when launched, supplies the print monitor (Lprmon.dll) that communicates with the LPD services (which are native to the UNIX host).

On the server side, Windows Server 2003 provides LPD services through Lpdsvc.dll. This service can support any print format, but it has no processing power. The client application must send the format expected by the printer.

To print from a UNIX client to a Windows Server 2003 printer, the client must have a supported version of LPR (not all flavors of UNIX support the LPR standards that are supported by Windows Server 2003). Lpdsvc on the print server receives the documents from the LPR utilities running on the client UNIX machine (the LPR utilities are native to the client, so you don't need to install them). The Windows Server 2003 print server must be running Print Services For UNIX.

To print from a Windows Server 2003 computer to a printer hosted by a UNIX print server, Lpr.exe supplies Lprmon.dll, which communicates with the native LPD UNIX service on the host. This also requires the installation of Print Services For UNIX.

Install Print Services for UNIX   To install Print Services For UNIX, follow these steps on the print server, which can be running on Windows Server 2003 or Windows XP Professional:

1. Open the Add or Remove Programs applet in Control Panel.

2. Click the Add/Remove Windows Components icon to open the Windows Components Wizard.

3. In the next wizard window, scroll through the Components list to locate Other Network File And Print Services. Select that listing, but don't click the check box to select the installation option.

4. Click Details to display the available services.

5. Select Print Services For UNIX and click OK.

6. Follow the additional prompts to install the services from the Windows CD-ROM.

Next, the LPD services must be started (client services are started by the Lpr executable), and an LPR port must be created for the printer.

Configure LPD Services LPD services (TCP/IP Print Server services) are started automatically when you install Print Services For UNIX. To make sure TCP/IP Print Server services are configured correctly, follow these steps:

1. Open the Services applet from either Control Panel or the Programs menu (if you installed Administrative Tools).

2. Scroll to the listing for TCP/IP Print Server. If you don't see its listing, choose Action | Refresh from the console menu bar.

3. Be sure the service is started.

4. Be sure the service is configured to start automatically.

Add an LPR Port To add a port to the Windows Server 2003 or Windows XP Professional print server that's providing print services for UNIX clients, follow these steps:

1. Open the Printers and Faxes folder and open the Add Printer object.

2. When the Add Printer Wizard appears, click Next to move past the introductory window.

3. Select Local Printer and be sure the option to autodetect the printer is not selected. Click Next.

4. In the next window, select the option Create A New Port to enable the Type text box.

5. Click the Down arrow next to the Type box and choose LPR port, which is listed as a result of installing Print Services For UNIX. Click Next.

6. In the Name Or Address field, enter the DNS name or the IP address of the host for this printer.

7. In the Name Of Printer Or Print Queue On That Server field, enter the name of the installed printer (the identification used by the host computer).

Third-Party Print Monitors

Several printer manufacturers provide their own print monitors. The Digital print monitor controls any Digital Network ports you install in order to use Digital Equipment Corporation (DEC) PrintServer devices. In addition, some individual DEC printers require this port and attendant port monitor. This monitor must be obtained from the manufacturer (www.hp.com). Use the Have Disk option to install the printer and port.

If you have Lexmark printing devices, you should have received the Lexmark print monitor software with the device. If not, try www.lexmark.com. The Lexmark print monitors control the advanced features available in the printers, all of which require communication with the port (which is, of course, the job of the print monitor). Use the Have Disk option to install the printer and print monitor.

AppleTalk ports can only be managed locally, on the print server.

Language Monitors

Language monitors are used to facilitate communications for bidirectional printing devices. To take advantage of bidirectional printing, you need a bidirectional printer, port, and port monitor.

The Windows Server 2003 language monitor is Pjlmon.dll, which resides in %SystemRoot%\System32. Pjlmon.dll uses Printer Job Language (PJL), and any bidirectional printer that uses PJL can use Pjlmon.dll. If a printer uses a different printer language, the vendor should be able to supply a language monitor.

Print Providers

The last component in Windows Server 2003 printing is the *print provider*. The print provider sends the job to the physical device, using the configuration options for that device. In effect, it implements the choices you make in the Properties dialog for the printer.

For example, if you've opted to print spooled jobs as soon as spooling begins, it sends the job to the printer immediately instead of waiting for the entire job to be received. Windows Server 2003 includes two print providers: local and remote.

Local Print Provider

The local print provider is Localspl.dll, which is in the %SystemRoot%\System32 directory. It sends print jobs to the locally attached printer. To accomplish this, it performs the following tasks (using RPC calls):

1. When the print job is received (from a local application or a remote user), it writes the job to disk as a spool file. It also writes the shadow file.

2. If there is a configuration option for separator pages, it processes them.

3. It checks to see which print processor is needed for the print job's data type and passes the job to that print processor. When the print processor finishes making modifications (if any are necessary), it passes the job back to the local print provider.

4. It checks the port for the target printer, and then passes the job to the print monitor attached to that port.

Remote Print Providers

Both of the remote print providers are .dll files in the %SystemRoot%\System32 directory. Remote print providers are employed when a Windows Server 2003 computer sends print jobs to a remote print server:

- Win32spl.dll moves print jobs to Windows print servers.
- NWProvau.dll moves print jobs to Novell NetWare print servers.

If the target printer is on a print server running a legacy Windows operating system (Windows NT and earlier), the Windows Server 2003 remote print provider contacts the Windows network redirector, which sends the job across the network to the appropriate print server. That server takes over the responsibility of printing the job.

Note *The Windows redirector is a component of the Windows Network APIs. It lets client computers have access to resources on other computers as if those accessed resources were local. Communication is accomplished via the protocol stack to which it is bound.*

The NetWare remote print provider takes control of a print job when the server name is recognized as a NetWare print server. The NetWare print provider turns the job over to the NetWare redirector, which passes the job to the print server.

Installing Local Printers

The installation of printers (which is really the installation of printer drivers) in Windows Server 2003 is a snap, especially if your printer is a Plug and Play device. You can install a local printer as long as you have administrative rights on the computer.

Plug and Play Printer Installation

After you physically connect the printer and start the computer, if your printer is detected by Plug and Play, it's automatically installed. The Found New Hardware Wizard runs automatically and installs the printer. The installation is totally silent, taking place in the background, and requiring no user action.

If Plug and Play doesn't detect the printer at startup, and you know that's because your printer is not Plug and Play, follow the instructions in the next section, "Manual Installation of Printers."

Note *Plug and Play may not work if your printer is a new model that the OS doesn't recognize. Check the Microsoft web sites for updated drivers.*

If you believe the printer should work with Plug and Play, you can try an automatic Plug and Play installation from the Printers and Faxes folder (on the Settings submenu, or in Control Panel). Open the Add Printer object to launch the Add Printer Wizard. Click Next in the first wizard window, which is an introductory window and performs no action. In the next wizard window, select Local Printer and check the option to Automatically Detect And Install My Plug And Play Printer. Then click Next.

When (or if) the Add Printer Wizard finds the printer, it displays a message telling you so, and asks if you want to print a test page (you should select Yes). Just follow the prompts for any additional configuration requests. When the installation is complete and the printer driver files are copied to your local drive, the test page prints.

If the Add Printer Wizard does not find the printer, a message displays telling you Windows was unable to detect any Plug and Play printers. Click Next to perform a manual installation of the printer (covered next). If you have drivers from the manufacturer, be sure they're handy (if they're on a floppy disk or CD-ROM) or that you know their location on your hard drive (if you downloaded them).

Manual Installation of Printers

If your printer is not Plug and Play, you must perform a manual installation with the following steps:

1. Open the Add Printer object in the Printers and Faxes folder to launch the Add Printer Wizard.

2. Click Next in the first wizard window, which is an introductory window and performs no actions.

3. In the next wizard window, select Local Printer and make sure the option to Automatically Detect And Install My Plug And Play Printer is cleared. Then click Next.

4. Select the port on which the printer is connected and click Next.

5. In the next window, select the manufacturer and model of your printer and click Next.

6. Enter a name for the printer and specify whether this printer is to be the default printer for Windows software applications.

7. The next window asks if you want to share the printer with other network users. If you do, select Share As and enter a share name for the printer (or accept the name suggested by Windows, which is usually the name of the printer model). You can add an optional description for the benefit of network users.

8. Specify whether you want to print a test page (it's always a good idea to say Yes).

9. Click Next to see the last wizard window, and click Finish.

The driver files are copied to your hard drive, and the printer's icon appears in the Printers and Faxes folder.

Printer Model Isn't Listed

If your printer model isn't listed, and you don't have drivers from the manufacturer, click Cancel and return to the wizard after you've contacted the manufacturer to get the drivers. If the printer is a new model, you can also try clicking Windows Update to see if the Microsoft web site has the driver.

The following options are available in this wizard window:

- **Have Disk**   Click this button if you want to use printer drivers from the manufacturer. See the following section, "Using Manufacturer Drivers."

- **Windows Update**   Click this button if you want to get a driver from Microsoft's web site.

Using Manufacturer Drivers

If you have printer drivers from the manufacturer, click Have Disk as described previously in the "Printer Model Isn't Listed" section. Specify the location of the drivers, and follow the rest of the prompts to finish installing the printer.

Installing USB Printers and IEEE Printers

If your printer connects to a Universal Serial Bus (USB) or IEEE 1394 port, Plug and Play detects it immediately. In fact, Plug and Play opens as soon as you plug the jack into the port; you don't even have to start the Add Printer Wizard. As soon as a USB or IEEE port is detected, that port is added to the list of ports available to the printer, and the automatic installation process selects the port without user intervention.

Installing Infrared Printers

Infrared printers are automatically detected and installed, as long as the printer and computer are both turned on and can see each other. Be sure to position the two devices within about three feet of each other. It takes a few seconds for the computer to find the printer, but then everything goes on autopilot and you don't have to do anything else.

If your computer is not infrared-capable but your printer is, you can add an infrared transceiver to your serial port to your computer. Then install the driver with these steps:

1. Open the Add/Remove Hardware applet in Control Panel and click Next to move past the opening window.

2. In the next window, select Add/Troubleshoot a device and click Next. Wait a few seconds until Windows searches in vain for Plug and Play devices.

3. When the next window appears, select A New Device (the first listing) and click Next.

4. In the next window, select I Will Select From A List To Manually Install My New Hardware; then click Next.

5. In the next window, select Infrared Devices and click Next.

6. In the next window, select a manufacturer and a device (or select Have Disk if you have manufacturer drivers).

7. Follow the remaining prompts to install the infrared device.

Now you can automatically install the infrared printer.

Install a Network-ready Printer

Printers that have their own network interface connections work faster than printers that are attached to computers via a parallel port. Most of today's Internet connection devices for printers are capable of using TCP/IP to communicate, and Windows Server 2003 is set up to take advantage of this. You can choose between two methods when you want to add a network-ready printer to the network:

- Add the printer to each user's computer, and eliminate printer-sharing management.
- Add the printer to a computer that acts as a print server, and set up printer sharing.

For administrators of small networks or small branch offices, it's tempting to believe it's less of an administrative headache to let each user install the printer and manage it directly. This passes the headaches to the users. The headaches include:

- No user knows the current state of the printer, because displaying the print queue shows only the user's print jobs.
- Setting print priorities is a useless exercise, because only the querying user's print jobs are involved in the settings.
- Printer errors (out of paper, jams, and so on) are only revealed to the user who sent the current print job. Everyone else just keeps sending jobs.

Administrators who think users will put up with these headaches either have a problem with reality or have done a heck of a job training users to solve their own problems.

Printers that are accessed by multiple users always benefit from the management advantages of printer sharing. Install the direct-connection printer to a print server. If the number of simultaneous accesses doesn't exceed ten, you can use a Windows XP Professional or Windows 2000 Professional workstation (unless you have to support Macintosh or NetWare services). Printing doesn't impose an enormous strain on a computer's processing or I/O levels, so you can use a computer that performs other chores.

Now that I've convinced you to attach the printer with a NIC to a print server (be sure the computer that's acting as a print server is running TCP/IP), here are the instructions for installing the printer:

1. Open the Printers and Faxes folder and then open the Add Printer object (click Next right away to move past the Add Printer Wizard welcome window).

2. Select Local Printer and clear the check box for automatic detection; then click Next.

3. In the Select the Printer Port window, select Create A New Port. Choose Standard TCP/IP Port from the drop-down list; then click Next to open a new wizard (this wizard adds and configures TCP/IP printer ports).

4. Enter a printer name or an IP address for the printer, name the port (the port and the printer can use the same name), and click Next.

5. Select the device type from the drop-down list or select Custom and configure the device manually.

 The protocol, port number, and data type for the printer are built into the device type, so if you need to perform a manual device installation, make sure you have this information at hand.

Sharing Printers

When you install a printer in Windows Server 2003, the default configuration is to share the printer. Windows XP Professional does not share printers by default during installation, and you must specifically elect to share the printer. It's common to share all the printers on a network—the exceptions are printers that hold checks or other specialized paper types that require security.

Create a Printer Share

If you elected not to share the printer during installation, you can share it at any time thereafter. Open the Printers and Faxes folder, right-click the printer's icon, and choose Sharing from the shortcut menu. The printer's Properties dialog opens to the Sharing tab. Select Shared As, and enter a name for the printer (or accept the default name, which is usually the printer model). The Sharing tab has additional options available, which you can use as follows:

- Select List in the Directory to publish the printer in the Active Directory.
- Click Additional Drivers to cover the needs of remote users who have different versions of Windows. See "Add Drivers for Other Windows Versions," later in this chapter.

On the General tab of the printer's Properties dialog, you can add optional descriptive comments (see Figure 9-1):

- Use the Location text box to describe the printer's physical whereabouts. This information is available to users who are searching for printers.
- Use the Comment text box to add information about this printer. The contents of this text box appear when a remote user hovers the mouse pointer over the printer's icon in My Network Places.

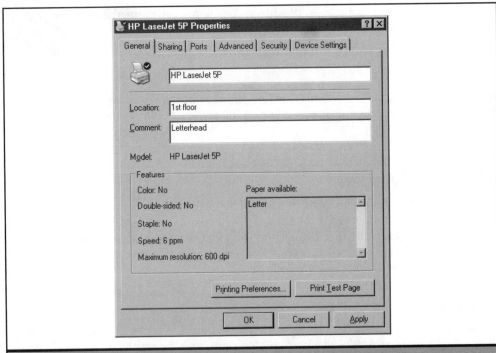

Figure 9-1.   *This printer always has letterhead loaded instead of plain paper, and it's important for remote users to know that.*

Set Printer Permissions

Printer permissions are set on the Security tab of the printer's Properties dialog (see Figure 9-2).

The default printer permissions are the following:

User or Group	Print	Manage Printer	Manage Documents
Everyone	Y		
Administrators	Y	Y	Y
Creator/Owner			Y
Power Users	Y	Y	Y

Each of the permission levels has a set of rights, as follows:

- Print:
  - Print documents

- ■ Pause, resume, restart, and cancel the user's own documents
- ■ Connect to the printer
- ■ Manage Documents:
    - ■ All permissions contained in the Print level
    - ■ Control job setting for all documents
    - ■ Pause, restart, and delete all documents
- ■ Manage Printer:
    - ■ All permissions contained in the Manage Documents level
    - ■ Share a printer
    - ■ Change printer properties
    - ■ Delete printers
    - ■ Change printer permissions

Use the Add button on the Security tab to give permissions to additional users and groups. You can use the listing for the domain or the entire Active Directory. Use the Remove button to delete a user or group from the list of permission holders for this printer.

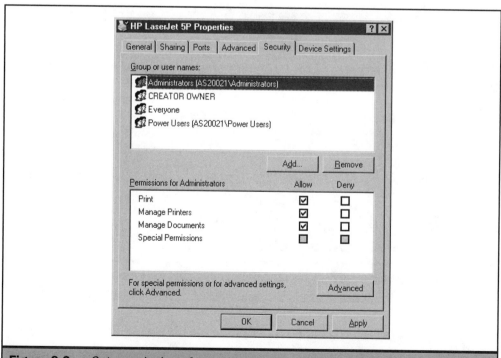

Figure 9-2.   *Set permissions for users and groups with the Security tab.*

Click Advanced to open the Access Control Settings dialog, shown in Figure 9-3, from which you can set more granular permissions, enable auditing, and change ownership.

If you have Macintosh clients on your network, you should be aware of the effect on security. If a Macintosh client can physically send a document to a printer, that's all the permission necessary to do any other manipulative action on the printer's settings. Macintosh clients ignore any permissions you've established for printer access, and you cannot impose any security for those clients.

Audit Printer Access

There may be some printers on your network that require auditing, either because of security concerns (for example, a printer that holds checks) or as a tool in troubleshooting inconsistent printer behavior.

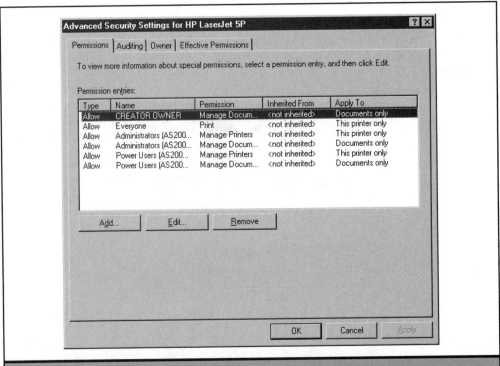

Figure 9-3.   *Tweak basic permissions to meet your own needs.*

Setting up printer auditing requires two procedures:

■ Enable auditing for the computer (assuming domain policies are configured to allow this).

■ Configure auditing on the printer(s).

Enable Auditing for the Computer

On the print server, open the Local Security Settings snap-in, which is available on the Administrative Toolsmenu. Expand Local Policies in the console pane, and select Audit Policy to display the available audit policies in the details pane.

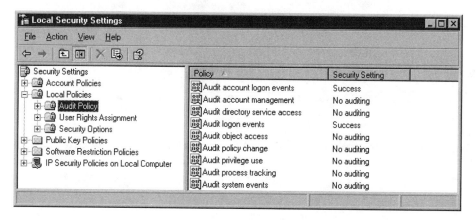

The policy you want to change is Audit Object Access, and by default, this policy has a security setting of No Auditing. If any other setting is displayed (Success, Failure, or both), either somebody with administrative privileges on this computer has beat you to it or a domain policy is in effect.

If a domain policy is in effect, you cannot change the settings. For example, a domain policy of auditing failure can't be changed on this computer to auditing success, or to auditing both failure and success. If you need a different setting for this computer, you must convince the system administrator to take one of the following actions:

■ Release the domain policy setting.

■ Change the domain policy setting to match what you need.

■ Apply the setting only to OUs to which this computer is not joined.

■ Move this computer into an OU that does not require this setting.

If no policy is in effect, double-click the Audit Object Access listing and select the attempts you want to audit: Success, Failure, or both.

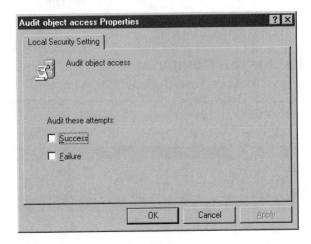

Configure the Printer for Auditing

To set up auditing for a printer, click the Advanced button on the Security tab of the printer's Properties dialog and move to the Auditing tab. You can audit the action of groups or individuals, or a combination of both. Click Add to open a window in which you can select the target users.

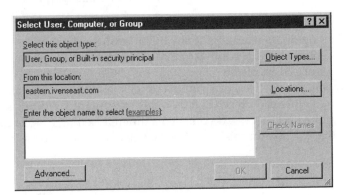

Click Object Types to select the types of objects you want to track:

- Built-in security principals
- Computers
- Groups
- Users

Click Locations to specify the range of your enterprise from which you want to track the object types you selected. The system presents the local computer, the domains the print server can access, the enterprise's OUs, and the entire Active Directory. Choose the appropriate location.

In the box labeled Enter the Object Name to Select, you must specify the names of the object types you selected. For instance, if you selected Users and specified a domain as the location, enter all the users in the domain you want to track as they access this printer. Unless you have a prodigious memory or your entire domain has only a handful of users (and you've memorized their logon names), you'll need some help to accomplish this.

Click Advanced to let the system find the targets for you, using the Select User, Computer, or Group dialog shown in Figure 9-4. You can apply filters to narrow the scope, which makes it easier to get a list of names that contains the objects you're looking for.

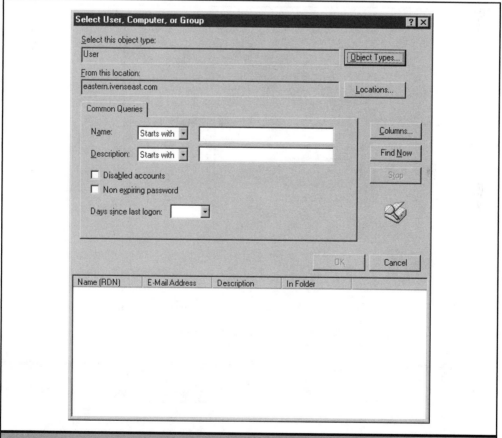

Figure 9-4.   *Select criteria to determine which objects are included in your audit policy.*

Click Find Now to produce a list that matches the selection criteria you established. The list appears in the bottom of the dialog. Select the first object you want to audit, and click OK. Click OK again to open the auditing configuration dialog for this object (see Figure 9-5). Select the audit options you want to impose and click OK.

For each additional user, group, or other object you want to audit, repeat the whole process, because you have to perform this procedure one object at a time.

Add Drivers for Other Windows Versions

If the printer you're configuring will be shared with users running other versions of Windows, you can install additional drivers for those users. The drivers are installed on the print server and are delivered to clients automatically when the printer is accessed. In effect, the print server becomes a network sharepoint for the distribution of printer drivers.

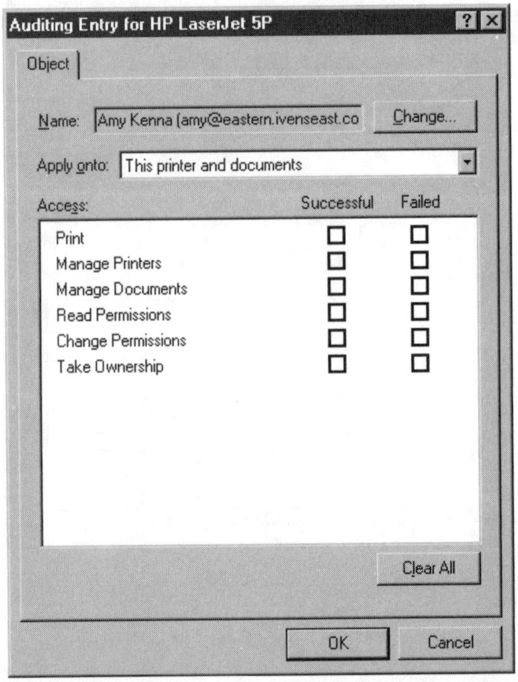

Figure 9-5. *Choose the access you want to audit.*

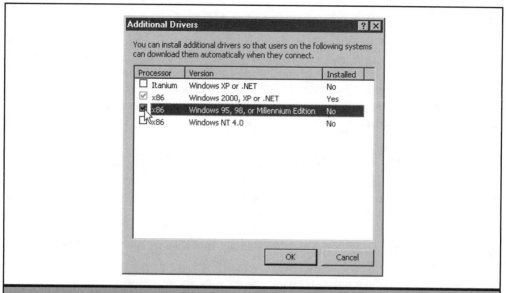

Figure 9-6. *Provide printer drivers for client computers that access this printer.*

To add drivers for additional clients, open the printer's Properties dialog and move to the Sharing tab. Click Additional Drivers to open the Additional Drivers dialog, shown in Figure 9-6. Select the drivers you want to install, click OK, and follow the prompts.

Printer drivers for Windows 2000/NT/Me/9*x* clients are included on the Windows Server 2003 Support CD.

If you have manufacturers' drivers, use the Have Disk option. Be aware that you may have to use the Have Disk option for printers that Windows 9*x* and NT 4 may have supported. You can use the CD from the operating system (for example, a Windows NT CD) as the disk in the Have Disk option.

Printer Drivers for Clusters

New in Windows Server 2003 is the ability to install a printer driver on one node of a cluster, and then relax in the knowledge that the clustering service will take care of propagating drivers to the other nodes. This is super cool! In earlier versions of Windows server products, you had to install the printer driver on every cluster node.

Using Printer Location Tracking

Windows Server 2003 supports Printer Location Tracking, which automates the process of finding and connecting to a remote printer based on location. Location Tracking is useful for large domains with multiple sites, because it relieves the user of the need to know the location of the target printer. When a user chooses to search the directory for a printer, the system identifies the user's location on the domain and automatically searches the directory for printers in the same location.

Printer Location Tracking Requirements

To use Printer Location Tracking, you need to prepare and configure your domain with this feature in mind, using the following guidelines:

- You have multiple sites in the domain, or multiple subnets in a single site.
- Your network IP addressing scheme is devised to correspond with the physical layout of your network.
- You have a subnet object for each site (created using Active Directory Sites and Services).

Only clients who participate in Active Directory can use this feature, which means your downlevel clients (Windows NT/Me/9x) must have the AD client installed.

You must create a subnet object for each subnet, using Active Directory Sites and Services. After you have created the site and subnet objects, you need to set the location string for each subnet. Then use the Location tab of the subnet Properties dialog to set the location string (see the next section).

 The directory service site name does not have to be the same as the location name.

Printer Location Naming Requirements

Because the process of locating printers is automated, and users must be able to count on the accuracy of the information in AD, you must devise a location naming protocol for all printers in AD. The protocol for naming locations must follow these rules:

- The location names take the form *Name/Name/Name/Name/*.
- The location name can consist of any character except the forward slash, which is used as a separator.
- The maximum length of each *Name* component is 32 characters.
- The maximum length of the entire location name string is 260 characters.

For example, in my organization, there are two domains (Eastern and Western) and each domain has two sites:

- Eastern has the sites Admin and Accounting.
- Western has the sites HR and Research.

The sites have subnets as follows:

- Admin has subnets for the 2nd Floor and the 3rd Floor.
- Accounting has subnets for the 5th Floor and 6th Floor.
- HR has subnets for West Bldg and West Bldg PH (penthouse is my hoity-toity way to name the top floor).
- Research has subnets for Lab and the 9th Floor.

The location naming for printers located in the Admin subnet on the 2nd Floor takes the form Eastern/Admin/Floor2. The protocol of using FloorX to designate floors was part of my general planning process for printing. I explained the protocol to users so that anyone who wanted to enter a location field in the Find Printers dialog knew the format of that data. It's important to make sure the Location field is filled in for each printer on the network.

Enabling Printer Location Tracking

Printer Location Tracking is enabled via three processes:

- Configure subnets.
- Create a group policy to enable the feature.
- Enter location information for each printer to match the location system for subnets.

Right-click each subnet you're using for location tracking and choose Properties. In the Location tab of the Properties dialog, enter the location of the subnet in the format *location/location*. For example, using the organization explained in the preceding section, I have a subnet named research/lab.

1. Open an MMC console and add a group policy for the appropriate container (domain or OU). Expand the console tree to Computer Configuration | Administrative Templates | Printers.

2. In the right pane, double-click Pre-Populate Printer Search Location Text to open its Properties dialog, and select Enabled on the Policy tab.

3. Open each printer in the AD and enter location information in the format *location/location* to match the location naming scheme for your subnets.

Tip   *Create an additional location set to give users very precise information about the printer—for example, /research/lab/room1 or research/lab/hallway.*

Installing Remote Printers

Now that your print servers have shared their printers, you and the users on your network can begin installing remote printers. To install a remote printer, you can use My Network Places, the Add Printer Wizard, Active Directory, or your browser.

Connect to Remote Printers

If you know the location of the printer you want to use, which means you know which computer is acting as the print server for the printer, open My Network Places. Expand the network to find the print server that has the printer you want to use. Right-click the printer object and choose Connect to automatically install the printer.

Alternatively, you can use the Add Printer Wizard. Open the Printers and Faxes folder and launch the Add Printer Wizard, clicking Next to move past the welcome window. Select the Network printer option and click Next to bring up the Locate Your Printer window, shown in Figure 9-7.

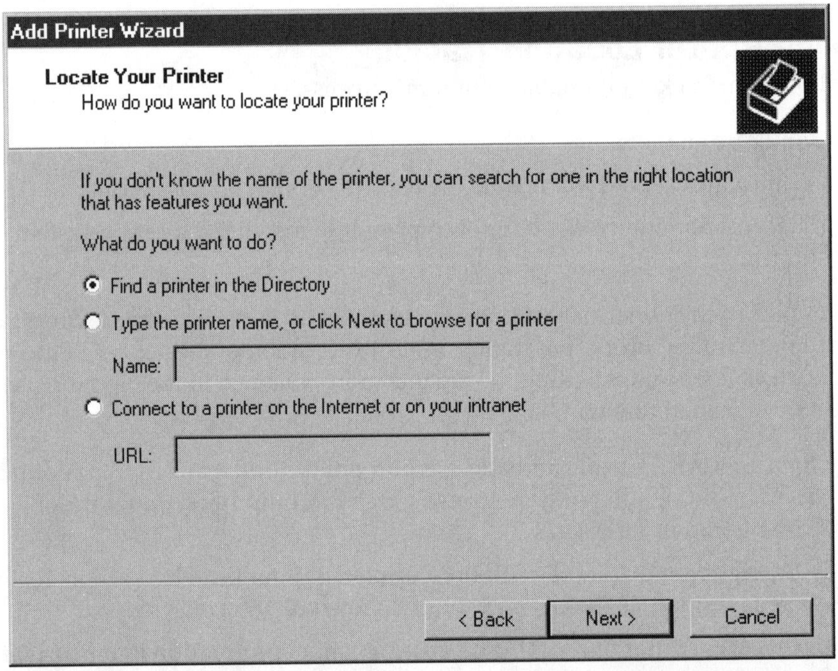

Figure 9-7. *The Add Printer Wizard offers multiple methods for finding a printer.*

The choice of methods offered in the wizard window is discussed in the following sections.

Search Active Directory

Using Active Directory is a nifty way to find a printer that has the options you need (I'm assuming that all of your shared printers are published to Active Directory). This feature uses the Find Printers dialog that is part of the Search function, which can be accessed using any of the following methods:

- Add Printer Wizard.
- Search command on the Start menu.
- Find Printer command on the Print dialog.

In the Add Printer Wizard, select Find A Printer In The Directory, and then click Next to locate a printer. The Find Printers dialog opens, and you can use the tabs on this dialog to specify the features you need.

Enter the Search Criteria

At the top of the dialog, select Entire Directory to search Active Directory for your organization, or select your domain. Usually, it's a good idea to select your domain because it's likely that other domains are located far afield, and you want to be able to go to the printer to retrieve your print job.

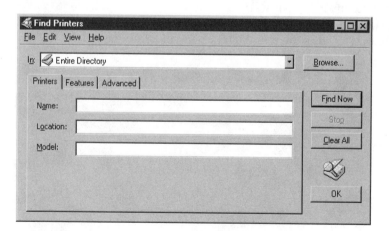

The information on the Printers tab is rather basic, and it's unlikely you'd know the printer name or model. Also, the location search succeeds only if you exactly match the information that was entered when the printer was set up for sharing.

More specific criteria are available in the Features tab. The information you enter is matched against the properties of all the network printers. For example, you might need a printer that is capable of color printing, or one that prints at a specific resolution.

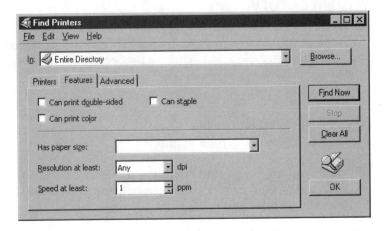

If you really need to narrow down the choices, you can move to the Advanced tab. Click Field to open a drop-down list of field names that describe printer characteristics. The list includes those criteria available on the other two tabs.

After you select a field, select the condition for the search. For some fields, the condition is True or False (such as support for color printing). For other fields, the choices are broad enough to cover any eventuality.

As you choose fields and set the conditions, click Add to build your list of criteria, an example of which is shown in the following illustration.

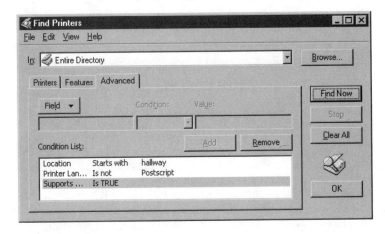

When you've completed your search criteria, click Find Now. The wizard returns all the printers that match the criteria. If no printers appear in the list, you can either enter different criteria or return to the Add Printer Wizard to change the way you're searching (the other search methods are discussed in the next sections).

Right-click the printer you want to use, and choose Connect from the shortcut menu. The printer is automatically installed and you can begin using it.

 You can click Find Now without entering any information to see a list of all the printers in the directory.

Sort and Filter the Search Results

If the search for printers results in multiple choices, you can sort and filter the results. Select the Details view of the Results box if it isn't already displayed.

Sorting To sort the display, click the column heading that has the criteria by which you want to sort. Click again to reverse the order of the sort scheme. For example, if you want to choose among the printers that are connected to a specific computer, click the Server Name column heading. Or, if you like a particular model, sort by the Model heading and then choose the server or location that you want.

Filtering Filtering makes it easier to choose a printer when the list of available printers is copious. To filter the display, choose View | Filter from the menu bar of the Find Printers dialog. This places a new row at the top of the results display, as shown in Figure 9-8.

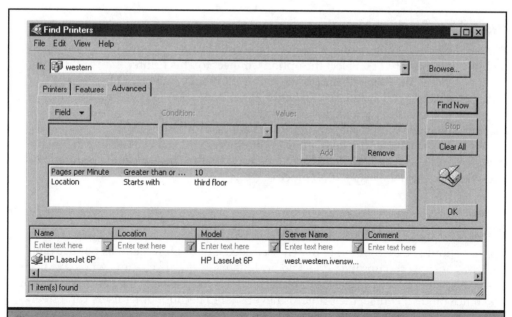

Figure 9-8. *Filter the search criteria for further refinement, and apply against the found printers.*

Filtering works by matching the text you enter for each column against the specifications you set for the filter. After you enter text, click the arrow next to the text box to choose the criterion to apply to your text from the drop-down list.

The default criterion (usually "contains") is applied as soon as you enter the text, so if that's your criterion, the column is already displaying your match. If you choose a different criterion, the column redisplays to match the information you want. You can filter as many columns as you need to. To turn off filtering, choose View | Filters again to deselect the option.

Save the Search

You can save the search information so that the next time you need to locate a printer with the characteristics you've described, you don't have to reinvent the wheel. To save the search, follow these steps:

1. Choose File | Save Search to open the Save Directory Search dialog.

2. Give the file a descriptive name (for example, Color-2ndFloor or LetterheadInTray). The extension .qds is automatically added to the filename.

You can distribute the search file to other users. If you selected printers from a domain instead of the whole directory, be sure the recipients are in the same domain. If you plan ahead, you can save users a lot of work by creating saved searches by location, paper type, color capabilities, and so on.

Browse the Network

Back in the Locate Your Printer window of the Add Printer Wizard, you can search by browsing the network. Select the option Connect to This Printer.

If you know the name of the printer, enter it in the Name box in the format *ServerName**PrinterShareName*, and click Next. If you don't know the name of the printer, leave the Name box empty and click Next to open a window that displays the name of every computer that is acting as a print server.

If you know which print server has the computer you want to connect to, open it. Otherwise, you'll have to open each one individually. Then select the printer and click Next to finish the installation process.

Planning Printer Deployment

Printers should be distributed to match user need, although sometimes political and security concerns can upset a perfect, logical plan. I know IT directors who have been told to place a printer in an executive office for the convenience of the person occupying that office (and, of course, the printer is never shared because other users can't freely enter the office to pick up print jobs). If that's the case in your organization, be sure to explain that such printers are additional budget items and you can't afford to use your "printer stock" in such a manner. Good luck!

One-to-One Printer Drivers

The standard relationship between a virtual printer (the printer icon displayed to users) and the physical printer is one-to-one. All users send print jobs to the virtual printer, which passes the jobs to the physical printer. Users can set print options in their software applications, and the virtual printer handles all the processing so the job prints correctly.

Printer Pools

A *printer pool* is a one-to-many relationship in which a single virtual printer can pass print jobs to multiple physical printers (see Figure 9-9). You can use printer pooling to ensure printing services in mission-critical operations. Pooling is commonly used to spread the printing load in situations where there is so much printing activity that users have to wait too long for documents to emerge from the printer.

To use printer pooling, all the physical printers have to be the same (or at least have an emulation mode that means the single printer driver works). The printers should be located together, because otherwise users will not know which physical printer received the job, and it's not cricket to force users to wander the halls looking for a print job.

To configure printer pooling, right-click the printer you want to use for pooling and choose Properties from the shortcut menu. Move to the Ports tab and select the Enable Printer Pooling check box. Then select the additional ports to which the printers in the pool are connected. You can add more parallel ports to this server, and/or select a port on another computer (using the UNC). That computer/printer combination becomes part of this pool.

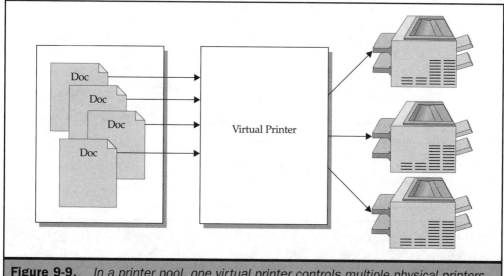

Figure 9-9. *In a printer pool, one virtual printer controls multiple physical printers.*

Many-to-One Printer Drivers

You can configure a many-to-one virtual-to-physical printer setup to take advantage of configuration options on a physical printer (see Figure 9-10). For example, a printer that has two trays may hold letterhead and plain paper (or purchase orders and sales orders). Creating a virtual printer that is configured for a specific form makes it easier for users who want to print to that form. Other reasons to create this scenario include the following:

- Printers accessed by groups who need banners and groups who don't
- Printers used for very large documents that should print at night (deferred printing)

To create multiple virtual printers, use the Add Printer Wizard in the Printers folder to create as many copies of the printer as you need (these are local printers, of course). When prompted about using the current driver, select the option to keep the current driver. The wizard's Name The Printer window displays the same name as the first printer, with the notation "(Copy 2)." You can rename the printer either at this point or later. The printer's final name should reflect its configuration. The wizard also asks for a share name and offers a comment field, and you have the same options—enter the information now or do it later.

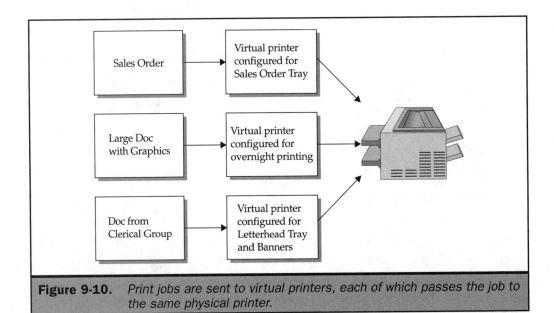

Figure 9-10. *Print jobs are sent to virtual printers, each of which passes the job to the same physical printer.*

Physical Security for Printers

Printer security is a concern when printers hold checks, purchase orders, or other paper types that can be dangerous in the wrong hands. In addition, users who print sensitive documents (especially the accounting and human resources departments) should have printers that are located in a secure manner. Secure printers should not be placed in hallways or rooms in which no supervisory users are working. It's best to attach them to the computer that is used by the person who sends sensitive print jobs. If other users must share the printer, you can use the printer permissions to restrict access.

Don't forget to secure the warehouse printers with strict permissions. Pick slips generate shipping, and I've had clients who suffered "shrinkage" (the polite term for employee theft) through the efforts of users who sent pick slips. The orders were picked and packed and shipped to the user's choice of cohorts. If pick slips require the existence of a sales order (a good security measure), be sure to secure your accounting software to prevent unauthorized users from getting to the Sales Order module. However, a clever user who knows how to format a word processing document can send a fake pick slip to the printer (it prints exactly as if it had come from the accounting software) and end-run the software's need to have a sales order before printing a pick slip.

For example, for my Lexmark printer, I have the following virtual printer objects:

- Lex-banners
- Lex-nights
- Lex-SO
- Lex-LH

SO indicates Sales Orders and LH indicates Letterhead. The Lex-LH printer is the original printer I installed, which I renamed to indicate its configuration.

Now you can configure each printer for its specific use. For example, using my Lexmark, the virtual printer for printing sales orders (which are in Tray #2) has Tray #2 configured for letter-sized paper and the other trays marked unavailable.

Printer configuration options are discussed later in this chapter, in the section "Configuring Printers."

Configuring Print Servers

You can set properties for a printer server by opening the Printers and Faxes folder and choosing File | Server Properties. The properties you set for the server are those that are not printer dependent, and are the defaults for all printers on this server.

Print Server Forms

Windows Server 2003 deals with paper sizes and formats as forms rather than printer tray options. A form is, by definition, a paper of a particular size. Forms give administrators a way to let users choose a form without having to worry about which tray is to hold which size form. Because most companies operate with network print servers, the printer is frequently not in sight, which means users can't lean over and see that the top tray contains letter-sized paper and the bottom tray contains legal-sized paper.

With configured forms, when a user chooses to print to legal paper, he or she merely picks the form. The system matches the form to the tray that holds it. Windows applications are capable of presenting different forms to the user, and when a selection is made that is other than a default, the spooler checks the printer's configuration options and includes the codes for the appropriate tray when the document is sent to the printer.

Select the Create A New Form check box, and then specify the measurements to match your creation. Give the form a name to make it available to all the printers on this print server (as long as they can physically handle the form).

Print Server Ports

The Ports tab displays the ports that are available on this print server. You can take the following actions on this tab:

- Choose Add to add vendor-specific ports and port monitors.
- Choose Delete to remove a port you are no longer using.
- Choose Configure Port to change port settings.

For parallel ports, you can change the timeout transmission retry period. This is the amount of time that elapses before it's assumed the printer isn't responding.

For serial ports, you can change the transmission settings for baud rate, data bits, parity, stop bits, and flow controls. The default settings are 9600, 8, N, 1, None. If you tinker with the settings (especially the Flow control) and the results are disastrous, there's a Restore Defaults button on the tab.

Print Server Drivers

The Drivers tab displays the printer drivers installed on the print server, including any additional drivers you loaded for legacy clients (see Figure 9-11).

You can add, remove, and update drivers for the printers installed on the server. (Adding and removing drivers launches a wizard.) Click the Properties button to see the driver files (including the help files) and to set permissions for accessing those files. Note that help files attached to printer drivers are not standard help files but the files that provide the text for the What's This? feature.

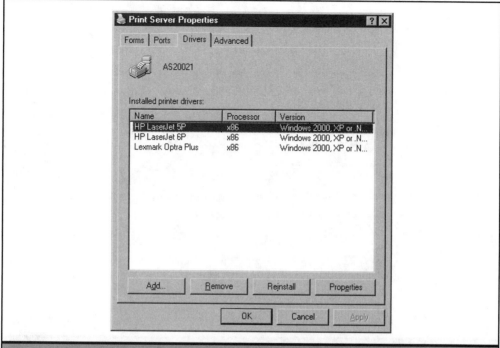

Figure 9-11. *These are the drivers for all printers on this print server.*

Server Spooler Options

The Advanced tab lets you set options for the spooler on the print server (see Figure 9-12). You can change the location of the spool folder (which affects all printers attached to this print server); see "Spooler" earlier in this chapter for instructions.

The configurable items that are turned on and off with check boxes on this dialog are self-explanatory. However, I'd like to point out that leaving the option to Log Spooler Warning Events may send more entries to the System Log in the Event Viewer than you're prepared for. Stick to error events only, or error and warning events. (A warning event is logged every time anyone with the appropriate permissions makes any changes to configuration options for a printer or the print server.) Unless you have a very good reason (such as a serious troubleshooting effort), don't elect to Log Spooler Information Events because every printing event will be recorded in the Event Viewer.

The option to notify users when remote documents are printed is a quick way to alienate users, and the fact that you can notify the sending computer instead of the user doesn't make this option more tolerable. It's not just that the system sends an annoying message to say the document has printed; remember that users also have to click OK to clear the message. Users do not enjoy this.

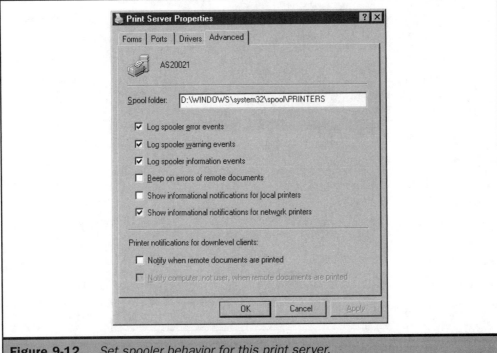

Figure 9-12.   *Set spooler behavior for this print server.*

Configuring Printers

You can set printing defaults with a printer's Properties dialog. The defaults you set can be changed by any users to whom you give permission to manage printers (see "Set Printer Permissions," earlier in this chapter). The configuration options vary from printer to printer, of course. Color printers have more options than monochrome, PostScript printers have unique options, duplex printers have special options, and so on. However, there are some settings that are global in nature, and those are covered in this section.

Printing Preferences

The Printing Preferences options are the defaults that appear in the Print dialog when a user chooses this printer. All of the options can be changed by the user for each individual print job; you are just configuring the default settings. To set the defaults, right-click the printer you want to configure and choose Printing Preferences from the shortcut menu. The Printing Preferences dialog for the selected printer opens, as shown in Figure 9-13.

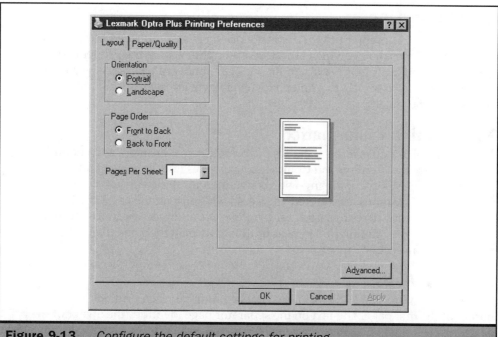

Figure 9-13. *Configure the default settings for printing.*

Note   *The same dialog is available on the Printer's Properties dialog by clicking Printing Defaults on the Advanced tab. The title bar says Printing Defaults instead of Printing Preferences, but the dialog is identical.*

The settings in the Layout tab of the Printing Preferences dialog should be set to default to those most users expect. The orientation, order of printing, and number of pages on a sheet of paper are standard settings. The Paper/Quality tab sets the paper source (the default setting of automatic selection is usually the best option). If the printer is capable of color printing, you can choose to use a default for gray scale printing instead of color. The Advanced button opens another dialog with printer-specific options for which you can configure the default settings.

These default settings are far more important if you are using multiple virtual printers to limit options. For example, you may want to give the word processing department a printer called "drafts," set the defaults for that virtual printer to print at lower resolution, and eschew color (if the printer is capable of color). Even if users can make changes on the Print dialog from the sending application, setting these defaults makes it more likely that the options you set will be used.

Printer Properties

The configuration of properties for a specific printer is accomplished through the printer's Properties dialog, which is accessed by right-clicking the printer object and choosing Properties from the shortcut menu. The number of tabs, and the contents of the tabs, varies from printer to printer. However, there are some global options you should examine and set.

General Printer Information

The General tab for all printers includes the printer name, location, and comments. You should use the Location and Comments text boxes to help users identify (and find) printers. Develop a company-wide convention for these entries; it's confusing if some printer locations are entered as "Room 304" and others as "305." In fact, to make it easier for users to search for printers, avoid unnecessary words (like "Room"). Click the Printing Preferences button to display the same dialog discussed in the preceding section.

Separator Pages

Separator pages are sent to the printer at the beginning of each print job, and they print in front of the first page. The text on the separator page identifies the owner of the print job (the user who sent the job to the printer). The separator page does not have any effect on the numbering or pagination of the print job it precedes. (Separator pages are also called *banners*, especially by those of us who spent many years with NetWare.)

When multiple users access the same printer, eventually they all mosey down the hall to get their printouts. Users have a habit of grabbing the sheets of paper emerging from the printer, glancing at them, and tossing them back into the printer tray if they belong to someone else. By that time, of course, the next page (or several more pages) has ejected and the print job is out of order, infuriating the print job owner who has to collate the pages. With separator pages, users can find their print jobs easily and they don't have to read each page to see when the job ends—they just look for the next separator page.

Tip   *Sometimes separator pages are more annoying than useful. If a printer is accessed by users who usually print one-page documents, the separator pages merely create trash.*

To enable separator pages, open the Properties dialog for the target printer, move to the Advanced tab, and click Separator Page. The Separator Page dialog appears so you can enter the name of the separator page file, or click Browse to find the file you want to use. Separator Page files are located in the %SystemRoot%\System32 directory and have the file extension .sep.

By default, Windows Server 2003 installs four separator page files:

- **Pcl.sep**   For printers that use PCL (printer control language). The separator file also switches dual-language printers to PCL printing before printing the separator page.

■ **Sysprint.sep** For printers that use PostScript. The separator file also switches dual-language printers to PostScript before printing the separator page.

■ **Pscript.sep** Does not print a separator page, and is used for switching dual-language printers to PostScript.

■ **Sysprtj.sep** Prints a separator page before each document and sets Japanese fonts if available.

It's reasonable to assume that you'll only be concerned with the first two separator files.

Schedule Printer Availability

A shared printer can be scheduled for use on the Advanced tab of the printer's Properties dialog. By default, printers are always available. If you want to change the printer's hours of operation, select the Available From radio button and specify a beginning and end time for this printer's availability.

This task is commonly performed when you're using multiple virtual printers for one physical printer. If the printer supports color and has other features that are needed for large, complex documents, you should set time limits for a virtual copy of the printer and have users send documents to the printer before they leave for the evening. This means that slow, complex documents will print during the night, and other users who need the printer won't be inconvenienced. Make sure there is plenty of paper in the printer before everyone leaves (in fact, don't use a printer for overnight printing unless its paper tray is capable of holding several hundred sheets of paper).

Another good use of a virtual printer that's configured for availability at specific times is for printers that are used for checks or other specialized paper. Set a company policy that checks are in the printer tray for a specific time period, and then match that time to the printer's availability.

Set Default Document Priorities

The Advanced tab also has a Priority text box, which represents the default priority level for each document sent to the printer. By default, the priority is 1, which is the lowest priority. You can change the default priority to any number between 1 and 99.

Setting a priority level for the documents that arrive at a printer is meaningless. The only way to make priority levels work is to establish multiple virtual printers and set a different priority for each. Print jobs that are sent to the virtual printer with high priority will print ahead of the jobs sent to the standard virtual printer. Then use one of these techniques to ensure that users employ printing priorities properly:

■ Explain that only higher-priority documents should be sent to the virtual printer marked for high priority (yeah, sure, that works).

■ Set permissions for the higher-priority printers so that access is limited to the groups and users that usually have realistic high-priority needs.

Set Spooling Options

There are a variety of spooling options available on the Advanced tab of the printer's Properties dialog (see Figure 9-14).

Set the Event That Begins the Printing Process   You can choose to start printing after the last page is spooled, or you can print immediately after the document has begun to feed data to the spooler directory. Opting for the former means the spooler does not begin processing the file until it has received the entire file (the application sends an end-of-file marker to indicate the entire file has been sent). The latter choice means the spooler sends pages through the printing process as they are received.

Waiting for the last page to spool before starting print processing means that there is a delay before the document emerges from the printer. However, it ensures that the whole document prints, and that the document is error-free, so a document with corrupt data isn't sent to the printer. This is actually a choice between speed and safety, and you should pick the option that matches your own philosophy.

Using or Bypassing the Spooler   There's an option on the Advanced tab to print directly to the printer. This means you bypass the spooler and move files directly from the application software to the printer. While this may sound terribly efficient, it's not a

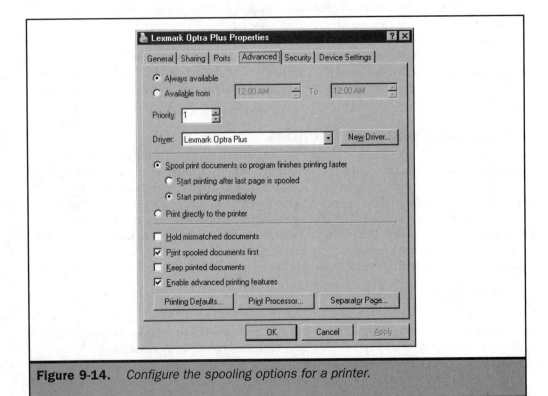

Figure 9-14.   *Configure the spooling options for a printer.*

good idea because the spooler keeps documents intact, separating multiple documents from each other.

If there's a problem with printing, however, use this option to determine whether the problem originates in the spooler. If a print job that didn't print (or didn't print correctly) prints properly when you bypass the spooler, then you should reinstall the spooler files (see the section "Spooler," earlier in this chapter).

Managing Mismatched Documents   The Advanced tab has an option to hold mismatched documents. A mismatched document is one in which the codes going to the printer don't match the printer's current configuration. For example, a document may be an envelope, and the target printer may not have an envelope tray, instead requiring manual insertion of envelopes.

Selecting the option to hold mismatched documents tells the spooler to move other documents (that are not mismatched) ahead of the document that requires special handling. Eventually, when the spooler is empty except for the mismatched document file, the document is sent to the printer. Most printers will blink some lights at that point to indicate there's a manual feed required to print the job.

By default, the option to hold mismatched documents is not selected, because most printers rarely have empty spoolers, and the user waiting for the mismatched document could be ready for retirement before the document is sent to the printer. However, it's imperative for users to understand that any time a paper form needs to be inserted, they must go to the printer and perform that task. Otherwise, all the jobs behind the mismatched job are held up.

Print Spooled Documents First   The Advanced tab has an option to print spooled documents first, and that option is selected by default. This means the spooler treats documents that have completed the spooling process with a higher priority than documents that are still in the process of spooling. Thus, a large document that is sent to the spooler from an application before another, smaller document is sent will print after the document that was sent later. This is usually just as efficient as it seems. In fact, sometimes a number of small documents arrive at the spooler after the large document is sent, and the small documents are placed in the queue as they finish spooling. When the large document has finished spooling, there may be four or five (or more) documents ahead of it in the queue. With this option enabled, the spooler prints the largest document first, then the next largest, and so on. This ensures that large documents don't receive a de facto low priority.

If you clear the option, the spooler looks at document priority before sending print jobs to the printer. If all documents have the same priority, the queue is printed in the order in which the documents finished spooling.

Keep Printed Documents   This option on the Advanced tab does exactly what it says it does—it tells the spooler to retain the spooler file for every document that is sent to the printer. The only way a spooler file is removed is manually: open My Computer or Windows Explorer and delete the file. You'll have to do this after every print job unless you have more disk space than you know what to do with.

The purpose of this option is to be able to reprint a file from the spooler instead of opening the application again. I'm willing to bet that the number of times administrators have needed this function is so small that it's safe to guess "never."

Enable Advanced Printing Features   This option on the Advanced tab is selected by default, and it makes any advanced features for this printer available to users. Some of those advanced features, such as booklet printing and multiple pages per sheet, require metafile spooling. If there are problems using advanced features (typically, problems only occur if you're using a printer driver that's an emulation instead of the real driver for the printer), you can deselect the option.

Metafiles are files that describe or specify other files. Microsoft uses metafiles for the Windows Metafile (WMF) format. A WMF file contains a sequence of Graphical Device Interface (GDI) commands that are commonly used for printing graphic images.

Color Management

For printers capable of color printing, you can take advantage of the Windows Server 2003 Image Color Management (ICM) feature. ICM provides a way to produce consistent color, regardless of the capabilities of a specific device. ICM maps colors and translates color types (RGB to CMYK, for example) to provide accurate and consistent colors. This means the screen color matches the print color, the scanner color matches the screen color, and so forth.

The Color Management tab of a color printer's Properties dialog provides the opportunity to supply profiles for users who access the printer. When you move to the Color Management tab (available only for color printers that support the color management features), you should see either of the following color profile configurations:

- No profiles are loaded for the printer.
- The sRGB Color Space Profile is loaded.

The sRGB profile is the default color profile for Windows Server 2003 and works with all devices that are capable of color management.

You can add a color profile to the printer by clicking Add and selecting a profile from the Add Profile Association dialog. Color profile files have an extension of .icm and are stored in %SystemRoot%\System32\Spool\Drivers\Color. You can add as many profiles as you wish, and then configure the printer to automatically select the best profile or let users select a profile.

If you have users who need the color-matching features to prepare high-end graphics or desktop publishing, read the next section.

An Overview of Color Management

While it's beyond the scope of this book to enter into a deep and detailed discussion of the color management utilities included in ICM, it seems worthwhile to present an

overview so you can decide for yourself whether you need to investigate this feature
more fully.

ICM uses APIs to configure colors for input and output devices (monitor, scanner,
and printer). You can assign color profiles to printers so that users can access those
profiles. The color profile has the data needed to send codes about color to the target
devices. You can also add a color profile to a monitor, using the Advanced button in
the Settings tab of the Display Properties dialog. In fact, if you add a color profile to
a printer, you should add the profile to the monitor (and vice versa). This means
that WYSIWYG displays match print jobs, which is important to the preparation
of high-end graphics.

Profiles can also be installed in the other direction, by opening the profile and
associating it with the monitor and printer. Right-click the profile's object and
choose Associate from the shortcut menu. Then add the monitor and printer(s)
to the associated devices list.

Without a color profile, color features can vary from job to job because of the
differences in the way hardware uses color. Users who have specialized needs
(graphics, desktop publishing, and so forth) can specify color profiles to match the
job they're working on, ensuring consistency across devices and computers. Because
profiles add overhead and can slow the printing process, day-to-day color printing
shouldn't involve the use of profiles.

The version of ICM included with Windows Server 2003 works with any scanners,
monitors, and printers that support color management. Only applications that are
written to support the ICM APIs work with color management. When you want to
invoke the color management features, choose File | Color Management from the
application's menu bar.

| **Note** | *Windows applications can support either of two levels of API: there is one set of APIs for RGB and another set for multiple color spaces. The APIs maintain device color profiles and provide color conversion procedures.* |

Scanners that support color management either create sRGB output or embed a
color profile into the image file. The former is preferable because the operating system
can work with sRGB output. An embedded color profile is not necessarily available to
the other devices. A scanner can create sRGB output in one of two ways:

- It can make a call to ICM, pass ICM the appropriate scanner profile, and point it
  to the sRGB profile. The Windows Server 2003 ICM then generates sRGB output
  that the device can pass onto the application.

- It can use a proprietary system that corrects from the scanner color space to
  sRGB standards. This isn't very flexible and usually requires software from
  the manufacturer to complete the process of passing the color data to the
  application. Unfortunately, some proprietary software isn't compatible with
  Windows ICM.

The importance of ICM and color profiles is that all components that use an associated color profile can let ICM manage color continuity throughout the entire editing process.

Administering Printers

With the proper permissions, you can manage printers on any print server. In fact, you can manage the print server properties for a remote computer. Windows Server 2003 is built for remote management of printing, which is why you must pay careful attention to permissions.

Managing Remote Printers

You can access a remote printer for management in My Network Places, or by using the Search command on the Start menu to locate a printer. You have the same powers for manipulating the properties of the Printers folder and the printers contained within it as you have for a local Printers folder.

If you manage a remote printer or a remote print server on a regular basis, you can bring the printers to your own computer. This is a nifty way to make your job easier. Create a folder for managing printers, or open the Printers and Faxes folder on your local computer. Then open My Network Places and expand the computer that is the print server you manage remotely. With the windows side by side, drag the Printers folder from the remote print server into your local folder. You can also open the Printers folder on the remote print server and drag individual printer objects to your own computer.

Redirecting Print Jobs

If a printer breaks down, you can move the print jobs that are waiting to print to another printer, as long as the other printer uses the same printer driver. The new printer can be on the same print server, or on another print server. The ability to redirect the documents means you don't have to kill the queue and tell users to reprint.

To accomplish this task, open the Printers and Faxes folder and open the printer that isn't working. The list of print jobs waiting to go to the printer displays in the Printer window. Choose Printer | Properties to open the Properties dialog, and move to the Ports tab. Then use the appropriate method to move the queue to another printer:

- To move the print jobs to another printer on the same print server, select the port to which the target printer is connected. Click OK.

- To move the print jobs to a printer on another print server, choose Add Port | Local Port | New Port. Then enter the UNC for the remote printer, using the format *PrintServer**PrinterShareName*.

The document that is showing an error message (the document that is currently printing) cannot be transferred and you must delete it. The user who owns the document must resend the print job.

Manipulate Print Jobs in the Queue

When you open a printer by double-clicking its icon in the Printers and Faxes folder, the window shows all the jobs in the queue, along with information about each job (document name, size, owner, and so on). With the appropriate permission level, you can perform the following actions on documents in the queue:

- Cancel the print job by right-clicking its listing and choosing Cancel.
- Pause the print job by right-clicking its listing and choosing Pause.
- Resume a paused print job by right-clicking its listing and choosing Resume.
- Restart a document that stopped (usually due to a printer jam or out-of-paper error) by right-clicking its listing and choosing Restart.
- Change the priority of a print job by right-clicking the job listing and choosing Properties. On the General tab of the Properties dialog, raise or lower the document's priority.

Note   *When you resume or restart a print job, it has to wait behind any documents with higher priority that may have arrived in the queue.*

To perform an action on all the documents in the queue, right-click the printer object in the Printers folder and choose the appropriate command from the shortcut menu:

- Pause printing
- Cancel all documents
- Resume printing

Note   *Users can manipulate only their own jobs, which they access by opening the printer icon that appears in the taskbar during printing.*

Printing to a File

The Windows Print dialog that appears when you choose File | Print in an application offers an option to print to a disk file. In addition, you can establish a printer that automatically prints to a disk file instead of a physical printer. There are several reasons you might want to do this:

- You want to print the document from another location.
- The printer is temporarily down.
- You want to give the file to another user.

It's a good idea to create a virtual printer that's preconfigured for disk files (see the section "Many-to-One Printer Drivers," earlier in this chapter). To do so, when you add the printer, use File as the port selection. When a user accesses this printer, he or she is prompted for a filename. The file is stored on the user's computer with the extension .prn.

To print a disk file, enter the following command at the command line:

```
print [/d:device] [[drive:] [path] [filename]]
```

where:

d:*device* is the output device, which can be a port (for example, lpt1) or a remote printer (*PrintServerName\PrinterShareName*).

drive:path filename is the path to the file you want to print.

The disk file only prints successfully to the printer that created it. In other words, you cannot configure your HP laser printer to print to a file, and then print the file to a Lexmark laser printer. The codes that the target printer expects are embedded in the disk file.

Printing from DOS

If your printer is connected to LPT1: on your own computer, you won't have a problem when you print from DOS software or from the command line. However, if you are using a remote printer, printing from DOS is not simply a matter of selecting a printer in the software. To print from DOS, you must manually redirect printing, using the following command:

```
net use lptx \\PrintServerName\PrinterShareName
```

where *x* is the port you want to redirect (usually lpt1).

You can make this a permanent command by adding the parameter **/persistent:yes**. For example, to use a printer named HPLJ6 that's connected to a computer named PrtSrv3, enter **net use lpt1 \\PrtSrv3\HPLJ6 /persistent: yes**.

After you've redirected the port, you can send files to the printer via the command line in addition to printing from DOS applications. The persistent parameter survives shutdown, so the remote printer is always available. However, the state of lpt port redirection is a user profile issue, so if multiple users access the computer, each user must invoke the redirection command.

If you have multiple remote printers to choose from, you can redirect lpt2 to one of them, lpt3 to another, and so on. Then, in your DOS software, be sure to establish the ability to print to those ports. For command-line printing, you need only name the port as the target of the command to send the DOS file to the right printer.

The Complete Reference

Chapter 10

Networking with TCP/IP

Windows Server 2003 is built from the ground up to communicate via TCP/IP. Many of the functions covered in this chapter are invisible to the user after TCP/IP has been properly configured, but you cannot fully understand administration of a Windows Server 2003 network until you examine the networking processes that run beneath the surface. This chapter presents an overview of many of these processes, including:

- The use of TCP/IP within the Windows Server 2003 networking model
- The TCP/IP protocols and their layered functionality
- The use of the Windows Server 2003 TCP/IP utilities

Understanding these subjects makes it easier to deal with TCP/IP communications problems when they arise.

The Ins and Outs of TCP/IP

The growth of Windows into an enterprise-class network operating system and the meteoric popularity of the Internet are two of the factors that have made the TCP/IP protocol the de facto networking standard that it is today. Enterprise networks have become more heterogeneous in recent years, either through the addition of new technologies or the consolidation of existing ones, and one of the problems resulting from this phenomenon has been the general increase in network traffic congestion due to the different protocol types used by different platforms.

To relieve this congestion, many network administrators have sought to standardize on a single set of network protocols, in the hope of making their network traffic easier to manage. For a number of reasons, the obvious protocol suite of choice is TCP/IP. Among these reasons are

- **Compatibility**   Most major network operating systems in use today are capable of using TCP/IP as a native protocol. Those that do not are now seen as being noticeably lacking in their support for industry standards.

- **Scalability**   TCP/IP was designed for use on what is now the world's largest internetwork, the Internet. It provides protocols to suit almost any communications task, with varying degrees of speed, overhead, and reliability.

- **Heterogeneity**   TCP/IP is capable of supporting virtually any hardware or operating system platform in use today. Its modular architecture allows support for new platforms to be added without reengineering the core protocols.

- **Addressability**   Every machine on a TCP/IP network is assigned a unique identifier, making it directly addressable by any other machine on the network.

- **Availability**   The TCP/IP protocols are designed to be open standards, freely usable by all, and are developed through an "open forum" approach in which contributions from all interested parties are welcome.

TCP/IP is partially responsible for the growing popularity that Windows enjoys today. Its predecessor, NetBEUI (Windows NT's original native protocol), falls short as an enterprise protocol because it has no network layer and is therefore not routable between network segments.

Microsoft's TCP/IP Rollout

Development of the TCP/IP protocols for use on the fledgling ARPANET (later called the Internet) began in the 1970s, but some of the innovations that have made it a practical choice for use on private enterprise networks were not conceived until much later. Microsoft's own adoption of TCP/IP for its global corporate internetwork was a telling case in point.

In the early 1990s, as Microsoft's Information Technology Group examined the various candidates that might replace the archaic XNS protocols it was then using, TCP/IP was a front-runner from the very beginning, but it presented certain major obstacles to a worldwide rollout of this size. Primary among these obstacles were the administration and configuration of IP addresses, network name resolution, and the use of broadcasts to locate other computers.

On a small or medium-sized network, the task of assigning IP addresses to workstations is an onerous one; but on a large internetwork spreading over 50 countries, it is a major administrative expense. Not only must the network address assignments be carefully planned and meticulous records be kept at a central location, but the task of actually configuring those thousands of nodes must be dealt with. Do you send trained personnel to every remote office? Do you train people who are already there? Do you develop documentation that will (hopefully) enable end users to configure their own workstations?

Name resolution on this scale is another difficult problem. To use TCP/IP with Microsoft operating systems prior to Windows 2000, you had to have a means of equating NetBIOS names with IP addresses. On a local network segment, this was done using broadcasts (which could cause network traffic problems themselves). Connections to machines on other networks required entries in an LMHOSTS file on each workstation, which listed NetBIOS names and their equivalent IP addresses. The task of maintaining these files on so many computers dwarfed even that of assigning IP addresses.

It was clear to Microsoft that the difficulties it was facing would afflict any large corporate adoption of TCP/IP to some extent. The results of Microsoft's efforts, in collaboration with other network engineers and product manufacturers, were the DHCP and WINS modules that provided IP address configuration and name resolution services, respectively, to network users. By using these services, you could greatly reduce the administrative overhead required by a large TCP/IP network and insulate your users from the need to know anything about protocols and IP addresses.

TCP/IP underwent a transformation for Microsoft with the development of Windows 2000, and now with the release of Windows Server 2003. It includes many new features and enhancements when compared to earlier implementations. In the purest sense, Windows Server 2003's TCP/IP implementation has standardized with the rest of the industry. It no longer has to rely on NetBIOS for name resolution. Instead, it uses the Domain Name System (DNS) as its primary name resolution mechanism.

The term TCP/IP is a misnomer. As it is generally used, the name actually refers to a collection of more than a dozen protocols and is taken from the two that are used most often. The standards on which the protocols are based are published by the Internet Engineering Task Force (IETF) and are known as Requests for Comments (RFCs). If you're interested in reading the RFCs, start at the IETF site, www.ietf.org/, from which you can travel to other sites that contain the RFCs. Most of the sites store the documents in a top-level directory called RFC. They are predominantly ASCII text files, and some contain illustrations available in PostScript format.

Windows Server 2003 TCP/IP Enhancements

Like almost everything else in the computer world, TCP/IP is continually undergoing changes and enhancements to meet ever-changing business needs. This section describes some of the new TCP/IP technologies that have been included in Windows Server 2003 (many of which were first introduced in Windows 2000, but are presented here as "new" for those of you who are moving to Windows Server 2003 from Windows NT).

IGMP Version 3

Internet Group Management Protocol Version 3 provides source-based multicast group membership reporting. Hosts can report interest in receiving multicast traffic from specified sources. This feature prevents multicast-enabled routers from delivering multicast traffic to a subnet where there are no listening hosts.

Alternate Configuration

Alternate TCP/IP configurations are new to the Windows family (Windows Server 2003 and Windows XP). *Alternate configuration* means a computer can have an alternate TCP/IP configuration—a manually configured IP address that can be used in the absence of a DHCP server. Without an alternate configuration, TCP/IP defaults to Automatic Private IP Addressing (APIPA) to assign a unique address from the range 169.254.0.1 to 169.254.255.254 and the subnet mask 255.255.0.0.

The ability to have an alternate setting is a nifty "two-for-the-price-of-one" advantage to users of computers that connect to more than one network, either or both of which may lack a DHCP server. For example, mobile users frequently attach to the office network, and also use their computers on their home networks. Many mobile users travel to company branch offices, or to client sites, and need to plug into the networks they find there. At one location, the user's laptop uses a DHCP-allocated TCP/IP configuration. At another location, if no DHCP server is present, the laptop automatically uses the alternate configuration, accessing home network devices and the Internet. The user has access to both networks without the need to reconfigure TCP/IP settings manually and then reboot.

While your Windows Server 2003 computer is unlikely to be a laptop, as an administrator you may need to configure a user's Windows XP Professional computer for alternate configuration. To accomplish this, follow these steps:

1. Open the Properties dialog for the Local Area Connection object.
2. On the General tab, select Internet Protocol (TCP/IP), and click Properties.
3. Select the option Obtain an IP address automatically (this action causes an Alternate Configuration tab to appear on the dialog).
4. Move to the Alternate Configuration tab (see Figure 10-1).
5. Select the option User Configured and enter the required information.

Disable NetBIOS over TCP/IP

Windows Server 2003 lets you disable NetBT for any individual network connection. This is useful for dual-homed computers that communicate with computers that have

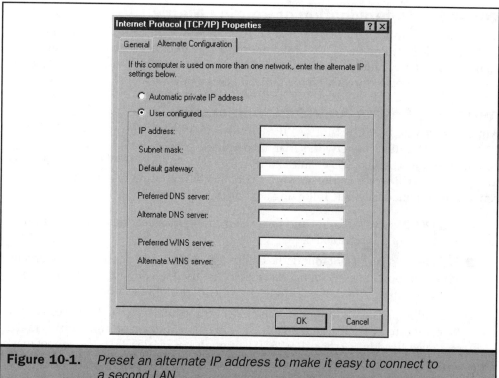

Figure 10-1.   Preset an alternate IP address to make it easy to connect to a second LAN.

NetBT disabled (such as proxy servers or bastion hosts in a firewall environment, where NetBT support isn't desirable).

For instance, dual-homed servers that connect to both the internal network and the Internet don't need NetBT on the Internet side. The ability to disable NetBT on the Internet connection means the computer can continue to function as a WINS server or client internally. This improves both performance and security.

By default, Windows Server 2003 sets the state of NetBT as "use DHCP, or else enable NetBT." To view or change this setting, follow these steps:

1. Open the Properties dialog for the target connection (usually you'd want to do this on the connection attached to the Internet).

2. Select Internet Protocol (TCP/IP) and click Properties.

3. Click Advanced to open the Advanced TCP/IP Settings dialog.

4. Move to the WINS tab to see the current NetBIOS settings (see Figure 10-2).

5. Make changes as necessary.

Automatic Determination of Routing Metric

If you have multiple interfaces, by default TCP/IP now automatically calculates a routing metric based on the speed of the interface. The interface metric determines the value of the Metric column for the routing table. This ensures that the fastest interface will be the one used to forward traffic to the default gateway.

Automatic Private Address Configuration

Automatic Private IP Addressing (APIPA) is a feature that lets you automate TCP/IP address configuration for networks that have a single subnet and no DHCP server. By default, Windows Server 2003 enables APIPA. The way it works is that a computer tries to contact a DHCP server on the network to obtain configuration for each network connection automatically. The following actions then take place:

- If a DHCP server is found and the leased configuration is successful, TCP/IP configuration is completed.

- If a DHCP server is not found, the computer interface is checked for an alternate configuration. If one is found, its settings are used to configure TCP/IP for the interface. (See "Alternate Configuration," earlier in this section.)

- If an alternate configuration doesn't exist for the interface, TCP/IP uses APIPA to configure TCP/IP automatically. This means Windows sets an address in the reserved IP address range (169.254.0.1 through 169.254.255.254). The subnet mask is set to 255.255.0.0. (Technically, this address is considered temporary until a DHCP server is located, and in fact, the system continues to search for one.)

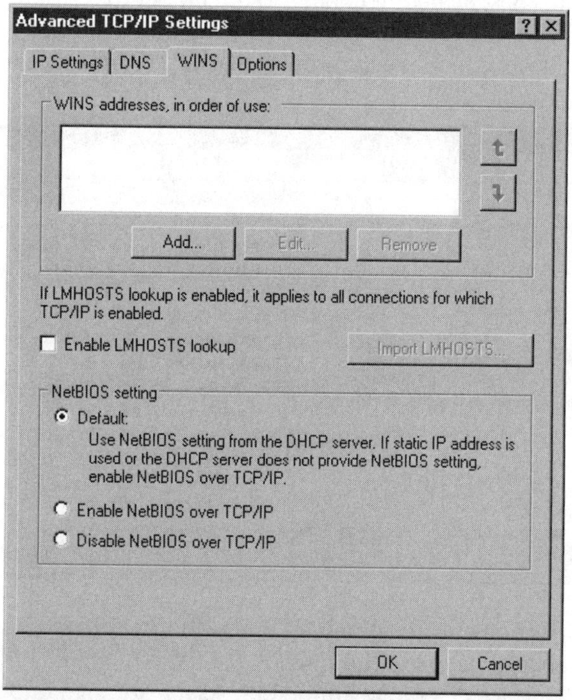

Figure 10-2.   *Manually disable or enable NetBT.*

You can disable APIPA on a computer by editing the registry as follows:

1. Go to HKEY_LOCAL_MACHINE\SYSTEM\CurrentControlSet\Services\
   Tcpip\Parameters.

2. Create a new REG_DWORD item named **IPAutoconfigurationEnabled**. (This
   data item doesn't exist unless you add it, because Windows automatically enables
   APIPA.)

3. Enter a value of 0 to disable APIPA.

4. To re-enable this feature later, change the value to 1.

To make this more complicated, you have to remember that this registry key contains settings that apply to the computer. However, the key has a subkey named Interfaces, which has additional subkeys for each individual TCP/IP interface in the computer.

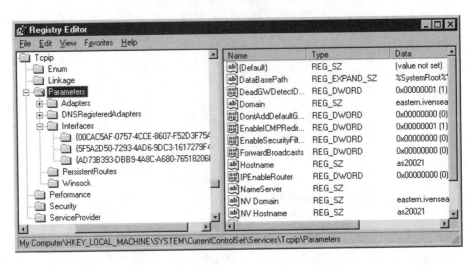

If the item IPAutoconfigurationEnabled exists in any *InterfaceName* subkey, its value takes precedence over the value in HKEY_LOCAL_MACHINE\SYSTEM\CurrentControlSet\Services\Tcpip\Parameters. As a result, it's important to check all the data items in all the subkeys to make sure the changes you're enabling will take effect.

Support for New TCP/IP Standards

New RFCs for TCP/IP appear constantly, and this section discusses some of the new RFCs that are supported in Windows Server 2003. You can obtain information on RFCs from the RFC Editor web site at www.rfc-editor.org/. The site is maintained by members of the Information Sciences Institute (ISI), who publish a classified listing of all RFCs.

Support for Large TCP Windows

Window size refers to the maximum number of packets that can be sent without waiting for positive acknowledgment. Without large window support, the maximum window size is usually fixed at 64KB. This is inefficient when large amounts of data are being transmitted between individual senders and receivers. With large windows, you can dynamically set the window size using TCP configuration options, thus increasing throughput when needed.

Large TCP windows are defined in RFC 1323, "TCP Extensions for High Performance."

Support for Selective Acknowledgments

Selective acknowledgments are a recently developed feature for TCP, and they permit the receiver to be selective about requests to a sender to resend data, limiting such requests to data that is actually missing.

Without this feature, acknowledgments are cumulative. TCP acknowledges only received segments that are contiguous with previous acknowledged segments. Segments that are received out of sequence aren't explicitly acknowledged. TCP requires that segments be acknowledged within a short period of time, or the missing segment and all the segments that follow it are retransmitted. This means that segments could be successfully received, but still retransmitted.

Selective acknowledgements means that only data that wasn't received needs to be retransmitted, increasing the efficiency of network bandwidth.

 Selective acknowledgements are defined in RFC 2018, "TCP Selective Acknowledgment Options."

Support for Improvements in Roundtrip Time Estimates

TCP uses roundtrip time (RTT) to estimate the amount of time required for roundtrip communication between a sender and a receiver. Windows Server 2003 supports the use of the new TCP RTT Measurement option, which improves the method for estimating the time. This in turn helps the setting of retransmission timers, increasing TCP speed and performance.

This new method is especially useful over longer roundtrip links, such as WANs that are widely separated, or that use wireless or satellite communication links.

 The improved TCP roundtrip time measurement is defined in RFC 1323, "TCP Extensions for High Performance."

Support for Internet Control Message Protocol Router Discovery

ICMP router discovery uses ICMP messages to discover the default gateway on a network segment, if a default gateway has not been configured manually, nor assigned via DHCP. Two ICMP messages are involved:

- A router solicitation, which is sent by a host to discover the routers on the network.
- A router advertisement, which is sent by a router. This message is sent in response to a solicitation, and is also sent periodically in order to notify hosts on the network that the router is available.

By default, Windows Server 2003 disables ICMP router discovery for hosts, unless the host gets a Perform Router Discovery option from a DHCP server. For Windows Server 2003 running RAS, you can enable support for ICMP router discovery as follows:

1. Open the Routing and Remote Access snap-in from the Administrative Tools menu.

2. In the console pane, expand the Server, then expand IP Routing, and select General.

3. In the details pane, right-click the appropriate NIC and choose Properties from the shortcut menu.

4. On the General tab, select the Enable Router Discovery Advertisements check box.

5. In Advertisement Lifetime (minutes), specify the time after which a router is considered down after hearing its last router advertisement.

6. In Level of preference, specify the level of preference for this router to be a default gateway for hosts.

7. In Minimum time (minutes), specify the minimum rate at which the router periodically sends ICMP router advertisements.

8. In Maximum time (minutes), specify the maximum rate at which the router periodically sends ICMP router advertisements.

   The router actually sends the periodic ICMP router advertisements at some random point between the minimum and maximum time settings.

   ICMP router discovery is described in RFC 1256, "ICMP Router Discovery Messages."

Support for IP Version 6

One of the primary reasons for IPv6 is to accommodate the explosive growth of registered IP addresses. The principles behind IPv6 are similar to the current IP addressing scheme (IPv4), but instead of using 32-bit addressing, it uses 128-bit addressing. As you can imagine, this significantly expands the number of available IP address. To accommodate the 128-bit addressing, IPv6 uses eight sets of four hexadecimal digits that are separated by a colon (:). So, an IPv6 IP address would look like this:

```
4321:0:1:2:3:4:567:89ab
```

IPv6 also defines a new resource record type, AAAA, that is equipped to handle the new 128-bit addressing format. In addition, it establishes ip6.int, which is the new reverse lookup (IP address to name mappings) namespace.

At the moment, the debate about whether we really need IPv6 is quite heated in the United States, and the primary argument against its adoption is the fact that fewer devices need public (Internet-accepted) IP addresses than the IPv6 proponents would lead us to believe. The "keep IPv4" supporters point to internal private IP address functions (such as DHCP) as a way to avoid running out of public addresses. The technicians I hear from in Europe and Asia seem to be more accepting of the move to IPv6 than administrators from the United States. They point out that the Internet may soon have a billion users, and each user may have more than one device that accesses the Internet. At that point, they argue, we definitely face an IP address shortage.

One interesting use of IPv6 is being developed, especially in Asia, for peer-to-peer networks that include non-computer devices. To communicate with your appliances, security systems, and other devices via your PC (either your home PC or a PC at a remote location such as your office), each device will have an IPv6 address. (In my imagination I picture my microwave oven displaying a time, a countdown while reheating my coffee, and its IPv6 address.)

Until it's widely accepted, there's no point in my spending lots of pages to cover all the details involved in running IPv6 on your network (you have to set up routers, DNS, and NICs). However, if you need IPv6 on your Windows Server 2003 computer (perhaps you have a home oven that uses IPv6 and you want to turn it on before you leave the office), I'll point out that you add IPv6 to your NIC by adding the protocol Microsoft TCP/IP version 6, which is available in the Select Network Protocol dialog box.

TCP/IP Enhancements

If you're moving to Windows Server 2003 from Windows NT, you should be aware of the TCP/IP enhancements that were added to Windows with the release of Windows 2000 (and are, of course, present in Windows Server 2003). Table 10-1 presents an overview.

Feature	Description
Internet Printing Protocol (IPP)	Enables you to print directly to a URL and manage print devices over an intranet or the Internet.
Quality of Service (QoS)	Supports QoS-related standards, such as Resource Reservation Protocol (RSVP), Differentiated Quality of Service, and 802.1p in order to obtain higher levels of service quality. Think of QoS as an agreement between two or more machines that guarantees a certain expected level of throughput, traffic control, and more. However, using this feature takes resources (you may be robbing Peter to pay Paul).

Table 10-1.   *TCP/IP Enhancements*

Feature	Description
Telephony Application Programming Interface (TAPI) 3	Increased support for telephony features.
IP Security (IPSec)	Encryption technology for IP. Often used in VPNs. Refer to Chapter 17 for more information on security-related topics.
Layer Two Tunneling Protocol (L2TP)	Provides enhancements for secure virtual private networking capabilities.
NDIS 5	New network architecture that supports a multitude of enhancements such as multicasts, bandwidth reservation, power management, and more.
Automatic Client Configuration	The ability of a DHCP client to configure itself to communicate on the network when no DHCP server can be contacted.
High-speed network support	Support for high-speed networks (defined in RFC 1323) for increased performance and scalability. This includes support for Selective Acknowledgements (SACK), IEEE 1394, wireless networks, IP over ATM (RFC 1577), and much more.
Internet Group Management Protocol version 2 (IGMPv2)	Allows computers to use multicasting-based technologies such as streaming media services.
Protocol Stack Tuning	Windows automatically adjusts protocol settings, such as increasing the default TCP window size, to increase network performance.
Plug and Play Networking	Automatic recognition of networking hardware, such as NICs and PCMCIA adapters, without manual intervention.
DHCP enhancements	New features for DHCP include integration with DNS, enhanced monitoring and reporting of usage, rogue DHCP server detection, and much more.

Table 10-1.   *TCP/IP Enhancements* (continued)

TCP/IP and the Windows Server 2003 Networking Model

Windows Server 2003's networking architecture is particularly well suited for use by different sets of protocols. With the Transport Device Interface (TDI) at the top of the OSI model's Transport layer, and the Network Device Interface Specification (NDIS) interface beneath the Network layer, the core transport protocols are largely isolated from the rest of the networking stack.

As long as they can address these two interfaces, any competent protocols can be used to send data over the network. Indeed, different transport protocols can function simultaneously in Windows Server 2003, resulting in the double-edged sword of platform interoperability and network traffic performance.

Above the TDI are the *user-mode interfaces* (also known as *application programming interfaces,* or *APIs*). These interfaces are addressed by applications when they require network services. Chief among these interfaces are the NetBIOS interface, which Windows Server 2003 still supports for file services, and Windows Sockets (Winsock), which is the standard interface for many TCP/IP and Internet utilities for backward-compatibility issues with down-level clients. Other supported APIs are

- Remote Procedure Calls (RPCs)
- Server Message Blocks (SMBs)
- Named Pipes
- Mail Slots

These APIs are not necessarily associated with a particular set of protocols. The original Windows NT release, for example, could only pass data from its APIs to the NetBEUI protocol and then to an NDIS driver. This simplified system lacked the functionality of TCP/IP but provided basic network services.

The TDI provides a distributed interface that enables network requests from different APIs to be directed to whichever protocol is needed to access the required resource. NetBIOS file requests, for example, can be directed to the TCP/IP protocols when accessing a Windows drive on the network, or to the NWLink protocol when the application needs a file from a NetWare server. Multiple applications running in Windows Server 2003 might be processing several network requests simultaneously, meaning that various function calls can be passing through the TDI to the TCP/IP protocol stack, or the NWLink stack, or both, at the same time.

All the protocol stacks operating on a Windows Server 2003 machine deliver their network service requests to the same place—the NDIS interface. NDIS is the standard used to create the device driver that provides access to the networking hardware. Thus the network architecture of Windows Server 2003 can be seen as a series of funneling procedures. Applications at the top of the model generate requests that can utilize any of a handful of APIs. The APIs then pass the requests on to a smaller number of protocols (usually one or two). Different kinds of requests might be intermingled in the individual protocol stacks; and at the NDIS interface, they are all funneled into a single stream and packaged into discrete packets that pass through the network adapter and out onto the network medium itself.

The TCP/IP protocols are therefore primarily occupied in moving the application requests from the TDI to the NDIS interface, packaging them into discrete units called *datagrams* so that they can be efficiently transmitted to their ultimate destination. The process is, of course, reversed when data arrives at the workstation. This packaging can be said to consist of three basic functions:

- **Addressing** To send data to another computer on the network, there must be a means by which the destination can be uniquely identified. TCP/IP provides its own identification system, in the form of an IP address for each machine on the network.

- **Routing** A Data Link-level protocol such as Ethernet is not concerned with the ultimate delivery of network packets, only with transmitting them to the next machine on the network. TCP/IP provides the means by which network traffic is efficiently and reliably routed through multiple network segments to its destination.

- **Multiplexing** Because an operating system like Windows Server 2003 can be running several programs at once, network requests are multiplexed over the cable (that is, packets with different origins and purposes are intermingled in the network data stream). Individual packets must therefore be identifiable in order for the requests to reach the appropriate application process in the destination computer. TCP/IP accomplishes this by assigning a port number to each process, which, in combination with an IP address, uniquely identifies the actual process on the network to which the packet must be delivered. The combination of an IP address and a port number is called a *socket*.

The TCP/IP Protocol Stack

The TCP/IP protocols, as realized on Windows Server 2003, can be broken down into four functional layers that roughly correspond to those of the OSI reference model:

- Application
- Transport
- Network (also known as the Internet layer)
- Network Access

As with the OSI reference model, the functionality of the various TCP/IP protocols is divided into layers that make the process of data encapsulation more comprehensible. As a message is passed down from the user interface at the top of the networking stack to the actual network medium (usually a cable) at the bottom, data processed by an upper-layer protocol is repeatedly encapsulated by protocols operating at each successive lower layer. This results in a compound packet that is transmitted to the destination system, where the whole process is repeated in reverse, as the message travels up through the layers.

Examining the layers at which the suite of protocols function is a way to understand how they have been adapted for use on Windows Server 2003 networks. The following sections present an overview of the TCP/IP layers.

The Network Access Layer

The Network Access protocols operate at the bottom of the TCP/IP protocol stack, working just above the Data Link layer to facilitate the transmission of datagrams over the network medium. TCP/IP has its own addressing system, by which it identifies the other computers on the network. Once the IP datagrams reach the NDIS interface, however, they are repackaged into frames that are appropriate for the network type being used.

Every network type, whether Ethernet or something else, has its own way of identifying the computers on the network. Most of the network types in use today accomplish this identification through the use of a hardware address that is coded into every network adapter by its manufacturer. This Media Access Control (MAC) address is used in the outermost frame of every network packet to identify the computer to which it should be sent.

Therefore, for an IP datagram to be sent out over the network, there must be a way of determining what hardware address corresponds to the given IP address. This is the job of the Network Access protocols, of which the most commonly known is the Address Resolution Protocol (ARP).

ARP

ARP functions between the Network and Data Link layers on Ethernet networks. It cannot operate until it is provided with the IP address of the computer to which a datagram is to be sent. No datagram can be transmitted over the network until ARP supplies the Data Link layer with a destination hardware address.

When ARP receives a datagram from the Network layer, it reads the IP address of the intended destination from the IP header and then generates an *address resolution request packet* (ARP packet), which is broadcast to the entire local network. The address resolution request contains the IP address of the destination computer (if the destination is on the same network segment) or the IP address of the workstation's default gateway (if it is not).

Each computer on the network segment processes the ARP packet and notes the IP address carried within. If a computer on the network detects its own IP address in an ARP packet, it responds to the sender with a reply containing the hardware address of its network adapter. ARP passes this address along to the Data Link layer protocol, which uses it to frame the packet and eventually transmit it over the network.

ARP also maintains a cache of IP addresses and their corresponding hardware addresses, to reduce the number of redundant broadcasts transmitted over the network. The cache is erased whenever the computer is shut down or rebooted, to prevent incorrect transmissions due to changes in network hardware.

ARP broadcasts are limited to the local network segment. A computer's Data Link protocol is concerned only with the transmission of the frame to the next computer down the line. In many cases, this could be a gateway to another network segment, not the computer whose IP address is specified as the final destination of the message.

ARP is only one of many Network Access protocols designed to support the extremely wide and varied array of platforms that can utilize TCP/IP.

The Network Layer

The Internet Protocol (IP), which operates at the Network layer of the TCP/IP stack, is the central protocol of the entire suite and the core of TCP/IP's functionality. All the upper-layer protocols in the suite are packaged within IP datagrams before being passed to the NDIS interface. IP performs many of the key functions that enable the TCP/IP suite to operate, including the following:

- The packaging of upper-layer traffic into datagrams, the fundamental TCP/IP transmission unit
- The implementation of the TCP/IP addressing system
- The routing of datagrams between networks
- The fragmentation and defragmentation of datagrams to accommodate the limitations of the network types between the source and the destination
- The passing of data between the Transport and Network Access layers (in both directions)

IP is a connectionless, unreliable protocol. *Connectionless* means that it transmits packets without first establishing that the destination computer is operating and ready to receive data; *unreliable* means that it has no inherent mechanisms that provide error detection and correction. These apparent deficiencies are not really a problem, because IP can always be used in conjunction with other protocols that can provide these services. As a basic carrier medium for network communications, the intention behind IP's design is to provide only the common services needed by all transmissions, so that an appropriate transport protocol can be selected to meet the specific needs of the data being transmitted.

IP Routing

IP is also responsible for the routing of datagrams to adjacent network segments. Every computer running TCP/IP on an internetwork has access to one or more gateways that it uses to transmit data to systems on other networks. A *gateway*, in TCP/IP parlance, is a device that passes packets between two or more networks. The term does not necessarily imply the existence of a protocol translation, as it does in the general networking vocabulary. A TCP/IP system that functions as a gateway between the source of a transmission and its destination is also known as an *intermediate system*. The source and destination themselves are called *end systems*.

TCP/IP traffic on an intermediate system travels up to the Network layer, and no higher. IP is aware only of the computers on its local network segment and the adjacent segments that can be accessed through local gateways. When it receives a packet destined for a computer on another segment, IP sends it to one of the local gateways to continue it on its way. That particular gateway is selected for one of the following reasons:

- It provides direct access to the network on which the destination computer resides.

- It is registered in the computer's routing table as the best possible route to the destination network.

- It is the computer's default gateway.

The IP Header

As with any network protocol, IP places its own header onto each packet it receives from the upper layers, encapsulating it for transmission and inserting the information needed to perform all the protocol's functions. The IP header is either 20 or 24 bytes long, depending on the inclusion of certain options. Bytes, in TCP/IP-speak, are referred to as *octets*, and the header is broken into 32-bit *words*, of which there are five or six. After the header is applied, the packet is referred to as a *datagram*, and it is passed down to the Network Access layer. The datagram will be encapsulated again by the Data Link layer, before it is actually transmitted over the network.

The IP header consists of the following fields:

- **First Word**

  - **Version (4 bits)**   Indicates the IP header version.

  - **Internet Header Length (4 bits)**   Specifies the overall length of the IP header (in 32-bit words), thus indicating whether the optional sixth word is present.

  - **Type of Service (8 bits)**   Indicates the desired network service priority for this datagram.

  - **Total Length (16 bits)**   Specifies the total length of the datagram in octets (bytes); can be used to determine whether fragmentation of datagrams is needed to complete the transmission.

- **Second Word**

  - **Identification (16 bits)**   When datagrams are fragmented or defragmented, this field specifies the datagram to which a particular fragment belongs.

  - **Flags (3 bits)**   Specifies whether the datagram can be fragmented and whether all the fragments composing the original datagram have been received.

  - **Fragmentation Offset (13 bits)**   Used to reassemble fragments in the proper order, this field provides the starting point (measured in 64-bit units) of this fragment in the datagram.

■ **Third Word**

  ■ **Time to Live (8 bits)**   Specifies how long (in seconds) the datagram can remain active on the internetwork. This allows undeliverable datagrams to be removed from the network after a set time period. Every system that processes the datagram decrements this value by at least one second.

  ■ **Protocol (8 bits)**   Indicates the protocol at the Transport layer of the destination computer for which this datagram is destined.

  ■ **Header Checksum (16 bits)**   Verifies that the IP header (but not the data) has been transmitted correctly. The checksum is verified by each intermediate system and recomputed before being sent to the next node.

■ **Fourth Word**

  ■ **Source Address (32 bits)**   The IP address of the transmitting computer.

■ **Fifth Word**

  ■ **Destination Address (32 bits)**   The IP address of the end system to which the datagram is being sent.

■ **Sixth Word (optional)**

  ■ **Options (variable)**   Provides routing, security, or time-stamp services for IP transmissions. The options field is itself optional, but must be supported by all implementations of IP.

  ■ **Padding (variable)**   Zeros added to fill out the sixth word to a full 32 bits.

Although it is the most heavily used of the TCP/IP protocols, IP by itself is not capable of coping with some of the situations that might be encountered during the transmission of datagrams. In these cases, a "helper" protocol is needed to perform additional transmission control functions.

Internet Control Message Protocol   ICMP operates at the Network layer. It is used to perform a number of diagnostic and administrative functions that aid in the transmission of IP packets. The ping utility, for example, uses ICMP packets to verify the existence of particular IP addresses on the network.

Similar ICMP packets are also used to provide a sending computer with reports on the status of its transmissions, such as:

■ Messages stating that a datagram's destination address is unreachable, specifying further whether it is the destination's network, host, protocol, or port that is unavailable.

■ ICMP Source Quench messages indicating that an intermediate or end system is being overwhelmed by incoming packets. This enables the sending node to initiate flow control procedures by slowing down its transmissions until the complaint messages cease.

- Reports that packets have been discarded by an intermediate or end system due to packet header corruption.

- Warnings that datagrams will have to be fragmented before they can be successfully transmitted to the destination.

Routing advice, in the form of ICMP Redirect packets, inform a sending node of conditions beyond the adjacent network segments. When the transmitting computer is on a segment with more than one usable gateway, these packets enable the sender to select the gateway that provides the most efficient route to the destination.

These functions should not be confused with those providing true connection-oriented service and error detection. ICMP aids in the delivery of IP datagrams to the destination but does not guarantee reliable service.

The Transport Layer

As in the OSI reference model, the TCP/IP Transport layer sits atop the Network layer. Transport protocols are encapsulated within IP datagrams for transmission over the network and provide different levels of service, depending on the needs of the application. The two main protocols that operate at the Transport layer are the Transport Control Protocol (TCP) and the User Datagram Protocol (UDP), both of which are profiled in the following two sections. TCP is used when more reliable service is required, and UDP is used when guaranteed delivery is less critical. The Protocol field of the IP header identifies which transport protocol is being carried within the datagram, so that the receiving workstation knows how to process the packet.

The Transport Control Protocol

TCP is the primary connection-oriented, reliable protocol used in TCP/IP communications. Applications use it in situations that require data transmissions that are verifiable as being absolutely accurate, such as ftp file transfers. Unlike IP, TCP data transmissions never begin until a three-way handshake with the destination system has been completed. This creates a virtual connection between the two systems, a prearranged agreement between the two machines for the exchange of packets. After the connection is established, all the datagrams transmitted during that session are considered to be *segments* of that transmission. The entire series of datagrams transmitted during the session is called a *sequence*.

The reliability of TCP communications is provided by an error detection and correction system called *positive acknowledgment with retransmission*. This means that the receiving computer examines the checksum included with each packet and sends requests for retransmission if the packet has errors (this is new in Windows Server 2003— previous versions send periodic acknowledgments back to the sender, indicating that the incoming packets up to a certain point have been received intact).

TCP also provides flow control and packet reordering services for every transmission. Even though a virtual connection exists between the two end systems, individual IP packets can travel different routes to the same destination, possibly even arriving in a different order from that in which they were sent.

TCP Header

The header of a TCP packet is complex, even though it is the same size as the IP header, because it has a great deal to do. The TCP header is carried within the IP header and is read only by the end system receiving the packet. Because the destination system must acknowledge receipt of the transmitted data, TCP is a bidirectional protocol. The same header is used to send data packets in one direction and acknowledgments in the other direction. The TCP header is formatted as follows:

- **First Word**
  - **Source Port (16 bits)** Specifies the port number of the application process at the source computer sending the transmission.
  - **Destination Port (16 bits)** Specifies the port number of the application process at the destination computer that will receive the transmission.
- **Second Word**
  - **Sequence Number (32 bits)** Ensures that segments are processed in the correct order at the destination by specifying the number of the first data octet in the segment out of the entire sequence.
- **Third Word**
  - **Acknowledgment Number (32 bits)** Specifies the sequence number of the segment that will next be received by the destination; indicates that all prior segments have been received correctly and acknowledged.
- **Fourth Word**
  - **Data Offset (4 bits)** Specifies the length of the TCP header in 32-bit words, thus indicating the beginning of the data field and whether the optional sixth word is present in the header.
  - **Reserved (6 bits)** Currently unused; the value must be zero.
  - **Control Bits (6 bits)** Binary flags that can be turned on to indicate the segment's function or purpose:
    - URG: Urgent Pointer field significant
    - ACK: Acknowledgment field significant
    - PSH: Push Function
    - RST: Reset the connection
    - SYN: Synchronize sequence numbers
    - FIN: No more data from sender

- **Window (16 bits)**   Provides flow control by specifying the number of octets (beginning at the sequence number in the Acknowledgment Number field) that the destination computer can accept from the source.

- **Fifth Word**

  - **Checksum (16 bits)**   Provides error correction by checking both the TCP header and data fields, as well as a pseudo-header containing the source address, destination address and protocol values from the IP header, and the overall length of the TCP packet. The pseudo-header enables the Transport layer to reverify that the datagrams have been sent to the correct destination.

  - **Urgent Pointer (16 bits)**   When the URG control bit is turned on, this field specifies the location of urgent data (in relation to the Sequence Number of this segment).

- **Sixth Word (optional)**

  - **Options (variable)**   Optional field used only to specify the maximum segment size allowed by the sending computer during the TCP handshake (when the SYN control bit is set).

  - **Padding (variable)**   Zeros added to fill out the sixth word to a full 32 bits.

Anatomy of a TCP Session

To begin a TCP session, one system transmits a packet that has the SYN control bit turned on and contains a randomly selected sequence number. The destination system replies to the sender with a packet that has the ACK control bit turned on and specifies its own beginning sequence number, and then returns a SYN. Each system maintains its own numbering of the bytes in the sequence, while remaining aware of the other machine's numbers as well.

The sequence numbering begun in the first packet is continually incremented by both systems during the entire duration of the TCP connection. When it actually begins to transmit data, the transmitting computer specifies in each packet the number of the first byte contained in that packet's data field. If packets should arrive at the destination in the wrong sequence, the receiving system uses the sequence numbers to reassemble them into the correct order.

During the data transmission, the transmitting system computes a checksum for each packet and includes the result in the TCP header. The destination computer recomputes the checksum for each packet received and compares the result to the value provided in the checksum field. If the values match, the packet is verified as having been transmitted without error.

When it has finished sending data, the transmitting node sends a packet with the FIN control bit turned on to the destination, breaking down the connection and ending the sequence.

The User Datagram Protocol

UDP provides a low-overhead alternative to TCP for use when the reliable transfer of data is not critical. It is connectionless, with each packet sent and processed independently of the others, and requires only a two-word header. There is no explicit acknowledgment of received packets during a UDP transmission (for example, a NetBIOS broadcast). Replies to UDP requests can be returned to the sender, but they are processed at the application level.

UDP is not typically used for the transfer of large binary data files, in which a single incorrect bit can cause the file to be ruined. UDP is more likely to be used for the transmission of a short query to another computer. If the sender receives no response, the entire request can usually be retransmitted using less overall traffic volume than the establishment of a TCP connection.

Some applications have begun to use UDP to stream audio and video over the Internet, because the control overhead is so much lower, and also because an audio or video stream can recover from an occasional lost packet more easily than most binary files.

Compared to the TCP header, UDP is simple and minimal. Its header layout is as follows:

- **First Word**
  - **Source Port (16 bits)**   Specifies the port number of the application process generating the UDP transmission (optional; padded with zeros if omitted).
  - **Destination Port (16 bits)**   Specifies the port number of the application process in the destination system to which the UDP transmission is directed.
- **Second Word**
  - **Length (16 bits)**   Specifies the overall length of the UDP packet in octets, including the data but excluding the IP header and any Data Link frames.
  - **Checksum (16 bits)**   Specifies the result of a checksum computation on the UDP header and data, plus a pseudo-header that consists of the IP header's Source Address, Destination Address, and Protocol fields.

The Application Layer

The TCP/IP suite includes many different protocols that operate above the Transport Device Interface. Some, like ftp and Telnet, are applications themselves, as well as protocols, and are included with most implementations of the TCP/IP suite to provide basic file transfer and terminal emulation services to users on any platform, with a standardized interface.

Common Layers   Other Application layer protocols are used to provide specific TCP/IP services to programs. Simple Mail Transfer Protocol (SMTP), for example, is used by many programs to send e-mail over TCP/IP networks. Other protocols, such as the Domain Name System (DNS), provide more generalized services. DNS is used by many applications to resolve Internet hostnames into IP addresses.

Obscure Layers   Although the examples cited thus far are rather well known, some application protocols operate almost invisibly to the user. The Router Information Protocol (RIP), for example, disseminates data to other computers on the network that helps them make more intelligent routing decisions.

How the Application Layer Works   Application protocols are, logically, closest to the user interface and are often directly involved with the process that generates the request for network resources. When such a request is processed, it is passed down the layers of the networking stack and encapsulated using the various protocols discussed in the preceding sections.

Thus, when you connect to an ftp server on the Internet and download a file, the ftp server at the remote site accesses the file and creates a packet by applying the header for the FTP application protocol. The entire packet is then passed down to the Transport layer, where it becomes the data field in a TCP packet. At the Network layer, the packet is divided up into units of the proper size to transmit over the network. An IP header is applied to each, and the packets can now properly be called a series of datagrams.

Except for minor changes to the IP headers while in transit, these datagrams will remain unopened until they arrive at their destination. While they are on the network, the outermost layer of the data packets, the Data Link frame, can change several times during the packets' journey from the ftp server to your workstation. The datagrams might arrive at your computer encased within Ethernet packets, and they might even start out that way when they leave the ftp server; but there could be 20 gateways or more between the source and the destination systems, running an untold number of different Data Link protocols.

After the packets arrive at your computer, the process begins in reverse. IP passes the datagrams up to the TCP protocol (which was specified in the IP header), where they are assembled into the correct order and fed to the FTP protocol (identified by its port number in the TCP header), which writes the received file to your hard disk drive.

All the TCP/IP protocols discussed in the preceding sections work together to transmit data over the network. By default, Windows Server 2003 installs them as part of the network communications stack. In Windows Server 2003, TCP/IP is often referred to as though it is a single protocol, when actually the entire family of protocols is implied.

Installing and Configuring TCP/IP

TCP/IP has been the preferred protocol since Windows NT 4 and is installed during the operating system's setup routine. However, with Windows Server 2003, TCP/IP is a prerequisite for you to log on, use Active Directory (AD), Domain Name System (DNS), and much more. The TCP/IP stack in Windows Server 2003 includes support for all the protocols discussed in the preceding sections, as well as a large collection of services and utilities that enable you to utilize, manage, and troubleshoot TCP/IP. Windows Server 2003 ships with many TCP/IP-based services that facilitate the administration of large numbers of TCP/IP users on a network.

TCP/IP can also, optionally, be installed after the operating system is already in place, by clicking the Add button on the Local Area Connections Property page. If you have been relying on other protocols, such as NetBEUI, to communicate with other Windows computers on your local network, I highly recommend removing them after all your machines have been configured to use TCP/IP. It's always a good rule of thumb to keep the number of protocols you're using to a minimum.

After TCP/IP is installed, whether through the installation program or the Local Area Connections Properties page, you must provide the settings needed to identify your machine and ready it for interaction with the rest of the TCP/IP network. Windows Server 2003 continues to include the Dynamic Host Configuration Protocol (DHCP), which can enable a Windows Server 2003 computer to automatically provide your systems with all the TCP/IP configuration settings they require. DHCP, discussed in Chapter 11, means you can skip the configuration settings covered in the following sections. However, to complete your education about TCP/IP, I'll discuss the settings required for effective TCP/IP communications, and how computers use them to communicate with the network.

The settings required to use TCP/IP on Windows Server 2003 are configured in the Internet Protocol (TCP/IP) Properties page of each network device:

- IP address
- Subnet mask
- Default gateway
- Preferred and alternate DNS servers

IP Address

The IP address is the means by which computers are identified on a TCP/IP network. It identifies both the host itself and the network on which it resides. Each computer must be assigned an address that is unique for the network, to prevent datagrams being delivered to the wrong system.

On a TCP/IP network, the term "host" is not necessarily synonymous with a computer. A host is a network interface, of which there can be more than one in a single system. In such a case, each host must have its own IP address.

IP addresses traditionally are 32 bits long and are expressed as four-decimal values from 0 to 255, representing 8 bits each, separated by periods. For example, the IP address 192.168.1.146 is equivalent to the following in binary

```
11000000.10101000.00000001.10010010
```

If your network is not connected to the Internet, the IP addresses can be assigned to individual hosts by network administrators. The actual addresses themselves can be any legal combination of numbers, as long as each assigned address is unique. This is known as an *unregistered* network because it is a wholly private arrangement within the confines of your enterprise.

If your network is connected to the Internet, however, you will have one or more machines with *registered* IP addresses. To prevent address duplication, you must register the IP addresses of Internet hosts with an Internet authority. A private network can elect to use registered IP addresses for all its hosts, or it can maintain an unregistered network for internal users and register only the machines directly accessible from the Internet, such as World Wide Web and ftp servers. In that case, users with unregistered IP addresses typically access the Internet through a firewall or proxy server that prevents unauthorized access to the local network from outside machines.

When you are configuring a computer to use TCP/IP, you should do so from a planned group of addresses, or use Windows Server 2003's DHCP server, which assigns addresses automatically from a pool you configure.

 The one thing that you should not do is select a random IP address just to see if it works. IP address conflicts are one of the most common problems on TCP/IP networks, and one of the most difficult to troubleshoot. Remember, the IP address that you just "borrowed" might belong to another system, and IP stacks shut down in the event of a duplicate.

Subnet Mask

The *subnet mask* is possibly the most misunderstood TCP/IP configuration setting. People see the values assigned to this setting, such as 255.255.255.0, and mistake them for actual IP addresses.

The subnet mask is actually based on a very simple concept. If you recall, in the last section you learned that the IP address identifies both the network and the actual host on that network. The only purpose of the subnet mask is to designate what part of the IP address identifies the network on which the host resides and what part identifies the host itself.

This is more easily understood if you think of the subnet mask in binary terms. All IP addresses are 32-bit binary values. They are notated in decimal form only for the sake of convenience. A subnet mask value of 255.255.255.0, when expressed in binary form, appears like this:

```
11111111.11111111.11111111.00000000
```

This value means that, for the IP address associated with this mask, all the digits with the value 1 identify the network, and all the 0's identify the host on that network (the 1's *mask* the network ID). Thus, if the machine's IP address is 123.45.67.89, then 123.45.67 identifies the network, and 89 identifies the host.

IP Address Types

When you understand what the subnet mask is used for, the next logical question is to ask why different networks require different numbers of digits to identify them. The answer to this, as with most TCP/IP questions, is found on the Internet. The TCP/IP protocols were designed for use on what is now known as the Internet. Although no one could have predicted its phenomenal growth, the Internet was designed to be a highly scalable network requiring a minimum of centralized administration.

TCP/IP's developers understood even in the early days that the idea of registering a unique address for every host on the network with some sort of administrative body was impractical. The cost would have been too high even then. They decided, therefore, that only networks would be registered and that the administrators of the networks would be responsible for maintaining the IP address assignments for the individual hosts.

Three different network classes were created, which would be registered to individual networks based on the number of hosts that connected to the Internet. Table 10-2 lists the classes, the subnet mask for each, the maximum number of possible networks of that class using the current system, and the number of unique host addresses available to a single network of each class.

> **Note** *Two additional address classes are D and E. Class D addresses are typically used for multicasting, and class E addresses are reserved for experimental use.*

On a practical level, this means that if you wanted to register your network in order to connect it to the Internet, you could obtain a class C address from an Internet authority. The authority assigns you a network address that you use for the first three octets of all your IP addresses, such as 199.45.67. You are then free to assign the 254 possible values for the fourth octet in any manner you wish, as long as there is no duplication. The subnet mask on all your machines is 255.255.255.0, indicating that only the last octet is being used to identify the host.

If you had more than 254 nodes on your network, you would have to get another class C address. If you had a sufficiently large network, you could get a class B address,

Address Class	Default Subnet Mask	Number of Networks	Number of Hosts
A	255.0.0.0	126	16,777,214
B	255.255.0.0	16,384	65,534
C	255.255.255.0	2,097,152	254

Table 10-2. *Address Class Characteristics*

which would support up to 65,534 hosts. You would then assign the last two octets yourself and use a subnet mask of 255.255.0.0.

Understanding a Subnet

Subnet masking is occasionally more complicated than the examples given thus far. Sometimes the dividing line between the network and the host portions of an IP address does not fall neatly between the octets.

A *subnet* is simply a logical subdivision imposed on a network address for organizational purposes. For example, a large corporation that has a registered class B network address is not likely to assign addresses to its nodes by numbering them consecutively from 0.0 to 255.555.

The more practical scenario would be to divide the network into a series of subnets, which are usually based on the wiring scheme of the facilities. By creating subnets corresponding to the networks that make up the enterprise, the task of assigning and maintaining the IP addresses can be divided among the administrators responsible for each network.

Therefore, in such a scenario, the class B network address would dictate the values of the first two octets of an IP address, and the subnet would dictate the value of the third octet, leaving the fourth to identify the host. The subnet mask in this situation would be 255.255.255.0 because the first three octets are defining the network address, regardless of whether it is registered.

Suppose, however, that you have a class C address and you find yourself in the same situation. The first three octets of your IP addresses are dictated by the registered network address, but you want to create subnets because your workstations are on several different network segments. You can still do this, if you again think of the subnet mask in binary terms. Instead of using the class C subnet mask as it stands, you can assign some of the bits in the fourth octet to the network address as well, like this:

```
1111111.11111111.11111111.11110000
```

Converting this address back to decimal form yields a subnet mask of 255.255.255.240. This arrangement enables you to define up to 14 network addresses (not 16, because values of all 0's or all 1's are not allowed) composed of up to 14 hosts on each. You can alter the bit arrangement in favor of more networks or more hosts as needed. To assign network and host addresses using this method, it is a good idea to work out the proper values in binary form and then convert them to decimals to avoid errors. Because few humans can think in binary terms, most of us need a calculator to accomplish this task.

In most cases, the value for your workstation's subnet mask is supplied to you along with your IP address, either by hand or through a DHCP server, especially if a complicated subnetting arrangement is in use. Remember, though, that subnetting is a local phenomenon—an administrator's device. TCP/IP applications treat all IP addresses alike, regardless of which bits are used to identify the network.

Default Gateway

The default gateway setting on the Internet Protocol (TCP/IP) Properties page is the address of a gateway system on your local network segment that provides access to the rest of the internetwork. The gateway can be a computer, a switch, or a router that joins two or more of the segments on your network. You can have more than one gateway on your local segment, but the default gateway is the one your computer uses by default when trying to connect to a computer on another network (frequently the Internet).

If you can connect to other systems on the local network, but not to those on other networks, then it is likely either that you have specified an incorrect value for the default gateway or that the gateway itself is malfunctioning.

The use of the default gateway to access certain destinations can be automatically overridden in your workstation by the receipt of an ICMP redirect message, which contains the address of another gateway that provides a more efficient route to the destination.

Advanced IP Addressing

A computer can have more than one network interface, each of which must have its own TCP/IP configuration settings. The Internet Protocol (TCP/IP) Properties page of the Local Area Connection Properties window contains a selector that enables you to make a selection from the network adapters installed in your machine, so you can configure the different settings needed for each.

For Windows Server 2003 family computers, you can assign more than one IP address to a single network host adapter. When you click the Advanced button on the Internet Protocol (TCP/IP) Properties page, you are presented with the Advanced TCP/IP Settings dialog box. On the IP Settings tab, you can enter additional IP addresses for each installed network adapter.

The most common scenario for assigning multiple addresses to a single adapter in a Windows Server 2003 computer is in the case of a machine used as a server on the Internet. You can, for example, run a World Wide Web (WWW) server, using IIS on a Windows Server 2003 machine directly connected to the Internet, and host web sites for different customers, providing each site with its own IP address. Internet users could then access the different sites associated with each of the IP addresses, never knowing that they were all running on the same machine.

The IP Settings tab in the Advanced TCP/IP Settings dialog also enables you to specify the addresses of additional gateways for each adapter. Unlike the additional IP addresses, however, which all remain active simultaneously, additional gateways are only used (in the order listed) when the primary default gateway is unreachable.

Preferred and Alternate DNS Servers

If you're moving to Windows Server 2003 from Windows NT, you haven't been as immersed in DNS as you will be now. You may be accustomed to using DNS mainly for external resolution, relying on NetBIOS and WINS, not DNS, to communicate with other computers on the network.

DNS has taken over the name resolution responsibility within Windows Server 2003 (actually, this started with Windows 2000). Anytime you request a contact to another computer on your network or on the Internet, DNS is the service providing the necessary name-to-IP address translation.

As a result of Windows Server 2003's dependence on DNS, you must configure all computers on your network to use a preferred DNS server. An alternate DNS server is recommended, but optional. You can either manually enter the preferred and secondary DNS servers' IP addresses or allow DHCP to pass the information to clients. Chapter 12 contains a more detailed explanation of DNS in Windows Server 2003.

Understanding Name Registration and Resolution

When it comes to network communications, the TCP/IP protocols are entirely reliant on IP addresses for the identification of other systems. In addition, hostnames and NetBIOS names are used to identify networked computers to make it easier for computers to contact each other. It would be extremely difficult, if not impossible, to remember the IP address for every computer or every web site that you want to contact.

Microsoft operating systems prior to Windows 2000 have always based their network communications on NetBIOS names. Windows Server 2003 still permits NetBIOS for compatibility, but it's designed to work with hostnames instead of NetBIOS names. Either way, there must be a method for equating these names with IP addresses.

You can use any of several mechanisms, with varying levels of sophistication, to accomplish these tasks; but they all can be reduced to what is ultimately a database containing the names and their equivalent addresses. The differences in the mechanisms center on the methods used to get the information into the database (*name registration*) and the ways in which it is retrieved (*name resolution*).

If you are running a Windows Server 2003 network with downlevel clients, you need to have at least two separate name resolution mechanisms. Hostnames and NetBIOS names are always treated separately in this respect, even if a computer uses the same name for both. If your network doesn't have downlevel clients or NetBIOS-based applications, you can dispense with the NetBIOS names.

- For hostnames, the available mechanisms are a HOSTS file and the Domain Name Service.

- For NetBIOS names, the available mechanisms are Network Broadcasts, WINS, and the LMHOSTS file.

All Windows-based computers use at least one of these mechanisms during every TCP/IP exchange that uses a name instead of an IP address. Understanding how they work can help you maximize the efficiency of your network, keep network traffic levels to a minimum, and troubleshoot communications problems. For a complete understanding of hostnames, domain hierarchy, DNS, and more, refer to Chapter 12.

Using a HOSTS File

The simplest way to resolve hostnames is to maintain a table of those names and their equivalent IP addresses. That's what a HOSTS file is—an ASCII file, stored on the local hard drive, that lists IP addresses on the left and hostnames on the right. When a user supplies an application with a hostname, the application looks it up in the HOSTS file. If the name is found, its equivalent IP address is used to create the network connection. If it is not found, the operation fails.

At one time, believe it or not, name resolution services for the entire Internet were provided through a single HOSTS table containing thousands of entries that had to be regularly downloaded by Internet users to upgrade their systems. The problems with this method are obvious. The name registration method—that is, the means by which the names and addresses are inserted into the file—is wholly manual. Users or administrators must individually modify or upgrade the HOSTS file on every network computer to include the name and address of every host to be contacted by name. Also, as the number of entries increases, the file can quickly become unwieldy and name resolution performance begins to suffer. Can you imagine trying to manage your company's HOSTS file with hundreds or thousands of name-to-IP-address mappings? Each change to the file would require all computers on the network to get an update, meaning that the entire HOSTS file would need to be transferred to each of them.

Using the Domain Name System

The Domain Name System, or DNS, is the more commonly used method of Internet hostname resolution because it enables users to connect to any site anywhere on the Internet, by name. This might seem like an incredible feat, particularly in light of the Internet's growth in the past few years, but DNS takes advantage of, and is indeed the primary reason for, the domain-based structure of Internet hostnames.

The Domain Name System consists of thousands of DNS servers located all over the Internet. When you register a domain name, you are required to specify a primary and a backup DNS server. These are known as the *authoritative servers* for your domain. A DNS server is a UNIX daemon or a Windows service that is responsible for maintaining and publishing a database of the hostnames and addresses in its own domain.

A domain's DNS servers do not necessarily have to be located on its local network, and in fact many Internet Service Providers (ISPs) run Web hosting services in which they provide the use of their DNS servers for a fee. What's important is that an Internet authority, or whatever other body has registered the domain name, has a record of the DNS servers responsible for that domain's hosts.

Because individual network administrators are responsible for assigning the hostnames within their domains, they must also be responsible for maintaining the DNS records of those names. Surprisingly, the registration of a domain's hostnames in its DNS servers is no less of a manual operation than in a HOSTS file. If you add a new ftp server to your network, for example, you must manually add or edit a DNS resource record, specifying the name and address of the new machine.

Windows Server 2003 DNS, however, has adopted the new technology of dynamically registering computers instead of tediously, manually updating resource records. Clients are able to have their host (A) and pointer (PTR) resource records registered automatically with the DNS server. Also, Windows Server 2003 DNS can be integrated with AD, which enhances security, replication of the DNS database, administration, and much more. Chapter 12 covers DNS and related topics in great detail.

NetBIOS Names

Although NetBIOS is no longer required on a Windows Server 2003 network, it is essential for backward compatibility with older Windows-based systems, such as Windows 9*x* and Windows NT, that use NetBIOS to communicate, and for applications that use NetBIOS. Therefore, Windows Server 2003 still supports NetBIOS.

NetBIOS is a software interface that has been used for many years to provide network communication capabilities to applications. Some of the original Windows NT networking architecture that has been incorporated into Windows Server 2003 relied solely on NetBIOS's own naming system to identify other computers on the network.

A NetBIOS name consists of 16 characters, the last of which Windows reserves to identify the special functions of certain computers, such as domain controllers or browsers. When NetBIOS is enabled, every computer is assigned a NetBIOS name by the operating system. The name might or might not correspond to the user's logon name or the computer's hostname. You use NetBIOS names whenever you type a UNC pathname that refers to a Windows network node.

NetBIOS is no longer a necessity unless you have downlevel clients or NetBIOS-dependent applications, but it is still an integral part of Windows networking. The Workstation and Server services that run on all Windows Server 2003/2000 computers use both NetBIOS and *direct hosting* to provide the core file-sharing services needed from any network operating system. Direct hosting is a protocol that uses DNS for name resolution rather than NetBIOS. The default configuration is that both NetBIOS and direct hosting are enabled and are used simultaneously to resolve names for new connections with other machines.

Because it runs above the Transport Device Interface, NetBIOS can theoretically use any compatible protocols for its lower-level communications needs. Originally, operating systems prior to Windows 2000 used NetBEUI (the NetBIOS Extended User Interface) to carry NetBIOS traffic. NetBEUI is not routable, however, so when TCP/IP was proposed as an alternative, networking authorities began work on an open standard (later published as an RFC) to define the way in which NetBIOS services could be provided using the TCP/IP protocols. This standard became known as NetBIOS over TCP/IP, or NetBT.

The NetBT standard defines two kinds of NetBIOS services: session and datagram. Session services use TCP to provide fully reliable, connection-oriented message transmissions, while datagram services use UDP and are subject to the low overhead and relative unreliability of the protocol.

The network service requests generated by the NetBIOS interface use the NetBIOS computer names to refer to other systems. For TCP/IP to carry requests over the network, the NetBIOS names, like hostnames, must first be resolved into IP addresses.

Because NetBIOS names are resolved into IP addresses before transmission, you can use them in place of hostnames on internal networks. To connect to an intranet web server, for example, a user can specify the server's NetBIOS name in a web browser, in place of the traditional hostname. In the same way, you can use a hostname in a UNC path rather than a NetBIOS name.

Node Types

There are several different methods by which computers can register and resolve NetBIOS names into IP addresses on a Windows Server 2003/2000 network. The methods vary in their capabilities and their efficiency. A computer can use network broadcasts to locate the system with a specific NetBIOS name, it can consult a NetBIOS Name Server (NBNS) on the network (such as WINS), or it can use a lookup table in a locally stored LMHOSTS file.

The NetBT standard defines several node types that specify which methods a computer should use and the order in which it should use them. Node types are either explicitly assigned to clients by a DHCP server or inferred by the TCP/IP options activated in the client configuration. The node defined in the NetBT standard document is as follows:

- **B-node**   The client uses network broadcasts for both name registration and resolution.

- **P-node**   The client directs unicast communications to a NetBIOS Name Server for name registration and resolution.

- **M-node**   The client uses broadcasts for name registration; for name resolution, the client uses broadcasts first and, if unsuccessful, directs unicast communications to a NetBIOS name server.

- **H-node**   The client directs unicast communications to a NetBIOS name server for both name registration and resolution; if the NBNS is unavailable, the client uses broadcasts until an NBNS is contacted.

Originally, operating systems prior to Windows 2000 provided enhanced B-node service for NetBIOS name registration and resolution. The service was considered enhanced because if the broadcast method failed to resolve a name, the computer's LMHOSTS file was consulted as an alternative. This enabled users to contact systems on other network segments, as long as those systems had been manually entered into LMHOSTS.

Windows Server 2003 still includes WINS, a NetBIOS name server that can store the NetBIOS names, and IP addresses for an entire internetwork in its database, making that information available to users all over the enterprise. Downlevel computers that use WINS are described as being *enhanced H-nodes*. These computers first attempt to resolve NetBIOS names using WINS, revert to broadcasts if WINS is unsuccessful or unavailable, and then consult the LMHOSTS file if broadcasts fail to resolve the name.

NetBIOS Name Registration

Whenever a downlevel machine logs on to the network, the NetBT standard requires it to register its NetBIOS name, to ensure both that no other system is using a duplicate name and that the IP address is correct. If you move a workstation to another subnet and manually change its IP address, the registration process ensures that other systems and WINS servers are all aware of the change.

The name registration method used by the workstation depends on its node type. B-nodes and M-nodes use broadcast transmissions to register their names, whereas H-nodes and P-nodes send unicast messages directly to the WINS server. These two methods are discussed in the following sections. One of the two is used by every downlevel system that is connected to the network.

Broadcast Name Registration

B-node and M-node systems that use broadcasts to register NetBIOS names don't perform registration in the same sense as the other node types. The name is not entered into a table, nor is it stored on other network systems. Instead, the system uses broadcasts to "claim" its NetBIOS name and check to see if any other system is already using it.

The registration process begins as soon as the computer logs on to the network. It broadcasts a series of NAME REGISTRATION REQUEST messages containing its proposed NetBIOS name and its IP address, using the UDP protocol. If any other machine on the network is already using that name, that machine transmits a NEGATIVE NAME REGISTRATION RESPONSE message as a unicast to the new machine's IP address. This causes the registration request to be denied. The broadcasting system must select another name and try again.

If the computer receives no responses to repeated NAME REGISTRATION REQUEST packets during a specified time-out period, the computer transmits a NAME OVERWRITE DEMAND message, announcing that it has successfully registered its name. That workstation is now responsible for responding to any requests directed at that NetBIOS name by other systems.

Like all broadcasts, these name registration messages are limited to the local network segment only. This means that it is possible for computers on different network segments to be using the same NetBIOS name. And therein lies an obvious problem. Only careful supervision by the networks' administrators prevents name conflicts and misdirected packets. This danger, as well as the excessive network traffic caused by all those computers sending broadcasts, provides the motivation for establishing WINS as a name registration solution.

WINS Name Registration

A WINS client computer begins its name registration procedure by generating the same NAME REGISTRATION REQUEST packet used in the broadcast method. This time, however, the packet is sent as a unicast directly to the WINS server specified in the WINS Configuration tab of the TCP/IP Properties dialog. If no other system is using the name, the WINS server returns a POSITIVE NAME REGISTRATION RESPONSE to the sender and writes the NetBIOS name and IP address to its database.

If the WINS server finds that another system has already registered that NetBIOS name, the WINS server challenges that system to defend its registered name by sending it a NAME QUERY REQUEST message. If the apparent nameholder doesn't respond, or sends a NEGATIVE NAME QUERY RESPONSE, then the WINS server registers the name to the new system and sends it a POSITIVE NAME REGISTRATION RESPONSE. If the challenged system returns a POSITIVE NAME QUERY RESPONSE, then it has successfully defended its name against the challenge. WINS then sends a NEGATIVE NAME REGISTRATION RESPONSE message to the original system, informing it that its registration attempt has failed.

When WINS successfully registers a NetBIOS name, it assigns an expiration date to the registration in the form of a time-to-live (TTL) value. Each time the system logs on to the network, the value is renewed. Until that time period expires, any attempt to register that NetBIOS name will be challenged. If no logons occur in the specified time period, however, the NetBIOS name is released and will be reassigned by the WINS server on demand, with no challenge. If the name remains unused for a specified time period, it is declared extinct and it's purged from the WINS database.

Notice that this entire transaction is conducted using unicast messages among the computers. There are no broadcasts flooding the network, which is one of the primary advantages of WINS.

NetBIOS Name Resolution

If NetBIOS is enabled, all Windows systems maintain a cache of NetBIOS names that they have previously resolved. When a computer has to resolve a NetBIOS name, the cache is always consulted first. If the name is not found in the cache, the next resolution method used is determined by the system's node type:

- A non-WINS client will proceed to use broadcasts to resolve the name and then consult its local LMHOSTS file.

- A WINS client can use all of the available methods to resolve NetBIOS names. It begins by consulting the NetBIOS name cache, and then proceeds to the WINS server. Broadcasts are sent if the WINS server fails, and if that produces no positive result, then the LMHOSTS file is consulted.

The following sections elucidate the possible NetBIOS name resolution methods in the order that they would be used by a WINS-enabled computer.

The NetBIOS Name Cache   During each network session, a client system stores all the NetBIOS names that it has successfully resolved in a memory cache so that they can be reused. Because it is stored in memory, the cache is by far the fastest and most efficient name resolution method available. It is the first resource accessed by all node types when they must resolve a name. You can view the current contents of your system's NetBIOS name cache at any time by entering **nbtstat -c** at the command prompt.

Wins Name Resolution   WINS is designed to be an enterprise network solution for the registration and resolution of NetBIOS names. It is the only mechanism available to a Windows Server 2003/2000 network that automatically maintains a database of a network's NetBIOS names and their IP addresses. Unlike the broadcast method, WINS uses only unicast network transmissions, enabling it to function irrespective of the boundaries between network segments. WINS unicast messages greatly reduce the network traffic generated by NetBIOS name resolution activities.

WINS is supplied with Windows Server 2003, and it runs as a service. A WINS snap-in manager application is included in your administrative tools suite, so you can manage all the WINS servers on an enterprise network from a central location. For speed (and also for fault tolerance), you can run several WINS servers on an enterprise network. The WINS databases can be automatically replicated among the servers at preset intervals or at specified times of day. You can schedule WINS replication to occur over WAN links during low-traffic periods, providing a unified enterprise database for a worldwide network.

WINS also provides its clients with the ability to browse machines on other network segments, without requiring the services of master browsers on those networks. This enables users to communicate with other machines at remote sites without wasting WAN bandwidth on browser traffic.

When a WINS client needs a NetBIOS name resolved, it sends a unicast NAME QUERY REQUEST to the first WINS server specified in the WINS Address page of its TCP/IP Properties dialog. The WINS server then replies with a POSITIVE NAME QUERY RESPONSE containing the requested name and its IP address, or a NEGATIVE NAME QUERY RESPONSE, signifying that there is no record of the name in the database.

If there is any delay in responding with the appropriate name query response, the WINS server sends WACK (or WAIT FOR ACKNOWLEDGMENT RESPONSE) packets to the client to prevent the client from moving on to the next resolution method.

If the WINS server fails to resolve the name, whether by sending a negative response or no response at all, the client contacts its secondary WINS server and repeats the process. If the secondary server fails, an H-node system proceeds to use broadcasts to resolve the name. If the WINS servers have failed to respond at all to resolution requests, however, the client will continue attempting to contact them and revert back to WINS name resolution at the earliest possible opportunity.

Broadcast Name Resolution

When NetBIOS names are resolved using broadcasts, it is the responsibility of all registered systems to respond to requests specifying their names. A computer using broadcast name resolution generates the same NAME QUERY REQUEST packet as a WINS client, except the query is broadcast to all the systems on the local subnet. Each system receiving the packet must examine the name for which the IP address is requested.

If the packet contains an unrecognized name, it is silently discarded. A computer recognizing its own name in a query request, however, must respond to the sender with a POSITIVE NAME QUERY RESPONSE packet containing its IP address. This response is sent as a unicast.

The broadcast method of name resolution is attempted by all downlevel systems that are not WINS clients, after the name cache is consulted. If the name to be resolved belongs to a system on another network segment, the broadcasts cannot reach it, and the method will fail after the broadcast timeout period is reached.

LMHOSTS File

When an attempt to resolve a NetBIOS name using broadcasts fails, the next alternative is to consult the LMHOSTS file on the local hard drive. Non-WINS clients do this automatically. For a WINS client to use LMHOSTS after both the WINS and broadcasts methods fail, you must check the Enable LMHOSTS Lookup check box in the WINS Address page of the TCP/IP Properties dialog.

Use of the LMHOSTS file is not included in the NetBT standard as part of the node type definitions. Clients that use LMHOSTS are therefore referred to as enhanced B-node and H-node systems.

An LMHOSTS file is similar to the HOSTS file used for hostname resolution except that it lists NetBIOS names. It is located in the same directory as HOSTS, %SystemRoot%\ System32\drivers\etc, and Windows provides a sample file named lmhosts.sam for you to use as a model for your own file (it's a text file, so you can use Notepad to view it).

For a system that is not a WINS client, LMHOSTS is the only name resolution method available for computers on other network segments. You register the NetBIOS names in LMHOSTS by manually editing the file and adding an entry for each system you will be contacting. Each entry should contain the system's IP address at the left margin followed by the associated NetBIOS name on the same line, separated by a space.

Unlike HOSTS, LMHOSTS files can contain additional options that aid in the name resolution process:

- **#PRE**   The #PRE tag, when added to an entry in the LMHOSTS file, causes that entry to be preloaded into the NetBIOS name cache whenever the system boots. Adding your most commonly accessed systems to the LMHOSTS file speeds up name resolution, even for WINS clients. The #PRE tag should be appended to the end of an LMHOSTS entry, with one or more spaces separating it from the NetBIOS name.

- **#DOM:***domain name*   The #DOM tag is used to associate an LMHOSTS entry with the Windows NT domain specified in the *domain name* variable. This causes the computer in this entry to receive the domain browse list from the specified domain's Primary Domain Controller (PDC). That way, computers that don't use WINS can browse the computers in the domain that are located on other network segments. The #DOM tag, with its variable, is placed at the end of an LMHOSTS entry, after a space.

- **#INCLUDE** *path name*   The #INCLUDE tag enables you to access an LMHOSTS file stored in another location. Typically, you would use this feature to access a file on a network drive, where it could be used by other clients at the same time. This means you can update a single, centrally located LMHOSTS file instead of updating workstation copies individually. The tag, followed by the full UNC path to the file, should be placed on a line of its own in the workstation's LMHOSTS file, as shown here:

```
#INCLUDE \\server1\share\etc\lmhosts
```

 Make sure the NetBIOS name used in the UNC path can be resolved by using the #PRE tag if the machine is on a different network segment.

- **#BEGIN_ALTERNATE/#END_ALTERNATE**   These tags are used to provide fault tolerance for the #INCLUDE tag. By placing several #INCLUDE statements between #BEGIN_ALTERNATE and #END_ALTERNATE tags, as shown, the #INCLUDEs will be processed in order until one is successfully accessed. After one #INCLUDE is successfully read, those following are ignored, and processing continues at the next line after the #END_ALTERNATE statement.

```
#BEGIN_ALTERNATE#INCLUDE\\server1\share\etc\lmhosts#INCLUDE\\
server2\share\etc\lmhosts#END_ALTERNATE
```

- **\Oxhh**   This tag is used to specify special characters in NetBIOS names by their hexadecimal values. If an application requires a certain character in the NetBIOS name's 16th position, you can supply it by enclosing the name in quotation marks and using \Oxhh (replacing *hh* with the hexadecimal value of the character needed) in the appropriate position. The \Oxhh replaces only a single character of the NetBIOS name. Be sure to include the proper number of spaces between the quotation marks to account for the 16 positions of the name, as shown:

```
139.41.129.18  "application    \ox14"
```

When to Stop Relying on NetBIOS

Microsoft is striving for a purer TCP/IP implementation in Windows network environments. It no longer requires NetBIOS to be overlaid on TCP/IP for name resolution; DNS has won that title. Also, NetBIOS is only supported because of legacy systems and applications.

DNS is simply better—it's a more scalable and reliable solution for name resolution. It has stood the test of time, and the Internet is the best example of its success. To familiarize yourself more with DNS and how it affects your Windows environment, see Chapter 12.

As you can probably already imagine, the sooner you stop using NetBIOS, the better off your Windows environment will be. The first step is to upgrade all your downlevel clients to the current version of Windows.

Unfortunately, upgrading doesn't quite complete your task. You also have to verify whether you're running applications that are dependent upon NetBIOS. If you do have NetBIOS-based applications, and you still need them, check with the vendor to see if it has an upgraded version that doesn't rely on NetBIOS (hint: check your version of Microsoft Office). Once you disable NetBIOS, any applications that rely on it will either stop working properly or not work at all. The final step is to actually disable NetBIOS on all Windows Server 2003/XP/2000 machines. To do so, follow these steps:

1. From the Start | Settings menu, select Network Connections.
2. Right-click the Local Area Connection icon and select Properties.
3. Select Internet Protocol (TCP/IP) and click Properties.
4. On the Properties dialog, click the Advanced button to display the Advanced TCP/IP Settings dialog.
5. Move to the WINS tab, and select the option Disable NetBIOS over TCP/IP.
6. Click OK twice, and then click Close.

TCP/IP Tools

The Windows Server 2003/2000 implementations of the TCP/IP protocols include a collection of tools and utilities that help you monitor and troubleshoot TCP/IP activities.

Ping

Ping is the most basic and most commonly known TCP/IP utility. Use it to determine whether the TCP/IP stack on your computer is functioning, whether another computer on the network can be contacted, or whether a DNS server can resolve a hostname into an IP address.

Ping operates by sending Echo Request packets to the destination specified on the command line using the Internet Control Message Protocol. The destination system returns an ECHO RESPONSE packet for each request it receives, and ping displays the size of each packet sent (in bytes), the round-trip time (in milliseconds), and the packet's time-to-live value.

The syntax for ping is

ping [**-t**] [**-a**] [**-n** *Count*] [**-l** *Size*] [**-f**] [**-i** *TTL*] [**-v** *TOS*] [**-r** *Count*] [**-s** *Count*] [{**-j** *HostList* | **-k** *HostList*}] [**-w** *Timeout*] [*TargetName*]

where:

-t tells ping to continue sending Echo Request messages to the destination until you stop the process. To interrupt the process and display statistics, press CTRL-BREAK. To interrupt and quit ping, press CTRL-C.

-a specifies reverse name resolution on the destination IP address.

-n *Count* specifies the number of Echo Request messages ping should send (the default is 4).

-l *Size* is the length, in bytes, of the Data field in the Echo Request messages sent. The default is 32. The maximum *Size* is 65,527.

-f sends Echo Request messages with the Don't Fragment flag in the IP header set to 1. This means the Echo Request message cannot be fragmented by routers that are in the path to the destination. Use this parameter when you're troubleshooting Path Maximum Transmission Unit (PMTU) problems.

-i *TTL* specifies the value of the TTL field in the IP header for Echo Request messages sent. The value defaults to the default TTL value for the host. For Windows Server 2003 hosts, this is usually 128. (The maximum *TTL* is 255.)

-v *TOS* specifies the value of the Type of Service (TOS) field in the IP header for Echo Request messages sent. The default is 0. (Specify the *TOS* value as a decimal value between 0 and 255.)

-r *Count* specifies that the Record Route option in the IP header is used to record the path taken by the Echo Request message and corresponding Echo Reply message. Each hop in the path uses an entry in the Record Route option. This works best if you specify a *Count* that is equal to or larger than the number of hops between the source and destination. (*Count* must be a number between 1 and 9.)

-s *Count* specifies that the Internet Timestamp option in the IP header is used to record the time of arrival for the Echo Request message and corresponding Echo Reply message for each hop. (*Count* must be a number between 1 and 4.)

-j *HostList* specifies that the Echo Request messages use the Loose Source Route option in the IP header with the set of intermediate destinations specified in *HostList*. Loose source routing operates with successive intermediate destinations, separated by one or more routers. The maximum number of addresses or names in the host list is nine. The host list is a series of IP addresses separated by spaces.

-k *HostList* specifies that the Echo Request messages use the Strict Source Route option in the IP header with the set of intermediate destinations specified in *HostList*. With strict source routing, each successive destination must be directly reachable (it must be a neighbor on an interface of the router). The maximum number of addresses or names in the host list is nine. The host list is a series of IP addresses separated by spaces.

-w *Timeout* specifies the amount of time, in milliseconds, to wait for the Echo Reply message that corresponds to a given Echo Request message to be received. If the Echo Reply message is not received within the time-out, the "Request timed out" error message is displayed. The default time-out is 4000 (4 seconds).

TargetName specifies the destination, either an IP address or a hostname.

Tracert

The *tracert* program, known as *traceroute* on UNIX systems, identifies the route taken by IP datagrams to reach a specified destination. Apart from being entertaining when you use it to trace Internet connections (especially connections that cross an ocean or a continent), it's useful for troubleshooting routing problems. When you have a multihomed Windows system, tracert is a sure way of determining which network the system is using to reach a specified destination.

Using the same ICMP packets as ping, tracert sends successive Echo Request messages to the destination address with incrementing time-to-live (TTL) values. Because each intermediate system that a packet travels through reduces the TTL value by one, each request times out one hop farther along the route to the destination.

As each successive packet times out, it returns a message to the source containing the address of the gateway where the TTL value reached zero. These addresses are resolved and displayed on the host computer, along with the time interval for each hop.

When used with Internet addresses, tracert provides a fascinating insight into the international telecommunications network. Because Windows resolves the IP addresses of each gateway, you can often identify the sites through which your packets are passing on the way to their destination. Trace the route from your United States system to a web server in Europe, and you can see from the elapsed times the point at which your signal crosses the ocean.

The syntax for tracert is

tracert [**-d**] [**-h** *MaximumHops*] [**-j** *HostList*] [**-w** *Timeout*] [*TargetName*]

where:

-d stops tracert from attempting to resolve the IP addresses of intermediate routers, which frequently speeds up the display of results.

-h *MaximumHops* specifies the maximum number of hops in the path to search for the target destination. (The default is 30 hops.)

-j *HostList* specifies that Echo Request messages use the Loose Source Route option in the IP header with the set of intermediate destinations specified in *HostList*. (See the discussion of the same parameter in the syntax for ping, in the previous section.)

-w *Timeout* specifies the amount of time (in milliseconds) to wait for the ICMP Time Exceeded or Echo Reply message corresponding to a given Echo Request message to be received. If not received within the time-out, an asterisk (*) is displayed. The default time-out is 4000 (4 seconds).

TargetName specifies the destination, either an IP address or a hostname.

Pathping

Pathping is the same as tracert, except it works only within your own enterprise. You can use this command to gain information about network latency and network loss at intermediate hops between a network source and destination. The syntax is

pathping [-n] [-h *MaximumHops*] [-g *HostList*] [-p *Period*] [-q *NumQueries* [-w *Timeout*] [-T] [-R] [*TargetName*]

where:

-n stops pathping from attempting to resolve the IP addresses of intermediate routers to their names, which frequently speeds up the display of results.

-h *MaximumHops* specifies the maximum number of hops in the path to search for the target destination. (The default is 30 hops.)

-g *HostList* specifies that the Echo Request messages use the Loose Source Route option in the IP header with the set of intermediate destinations specified in *HostList*. (See the discussion of Loose Source Route in the previous sections.)

-p *Period* is the number of milliseconds to wait between consecutive pings. The default is 250 milliseconds (1/4 second).

-q *NumQueries* sets the number of Echo Request messages sent to each router in the path. The default is 100 queries.

-w *Timeout* is the number of milliseconds to wait for each reply. The default is 3000 milliseconds (3 seconds).

-T attaches a layer-2 priority tag (for example, 802.1p) to the Echo Request messages that it sends to each of the network devices along the route. This is a way to identify network devices that don't have layer-2 priority capability. Mostly, you'll use this parameter to test for Quality of Service (QoS) connectivity.

-R specifies whether each network device along the route supports the Resource Reservation Protocol (RSVP), which allows the host computer to reserve a specified amount of bandwidth for a data stream. This parameter is also used to test for QoS connectivity.

TargetName is the destination, an IP address or a hostname.

Ipconfig

Ipconfig is a command-line utility that displays the current IP configuration settings for your computer. When you use ipconfig with the /all switch, it displays the current IP configuration settings for each of the network adapters installed in your computer. This is particularly useful on DHCP client systems, where there is no other way to determine this information without access to the DHCP Manager program on the server. The syntax is

> **ipconfig [/all] [/renew** [*Adapter*]] **[/release** [*Adapter*]] **[/flushdns] [/displaydns]**
> **[/registerdns] [/showclassid** *Adapter*] **[/setclassid** *Adapter* [*ClassID*]]]

where:

/all displays the full TCP/IP configuration for all adapters. If omitted, ipconfig displays only the IP address, subnet mask, and default gateway values for each adapter. An adapter can be a physical interface (such as a NIC) or a logical interface (such as a dial-up connection).

/renew [*Adapter*] renews DHCP configuration for all adapters (if an adapter is not specified) or for a specific adapter if the *Adapter* parameter is included. This parameter is only available if you have configured the system to obtain an IP address automatically. (To specify an adapter name, type the adapter name that appears when you use ipconfig without parameters.)

/release [*Adapter*] sends a DHCPRELEASE message to the DHCP server to release the current DHCP configuration and discard the IP address configuration for either all adapters (if an adapter is not specified) or for a specific adapter if the *Adapter* parameter is included. This parameter disables TCP/IP for adapters configured to obtain an IP address automatically.

/flushdns flushes and resets the contents of the DNS client resolver cache. This is useful if you're troubleshooting problems with DNS.

/displaydns displays the contents of the DNS client resolver cache, which includes both entries preloaded from the local HOSTS file and any recently obtained resource records for name queries resolved by the computer.

/registerdns performs a manual dynamic registration for the DNS names and IP addresses that are configured on the computer. This parameter is useful for troubleshooting a failed DNS name registration. It can also be used to resolve a dynamic update problem between a client and the DNS server without the need to reboot the client.

/showclassid *Adapter* shows the DHCP class ID for a specified adapter (or all adapters if you substitute an asterisk, *, for *Adapter*).

/setclassid *Adapter* [*ClassID*] configures the DHCP class ID for a specified adapter (or for all adapters if you substitute an asterisk, *, for *Adapter*).

See Chapter 11 for more information about using classid.

Netstat

Use netstat to display the TCP/IP connections currently in use by the computer, as well as communications statistics for the network interface and for the IP, TCP, and UDP protocols. The syntax is

netstat [**-a**] [**-e**] [**-n**] [**-o**] [**-p** *protocol*] [**-r**] [**-s**] [*interval*]

where:

-a lists all active TCP connections, along with the TCP and UDP ports on which the computer is listening.

-e shows Ethernet statistics, such as the number of bytes and packets sent and received (you can combine the -e parameter with the -s parameter).

-n lists active TCP connections, with addresses and port numbers shown numerically (no attempt is made to determine names).

-o lists active TCP connections and includes the process ID (PID) for each connection. You can find the application based on the PID on the Processes tab in Task Manager. (This parameter can be combined with -a, -n, and -p.)

-p *protocol* displays connections for the specified *protocol* (tcp or udp). If you combine this parameter with the -s parameter, the protocol can be tcp, udp, icmp, or ip.

-s shows statistics by protocol. By default, statistics are shown for the tcp, udp, icmp, and ip protocols.

-r shows the contents of the IP routing table.

interval redisplays the selected information every *interval* seconds. Press CTRL-C to stop the action.

Caution *You cannot substitute a forward slash for the hyphen when entering parameters.*

ARP

The ARP utility displays the current contents of the system's Address Resolution Protocol cache. This cache contains the MAC addresses and IP addresses of the machines on your local network that have recently been involved in TCP/IP communications. The syntax is

arp [**-a** [*InetAddr*] [**-N** *IfaceAddr*]] [**-g** [*InetAddr*] [**-N** *IfaceAddr*]] [**-d** *InetAddr* [*IfaceAddr*]] [**-s** *InetAddr EtherAddr* [*IfaceAddr*]]

where:

-a [*InetAddr*] [**-N** *IfaceAddr*] lists current ARP cache tables for all interfaces. To display the ARP cache entry for a specific IP address, use **arp -a** with the *InetAddr* parameter (the IP address). To display the ARP cache table for a specific interface, use the **-N** *IfaceAddr* parameter, where *IfaceAddr* is the IP address assigned to the interface.

 The -N parameter is case-sensitive.

-g [*InetAddr*] [**-N** *IfaceAddr*] is the same as **-a**.

-d *InetAddr* [*IfaceAddr*] deletes an entry with a specific IP address, where *InetAddr* is the IP address. To delete an entry in a table for a specific interface, use the *IfaceAddr* parameter, where *IfaceAddr* is the IP address assigned to the interface. To delete all entries, use an asterisk (*) instead of *InetAddr*.

-s *InetAddr EtherAddr* [*IfaceAddr*] adds a static entry to the ARP cache that resolves *InetAddr* to *EtherAddr*.

The cache contains entries for the system that your workstation has contacted, as well as others, because the reply packets generated by computers in response to ARP requests are transmitted as broadcasts. This enables all the systems on a network to benefit from one machine's request.

The ARP cache is purged periodically to ensure that the data remains current. However, using the -s parameter to add entries to the ARP table makes those entries permanent.

Route

Your Windows Server 2003 system maintains a table that contains a record of the routing information received from other systems, in the form of ICMP Redirect packets. You can use the route command to view or manipulate network routing tables. For example, you could specify that a gateway other than the default be used when transmitting to a specific destination. The syntax is

route [**-f**] [**-p**] [*Command* [*Destination*] [**mask** *Netmask*] [*Gateway*] [**metric** *Metric*]] [**if** *Interface*]]

where:

-f clears the routing table of all entries that are not in the following categories:

■ Host routes (routes with a netmask of 255.255.255.255)

■ The loopback network route (routes with a destination of 127.0.0.0 and a netmask of 255.0.0.0)

■ Multicast routes (routes with a destination of 224.0.0.0 and a netmask of 240.0.0.0)

Note *If you use the -f parameter along with one of the commands (such as add, change, or delete), the table is automatically cleared before the command runs.*

-p is used with a *command* parameter, as follows:

■ Use -p with the add command to add the specified route to the registry. The registry entry initializes the IP routing table when the TCP/IP protocol is started. (By default, added routes are not persistent.)

■ Use -p with the print command to display a list of persistent routes.

■ Persistent routes are stored in the registry location in the subkey HKEY_LOCAL_MACHINE\SYSTEM\CurrentControlSet\Services\Tcpip\ Parameters\PersistentRoutes.

Command specifies one of the following commands:

■ **add**   Adds a route
■ **change**   Modifies an existing route
■ **delete**   Removes a route
■ **print**   Prints a route

Destination specifies the network destination of the route. This is an IP network address (where the host bits of the network address are set to 0), an IP address for a host route, or 0.0.0.0 for the default route.

mask *Netmask* specifies the netmask (subnet mask) associated with the network destination. The subnet mask can be the appropriate subnet mask for an IP network address, 255.255.255.255 for a host route, or 0.0.0.0 for the default route.

Gateway specifies the forwarding IP address over which the set of addresses defined by the network destination and subnet mask are reached (it's the next hop).

Note *For local subnet routes, the gateway address is the IP address assigned to the interface attached to the subnet. For remote routes (crossing one or more routers), the gateway address is a directly reachable IP address that is assigned to a neighboring router.*

metric *Metric* is an integer cost metric (ranging from 1 to 9999) for the route. This is used when choosing among multiple routes in the routing table (the system chooses the route with the lowest metric).

The metric can be the number of hops, the speed of the path, path reliability, path throughput, or administrative properties.

if *Interface* specifies the interface index for the interface over which the destination can be reached. If omitted, the interface is determined from the gateway address.

You can see the list of interfaces and their corresponding interface indexes by entering **route print**.

If you're using Routing and Remote Access, you should only use the RRAS snap-in to manipulate routes.

Nbtstat

Use the nbtstat command to display statistics about the NetBT activity on a computer. With nbtstat, you can display the contents of the NetBIOS name cache, list the current NetBT sessions in progress, show protocol statistics at regular intervals, and even reload the cache by processing the LMHOSTS file (you can make changes to the file that take effect immediately).

The syntax is

nbtstat [-a *RemoteName*] [**-A** *IPAddress*] [**-c**] [**-n**] [**-r**] [**-R**] [**-RR**] [**-s**] [**-S**] [*Interval*]

where:

-a *RemoteName* lists the NetBIOS name table of a remote computer (use the NetBIOS computer name for *RemoteName*).

-A *IPAddress* shows the NetBIOS name table of a remote computer, using the remote computer's IP address.

-c shows the contents of the NetBIOS name cache, the table of NetBIOS names and their resolved IP addresses.

-n shows the NetBIOS name table of the local computer. The status Registered means the name is registered either by broadcast or with a WINS server.

-r shows NetBIOS name resolution statistics. On a Windows Server 2003/XP Professional computer that is configured to use WINS, this parameter returns the number of names that have been resolved and registered using broadcast and WINS.

-R removes the contents of the NetBIOS name cache and then reloads the #PRE-tagged entries from the LMHOSTS file.

-RR releases NetBIOS names and then refreshes the names that are registered by the local computer.

-s shows NetBIOS client and server sessions, and attempts to convert the destination IP address to a name.

-S shows NetBIOS client and server sessions, listing the remote computers by destination IP address only.

Interval redisplays your selected statistics every *Interval* (in seconds). Press CTRL-C to stop the action.

A great deal of the information you've absorbed about TCP/IP in this chapter is useless unless you also understand the way you'll use TCP/IP features in your enterprise: DHCP and DNS. The following chapters contain information about those important tools.

Chapter 11

DHCP and IP Addressing

W̲e discussed the concepts for how to apply IP addressing in your network environment in Chapter 10. In this chapter we will go over *public* and *private* *IP addresses*. We will also discuss DHCP installation and configuration.

Public IP Addresses

Any computer that is directly connected to the Internet is assigned a public IP address. A public IP address is one that is routable through the Internet using different classes of addresses that make up a network ID and a node address (discussed in Chapter 10). The *Local Internet Registry* (*LIR*), *National Internet Registry* (*NIR*), or *Regional Internet Registry* (*RIR*) assigns public IP addresses to Internet Service Providers. Following is a list of available RIRs:

- **APNIC**   www.apnic.net (Asia/Pacific Region)
- **ARIN**   www.arin.net (Americas and sub-Sahara Africa)
- **LACNIC**   www.lacnic.net/en/index.html (Latin America and some Caribbean Islands)
- **RIPE NCC**   www.ripe.net (Europe, Middle East, Central Asia, and African countries north of the equator)

As the Internet continues to grow, public IPv4 address availability decreases rapidly. Proxy servers and several protocols used on routers such as *Network Address Translation* (*NAT*) and *Port Address Translation* (*PAT*) were created to enable multiple nodes on a network that use private addresses to use one public IP address. NAT and PAT do this by appending a port number to the IP address on incoming and outgoing packets. The routers then keep track of the port numbers assigned to destinations, and the workstation or device that is the receiver on the inside network. These protocols allow hundreds of workstations in one network to simultaneously access the Internet using the same public IP address.

From the outside world every PC in your network appears to use the same IP address; this offers an additional layer of security and anonymity when accessing Internet servers that require certain ports to have a one-to-one address mapping. Some examples are Simple Mail Transfer Protocol (SMTP), Post Office Protocol version 3 (POP3) server, and FTP servers, all of which can be statically mapped with NAT or PAT using the same address as your other nodes on the network.

For example, let's say you have two servers on the inside network. One is a Windows Server 2003 providing FTP (Ports 20 and 21) services; it is assigned the private IP address 10.1.2.1. Another Windows 2003 server running Exchange 2003 providing SMTP (Port 25) and POP3 (Port 110) mail services is assigned the address 10.1.2.2. Using NAT and the single routable public address 207.212.78.108, anything coming in for ports 20 and 21 is sent to the FTP server, and anything coming in for ports 25 and 110 is sent to the server running Exchange 2003. Every other node on the network can use other port numbers utilizing the same IP address. Look at all the public IP addresses we just saved—even in a network of ten PCs and two servers.

Private IP Addresses

Private IP addresses are used on the inside network and assigned at your discretion. The addresses are nonroutable on the Internet. Depending on the number of locations, workstations, and devices needing IP addresses in your network, there are three different address ranges reserved for Private IP addresses:

- **Class A 10.0.0.0 to 10.255.255.255**   For large enterprises
- **Class B 172.16.0.0 to 172.31.255.255**   For medium enterprises
- **Class C 192.68.0.0 to 192.68.255.255**   For smaller enterprises

Understanding DHCP

TCP/IP users and administrators can avoid manually configuring IP addresses, the subnet mask, DNS server addresses, WINs server addresses, and other TCP/IP addressing chores by using a Dynamic Host Configuration Protocol (DHCP) server to assign the configuration settings automatically.

To resolve the problem of IP address assignment and administration on a large scale, Microsoft worked with other networking professionals to create the Dynamic Host Configuration Protocol. DHCP is an open standard defined in the IETF's Requests for Comments 2132. Other manufacturers market DHCP servers, but Microsoft includes its DHCP server in the Windows Server 2003 package.

DHCP resolves some of the biggest problems inherent in TCP/IP, as it was originally conceived. It eliminates the chore of individually configuring every workstation and makes the assignment of duplicate IP addresses virtually impossible. DHCP is recommended on all Windows 2003 networks, but only when it is used on all of the network's systems.

You can encounter problems when IP addressing *overlaps*, meaning the same address is assigned to multiple devices in a mixed environment. A mixed environment is created when some computers use DHCP and others use IP addresses manually assigned. Even when you have systems that must be assigned a specific IP address, assign it using DHCP for efficient record keeping.

Origins of DHCP

DHCP has its origins in BOOTP, which is a legacy protocol designed for use with diskless workstations. A BOOTP server stored IP addresses and other configuration settings for workstations, keyed according to the MAC address hard-coded into each workstation's network interface adapter. As each computer on the network booted, its TCP/IP settings would be delivered to it by the server. Once the TCP/IP stack was operational, BOOTP would transfer an executable operating system boot file to the workstation using TFTP (the Trivial File Transfer Protocol, a UDP version of FTP); then the workstation would be ready for use.

BOOTP resolved one of TCP/IP's basic problems by eliminating the need for each workstation to be manually configured by an administrator or an end user. However, it did not really alleviate the administrative problem of IP address assignment because it provided only a central location for the storage of the configuration settings. The IP settings for each individual workstation still had to be specified by the administrator and manually stored on the server. If duplicate IP addresses were accidentally entered into the configurations of two different machines, BOOTP could do nothing to detect, prevent, or remedy the situation.

IP Address Allocation

DHCP was designed to be an improvement over BOOTP. It retains the best aspects of its predecessor, which are the storage and automatic delivery of TCP/IP configuration data, and expands to create an even better solution.

DHCP can assign IP addresses to its clients in three different ways:

- **Manual allocation**   Essentially the equivalent of the BOOTP service; IP addresses and other configuration settings are individually entered by the administrator, stored on the server, and delivered to predetermined clients.

- **Automatic allocation**   This is what we call using a *static pool*. As a DHCP client workstation boots on the network for the first time, the DHCP server assigns it an IP address and other configuration settings from a pool of available addresses that the administrator has configured the server to use; these become the permanent settings for the machine. This is called *mapping a reservation*.

- **Dynamic allocation**   This is the same as automatic allocation, except that the TCP/IP settings are not permanently assigned; they are only leased for a specified amount of time. The lease must be periodically renewed through (automatic) negotiations between the DHCP client and the server.

These three methods can be used simultaneously, providing all the options network administrators should require. Manual allocation is a necessary holdover from BOOTP because often certain computers on the network must have a particular IP address permanently assigned, such as World Wide Web and FTP servers. The advantages to using DHCP for such computers (rather than simply manually configuring them) are that all IP address information for the entire network can be stored in one place, and DHCP will prevent any other DHCP client from using the addresses that have been manually allocated.

A network that rarely changes can use DHCP to automatically allocate IP addresses, creating a permanent network configuration. If a computer is moved from one subnet to another, it will automatically be assigned a new IP address for that subnet; however, the address on the old subnet will remain allocated until the administrator manually deletes the assignments from the DHCP table.

When a computer is dynamically allocated an IP address, its lease must be renewed periodically or it will expire, causing the address to be returned to the pool of available addresses. The lease renewal process is automatic and invisible to the user—unless it fails. If the computer is moved to a different subnet, it is assigned an appropriate IP address for its new location. The old address assignment is returned to the pool when its lease expires.

Thus, dynamic allocation resolved the problem of the "roving user," the portable computers that can be logged onto the network from different offices, different buildings, or even different cities.

Other DHCP Capabilities

The controlled allocation of IP addresses clearly is DHCP's primary strength, but an IP address alone is not sufficient to fully configure a client's TCP/IP stack. DHCP also can supply a client with settings for more than 50 other TCP/IP-related parameters, many of which are intended for use with only non-Microsoft clients.

A Windows 2003 or down-level DHCP client can be furnished with any or all of the following configuration parameters (these are the most common parameters passed to clients):

- **IP address**   A 32-bit dotted with 4 octets decimal address used to identify a particular host on an IP network.

- **Subnet mask**   A 32-bit dotted decimal value with 4 octets used to differentiate the network address bits of an IP address from the host address bits.

- **Router**   The IP addresses of the default gateway that a client will use to access remote networks (accessed in the order in which they are listed).

- **DNS servers**   The IP addresses of the DNS servers that will be used by a client to resolve Internet host names into IP addresses (accessed in the order in which they are listed).

- **Domain name**   The name of the client's domain.

- **WINS/NBNS (Windows Internet Naming System/ NetBIOS Name Server) addresses**   The IP addresses of the WINS servers that the client will use for NetBIOS name registration and resolution services.

- **WINS/NBT (Windows Internet Naming System/NetBIOS over TCP/IP) node type**   A code used to specify which name resolution techniques will be used by the client, and in what order.

- **NetBIOS scope ID**   A character string used to identify a group of NetBIOS machines that can communicate only with each other. (This is one to avoid; it almost always causes more problems than it's worth.)

There are several other parameters that are less commonly used than those listed above; nonetheless they might be useful to clients, depending on the environment. To name a few:

- Cookie servers
- LPR servers

- Impress servers
- Resource location servers
- Host name

New Features for DHCP in Windows Server 2003

If you are upgrading from Windows NT Server 4.0, the following is a list of improvements made to DHCP. (All of these improvements were included in Windows 2000.)

- Integration of DHCP with DNS
- Enhanced monitoring and reporting
- Support for vendor-specific and user-class options
- Multicast address allocation
- Detecting and preventing unauthorized DHCP servers
- AD integration
- Support for Windows 2000 Clustering Service
- Automatic client configuration

Automatic Client Configuration

Another noteworthy enhancement to Windows Server 2003's DHCP involves the DHCP client. Windows 2000 and Windows 98 clients configured to use DHCP can automatically configure themselves with an IP address and subnet mask if a DHCP server can't be contacted. The procedure that the DHCP client service goes through before actually assigning itself this information depends on whether a DHCP server has been contacted previously.

After a fresh installation attempt, the DHCP client service attempts to find a DHCP server to get all the TCP/IP information necessary to function on the network. If the search fails, the client automatically configures itself with a Class B IP address and subnet mask. More specifically, it assigns itself with an IP address within the 169.254.0.0 to 169.254.255.255 address range with a subnet mask of 255.255.0.0. It then announces this address to the world to see whether another computer already has taken this address. The client periodically tries to contact a DHCP server until it's successful (the default is every five minutes).

The last procedure involves a client that has previously contacted and received TCP/IP information from a DHCP server. In this case, the client is contacting the DHCP server to renew a lease. If the client fails to contact the DHCP server, it pings its assigned default gateway. When the ping is successful, the client treats the failed communication with the DHCP server as a temporary setback and continues to use the lease it has. For instance, the DHCP server could be down for maintenance or might have connectivity problems of its own. The client also continues to try to contact the DHCP server for a lease renewal. Only when the ping fails will the client automatically configure itself with the aforementioned Class B IP address.

Disabling Automatic Client Configuration

Automatic client configuration definitely is an improvement to the DHCP service; however, it does have its drawbacks. For example, would a client be able to contact other machines with the Class B IP address? In most cases the answer is no, because of the subnet differences. The client would be able to contact only those computers on the same subnet. Also, the client is unable to automatically configure itself with a default gateway or DNS server IP address that would help it communicate. Therefore, this feature generally is useful only in very small environments.

If you feel this feature does not bring added benefit to your environment, you have the option to disable it. To disable automatic client configuration on a Windows 2000/XP computer, do the following:

1. From the Start | Run menu, type **regedit** to start the Registry editor as shown in Figure 11-1.

   ```
   Open HKEY_LOCAL_MACHINE\SYSTEM\CurrentControlSet\Services\Tcpip\Parameters\
   ```

2. Add the value IPAutoconfigurationEnabled and set it to 0.

For more information see http://www.microsoft.com/technet/treeview/default.asp?url=/technet/prodtechnol/windowsserver2003/proddocs/datacenter/sag_TCPIP_pro_DisableAutoConfiguration.asp

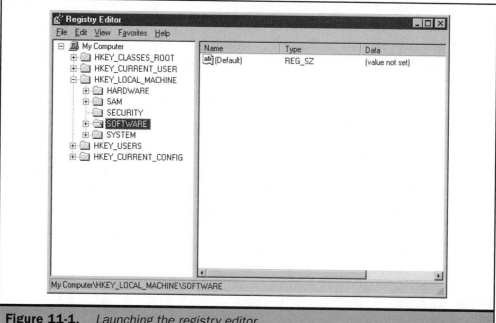

Figure 11-1.   *Launching the registry editor*

Detecting and Preventing Unauthorized DHCP Servers

The DHCP service is a tremendous improvement over manually configuring IP addresses and other TCP/IP-related settings for every computer on the network. However, network administration can get pretty hairy when you have unauthorized DHCP servers contending with authorized DHCP servers over rights for who gets to pass information to clients. For instance, a user decides to install the DHCP Server service on his/her computer to pass information to a select few computers in a lab. As it turns out, what was intended to be a local DHCP server actually services other clients on the network. The change might render the clients useless.

Most of the time these situations are accidental, but they affect the network nonetheless. Previous versions of DHCP weren't able to adequately cope with such problems. Administrators had to keep on their toes to ensure that only the DHCP Servers they created or managed were allowed on the network.

One of the many enhancements to DHCP is the capability to detect and prevent unauthorized DHCP servers on the network. Each DHCP Server installation must go through an authorization step by either checking with AD or being led by someone with administrative privileges. Otherwise, the DHCP Server is not allowed to service clients.

AD can store a list of authorized DHCP servers so that when a new DHCP server starts up, it tries to find out whether it's authorized. If it is authorized, it sends out DHCPINFORM messages to find out whether it is authorized in other directory services as well. If the DHCP server isn't authorized but needs to be, you must do the following:

1. Within the DHCP snap-in, select the unauthorized DHCP server in the left pane.

2. Select Authorize from the Action menu.

3. You might have to wait several minutes before the authorization process finishes. If you're impatient like I am, you might want to hit F5 to refresh the DHCP snap-in window until you've been authorized.

DHCP Communications

When a Windows 2000/XP or down-level client is configured to use DHCP to obtain its TCP/IP configuration settings, it undergoes a negotiation process with a DHCP server that results in a lease arrangement. The communications with the server are carried out using the protocol defined in the DHCP Request for Comment, published by the Internet Engineering Task Force (IETF).

The actual Dynamic Host Configuration Protocol consists of a single packet type that is used for all DHCP client/server communications. Carried by the User Datagram Protocol (UDP), the packet header contains a DHCP Message Type field that identifies the function of that packet from among the choices shown in Table 11-1.

As detailed in the following sections the various message types communicate among DHCP servers and clients to allot IP addresses and periodically renew them.

Value	Message Type	Purpose
1	DHCPDISCOVER	Used by clients to locate DHCP servers
2	DHCPOFFER	Used by servers to offer IP addresses to clients
3	DHCPREQUEST	Used by clients to request a specific IP address
4	DHCPDECLINE	Used by clients to reject an offered IP address
5	DHCPACK	Used by servers to acknowledge a client's acceptance of an IP address
6	DHCPNAK	Used by servers to reject a client's acceptance of an IP address
7	DHCPRELEASE	Used by clients to terminate the lease of an IP address

Table 11-1.   *Dynamic Host Configuration Protocol*

Lease Negotiations

Before a lease has been negotiated, a potential DHCP client is operating a TCP/IP stack without an IP address, so its communication capabilities are obviously limited. However, it is able to broadcast a DHCPDISCOVER message hoping to locate a DHCP server. Broadcasts are normally limited to the local network segment but being an open standard, DHCP is supported by many of the routers on the market, enabling them to propagate DHCP broadcasts across network boundaries. In this way, a single DHCP server can maintain clients on multiple network segments.

The DHCPDISCOVER packet contains the MAC address of the workstation, enabling DHCP servers to reply using unicasts rather than broadcasts. All DHCP servers receiving the broadcast are obliged to reply to the client with a DHCPOFFER packet containing an IP address and other configuration settings for the client's consideration. If the client receives multiple DHCPOFFER packets, it selects one and broadcasts a DHCPREQUEST containing the IP address and settings that it intends to accept. This message is broadcast both to inform the selected server of its acceptance and to notify the other servers that their offers are being rejected.

During this period, the IP address offered by the server is not yet fully committed to that client. Under certain circumstances, those same settings might be offered to another potential client in the interim. However, upon receiving a DHCPREQUEST, the server commits the offered settings to the client, writing them to its database and creating a *bound client*. It then sends a DHCPACK packet to the client, informing it of its acknowledgment. The exchanges involved in a successful lease negotiation are shown in the following illustration. If for any reason the lease cannot be finalized, the server sends a DHCPNACK packet, and the client begins the entire process again with a new DHCPDISCOVER packet.

On receipt of the DHCPACK, the client performs a final check of the offered IP address using the Address Resolution Protocol to look for a duplicate address on the network. If one is found, the client sends a DHCPDECLINE packet to the server, nullifying the entire transaction. Otherwise, the settings are used to configure the TCP/IP stack and a network logon can commence.

Lease Renewal

After a lease has been negotiated, the DHCP client has the right to utilize the settings allocated to it for a period of time that is configured at the server. The default lease period is eight days. Each time the workstation logs onto the network, it renews the lease by broadcasting a DHCPREQUEST message containing the *lease identification cookie*, the combination of the workstation's MAC address and IP address that uniquely identifies the lease to the server.

Under normal conditions, the server replies with a DHCPACK message as before. If the server detects that the client is on a different subnet from the one where the lease was negotiated, it will issue a DHCPNACK message, terminating the lease and forcing a renegotiation. If the client receives no response to the request after ten attempts, it will broadcast a DHCPDISCOVER in the hope of negotiating a new lease.

If the client reaches the time at which 50 percent of its current lease period has expired, it moves from the *bound* state to the *renewing* state. DHCPREQUEST messages then are sent as unicasts to the server holding the lease rather than broadcasts. At 87.5 percent of the lease period, the client moves into the *rebinding* state, in which it begins broadcasting DHCPREQUEST messages again, soliciting a response from any DHCP server. If the entire lease period expires without a response from a DHCP server, the client enters the *unbound* state, and it goes through the process of automatically configuring itself with a Class B IP address and subnet mask.

Running the Microsoft DHCP Server

Microsoft's DHCP server consists of an application for managing, tracking, and allocating TCP/IP configuration settings and a protocol for delivering those settings to DHCP clients. The DHCP server that ships with Windows 2000 Server runs as a service after being installed through the Local Area Connections Properties page or through the Add/Remove Programs applet in the Control Panel. Also included is the DHCP snap-in, an application that network administrators use to define the configuration settings to be furnished to DHCP clients.

As mentioned in previous chapters a new tool for Windows Server 2003 administrators is the Manage Your Server Wizard. We will talk about how to install DHCP with the Manage Your Server Wizard, and also through the Add/Remove Windows Components in the control panel.

To install a DHCP Server with the Manage Your Server Wizard, do the following:

1. Open the Manage Your Server Wizard (which automatically launches on startup) from the administrative tools menu.
2. Select Add or remove a role. The wizard will make sure your network connection is functioning properly; select Next.
3. Select DHCP server on the Server Role Menu.

From there, the wizard launches the New Scope Wizard.
To install DHCP server, through the control panel do the following:

1. Double-click the Add/Remove Programs applet within the Control Panel.
2. Select Add/Remove Windows Components in the Add/Remove Programs window as shown in Figure 11-2.
3. Select Networking Services in the Windows Components Wizard window and click the Details button.
4. Check the box beside Dynamic Host Configuration Protocol (DHCP) as shown in Figure 11-3, and click OK.
5. Click Next in the Windows Components Wizard window to install the service.
6. Click Finish to complete the installation. You are ready to configure the DHCP server.

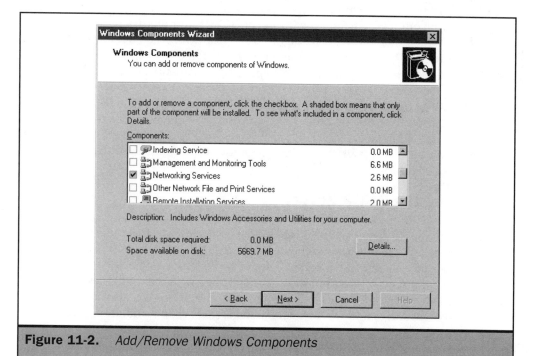

Figure 11-2. *Add/Remove Windows Components*

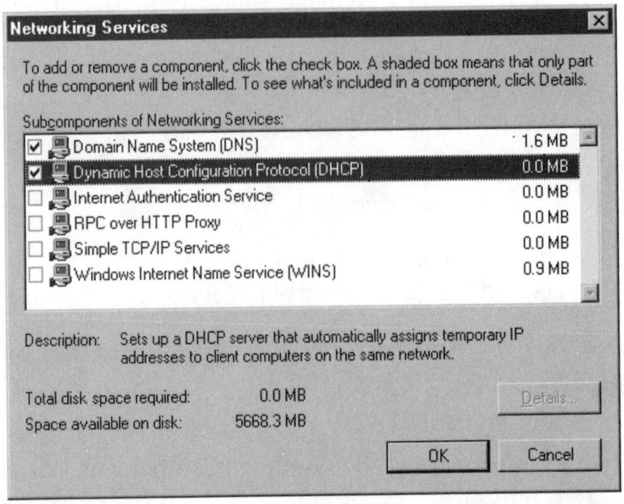

Networking Services

To add or remove a component, click the check box. A shaded box means that only part of the component will be installed. To see what's included in a component, click Details.

Subcomponents of Networking Services:

☑ 🖳 Domain Name System (DNS)	1.6 MB
☑ 🖳 Dynamic Host Configuration Protocol (DHCP)	0.0 MB
☐ 🖳 Internet Authentication Service	0.0 MB
☐ 🖳 RPC over HTTP Proxy	0.0 MB
☐ 🖳 Simple TCP/IP Services	0.0 MB
☐ 🖳 Windows Internet Name Service (WINS)	0.9 MB

Description: Sets up a DHCP server that automatically assigns temporary IP addresses to client computers on the same network.

Total disk space required: 0.0 MB

Space available on disk: 5668.3 MB

[OK]   [Cancel]

Figure 11-3.   *Selecting DHCP*

Configuring a Client to Use DHCP

When you elect to make a Windows XP/2000 machine into a DHCP client, you need to click the radio button on the Internet Protocol (TCP/IP) Properties page to have all the required TCP/IP configuration settings automatically assigned to your machine (as shown in Figure 11-4). In addition, all the settings are stored in a central location—the DHCP server—which eliminates the need to manually maintain a record of IP address assignments.

Client settings for many parameters of the DHCP client (except the IP address and subnet mask) also can be applied at the client computer. A client-specified setting will always override one supplied by DHCP. For this reason, if you are converting computers from local configurations to DHCP, be sure to remove the existing, hard-coded TCP/IP settings on the client.

Configuring the DHCP Server

You configure TCP/IP settings in the DHCP Manager by creating *scopes* and then assigning properties to them. A scope is a collection of IP addresses that can be dynamically or automatically allocated to DHCP clients as needed. You create a scope by defining a range of consecutive IP addresses in the New Scope Wizard dialog box (see Figure 11-5) and specifying the subnet mask that should be supplied with them. If necessary, you can exclude some of the addresses in the range from allocation. You also can modify the duration of the leases that will be negotiated between clients and the server.

Note   *You can configure the DHCP server, but it won't start servicing clients until you authorize it.*

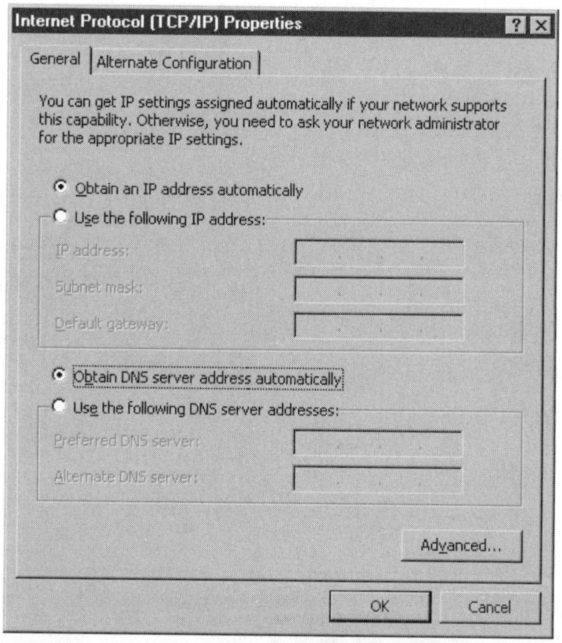

Figure 11-4. Configuring DHCP on the client

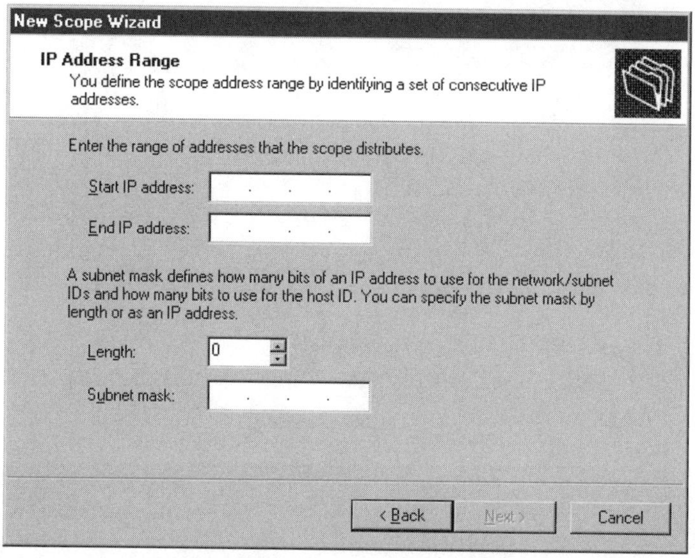

Figure 11-5. New scope configuration

After you have created a scope, you define the additional settings (from the list shown in the earlier section "Other DHCP Capabilities") that you want to deliver along with scopes, or specify only the options to be delivered with the addresses of a particular scope. The reason for these options is that separate scopes typically would have to be defined for each subnet on your network because certain settings (such as default gateways) would necessarily differ.

For example, a typical medium-sized network might consist of several subnets and for each you would create a scope. Settings like those for the domain name, the DNS servers, and the WINS/NBT node are probably going to be the same for all the clients in the enterprise, so they are best defined as global options. Routers and WINS/NBNS servers will more likely have to be defined as scope options, as there might be different values for different scopes. Figure 11-6 shows an example of the options that can be defined within a scope.

It is up to the administrator to supply correct settings for all the required TCP/IP configuration parameters. The objective is usually to provide clients with a complete TCP/IP configuration solution, but any settings that are omitted or incorrectly configured will cause TCP/IP communications at the client to malfunction without warning.

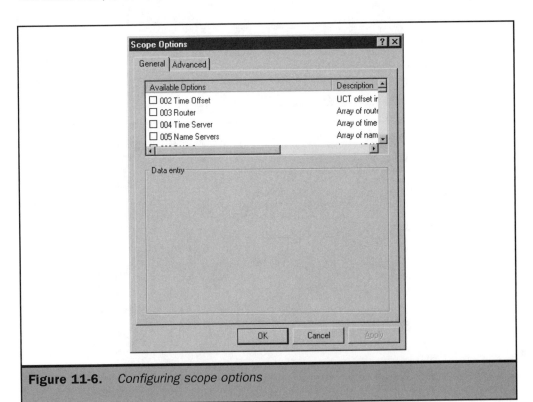

Figure 11-6. *Configuring scope options*

A DHCP server cannot itself use DHCP to obtain its own TCP/IP configuration (even from another DHCP server). Its settings must be manually configured in the Internet Protocol (TCP/IP) Properties dialog box.

DHCP and Name Resolution

As you will learn in the following sections, another major concern when using TCP/IP on the enterprise internetwork is name resolution. Just as DHCP maintains a listing of its clients' MAC addresses and their corresponding IP addresses, there must be a means to align IP addresses with host names assigned to all computers in a Windows 2003 network environment. Equally important is equating IP addresses with any NetBIOS names from down-level clients.

DHCP and DNS

DHCP has a rather interesting relationship with DNS because it isn't necessarily just responsible for passing an IP address to the client. Instead, DHCP can be made responsible for registering clients when Dynamic DNS (DDNS) and the DHCP option code 81 are enabled. Option code 81 allows for DHCP clients to return their fully qualified domain name (FQDN) to the DHCP server. In turn, the DHCP server can register clients with DDNS or the clients can register with the name resolution service. This option code gives the DHCP server three options for processing DDNS information for a DHCP client:

- It always registers the DHCP client's A and PTR resource records with DDNS.
- It never registers the DHCP client's A resource record.
- It registers the DHCP client's A and PTR resource records with DDNS only at the client's request.

DDNS allows DHCP servers and clients to dynamically update the DNS database. In particular, they are allowed to update A (the name maps to an IP address) and PTR (the IP address maps to a name) records. When a DHCP client contacts a DHCP server to obtain network configuration parameters at startup, the DHCP server registers the client's A and PTR resource records with DDNS from the client's FQDN. With one exception, the same process applies when a DHCP client tries to renew a lease. It contacts the DHCP server to get a renewal, but then the client's DHCP service can perform the update with DDNS.

 It is imperative that you test the DHCP and DDNS interactions with down-level clients.

For more information on DHCP interacting with DNS as well as more information on DNS, refer to Chapter 12.

DHCP and WINS

By resolving the problem of IP address administration, DHCP exacerbates the problem of NetBIOS name resolution. When IP addresses are automatically or dynamically allocated to network clients, it becomes all but impossible for the network administrator to keep up with the ever-changing assignments. For that reason, WINS, the Window Internet Naming System, works together with DHCP to provide an automatic NetBIOS name server that is updated whenever DHCP assigns a new IP address. On a Windows 2003 network running DHCP, WINS is necessary only when NetBIOS is still present (the presence of down-level clients).

The Complete Reference

Windows Server 2003

Chapter 12

Understanding DNS

Introduction to the Domain Name System

The Domain Name System (DNS) was developed by Paul Mokapetris, who, in the fledgling days of the Internet (the early 1980s) found himself asked to work on what became DNS, the system that translates a Web address into the four-octet IP address that networked machines use to communicate on TCP/IP (this is discussed in Chapter 10). Mokapetris came up with a hierarchical name space that assigned certain user-friendly names to machines and associated those names to IP addresses. These groups of machines were subdivided into domains, and each domain bears responsibility for its own management.

DNS can also help in the location of items stored in an LDAP database. DNS is a client/server process that reads a flat file (like the HOSTS files you sometimes see today). In Windows, DNS dates back to NT4 and became an integral part of the operating system in Windows 2000. This was largely due to the fact that Microsoft changed its default method of name resolution from NetBIOS names and Windows Internet Naming Service (WINS) to Fully Qualified Domain Names (FQDN) and DNS. Active Directory changed things further still, along with DNS RFC 2136 (dynamic record update). Much has changed, and much more will, with proposals on the table for DNSSEC extensions (RFC 2541). DNS is still a service, with server and client (resolver) pieces. The interactions between it and Active Directory are interdependent, suggesting one system instead of two.

This AD integration sounds as if it is mandatory; it isn't, though, unless you plan on constructing domains and forests (more on these in Chapter 19). It isn't mandatory even then, but you should integrate the two if you want to minimize administration. You may have UNIX boxes; it is possible to use DNS on Microsoft boxes in a standard primary and secondary (classic) DNS configuration if you're a purist or don't need/ want a domain in the neighborhood. However, the preferred method is forest/domain constructs and propagation through the Domain Controllers via Active Directory.

This chapter aims to impart an understanding of name resolution in general, and DNS in particular, with emphasis on the contrasts between Windows 2000 and 2003. You'll also learn about another, earlier form of name resolution used by Microsoft: NetBIOS name resolution, as serviced by Windows Internet Naming Service, or WINS.

How Did This Begin?

It all began with HOSTS files. These are flat ASCII text files that contain a line-by-line set of records. These records were really nothing more than an association of an IP address to a machine name, e.g., 192.168.1.1 Trucker.Truckstp.com. The idea was that Trucker was an easy-to-remember machine name (good for humans), and the resolver (a piece of software and libraries on the client system) would read this file, find the machine name, pick up its IP address, and go find it.

You can still use these HOSTS files; they are usually found in %SYSTEMROOT\ system32\drivers\etc subdirectory. You can edit one with Notepad and add any machine you need to, as long as you get the machine name and IP address right and are aware of changes on the network that might affect these records. Use of a HOSTS file is liable to errors, such as duplicated names or addresses. This approach does not scale well; just think how much trouble it would be to maintain a large environment of these files. On each machine! No security! The implications for calamity boggle the mind.

Name Resolution in General

HOSTS files are a dangerous way to do things, and the name resolution function had to be implemented in a reliable manner. DNS was the answer. With its own database and tools, plus its distributed nature, a good DNS design would ensure name resolution redundancy, consistency, and accuracy. There is some form of name resolution on any network that has more than one segment. If a LAN is only one segment without name resolution, broadcasts are used. On a network, broadcasts are used by computers to find other computers. Unfortunately, the source computer does not know the location of the target computer, so the source computer will broadcast for the target—this is like finding a friend in a crowded room by yelling his name. All parties in the room, much like all computers on the segment, will hear the broadcast, but only the target computer will respond to the broadcast. Once the relationship is established between target and source, then the communication carries on in directed datagrams.

Computers also do this if they are on small nonrouted LANS. LANS do not stay small: broadcasts are one of the reasons they are routed when they get large. Name resolution almost always involves the association of an IP address and a machine name, with intent to locate and connect to some service that machine offers. In TCP/IP, the connection is to a machine, and then to a port in the protocol stack to which the message is directed (say port 80, for a visit to a web site). All this so you can have an easy-to-remember machine name like www.skillet.com. Oh, remember the resolver? Let's look at the process of resolving a trip to www.skillet.com.

You want a new skillet. You're online, so you fire up the browser and type in www .skillet.com, which the browser passes to the resolver, whose job it is to do the legwork and find the Skillet server. The resolver is a set of libraries that takes the friendly name www.skillet.com and runs to the DNS server. The resolver has a specific order in which it does things. It will always look locally (that is, in your system first), so if you have anything in the HOSTS file, it will be processed, for better or worse.

The resolver will next look at your TCP/IP configuration, discover who the preferred DNS server is, and then query that server. Your downlevel clients won't behave this way; Windows 9x (DOS)–based products will look for NetBIOS names first. They will try DNS if NetBIOS fails, but in some cases waiting for NetBIOS to time out will add a noticeable delay. The reason is simple: these systems were built to run primarily on NetBIOS name resolution serviced by WINS. In time, DNS caught on, and these downlevel operating systems' search order is now out of date, failing to reflect how a TCP/IP network resolves hostnames.

NT4 will even resolve in this manner unless the NetBIOS name is over 15 characters or it finds a dot in the name it's looking for. If either of these conditions is true, it tries DNS first. Meanwhile, we aren't at Skillet.com yet.

Remember our resolver? It's busy asking the primary DNS server if it can translate the name. The DNS server checks its zone and cache, finds no match, and fails to resolve the name. Then this DNS server will seek out another DNS server and query it. A DNS server is typically installed at the edge of the company network, and all it does is forward queries to a DNS server outside. This type of DNS server is called a forwarder. The internal DNS server queries the forwarder, which first checks to see if it can resolve the name. If not, it passes the query to other DNS servers on the Internet until either a match is made or the query fails. A successful name resolution comes back to the local DNS server's cache so that when others attempt to go to Skillet's web site, the resolution will be faster.

Okay! That skillet is on order now; thanks to DNS, we have found our way to Skillet.com, and we got a look at the name resolution process as we went. DNS is a fascinating creature, and it has ways of finding what it wants to know, which are called *queries.* Here are the types of queries it conducts:

■ **Recursive**   A resolver has made a query of a DNS server and expects no more interaction in attempting to find the answer. The DNS server is responsible for the completion of the search, and it will start using other DNS servers, issuing queries, acting as the benefactor to this resolver. These further queries are iterative.

■ **Iterative**   An iterative query is the opposite of a recursive query (it is also called a nonrecursive query); it asks a DNS server for its best answer, and it has to respond without any queries to any other DNS servers.

■ **Inverse**   This type of query is issued by a machine that is looking for a hostname and sends an IP address in hopes of getting that hostname. This query is unusual in that the DNS server will check only its own zone. The search will conclude there, successful or not. This query is rare and is supported only with Windows DNS to provide backward compatibility with older DNS versions.

■ **Caching-only server**   This DNS function isn't technically a query, but it has to do with queries. This server has no authority, nor does it host any zone. It receives a query from a client and hands off the query to the DNS network for a resolution. Once it receive this resolution, it caches it for some amount of time in case some other client should repeat the same query. This speeds name resolution.

Through these methods, a DNS server will doggedly chase down the IP address from the URL (Uniform Resource Locator) your browser fed to the resolver. One of two things will be returned, what you were looking for, or an error. Just think of it as Rover the bloodhound.

The Domains

To understand DNS, it is helpful to be familiar with the environment in which it performs its work. Start by considering the DNS hierarchy. The root domain is known simply as ".". The top domain is the next level down, and a number of DNS domains live on this level. You'll know their suffixes: .COM (commercial), .GOV (government), .EDU (educational), .INT (international), .ORG (organization), .NET (Net providers, ISPs, and the like), and .MIL (military). Interestingly enough, ICANN refers to these as "generic" top-level domains, and between 2000 and 2002 it introduced seven more: .BIZ, .INFO, .NAME, .PRO, .AERO, .COOP, and .MUSEUM. Not all the new names are rolled out yet.

The next level down is usually a domain run by a private concern; I will use a corporate .COM. domain for my examples, but it could be a name from any of the operating domains just listed. You can view DNS domains as analogous to a directory structure on a hard drive in the way the DNS namespace is divided, or partitioned. The "." domain is the root directory; the next level down is the top level (.COM), and the next is a folder representing a corporate (private or public) entity of some sort. The top-level name (.COM) and the corporate "folder," let's say, Microsoft, together constitute a domain name. The Microsoft namespace can become further subdivided (subfolders, if you will) under the corporate folder, with smaller AD/DNS domains from within Microsoft representing different divisions or services, such as accounting.microsoft.com. This would normally not be accessible from the Internet the way microsoft.com would be; however, there are exceptions. For example:

```
http://support.microsoft.com/default.aspx?scid=fh;[ln];kbhowto
```

will take you to the support side of Microsoft. The Knowledge Base lives here, along with various pieces of guidance from MS Support. Each subzone is responsible for its own correct operation.

This is the normal DNS namespace, known as a *forward lookup zone*. There is also a *reverse lookup zone*, also known as in-addr.arpa, which is its technical name. When a reverse lookup is issued, instead of calling for the user-friendly name (and conducting a search in the forward lookup zone), it is actually looking for the IP address of the system instead. Records in the reverse lookup zone are listed IP address to machine name. The resolver is able to see if a specific IP address that is reporting itself to be a user-friendly name is indeed who it says it is. Since IP addresses are registered in association with DNS domain names, looking up the IP address should tell you what domain the IP address is coming from. If it isn't what it should be, you may have an intruder.

The design of IP addresses is such that they become more significant from left to right, whereas domain names get less significant from left to right, but IP addresses in the in-addr.arpa (reverse lookup zone) domain are listed in reverse order. Pointer records are added to the reverse lookup zone listing IP address to hostname, as opposed to a forward lookup zone, that will list hostname and then IP address. To perform a successful reverse lookup of a given IP address, such as 121.41.113.10, the DNS server performing the query looks for a PTR record for 10.113.41.121.in-addr.arpa, which will have the host name and IP address 121.41.113.10.

FQDN (Fully Qualified Domain Name)

Let's suppose that we know of a host inside a domain like this. We'll go back to our example, in the accounting subdomain at Microsoft. A domain under a domain like this is called a *child domain,* where microsoft.com is the *parent domain.* The hostname is Syscrusher. It would look like syscrusher.accounting.microsoft.com. Any hostname expressed in this manner is considered a *fully qualified domain name (FQDN).*

The Zones

Now is a good time to discuss zones. Each domain is a self-policing entity. If we took a look into one of the DNS servers inside Microsoft, we would see zones through the DNS snap-in. In a zone, you may find a domain, a part of a domain, or a number of domains; each has a DNS server or servers responsible for those zones. There will be at least one DNS server hosting each zone. Each zone has a set of records it houses. These are known as *resource records.* The DNS server that handles a given zone is said to be "the authority" for that zone, or "authoritative" for that zone. It will answer any queries delivered to it for that zone. That being understood, let's see what kinds of DNS zones there are. This refers to their storage, access, and replication, not their content (the records—we'll get to those soon). Classic DNS zones were, and still are, hosted in text files with a .dns extension in Windows.

Primary Zone

The first zone is called the *primary zone.* This zone is set up on the primary server and is the only writable copy of the database. At the minimum, this zone will have two records in it, an SOA (Start of Authority) record, and an NS (name server) record. In classic DNS, this zone file would have to be edited by hand, but later versions of DNS found in Windows 2000 and 2003 allow secure and nonsecure dynamic updating. Most of the records will be "A" records representing hosts that have been added by hand or have registered themselves; however, there are many kinds of records. We'll get to the more popular ones shortly. Classic DNS in Windows Server 2003 allows two choices: disallow dynamic updates, or allow secure and nonsecure updates.

Secondary Zone

The *secondary zone* is pulled from the primary and is read-only. This server should be on a different subnet and is provided for redundancy in a smaller environment; in larger ones, it allows secondary DNS servers to be distributed to remote sites for better performance.

Active Directory Integrated

This version of the zone lives within Active Directory on each domain controller. The master copy of the DNS database is replicated to each domain controller and can be altered by each domain controller, with proper authentication, of course. One must be careful with how many records/zones one uses in AD; a very large number can degrade performance.

Stub Zone

This is new to Windows 2003. It is a copy of a child zone with records that identify a child name server that is authoritative for that child zone. It has an SOA record, an NS record, and a glue A record. This is known as *delegation.* The parent zone's server can receive updates from the child zone, which will be stored in the cache of the parent zone's server. The records in the stub zone won't change. The purpose is to "glue" the two namespaces together so that proper referral will occur from the parent to the child zone.

Okay, delegation is not new, fair enough. Stub zones correct an issue that has existed with delegation, and I'll detail that for you now. We have a parent domain, microsoft.com. We also have a child domain, accounting.microsoft.com. When the child zone was first delegated, there was only one authoritative DNS server in the accounting zone. Since the accounting namespace has grown over time, administrators have come along and installed two new DNS servers for this child domain.

The DNS server hosting the parent zone, microsoft.com, remains blissfully unaware of their existence, however, and continues to beat the original DNS server (authoritative) for accounting.microsoft.com senseless. To get around this load balancing issue, the parent is configured to host a stub zone for the child domain, and when that zone is updated, it will query the zone's authoritative server, and the parent will learn about the two new DNS servers and can do recursion on all of them.

Delegation

To continue with our example, a parent zone, microsoft.com, has a child zone, accounting .microsoft.com, and control of this child zone is said to be *delegated* from the parent zone. Delegation, which transfers authority across a divided namespace, can be done for a number of reasons, such as a need for another department to manage a separate management zone, or for load balancing and fault tolerance. The child zone will be authoritative for itself. It is important to remember that one can create child zones without delegating to them. In that case, authority rests with the parent.

The Records

There are many types of records in DNS, but space, time, and relevance prohibit listing them here, so we'll go over those most commonly found in a given zone.

- **A record** This specifies a host address. It maps a hostname to an address and look like this:

```
Myhost.mycompany.com  IN A 192.168.0.1
```

- **AAAA record** This is not a common record but was expected to become so with the advent of IP6. People thought we would all run out of domain names and IP addresses by now because of the rate of consumption. That never happened, and IPv4 is still around. Here is an example of a host record from a zone hosted in an IPv6 environment.

```
IN AAAA 1234:1:2:3:4:567:89cd
```

- **CNAME record** This is the canonical record, commonly used for aliases. It allows you to map multiple hostnames to a given IP address. Many companies use this technique to make sure they capture the intended customer's visit, even if the visitor misspells something in the URL, or if there are multiple ways to spell a company's URL. This way, the customer is sure to arrive at the correct site.

- **SRV record (service locater)** This record is particularly important to Windows 2000 and 2003, in a forest/domain configuration. It is used to register DCs in DNS, and to advertise several servers providing a given TCP/IP service. If you attempt to create a new record, you will have the option of assigning a particular TCP/IP service to it. Once that record is in place, a client using an SRV query can use a particular TCP/IP service offered in a given domain by multiple servers. If you cannot get DC to join a domain, this is one of the things you should look at. This record will locate domain controllers that use the LDAP (AD) service over TCP port 389.

- **NS record** This record identifies the name server(s) for a given DNS domain. NS records list primary and secondary servers for a namespace, plus child zones emanating from it.

- **SOA (Start of Authority) record** This record defines the zone for which this server is authoritative. It has config parameters for the server such as time to live, who is responsible for said server, NS server names, refresh rates, the serial (or magic) number used to mark zone changes, and trigger replication.

- **PTR record** This record enables quick reverse lookups using inaddr.arpa. It is thought of as a reverse A record, but it does not look like one because of the use of inaddr.arpa in the actual record. The record for a host at syscrusher.skillet.com, with an IP address of 100.200.252.1, would look like 1.252.200.100.in-addr.arpa IN PTR syscrusher.skillet.com.

- **MX record** This record facilitates e-mail exchanges. You can have multiple records pointing to multiple mail servers out there, and you can have them tapped in an order of your choosing, if you wish.

Microsoft has a few records that are specific to it; these records are a sort of glue for surviving WINS environments. They are

- **WINS** This allows MS DNS to use a WINS server to get a resolution to a hostname. This is helpful if you have a bunch of downlevel clients that don't have registration in a DNS zone. This record will be found, and the WINS server will be queried.

- **WINS-R** This record allows reverse lookup.

These are MS-only records, and they can be restricted in a zone transfer.

Zone Transfer/Replication

DNS servers replicate their zones. They do this for a number of reasons depending on network design, but the two most prevalent reasons are fault tolerance and performance. In the early DNS days, there were the primary and the secondary. They both carried identical copies of their zones, and the secondary was generally put on another network so that either a failure of the primary's network or a failure of the server would not cause the network to lose name resolution. They replicated via a trigger, such as the start-up of the servers, or when the zones on the primary were updated, so if there was a "magic number" in the Start of Authority record, the secondary would look for this and pull the database if there was a difference.

The magic Number is from BIND DNS nomenclature. It refers to a serial number which is incremented each time an update is made to a primary zone. This is referred to by the secondaries, and if changed, will trigger a zone replication. This is a called a zone transfer.

Changes could be made only on the primary; all secondary systems were copies of that primary. This reduced the risk of database corruption. This type of configuration is typical of a UNIX environment but can be set up using Windows 2003. As I had mentioned earlier, the preferred method of use is with forests and domains. Replication takes on a different meaning here; the concept of primary and secondary go out the window in an AD/DNS-based domain. In AD, there are only AD zones.

In this configuration, called *multimaster replication,* DNS zones exist on domain controllers, and the zones are replicated via Active Directory. Their relationship is symbiotic: AD needs DNS to find objects, other DCs, and sites in the tree; DNS needs AD to replicate to the rest of the DCs in each domain. It works something like this: Once the zone is created, it is stored using directory-integrated zone storage. These are stored in the Active Directory tree under the domain or application directory partition.

An application partition is new to Windows 2003; it houses application data that can be selectively replicated to specific domain controllers (more in Chapter 19, and we'll discuss the tool that makes this possible, DNSCMD, under "DNS Tools," later in this chapter). In classic DNS, full zones were replicated all the time. Starting with Windows 2000, replication of the zones can be configured for full replication (the entire zone gets copied via an AXFR request) or an incremental form of zone transfer can happen (using an IXFR request). As you may guess, only changes are replicated here. This process is documented in RFC 1995, if you need more info.

All this buys you a selective form of multimaster replication: all or selected DCs have copies of the zone and can resolve names, plus zone security. What kind of security? Check this: You can use access control list (ACL) editing to secure a dnsZone object container in the directory tree. This will give you complete control over access to either the zone or a specified RR in that zone. With an ACL, you can prohibit dynamic updates to any RR (resource record) the zone has by groups and/or hosts.

If you add a DC to the domain, the zone will get replicated to it with no further effort. You can also choose to replicate all or part of a zone. That wasn't possible with your father's DNS!

The Files

DNS is composed of a number of files. The following list identifies them and explains their uses.

- **Cache.dns**   This file could also be known as "root hints." It contains the root servers for the Internet. If you are connected to the Internet, this is fine, but if not, it will take a little tweaking. Simply replace the Internet servers with the SOA and NS records for the DNS server authoritative for your zone. This file's purpose is to help locate those root servers for use in server cache initialization. If you're on the Internet, using the servers that come in this file, you can even easily update it from the Root Hints tab located under your server properties.

- **Root.dns**   This file is used if your DNS server is a root server for your network.

- **Your_Zone.dns**   You will see this file only if you are using a standard primary or secondary zone. You won't see this if you are using Active Directory–integrated DNS.

- **Boot**   You might know this one as named.boot, if you've used BIND DNS. You won't get it by default, but if you have a BIND box you would care to import it from, use the From File option under server properties in the DNS snap-in.

There are also the executables (DNS.EXE) and the resolver running on the client.

Windows Server 2003 DNS

It's time to talk about the new stuff! There are quite a few differences you will notice in 2003 DNS. Here are the improvements:

- **Round robin update**   In DNS, normal behavior is to have a round robin effect when the server is queried for resource records of the same types for the same domain name. If this causes an issue in your environment, it can be adjusted such that round robin will not be used for certain record types. It's done using a registry tweak:

  - HKLM\System\CurrentControlSet\Services\DNS\Parameters\
  - DoNotRoundRobinTypes
  - Type: REG_DWORD
  - Valid Range: any RR type (SRV, A, NS)

- **Disjoined namespace**   If you upgrade an NT4 server to Windows 2003, and you want to use an Active Directory name that is different from the previous NT4 primary suffix, the current primary suffix of the FQDN will always match the domain name. If you have not run into this one yet and want to know more, check Knowledge Base Article Q257623, "Domain Controller's DNS Suffix Does Not Match Domain Name."

- **Root zone**   Since NT4, MS DNS has automatically been adding root zones to DNS servers. In Windows 2003, this practice has stopped; In NT4, it was initiated when a DNS server first came online and could not prime any of the root hints servers on the Internet. This caused a couple of issues, most notably the inability to set up forwarding, or to talk to those servers. Now, if you want a root zone ".", you can do it manually.

- **Zone replication options**   You can now choose replication on one of four ways. You can choose them when you create your zone, or when you want to change the storage method for a zone. Here are your choices; read carefully, as the differences are subtle. Also, consider what impact your choice will have on bandwidth and network load:

  - **All DNS Servers in AD Domain**   This choice replicates all your zone data to every DC in the AD domain. This is the default choice when you set up integrated DNS zones in the Windows Server 2003 product.

  - **All DNS Servers in AD Forest**   In about the largest scope available, this choice replicates your zones to every DC in the forest. The act of replication eats bandwidth. The purpose of these options is to give the administrator control over the properties of replication so that not so much bandwidth is used, or to tune a low bandwidth connection. In this example, every DNS server in a given forest would be replicated to, maximizing traffic. It is the largest replication scope available.

  - **All DCs in AD Domain**   Zone data gets replicated to all your DCs in an AD domain. This is a setting that you must check if you want Windows 2000 DNS servers to load an AD zone.

  - **All DCs Servers in a Specified Application Directory Partition**   You can replicate zone info according to a replication scope of a specified application directory partition. If you choose to do this, the DNS server hosting your zone must be registered in the application directory you have chosen. You can use DNSCMD to do this (more on DNSCMD in the section "DNS Tools," later in this chapter) by using this:

    ```
    dnscmd Yourservername /CreateDirectoryPartition
    yourdc.yourdomain.com
    ```

You have to use an FQDN here. Registering your DNS server in the new partition is just about the same:

```
dnscmd Yourservername /EnlistDirectoryPartition yourdc.yourdomain.com
```

Finally, if you choose to use AD partitions, all DNS objects are removed from the Global Catalog. DNSCMD does not come installed by default; you have to do it. Here's how:

1. Get your distribution CD.

2. Look in the support\tools folder.

3. Click suptools.msi. This starts the installer, and you will have installed support tools.

   - **DNS Auto Configuration in DCPromo**   This will set your client DNS settings automatically if the following conditions are met:

     - There is a single net connection.

     - The preferred and alternate DNS settings match.

     - DNS settings exist on one connection only.

This will query current DNS servers specified in network settings, update root hints, configure forwarders with the current preferred and alternate DNS servers, set up DNS settings with 127.0.0.1, and then configure all previous preferred and alternate DNS servers. If it all succeeds, a log is written in Event Viewer.

- **Stub zones**   You looked at stub zones earlier; these are essentially child zones that are delegated and contain SOA, NS, and host A records. They glue the namespace together. The DNS server can query NS directly instead of through recursion. The changes to zones are made when the master zone is updated or loaded. The local list of master zones defines physically local servers from which to transfer.

- **Conditional forwarders**   When a DNS server gets a query from a client, the server looks locally; that is, it will check its zone info, or any info it has in its cache. If it does not have the reply and it is configured to do so, it will forward that query to the DNS servers it has been configured for. Conditional forwarding is more granular in that instead of simply forwarding the query to any server, it can actually do the forwarding according to specific domain names found in those queries. The Conditional Forwarders tab (right-click the DNS server name in the DNS management snap-in) shows that the conditions can be set by specific domain name or the domain forwarder's IP address.

- **Group policy**   This is a client configuration tool. One thing about an environment with many DNS clients is that there is no way to configure them all via any tool, and this configuration historically has been done on a system-by-system basis. Things like domain suffixing and whether or not a client could dynamically update its records have been done by hand. The group policy tool will allow a group of clients to be configured identically via a group policy. The actual settings include enabling/disabling dynamic update, listing DNS servers for a client to use, providing DNS suffix lists, and devolving the primary DNS suffix in the name resolution process. If you're troubleshooting an issue and using a group policy, remember that the group policy will supersede any other settings, e.g., local settings and/or DHCP settings. If you need it, there is a way around this problem via the registry, although it addresses dynamic registration only:

- **Name**   DoNotUseGroupPolicyForDisableDynamicUpdate
- **Key**   HKLM\SYSTEM\CurrentControlSet\Services\Tcpip\Parameters
- **Data type**   REG_DWORD
- **Valid Range**   0x0 (use group policy) and 0x1 (use local)
- **Default**   0x0

Client-Side Registry Entries

Here is a more inclusive list of the client-side registry entries.

Dynamic Update

This policy setting determines if dynamic update is enabled. Computers configured for dynamic update automatically register and update their DNS resource records with a DNS server.

Name: RegistrationEnabled

Key: HKLM\Software\Polices\Microsoft\Windows NT\DNSClient

Type: REG_DWORD

Valid Range: 0x0 (disable) and 0x1 (enable)

DNS Suffix Search List

Group policy for the DNS suffix search list is considered important to the future transition to a NetBIOS-free environment. When you use this setting as enabled, a user submits a query for a single-label name (such as "widgets"), and a local DNS client attaches a suffix (such as "microsoft.com"), resulting in the query "widgets.microsoft.com," prior to sending the query to a DNS server.

Name: SearchList

Key: HKLM\Software\Polices\Microsoft\Windows NT\DNSClient

Type: REG_SZ

Valid Range: comma-separated strings of DNS suffixes

Primary DNS Suffix Devolution

This policy setting determines whether the DNS client performs primary DNS suffix devolution in a name resolution process. When a client sends a query for a single-label name (such as "mybox"), a local DNS client attaches a suffix (such as "skillet.com"), resulting in the query "test.microsoft.com," prior to sending the query to a DNS server.

The primary DNS suffix is devolved until the query is successful or the DNS suffix has two labels (for example, "skillet.com"). The primary DNS suffix cannot be devolved to less than two labels.

Key: HKLM\Software\Polices\Microsoft\Windows NT\DNSClient

Type: REG_DWORD

Valid Range: 0x0 (disable) and 0x1 (enable)

Register PTR Record

This policy setting will allow or disallow whether a client can register PTR records. In the default state, DNS clients configured to perform dynamic DNS registration attempt PTR resource record registration only if they successfully registered the corresponding A resource record. To enable this policy, select Enable and choose one of the following values:

- **Do not register**   Computers never attempt PTR resource records registration.

- **Register**   Computers attempt PTR resource records registration regardless of the success of the A records' registration.

- **Register only if A record registration succeeds**   Computers attempt PTR resource records registration only if they successfully registered the corresponding A resource records.

    Name: RegisterReverseLookup

    Key: HKLM\Software\Polices\Microsoft\Windows NT\DNSClient

    Type: REG_DWORD

    Valid Range: 0x0 (disabled), 0x1 (enabled)

Registration Refresh Interval

This policy setting dictates the Registration Refresh Interval of A and PTR resource records for computers. This setting can be applied to computers using dynamic update only. If the DNS resource records are registered in zones with scavenging enabled, the value of this setting should never be longer than the Refresh Interval configured for these zones. Setting the Registration Refresh Interval to longer than the Refresh Interval of the DNS zones may cause the premature deletion of A and PTR resource records. That could be a problem.

    Name: RegistrationRefreshInterval

    Key: HKLM\Software\Polices\Microsoft\Windows NT\DNSClient

    Type: REG_DWORD

    Valid Range: larger than or equal to 1800 (seconds)

Replace Addresses in Conflicts

This policy setting determines whether a DNS client that attempts to register
its A resource record should overwrite an existing A resource record(s) containing a
conflicting IP address(es). During dynamic update of a zone that does not use Secure
Dynamic Update, a DNS client may discover that an existing A resource record associates
the client's host DNS name with an IP address of a different computer. According to the
default configuration, the DNS client will try to overwrite that existing A resource record
with an A resource record associating the DNS name with the client's IP address.

> Name: RegistrationOverwritesInConflict
>
> Key: HKLM\Software\Polices\Microsoft\Windows NT\DNSClient
>
> Type: REG_DWORD
>
> Valid Range: 0x0 (disable) and 0x1 (enable)

Register DNS Records with Connection-Specific DNS Suffix

This policy setting determines if a computer performing dynamic registration may
register its A and PTR resource records with a concatenation of its Computer Name
and a connection-specific DNS suffix, in addition to registering these records with
a concatenation of its Computer Name and the Primary DNS suffix.

> Name: RegisterAdapterName
>
> Key: HKLM\Software\Polices\Microsoft\Windows NT\DNSClient
>
> Type: REG_DWORD
>
> Valid Range: 0x0 (disable), 0x1 (enable)

 *If dynamic DNS registration is disabled on a computer (or is disabled on a specific
network connection to which this setting is applied), a computer will not attempt
dynamic DNS registration of its A and PTR records regardless of this policy setting.*

TTL Set in the A and PTR Records

This policy setting specifies the value for the time-to-live (TTL) field in A and PTR
resource records registered in the computers to which this setting is applied.

> Name: RegistrationTTL
>
> Key: HKLM\Software\Polices\Microsoft\Windows NT\DNSClient
>
> Type: REG_DWORD
>
> Valid Range: 0-4294967200 (seconds)
>
> Default: 600

Update Security Level

This policy setting specifies whether the computers to which this setting is applied use secure dynamic update or standard dynamic update for registration of DNS records.

To enable this setting, select Enable and choose one of the following values:

- **Unsecure Followed By Secure**   If this option is chosen, then computers send secure dynamic updates only when nonsecure dynamic updates are refused.

- **Only Unsecure**   If this option is chosen, then computers send only nonsecure dynamic updates.

- **Only Secure**   If this option is chosen, then computers send only secure dynamic updates.

     Name: UpdateSecurityLevel

     Key: HKLM\Software\Polices\Microsoft\Windows NT\DNSClient

     Type: REG_DWORD

     Valid Range: 0 (UnsecureFollowedBySecure), 16 (OnlyUnsecure), 256 (OnlySecure)

Update Top-Level Domain Zones

This policy setting specifies whether the computers to which this policy is applied may send dynamic updates to the zones named with a single label name (also known as top-level domain zones, e.g., "com").

By default, a DNS client configured to perform dynamic DNS update will send dynamic updates to the DNS zone(s) authoritative for its DNS resource records, unless the authoritative zone(s) is a top-level domain and a root zone.

If this policy is enabled, then computers to which this policy is applied will send dynamic updates to any zone authoritative for the resource records that the computer needs to update, except the root zone.

     Name: UpdateTopLevelDomainZones

     Key: HKLM\Software\Polices\Microsoft\Windows NT\DNSClient

     Type: REG_DWORD

     Value: 0x0 (Disable) and 0x1 (Enable)

Basic Support for DNSSEC (RFC 2535)

It is important to note that Windows Server 2003 does not fully support the DNSSEC standard, but its intent is to use cryptography to assure data protection as the zone information is crossing the wire (or air, in the case of wireless connectivity). This is important, because someone with malicious intent could intercept this information and locate strategic servers, and then either impersonate or compromise them. There are public and private keys that are associated with zones, so that if the DNS server is compromised, the resolvers can still authenticate resource records from those zones (e.g., the keys apply to the zones and not the server).

This service uses encrypted digital signatures using private keys, which are sent as resource records from DNS servers that host these signed zones. These records go to resolvers that can authenticate them via public key. Digital signatures and public keys are added to a signed zone as resource records. If you want to use this service, note that you won't find it in the DNS snap-in. Look instead to the registry:

HKEY_LOCAL_MACHINE\SYSTEM\CurrentControlSet\Services\DNS\ Parameters

Add EnableDnsSec in the DWORD field.

This field takes one of three arguments, depending on what you want to do:

- **0x0**   This excludes DNSSEC RRs in query responses unless one of three records is a NXT, SIG, or KEY record. If this is the case, the appropriate RRs will be sent in responses to NXT, SIG, or KEY records only.
- **0x2**   This includes the DNSSEC RRs in all responses.
- **0x1 (or blank field)**   If you need DNSSEC records included in responses where the client query contains the OPT record, either add 0x1 or leave this field blank; either will do.

There are times when you may have a multihomed DNS server, and would like the DNS server to listen and respond on one NIC only. If the system is multihomed (two NICS on different networks) and one of the NICs is facing the Internet, another security option to consider is to configure DNS to listen only on the private network. This can be done through a GUI. You will use the Microsoft management console GUI for this activity. Load the DNS snap-in and go to the Actions pull-down menu. Click Properties. Click the Interface tab, choose Only The Following IP Addresses, and add your IP address. When you're done, click Add.

Extension Records for DNS (EDNS0)

The original specification for DNS limited the packet size to 512 octets. EDNS0 (RFC 2671) allows the transfer of larger packets. When DNS server gets a request (UDP is used), it looks at the client's OPT resource record and changes its response to allow the transfer of as many resource records as the client specified in the OPT record (UDP size is specified in the OPT record).

DNS Logging

The DNS logging options have not changed much since Windows 2000, but they have been made nice through the use of a GUI, which is now part of the Event Viewer. You can filter by user, computer, event ID, category, or event source, from first to last event, and according to the usual information, warning, and error event types. DNS logging will appear either through the DNS snap-in, or the normal Event Viewer included in Administrative Tools. You can choose event logging and debug options by right-clicking the server in the DNS snap-in and choosing Properties. Debug logging selections and event logging selections tabs will be exposed, and you can make your selections. Those selections are Query, Notify, Update, Questions, Answers, Send, Receive, UDP, TCP, Full Packets, and Write Through.

DNS Tools

Windows Server 2003 has many built-in tools that can be used to monitor, manage, and troubleshoot DNS. These tools are described in the following sections.

NSLOOKUP

This command-line utility allows query of the DNS namespace, and allows you to troubleshoot common DNS issues. It has an interactive mode, and you can examine resource records in a given server with it. The syntax is:

```
Nslookup -Subcommand hostname | -Server
```

Server uses the server you specify, but its default is the DNS server in your TCP/IP Properties sheet.

IPCONFIG

This tool can't be used unless your system is also using DHCP. It has three parameters that relate to DNS, /registerdns, / flushdns, and /displaydns.

The /registerdns parameter refreshes DHCP lease and forces a client to reregister with the DNS server. The /flushdns parameter will clear the resolver cache, and /displaydns shows what is in the resolver cache.

PING

This is a TCP/IP utility and should be used first, to establish that connectivity between client and server exists. If it does not, there is no need to troubleshoot DNS, as the issue is at a lower level. Also, for a quick check of PTR resolution, you can ping an IP address, and you should be able to verify connectivity and hostname.

DNSCMD

This is a command-line tool that will let you do quite a bit. Most of the things that can be done through the DNS snap-in can be done using DNSCMD, including scripts, creation of AD partitions, enlisting of those partitions, setup and configuration of DNS servers, and management. It does not come installed by default; you have to do it. Here's how:

Go to the OS distribution CD, look under support\tools, and click suptools.msi. This starts the installer, and you will have installed support tools. This is a very powerful tool—typing **DNSCMD** at a DOS prompt will give you a sense of awe—the real question is what doesn't it do? Most, if not all, of the functionality that you have with the GUI is available with DNSCMD.

NETDIAG

This tool is not solely dedicated to DNS—it has many network functions—but it can fix a number of mystery ailments and give you a status report on what it has found for DNS records after it has looked at the registrations. To see what NETDIAG thinks about a given issue, go to the command prompt and type **netdiag /fix** for all network-related functionality to be checked, or **netdiag /DNS**. To get a look at what it can do, go to the Microsoft Knowledge Base and look at article number 321708. (MS recently dropped the "Q" preceding the article numbers.) You will find NETDIAG in the Support Tools folder of your distribution CD.

RENDOM

This tool allows the renaming of domains in Windows 2003. It also has the desirable side effect of checking domain integrity by looking for needed DC Locator Source records on authoritative DNS servers. This is done to make sure proper replication and authentication will happen after the rename. In short order, it renames DC locater records at the DNS server authoritative for the zone and then checks domain integrity. If a record is missing, it is able to tell you which one so that troubleshooting is not quite as tedious.

DNSlint

This is a command-line tool that should encompass most DNS diagnostics. It can be used to diagnose common DNS name resolution issues. It has three main functional areas: dnslint /ql (verifies user-defined records on a DNS server), dnslint /ad (verifies records specific to Active Domain), and dnslint /d (checks for "lame delegations"). You can download this tool from the Microsoft Web site.

Installing DNS

Installing DNS depends on what you are planning to do with the namespace and AD. Integration of the two is the preferred method, calling for AD installation, and AD-integrated zones. This is in contrast to installing classic DNS on an active directory based domain controller. You would perform the necessary steps either at install time, or using DCPROMO from the Start/Run menu. Make sure the system is configured with a static IP address before you start this, or you won't get your SRV records. These are created in your AD zone, and the other DCs look for them when joining a domain.

In Windows 2003, you're greeted by a new dialog box indicating that there may be operating system issues with this domain controller if you have machines running Windows 95 or NT4 SP3 or earlier. The reason for this is SMB (Server Message Block) signing and a more secure connection regarding the DC and its clients. It provides sharing of printers and files, administration, and logon authentication for Miocrosoft operating systems. SMB has been enhanced in Windows 2003. In short, it is incompatible with the earlier forms of Session Message Block Protocol, and will not allow these down-level clients to authenticate to the domain. You've been warned!

Another dialog box for DNS that has changed is incorporated into the DCPROMO dialog process. It's the one that used to tell you that the DNS server for this domain cannot be contacted. The wizard will ask if you would like to install and configure DNS on this server, or if you'll do it manually later. Now it's called the DNS registration diagnostics screen. It describes what record it cannot find (SRV), suggests what to do about it, and gives you the following three choices:

- I have corrected the problem, test again.
- Install and configure DNS server on this computer and set this computer to use its own DNS service.
- I'll correct this later by installing DNS manually.

DCPromo will act as a wizard, asking for information and creating DNS zones for you, and configuring some settings. The wizard obtains these from you, turns the crank, and soon you will have a DC running AD DNS. This gives you dynamic update capability, plus forward and reverse zones.

Installing DNS Manually

This is straightforward. Here's how:

1. Go to Control Panel, Add or Remove Programs.
2. Click Add/Remove Windows Components, go to Networking Services and drill down to the checkboxes checking the Domain Name System (DNS).
3. Click OK. The system will go about installing code and may ask you for the CD. Once it's finished, you will find it has installed the DNS manager snap-in, created the DNS directory located under %SYSTEMROOT%\System32, and added the DNS service to the registry.

Installing DNS Using the Manage Your Server Wizard

Here is how you can install DNS from the Manage Your Server Wizard:

1. Once the Manage Your Server Wizard starts, you will see two choices. They are "Adding Roles To Your Server" and "Managing Your Server Roles."
2. Choose Add Or Remove A Role. You will see the Preliminary Steps screen.
3. The Wizard starts scanning your network interfaces.
4. Once this is done, you are offered two choices, Typical Configuration Of First Server, or Custom Configuration. Typical is a turnkey solution that will install DNS, DHCP, and DCPROMO the system as a domain controller.
5. Choose Custom Configuration.

6. Select DNS Server from the Server Role list. The Summary Selection screen appears.

7. Files will be installed. Have your source CD ready, the server will be looking for it. If the system does not have a static IP address, you will be prompted to change that now. Once in the TCP/IP Properties page, you may leave the DNS address empty. If you do, it will fill in its own address (point back to itself) for name resolution.

8. The Configure DNS Server Wizard appears.

9. The Wizard presents a screen asking how you would like to configure DNS. You can create a forward lookup zone, create forward and reverse lookup zones, or configure root hints only. Choose Forward Lookup Zone.

10. The next screen asks for your zone name.

11. The zone file is created, and its name displayed for your approval.

12. You will now be given a choice as to whether you will allow nonsecure and secure dynamic updates, or will not allow dynamic updates.

13. The Reverse Lookup Zone screen comes up; you may or may not choose to create a reverse lookup zone here. If you do, you will be presented with the proposed .dns filename.

14. On the following screen, you can choose whether or not to allow nonsecure and secure dynamic updates.

15. The Forwarders screen appears. You may choose not to forward at all, or if you do choose to forward, the server IP addresses of the server you plan to forward to must be given. Clicking Next will give you a summary of your choices and search for root hints. Once it has done that, you have a DNS server.

Setting a Forward Lookup Zone

To configure a forward lookup zone, do the following:

1. Start the DNS snap-in and right-click the Forward Lookup Zone.

2. Select "New Zone" and add the name for the new zone. You will have three or four choices here depending on whether this system is AD integrated or not. The first three you get in any event, the Primary Zone, Secondary Zone, and the Stub Zone. The fourth (if the system is a DC) is Store Zone In Active Directory.

3. Take the Primary selection. Now you'll be asked to choose a replication scheme—to all DNS servers in the AD forest myforest.com, to all DNS servers in the AD domain mydomain.com, or to all DCs in the Active Directory domain. Type in the zone name, click OK, and you will be asked about the kinds of updates your new zone should allow. You can choose between Only Secure Updates; Allow Both Secure And Nonsecure Updates; or Do Not Allow Dynamic Updates.

Now you can add records, but the way to do this right is to configure the zone to accept dynamic updates and configure the clients to register themselves. If you need to add a record manually, right-click your newly created zone, choose Add A Record, and scroll the list until you find the record that suits your needs.

Testing: Let's See If This Works

To test whether or not the forward lookup zone is configured properly, do the following:

1. Open the DNS snap-in: from the Start | Administrative Tools menu, choose the DNS Snapin.

2. In the left pane, select your primary DNS server for the zones you need to check and select Properties from the action menu.

3. Under the Monitoring tab, choose the test you want to perform. Those choices would be A Simple Query Against This DNS Server, or A Recursive Query To Other DNS Servers.

4. Choose Test Now, or Perform Automatic Testing The Following Interval, and choose the interval you need.

Security Options

DNS has the ability to delegate permissions to users and groups for administration and management. Review your permissions needs and select the level of security you need. To get to the Security page, right-click the DNS server in the DNS server snap-in and choose Security from the properties sheet.

DHCP Integration

DNS and DHCP can work together. In this configuration, clients and servers are allowed to update A (host) and (PTR) reverse-lookup records. DHCP will give leases and update DNS records accordingly.

RFCs

Need more information on the specifications? The RFC (Request for Comment) is the place to go. Here are all the RFCs for Windows Server 2003 and its clients:

- 1034 Domain Names—Concepts and Facilities
- 1035 Domain Names—Implementation and Specification
- 1123 Requirements for Internet Hosts—Application and Support
- 1886 DNS Extensions to Support IP Version 6
- 1995 Incremental Zone Transfer in DNS
- 1996 A Mechanism for Prompt Notification of Zone Changes (DNS NOTIFY)
- 2136 Dynamic Updates in the Domain Name System (DNS UPDATE)

- 2181 Clarifications to the DNS Specification

- 2308 Negative Caching of DNS Queries (DNS NCACHE)

- 2535 Domain Name System Security Extensions (DNSSEC)

- 2671 Extension Mechanisms for DNS (EDNS0)

- 2782 A DNS RR for Specifying the Location of Services (DNS SRV)

- Internet drafts for DNS

The following Internet drafts contain specifications used to design and implement the DNS server and client services:

- Draft-skwan-utf8-dns-02.txt Using the UTF-8 Character Set in the Domain Name System

- Draft-ietf-dhc-dhcp-dns-08.txt Interaction Between DHCP and DNS

- Draft-ietf-dnsind-tsig-11.txt Secret Key Transaction Signatures for DNS (TSIG)

- Draft-ietf-dnsind-tkey-00.txt Secret Key Establishment for DNS (TKEY RR)

- Draft-skwan-gss-tsig-04.txt GSS Algorithm for TSIG (GSS-TSIG)

- Other specifications for DNS

The following additional specifications are used to design and implement the DNS Server and Client services:

- **af-saa-0069.000.doc ATM Name System Specification version 1.0**   This specification is published by the ATM Forum. For more information, you can obtain this specification by downloading it from the ATM Forum FTP site. You can get it at http://www.gmd.de/ftp/mirrors3/atmforum/approved-specs/

WINS

WINS does for NetBIOS names the same thing DNS does for hostnames; the major difference is the namespace structure. WINS is a distributed database, or it can be. WINS maps IP addresses to NetBIOS names. WINS is a flat namespace when compared to DNS, which is a hierarchy; in WINS there is no hierarchy, expressed or implied. Whereas in DNS, a machine located in accounting at skillet.com would be myhost .skillet.com, the domain NetBIOS name would be SKILLET.

WINS was originally intended to provide NetBIOS name resolution on a nonrouted network. Without WINS, systems would simply broadcast across the wire. That is the problem with NetBIOS—using it, broadcasts would flood a large network and eat net bandwidth. NetBIOS is nonroutable and is on the wire by running on top of TCP/IP.

NetBIOS is a presentation layer (see OSI model) application programming interface (API) developed by IBM in 1983. It allows programs to give instructions to underlying network protocols; as old as it is, that is precisely why it is still with us. Legacy applications and numerous network administration tools still use that API and would not function without NetBIOS name resolution to communicate with. Remember in the DNS name resolution example, we alluded to a browser that passed a name query down to the resolver for name resolution. NetBIOS does much the same thing: an application needing to find a service running on another system (file and print services) sends a request for a NetBIOS name. This now has to be translated to an IP address. The example application may not know how to use DNS for the same function.

Two immediate examples of this are browsing and file and print services. NetBIOS names can be resolved in different ways, depending on how the client is configured (see the next section).

As you might expect, this flat namespace will have a WINS server, which will contain records. They are quite a bit different than DNS records, and the database format and method of storage are all different. In WINS, there is no ASCII file. The database is an MS database known as Jet, used in Access as well. It can and does corrupt and is sensitive to a great many things. As we go, you will see a few parallels with DNS.

NetBIOS names

NetBIOS names can be unique or a part of a group. They are 16-byte addresses, and they will have one position reserved for the type of service they represent. If your name is shorter than 16 bytes, the remaining bytes will be padded until 16 are used. This is important to know if you are editing an LMHOSTS file (see "LMHOSTS" later in this chapter). A record for the workstation service may look like this:

```
Machinename    <00>    UNIQUE
```

This represents a system's record in WINS for the Workstation service. The way you tell is by the suffix (<##>) designation, which will contain alphanumeric characters. You also can see Machinename   <00>   GROUP, and this is valid as well. Unique names are used to access services on individual systems; groups are used for groups of systems. Those are the record types—there are a lot of them—this list isn't all inclusive. There isn't any way it can be, because third-party vendors have their own suffixes that are registered with their applications. To see those, look at the two very last entries for Irmalan and Lotus Notes.

```
<computername>    00  U Workstation Service
<computername>    01  U Messenger Service
<\\--__MSBROWSE__>  01  G Master Browser
<computername>    03  U Messenger Service
<computername>    06  U RAS Server Service
<computername>    1F  U NetDDE Service
<computername>    20  U File Server Service
<computername>    21  U RAS Client Service
```

```
<computername>    22  U Microsoft Exchange Interchange (MSMail
          Connector)
<computername>    23  U Microsoft Exchange Store
<computername>    24  U Microsoft Exchange Directory
<computername>    30  U Modem Sharing Server Service
<computername>    31  U Modem Sharing Client Service
<computername>    43  U SMS Clients Remote Control
<computername>    44  U SMS Administrators Remote Control
          Tool
<computername>    45  U SMS Clients Remote Chat
<computername>    46  U SMS Clients Remote Transfer
<computername>    4C  U DEC Pathworks TCPIP service on
          Windows NT
<computername>    42  U mccaffee anti-virus
<computername>    52  U DEC Pathworks TCPIP service on
          Windows NT
<computername>    87  U Microsoft Exchange MTA
<computername>    6A  U Microsoft Exchange IMC
<computername>    BE  U Network Monitor Agent
<computername>    BF  U Network Monitor Application
<username>        03  U Messenger Service
<domain>          00  G Domain Name
<domain>          1B  U Domain Master Browser
<domain>          1C  G Domain Controllers
<domain>          1D  U Master Browser
<domain>          1E  G Browser Service Elections
<INet~Services>   1C  G IIS
<IS~computer name> 00  U IIS
<computername>    [2B]  U Lotus Notes Server Service
IRISMULTICAST    [2F] G Lotus Notes
IRISNAMESERVER   [33] G Lotus Notes
Forte_$ND800ZA   [20 U DCA IrmaLan Gateway Server Service
```

These are exactly the kinds of records you could expect to see in a WINS database. (Another one is called "static entry.") Most WINS registrations are dynamic and behave similarly to a DHCP lease. A static entry is used for systems like UNIX that are not NetBIOS aware. As a troubleshooting aside, never use these for NetBIOS-aware clients, because they will attempt to register themselves and be denied. This generally means that the client won't get resolution, and you'll get the call: Duplicate name on network! Static entries can be used for systems that are not capable of registering a NetBIOS name, and the records that can be manually added are of the same types that would normally be dynamically entered by a NetBIOS aware client: Unique, Group, Domain Name, Internet Group, and Multihomed.

LMHOSTS

When a NetBIOS broadcast fails, the next alternative is to consult the LMHOSTS file on the local computer. You can see an example in the %systemroot%\system32\drivers\ etc folder. Unlike HOSTS files, LMHOSTS files have additional options for name resolution, including but not limited to the following:

- **#PRE**   An entry preceded with this keyword will be preloaded into cache on system startup.

- **#DOM [domain name]**   This keyword is needed for domain validation across a router, and for domain browsing, and account synch.

- **#INCLUDE <path name>**   The #INCLUDE tag enables you to access the LMHOSTS file stored in another location other than the default.

Resolution Types

The setup of the client in WINS/NetBIOS name resolution will determine its behavior. There are four methods of resolution, called *node types*. Here is what they do:

- **B-node**   Remember, B is for Broadcast. It's generally what you would use if you had a one segment network, because it broadcasts, which bothers other clients, and most routers won't pass broadcasts anyway, which is how it should be.

- **P-Node**   This is what you would use if you had a WINS server; it does not broadcast but queries a WINS server directly for its name resolution.

- **M-Node**   This is mixed mode, so known because it uses a combination of B and P nodes. By default, it uses B-Node operation; if it gets no answer (the resource it wants is on another subnet), it flips to P-Node and queries the WINS server.

- **H-Node**   This is known as hybrid node. Actually an inverse version of M-Node, it will query the WINS server first, and if it gets no answer, it will go to B-Node and broadcast. This is the default.

Name Registration, Renewal, and Release

When they start up, WINS clients contact a WINS server and register their names and IP addresses. If a name is not in use (WINS does not care about IP addresses; you can duplicate those all day long), the server will allow the client to register its services with the WINS server. The client will get a positive name registration message. A bare minimum for a system coming online with nothing but an operating system will usually register <00> (Workstation service), <20> (Server service), and <03> Messenger service. If the name is in use, then the server will send a challenge to the last system that had registered it. It will do this three times, at predefined intervals, and if that challenge is responded to, the client is sent a negative registration response message.

The user will see a pop-up box indicating "Duplicate name on network." If the challenge is not responded to, then the client will be allowed to register. These registrations are not permanent but have a TTL (time to live) assigned to them. They have to renew these registrations. In *name renewal,* if a client is challenged as I just described, and it does not respond, then that client gives up the name for another system to use. To do a name refresh, which a client will try to do when 50 percent of its lease has expired, it will send a name refresh request. This request has the IP address and NetBIOS name of the system that wants to refresh, and the WINS server responds by sending back a new time lease (TTL) on the record. That's in a perfect world.

What happens when the client can't find the server is that the server will try to refresh every ten minutes for one hour on the primary WINS server. Then it will switch to the secondary WINS server and try at ten-minute intervals for another hour. If it still has not renewed, it will go back to the first server and try again. It will keep this up until the lease is exhausted; if it still has not renewed by that time, it will release the name. Another way for the name to be released is a system shutdown (proper, just powering down the box won't do it), when a request is sent to the WINS server. The WINS server will check the database, and if it finds the record (it should), it will return a positive release with a TTL of zero. If it finds an IP address/name mismatch, it will send a negative release.

The Name Resolution Process

When a client issues a need to get a NetBIOS name resolved, it looks locally first. It will check its cache for the name/IP address. If the name isn't resolved, the client queries the WINS server directly. It will look for this server for three more tries, and if it gets no answer, it will revert to the secondary server and repeat the process. If either server resolves the request, the client gets a success message, and the IP address for the proper NetBIOS name is returned to it. If neither resolves it, a "requested name does not exist" message is sent to the client. The client will begin using broadcasts at this point.

Database Replication

The WINS servers replicate their databases, and as in the case of DNS, how they do so is regulated by your configuration options. Remember, WINS is a *flat* namespace, so its replication topology is remarkably simple. I've seen and consulted many a customer who tried to employ a hierarchy in a WINS namespace. In terms of database replication, there is usually one design that works well and is generally low maintenance. The actual replication scheme is called *push/pull* replication, which we'll get into soon. Figure 12-1 shows the prescribed network topology regarding the manner in which the WINS servers are set up to replicate.

This is called *hub and spoke* replication. A group of WINS servers does replication with a central primary; the same design is used with a secondary, and the primary and secondary replicate between each other. They do this using push/pull replication. Let's nail down what this is.

A *pull partner* is a WINS server that asks for replicas from its push partners. The push partners know what to replicate because the version number should be higher that what the pull partner last received in the preceding replication session. A *push partner* is a WINS server that sends a replication request to its pull partners letting them know that

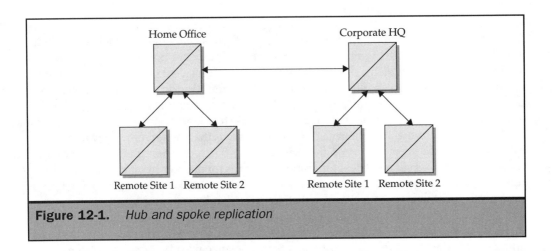

Figure 12-1. *Hub and spoke replication*

its database has been updated. They will pull replicas at that point, and your choice of push/pull replication should have two primary considerations: your WAN link speeds, and what systems need to communicate which what sites.

If your machine is in Remote Site 1 (as in Figure 12-1), which pushes/pulls with the Home Office server, and needs to communicate with a system in Remote Site 2, which replicates with the Corporate Office, it will never see the records it needs to do this unless the records are part of a replica that pulls from Remote Site 1 to the Corporate Office, which are then replicated to the Home Office. A replica is a copy of WINS records replicated from a push/pull partner. Since the Home Office replicates back to its Remote Site 1, the records are part of the WINS server in Remote Site 1 services by the Home Office.

WINS is not a difficult technology (although it does not scale well), and a common-sense approach to it will normally work well. Most issues come when designers try to do complex things with something that was not meant to be complex. If the bandwidth is available, push/pull replication between each server is preferred, since all records will be replicated to all points. Always configure the WINS server to point to itself for resolution.

Automatic Replication

WINS can detect and set up its replication partners automatically if your network is set up for multicasting. WINS will multicast every half hour or so to an IP address of 224.0.1.24. Any WINS server located will configure itself as a push/pull partner.

WINS capacity planning is one server per 10,000 clients, in less complex networks. This can be realistically achieved, but most of the time certain considerations are not taken—e.g., WINS will be put on a system that is a DC, print server, and application server.

This degrades performance, and if WINS does not perform well, then connectivity issues will arise. If you plan to use WINS in a 1 to 10,000 configuration, do not tax the system with any other processes, make sure it has fat pipes and good network capacity, use a high-speed LAN connection (prevent bottlenecks), don't multihome the server, and make sure the server has a high-performance disk subsystem. It sounds odd, but the biggest issues with these configurations have involved a disk subsystem overwhelmed with writes it can't get to the disk. In these cases, Performance Monitor (more on PM in Chapter 25) indicated that the writes were pegged, and when the disk subsystem was replaced with a SCSI RAID 0 one, performance then became very good.

Performance problems also arise when the WINS server is overburdened by being placed on a system performing many other functions. One of the classic cases I have seen was a third-party virus scanner on a large corporate network, which polls the WINS clients every so often for some reason, presumably to check if updates are needed. Such software typically has a configuration console, and the customer had configured it to check on these clients every 20 minutes. The big problem was that this server had 5000 clients depending on it, so the virus scanning software effectively tied up WINS cycles resolving names for the virus scanning software, so it could go poll all the clients! This taxed the server so heavily that no normal network name resolution could take place, and the business aspect of the network was effectively shut down. It could be more easily understood when thought of as a denial of service attack; it had the same effect.

Automatic Backup

WINS can be configured to back its database up to a location of your choosing. The Directory is chosen through the WINS snap-in, and once this is done, WINS will back up the databases every three hours. On paper, this sounds good; in practice, what happens is that the production database will corrupt for some reason, and the problem won't be discovered in the three hours before the next backup cycle, so the backup is now also corrupted.

A better practice, although more trouble, might be to use the Jetpack utility to verify the database integrity before backing it up. Jetpack has the capability to establish database integrity, or to reestablish it provided the database file is not too corrupted. Once this is done, do a manual backup. You might wonder why a backup is needed. It's more for quick recovery in the event of. . .database corruption! When WINS corrupts, there are two choices left if Jetpack can't recover the file: 1) Delete the file, stop WINS, and start WINS; this will create a fresh database. Sounds good until you realize all systems are going to have to reregister. That usually means a reboot. 2) Reload a backed-up WINS database, and only machines that need updating will be in limbo, which is better than the entire system being down.

Primary tools for troubleshooting are NBTSTAT and JETPACK.

The
Complete
Reference

Chapter 13

Routing and Remote Access Service

R outing and Remote Access Service (RRAS) has traditionally been an intriguing yet complicated technology for many administrators. RRAS overcomes the physical boundaries of your network environment by enabling remote clients to connect and use resources on your network. It also provides a way to connect network resources so that users can access resources on otherwise disjointed networks.

RRAS is a feature-rich service that includes support for sharing an Internet connection, dialing into the server, routing information from one network to another, protecting data through the use of a virtual private network (VPN), and more. This chapter gives you an overview of the technologies that RRAS offers and explains how to configure and manage solutions for your Windows Server 2003 network environment.

Changes in Routing and Remote Access for Windows Server 2003

The Windows Server 2003 version of RRAS is slightly different from the Windows 2000 version, and most of the differences are seen in the interface rather than the functions. For Windows NT administrators, the new version of RRAS provides more power and easier management.

The major functional changes in the Windows Server 2003 version of RRAS are due to changes in protocol support:

- Support for the NetBEUI protocol has been removed from Windows Server 2003, and so is no longer supported by RRAS.

- While the 32-bit versions of Windows Server 2003 still support IPX/SPX as a network protocol, RRAS will no longer route it.

A few new features have been added:

- Support for pre-shared keys in L2TP/IPSec authentication

- Integration of Network Address Translation (NAT) and static and dynamic packet filtering

- Support for L2TP/IPSec connections over NAT

- Broadcast name resolution for small networks without a local WINS or DNS server

IP Routing Overview

Network environments are often segmented for a variety of reasons, including the following:

- The number of available IP addresses in a TCP/IP-based network environment

- Separation of administration and management

- Security

- Ownership of the network

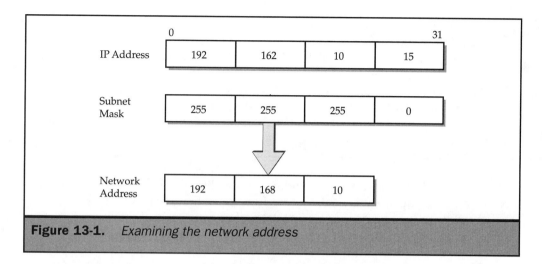

Figure 13-1.   *Examining the network address*

Many routers can route TCP/IP, IPX, and AppleTalk. However, since Windows Server 2003 and the Internet rely on TCP/IP, the focus of this section is TCP/IP routing.

With TCP/IP, the IP address, combined with the subnet mask, defines a network address. The network address identifies the network where the device resides (see Figure 13-1). More information on TCP/IP can be found in Chapter 10.

These networks, although disjointed, may require inter-communication, and this is where routing comes into the picture. *Routing* is the process of passing information across an internetwork boundary. The origination point is called the *source,* and the receiving end is the *destination*. An intermediary device, usually a router (and sometimes multiple devices), is responsible for passing the information from one network to another until the information reaches the intended recipient, as illustrated in Figure 13-2. For instance, when a computer on one network wants to send information to a computer located on a different network, it forwards the information to the router. The router then examines the packet and uses the destination address in the packet header to pass the information to the appropriate network.

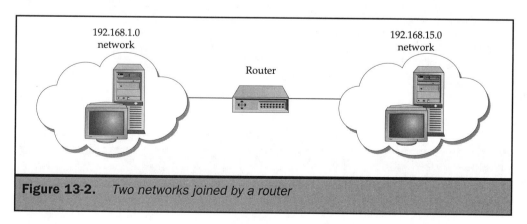

Figure 13-2.   *Two networks joined by a router*

Routing vs. Bridging

Routing is sometimes confused with bridging. The two technologies essentially take care of the same thing, passing information across an internetwork from source to destination, but the mechanisms used are quite different. Routing occurs at the Network layer, while bridging occurs at the Data Link layer in the OSI layer model. Operation at the different OSI layers has an effect on the way the information is processed and passed from source to destination.

While it's typical to use a router, Windows Server 2003 allows you to configure the server as a routing device as well. A router's function in life is to route packets from one network to the next. It does so by first determining the optimal routing paths using routing algorithms. *Routing algorithms* determine the shortest distance or the path of least resistance between a packet's source and its destination, as well as maintain routing tables that contain route information to help optimize the transfer of information. Figure 13-3 shows a sample routing table that informs the router how it might send packets of information.

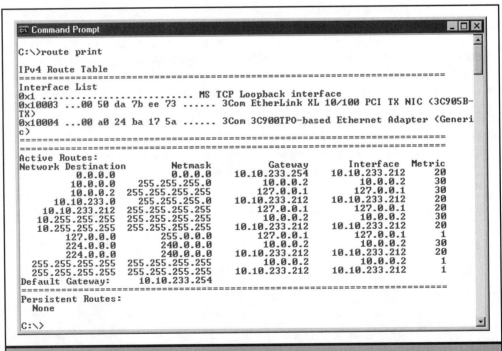

Figure 13-3. *Sample routing table*

Routers can also use a *router update message* to communicate with other routers to find the optimal paths for information being transferred from one network to another. Employing router update messages allows routers to compare and update their routing tables with information about paths to other networks.

Routing Algorithms

Routers, and Windows Server 2003 computers configured as routers, typically use either static or dynamic routing algorithms, but demand-dial routing is also supported. All of these routing algorithms basically serve the same purpose, although they have different mechanisms for moving information from a source to a destination.

Static Routing

A static route specifies a single path that information must use to travel from any two points. An administrator must identify and configure static routings in routing tables, and they don't change unless the administrator changes them. Statically routed network environments are relatively simple to design and maintain and are particularly well suited for small environments that experience little change in their routing topology.

Note	*Specific routes are not necessarily persistent routes in Microsoft Windows operating systems. In other words, you must specify that a route is persistent using the –p switch so that when the server is restarted for any reason, the static route will stick to the routing table.*

The major downfall of statically routed network environments is that they don't adapt to changing network conditions. For instance, if a router or link goes offline, the static routes won't be able to reroute the packets to other routers to get to the intended destination. Also, when a network is added or removed from your environment, an administrator has to identify possible routing scenarios and configure them accordingly. Therefore, statically routed network environments, especially the ones undergoing constant change, aren't a viable routing choice for larger networks. The cost in administration alone should cause you to avoid using static routing for anything other than small environments.

As a general rule of thumb, use static routes only for the following conditions:

- Home or branch offices
- Network environments with a very small number of networks
- Connections that aren't going to change in the near future (for example, a router that is used as a last resort when the information can't be routed otherwise)

Auto-Static Routing   Windows Server 2003 routers that use static routes can have their routing tables updated either manually or automatically. Automatically updating static routes is referred to as *auto-static* routing. Auto-static updates can be configured either through the RRAS interface, as shown in Figure 13-4, or by using the NETSH

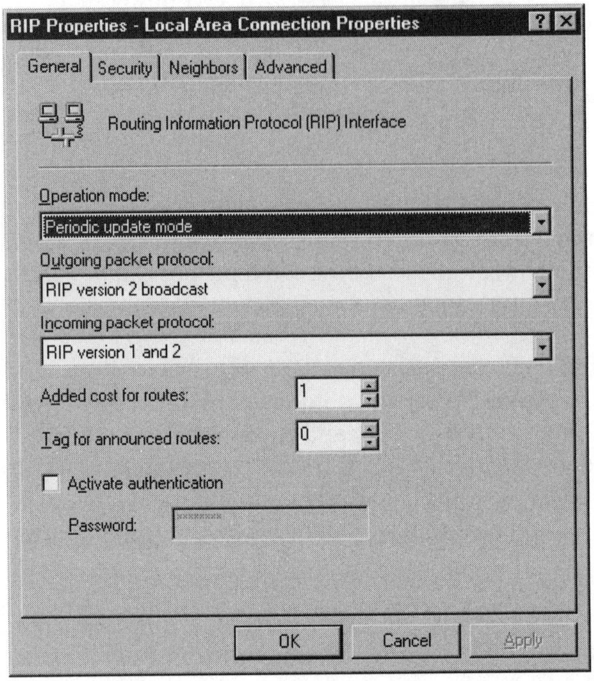

RIP Properties - Local Area Connection Properties

General | Security | Neighbors | Advanced

Routing Information Protocol (RIP) Interface

Operation mode:
Periodic update mode

Outgoing packet protocol:
RIP version 2 broadcast

Incoming packet protocol:
RIP version 1 and 2

Added cost for routes: 1

Tag for announced routes: 0

☐ Activate authentication

Password:

OK   Cancel   Apply

Figure 13-4.   *Auto-static routing using the RRAS interface*

utility. This allows you to update Windows Server 2003 routers only at desired times, to save connection costs and/or link bandwidth.

When you specify to have static routes updated, the router sends a request across an active connection to update all of the routes on the connection. The receiving router deletes any existing auto-static routes and then enters the new auto-static entries as static, persistent routes.

Auto-static updates are supported only if you're using RIP for IP.

Dynamic Routing

As the name implies, dynamic routing algorithms adapt to change in the network environment without manual intervention. Changes that are made are reflected almost instantaneously in the router. The following is a list of conditions for which dynamic routing is beneficial:

- A router or link goes down and the information must be rerouted
- A router is added or removed in the internetwork
- Large network environments that have many possible routing scenarios
- Large network environments that frequently undergo changes in network topology

Dynamic routing algorithms are able to adapt, in real time, to changing conditions by communicating with other routers. When the router is notified that a network change has occurred, the router recalculates routes and notifies other routers. This allows all routers on the internetwork to be aware of the entire network topology even as it changes. Most routers today use dynamic routing algorithms and are well suited for any size network.

Demand-Dial Routing

The most common routing protocols (RIP, OSPF, and so forth) that are used to communicate with other routers periodically send routing information to help adapt to dynamically changing network conditions. Generally speaking, this communication is an immense benefit for keeping track of changes so that information is routed through the path of least resistance. There are situations, however, when periodic router updates are less than desirable. For instance, you may be charged each time the link is activated.

To avoid these shortcomings, you can use *demand-dial routing*. Demand-dial routing activates a link only when information has to be passed through to the other side of the connection, which ultimately saves connection charges. Static routing or auto-static routing is used to keep the routers updated.

Routing Protocols

Routing protocols are a special type of protocol in that they keep track of the overall network topology in a routed network environment. They dynamically maintain information about other routers on the network and use this information to accurately predict the best route information should take.

Routing protocols use algorithms that can impact the router as well as influence how information is routed from one network to the next. Each routing protocol has characteristics that differentiate it from other routing protocols, but the primary goal for all of them is to provide simplicity, optimality, stability, and flexibility.

Routed vs. Routing Protocols

You've probably heard the terms "routed" and "routing protocols" used interchangeably. For instance, you probably know that TCP/IP, IPX/SPX, and so forth are routable protocols. Then, when you hear about routing protocols, you get confused on how the two types of protocols are different and how they are used. This mesh of terminology is quite common, but there is an important difference between the two.

Simply put, routing protocols route routed protocols such as TCP/IP, IPX/SPX, AppleTalk, and more. They are the missing link for getting information from one network to another. There are many routing protocols in use today, including but not limited to the following:

- Border Gateway Protocol (BGP)
- Enhanced Interior Gateway Routing Protocol (EIGRP)
- Exterior Gateway Protocol (EGP)
- Interior Gateway Routing Protocol (IGRP)
- Open Shortest Path First (OSPF)
- Routing Information Protocol (RIP)

Windows Server 2003's RRAS routers include built-in support for OSPF and RIP. In addition, RRAS can support third-party routing protocols, such as BGP, EIGRP, EGP, and IGRP, through its set of application programming interfaces (APIs). The routing protocols that Windows Server 2003 supports are explained next.

RIP

RIP is a distance-vector routing protocol that is relatively simple to use and configure. Distance-vector routing protocols send router updates to adjacent routers only. RIP has been widely adopted by the industry and has been in use with TCP/IP networks for almost two decades. RIP is described in several RFCs, which are listed in Table 13-1.

As you can see from Table 13-1, there are two versions of RIP. Version 1 uses broadcast messaging while version 2 uses multicast messaging for router update messages. RIP dynamically maintains routing information by sending routing update messages to other routers using RIP on the internetwork every 30 seconds.

RFC	Description
1058	Routing Information Protocol
1721	RIP version 2 protocol analysis
1722	RIP version 2 protocol applicability statement
1723	RIP version 2 carrying additional information

Table 13-1.   *RFCs Associated with RIP*

In addition to router update messages, RIP features several other mechanisms that fortify reliability and ensure that its routing tables are up-to-date. These include the following:

- **Hop-count limit**   The trip between one router and another is considered a hop. RIP's hop-count limit limits the number of hops to a destination to 15. Destinations that require more than 15 hops are considered unreachable.

- **Hold-downs**   Hold-downs ensure that old, unroutable routes aren't used in the routing table.

- **Split horizons**   Split horizons prevent redundancy of routing update messages (routing loops) to the router from which the message was sent.

- **Poison reverse updates**   Poison reverse updates prevent routing loops on the internetwork.

Despite these features, RIP still has its limitations. It can become cumbersome in large enterprise networks because its router update messages tend to eat away at bandwidth. Also, information is considered unroutable after 15 hops, which may cause problems in such environments.

OSPF

The OSPF routing protocol was developed by the Internet Engineering Task Force (IETF) specifically for TCP/IP environments such as the Internet. It is an efficient yet complex routing protocol, and it maintains both link states and routing tables. As a link routing protocol, OSPF retains information from all other routers in the internetwork and uses this information to calculate the shortest path to each router. This is in contrast to distance-vector routing protocols, mentioned earlier, which send router update messages only to adjacent routers.

OSPF was designed to overcome the limitations of other routing protocols, such as RIP. It is designed to scale without accruing large amounts of overhead. As a result, it meets the requirements for large enterprise internetworks. The RFCs for the OSPF routing protocol are 1247 for OSPF and 2328 for OSPF version 2.

OSPF Hierarchy   Another differentiating feature of OSPF is that it can operate hierarchically, as shown in the following illustration. Each OSPF router sends and receives routing information to all other routers in the *autonomous system (AS)*, a collection of routers (networks) that share a common routing strategy. Each AS can be divided into smaller groups called *areas*, which are essentially contiguous networks according to their network interfaces. Some routers may have multiple interfaces, and those that do can participate in more than one area. These routers are appropriately called *area border* *routers (ABRs)*, and they are responsible for passing routing information from one area to another, which reduces routing traffic in the AS.

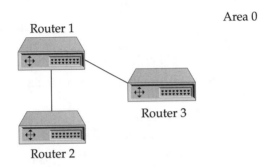

An AS containing multiple areas requires a *backbone* for structural and managerial support. The backbone connects ABRs and any networks that aren't totally contained in any specific area. Figure 13-5 shows an AS comprised of more than one area and a backbone. The backbone is in area 0.

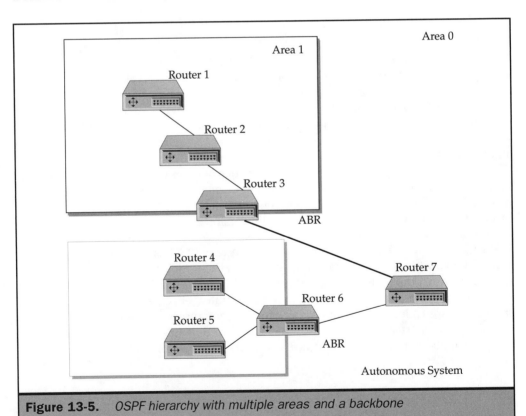

Figure 13-5. *OSPF hierarchy with multiple areas and a backbone*

Routing and Remote Access Service Fundamentals

RRAS (formerly code-named "Steelhead") was first introduced with the Windows NT 4 Option Pack as an add-on feature that essentially allowed the operating system to serve as a software-based router. It was designed to extend the current implementation of RAS that was built into Windows NT. The Windows NT 4 implementation provided multiprotocol routing and enhanced enterprise networking. It enabled remote site connectivity (LAN to LAN, LAN to user, and so on) via a wide area network (WAN) or through a VPN connection over a public network such as the Internet.

In Windows 2000 and Windows Server 2003, RRAS is no longer an add-on service. Instead, it is a single, unified service that combines the functionality of Windows NT's RAS and RRAS. It also improves upon the earlier implementations with increased support for industry standards and furnishes usability enhancements that reduce administration costs. You can configure and manage an Internet Connection Server, a Remote Access Server, or a VPN Server, all from a single interface.

Although RRAS is a single service, it operates as a client/server service. A *client* is any entity that connects through the RRAS server service to access resources, while the server side provides that connectivity. If you've used Windows NT versions of RAS or RRAS, you're probably already familiar with the concept of clients working from home or traveling using their modems to dial into an RRAS server. Windows 9*x* client machines configure a connection through Dial-Up Networking (DUN) to the RAS or RRAS server, and they're on their way. Other clients, such as Windows 3.1 and non-Microsoft operating systems, have other client-side software that allows them to connect remotely to resources through RAS or RRAS.

Windows Server 2003 changes the remote connectivity definition ever so slightly by extending the definition of a client. It's important to note that the most common (and supported) access methods from previous versions are still intact. Users can still connect using modems (see Figure 13-6), X.25 connections, VPNs, and more. However, RRAS clients now include network-connected clients in home offices or small businesses when you configure Internet connection sharing in RRAS. Moreover, configuring the RRAS server as a VPN server extends the definition of a client to include a remote office.

Remote Connectivity vs. Remote Control

Before discussing Windows Server 2003's RRAS any further, it would be useful to clear up a common misconception about remote connectivity and remote control. Remote connectivity is exactly what RRAS provides. It boils down to RRAS providing a network connection so that users can access resources—such as printers, network shares, and so on—remotely. It's also possible, but generally not recommended, to run applications over the WAN link. The reason to avoid running applications over the WAN link is that WAN links are typically slow connections. Depending on the size and type of application you're trying to run, you may find that it's excruciatingly slow.

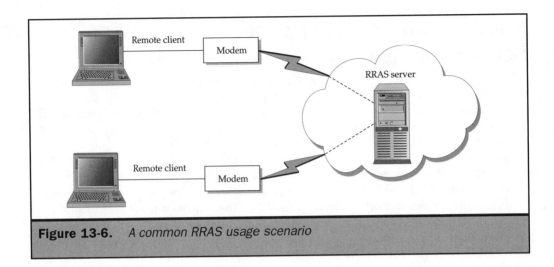

Figure 13-6.   *A common RRAS usage scenario*

With remote control, on the other hand, clients see a redirected screen output from the server exactly as it shows on the server's monitor. Every operation that is performed in the remote control session is actually being performed on the server end. Only the screen information is being sent across the connection. Remote control lets you, the client, feel as if you were right there on the server.

Said another way, remote connectivity makes your computer a part of the remote network, while remote control makes it seem like you are sitting at a remote computer.

Windows Server 2003 does provide remote control operations as well, just not through RRAS. Instead, you use Terminal Server, which comes bundled with the operating system. For more information on remote control and Terminal Server capabilities of Windows Server 2003, refer to Chapter 3.

Network Protocols

Language is fascinating because of its diversity. Even when you're speaking the same language with someone, there may be different dialects or accents that you'll interpret. Communicating (speaking, listening, and so forth) with others in our native language is something that all of us do (some of us better than others) on a daily basis and is usually taken for granted. Only when you are trying to communicate with someone who can't speak your native language do things get difficult, and you probably resort to other forms of communication like hand gestures to get the other person to understand what you're trying to communicate.

Now, network protocols, such as TCP/IP, IPX/SPX, NetBEUI, and AppleTalk, are the basis for communication for computers whether they're on a LAN or connecting remotely. These protocols are different languages that computers use to talk with one another. The key difference is that if the computer is not set up to speak a certain language (protocol), it simply won't try, and it can't rely on hand gestures or other forms of communication to communicate with the other computer. So, if one computer speaks only TCP/IP and another speaks only IPX/SPX, the two won't be able to talk to each other.

Two of the network protocols previously mentioned—TCP/IP and AppleTalk—are also supported by RRAS. It supports these network protocols for use with a variety of clients. What you decide to use not only must be loaded on both the client and server but, more importantly, the protocol or protocols should also match what you use in your Windows Server 2003 network environment. Because most Windows Server 2003 services depend on TCP/IP, the TCP/IP protocol should be your first choice and possibly the only protocol that you use with RRAS. If you have Macintosh clients, AppleTalk is a useful addition.

TCP/IP

Windows Server 2003 has standardized on using the popular TCP/IP protocol. As you saw after reading about TCP/IP in Chapter 10, TCP/IP has rooted itself as the protocol of choice for Windows Server 2003 network environments and has become widely adopted by all companies on the Internet. There are many reasons why TCP/IP has become the de facto standard for networking and for Windows Server 2003. The most notable reasons are its routing capabilities, its flexibility, its reliability, and its scalability.

With TCP/IP-enabled RRAS, you must provide IP addresses to clients. Clients can either get an IP address directly from the RRAS server's static pool of addresses or use DHCP (described in Chapter 10) to get the necessary TCP/IP information.

RRAS can be configured to assign an IP address from a pool of one or more static IP addresses. Each subsequent client connecting through RRAS is assigned the next available IP address in the pool and is freed up only when the client disconnects.

Using RRAS to assign IP addresses to clients is recommended only for small environments that aren't using DHCP in the Windows Server 2003 network environment. The reason for this is twofold. First, the client is given a limited amount of information. You must manually configure other TCP/IP configuration parameters on the client side in order for it to effectively communicate with other machines and use resources on your network. In addition, you must ensure that each client is given a unique IP address so that there aren't any IP address conflicts on the network. As the number of clients connecting through RRAS increases, so does the amount of work you'll be doing to configure client TCP/IP configuration settings. The second reason is that when TCP/IP information changes, such as adding or changing a WINS or DNS server, that information is not propagated to the client. Each change in your network environment could potentially mean that you must reconfigure each client machine connecting through RRAS. Of course, you could write a script that would change TCP/IP configuration settings as they log on to the network through RRAS, but this is still much more difficult and time-consuming than using DHCP.

To overcome the limitations inherent with RRAS assigning an IP address to RRAS clients, you can use DHCP to dynamically assign them an IP address as well as other TCP/IP configuration parameters. The benefits are enormous, but it boils down to greater flexibility and control over your environment without placing more work on your already hectic schedule. DHCP can pass many TCP/IP configuration settings—an IP address, subnet mask, default gateway, DNS servers, WINS servers, and more—to the RRAS client upon connecting to the RRAS server. Also, if the network configuration changes (if you get a new default gateway, a new DNS server, and so forth), then the change has to be made in only one place, the DHCP server.

Name Resolution   Clients logging on to the Windows Server 2003 network through RRAS using TCP/IP also require a naming service or a method for name resolution. More specifically, to use resources on the network, they need name to IP address resolution and vice versa. For example, when a client wants to use a shared resource (such as a printer) on a computer named DR-K, it must use a service that translates the computer name to its corresponding IP address in order to connect to the computer.

There are five name resolution mechanisms that clients can use to locate and use resources:

- DNS
- WINS
- HOSTS
- LMHOSTS
- Broadcasts

These are covered in detail in Chapter 11.

IPX/SPX

Internetwork Packet Exchange/Sequenced Packet Exchange (IPX/SPX) is the protocol developed by Novell to be used on Novell NetWare networks, and it was derived from Xerox's Xerox Network Systems (XNS) protocol. Although its design is best suited for LAN environments, IPX/SPX is routable and can therefore be used in enterprise-wide internetworks. IPX/SPX can use either of two routing protocols, RIP or NetWare Link Services Protocol (NLSP), to pass information to other routers.

Compared to TCP/IP, configuring and using the IPX/SPX protocol is a cakewalk. For starters, it doesn't rely on complex numbering systems that you need to configure to communicate, and it doesn't need to rely on other services for name resolution. In fact, very little configuration is needed once you install the protocol. This also makes IPX/SPX easy to install.

However, while RRAS in Windows NT 4 and Windows 2000 supported IPX routing, Windows Server 2003 does not. Keep in mind, though, that you're already running TCP/IP in your Windows Server 2003 network, so your only compelling reason for using IPX/SPX is to support Novell NetWare connectivity. It is also important to point out that the

IPX/SPX protocol broadcasts using the Service Advertisement Protocol (SAP) to identify resources on the network. Broadcasts, by definition, increase the amount of traffic generated on the network. Avoiding the use of this protocol helps you keep the number of protocols used in your network environment to a minimum and consequently reduces administration as well as traffic on the network.

NetBEUI

The NetBIOS Extended User Interface (NetBEUI) protocol was designed in the late 1980s as an extension to NetBIOS. NetBEUI is a relatively simple protocol that is best suited for small network environments only. In small network environments it provides quick response times when trying to locate services, but as the size of the network grows, performance diminishes because of the way it manages name resolution. Support for NetBEUI has been removed from Windows Server 2003.

For many networks, NetBIOS is an integral part of the communication between computers and other network devices. Each device, whether a computer or printer, has a NetBIOS name associated with it. NetBEUI uses these NetBIOS names to locate resources on the network by broadcasting. So, when a computer wants to locate a printer, for example, it sends a broadcast out across the network to find the device attached to the NetBIOS name that it's looking for. As you can see, the more devices on the network using NetBEUI, the more traffic that will be clogging the network. A large number of broadcasts may even result in a broadcast storm, which can easily cripple a network. I have personally witnessed a 10,000-node network shut down due to a broadcast storm (no, I wasn't responsible for configuring the network).

AppleTalk

AppleTalk is the network protocol for Apple Macintosh computers and is supported in Windows Server 2003 RRAS. This network protocol dynamically assigns all devices (computers, printers, and so forth) on the network a unique node number to distinguish them from other devices. It does so by the use of broadcasts.

Communication between computers and other network devices using AppleTalk relies on broadcasts, which is similar to a mass mailing. Every device speaking AppleTalk receives the message. When a successful name resolution occurs after a broadcast, the information is stored in the computer's AppleTalk Address Resolution Protocol (AARP) cache. The next time the computer needs name resolution, it checks its AARP cache before broadcasting.

Although your network may support Macintosh clients, you should configure RRAS to support AppleTalk only if some AppleTalk clients need to remotely connect to the Windows Server 2003 network.

Access Protocols

Access protocols, also known as encapsulation protocols, establish and control the transmission of information over a WAN link between the RRAS server and client. These protocols are vendor independent, which means that they foster communication between dissimilar vendor technologies and operating system platforms. As a result, many different types of clients (such as Macintosh, UNIX, and so on) can connect through RRAS.

Access protocols live and work in the Data Link layer of the OSI model, while the network protocols, previously described, operate at the Network layer of the OSI model. The layer in which access protocols operate is the basis for their vendor independence. The primary responsibility of these protocols is to maintain the remote access session by providing compression, packetization of data, and error control. Some access protocols can also provide security by encrypting data before it is sent over the WAN link.

Point-to-Point Protocol (PPP)

PPP is one of the most common access protocols in use today and is the default for Windows Server 2003. It is actually a suite of standardized protocols, much like TCP/IP, that work together to provide a multitude of services used to establish and maintain point-to-point connections. PPP provides many features, including

- Encapsulation (tunneling) of data
- Compression of data
- Multiplexing (multilink) to combine two or more WAN links
- Reliability by using the High-Level Data Link Control (HDLC) protocol to configure framing of data
- Network configuration negotiation

PPP uses two other protocols, the Link Control Protocol (LCP) and the Network Control Protocol (NCP), to establish and maintain the point-to-point connections. LCP is primarily used to establish the connection and configure link parameters such as frame size. NCP, on the other hand, is primarily responsible for negotiating network configuration parameters, such as encapsulation and compression, for the network protocols (AppleTalk, TCP/IP, and NetBEUI) on the WAN link. Each network protocol has its own version of an NCP to be used. They are listed with their corresponding network protocol in Table 13-2.

As you might expect, PPP is defined in a series of RFCs. Table 13-3 lists the PPP RFCs, which can all be found at www.rfc-editor.org.

Note   *PPP is the standard from which the PPTP and L2TP protocols were derived. These protocols are explained in the following sections.*

Point-to-Point Tunneling Protocol (PPTP)

A popular remote access subject that has received a lot of attention in the past couple of years is virtual private networking, and PPTP started it all. More information on VPNs can be found later in this chapter. PPTP extends the PPP protocol by enhancing many of PPP's features, such as security and multiprotocol support. PPTP can encapsulate

NCP	Network Protocol
AppleTalk Control Protocol (ATCP)	AppleTalk
Internet Protocol Control Protocol (IPCP)	TCP/IP
Internet Packet Exchange Control Protocol (IPXCP)	IPX/SPX
NetBEUI Control Protocol (NBCP)	NetBEUI

Table 13-2.   *NCPs and Corresponding Network Protocol*

TCP/IP, and NetBEUI protocols within PPP *datagrams*. Datagrams are associated with connectionless delivery methods that may or may not reach the intended recipient. PPTP is also a set of standardized protocols that work together to provide remote clients with a secure communications channel through a TCP/IP-based network, such as the Internet, to a private network.

RFC Number	Description
1549	Information regarding PPP in HDLC framing
1552	Information regarding PPP IPXCP
1334	Information regarding PPP authentication protocols
1332	Information regarding PPP IPCP
1661	Information regarding LCP
1990	Information regarding PPP Multilink Protocol
2125	Information regarding PPP Bandwidth Allocation Protocol (BAP) and PPP Bandwidth Allocation Control Protocol (BACP)
2097	PPP NetBIOS Frames Control Protocol (NBFCP)
1962	PPP Compression Control Protocol (CCP)
1570	PPP LCP Extensions
2284	PPP Extensible Authentication Protocol (EAP)

Table 13-3.   *PPP-Related RFCs*

A PPTP connection is typically encrypted with either RC4 or DES 40-bit encryption schemes, but a 128-bit encryption version can also be obtained if it's kept within the United States.

Several practical implementations stem from PPTP connections. For example, while on the road, clients can establish a secure connection to their company through the Internet. This enables them to utilize resources on the company network without accruing long-distance phone costs. Another example is using PPTP connectivity to link various company sites securely and inexpensively, as in the configuration shown in Figure 13-7. As you can see from these examples, PPTP can be used with a dial-up connection, but it isn't required. All that is necessary is IP connectivity between two points.

Extensible Authentication Protocol (EAP)   With help from EAP, security with PPTP connections is tightened. As the name implies, EAP is an authentication protocol that adds to and enhances authentication mechanisms with a PPTP connection. In particular, EAP brings to PPTP several authentication mechanisms, including these:

- Token card authentication
- Public key authentication using smart cards and certificates
- One-time passwords

Depending on which implementation of EAP you use, the client, not the server, may be the only party obligated to prove its identity. However, with Windows Server 2003, both the client and server are obligated to prove to one another that they are who they say they are.

Layer Two Tunneling Protocol (L2TP)

L2TP promises to be the PPTP's replacement as the tunneling protocol of choice. It is supported by vendors such as Cisco, Microsoft, 3Com, and others. L2TP is based on PPTP and the Layer Two Forwarding (L2F) protocol. L2F was designed by Cisco and

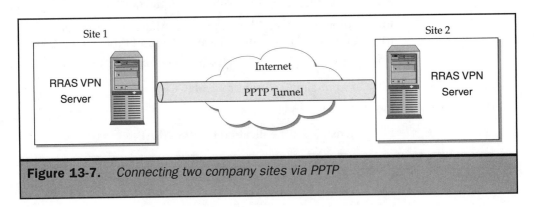

Figure 13-7.   *Connecting two company sites via PPTP*

is a more robust tunneling protocol that supports the encapsulation of many more protocols than PPTP, including AppleTalk and SNA. This allows for a broader coverage of the operating system platforms that can be supported.

Like PPTP, L2TP can be used to create a secure, reliable communications channel between two endpoints, such as a remote client and server or site to site. It uses Internet Protocol Security (IPSec) for authentication and encryption to protect data traversing the connection. IPSec is covered in more detail later in this chapter. L2TP encapsulates PPP packets just like PPTP does in order to secure the connection. Recall that PPP packets essentially encapsulate or wrap up network protocols (TCP/IP and so forth). Figure 13-8 illustrates how L2TP encapsulates the packets.

L2TP is frequently used for dial-up connections because its design is optimized for dial-up connections rather than site-to-site implementations. Moreover, the L2TP implementation in Windows Server 2003 is also designed primarily over IP networks, and it doesn't support native tunneling over X.25, Frame Relay, or ATM networks.

Serial Line Internet Protocol (SLIP)

SLIP is the oldest type of access protocol for point-to-point connections. It encapsulates network protocols so that they can be transmitted over the link, but it lacks many of the features of its protocols, including compression and error checking. As a result, SLIP does little to ensure the quality of data that is being transmitted and should therefore be used only as a last resort.

Windows Server 2003 no longer supports SLIP for incoming connections, but does support it for outbound connections only for backward compatibility with older systems that don't support the more robust PPP communications. SLIP is all but phased out as a means of point-to-point communications.

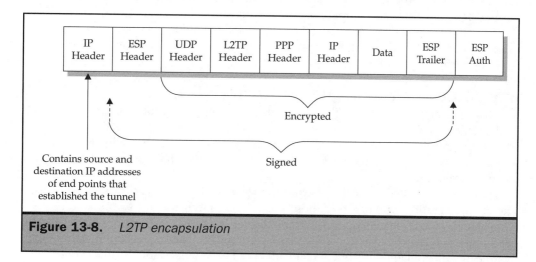

Figure 13-8. *L2TP encapsulation*

Access Methods

Having discussed the various network and access protocols that RRAS supports, it's time to examine the methods that use the physical layer protocols for communication.

Analog Connections

The Public Switched Telephone Network (PSTN) is the standard telephone service that you're accustomed to using and is also known as the Plain Old Telephone System (POTS). POTS uses analog lines that were designed primarily for voice communications, but they are now also commonly used for data transmission. Modems allow you to transmit data over the analog system. Chances are that anywhere there is a telephone, you will be able to use a modem to make a remote connection to your own network. Because POTS was designed for voice communications, there are limitations on the rate at which data can be transmitted.

Modems convert digital signals to analog to be transmitted across the link, and convert analog signals being received back to digital signals so that the computer can understand them. Generally speaking, modems are categorized by the standards they support (such as V.32, V.32bis, and V.90) and the speed at which they send and receive data. Modems can operate at speeds up to 56 Kbps using the V.90 modulation standard. However, the Federal Communications Commission (FCC) power rules limit the ability to send data faster than 33.6 Kbps and receive data at 53 Kbps. The conversion, along with other factors such as noise that are inherent to POTS, chokes the amount of data that you can send and receive over the connection.

There are many vendors that supply modems, and Windows Server 2003 supports tons of them. This includes, for instance, most if not all of the major brands of modems, such as 3Com/US Robotics, and Hayes. However, to be on the safe side, you should verify that your modem is compatible. Check Microsoft's Hardware Compatibility List (HCL) at www.microsoft.com/HCL. After you install the modem, Windows Server 2003 is likely to detect it and install the appropriate drivers, because Windows Server 2003 fully supports Plug and Play.

Integrated Services Digital Network (ISDN)

ISDN is a digital version of POTS. It can transfer data at a rate much higher than the analog phone system because the line is much cleaner (higher clarity, less noise, and so forth). Typically, phone lines transmit at up to 53 Kbps, with a 56 Kbps modem, whereas ISDN transmits data at either 64 or 128 Kbps depending on how many ISDN channels are used.

ISDN uses two B-channels for transferring data. Each channel operates at 64 Kbps. Therefore, operating with one B-channel allows you to transmit at 64 Kbps, and using two channels boosts speeds up to 128 Kbps through channel aggregation. ISDN also has a third channel, the D-channel, that isn't used for transmitting data but rather for overseeing and managing the two B-channels. The D-channel establishes the connection and controls data transfer such as signaling.

Two protocols are used with ISDN. They are Basic Rate Interface (BRI) and Primary Rate Interface (PRI). The type of protocol you use depends on how the phone company is providing the ISDN service to you. The most common ISDN protocol used is BRI. It defaults to using two B-channels and a D-channel. PRI is a little less common because it uses a portion of a T1 data circuit. A T1 circuit (or line) is an aggregation of twenty-four 64 Kbps channels. When you use PRI, it can take three of those channels (two are used as B-channels and one as a D-channel).

Several years ago, ISDN was typically used only for businesses, because of its high price tag. However, ISDN is now becoming an affordable and widely available option for home use as well.

X.25

X.25 is a global standard developed in the 1970s for data communications over a telephone network or packet-switched networks (PSNs). Although X.25 implementations are gradually being replaced with other low-cost alternatives, it is often the best choice in underdeveloped areas around the world.

X.25 communications are very similar to telephone use or dial-up connections. A host calls another computer to request a connection, and if it's accepted, information can then be transferred. More specifically, data terminal equipment (DTE) connects to data circuit-terminating equipment (DCE) within a PSN.

In Windows Server 2003, network and dial-up connections support X.25 by using packet assemblers/disassemblers (PADs) and X.25 cards. RRAS clients may also use a modem to dial into a Windows Server 2003 server using X.25, but the server must use an X.25 card to accept the call.

Asymmetric Digital Subscriber Line (ADSL)

ADSL is a new access method (and one of the most talked about) that has found its way into many small businesses and residential areas because of its relatively low cost and high bandwidth capabilities. ADSL provides high-speed data connections using the same copper phone lines that are used in POTS.

Although ADSL promises high bandwidth, the upstream (client-to-service) is slower than the downstream (service-to-client) data transfer rate. Typically, upstream transfer rates range from 64 Kbps to 256 Kbps, while downstream boasts an impressive 1.544 Mbps for data transmission. The downstream transfer rate is equivalent to a T1 line. There are also variations of ADSL, such as HDSL and VDSL, that claim substantially higher upstream and downstream transfer rates.

When you install an ADSL network adapter in Windows Server 2003, the adapter appears as either an Ethernet or a dial-up interface. The connection configuration depends on the interface it uses. For instance, if ADSL appears as an Ethernet interface, the connection operates just as it would with an Ethernet connection, but if it appears as a dial-up interface, ADSL uses ATM.

Asynchronous Transfer Mode (ATM)

ATM is a collection of technologies that provides robust, high-quality networking services for voice, video, and data. ATM uses very large-scale integration (VLSI) technology to segment data at high speeds into packets called *cells*. Each cell is 53 bytes in length and consists of 5 bytes of header information and 48 bytes of data.

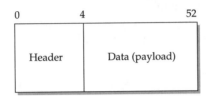

ATM is *connection oriented*, meaning that a path from source to destination is established before data is sent across the connection. This path is commonly referred to as a *virtual circuit (VC)*. Also, during the establishment of the connection, Quality of Service (QoS) parameters are negotiated to provide the highest level of accuracy and guarantee quality for the connection regardless of whether it's LAN based or WAN based.

When comparing ATM with Ethernet or Token Ring, you'll notice many differing characteristics between the technologies, most notably these:

- **Connection oriented**   ATM is connection oriented while Ethernet and Token Ring are connectionless oriented. Connectionless-oriented technologies do not establish a connection prior to sending data across the connection, but they do have other mechanisms within the upper-level, network protocols to ensure that data reaches the intended recipient.

- **Packets**   ATM packets are called *cells,* and each cell has a fixed length of 53 bytes. This is in contrast to Ethernet's or Token Ring's variable packet length structure. Because the ATM cell is fixed in length, it's predictable. The network doesn't spend time determining where a particular cell begins or ends, and the overall transmission of the data is optimized.

Internet Connection Sharing

Internet Connection Sharing (ICS) is an invaluable service provided in Windows Server 2003. Basically, it allows you to share a dedicated or dial-up Internet connection with other machines in small office/home office (SOHO) environments. It also provides a low-cost alternative for the SOHO.

Traditionally, you were required to configure each machine in the SOHO with a registered IP address or a separate dial-up connection to get out onto the Internet. There are two inherent problems with this situation. First, registering IP addresses and buying additional equipment (routers, hubs, and so on) to connect the SOHO to the Internet is an expensive solution for this type of environment. Only larger environments could make this investment worthwhile. Also, creating separate dial-up connections requires additional expenses (phone lines, modems, and possibly several Internet accounts from your ISP) and your time, but more importantly, it patches up the problem rather than solving it. ICS removes these limitations by serving as a centralized, low-cost mechanism for connecting your environment to the Internet.

Following are two methods in which you can configure ICS:

- **Routed connection**   Configuring ICS as a routed connection allows the server to act as a router that forwards packets from a single SOHO network to the Internet. This option is performed through the Network And Dial-Up Connections interface.

- **Translated connection**   This option, performed through the RRAS management console using the NAT configuration path, configures the Windows Server 2003 server again as a router that forwards packets from a network to the Internet. The difference between this option and the first one is that it affords much more flexibility in the way you configure Windows Server 2003 as a router.

Both methods perform network address translation (NAT), but the NAT capability of the translated connection is more sophisticated because it can route more than one IP address. NAT hides the private IP address or addresses on the internal network behind one or more public IP addresses. For instance, your computer on the internal network has an IP address of 192.168.1.10 (private IP address), but when you jump onto the Internet, the server translates it into a public IP address. A public IP address is needed in order to use Internet resources such as the Web.

Securing RRAS

Securing remote access connections is key to successfully deploying remote access solutions. If you don't properly secure remote connections, you'll risk leaving your Windows Server 2003 network environment wide open. Windows Server 2003's RRAS provides many security features, including encryption, authentication, callback, and caller ID, which help fortify your remote connections and consequently your network.

Authentication Methods

There are several authentication methods that you can use with remote connections. By default, RRAS uses MS-CHAP and MS-CHAPv2 authentication. Selected authentication methods are used in the following order:

1. Extensible Authentication Protocol (EAP)

2. Microsoft Challenge Handshake Authentication Protocol version 2 (MS-CHAPv2)

3. Microsoft Challenge Handshake Authentication Protocol (MS-CHAP)

4. Challenge Handshake Authentication Protocol (CHAP)

5. Shiva Password Authentication Protocol (SPAP)

6. Password Authentication Protocol (PAP)

7. Unauthenticated access

These authentication methods, illustrated in Figure 13-9, can be found within the RRAS management console by selecting the appropriate server in the right console and selecting Properties. Then, under the Security tab, select the Authentication Methods button. To use any of the authentication methods, you simply check the box beside them.

EAP

EAP is an extension to PPP that allows an arbitrary authentication method to be negotiated between the remote client and server. Once the link is established, the client and server negotiate which EAP type of authentication mechanism will be used. These options include EAP-MD5 CHAP, EAP-TLS, smart cards, and more. After a decision is made, the client uses the selected authentication mechanism to gain access to the RRAS server and network.

As the name implies, EAP is extensible, meaning that any number of EAP types can be added at any time. To see which EAP methods you're currently using, do the following:

1. Open the RRAS management console from the Start | Programs | Administrative Tools menu.

2. In the right console, right-click a RRAS server and select Properties.

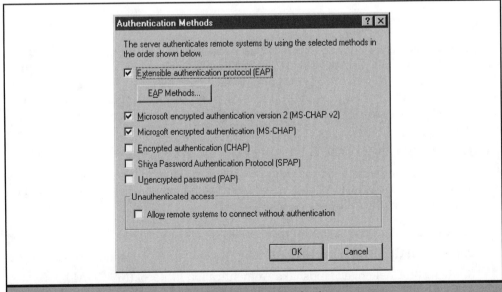

Figure 13-9.   *Remote access authentication methods*

3. Under the Security tab, click the Authentication Methods button to display the Authentication Methods window.

4. Click the EAP Methods button to see the EAP methods that are currently installed, as shown in Figure 13-10.

EAP Methods   Windows Server 2003 can support any EAP method types (such as smart cards) as plug-ins, but it automatically provides the following two EAP methods:

- **EAP-MD5 CHAP**   EAP-Message Digest 5 CHAP is a required EAP method that retains many of the same attributes as CHAP but also sends the challenges and responses as EAP messages.

- **EAP-TLS**   The EAP-Transport Level Security method is certificate-based authentication. This method is required if you're using smart cards. EAP-TLS is currently the strongest type of authentication, and it requires that the RRAS server be a member of a domain. It provides mutual authentication (both client and server are authenticated), encryption, as well as secured private key exchange.

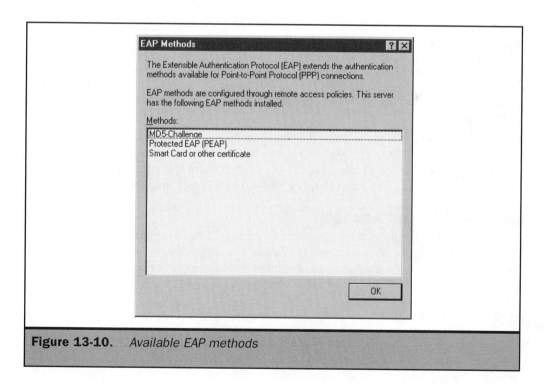

Figure 13-10.   *Available EAP methods*

CHAP

CHAP is probably the most common authentication protocol in use today. Three versions of CHAP are supported by Windows Server 2003's RRAS:

- **CHAP** As an industry standard, CHAP is a challenge-response authentication protocol that supports one-way encryption of responses to challenges. The authentication process uses three steps to completion. First, the server challenges the client to prove its identity. Then, the client sends an encrypted CHAP message in response to the challenge. The server then verifies the response, and if it's correct, the client is granted access.

- **MS-CHAP** MS-CHAP is a modified, proprietary version of CHAP. The major difference between MS-CHAP and CHAP in Windows Server 2003 is that the user's password is in a reversibly encrypted form.

- **MS-CHAPv2** Version 2 of MS-CHAP is a stronger, more secure authentication method than previous implementations. Some of the most notable differences are that it no longer supports NTLM (it can be used only with Windows Server 2003), it provides mutual authentication, and separate cryptographic keys are used for sending and receiving data.

SPAP

Shiva is an older, yet widely accepted, remote access solution. Clients using Shiva client software must be authenticated using SPAP. SPAP is a rather simple authentication method that encrypts passwords traveling across the link. This authentication option is supported by Windows Server 2003 only for Shiva clients that you may need to service.

PAP

PAP is actually a misnomer because it is the most insecure authentication method available today. Both the username and password are sent across the link in clear text. Anyone snooping the connection could easily grab and use the information to gain access to your network. As a result, using PAP for authentication is not advisable.

Unauthenticated Access

This option is pretty obvious, so there's really no need to go into much depth about it. All that need be said is that you should never use this option unless you absolutely don't care about securing your environment. You're essentially opening access to anyone who wants to connect remotely.

Callback

Callback means just what the word implies. A remote client dials the RRAS server, and the client's credentials (username and password) are verified. Once the credentials are verified, the connection is dropped so that the RRAS server can call the remote client back. The number that the RRAS server calls can either be specified during the initial call or you can require that RRAS call a specific number. The latter of the two is the most secure method because it restricts remote connectivity locations. Another benefit of callback is to save on the remote client's connection charges.

Caller ID

Most, if not all, of you are already familiar with caller ID on your phone systems at home. Someone calls you, and his or her telephone number is displayed. This same functionality can be applied to remote access to offer heightened security.

Caller ID can be used to verify that a remote client that dials into RRAS is calling from a specified number. If the client isn't calling from the specified number, the connection is denied and dropped. Sometimes you may find that the phone company can't provide you with a caller's number because somewhere POTS isn't equipped to handle caller ID or the caller has blocked the number from being displayed. When the number can't be displayed, for whatever reason, the connection is denied.

Virtual Private Networking Fundamentals

VPNs are probably one of the most talked about but, surprisingly, least understood concepts relating to the Internet and remote access. VPNs have been around for years, but they haven't received a lot of attention until now. They have been supported by Microsoft since the Windows NT 4 implementation of RRAS and continue to be supported in Windows Server 2003's RRAS.

Part of the confusion stems from what the word "private" means. For instance, companies have long given their sites, such as branch offices, connectivity through dedicated leased lines. This is in fact a private network that has been extended to reach remote areas. This is also commonly referred to as a *carrier-based VPN*. The ISP (or phone company) sets up virtual circuits between sites. In this case, there are two types of virtual circuits, permanent virtual circuits (PVCs) and switched virtual circuits (SVCs), that provide private connectivity. The most common of these is the PVC.

In the following discussion, we won't be discussing carrier-based VPNs. RRAS supports the *Internet VPN*. An Internet VPN is a means by which two computers or networks can communicate privately through an otherwise shared or public network such as the Internet. It is also an extension to your private network, but it doesn't require an ISP or phone company to place a separate, additional link to provide the connectivity, which can potentially save you tons of money. VPNs aren't limited to site-to-site connections. They also allow remote clients, such as road warriors and telecommuters, to connect securely to the company's network. For example, a remote client dials his or her local ISP (saving phone charges) and then establishes a VPN through the Internet to his or her company's network.

VPNs provide security and reliability to what would otherwise be an insecure connection through a public network. A VPN is basically composed of three technologies that, when used together, form the secure connection. They are *authentication, tunneling,* and *encryption.*

Authentication

The primary reason for authentication with VPNs is to have a method ensuring that the client and server are who they say they are before the VPN session is established. This doesn't necessarily imply that mutual authentication is required. Successful authentication is required before the tunnel can be established and data is transmitted, but the type of authentication used depends on the types of clients in your environment and your choice of authentication methods.

Any of the authentication methods described earlier in the "Securing RRAS" section of this chapter can be used. The only drawback, though, is that if remote clients are down-level clients, they probably don't support EAP. In fact, Windows NT and Windows 9*x* clients don't support it. When you're deciding which ones to use, keep in mind that it's important to provide the strongest level of authentication possible. This means using authentication protocols such as EAP, MS-CHAP, or MS-CHAPv2.

Tunneling

Tunneling is used to encapsulate network protocols (TCP/IP, AppleTalk, and NetBEUI) into an IP packet that can travel across the Internet. Yes, TCP/IP can travel across the Internet on its own, but then it wouldn't be a part of the tunnel or the VPN. Think of tunneling as a mole burrowing through the ground making a path from one site to the next.

Before the tunnel can be created, it must be verified that the two endpoints are who they say they are. Once they're authenticated, the tunnel is created and information between the two ends is sent, as illustrated in Figure 13-11. The two protocols that are responsible for creating the VPN tunnels in Windows Server 2003 are PPTP and L2TP, which were explained earlier. L2TP is an advancement over the PPTP tunneling protocol, and it uses the IPSec authentication and encryption protocol.

L2TP is available only in the Windows 2000 and Windows Server 2003 version of RRAS, and Windows 2000 and later clients are the only ones equipped to use it. Table 13-4 outlines which clients support the different tunneling protocols. You can add L2TP/IPSec support to Windows 98, Windows Me, and Windows NT 4 by downloading and installing the L2TP/IPSec VPN Client from the Microsoft web site.

Encryption

The third major component of a VPN is encryption. Encryption is an extra precautionary measure that protects the data that is sent through the tunnel. Data is encrypted before it's encapsulated to reduce the risk that someone might tamper with it if the tunnel is breached.

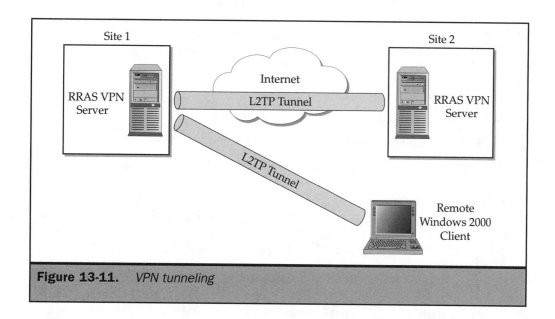

Figure 13-11. *VPN tunneling*

Windows Server 2003 supports two encryption technologies, Microsoft Point-to-Point Encryption (MPPE) and IPSec. Both methods use an encryption key to encrypt and decrypt information at the sender and receiver ends. You can require that remote clients or sites use either method. If they don't use the encryption method you specify, you can configure RRAS to deny the connection.

VPN Client	Tunneling Protocols Supported
Windows Server 2003	PPTP, L2TP
Windows XP	PPTP, L2TP
Windows 2000	PPTP, L2TP
Windows NT 4	PPTP
Windows 98	PPTP
Windows 95	PPTP with Windows Dial-up Networking 1.3

Table 13-4. *Clients and the Tunneling Protocols They Support*

MPPE

MPPE can encrypt data in PPTP VPN connections. It supports the following encryption schemes:

- Standard 40-bit encryption
- Standard 56-bit encryption
- Strong 128-bit encryption for use only within the United States and Canada

To use MPPE, you must use either MS-CHAP or MS-CHAPv2 authentication protocols.

IPSec

Despite popular belief, IPSec is actually a collection of cryptography-based services and protocols. It provides authentication as well as encryption to a VPN connection that uses L2TP. However, L2TP still uses the authentication methods, such as EAP and MS-CHAP, described earlier.

IPSec, in Windows Server 2003 implementations, uses either the Data Encryption Standard (DES) or Triple DES (3DES). DES uses a 56-bit encryption key and can be used internationally. 3DES, on the other hand, uses two 56-bit encryption keys and cannot be exported outside the United States. The type of IPSec encryption used is determined by the *security association (SA)*. An SA is set up between the two endpoints in the VPN, and it establishes the common security measures to be used.

VPN Implementation Considerations

Just because VPNs are one of the hottest technologies for remote access doesn't mean that a VPN is the right solution for you. Before you actually implement it as a solution in your Windows Server 2003 network environment, you need to consider the following:

- **Security**   Security concerns should be one of the major deciding factors that lead you to use a VPN solution. There are two questions that you should ask yourself. First, "Will a VPN be overkill for the type of information that I'm transmitting?" For instance, are you just sending nonconfidential e-mail? Second, "Is a VPN going to satisfy my security requirements?" Government agencies are often used in examples concerning security. The military, for instance, probably won't even consider using a VPN over a public network no matter how good the security it claims to provide.

- **Budgetary concerns**   Initial and ongoing costs for setting up a VPN solution in your Windows Server 2003 network environment is miniscule compared to leased lines. A VPN clearly gives you the cost advantages because now sites and remote clients can connect to the company's network securely without additional charges such as connectivity hardware, phone costs, and so on.

It's true that remote users could use an 800 number to dial in, but that doesn't totally solve the problem, and it's expensive.

■ **Throughput** Because VPNs require authentication and encryption, the rate at which data is transmitted is, by definition, going to be slower than without it. You can count on as little as 30 to as much as 50 percent degradation in performance using a VPN. You'll have to weigh the costs of throughput versus security.

These are just a few of the things you need to ponder before implementing a VPN solution. However, if you consider these three issues, you'll be prepared and more confident of your decision on whether or not to provide VPN capabilities to your Windows Server 2003 network.

Choosing a VPN Solution

There are basically two types of VPN solutions, dial-up VPN and site to site. A combination of the two can be categorized as a third type.

■ **Dial-up VPN** Typically, remote clients dial their local ISP and then "dial" the Windows Server 2003 VPN server to establish a VPN connection between the VPN server and remote client. This saves long-distance phone charges for the remote client, and also saves money at the VPN server site because, in many cases it can replace the need for large numbers of modems and other remote access devices for connectivity.

■ **Site to site** The most commonly used VPN solution is the site-to-site implementation. In this scenario, you use two or more Windows Server 2003 VPN servers to establish a VPN between them. Communication is securely defined between the two sites. Users on either network can communicate with the other remote site.

■ **Combining solutions** As the name implies, Windows Server 2003 environments that have both remote clients and sites can create a VPN solution to service both of them.

Installing RRAS

Installing RRAS is such an easy, straightforward topic that it may seem too obvious to mention. When you install Windows Server 2003 Server, RRAS is automatically installed for you but in a disabled state. This means that it's not taking up precious resources if you're not using it.

To start using RRAS, whether it's for remote access, routing, or setting up a VPN between sites, you first need to enable it.

Enabling RRAS

Your next step in getting RRAS up and running is almost as straightforward as installing it. Since it's disabled by default after you install Windows Server 2003 Server, you'll need to enable the service. Before doing so, you must have administrative privileges or be a member of the RAS and IAS Servers security group for the domain. To enable RRAS, do the following:

1. From the Start | Programs | Administrative Tools menu, select Routing and Remote Access to start the Routing and Remote Access snap-in manager, shown in Figure 13-12.

2. In the right pane, select the server you want to enable, and then click Configure and Enable Routing and Remote Access from the Action menu. At this point the Routing and Remote Access Server Setup Wizard appears, and you can begin configuring RRAS.

Next, you need to configure the functionality you want to use with RRAS.

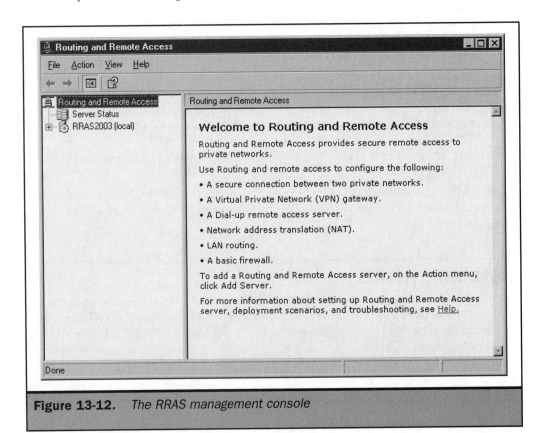

Figure 13-12.   *The RRAS management console*

Configuring RRAS

The Routing and Remote Access Server Setup Wizard abolishes much of the pain that you may have experienced with earlier versions of RAS or RRAS. This wizard holds your hand each step of the way, whether you're configuring an Internet connection server, a remote access server, or a VPN solution. It is important to note here that the following sections on configuring the server assume that you already have installed a modem or other devices used for remote connections. The principles behind configuring a RAS server in Windows NT or Windows 2000 haven't changed much in Windows Server 2003. However, the structure of the RRAS Setup Wizard has changed somewhat.

The Routing and Remote Access Server Wizard (shown in Figure 13-13) offers four choices for common configurations, and a fifth, Custom configuration option. The wizard is available only for the initial configuration of RRAS on a server. After gaining an understanding of each of the wizard's initial configuration options, choose the one that most closely resembles the configuration you want to end up with. The wizard will generate a default configuration, which you can subsequently modify to conform to local requirements.

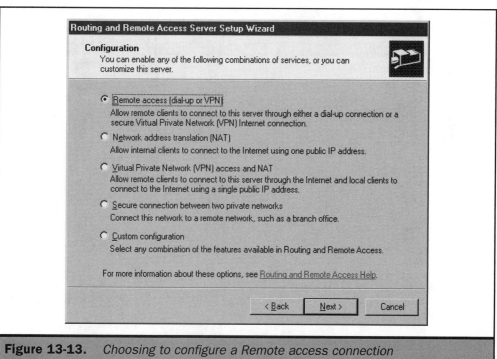

Figure 13-13.   *Choosing to configure a Remote access connection*

Configuring Remote Access (Dial-up or VPN)

This option configures the Windows Server 2003 server to accept incoming dial-up connections from remote clients. Alternatively, the clients can connect using a VPN connection. By configuring RRAS as a VPN server, you are allowing remote clients to pass through a public network, such as the Internet, through an encrypted tunnel to your Windows Server 2003 network environment.

To configure this option, do the following:

1. Open Routing and Remote Access from the Start | Programs | Administrative Tools menu.

2. From the Action menu, select Configure and Enable Routing and Remote Access. When the Routing and Remote Access Server Setup Wizard window pops up, click Next to continue.

3. Select Remote Access (Dial-up or VPN), as shown in Figure 13-13, and click Next.

4. The next screen, shown in Figure 13-14, offers two options: VPN and Dial-up. Select one or both of these options, depending on how you want remote users to connect to your network, and then click Next.

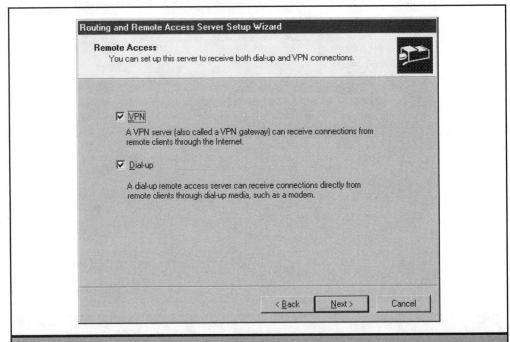

Figure 13-14. *Allowing the server to receive either dial-up or VPN connections, or both*

5. If you have selected both options, the VPN connection screen, shown in Figure 13-15, displays next. This screen shows the network interfaces that are installed on the server. Select the one that remote users will connect to— that is, the interface owning the IP address or DNS name that a user's VPN client will connect to. If the network interface you select is dedicated to VPN access—that is, no one will connect to the server through the interface except by using a VPN connection—then you can select the Enable security on the selected interface by using static packet filters option. With this option enabled, only packets sent the TCP and UDP ports used by the server's VPN configuration will be allowed through; all other packets will be deleted. After making your selections, click Next.

6. Choose how you'd like to assign IP addresses to remote clients. If your network uses a DHCP server to assign client addresses, this option is highly recommended. Otherwise, identify a range of IP addresses that RRAS can assign and select the option From a specified range of addresses. If you select the From a specified range of addresses option, click Next and enter the range on the next screen. Click Next to continue.

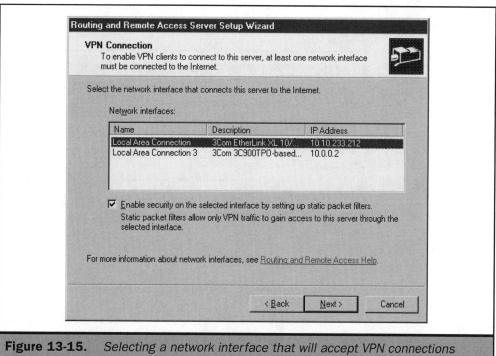

Figure 13-15.   *Selecting a network interface that will accept VPN connections*

7. Choose whether or not you want to configure a RADIUS server now (the default is no). If remote clients aren't going to use a VPN to connect, keeping the default is recommended.

8. If you've chosen to configure a RADIUS server, the RADIUS Server Selection screen, shown in Figure 13-16, displays next. Enter the name or address of your RADIUS server(s) and its password, and click Next to continue.

9. Click Finish and you're done.

Configuring a Router with Network Address Translation

A router with NAT enabled enhances the security of client-to-Internet communications. Normally, all IP packets include the IP address of the computer that created the packet—the source IP address and port number. A router with NAT enabled will keep track of a packet's true IP address and port, and substitute a fixed public IP address and a port that isn't otherwise used at the router. When the router receives an inbound packet at the public IP address, it uses the port—now in the destination port field of the packet—to translate the destination IP address and port field of the packet back to the client's original IP address and port information. NAT effectively hides a client's true IP address for all outbound communications, and only forwards inbound packets to the internal network when they are, or appear to be, a response to an active client application request.

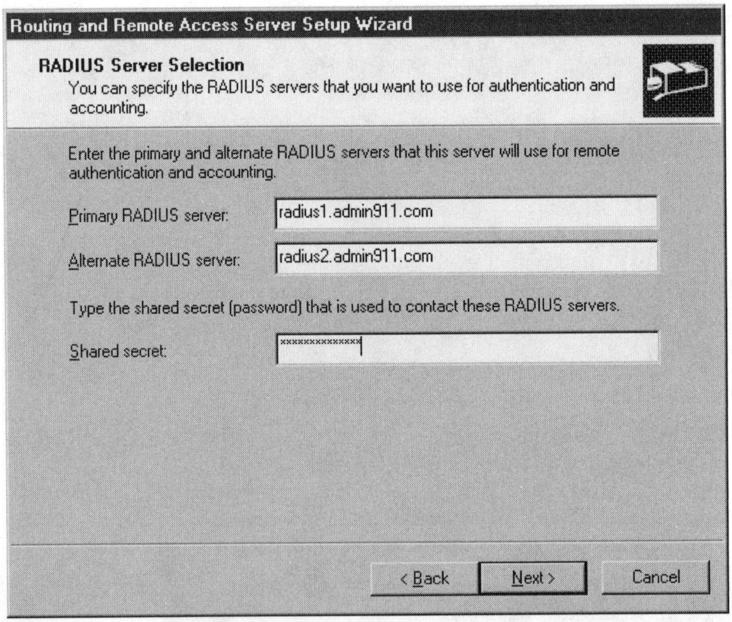

Figure 13-16. *Specifying RADIUS servers to authenticate remote access*

The second option presented involves configuring Windows Server 2003 as an Internet Connection Server router using NAT connecting through a NIC. This option supports the following:

- Multiple public IP addresses
- Multiple SOHO interfaces
- Configurable IP address range for network clients

 Use this option in an existing network with other domain controllers (DCs), DNS servers, or DHCP servers.

Here's how you can configure a Windows Server 2003 server as a router using NAT:

1. Open Routing and Remote Access from the Start | Programs | Administrative Tools menu.

2. From the Action menu, select Configure and Enable Routing and Remote Access. When the Routing and Remote Access Server Setup Wizard window pops up, click Next to continue.

3. Select Network Address Translation (NAT), as shown in Figure 13-17, and click Next.

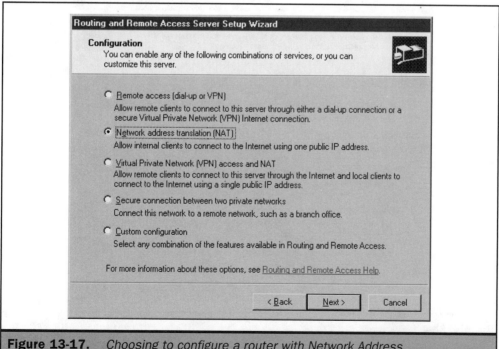

Figure 13-17. *Choosing to configure a router with Network Address Translation (NAT)*

4. Select Use this public interface to connect to the Internet, and then click the desired interface, as shown in Figure 13-18. Click Next to continue.

5. If the wizard fails to detect DNS and/or DHCP servers on your network, it will present a screen offering you the option to set them up on this server, or to configure them later. I recommend that you select the option I will set up name and address services later, and ensure the availability of both DNS and DHCP on your network after the RRAS Setup Wizard completes. Click Next to continue.

6. This completes setting up the router with NAT. Click Finish.

7. This example uses the latter option, which starts the Demand-Dial Interface Wizard.

Creating a Demand-Dial Interface

You can also use NAT when connecting to the Internet using the features of dial-up networking. Windows Server 2003 supports demand-dial connections using dial-up modems, ISDN or other supported physical devices, VPN connections, and Point-to-Point Protocol over Ethernet (PPPoE).

To configure a demand-dial interface with NAT, begin the process as described in the previous numbered list. In Step 4, select Create a new demand-dial interface to the

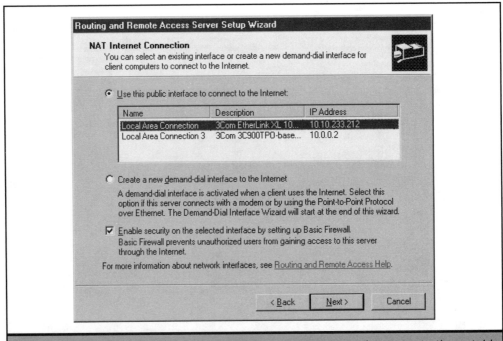

Figure 13-18. *Selecting a network interface that connects the router to the outside network*

Internet, as shown in Figure 13-19. When the RRAS Setup Wizard completes, the RRAS service will start and then the Demand-Dial Interface Wizard will start. After it opens, follow these steps:

1. Click Next to continue.

2. Specify the name of the interface and click Next.

3. The next window, shown in Figure 13-20, asks you to specify the connection type (modem or other adapter; use a VPN; or use PPPoE). Click Next to continue.

   ■ If you selected a modem or other physical device, specify the device from the list to be used and click Next. Enter the phone number (and alternates) for the router you are dialing into, and click Next.

   ■ If you selected a VPN connection, select the VPN type (Automatic selection, PPTP, or L2TP) and click Next. Then, enter the VPN server name or address and click Next.

   ■ If you selected PPPoE, enter the service name (or leave it blank for Windows to automatically detect and configure the service when you connect).

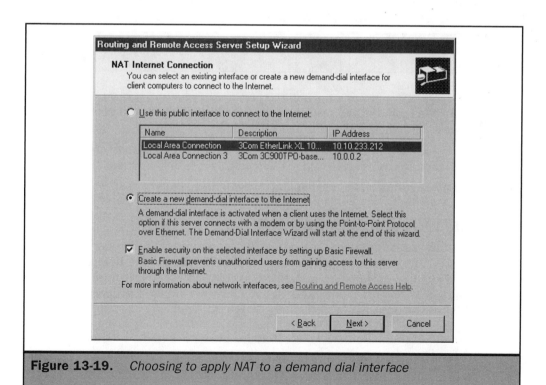

Figure 13-19.   *Choosing to apply NAT to a demand dial interface*

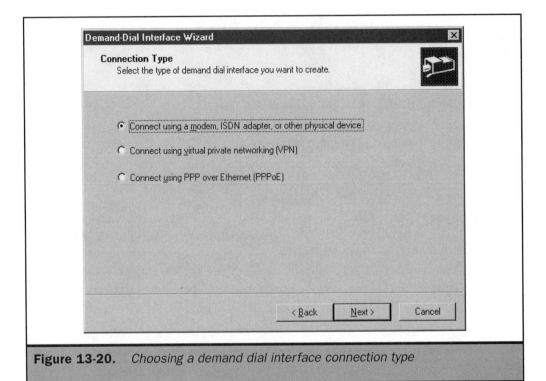

Figure 13-20.   *Choosing a demand dial interface connection type*

4. Specify the protocols and security settings for the interface, as illustrated in Figure 13-21. When you're finished, click Next to continue.

5. Specify the dial-out credentials. In particular, specify the username, domain, and password that will be used to dial out. Click Next to continue.

6. Click Finish to complete the demand-dial interface setup.

Configuring VPN Access and NAT

The RRAS Setup Wizard offers an option to easily configure a Windows Server 2003 server both as a VPN server and as a router with NAT. This setup option combines elements of the setup procedure for remote access using VPN and the procedure for setting up a router using NAT. Both were described earlier in this chapter, and there is little need to go over the details again here. To get started:

1. Open Routing and Remote Access from the Start | Programs | Administrative Tools menu.

2. From the Action menu, select Configure and Enable Routing and Remote Access. When the Routing and Remote Access Server Setup Wizard window pops up, click Next to continue.

3. Select Virtual Private Network (VPN) Access and NAT, as shown in Figure 13-22, and click Next. The subsequent steps are similar to those described in the preceding sections. See the sections entitled "Configuring Remote Access (Dial-up or VPN)" and "Configuring a Router with Network Address Translation" for a description of the configuration options.

Configuring a Secure Connection Between Two Private Networks

The RRAS Setup Wizard offers an option to configure a Windows Server 2003 server for a secure connection to another Windows Server 2003 server running RRAS on a remote network. This RRAS Setup Wizard option supports a VPN connection to the remote network either through the Internet or via one of the supported demand-dial connections. The part of the setup procedure covered by the RRAS Setup Wizard is elementary—it installs RRAS with VPN support, and starts the Demand-Dial Interface Wizard if you selected that option. Following completion of the wizards, you still need to configure other properties of the link.

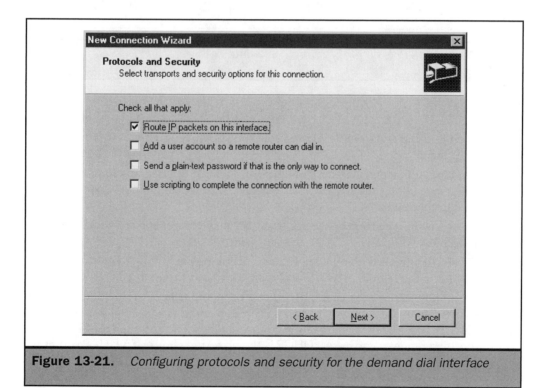

Figure 13-21.   *Configuring protocols and security for the demand dial interface*

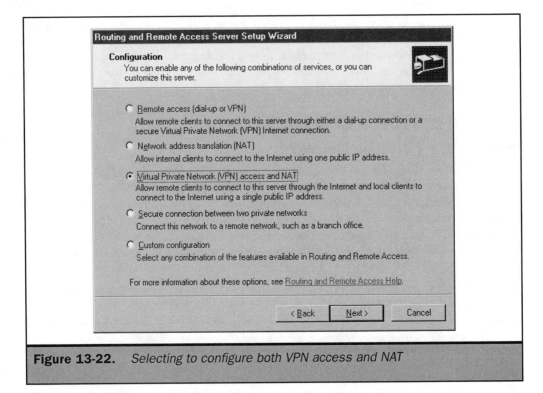

Figure 13-22. *Selecting to configure both VPN access and NAT*

To enable RRAS for a secure link between two private networks:

1. Open Routing and Remote Access from the Start | Programs | Administrative Tools menu.

2. From the Action menu, select Configure and Enable Routing and Remote Access. When the Routing and Remote Access Server Setup Wizard window pops up, click Next to continue.

3. Select Secure connection between two private networks, as shown in Figure 13-23, and click Next.

4. Chose whether or not you want to use a demand-dial interface connection to connect to the remote network, and then click Next to continue.

5. If you chose to use a demand-dial interface connection, the IP Address Assignment screen displays, asking you to choose between using an automatically assigned (DHCP) IP address for the remote connection or an address selected from a specified range of addresses. DHCP is the preferred choice, if a DHCP server is available. After making your selection, click Next to continue. The RRAS Setup Wizard completes when you click Finish.

6. If you chose to use a demand-dial interface connection, the Demand-Dial Interface Wizard starts now.

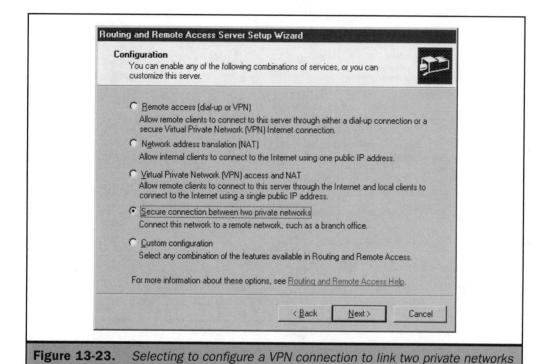

Figure 13-23.   *Selecting to configure a VPN connection to link two private networks*

Configuring a Custom RRAS Configuration

The last path through the RRAS Setup Wizard allows you to create a custom configuration using any of the available RRAS features. When you use the Custom configuration path through the RRAS Setup Wizard, the wizard installs the RRAS components necessary to support the connection types you request, but does not prompt for any information to set up specific connections—this task is left to your discretion following completion of the wizard.

To enable RRAS with a custom configuration:

1. Open Routing and Remote Access from the Start | Programs | Administrative Tools menu.

2. From the Action menu, select Configure and Enable Routing and Remote Access. When the Routing and Remote Access Server Setup Wizard window pops up, click Next to continue.

3. Select Custom configuration, as shown in Figure 13-24, and click Next.

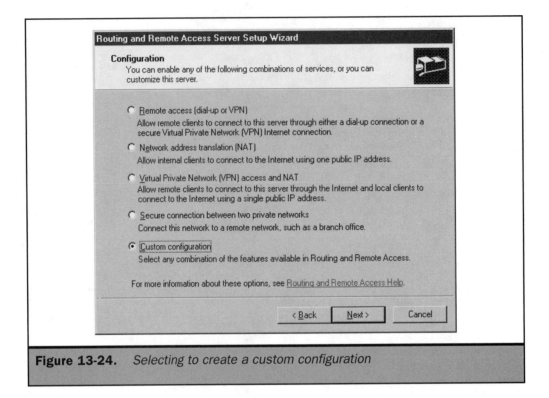

Figure 13-24. *Selecting to create a custom configuration*

4. The Custom Configuration screen displays, as shown in Figure 13-25, allowing you to chose from the following options:

- VPN access
- Dial-up access
- Demand-dial connections
- NAT and basic firewall
- LAN routing

5. Select any or all of the options as you wish, and click Next to continue. The completion screen displays now—after reviewing its summary of actions, click Finish to complete the wizard.

Configuring Internet Connection Sharing

Looking for a simpler way to configure an Internet-connected computer as a router with NAT, in order to share that Internet connection? Internet Connection Sharing (ICS)

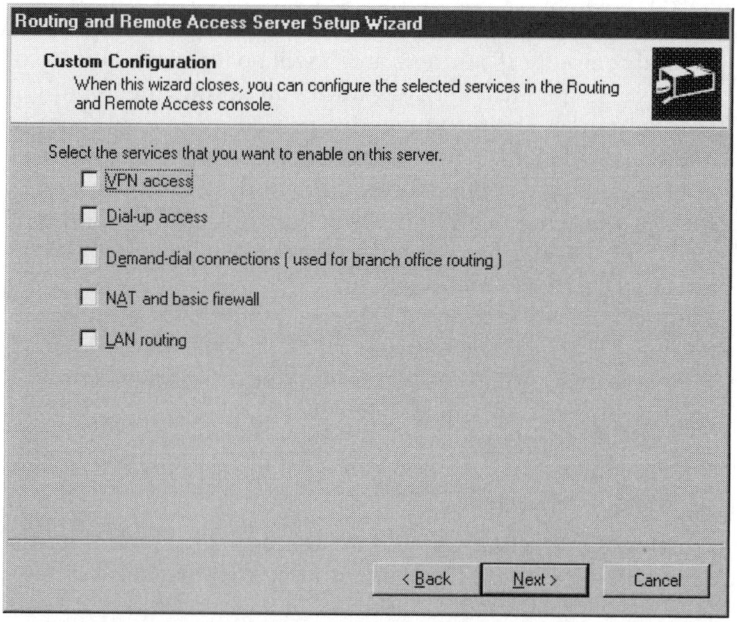

Routing and Remote Access Server Setup Wizard

Custom Configuration
When this wizard closes, you can configure the selected services in the Routing and Remote Access console.

Select the services that you want to enable on this server.

☐ VPN access

☐ Dial-up access

☐ Demand-dial connections (used for branch office routing)

☐ NAT and basic firewall

☐ LAN routing

[< Back] [Next >] [Cancel]

Figure 13-25.   *Selection custom configuration options*

may be just the ticket. ICS is a simple alternative to RRAS, intended for SOHO. In a simple one-step process, ICS does the following:

1. Reconfigures the IP address of the LAN adapter that connects to the local network to 192.168.0.1, with a subnet mask of 255.255.255.0 (or 192.168.0.1/24 in CIDR notation).

2. Adds a static (but not persistent) route to the Internet to the routing table when the Internet connection is established.

3. Starts the Internet Connection Sharing Service.

4. Configures and starts DHCP services to allocate addresses in the range 192.168.0.2 to 192.168.0.254 to clients on the local subnet.

5. Enables DNS Proxy, forwarding DNS name resolution requests from clients on the local network to the DNS server provided by the ISP when the Internet connection is established.

You cannot override the way ICS configures the network. If you want a setup other than the ICS configuration, you must use RRAS. Remember when implementing ICS that ICS changes the local computer IP address, and it will no longer be able to communicate with other computers on the local network until you update their configuration to match the ICS configuration. The recommended procedure is to set client computers to obtain their IP addresses via DHCP (or Automatically, as some IP configuration panels describe it) and to remove any existing DNS server addresses from a client IP. You can configure ICS as described here on Windows Server 2003 and Windows XP systems. Any computer running a desktop or server version of Windows from Windows 98 on can be configured as a client on an ICS network.

Want to configure ICS? In Windows 2000 Server, the RRAS Setup Wizard provided some guidance in the ICS setup when you selected an option under its Internet connection server setup path. This guidance is missing from Windows Server 2003's RRAS Setup Wizard, but the procedure is very similar. Here it is:

1. Verify that the Internet connection you want to share is fully configured and working, but not connected.

2. Open Network Connections, shown in Figure 13-26, which is accessible either by selecting Start | Control Panel and double-clicking Network Connections,

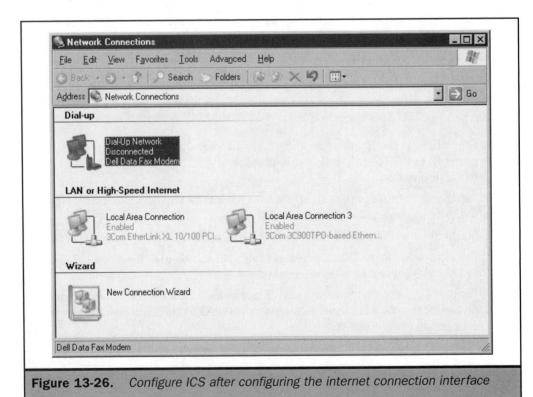

Figure 13-26.   *Configure ICS after configuring the internet connection interface*

or, from Windows Explorer, by right-clicking My Network Places and selecting Properties from the Action menu.

3. Right-click the network interface that connects to the Internet, often a dial-up modem or LAN connection to a broadband modem. Select Properties from the Action menu. (Windows 2000 users will see a Sharing tab that provides options similar to those described next.)

4. Click the Advanced tab to display the screen shown in Figure 13-27.

5. In the Internet Connection Sharing section, select the check box Allow other network users to connect through this computer's Internet connection.

6. If this adapter doesn't establish a permanent connection, and the user ID and password necessary to make the connection haven't been saved for use by anyone, you will be reminded to do so. This is an option on the screen that displays when you select Connect for the adapter. Saving the user ID and password for use by anyone allows anyone logged on to the ICS gateway computer to make an Internet connection, and allows ICS to automatically make the connection when the option described in step 8 is selected.

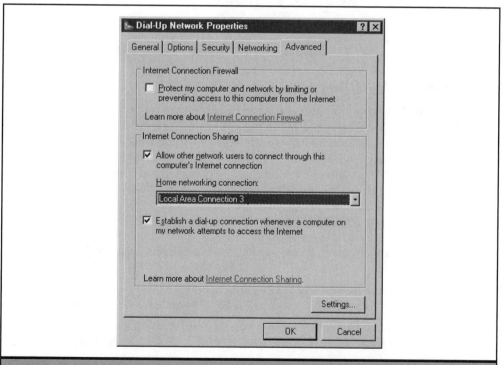

Figure 13-27.   *Internet Connection Sharing is a checkbox in the network interface properties*

7. If this computer has more than two network adapters, the Home networking connection drop-down box shown in Figure 13-27 will also display. Select the interface that connects to the local network. This is the interface that ICS will reconfigure to an IP address of 192.168.0.1.

8. If this adapter doesn't by nature establish a permanent connection, the Establish a dial-up connection whenever a computer on my network attempts to access the Internet check box will be available. Check the box if you want to have ICS make the connection automatically, or leave it unchecked if you want always to manually initiate an Internet connection.

9. Click OK. At this point you will see a panel reminding you that the IP address of the local interface will change to 192.168.0.1, and recommending that you configure other computers on the same network to obtain an IP address automatically. Click Yes.

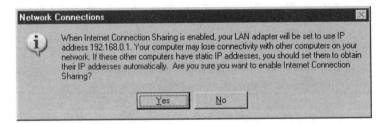

Configuring RRAS Clients

Configuring clients to connect remotely is a relatively simple procedure with Windows Server 2003. RRAS does support other client operating systems, including, but not limited to, Windows NT, Windows 9x, UNIX variants, Macintosh, and others connecting remotely, but the focus of this section is on Windows 2000 and Windows XP clients.

After you've installed a modem on the client, you're ready to configure a connection to the RRAS server. This requires the following steps:

From a Windows 2000 Client:

1. From the Start | Settings menu, open the Network and Dial-Up Connections folder.

2. Double-click the Make New Connection icon to start the Network Connection Wizard. Click Next when you see the wizard's window.

3. Figure 13-28 shows the choices that you have for making a connection. The choices that are relevant to connecting to the RRAS server are Dial-up to private

network and Connect to a private network through the Internet. Choose either of these options. For simplicity, this example will use the first option. Click Next to continue.

4. The next screen prompts you to supply a phone number to dial. If you'll primarily be making local calls, just specify the local number. Otherwise, check the option Use dialing rules to allow Windows Server 2003 to dial the area code. Click Next to continue.

5. Choose whether or not this connection is intended to be used by everyone or just yourself. Click Next to continue.

6. On the next screen, make sure that the Enable Internet Connection Sharing for this connection option is unchecked and then click Next. You don't want to enable this option.

7. Type in the name for the connection and then click Finish. You can optionally add a shortcut on the desktop for accessibility.

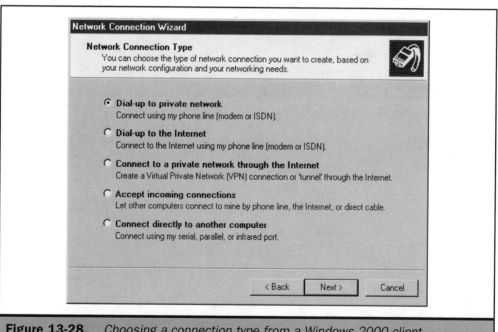

Figure 13-28.   *Choosing a connection type from a Windows 2000 client*

From a Windows XP Client:

1. From the Start | Settings menu, open the Network Connections folder.

2. Double-click the New Connection Wizard icon to start the New Connection Wizard. Click Next when you see the wizard's window.

3. Figure 13-29 shows the choices that you have for making a connection. The choice that is relevant to connecting to the RRAS server is Connect to the network at my workplace, which supports creating either dial-up or VPN connections. Click Next to continue.

4. The Network Connection screen asks you to choose between a dial-up or a VPN connection. Click Next after making your selection.

5. The next screen prompts you to supply a name for the connection. Click Next after completing the screen.

6. If you are configuring a VPN connection, a Public Network screen may display, asking whether you want to dial into the network before attempting to make the VPN virtual connection. If you choose to dial into the network first, you can choose an existing dial-up connection, or choose to dial manually. Click Next to continue.

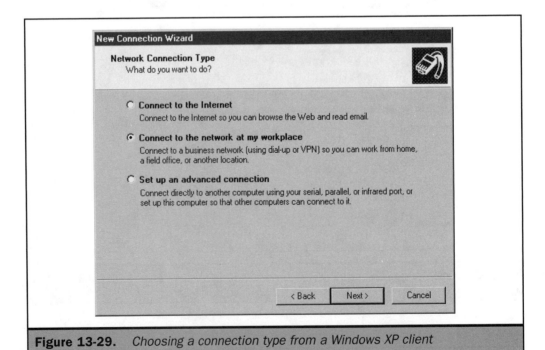

Figure 13-29.   *Choosing a connection type from a Windows XP client*

7. The next screen prompts you to supply a phone number to dial, or a hostname (or address) for a VPN connection. If entering a phone number, enter it as you would dial it from your phone. Click Next to continue.

8. Choose whether or not this connection is intended to be used by everyone or just yourself. Click Next to continue.

9. The completion screen displays. Click Finish after reviewing it.

Specifying a Connection's Security Settings

At this point you're done, unless you want to configure the connection's security. This is a good idea, because the default setting for the client is to allow unsecured password validation.

1. Return to the Network Connections or Network and Dial-Up Connections folder, right-click the connection you just finished configuring, and select Properties.

2. Under the Security tab, you can choose your security options, as shown in Figure 13-30. The best procedure here is to configure the client to use the security

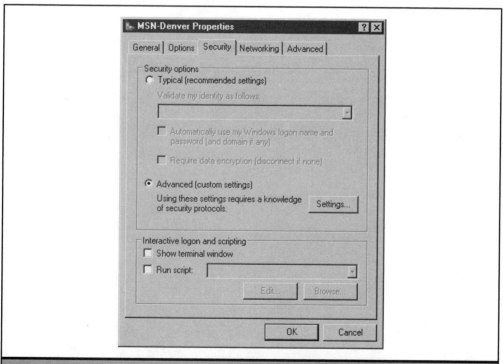

Figure 13-30.   *Finding the Advanced (custom settings) button on the connection's Security tab*

mechanisms used by the server. For example, a client should be told to use EAP if the server is using EAP. In this particular case, you would click the Advanced (custom settings) option, click the Settings button, and click Use Extensible Authentication Protocol (EAP), as illustrated in Figure 13-31.

Configuring Remote Access Policies

Remote access connections are granted access based on a user's account and remote access policies. Basically, a remote access policy defines the connection by imposing a set of conditions. Table 13-5 lists the most common remote access policies and provides a brief description of each.

When you're adding remote access policies, you aren't limited to using one per remote client. You can add as many as you'd like, but it's best to minimize the number of policies you use to keep the configuration as simple as possible. The New Remote Access Policy Wizard will guide you through configuring a policy for one of several common connection types. The wizard also allows you to create a custom policy that compares the parameters of a connection attempt to any of the available policy and profile attributes. I'll describe creating a custom policy first.

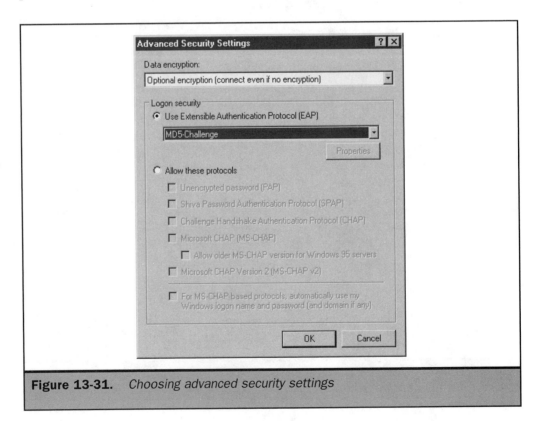

Figure 13-31. *Choosing advanced security settings*

Policy Name	Policy Description
Called-Station-ID	Phone number dialed by user
Calling-Station-ID	Phone number from which call originated (caller ID)
Day-And-Time-Restrictions	Time periods and days of week during which user is allowed to connect
Framed-Protocol	The protocol to be used during the connection
Tunnel-Type	The tunneling protocols to be used during the connection
Windows-Groups	The Windows 2000 groups to which the user belongs

Table 13-5.   *Common Remote Access Policies*

Configuring a Custom Remote Access Policy

To add a remote access policy, do the following:

1. Open Routing and Remote Access from the Start | Programs | Administrative Tools menu.

2. In the left pane of the console window, right-click Remote Access Policies and select New Remote Access Policy. This starts the New Remote Access Policy Wizard. Click Next to move from the opening screen to the Policy Configuration Method screen, shown in Figure 13-32.

3. Select the Set up a custom policy option, specify a name for the policy, and click Next.

4. Click the Add button to bring up the Select Attribute window, shown in Figure 13-33. After selecting the attribute, click the Add button.

5. Type in the parameter corresponding to the condition you're specifying. For example, for Caller-Station-Id, type in a phone number. It is important to note that the information you provide here depends on which condition you're trying to add. Click OK when done.

6. Repeat Steps 4 and 5 until you're done adding conditions. At that time, click Next to continue.

7. The next window in the wizard asks you if you want to grant or deny access to the user when the specified conditions are met. Choose either Grant or Deny and click Next.

8. At this point, you can either edit the policy, by clicking the Edit Profile button, or finish configuring the policy, by clicking the Finish button.

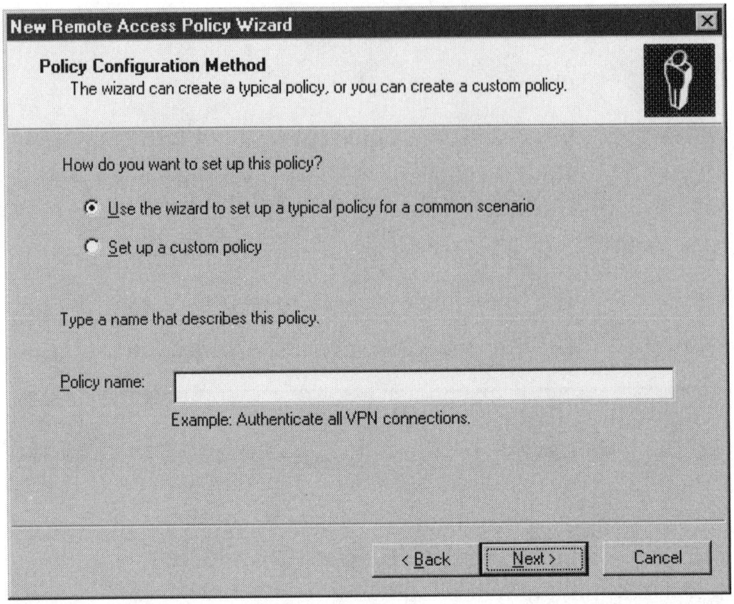

Figure 13-32. *Choosing Set up a custom policy*

Editing the remote access policy profile displays a number of different options. It allows you to configure dial-in constraints, IP, multilink, authentication, encryption, and other attributes' settings. As you can see, remote access policies are extremely customizable, to meet and exceed your environment's needs.

Remote Access Policy Wizard: Using the Typical Policy for a Common Scenario Path

Choosing the first option shown in Figure 13-32 to set up a typical policy for a common scenario is an easy path to make a policy for dial-up, VPN, wireless, and Ethernet LAN connections. This path through the wizard works like this:

1. Open Routing and Remote Access from the Start | Programs | Administrative Tools menu.

2. In the left pane of the console window, right-click Remote Access Policies and select New Remote Access Policy. This starts the New Remote Access Policy Wizard. Click Next to move from the opening screen to the Policy Configuration Method screen, shown previously in Figure 13-32. Select the Use the wizard to set up a typical policy for a common scenario option, specify a name for the policy, and click Next.

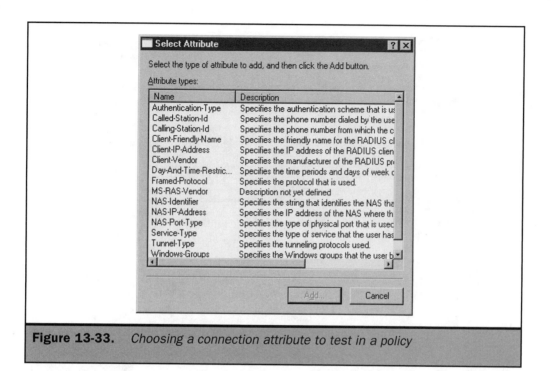

Figure 13-33.   *Choosing a connection attribute to test in a policy*

3. The User or Group Access screen, shown in Figure 13-34, determines who the policy will apply to. When User is selected, the policy will apply to users based solely on the access permissions found on the Dial-in tab of the user's account properties. When the Group option is selected, the policy will apply to user accounts who are members of one of the groups listed on this page, as long as their account-level permissions have Control access through Remote Access Policy selected. Grant or Deny permissions in the account will override the policy. Select User, or select Group and fill in the group or groups to control access. Click Next to continue.

4. The Authentication Methods screen is next. Select one or more of the available authentication methods for the connection type that you will allow to authenticate a connection. It is advisable to require the strongest authentication type that works in your environment. Click Next to continue.

5. The Policy Encryption Level screen allows you to choose to support 40-bit, 56-bit, and/or 128-bit encryption levels. The policy defaults to supporting all three. Click Next to continue.

6. Review the Policy summary page and click Finish.

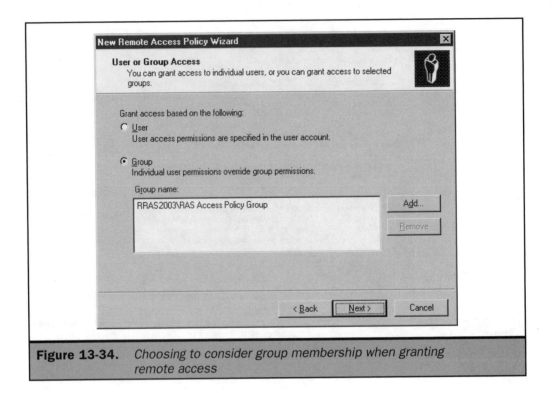

Figure 13-34. *Choosing to consider group membership when granting remote access*

Editing a Remote Access Policy

Once created, you can view the policy settings using the RRAS console:

1. Open Routing and Remote Access from the Start | Programs | Administrative Tools menu.

2. In the left pane of the window, click Remote Access Policies.

3. In the right pane, right-click the policy you want to view or modify, and select Properties from the shortcut menu.

4. The Policy Properties dialog box, shown in Figure 13-35, displays the Policy Conditions, which you can modify using the Add, Edit, and Remove buttons. The Grant/Deny parameter can be changed from this page.

5. To edit other policy parameters, click the Edit Profile button. Using the Edit Dial-in Profile page, shown in Figure 13-36, you can modify the other parameters of the policy.

The ability to easily create a typical policy for common remote access scenarios combined with the powerful policy edit interface makes it easy to configure basic as well as custom policies.

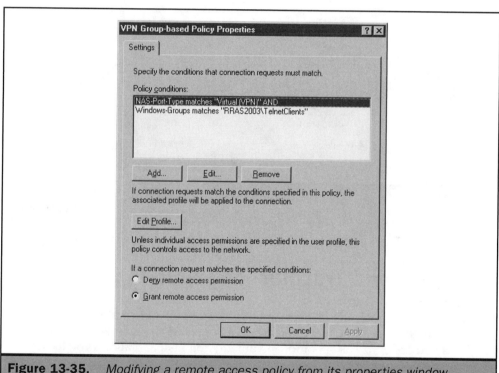

Figure 13-35.   *Modifying a remote access policy from its properties window*

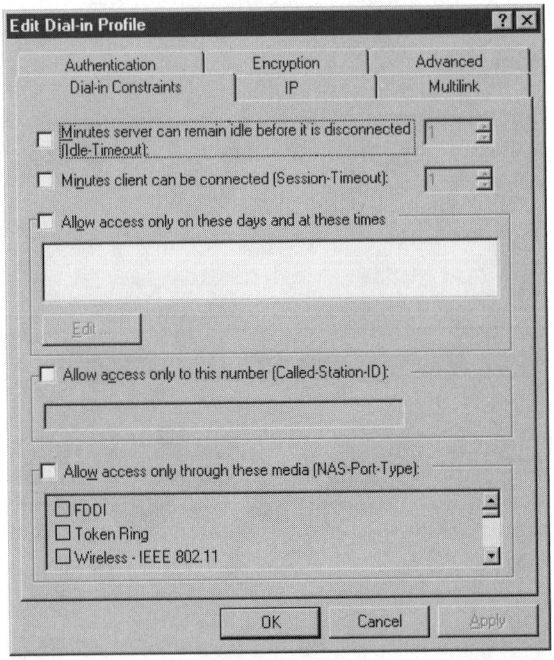

Figure 13-36. *Modifying other policy parameters through the Edit Dial-in Profile window*

Managing and Troubleshooting RRAS

As with many services in Windows Server 2003, after you install and configure RRAS, you may need to periodically manage and troubleshoot it. For instance, you may want to reconfigure RRAS settings, add resources, monitor connections, and so on. Managing RRAS lets you customize its operation in your environment and allows you to keep up-to-date with its implementation.

Managing Multiple RRAS Servers

Managing a Windows Server 2003 network environment that has more than one RRAS server would get a bit overwhelming if you had to jump from machine to machine to manage them. By default, the Routing and Remote Access snap-in displays only the local computer in its server list. However, for simplicity and ease of use, you can add other RRAS servers to the snap-in so that you can manage them from a single location.

To add another server to the Routing and Remote Access snap-in, do the following:

1. Within the right pane of the Routing and Remote Access snap-in, right-click Server Status and select Add Server, as shown in Figure 13-37.

2. In the Add Server dialog box, select one of the four options for locating and adding another RRAS server:

   ■ **This computer**   This option is self explanatory.

   ■ **The following computer**   This option gives you the opportunity to specify the computer name that you wish to add.

   ■ **All Routing and Remote Access computers**   You must specify the domain name from which to add all RRAS servers. This option is useful when you have many RRAS servers and want to manage them all in one central location. It's also useful when you don't know the RRAS server's name.

   ■ **Browse Active Directory (AD)**   Use this option when you want to browse the directory service to find one or more RRAS servers in the domain or tree.

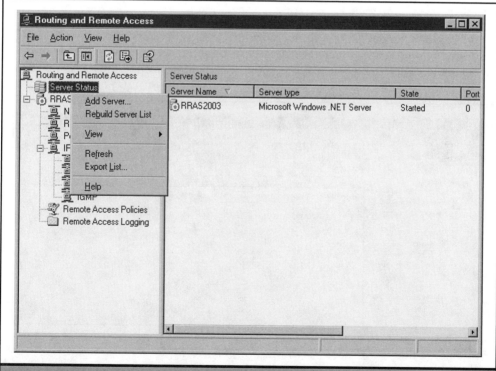

Figure 13-37.   *Adding a server to the RRAS management console*

Monitoring Connections

A good habit to start practicing is periodically monitoring RRAS connections. The RRAS management console allows you to easily check the status of the service and any active connections. By doing so, you are able to get an accurate picture of RRAS in real time, and it's also an excellent way of troubleshooting any problems you may encounter. Checking server status is as simple as opening the RRAS management console and clicking Server Status. The right console window, pictured in Figure 13-38, displays the status reports. In particular, it shows the following statistics:

- The server name
- The state of the RRAS service (started or stopped)
- The total number of ports on the server
- The number of ports in use
- The amount of time that the server has been up since the RRAS service was last started

Viewing Routing Tables

Every Windows Server 2003 computer, with an installed network interface card (NIC), has a simple routing table created by default. You can view a computer's static routing entries in the routing table either through the command prompt or the RRAS interface.

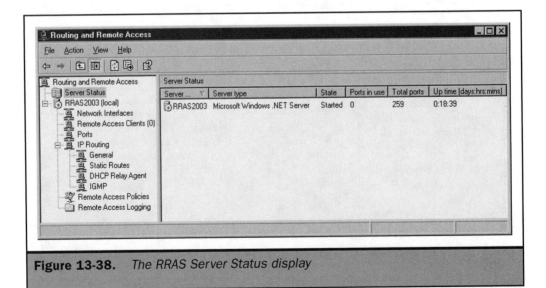

Figure 13-38.   *The RRAS Server Status display*

To view the routing table from the command prompt, you simply type **route print**. You may also view the routing table using the RRAS interface by doing the following:

1. Open Routing and Remote Access from the Start | Programs | Administrative Tools menu.

2. In the left pane of the console window, expand the console tree to expose the Static Routes entry underneath the IP Routing subtree.

3. Right-click Static Routes and select Show IP Routing Table to display the routing table.

RRAS2003 - IP Routing Table

Destination	Network mask	Gateway	Interface	Metric	Protocol
0.0.0.0	0.0.0.0	10.10.233.254	Local Area C...	20	Network management
10.0.0.0	255.255.255.0	10.0.0.2	Local Area C...	30	Local
10.0.0.2	255.255.255.255	127.0.0.1	Loopback	30	Local
10.10.233.0	255.255.255.0	10.10.233.212	Local Area C...	20	Local
10.10.233.212	255.255.255.255	127.0.0.1	Loopback	20	Local
10.10.250.0	255.255.255.0	0.0.0.0	DialingOut	1	Static
10.255.255.255	255.255.255.255	10.10.233.212	Local Area C...	20	Local
10.255.255.255	255.255.255.255	10.0.0.2	Local Area C...	30	Local
127.0.0.0	255.0.0.0	127.0.0.1	Loopback	1	Local
127.0.0.1	255.255.255.255	127.0.0.1	Loopback	1	Local
224.0.0.0	240.0.0.0	10.10.233.212	Local Area C...	20	Local
224.0.0.0	240.0.0.0	10.0.0.2	Local Area C...	30	Local
255.255.255.255	255.255.255.255	10.10.233.212	Local Area C...	1	Local
255.255.255.255	255.255.255.255	10.0.0.2	Local Area C...	1	Local

Viewing the static routes in the routing table can be an extremely useful troubleshooting tool when you are presented with a possible routing problem. Examining the routing table helps you determine whether or not the server is properly sending or receiving routed information. This is especially useful when your network environment consists mainly of static routes.

Adding Static Routes

For small network environments such as a home office or small business, you may want or need to manually add a static route to the routing table to connect to another network. You can accomplish this in two ways: using the Route Add command at the command prompt (for example, route add 192.168.1.0 192.168.3.0) or using the RRAS interface. The easiest (and laziest) way to configure a static route is through the RRAS interface. Using the RRAS interface is recommended, especially if you're not familiar with the route command. Besides, you're less likely to make a syntax error or, even worse, a configuration error.

To add a static route using the RRAS snap-in, do the following:

1. Open Routing and Remote Access from the Start | Programs | Administrative Tools menu.

2. In the left pane of the console window, expand the console tree to expose the Static Routes entry underneath the IP Routing subtree.

3. If you're adding a static route for IP routing, select New Static Route to display the Static Route window (see Figure 13-39).

4. Fill in the appropriate information for the following (for an IP static route):

   - **Interface**   The network interface to use to configure a static route

   - **Destination**   The computer or router in which to route the information

   - **Network Mask**   The network address that will use the route

   - **Gateway**   An IP address that the packets must be sent to in order to get routed; this is typically the default gateway

   - **Metric**   The number of hops to reach the destination

5. Click OK.

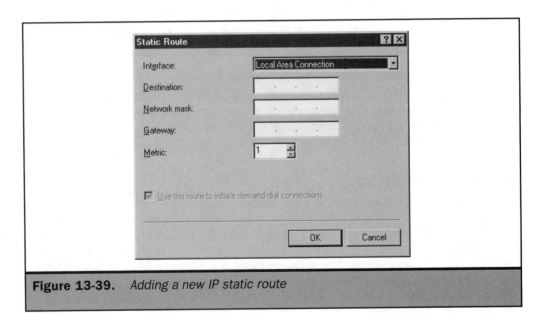

Figure 13-39.   *Adding a new IP static route*

Event Logging

Windows Server 2003 documents events that occur on the system, including those relating to the RRAS service. The events may be errors, warnings, or purely informational messages such as accounting logging. The messages can be viewed in the Windows Server 2003 system event log.

Reviewing the events in the system event log provides an invaluable means to keep track of the RRAS service and is especially useful when you need to troubleshoot a problem. Figure 13-40 shows you the various configurations for event logging. By default, RRAS records errors and warnings.

To modify the default logging parameters, do the following:

1. Open Routing and Remote Access from the Start | Programs | Administrative Tools menu.

2. In the left pane, right-click the RRAS server and select Properties.

3. Under the Logging tab, you can select how you'd like to log events, and you may even disable logging altogether for RRAS (not recommended).

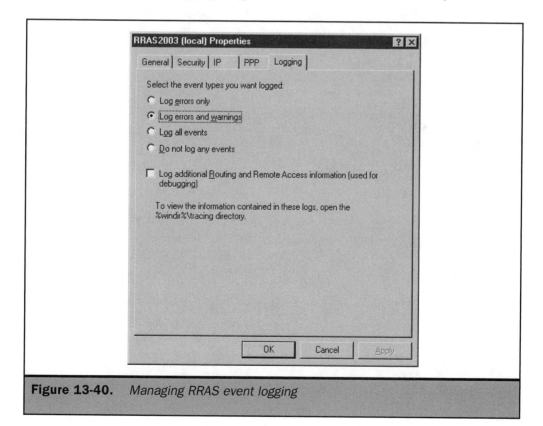

Figure 13-40.   *Managing RRAS event logging*

You can also choose to enable extended logging to a file, or to a SQL Server database. With extended logging, you can record accounting requests, authentication requests, and periodic status. To enable extended logging:

1. Open Routing and Remote Access from the Start | Programs | Administrative Tools menu.

2. In the left pane, right-click Remote Access Logging. (If it doesn't appear, then Windows Accounting is not enabled.)

3. In the right pane, right-click the log file type you want to enable, and select Properties from the Action menu.

4. On the Settings tab, select the types of information you want to be logged.

On the Log File tab (Local File only), shown in Figure 13-41, select the log file location (the default is %windir%\system32\LogFiles), the log file format, and how often you want the information logged to a new file.

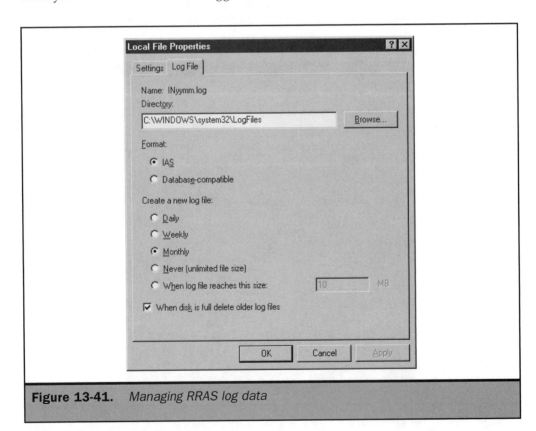

Figure 13-41. *Managing RRAS log data*

Where Did My Options Go?

After reading this chapter, you may be wondering why you don't have some of the options described. In particular, you may notice that some dial-in options for user accounts in AD are unavailable. This occurs when AD Domain Functional Level is in Windows 2000 mixed mode (refer to Chapter 18 for more information on AD modes of operation).

The following options are not available while you're running in mixed mode:

- The ability to control access through remote access policy
- Verifying a caller with caller ID
- Assigning a static IP address
- Applying static routes

RRAS and 64-bit Versions of Windows Server 2003

Several networking and Routing and Remote Access Service features are not included in the 64-bit versions of Windows Server 2003. These include:

- Internet Connection Sharing (ICS)
- Internet Connection Firewall (ICF)
- Earlier transports:
  - IPX/SPX LAN and WAN
  - Client Service for NetWare
  - Services for Macintosh
  - NetBIOS
  - Open Shortest Path First (OSPF) routing protocol
  - Simple Network Management Protocol (SNMP) over IPX/SPX
- Network Bridge
- Network Setup Wizard

Chapter 14

Client Networking Services

Many network environments have Windows Server 2003 systems operating with both Windows and non-Windows computers. In this chapter, I'll go over client services for Windows clients, as well as networking services for the non-Windows computers in your enterprise.

The administrators I talk to cite a wide variety of reasons for maintaining a heterogeneous network environment, and if your enterprise fits that description, your reasons probably match those I've heard. One scenario I hear about often is the need to support Macintosh clients in certain corporate departments (those that produce graphics, advertising, and other similar work). Also, it's not uncommon for a company to experience mergers or acquisitions that force Windows administrators to learn to work with Novell NetWare or UNIX (and also force the NetWare and UNIX administrators to learn to work with Windows).

Whatever your reason for supporting a heterogeneous environment, you'll find that Windows Server 2003 is prepared to offer services that ensure its integration with non-Microsoft client systems.

Windows Client Networking Service

Configuring Windows clients to connect to a Windows Server requires several steps. You must install and configure client software, install one or more protocols on the client computer, and create user and computer accounts for the network. This section covers the client software that's needed to communicate across the network.

Client for Microsoft Networks

Client for Microsoft Networks is a software component that allows a computer to access resources, such as file and print services, on a Microsoft network. When you install networking components (hardware and drivers for network interface devices), this client is installed automatically. Client for Microsoft Networks is independent of the protocol that you choose to use for network communication (although Windows also installs TCP/IP by default).

Note *Client for Microsoft Networks is actually the Common Internet File System (CIFS) protocol that rides on top of TCP/IP (or any other protocol). A newer version of the Server Message Block (SMB) protocol, CIFS is a file and print service protocol that allows computers to access resources located on remote computers transparently.*

Client for Microsoft Networks uses a remote procedure call (RPC) to call services on other computers on the network. RPC is nothing more than a message-passing facility; it performs no name resolution. By default, Windows Server 2003 uses the Windows Locator RPC, but if you have some reason to do so, it is also possible to use the Distributed Computing Environment (DCE) Cell Directory Service.

DCE, which is seen less and less these days, is typically used to connect systems that are widely scattered. Because DCE uses the client/server model, it was frequently deployed in enterprises where users needed to access applications and data on servers that were at remote locations. When I was administering (and writing about) Windows NT networks, I covered DCE in more detail. Today, if I face a scenario where users need to access applications and data on remote servers, I use Terminal Server.

 Client for Microsoft Networks is the equivalent of the Workstation service you were used to in Windows NT.

File and Printer Sharing for Microsoft Networks

File and Printer Sharing for Microsoft Networks is a service component that complements the Client for Microsoft Networks service. It allows computers on the network to access files and printers that you configure for sharing. This service is also installed and enabled by default when you install networking services.

 File and Printer Sharing for Microsoft Networks is the equivalent of the Server service in Windows NT.

You can optimize the way a Windows Server 2003 performs when it's set up for File and Printer Sharing. This lets you use the server in a manner that's appropriate for the services it provides to network clients. To configure File and Printer Sharing performance, take these steps:

1. Choose Start | Control Panel | Network Connections | Local Area Connection.

2. Click Properties.

3. Select File And Printer Sharing For Microsoft Networks, and click the Properties button.

4. Use the options in the File And Printer Sharing For Microsoft Networks Properties dialog (see Figure 14-1) to optimize the service, as follows:

   ■ Select Minimize Memory Used to optimize the server for a small number of clients.

   ■ Select Balance to optimize the server for a mixed usage of file and printer sharing in addition to other services.

   ■ Select Maximize Data Throughput For File Sharing to dedicate as many resources as possible to file and print server services.

   ■ Select Maximize Data Throughput For Network Applications to optimize server memory for network applications such as Microsoft SQL Server.

   ■ Select Make Browser Broadcasts To LAN Manager 2.*x* Clients to allow LAN Manager 2.*x* clients (Windows NT and earlier) to browse for shared resources on this computer.

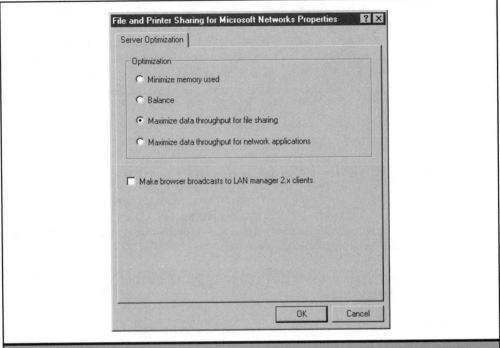

Figure 14-1.   *Optimize computer performance by selecting the appropriate option.*

Browser Service

Downlevel clients use the Browser service to announce themselves and their shared resources on the network. When you use earlier versions of Windows (NT 4 and 9x), double-clicking the Network Neighborhood icon on the desktop results in a list of computers within the domain or workgroup. Selecting a computer displays its shared resources. The Browser service is responsible for these features. It uses broadcasts during Windows startup, and then at specified intervals, to make the announcements.

Unfortunately, the initial implementation of the Browser service frequently hindered performance by clogging the network with unnecessary broadcast messages. To minimize the browser service's impact on the network, Windows moved to the use of a *domain master browser (DomMB)* and a *segment master browser (SegMB)*. The master browsers are responsible for receiving announcements to help reduce clutter on the network, as well as keeping an accurate listing of the computers and shared resources. By definition, a Windows NT 4 Primary Domain Controller (PDC) is the DomMB.

For Windows NT networks with multiple segments, the browser concept was extended slightly with the SegMB. In this case, each segment contains a SegMB that is responsible for maintaining a browse list of the computers on the local segment. Computers on that segment would query and obtain their browse list from the SegMB. The SegMB is also configured to forward the browse list to the DomMB and to request the domain browse list. The SegMB then makes the complete list available to its local clients.

Starting with Windows 2000, the Browser service was replaced by Active Directory (AD) services. As a result, although you may have the Browser service running on Windows Server 2003, it's only there for backward compatibility with downlevel clients. When you finally upgrade all downlevel clients, and remove NetBIOS, the browser service will no longer be needed, because you can rely solely on AD to locate and announce resources. This will improve performance, because AD doesn't impose the toll on network traffic that the browser service does.

Novell NetWare Services

Novell NetWare once held the greatest market share for Intel-based computers. Today, it is no longer dominant, but it still has a presence in many network environments. Because of this, ever since Windows NT 3.5, Microsoft has built services into the operating system that allow the two environments to communicate.

Windows Server 2003, and its client system, Windows XP, continue to provide some interoperability services for NetWare, namely Client Service for NetWare (CSNW), which is built into the operating system. In addition, there are several add-on and third-party solutions. In this section, I'll present an overview of some of the interoperability features that permit communication between these dissimilar network environments.

> **Note** *NetWare-related protocols and services are supported only in 32-bit versions of Windows. The 64-bit versions of Windows don't support the IPX/SPX protocol, and therefore cannot support the NetWare-related services that rely on it.*

Windows vs. NetWare Communications

The way in which Novell NetWare and Windows Server 2003 communicate with machines within their own respective environments is fundamentally different. NetWare clients typically use IPX/SPX (although TCP/IP is also common starting with NetWare 5.x) and the Network Core Protocol (NCP) to function within their own environment. Windows clients rely on CIFS. Therefore, communication between the two systems requires additional services and/or multiple protocol stacks.

The NCP and CIFS architectures are incompatible, in spite of the fact that they share a common function—letting clients request services from a server. To overcome the incompatibility, you need to install and configure additional services.

Historically, as a Windows administrator, you've commonly bridged the communication barrier by configuring clients with multiple protocols in conjunction with CSNW, and by configuring Windows servers as NetWare gateways.

However, Windows Server 2003 does not include Gateway Services for NetWare, and if you require this feature, you need to install Services for NetWare, which is a separate product you can obtain from Microsoft. See the section "Services for NetWare," later in this chapter, for more information.

NWLink

Windows Server 2003, like earlier versions of Windows, includes an IPX/SPX-compatible protocol called NWLink, which is Microsoft's implementation of the IPX/SPX protocol. NWLink allows computers running Windows to communicate with computers running NetWare. It supports WinSock and NetBIOS over IPX APIs.

 You can also use the NWLink protocol to connect computers running Windows to computers running MS Client for DOS.

Installing NWLink

The NWLink protocol is required for communication with NetWare environments, and must be installed if you want to use Client Service for NetWare. To install NWLink, do the following:

1. Choose Start | Control Panel | Network Connections | Local Area Connection.

2. Click Properties.

3. Click Install.

4. Select Protocol and then click Add to open the Select Network Protocol dialog.

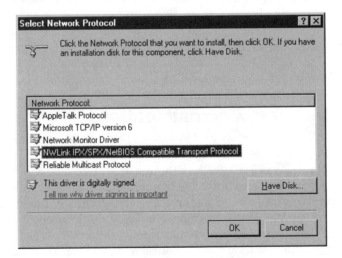

5. Select NWLink IPX/SPX/NetBIOS Compatible Transport Protocol, and click OK.

This adds the following two components to every LAN connection installed on the computer:

- NWLink NetBIOS
- NWLink IPX/SPX/NetBIOS Compatible Transport Protocol

If NWLink is not installed prior to installing the Client Service for NetWare, Windows installs it automatically.

Configuring NWLink

After installation is complete, configure the parameters for the NWLink IPX/SPX/ NetBIOS Compatible Transport protocol (see Figure 14-2).

NWLink Frame Type   The Frame Type parameter defines the way data is formatted as it travels across the network. Servers and workstations cannot communicate with one another over NWLink when they use different frame types.

By default, Windows Server 2003 detects the frame type for you. Automatic frame detection configures NWLink to receive only one frame type—the one that NWLink detects in use on the network:

- NetWare 3.11 and earlier servers are commonly configured to use the 802.3 frame type.

- NetWare 3.12 and later servers default to the 802.2 frame type with the IPX/ SPX protocol.

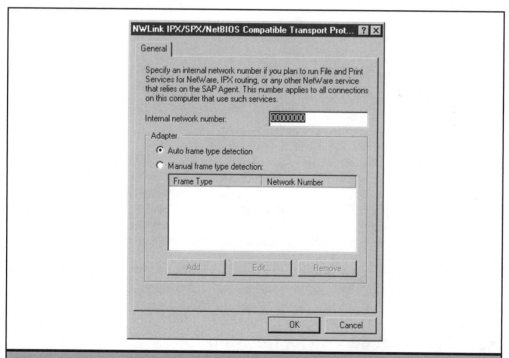

Figure 14-2.   *Configure NWLink to enable communication.*

- Ethernet_II is used with the TCP/IP protocol.
- The Ethernet_SNAP frame type is favored for use with AppleTalk under NetWare.

If you need to access multiple NetWare servers on your network, and they use different frame types with IPX/SPX, you must manually configure NWLink to specify the frame types in use on your network. To determine the frame type your routers are using, enter **ipxroute config** at a command prompt.

If you don't use autodetection for frame type, all the server computers on your network that use IPX/SPX must be using the same frame type. If they're not, you must use autodetection.

NWLink Network Number   Network numbers are associated with the frame type. The network number is used to segment different frame types that may exist on the network. For example, every machine using a specific frame type also uses the same network number. This parameter is automatically detected by Windows Server 2003.

NWLink Internal Network Number   The internal network number is a hexadecimal identifier that is unique for each computer using NWLink. If you do not know what the internal network number should be, accept the default value of 00000000. You can determine the internal network number your routers are using by entering **ipxroute config** at a command prompt.

Client Service for NetWare

In addition to NWLink, clients need CSNW to access file and print resources on NetWare servers. CSNW, which is included with all versions of Windows, provides the redirector services that NWLink lacks. You can use CSNW to connect to NetWare servers (versions 2.*x* to 5.*x*) for file and print services, as well as to access Novell Directory Services (NDS) or bindery information.

Clients communicating in a Windows Server 2003 network using the TCP/IP protocol must use NWLink and CSNW in order to use file resources on NetWare servers. When a machine is configured with both sets of protocols (TCP/IP and NWLink) and CSNW, clients can access NetWare server resources directly. As a result of this direct access, your system suffers no degradation in performance due to protocol translation.

CSNW can only connect to NetWare servers that use the IPX/SPX protocol. CSNW will not connect to NetWare servers that use only the TCP/IP protocol. Use one of the Novell Clients for Windows to access IP-only NetWare servers.

Installing Client Service for NetWare

To begin, you must install CSNW by taking the following steps:

1. Choose Start | Control Panel | Network Connections | Local Area Connection.
2. Click Properties.
3. Click the Install button to display the Select Network Component Type dialog.
4. Select Client and click the Add button.
5. Select Client Service for NetWare and click OK.

You need to restart Windows to complete the installation.

Configuring Client Service for NetWare

While you configure many of the networking components displayed on a Local Area Connection Properties dialog using the component's Properties dialog, this is not true for CSNW. Instead, you configure CSNW via the CSNW Control Panel applet.

To access NDS servers, CSNW uses the NetWare server's bindary-mode emulation feature. The CSNW Control Panel applet gives you two ways to designate the NetWare server you want to access:

- To access a NetWare 3.1x server, you must specify a Preferred Server.
- In an NDS environment, you can specify either a Preferred Server or the name of the NDS Tree and Context where your NetWare user ID is defined—that is, the name of the NDS container that holds your user ID.

Use the following steps to configure CSNW:

1. Open the CSNW applet in Control Panel.
2. To use the Preferred Server option, enter the name of your NetWare server.
3. To use the Default Tree and Context, enter the name of the NDS tree, and the Context within the tree. The context can be in either label or label-less format.
4. Select the desired printing options.
5. Select Run Login Script, if you want CSNW to run the login script that the NetWare Administrator has associated with your NetWare User ID.
6. Click OK to save your selections and close the window.

Services for NetWare

Microsoft Services for NetWare version 5 (SFNW5) is an add-on product with components for Windows NT/2000/2003. The product includes three components for Windows 2000/2003 servers:

- Microsoft Directory Synchronization Services (MSDSS)
- File Migration Utility (FMU)
- File and Print Services for NetWare version 5 (FPNW5)

In addition, SFNW5 includes two components for use with Windows NT 4 servers:

- File and Print Services for NetWare version 4
- Directory Service Manager for NetWare

All of these features are covered in this section.

Microsoft Directory Synchronization Services

Microsoft Directory Synchronization Services (MSDSS) is an add-on service that provides migration support and bidirectional synchronization of directory information with AD and other directory services. Most importantly, it functions with NDS for true enterprise management of directories. MSDSS supports all versions of NDS as well as older NetWare bindery services, allowing you to preserve your NetWare investment (until you migrate NetWare to Windows, of course).

In the capacity of serving more than one directory service, MSDSS also serves as a metadirectory utility. Metadirectories glue various directory services into a unified, manageable service, while at the same time allowing the directory services to be managed separately. MSDSS can be configured and managed through its MMC snap-in. This allows you to easily manage shared information, such as user accounts, from a single interface.

File Migration Utility

Use the File Migration Utility (FMU) in conjunction with MSDSS to migrate files from any NetWare bindary-mode or NDS server to an NTFS volume, while retaining all the original file access rights. Because access rights depend upon User and Group accounts, you must first use MSDSS to migrate NDS directory or Bindary objects to Active Directory, selecting the Migrate Files option when synchronizing the directories.

With the Migrate Files option selected, MSDSS creates a migration log that FMU will use when migrating the files and access rights to an NTFS share.

FMU will also migrate files to a FAT volume, discarding the associated access rights that the FAT file system does not support. However, there are very few acceptable reasons for using a FAT volume in a network.

File and Print Services for NetWare

File and Print Services for NetWare is focused on interoperability for NetWare clients accessing a Windows Server 2003/Windows 2000 network. FPNW lets a NetWare client access file and print services on a Windows server. No configuration on the client is necessary, because the client views the Windows server as a NetWare server. However, FPNW does not include the capability to manage permissions associated with the NetWare clients in the Windows network.

With FPNW, the Windows server appears as a NetWare server that supplies file and print services to NetWare clients. FPNW supports bindary-mode emulation only, making a Windows server appear as a NetWare 3.12 server to NetWare clients. Client applications written to NetWare that require NDS support will fail when used with an FPNW server.

Services for Macintosh

Windows Server 2003 continues to foster interoperability between Intel-based PCs and the Macintosh platform with Services for Macintosh (SFM), which is sometimes referred to as AppleTalk network integration services. SFM is a collection of services that can be individually or collectively installed. The following three components are in SFM:

- AppleTalk Protocol, which is the set of network protocols on which the AppleTalk network architecture is based.

- File Services for Macintosh (sometimes called *MacFile*), which allows Macintosh clients to access files on Windows servers that are running SFM.

- Print Services for Macintosh (also known as *MacPrint*), which enables Macintosh clients to send and spool documents to printers attached to a Windows server (and to any printer on an AppleTalk network).

I'll discuss these components, along with other issues involved with servicing Macintosh clients, in this section.

Macintosh Network Protocols

Integrating Macintosh and Intel-based computers isn't as simple as loading SFM on a Windows Server 2003 computer and expecting the two operating systems to talk to each other. You must also consider the network topologies that are being used, to overcome any problems that arise from network hardware differences.

For Windows Server 2003, the most common network topology is Ethernet, but the OS also supports Token Ring, LocalTalk, FDDI, and ATM. A Macintosh computer can also be equipped to use Ethernet but many still use LocalTalk (used in AppleTalk networking), because LocalTalk networking equipment is built into every Macintosh machine.

If everyone is using the same network media, such as Ethernet, then you're in luck. Otherwise, you'll need to take into consideration the number of Macintosh clients you have. The two most common scenarios are the following:

- Administrators install Ethernet adapters in all the Macintosh computers.

- Administrators install a LocalTalk adapter in the Windows Server 2003 that is running SFM.

There may be other scenarios (sometimes I come across Macintosh computers using Token Ring), but the point is that there must be some common ground between all of this hardware.

AppleTalk and Apple File Protocol over TCP/IP

For a long time, AppleTalk has been the network protocol for enabling Macintosh computers to communicate with each another. Although it's still in use today for many Macintosh LocalTalk networks, it's used primarily with older Macintosh systems.

Much like every other operating system platform and the Internet, newer Macintosh systems have adopted TCP/IP as the protocol of choice.

Macintosh computers that use TCP/IP support file sharing via Apple File Protocol (AFP) over TCP/IP. AFP over TCP/IP is not a full implementation of AFP. AFP/IP Windows servers don't appear in the Macintosh Clients Chooser, because AFP/IP does not broadcast advertisements of network services (AppleTalk does). However, clients can still connect to the SFM volume using the server's IP address.

Windows Server 2003 supports both AppleTalk and AFP over TCP/IP to ensure compatibility with all Macintosh systems. Since Windows Server 2003 relies on TCP/IP, you should standardize on the TCP/IP protocol on Macintosh systems, if possible. Reducing the number of protocols supported in a network environment also reduces the total cost of administration.

If the AppleTalk and/or the AFP over TCP/IP protocols aren't installed before you install file or print services for the Macintosh, Windows Server 2003 installs them automatically. However, if you merely want to install the protocols, you can do so manually with the following steps:

1. Choose Start | Control Panel | Network Connections | Local Area Connection.

2. Click Properties.

3. On the General tab, click the Install button.

4. In the Select Network Component Type window, click Protocol and then click Add.

5. In the Select Network Protocol window, select the AppleTalk Protocol and then click OK.

AppleTalk Routing

After you install AppleTalk on a Windows Server 2003 computer, you can enable AppleTalk routing and create a *zone* (a collection of computers similar to a workgroup) so that the server can act as an AppleTalk router.

AppleTalk routing uses network number ranges to define a segment (a physically connected network). This is analogous to the network portion of an IP address. Two numbers separated by a dash (for example, 10-11) can represent network ranges on an AppleTalk router. The number range tells the router which network addresses to advertise on the segment. (Network numbers can range from 1 to 65,279.)

Each network number can accommodate up to 253 node numbers. A node number corresponds to the host portion of an IP address. Macs on an AppleTalk segment are dynamically given node numbers during startup.

This combination of a network number range and a specific node number identifies an AppleTalk device to the network.

By enabling AppleTalk routing on your Windows Server 2003 computer, you're defining a network much as you do with TCP/IP. Each network is defined by a *network address range* where the number of numbers in the address range times 253 possible nodes per network address ($n \times 253$) defines how many devices you can have in the segment.

Seed Routers

A *seed router* is responsible for broadcasting routing information such as network addresses on the segment (this is called *seeding the network*). Enabling AppleTalk routing on a Windows Server 2003 computer turns that computer into a seed router for Macintosh clients. If you have more than one NIC in the computer, you can seed more than one AppleTalk network.

The AppleTalk environment can include different kinds of routers, all of which forward data from one physical network to another (which is what routers do, of course). Seed routers, however, also have the onus of initializing and broadcasting information about the physical networks. That information lets any other routers on the network know where to send each packet of data.

Each physical network must have at least one seed router. The seed router must be booted first to make sure that any other routers (including Internet routers) are initialized with the correct information about the network.

You can have more than one seed router, and this is handy if your Macintosh clients are scattered across a WAN. Each WAN can have a seed router, so users in one area don't have to wait for seed routers in remote locations to boot up and seed the network.

However, it's urgent that you realize that multiple seed routers must all contain identical seeding information. If there's a difference in information between seed routers, the first router that boots becomes the only seed router—the next seed router that boots notices the differences, and shuts down its seeding services. If the first router to boot isn't the one with the correct information, your network communications are compromised.

Zones

A *zone* is a contiguous range of networks. The zone defines where the Macintosh clients look to find Macintosh-accessible volumes and printers in the Windows environment. This is similar to the principles behind DNS zones (see Chapter 12) where a zone segments the network into manageable pieces. You can have one or more zones defined per segment.

Configuring Routing and Zones

To configure a network adapter in a Windows Server 2003 computer with a Macintosh zone, and enable the computer to act as a seed router, use the following steps:

1. From the Administrative Tools menu, open the Routing And Remote Access Management Console.

2. Expand the RRAS server, right-click AppleTalk Routing, and select Enable AppleTalk Routing.

3. Select AppleTalk Routing in the left pane to display the connections that apply to AppleTalk Routing in the right pane.

4. Right-click the connection (for example, Local Area Connection) and choose Properties.

5. Select the Enable Seed Routing On This Network check box, which enables configuration of AppleTalk Routing parameters.

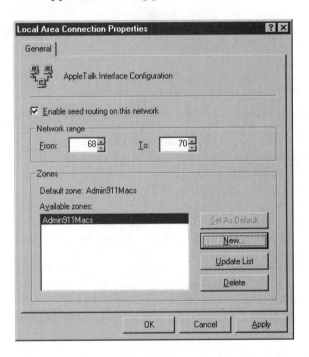

The first parameter to configure is the Network Range of numbers. The numbers you specify can be arbitrary, as long as they're contiguous. Keep in mind that the number of AppleTalk nodes (such as computers, printers, and so on) that can be supported is 253 times the number of numbers in the network range. For example, a network range of 100 to 101 can support 506 (2×253) nodes.

If there aren't any default zones listed, you can create a new zone by clicking the New button, and entering the name of the zone in the New Zone dialog.

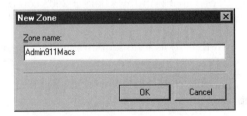

Click OK to create the zone, and repeat the steps to create as many zones as you require. The first zone you create becomes the default zone. To make a different zone the default, select it and click Set As Default. Click Apply to save your changes, and then click OK to close the window.

Remote Access

In addition to supporting Macintosh clients on a LAN, Windows Server 2003's RRAS allows Macintosh clients to connect from remote locations using the AppleTalk Control Protocol (ATCP). ATCP dynamically configures a remote Macintosh client through a PPP link by negotiating various AppleTalk-based parameters, such as an AppleTalk network address.

Once connected, Macintosh users can access Windows resources by using the Guest account or by authenticating using the UAM.

To begin, configure RRAS on the server by doing the following:

1. From the Administrative Tools menu, open the Routing And Remote Access Management Console.

2. In the left pane, right-click the RRAS server object and select Configure and Enable Routing and Remote Access. This launches the Routing and Remote Access Server Setup Wizard.

3. Click Next to skip past the Welcome screen.

4. In the Configurations window, select Remote Access Server and click Next.

5. In the Remote Access window, select dial-up and click Next.

6. In the IP Address Assignment window, click Next to accept the RRAS default. RRAS needs to assign a local network IP address to each remote client connecting through RRAS. RRAS will use addresses supplied by the network's DHCP server, or will generate its own addresses if it doesn't find a DHCP server on the network.

7. The next window, Managing Multiple Remote Access Servers, allows you to choose a RADIUS server to authenticate access to multiple RRAS servers. Unless you have some configuration that requires a RADIUS server, you should accept the default selection to skip it.

8. Click Finish in the next window to complete the installation process.

Then, to configure RRAS to allow Macintosh clients remote access, do the following:

1. From the Administrative Tools menu, open the Routing And Remote Access Management Console.

2. In the console pane, right-click the RRAS server and select Properties from the shortcut menu.

3. In the AppleTalk tab, select Allow AppleTalk-based remote clients to connect to this server.

Authenticating Macintosh Clients

Macintosh clients are required to log on to the Windows Server 2003 network before they can use resources such as file and printer services. The logon mechanism is slightly different than for Windows clients. Macintosh clients use their built-in user authentication module (UAM), which can be configured from their Chooser to log on to an AppleShare Server. However, they have additional options when they log on to Windows Server 2003, which supports the following UAM authentication methods:

- **Guest**   This allows Macintosh clients who don't have a user account and password to log on.

- **Client's AppleShare Authentication**   This prompts Macintosh clients for a username and password (which is sent as cleartext). It's important to note that Apple's built-in Random Number Exchange security method isn't supported by Windows Server 2003, which stores account information in a manner that's incompatible.

- **Microsoft UAM (MS UAM)**   When Macintosh clients log on to a Windows Server 2003 environment, they can optionally use Microsoft's UAM, which offers a higher degree of security than those mechanisms built into the Macintosh Chooser's UAM. There are two versions of Microsoft's UAM, version 1 and version 5. The later version is available only with Windows Server 2003.

Note   *MS UAM 5 requires the client to have AppleShare Client 3.8 or greater, or Mac OS 8.5 or greater. Otherwise, MS UAM version 1 is used.*

Note   *When you install File Services for Macintosh, Windows Server 2003 automatically creates a directory called Microsoft UAM Volume. It shares this directory as a read-only Macintosh volume, and allows guests to access the directory. Macintosh clients connect to this share to get the MS UAM and install it on their computer, after which they can log on securely using MS UAM.*

If you tighten security by using MS UAM, you also need to configure Macintosh clients to install the MS UAM. To configure Macintosh clients to access the authentication files located in the Microsoft UAM Volume, do the following:

1. On the Macintosh Apple menu, double-click Chooser.

2. Double-click the AppleShare icon, and then click the AppleTalk zone you configured on Windows Server 2003.

3. Select the server, and click OK.

4. Click Guest, and click OK.

5. Click the Microsoft UAM Volume, and click OK.

6. Close the Chooser dialog.

7. Connect and select the Microsoft UAM Volume.

8. On the Macintosh Desktop, double-click the Microsoft UAM Volume to open it.

9. Double-click MS UAM Installer.

File Services for Macintosh

File Services for Macintosh (also called MacFile) lets you designate a directory that can be accessible to Macintosh as well as Windows users. For compatibility reasons, a Macintosh-accessible volume requires NTFS to ensure that filenames are set properly for both environments, and to make sure proper security permissions are invoked.

 CDFS (for CD-ROM drives) is also a supported file system that can be used for sharing between platforms. Permissions are always read-only on CDFS drives.

To install File Services for Macintosh, take the following steps:

1. In Control Panel, open Add or Remove Programs.

2. Select Add/Remove Windows Components.

3. Select Other Network File and Print Services (don't put a check mark in the check box), and click the Details button.

4. Select the File Services For Macintosh check box.

5. Click OK, and then click Next.

6. Click Finish to complete the installation.

The installation process is easy, because Windows Server 2003 does most of the work for you. Some important installation issues the OS takes care of include the following:

■ When File Services for Macintosh and TCP/IP are installed, the Apple File Protocol (AFP) over TCP/IP is enabled automatically.

■ If the AppleTalk protocol is not installed before you attempt to install File Services for Macintosh, it is installed automatically.

■ The Microsoft User Authentication Module (UAM) Volume is created automatically.

Windows Server 2003 offers a new way to configure and manage File Services for Macintosh. Instead of using the File Manager you used in Windows NT, you use the Shared Folders snap-in in the Computer Management Console. To open the Computer Management Console, right-click My Computer and choose Manage from the shortcut menu.

Creating Other Macintosh Volumes   Besides the Microsoft UAM Volume, other
Macintosh-accessible volumes can be created to share files among Macintosh and
Windows Server 2003 computers. To create a Macintosh-accessible volume, do the
following:

1. Open Computer Management from the Start | Programs | Administrative
   Tools menu, and expand Shared Folders (either double-click Shared Folders
   or click the +).

2. Right-click Shares and select New File Share to launch the Share a Folder Wizard.

3. Click Next to skip the Share a Folder Wizard welcome screen.

4. In the Folder Path window, enter the drive and path to the folder you want to
   make Macintosh accessible in the Folder to share dialog. You can also use the
   Browse button to find the folder.

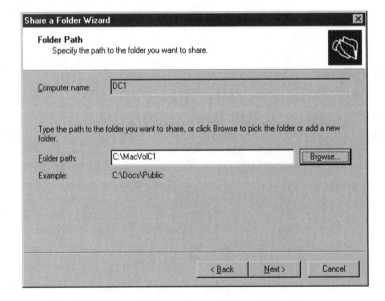

5. In the Name, Description, and Settings window, type the name of the share in
   the Share Name box, and optionally enter a description.

6. Select the Apple Macintosh Users check box to populate the Macintosh Share
   Name dialog with the sharename.

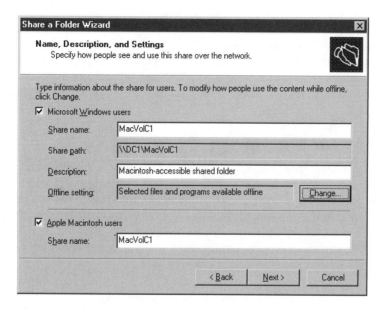

7. The wizard prompts you to set permissions for the shared folder, offering the following options:

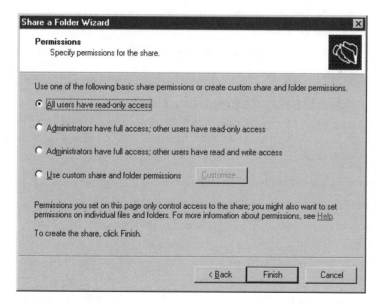

- All users have read-only access
- Administrators have full access; other users have read-only access
- Administrators have full access; other users have read and write access
- Use custom share and folder permissions

Optionally, select Customize Share And Folder Permissions, and then click the Custom button to customize permissions.

You can add users or groups and customize their permissions; select a user or group and set advanced, more granular, permission; and use the Security tab to enable auditing.

Click Finish to close the wizard and see a display of the type of clients that can access the folder.

Print Services for Macintosh

Print Services for Macintosh (also called MacPrint) lets Macintosh users print to shared printers installed on a Windows Server 2003 computer, and also lets Intel-based clients print to AppleTalk PostScript printers. This service can be configured and managed within the Printers folder.

Note   *If you haven't already installed the AppleTalk protocol, it is installed automatically during the Print Services for Macintosh installation.*

To install Print Services for Macintosh, do the following:

1. In Control Panel, open Add or Remove Programs and select Add/Remove Windows Components.
2. Select Other Network File and Print Services (don't put a check mark in the check box) and click Details.
3. Put a check mark into the check box next to Print Services For Macintosh.
4. Click OK, click Next, and then click Finish.

Creating a Macintosh-Accessible Printer

Before Macintosh clients can use printers that are defined on a Windows Server 2003 computer, you must add the printer and configure it for AppleTalk. Use the following steps to accomplish this:

1. Open the Printers and Faxes folder.
2. Choose Add Printer to start the Add Printer Wizard.
3. Click Next to begin configuring a Macintosh-accessible printer.
4. Select Local Printer. If the printer is directly attached, be sure to check Automatically Detect And Install My Plug And Play Printer check box to install the printer. Click Next to continue.
5. Click Create A New Port, and select AppleTalk Printing Devices. Click Next.

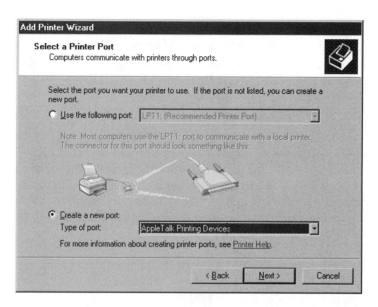

6. In the next window, expand the AppleTalk zone where the printer is located, select the printer, and click OK.

7. Click Next and then click Finish to complete the installation.

UNIX Integration Services

UNIX has been around for decades (much longer than Windows Server 2003 and earlier Windows versions) and has established itself in many network environments. As a result, Microsoft has realized the importance of fostering interoperability with UNIX so that clients of those environments can communicate with both platforms.

Windows Server 2003 has a set of built-in components that enhance interoperability between the two environments, including file, printer, and network connectivity. I'll go over these components in this section.

Microsoft also offers Services for UNIX version 2, which is an add-on product with advanced UNIX interoperability and migration components.

POSIX

The Portable Operating System Interface for UNIX (POSIX) subsystem allows applications written to the POSIX standard to run on Windows Server 2003. POSIX is an Institute of Electrical and Electronics Engineers (IEEE) standard that defines a set of operating-system services that make it easier to port services from one system to another. This set of application portability standards has evolved ranging from POSIX.1

to POSIX.2. Windows Server 2003 uses the POSIX.1-compliant subsystem, meaning that it complies with the basic POSIX standards. These standards include case sensitivity and support for multiple filenames. Applications conforming to this standard can execute within the POSIX subsystem in their own protected memory space.

Print Services for UNIX

Print Services for UNIX gives Windows Server 2003 the ability to send and receive print jobs to and from UNIX clients and servers. The line printer remote (LPR) service is used for sending print jobs, and the line printer daemon (LPD) service is used to receive them.

Another useful service that Windows Server 2003 provides with Print Services for UNIX is the line printer query (LPQ) service. This service emulates the features you gain when you double-click a printer icon in the Printers and Faxes folder to retrieve information about the printer's status.

Note *For more information on printing and related services, refer to Chapter 9.*

Installing Print Services for UNIX

Print Services for UNIX (PS-UNIX) requires TCP/IP, which I'm assuming is installed on your network. If it's not, you can't install Print Services for UNIX. To install the service, take the following steps:

1. In Control Panel, open Add or Remove Programs, and choose Add/Remove Windows Components.

2. Select Other Network File And Print Services (don't insert a check mark in the check box), and click Details.

3. Put a check mark into the check box next to Print Services For UNIX, and click OK.

4. Click Next to install the files, and then choose Finish.

Creating a UNIX-Accessible Printer

After you install Print Services for UNIX, you can configure printers to accept LPR print jobs. Configuring a UNIX-accessible printer is basically the same as configuring a local printer, except that you'll create a LPR port, using the following steps:

1. Open the Printers and Faxes folder.

2. Double-click Add Printer to start the Add Printer Wizard.

3. Click Next to begin configuring a UNIX-accessible printer.

4. Select Local Printer. If the printer is directly attached, be sure to check Automatically Detect And Install My Plug And Play Printer check box to install the printer. Click Next to continue.

5. Select Create A New Port, select LPR Port, and then click Next.

6. In the Add LPR Compatible Printer window, enter either the hostname or the IP address of the computer hosting the printer. Then enter the name of the printer as it's defined on the UNIX machine (unless your memory is much better than mine, you'll have to look it up). Alternatively, if the printer is directly attached to the network, enter the IP address.

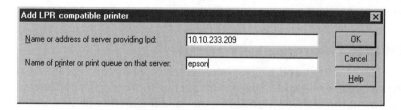

7. Click OK to let Windows Server 2003 try to communicate with the printer. Follow the wizard's prompts, and click Next when you're done.

8. Choose an appropriate name for the printer and click Next.

9. Specify whether or not you want to share this printer (the default for Windows servers is to share printers), and click Next.

10. Optionally, enter the printer's location information in the Location field, and a descriptive phrase in the Comments field. Then click Next.

11. Select Yes to print a test page.

12. Click Finish to complete the installation.

Now that you've installed and configured the printer, it's ready to accept print jobs. Windows Server 2003 and downlevel clients can connect to the printer using Active Directory.

In addition, clients can print using LPR commands in the same way UNIX clients can. The LPR command syntax is

lpr -s server -p printer

For example, to print the document named resume.txt on the printer named sharedprinter, enter the following command:

lpr –s unix.mydomain.com –p sharedprinter c:\resume.txt

Using Print Services for UNIX with Windows Printers

When you install Print Services for UNIX on Windows Server 2003/2000 computers, PS-UNIX exposes all local printers as LPR-compatible printers. You can use this feature to access shared Windows printers in some routed networks where NetBIOS name resolution fails to locate the server hosting the printer, or where NetBIOS traffic through the router is disallowed.

After you install PS-UNIX on the computer that hosts the printer, you can use PS-UNIX on a remote network to create a UNIX-accessible printer, as described in the preceding section. This creates a printer share for users on the remote network that routes print jobs to the printer on the local network. Because PS-UNIX creates UNIX-compatible printers, Windows security is not active, and any LPR-compatible program can print to the printer. Be sure to understand the lack of security for Windows printers in your environment before installing PS-UNIX.

UNIX Network Connectivity

Fortunately, the Windows and UNIX platform advocates are in agreement about which underlying network protocol is most advantageous for network connectivity—TCP/IP.

What rides on top of TCP/IP still remains fundamentally different for the different platforms—hence the need for interoperability services from the operating system developers as well as third-party vendors. To advertise services on the network, Windows Server 2003 uses CIFSs, while UNIX variants have standardized on the Network File System (NFS).

To make sure clients on both sides can access file and other services, you should consider add-ons and/or third-party solutions. Microsoft has an add-on called Services for UNIX Version 2 that enables you to share resources, administer machines remotely, synchronize Windows Server 2003 and UNIX passwords, and much more.

The choices you'll face when trying to integrate the two platforms are numerous, and I could probably write an entire book on the choices alone. Following are some of the common choices you may have to make, and some possible vendors to contact for solutions.

To install NFS client software on Windows Server 2003 and downlevel client computers, check the following vendors:

- Microsoft (www.microsoft.com)
- HummingBird Communications (www.hummingbird.com)
- FTP Software (www.netmanage.com)

Platform Wars about DNS

Windows and UNIX advocates agree that DNS is one of the most efficient mechanisms for name resolution. However, choosing a specific DNS solution is definitely not an issue on which differing platform advocates agree. When you're investigating DNS integration issues, be warned that you may find yourself in some rather heated (almost religious) battles. I'm not going to get into all the details and arguments about DNS platform issues here, but take my advice and do your homework before you make decisions. In the end, of course, the DNS solution you choose depends on the features that best serve your infrastructure.

To install SMB client software on UNIX clients and servers, contact SAMBA (http://samba.anu.edu.au/samba).

To use application servers to share applications across both platforms, check the following vendors:

- Microsoft (www.microsoft.com)
- NetManage (www.netmanage.com)
- Citrix Systems (www.citrix.com)

Telnet

Telnet is a client/server service that lets a telnet client connect and log on to a server that's running the telnet daemon. From a telnet window, you can manage and configure just about anything for which you have appropriate permissions.

Telnet is useful for accessing UNIX servers, and for letting UNIX computers contact Windows Server 2003 computers that are running as telnet servers.

Caution   *One large drawback to telnet is that it sends passwords across the network in plain text, so that anyone sniffing the network can grab the password and use it to their advantage. For this reason, UNIX administrators usually implement security measures such as Secure Shell (SSH) when they perform remote management and configuration tasks.*

Windows Server 2003 can be a telnet server and a telnet client. The version of telnet that comes bundled in Windows Server 2003 is fundamentally different from the telnet versions you may have used in earlier versions of Windows. In the following sections, I'll go over the Windows Server 2003 implementation of telnet.

Telnet Server

Windows Server 2003 includes a telnet server, so it can accept incoming telnet connection requests. In earlier versions of Windows, the telnet service didn't provide this feature, so you had to use third-party telnet servers.

The Windows Server 2003 telnet server can be configured to use standard authentication methods (username and password), or domain user account information, to grant clients access to the server. Each telnet server is configured for a maximum of two concurrent connections, but you can change that default with the telnet administration tool tlntadmn.exe (see the section "Tlntadmn.exe," later in this chapter).

The telnet server service doesn't start automatically; in fact, its default status is "disabled." To change the service to start automatically (or manually), open the Services snap-in from the Administrative Tools menu and double-click the telnet listing. On the General tab, select Automatic from the Startup Type drop-down list.

Note   *If the service is set for manual startup, you can also start the telnet service from the command line by entering **start telnet**.*

HyperTerminal Replaces Telnet Client

The GUI-based telnet client you may have used in Windows NT is not included in Windows Server 2003 (nor in Windows 2000). Instead, you have an enhanced version of HyperTerminal, which you can use to connect to a server using TCP/IP (Winsock) in addition to the familiar COM ports.

*The text-based telnet client is still included with Windows Server 2003, and can be launched by entering **telnet** at a command prompt. Don't forget that "exit" doesn't work; you must type **quit** to end the session, and then type **exit** to close the command window.*

HyperTerminal is not installed by default when you install Windows Server 2003. To add the service, you need the Windows Server 2003 CD, or access to the shared folder you used as a distribution point. Then take the following steps:

1. Open Add or Remove Programs in Control Panel, and click Add/ Remove Windows Components.

2. Select Accessories and Utilities and click Details.

3. Select Communications and click Details.

4. Select HyperTerminal and click OK.

5. Click OK twice to return to the Add/Remove Windows Components window, and then click Next to install the software.

6. After the files are copied, click Finish, and close the Add or Remove Programs window.

The HyperTerminal program listing is installed in the Communications submenu of the Accessories submenu. The first time you launch HyperTerminal, the following events occur:

1. You're asked if you want to make HyperTerminal your default telnet program. Unless you have another telnet program you prefer, answer Yes and select the option to stop asking.

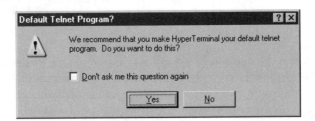

2. The standard Windows Server 2003 Location Information dialog appears, so you can set the configuration options for connecting to a telnet server.

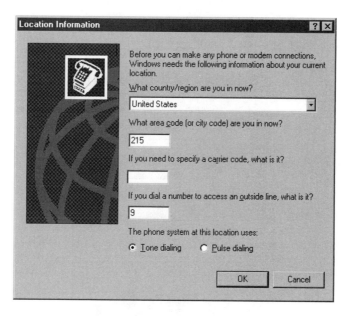

3. The Phone and Modem Options dialog appears, so you can edit the location you just created (for example, setting up dialing and long distance rules).

4. The Connection Description dialog appears, where you can establish the settings for the telnet server you're setting up as a connection.

5. The Connect To dialog appears, and the options change depending on the specification you select from the drop-down list in the Connect Using field:

   ■ If you select a COM port, enter the area code and telephone number.

■ If you select TCP/IP (Winsock), enter the server's IP address and the port number (Port 23 is the default section).

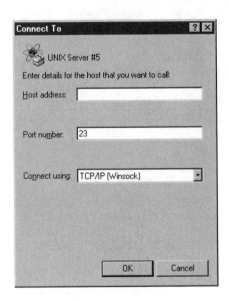

6. Finally, the HyperTerminal window opens, and you're connected to the telnet server.

After you finish your tasks and close the HyperTerminal window, you're given an opportunity to save the connection, so it's available the next time you want to dial into that server.

 For detailed information on using HyperTerminal, choose Help in the HyperTerminal window.

Telnet Security

By default, only members of the local Administrators group can connect to the Windows Server 2003 telnet server. When a client connects, the remote user must enter a username and password that is valid on the server, and has administrative permissions. A command window opens and the client user can perform tasks, but cannot use any applications that interact with the desktop.

If you create a local group named TelnetClients, any member of that group is also allowed to connect to the telnet server. You have to add users or groups to the TelnetClients group manually. You can then use NTFS security to set permissions on the computer for the TelnetClients group.

Whether the telnet server will accept NTLM authentication, clear text authentication, or both is set in the registry key HKLM/Software/Microsoft/ TelnetServer/1.0/SecurityMechanism:

- A value of 2 allows NTLM security
- A value of 4 allows clear text authentication
- A value of 6 allows both (or either, depending on how you look at it)

Tlntadmn.exe

Tlntadmn.exe is a command-line program you can use to manage telnet server services. After you issue a command, you must stop and restart the telnet service to have your changes take effect. Most of the time, telnet server is administered locally, but you can use tlntadmn.exe from a remote computer if you have administrative permissions on the target telnet server. (The remote computer must have tlntadmn.exe available, which means it's running Windows NT or a later version of Windows.)

Complete documentation for tlntadmn.exe is available in the Windows Server 2003 Help and Support Center, but I'll go over a few of the common tasks here.

Increase the Number of Concurrent Connections Permitted   The syntax is **tlntadmn config maxconn=***PositiveInteger*. The maximum value of *PositiveInteger* is in the millions, but you shouldn't permit more concurrent connections than the computer's resources (especially RAM) and your Microsoft license agreement permit. If you are working from a remote computer, the syntax is

tlntadmn [*RemoteServer*] **config** [**maxconn=***PositiveInteger*] [**-u** *UserName* **-p** *Password*]

where:

RemoteServer is the name of the Windows Server 2003 computer operating as a telnet server.

-u *UserName* **-p** *Password* is a username and password of an account that has administrative privileges on the remote server.

Use the additional parameters for all tlntadmn.exe commands if you're working remotely.

Set the Maximum Number of Failed Logon Attempts Before a User is Disconnected   The syntax is **tlntadmn config maxfail=***PositiveInteger*. The maximum *PostitiveInteger* is 100.

Set the Telnet Port   The syntax is **tlntadmn config port=***IntegerValue*. The value of *IntegerValue* is the port number on the computer.

Set the Time-Out for Idle Sessions   The syntax is **tlntadmn config timeout=***hh:mm:ss*.

Tip   *Tlntadmn.exe is also available on Windows XP, so you can manage telnet servers from the comfort of your own XP workstation.*

The Complete Reference

Chapter 15

File Systems
and Functions

Y ou can choose among three file systems for disk partitions on a computer running Windows Server 2003: FAT, FAT32, and NTFS. This chapter discusses these file systems, as well as some of the features available in NTFS.

FAT and FAT32

The FAT (File Allocation Table) is a table of links that holds information about the data blocks that make up a file. The first FAT file system (which used 12-bit entries) was introduced with DOS. The first DOS version (1.0) didn't support subdirectories, and as DOS improved, the FAT file system was altered so it could handle the new features. For example, when DOS 4.0 was released, FAT entries were increased to 16 bits to handle partitions that were larger than 32MB.

The FAT is on the disk, along with a duplicate FAT, which is an effort to provide an element of fault tolerance (however, a damaged FAT is rarely successfully repaired). The system also contains a root directory section that has a fixed size, limiting the number of files that can be located in the root directory.

The FAT contains entries for filenames and file attributes such as the size, the attribute byte (an 8-bit entry for information such as hidden, read-only, and so on), the last modification time/date (16-bit entries), and the starting allocation unit, which is a pointer to the file's entry in the FAT. If the file is not contiguous, there are FAT entries pointing to each block that contains an allocation unit for the file. This is called a *chain*. The last, or "end of file," entry contains the hexadecimal pattern FFFF, to indicate that it's the end of the chain. When the file is loaded or saved, the operating system uses the chain to track the location of the file fragments. As the chain grows longer (the disk is highly fragmented), performance suffers.

The files themselves are stored in clusters, the size of which depends on the size of the drive. Because the size of the FAT itself is fixed, the adjustments for handling large drives are made by changing the cluster size. The size of a cluster can be 2048 bytes, 4096 bytes, or 8192 bytes. The 16-bit length of the FAT entries limited the size of hard disks to 128MB (assuming a 2048-byte cluster). Theoretically, FAT could support a 512MB drive, but the cluster size would have to be 8192, which is highly inefficient. Starting with DOS 5.0, partitions up to 2GB were supported by creating separate FATs for each drive partition (up to four partitions).

FAT32, a table that held 32-bit entries, was introduced in Windows 95 OSR2. This new design brought a number of features to FAT file systems:

- The 32GB partition size limit was eliminated.
- The root directory isn't placed in a fixed position and can be relocated.
- There is no limit on the number of entries that can be placed on the root directory.
- The backup copies of the FAT actually manage to resolve crashes.
- FAT32 permits far more clusters on a disk by allowing 4096 bytes in a cluster, even for large drives.

FAT32 also introduced the ability to handle filenames longer than the previous limit of 8.3. For users, long filename support was probably the most noticed, and most appreciated, function. Microsoft used a Virtual File Allocation Table (VFAT) in Windows 95 to handle long filenames, a 32-bit utility that runs in protected mode. Microsoft actually calls the VFAT extension a driver, because it's installable, and it was assumed it would be installed into any operating system.

NTFS

Windows Server 2003 uses the same NTFS system that was introduced in Windows 2000 (sometimes referred to as NTFS 5). This file system has built-in support for a variety of features that help you manage domains, user accounts, and security features. This is not the same NTFS system available in Windows NT 4. The features that NTFS 5 supports are part of the core design of Windows Server 2003 (and Windows 2000), and include, but are not limited to, the following:

- **Active Directory**   Holds all the objects in the operating system, allowing and preventing access through permissions. See Chapter 19 to learn about Active Directory.

- **Disk quotas**   Limits the use of disk space on a per-user or per-group basis. See Chapter 16 for detailed information on disk quotas.

- **Encryption**   Provides automatic encryption and decryption of file data as files are written and read. See Chapter 17 for information about using Encrypting File System (EFS).

- **Distributed File System**   Lets you use a single directory tree to include multiple servers and shares. See Chapter 16 for more information on setting up and maintaining DFS.

In addition to the powerful tools and features that make managing an enterprise easier for administrators, NTFS has one feature that end users enjoy and appreciate—the ability to follow a location change in a document shortcut. This nifty function, which many administrators aren't even aware of, is terrific for users who maintain shortcuts for frequently accessed documents. I, for example, keep document shortcuts on my Quick Launch toolbar for documents I work on over a long period of time (such as chapters for books). These shortcuts are created and removed as needed. In addition, I keep a shortcut to any document that requires constant updating—such as the document I keep that has my passwords for web sites.

The Properties dialog for a document shortcut displays the path to the document. If you move the document to another folder, and then click the shortcut, the document opens. The next time you check the Properties dialog, you see that the location path has been updated.

NTFS Master File Table

Instead of a File Allocation Table, NTFS uses a special file called the Master File Table (MFT) to track all the files and directories on a volume. The size of the MFT is dynamic, and is automatically extended when necessary. The MFT is really an array of records, which you can think of as a database of all the files on the system.

Each record in the MFT is usually fixed at 1K, and the first 16 records contain information about the volume. These volume-specific records are called the *metadata files*, which is the terminology used for overhead structures in the file system.

Normally, each record in the MFT corresponds to one file or directory in the file system. The record contains the file's attributes, including items such as read-only and archive flags, creation and last-accessed dates, the filename, and a security descriptor.

Note	*The filename's record usually contains two filenames: a long filename and a DOS-compatible filename (8.3).*

More important, and certainly far different from FAT, the file data is just another attribute of NTFS. There is a limit to the amount of data that can fit in the MFT record, and anything over that limit is replaced in the record with pointers to where the file data resides on the disk. The MFT record can hold about 750 bytes of file data (the actual amount depends on the number of attributes being stored in the MFT record). Small data files (under 750 bytes) can fit entirely within their MFT entries, providing incredibly good performance and no risk of fragmentation for those files.

There is at least one entry in the MFT for each file on the NTFS volume, including the MFT itself (which is a file) and other metadata files, such as the log file, the bad cluster map, and the root directory.

Of course, most files are not small enough to fit their data into their MFT entries, so the MFT stores their data on the disk. NTFS allocates files in units of clusters, which are referenced in two ways:

- Virtual Cluster Numbers (VCNs), from 0 through $n-1$, where there are n clusters in the file.
- Logical Cluster Numbers (LCNs), which correspond to the clusters' numbers on the volume.

VCNs are the analog for file offsets requested by applications. An application knows the format of the data it uses in a file, and uses it to calculate a byte offset within the logical format of the file. When the application requests a read or write at that address of the file, NTFS divides that number by cluster size to determine the VCN to read or write.

LCNs are an index to the clusters on a volume, and when there is a need to read or write, NTFS uses an LCN to calculate an address on the disk. The calculation involves multiplying the LCN by the number of sectors per cluster, and then reading or writing sectors starting at that address on the disk. By associating VCNs with their LCN, NTFS associates a file's logical addressing with the physical locations on disk.

If any attribute doesn't fit in the MFT record, NTFS stores it in a new, separate set of clusters on the disk, called a *run* or an *extent*. Usually, the file data attribute is the attribute that is too large for the MFT record. However, other attributes besides the data attribute could become large enough to force new extents. For example, long filenames can be up to 255 characters that consume 2 bytes apiece (caused by the fact that filenames are stored in Unicode).

An attribute that is stored within the MFT entry is called a *resident* attribute. When an attribute is forced out to an extent, it is called a *nonresident* attribute. This means that unless users consistently create extremely small files with short names, the majority of the files on a volume have data that is a nonresident attribute.

When the extent needs to be enlarged (usually because a user adds data to a file that's already large), NTFS attempts to allocate physically contiguous clusters to the same extent. If there is no more contiguous space available, NTFS will allocate a new extent elsewhere on the disk, separating the file into two fragments. If the new extent also fails to provide enough contiguous space, the action is repeated. The data attribute header (kept within the MFT record) stores that information in the form of LCNs and run lengths, and NTFS uses the information to locate the extents.

In some cases, usually when the number of attributes is extremely large, NTFS may be forced to allocate an additional MFT entry for the file. If this occurs, NTFS creates an attribute called an *attribute list*, which acts as an index to all the attributes for the file. While this is an unusual situation, the presence of additional MFT entries can greatly slow the performance of operations on the affected files.

Directories are handled very much like files in NTFS. If a directory is small enough, the index to the files to which it points can fit in the MFT record. This information is an attribute, called the Index Root attribute.

If more entries are present than can fit in the MFT record, NTFS creates a new extent with a nonresident attribute called an *index buffer*. For those directories, the index buffers contain what is called a *b+ tree*, which is a data structure designed to minimize the number of comparisons needed to find a particular file entry.

A b+ tree stores information (or indexes to information) in a sorted order. A request for a sorted list of the entries in a directory is satisfied quickly, because that is the order of storage in the index buffer. To find a particular entry, the lookup is quick, because the trees tend to get wide rather than deep, which minimizes the number of accesses necessary to reach a particular point in the tree.

NTFS Fragmentation

Any rumors you've heard that NTFS prevents fragmentation are untrue. Windows Server 2003, Windows 2000, and Windows NT are much smarter than earlier versions of Windows (and DOS) in allocating disk space to files, and as a result, systems are less prone to fragment files.

However, NTFS is not immune to the forces that fragment individual files, and over time, files on an NTFS volume will become fragmented. In addition, a side effect of the operating system's efforts to prevent file fragmentation is fragmentation of the system's free space.

When you format a volume with NTFS, you have a choice of cluster size to use. Windows NT offers a default cluster size, based on the size of the volume, but if you have some knowledge about the way the volume is used, you can choose a cluster size that works better for that usage. However, you have to be very careful if you opt to bypass the default size. Choosing a smaller cluster size will waste less space but is more likely to cause fragmentation. Larger cluster sizes are less likely to cause fragmentation but will waste more space.

Caution *Choosing 512-byte clusters can be problematic, since the MFT consists of records that are always 1024 bytes. It is possible, with 512-byte clusters, to have individual MFT entries fragmented. This is not possible on larger sizes, which can hold more than one MFT entry with no waste.*

If a file or directory is contiguous, the cluster size doesn't matter, unless you choose to be upset about wasting a small amount of space. If you know that the volume will hold a very large number of small files, or if you know that almost all of the files will be very large, you have information you can use for a better cluster decision. Also, a very large absolute number of files (on the order of 100,000) will make fragmentation of the MFT more likely. In this case, a larger cluster size will limit the fragmentation in the MFT as it grows to accommodate the files.

Note *It's possible to create an NTFS volume with a cluster size greater than 4K, but you will not be able to defragment the volume using the built-in defragmentation program. You will also not be able to use NTFS compression.*

It's important to note the distinctions between fragmentation at different levels of data storage. Individual applications, such as Microsoft Office, and database servers, such as Oracle, have fragmentation issues within their own data storage. These issues are present regardless of the file system or operating system.

NTFS is not aware of the logical organization of user data. Wherever the file may exist on the disk, and whether or not the file is fragmented, the file system presents it to the application as a single contiguous area of storage. The application's view of the data in the file, however, has a logical structure. For mailing list software, a file is a group of first names, last names, addresses, and so forth. To NTFS, it is just a group of clusters of data.

Applications, in their own internal organization of data, may create gaps in the data, which effectively fragments the data. Like a file system, when you delete data in an application, it may not actually remove the data, but only mark it as deleted. The resulting gaps in the logical storage of data are known as *internal fragmentation*. To combat internal data fragmentation, some applications, such as Microsoft Access, provide utilities to compact the data in the file—in effect, a defragmentation of an internal file. Ironically, these compaction utilities frequently increase the level of fragmentation at the file system level, because they usually create an entirely new copy of the file, consuming large amounts of disk space in the process. Thus, regular defragmentation of your data files may exacerbate fragmentation of your file system.

Applications frequently create temporary files, which occupy space while the user works with the software, opening and saving files. The temporary files are deleted when the software is closed, leaving behind the empty allocated space. Data files may also have allocated but unused space, as programs allocate space for their own organizational or performance reasons. Also, the individual files associated with an application can, over time, become physically dispersed across a disk. This type of fragmentation, known as *usage fragmentation,* is an especially difficult problem for a defragmentation program, because normal methods of fragmentation analysis may not identify it.

Fragmentation and defragmentation of directories work similarly to that of files. In fact, to NTFS, a directory is just another file, although directories have special types of attributes in their MFT records. While applications manage the contents of data files, NTFS manages the contents of directories, which are b+ trees that provide an indexed access to files contained in the directories.

Directories that hold program files don't grow or shrink much over their lifetimes. But user document directories, and the system's TEMP directory, change size quite a bit. As the number of files in a directory grows, NTFS can accommodate the growth by growing the directory storage. If the contents of the directory shrink, NTFS can also free up the unused space in the directory, but this doesn't always happen, because it's a complicated maneuver. The directories that are most likely to grow and shrink are usually those that were created early in the system's configuration, such as My Documents and the TEMP directory. It is quite likely that the growth of these directories is noncontiguous. Because these directories are heavily used, their fragmentation has a real impact on the system's performance.

Speaking of performance, you should be aware that deeply nested directories may present an organizational convenience, but you're paying a performance penalty for them. When NTFS searches its b+ trees for data, it performs the search from the beginning for each level in the directory subtree. Therefore, performance may be better with flatter trees that have larger numbers of files in them than with deeper trees that have fewer files in each. Very deep subtrees can also create problems for applications that have limits to the number of characters in a complete file path (a limit of 255 characters is not unusual).

Note   *You can find information on using the Windows 2000 defragmentation program in Chapter 8.*

NTFS Compression

NTFS file compression is a built-in function of the file system. You can compress the data on an entire volume, in a specific directory, or in a specific file. To enable compression, open the Properties dialog of a volume, directory, or file, and use the General tab as follows:

- For a volume, select the option Compress Drive To Save Disk Space. You are asked if you want to apply compression only to the root, or include all the folders.

- For a folder, click Advanced, and then select the option Compress Contents To Save Disk Space. You are asked if you also want to apply compression to subfolders.

- For a file, click Advanced, and then select the option Compress Contents To Save Disk Space.

When you view a compressed object's properties in My Computer or Windows Explorer, you see both sizes (see Figure 15-1).

The NTFS compression scheme uses both VCNs and LCNs. In a file that has data stored in nonresident attributes or in extents, the data attribute contains mappings for the starting VCN and starting LCN in the extent, as well as the length in clusters. NTFS manipulates these cluster numbers to achieve compression, using one of two approaches: sparse storage or divided data.

Sparse storage is a way to commit disk space so that null data blocks aren't stored on the disk. Sometimes, big files have large blocks of nulls (bytes of value 0). NTFS calls these files *sparse files*, and only stores the nonzero data. For example, you may have a 100-cluster file that contains real data in only the first 5 and last 5 clusters—the middle 90 clusters are all 0's. NTFS can store two extents for this file, each of which is five clusters long. The first extent will have VCNs 0 through 4, and the second will have VCNs 95 through 99.

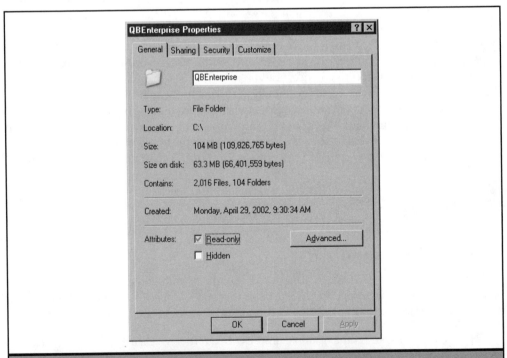

Figure 15-1.   *The size of the file on disk indicates the compression.*

NTFS infers that VCNs 5 through 94 are null and do not need physical storage. If a program requests data in this space, NTFS simply fills the requesting program's buffer with nulls. When (or if) the application allocates real data (nonzero data) to this space, NTFS creates a new extent with the appropriate VCNs.

If a file is not predominately null, NTFS does not try to write the file data inside one extent; instead, it divides the data into runs of 16 clusters each. In any particular extent, if compressing the data will save at least 1 cluster, NTFS stores the compressed data, resulting in 15 or fewer clusters. If the data cannot be effectively compressed (random data, for example, is generally not compressible), NTFS simply stores that entire extent as it normally would, without compression. In the MFT record for a compressed file, NTFS can see that there are missing VCNs in the runs, and knows that the file is compressed.

When data is stored in a compressed form, it is not possible to look up a specific byte by calculating the cluster in which it is stored. Instead, NTFS calculates in which 16-cluster run the address is located, decompresses the run back to 16 uncompressed clusters, and then calculates the offset into the file using valid virtual cluster numbers. To make this addressing scheme possible, NTFS ensures that all these runs begin with a virtual cluster number divisible by 16.

NTFS tries to write these runs in a single contiguous space, because the I/O system is already encountering enough added processing and management burden using compressed files without having to fragment individual extents. NTFS also tries to keep the individual, separate runs of the file contiguous, but this is a harder job. As a result, compressed files are more likely to be fragmented than noncompressed files.

Note *NTFS compresses only the file's data attribute, not the metadata.*

Upgrading to NTFS

When you install Windows Server 2003 over an existing Windows NT 4 NTFS volume, the volume is automatically upgraded to the newer NTFS file system. The upgrade is mandatory, and you have no control over the process. The file system upgrade is not a process that's spawned by Windows Server 2003 Setup; it is launched by the NTFS driver after installation is complete. All locally attached NTFS volumes are upgraded to the new version of the NTFS file system, including removable media. Windows NT 4 NTFS volumes that are removed or powered off during installation are upgraded automatically when the drives are next mounted. Any Windows NT 4 NTFS volumes that are not upgraded will not be mounted under Windows Server 2003.

Caution *If you want to dual-boot between Windows NT 4 and Windows Server 2003, the NT 4 system must be at Service Pack 4 or better, and running NTFS. The new features supported by NTFS change the data structure on disks, and the ntfs.sys file in SP4 (and higher) can handle the changes.*

When you upgrade over any Windows operating system that is not running NTFS, you are offered an option to convert the hard disk from FAT or FAT32 to NTFS during the text-based phase of Windows 2000 Setup. The screen displays the following message:

```
Upgrading to the Windows NT File System
Do you want Setup to upgrade your drive to NTFS?
Yes, Upgrade my drive
No, Do not upgrade my drive
```

The default selection is Yes.

You can convert from FAT/FAT32 after you've installed Windows Server 2003. See the section "Converting to NTFS," later in this chapter.

Deciding on a File System

Apart from domain controllers, which must run NTFS, you may want to decide on a file system instead of automatically installing NTFS. This is commonly an issue if you need to dual-boot. This section presents some guidelines for making these decisions.

Years ago, when I was writing about Windows NT, I used to advise readers to format the system partition with FAT. If the system wouldn't boot, and the cause was a corrupted or missing system file, you could replace the file easily by booting to DOS and copying the file.

However, I now strongly advise that all Windows Server 2003 computers, as well as Windows XP and Windows 2000 computers, be formatted with NTFS. Two developments spurred my change of mind:

- The size of an installation of the OS is so enormous that FAT/FAT32 volumes, with their wasteful use of space, just aren't efficient.

- The Recovery Console, an NTFS-compatible command-line application introduced in Windows 2000, provides access to a damaged system partition.

There are some instances in which you may want to select FAT or FAT32 as the file system, and most of the time (if not always) this decision applies to workstations on which you are installing Windows XP Professional (or Windows 2000 Professional):

- If you choose FAT, access to the computer and its files is available from every operating system: MS-DOS, any version of Windows, Windows NT, Windows 2000, and OS/2.

- If you choose FAT32, access to the computer and its files is available through Windows 95 OSR2, Windows 98, and Windows 2000.

Dual-booting is commonly utilized if a computer needs to support applications that don't run in both of the operating systems installed on the machine. You can reboot the computer and choose the appropriate operating system to use a particular application. For workstations, I've seen dual-booting used to allow multiple users to get to the operating system and applications needed by each specific user. However, before deciding on a dual-boot system, you must be aware of the compatibility issues between NTFS and other file systems.

The primary rule to remember is that, unlike Windows NT, Windows Server 2003 (and Windows 2000) must be installed on its own partition; selecting a new installation directory on the partition that holds another operating system is no longer an option. This means that if your disk doesn't currently have two volumes, you must partition and format it, and then install the operating systems.

If you are dual-booting between Windows NT 4 and Windows Server 2003 (or Windows 2000), and want to use NTFS as the file system, Microsoft recommends upgrading Windows NT 4 to SP4 or higher. However, I've found occasions when that didn't solve the potential problems of file access. I've found it better to dual-boot between these operating systems using FAT partitions. Well, that's not totally true—I actually stopped dual-booting between Windows NT and later versions of Windows when I became "sold" on Windows 2000, and moved my domain to Windows 2000.

Converting to NTFS

If you have an existing FAT/FAT32 volume, you can convert it to NTFS without backing up the files, reformatting the disk, and starting all over with NTFS. Windows supplies a command-line tool, convert.exe, to convert the file system without messing around with data. The basic syntax for using convert.exe is

convert *driveletter*: **/fs:ntfs**

The parameter /fs:ntfs is required, even though there aren't any other conversion options—convert.exe only converts to NTFS. Convert.exe doesn't work in the opposite direction—you cannot convert an NTFS drive to FAT/FAT32.

Convert.exe has to lock the drive to perform its tasks, so you cannot convert the current volume (the volume you're on when you issue the command) immediately, because it's in use. Convert cannot lock the system volume, either, because it's always in use. (In many cases, the system volume is also the current volume.) Instead, the conversion process takes place during the next boot. Be aware that the next boot will take considerably longer than usual, because conversion isn't a quick process.

If you're converting another volume on the computer, and that volume isn't the system drive, the conversion takes place immediately. For example, entering **convert d: /fs:ntfs** produces a series of onscreen messages:

```
The type of the file system is FAT32
Determining disk space required for filesystem conversion
Total disk space: (size of drive in KB)
Free space on volume: (free space in KB)
Space required for conversion: (required space in KB)
```

```
Converting file system
Conversion complete.
```

The time elapsed between the appearance of the messages "converting file system" and "conversion complete" varies, depending on the size of the volume.

The space required for conversion is taken from free space, and if insufficient free space is available, convert.exe won't convert the volume. Clean off unused files before trying again.

Tip   *It's a good idea to defrag the volume before converting, because the system will be able to find more contiguous free space, and also because the conversion process will move a bit faster.*

Convert.exe has a couple of additional parameters that are sometimes used:

- **/v** specifies verbose mode, which means that all messages (mostly progress reports) are displayed during the conversion process (this parameter is for the terminally curious).

- **/nosecurity** is used to specify that the converted files and directory security settings are set so that everyone can access everything (not a good idea if you're converting a server).

Because the volume already has files and boot records, when you use convert.exe to install NTFS, the MFT is created in a different location than it is when you format a volume with NTFS. This could result in lower performance, especially if the volume is large and holds a lot of files. If you're going to use the computer as a file server, and a great many users access this server (and each user creates a lot of files), the performance hit could be quite noticeable. In that case, I suggest you back up the existing data, and format the volume with NTFS instead of using convert.exe.

Formatting a Volume for NTFS

You can format a FAT/FAT32 volume for NTFS as long as it's not the system volume or the boot volume. This means you can format a volume on computers that have multiple volumes (otherwise you must use the convert.exe utility, or reinstall the operating system). To accomplish this, you can use the Disk Management snap-in, or the command-line tool format.com.

Formatting a Volume with the Disk Management Snap-in

To open the Disk Management snap-in, right-click My Computer and choose Manage from the shortcut menu to open the Computer Management (Local) MMC. Expand the Storage object in the left pane (if it isn't already expanded) and select Disk Management to view information about the volumes in the system.

Right-click a FAT/FAT32 volume that is neither a boot nor system volume, and choose Format from the shortcut menu to open the Format dialog. Format the disk using the following guidelines:

- Enter a Volume Label if you want to label the volume (I usually use the drive letter)
- Select NTFS as the file system
- Select Default for the Allocation Unit Size

The dialog also contains an option for performing a quick format, which means the disk isn't checked for errors. As long as you're wiping the disk, it's silly to skip the error check that a full format performs on the physical disk.

You can also enable folder and file compression during the format, but this is rarely a good idea. It's usually better to compress folders after the disk is running NTFS.

Formatting a Volume with Format.com

If you're a command-line junkie (as I am), you can use format.com to format a volume that isn't a system or boot volume. The syntax for formatting a volume with NTFS is

format *driveletter:*

[/fs:NTFS] [/v:*label*] [/q] [/a:*UnitSize*] [/c]

where:

driveletter is the drive letter (be sure to enter the colon).

/fs:NTFS specifies the NTFS file system.

/v:*label* specifies the volume label *label*. If you omit this parameter, you are prompted for a volume label after the format is complete (press ENTER at that point to omit the volume label).

/q specifies a quick format.

/a:*UnitSize* specifies the size of the allocation units. If you omit this parameter, the system installs the allocation unit size using default values that are based on the size of the volume.

/c turns on folder and file compression for the entire volume.

After typing the command, pressing ENTER displays the following warning:

```
WARNING, ALL DATA ON nonremovable DISK
DRIVE x: WILL BE LOST!
Proceed with Format (Y/N)?
```

Type Y to begin the format. When the process is complete, the system displays messages showing the total disk space, any space marked as defective, and the total space available for files.

NTFS Permissions

On a day to day basis, administrators (and, for that matter, users) don't think much about the functions and features built into NTFS, with the exception of the folder and file security that NTFS provides. To make sure your users can perform the actions they need to, and to prevent them from performing actions that could be detrimental to your systems, you have to understand the NTFS security paradigm, and how it affects user actions.

When you format a drive with NTFS, you can configure user permissions for the resources on that computer. Those permissions determine, for example, whether users can access a folder or file, view or open files, modify files, or create files.

Incidentally, just to keep the terminology straight, let's discuss the difference between *permissions* and *rights*. The simple explanation is that permissions are the tasks users can perform within objects on an NTFS drive. Rights are the tasks users can perform on the system's or domain's settings.

NTFS Permissions vs. Share Permissions

When you share a resource (for example, a folder), you can set permissions for the share, even if the volume on which the share resides is formatted with FAT or FAT32. Share permissions apply to any user accessing the share from a remote computer—they're ignored for local users. NTFS permissions, on the other hand, affect every user, whether local or remote.

To set share permissions, click the Permissions button on the Sharing tab of the share's Properties dialog. By default, the Permissions dialog, shown in Figure 15-2, lists only the Everyone group.

The default Read permission in Windows Server 2003 is new; in Windows 2000, creating a share automatically set Full Control permission for the Everyone group. I suggest you change the permissions on shares to Full Control for Everyone on your Windows Server 2003 computers. That's because, for remote users, the actual permissions are determined by taking into consideration both the Share permissions and the NTFS permissions, and the more restrictive permissions are applied. This means you can make sure users have the permissions they need to get their work done by giving the Everyone group Full Control for share permissions, and then carefully applying NTFS permissions. For local users, the share permissions don't count, and only the NTFS permissions affect access.

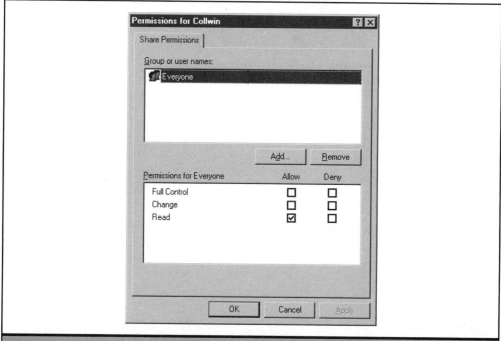

Figure 15-2. *Share permissions are automatically configured as Read permissions for the Everyone group.*

Default Permissions

When you work with folder permissions, the terminology you encounter seems simple and straightforward. Following are the permissions you can allow or deny as you configure users and groups for file and folder permissions:

- Full Control
- Modify
- Read & Execute
- List Folder Contents
- Read
- Write

However, those permissions are really collective terms, because each one of them represents a set of one or more specific, more granular, permissions. Table 15-1 describes what's really contained in a permission you allow or deny.

	Full Control	Modify	Read & Execute	List Folder Contents	Read	Write
Traverse Folder/ Execute File	Y	Y	Y	Y		
List Folder/ Read Data	Y	Y	Y	Y	Y	
Read Attributes	Y	Y	Y	Y	Y	
Read Extended Attributes	Y	Y	Y	Y	Y	
Create Files/ Write Data	Y	Y				Y
Create Folders/ Append Data	Y	Y				Y
Write Attributes	Y	Y				Y
Write Extended Attributes	Y	Y				Y
Delete Subfolders and Files	Y					
Delete	Y	Y				
View Permissions	Y	Y	Y	Y	Y	Y
Change Permissions	Y					
Take Ownership	Y					
Synchronize	Y	Y	Y	Y	Y	Y

Table 15-1.   *Details of Granular Permissions That Are Invoked by Permissions You Set*

Some of the granular permissions aren't easily figured out, so here's an overview of what actions they enable the permission holder to perform:

■ **Traverse Folder**   Move through folders to reach other folders, or files, even if the user has no permissions to manipulate the traversed folders.

■ **Execute File**   Launch program files.

- **List Folder**   View filenames and subfolder names within a folder.
- **Read Data**   View the data in files (and, implicitly, open data files).
- **Read Attributes**   View the operating system attributes attached to a file or folder.
- **Read Extended Attributes**   View the extended attributes, set by applications, for a file or folder.
- **Create Files**   Create files within a folder.
- **Write Data**   Make changes to a file, overwriting existing content.
- **Create Folders**   Create a subfolder within a folder.
- **Append Data**   Make changes to the end of the file (but cannot change, delete, or overwrite existing data).
- **Write Attributes**   Change the operating system attributes of a file or folder.
- **Write Extended Attributes**   Change the extended attributes, which were established by an application, of a file or folder.
- **Delete Subfolders and Files**   Delete subfolders and files, even if the Delete permission is not granted for the current folder.
- **Delete**   Delete the folder or file.
- **Read Permissions**   View the permissions for the folder or file.
- **Change Permissions**   Change the permissions that are set for the folder or file.
- **Take Ownership**   Name yourself as the owner of the folder or file.
- **Synchronize**   Have different threads wait on the handle for the file or folder, and synchronize with another thread that may signal it. This permission is used only by multithreaded, multiprocess programs.

Inherited Permissions

When you set permissions on a parent folder, all files and subfolders created in that folder inherit these permissions. You have three ways to interrupt that inheritance:

- Remove the inheritance at the parent level, which prevents all child objects from inheriting the permissions
- Remove the inheritance at the child object
- In a child, explicitly allow or deny a permission setting from a parent

On the whole, inherited permissions are a good idea, because they're easy to set up and maintain, and because they're generally safer and more secure than permissions that are individually manipulated. If you find yourself changing and tweaking the inherited values, perhaps you should reexamine the way you designed the folder structures on the server. When you set up a folder, create subfolders that should logically contain the same permissions as the parent folder.

Explicit Permissions vs. Inherited Permissions

Explicit permissions are those that are specifically set, either automatically by the operating system or manually by an administrator. Inherited permissions are those that were set at a parent level and are automatically inherited (okay, I know, you could have figured that definition out yourself). I'm providing these definitions for a reason, and it's not because I enjoy stating the obvious—it's because you need to implant in your mind the fact that there are two types of permissions, and explicit permissions have precedence over inherited permissions.

If you think about that for a minute, you'll realize that you don't have to interrupt the chain of inheritance to provide needed permissions on a child object; you only need to set an explicit permission to deny/allow a permission that's inherited. This is much easier (and safer) than giving up the ease and security of the inherited permissions paradigm.

Remove Inheritance from a Parent Object

To change the default behavior of a parent object, so that child objects don't automatically inherit permissions, open the Security tab of the parent object and click Advanced. In the Advanced Security Settings dialog, select an entity (usually a group) and click Edit. Select the Apply These Permissions To Objects And/Or Containers Within This Container Only check box. If you wish, you can change the permissions before stopping the inheritance.

Changing Inherited Permissions on a Child Object

If you view permissions on a child object that's inheriting permissions, the first thing you notice is that the check marks for permissions are grayed out and inaccessible (see Figure 15-3).

Even though you have no ability to change a permission with a grayed-out check mark, you do have ways to make changes to inherited permissions. You could, of course, make changes to the permissions on the parent object, and then the child object would inherit those permissions. However, under most circumstances this is unwise, and even dangerous.

You can select the opposite permission (Allow or Deny) in the child object. That action creates an explicit permission, which overrides the inherited permission. For example, in Figure 15-3, I could explicitly deny the Read & Execute permission.

Another approach is to click the Advanced button and select the entity whose permission levels you want to remove from inheritance (see Figure 15-4). Deselect the option that forces inheritance.

Windows displays a Security dialog that explains what interrupting inheritance means, and offers the following three options for proceeding:

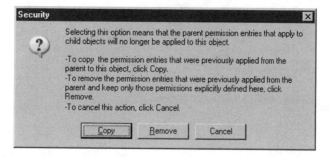

- **Copy**   Duplicates the inherited permissions, but they're now explicit permissions instead of inherited permissions, so all the selections are accessible, and you can change any permission at will.

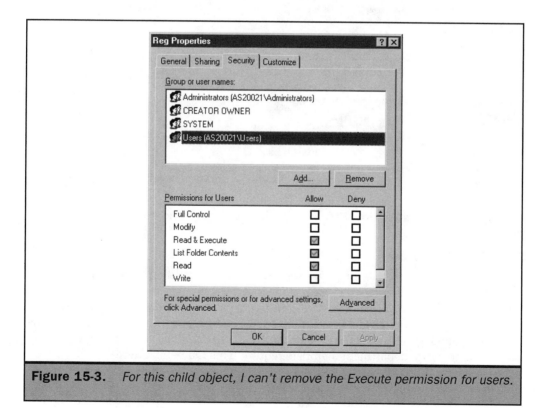

Figure 15-3.   *For this child object, I can't remove the Execute permission for users.*

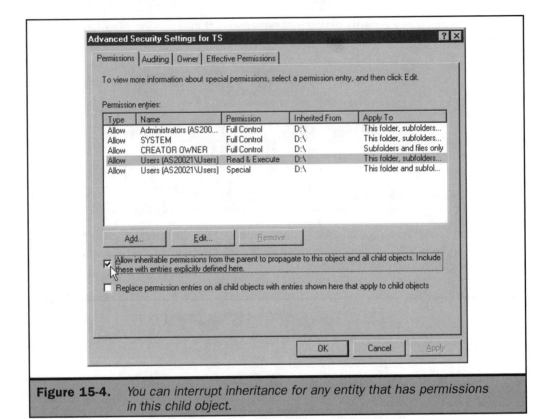

Figure 15-4.   *You can interrupt inheritance for any entity that has permissions in this child object.*

- **Remove**   Deletes all inherited permissions, and you must create explicit permissions.
- **Cancel**   Tells Windows that you've changed your mind, forget about it.

Tweaking Permissions

You can make NTFS security more granular by creating security groups and then adding specific permissions for those groups to drives, folders, and files. The users who need the customized set of permissions you create can obtain them by being added to the group. For example, you may want to add groups for certain departments (such as accounting, research, IT, and so on) and then provide more powerful permissions on the folders those department members require. This is a better alternative than increasing permissions by moving users into administrative-level groups, which would give them increased permissions on all objects.

Create a Security Group for Customized Permissions

You can create a new security group for the domain, and then populate that group with members who need the permissions you'll assign the group in certain folders. In Active Directory Users and Computers, go to the level at which you want to create the group. You can create a group in a domain, in an OU, or in a domain folder (such as the Users folder). You can even create a group in the Built-in folder for the domain, but I generally avoid that, just to keep things "pure," and instead create my new groups in the Users folder. Right-click the container and choose New | Group from the shortcut menu, to open the New Object-Group dialog.

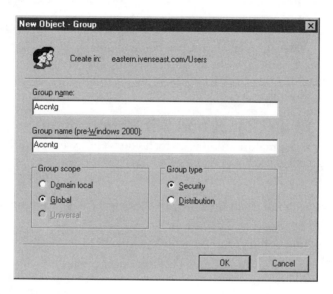

Name the group and select a scope and a type. Groups you create in order to set permissions and user rights are always Security groups, while groups you create to facilitate communication (for example, for your e-mail program) are Distribution groups. The group scope varies, depending on the way you want to use the group, and the current configuration of your enterprise.

Global Groups   Global groups can be populated with users from the domain. You can nest global groups, as long as all the global groups are in the same domain. You can put a global group into a local group on any server. You can also put a global group inside a local group of a trusting domain (which really means you can put a global group almost anywhere in a forest).

Domain Local Groups   Domain local groups are global groups that can't be put into local groups on trusting domains. Otherwise, within their own domain, you can create them within other group types.

If you're creating a group on a computer that isn't a domain controller, you also have the option to select the group type "local." The group only exists on the computer, and can only be populated with local users.

Universal Groups   Universal groups have a lot more power, because they're a lot more flexible about where they live, and what they can contain:

- You can put any global group from any domain in the forest into any universal group.
- You can put any universal group into any other universal group.
- You can put any universal group into any local or domain local group.

The option to create a universal group is not available until you are operating your domain in *native mode,* which means all domain controllers are running Windows 2000 or Windows Server 2003. See Chapter 20 for more information about creating, using, and manipulating groups.

Add a Group to an Object and Set Permissions

After you create and populate a group for which you want to set specialized permissions, you can add the group to the list of entities that have permissions set for the object, using these steps:

1. On the Security tab, click Add to open the Select Users, Computers, or Groups dialog.
2. Enter the name of the group for which you want to set permissions.
3. Click OK to add the group to the Group or user names list.

After the group is added to the Security tab list, you can set permissions. Click the Allow or Deny check boxes next to each permission you want to allow or deny. Then Click OK.

Effective Permissions

One nifty new feature in Windows Server 2003 is that the Security tab of an object's Properties dialog displays the effective permissions for users and groups that are defined for the object. The concept isn't new—it's always been the important factor in determining access for a given user—but now you can see the information instead of having to figure it out. *Effective* permissions are exactly what the term implies: the "real" permissions a user has as a result of her group membership.

To get to the Effective Permissions tab, click Advanced on the Security dialog, and move to the Effective Permissions tab. Click Select, enter the name of a user or group, and click OK. The check boxes indicate the effective permissions of the user or group for this object.

The permissions are calculated, taking into consideration group membership and inherited permissions. The system also checks all the domain and local groups that a user or group belongs to. Share permissions are not used in the calculation.

Understanding the Deny Permission

If you view the effective permissions for a user, and the results don't look right to you, or if users are complaining about insufficient rights, check all the permissions on the object to see if you selected Deny for any permission for any group. Most administrators use Deny to override a setting they think is too generous for a certain group. However, this action can be dangerous if you don't understand that deny permissions are enumerated first when Windows determines whether a user can perform a specific task. When a Deny is encountered, it may mean that other rights you meant to assign can't be enumerated.

Avoid using explicit Deny permissions unless you've decided that you have no other way to obtain a specific level of permissions that are required for a certain group. Then, carefully examine inherited permissions, and make sure your deny permissions don't shut out basic permissions, such as Read.

The
Complete
Reference

Chapter 16

Disk and File
Management

Windows Server 2003 contains a wide variety of features and tools designed to fulfill two important functions: to make it easier for users to access what they need to do their work; and to make it easier for administrators to manage and secure the resources users access. This chapter covers disk and file management tools built into Windows Server 2003.

Distributed File System

The Distributed File System (DFS) is not really a file system, but it acts enough like one to think of it as an ersatz file system ("I'm not a file system, but I play one on television?"). DFS provides a way to display a logical, hierarchical structure of a file system to users, even if the components of the file system are scattered throughout the enterprise. DFS is installed automatically with Windows Server 2003, and the DFS service starts automatically.

When to Use DFS

The best way to visualize a need for DFS is with a real example, so here's the scenario that existed when I set up my first DFS system. My client had a human resources department that was divided into departments and scattered across sites (main office, Midwest headquarters, and West Coast headquarters). Each department saved documents to different file servers, in discrete directories that held specific types of documents. Some of the directories were not available to users (for example, payroll records), but most of them were. For instance, users could access documents explaining the company pension plan, benefits package, employee rules and regulations; forms for making changes to pensions and benefits; application forms for job openings (also available to Internet visitors); and so on.

An employee who wanted to view a document would send an e-mail message to the HR department, which would reply with the appropriate attachment. Documents that were forms were opened, filled in, and returned by e-mail, and were then forwarded to the appropriate HR specialist. Members of the HR department complained that the amount of time they spent finding the right documents, and working in e-mail, was excessive and wasteful. The Exchange Server administrator was complaining about the size of mailboxes resulting from all the attachments.

The IT department e-mailed a list of employee-accessible documents and their UNCs to every employee, and some employees actually paid attention. E-mail replies to employees who continued to e-mail the HR department contained the list, and eventually anyone who needed a particular document, or wanted to fill in an online form, headed to the appropriate directory. Some employees even mapped drives to oft-used documents (such as the new online fill-in form for entering hours worked).

However, the system started to fall apart, because servers were added, servers were replaced with computers that had different names, directories were moved among servers, and the growing assortment of documents were frequently moved around the enterprise as the company grew.

DFS fixed all of this, because access no longer depended on having an accurate UNC, meaning administrators could change servers and move documents transparently—the employees saw only a single hierarchy for all the directories and documents. Directories and documents that were frequently accessed by thousands of users were duplicated on multiple servers, DFS replication kept everything up to date, and users saw only one listing (representing multiple locations) in the hierarchy.

In your enterprise, if it isn't the HR department that needs access to documents that are scattered throughout the enterprise, substitute the folks who have to put together the company budget, the annual report, the documentation of help desk requests, or have any other need to access lots of documents that are in different places.

DFS Terminology

To plan a DFS implementation, you have to understand the following DFS components:

- **Root** The name (in DFS lingo, a *namespace*) that's visible to users. It's the starting point of the DFS hierarchy. The root can have subdirectories, or one or more root targets, each of which corresponds to a shared folder on a server. You can have multiple roots in your enterprise, with the following rules:

  - Windows Server 2003 Standard Edition can house only one root per server.

  - Windows Server 2003 Enterprise Edition and Datacenter Edition can house multiple roots on each server.

- **Link** The element that lies below the root and maps to the targets, each of which is either a shared folder on a server or another DFS root.

- **Target** The destination (a folder that has been shared on a server) of a link.

- **Referral** The list of targets a client receives from DFS when the user is accessing a root or a link in the DFS namespace. This list is not seen by the client, and is cached on the client computer for a time period specified in the DFS configuration.

- **Replica** An identical share on a different server. The two shares are grouped as a single link (called *DFS replica members*). A replica can be a root or a link. When you configure replicas, the File Replication Service (FRS) takes care of keeping the contents in sync. Replicas provide load balancing and fault tolerance for your DFS.

Stand-alone vs. Domain DFS

Windows Server 2003 provides two types of DFS implementation: stand-alone and domain-based. The domain-based DFS is housed in Active Directory, so if you're using Windows Server 2003 computers in a network that isn't using Active Directory, you can only implement a stand-alone DFS. Even if you're running Active Directory, you can use a stand-alone DFS root, but for very large enterprises, it makes more sense (and delivers more power) to use a domain-based DFS.

Stand-alone DFS

In a stand-alone system, the root is stored in the host server, and the path to access the root (or a link) starts with the host server name. A stand-alone root has only one root target, and there can be no replicas. When the root target is unavailable, the entire DFS namespace is inaccessible.

Domain DFS

In a domain-based DFS, the configuration information is stored in Active Directory, and the path to access the root (or a link) starts with the domain name. A domain root can have replicas, and you can set a replication schedule. Replication is handled by the File Replication Service (FRS), which is the replication engine for Active Directory and DFS.

In a domain DFS, fault tolerance is managed by FRS, which automatically moves users to the replica data. Load balancing is handled by DFS, and doesn't require Windows Network Load Balancing. With a domain DFS, users don't know which servers house the shared directories, and they don't know which servers host DFS. It's all transparent.

Creating a DFS Root

Before you can make DFS shares accessible to users, you must create a DFS root object. This object is a container: it holds the links to shares and files that users access. To create the root, you're asked to enter the name of a shared folder on the server that will hold the root, and that folder should be empty—it exists only to provide the root, not to provide documents. (If the shared folder doesn't exist before you start creating the root, you can create the folder and share it on-the-fly.)

When you create a DFS root, the computer that holds the root must meet the following criteria:

- The computer must be a server (either a member server or a domain controller)
- The computer must be running NTFS

To create a root object, choose Distributed File System from the Administrative Tools menu to open the DFS snap-in. Right-click the Distributed File System object in the console pane and choose New Root to launch the New Root Wizard. Click Next to move past the introductory window, and then select either a stand-alone or domain DFS root.

Creating a Stand-alone DFS Root

If you're creating a stand-alone DFS root, the next wizard window asks you to specify the host server. Enter the computer name of the server you want to contain the root, or click Browse and select the server from the list of computers. Click Next, and name the root, optionally providing a description (see Figure 16-1).

Notice that the wizard automatically enumerates the complete path, starting with the server name, and using the root name you enter as the folder name at the end of the path. The wizard doesn't check to see if a share exists with that name until you click Next. At that point, if the name of your root is the share name of a folder on the target computer, that's all you have to do. Click Next, and then click Finish to create the stand-alone DFS root.

If your root name doesn't match the name of an existing share on the target computer, when you click Next, you're asked to create a share that matches the root's name.

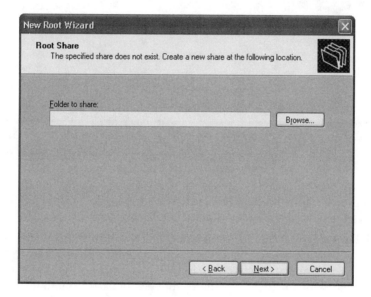

You can create a sharename that matches the root name in any of the following ways:

- Enter the full path to an existing folder on the computer. The wizard shares the folder, using the root name as the sharename.

- Enter the full path, using the name of a new (nonexistent) folder on the computer. The new folder name does not have to match the root name, because only the sharename is linked to the root. The wizard displays a message telling you the folder doesn't exist, and asking if you want to create it. Click Yes to have the wizard create the folder, and share it using the root name as the sharename.

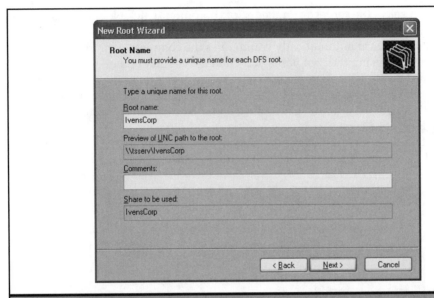

Figure 16-1.   *Enter a name for the root, which is the name users see at the top of the DFS hierarchy.*

- Click Browse, and expand the hierarchy of the target computer. Select a folder to have the wizard share the folder using the root name as the sharename.

- Click Browse, select the parent of a new folder you want to create (the parent can be a drive or an existing folder), and click Make New Folder. Name the folder, and the wizard shares it, using the root name as the sharename. (You don't have to use the root/share name for new folder, because only the sharename is linked to the root.)

In the next wizard window, click Finish to create the stand-alone root, and place its listing in the console pane of the Distributed File System snap-in. Because this is a stand-alone root, this is the only target you can create for your root (domain roots, however, can contain multiple targets).

Creating a Domain DFS Root

If you select a domain root, the wizard asks you to select a domain (a list of available domains is displayed in the Trusting Domains dialog). In the next wizard window, enter the name of the computer that holds the directory for your root, or click Browse and select the server from the list of computers. If you enter the name directly, you can enter either the NetBIOS name or the FQDN; the wizard automatically expands the NetBIOS name to the FQDN.

Click Next, and name the root, optionally providing a description. As you can see in Figure 16-2, the wizard automatically enumerates a path using the format *DomainName*\ *Root*. The server name doesn't appear, because this is a domain root, not a stand-alone root, and is not server-based like a stand-alone root.

This is where the additional power of domain roots is evident—not linking the root to the server means that you can move the root's shared folder to another server, or even duplicate it on multiple servers. The root you're creating, along with its domain-based path, is what the users see, and DFS tracks your changes to make sure users can connect.

The wizard doesn't check to see if a share exists with that name until you click Next. At that point, if the name of your root is the name of a shared folder on the target computer, that's all you have to do. Click Next, and then click Finish to create the stand-alone DFS root.

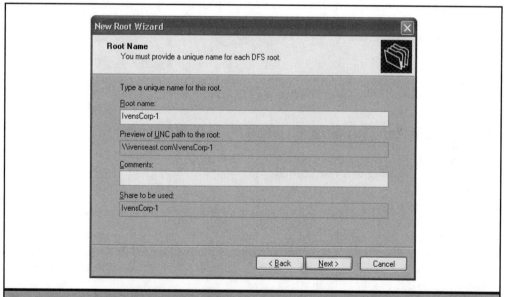

Figure 16-2. *The path to a domain root doesn't include the name of the server that currently holds the shared folder, because you're free to change the server whenever you wish.*

If your root name doesn't match the name of an existing share on the target computer, when you click Next, you're asked to create a share that matches the root's name. You can create a sharename that matches the root name in any of the following ways:

- Enter the full path to an existing folder on the computer. The wizard shares the folder, using the root name as the sharename.

- Enter the full path, using the name of a new (nonexistent) folder on the computer. The new folder name does not have to match the root name, because only the sharename is linked to the root. The wizard displays a message telling you the folder doesn't exist, and asking if you want to create it. Click Yes to have the wizard create the folder, and share it using the root name as the sharename.

- Click Browse, and expand the hierarchy of the target computer. Select a folder to have the wizard share the folder using the root name as the share name.

- Click Browse, select the parent of a new folder you want to create (the parent can be a drive or an existing folder), and click Make New Folder. Name the folder, and the wizard shares it, using the root name as the sharename. (You don't have to use the root/share name for new folder, because only the sharename is linked to the root.)

Click Next to see a summary of the settings for the DFS root. Click Finish (or go back to make any necessary corrections) to create the root and place its object in the console pane of the Distributed File System snap-in.

Adding a Link to the Root

At this point, you have an empty DFS root, which means you have a DFS namespace. From here on, I'm going to move through the rest of the steps assuming you're building a domain root. (If you're creating a stand-alone root, the steps are similar, but much narrower in scope.)

For this share to be useful, you need to populate it with content. This means creating one or more links for the root. A *link* is a pointer to a target, which is usually a folder that contains the documents you want to make available via DFS. In fact, it works very much like a link on a web page—click it to travel to another location (to save the work of entering the path to that location).

Your link should have a name that hints at the contents of its target. For example, if you're creating a link to a target that contains the documents your accounting department needs to create the company budget, you can name the link Budget.

Right-click the DFS root you created, and choose New Link from the shortcut menu to open the New Link dialog (see Figure 16-3). Then follow these steps:

1. In the Link Name field, specify the share that's using the link name. The share can be on any server on the network. If you didn't create and share the directory

ahead of time, you'll have an opportunity to create it on-the-fly. However, most of the time links point to targets that are existing shares that hold files.

2. In the Path to Target field, enter the UNC (*ServerName**Sharename*) to the share for this link:

   ■ If you created the share ahead of time, either enter the UNC or click Browse to open a hierarchical view of My Network Places and select the share.

   ■ If you haven't yet created the share, enter the UNC. When you click OK, you'll have an opportunity to create the share.

3. Enter a description of the link (this is an optional field).

4. Enter a cache time-out value, which is the amount of time the client retains the information about the link to this share. When the time expires, the client has to reselect the share from the DFS root. The limited time for caching the link means the client won't see old information when returning to the share. In fact, for links that point to targets with content that changes quite frequently, use a short cache time-out value to make sure clients always see the latest and greatest content when they access the target.

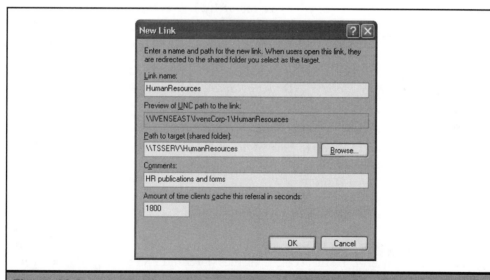

Figure 16-3.   *Configure the link to the network shares you want your users to be able to access.*

Click OK. If the share didn't exist on the server, you're asked if you want to create it.

Click Yes to create the directory on the target server, and automatically share it. (The name you entered is both the directory name and the sharename.)

 The shared folders holding data must be configured for appropriate permissions for users (often including Write permissions).

Mapping Drives to the Root for Users

Users can't travel to the folders in your domain-based DFS root in the normal fashion, such as using Windows Explorer or a UNC that points to any individual folder. After all, a folder may not be in the same place on Wednesday that it was on Monday. In addition, if you create replicas of your DFS hierarchy, DFS is capable of performing load-balancing chores to make sure user referrals don't overwhelm a particular server.

In the absence of knowing exactly where the folder and its data reside, users must access the DFS root, which is accomplished by drive mapping. You can provide instructions to users, or you can map a drive to the root in a logon script. The following command does the trick: **net use** *driveletter*: *DomainName**DfsRootName*.

Managing DFS

It's beyond the scope of this book to present detailed instructions for all the available features of DFS (that information could fill a book), but it seems appropriate to mention some of the other functions you can add to your DFS structure. All of the commands you need are available in the Distributed File System snap-in.

DFS Replicas

You can create replicas of your DFS roots and targets on additional servers. If one of the servers goes down, users can still access their files (DFS and FRS manage the failover functions). In addition, DFS manages load balancing for duplicate sets of folders.

Right-click the link you want to duplicate, and choose New Replica. In the dialog that appears, specify the location of the shared folder that is a replica of the original link, and select a replication method. You can schedule and manage FRS replication right from the DFS snap-in.

Use the Distributed File System console window to manage the objects in your DFS tree. You can use the toolbar to delete a link, take a link offline, check the status of replication, remove a link from the namespace, add replicas, or set replication policy.

Keep an eye on the way contents change, and tweak your links to maintain efficiency. If a link is busy and contents change frequently, shorten the cache timeout interval to make sure users get the latest version of any file they access. If contents don't change often (for example, a folder that holds boilerplate documents), lengthen the cache timeout to reduce network traffic.

DFS use on your network can be as complex and as widespread as you want to make it. I suggest that you set up DFS in a lab environment (the best test setup is two servers and one client). The more you experiment with DFS, the more you'll understand its capabilities. You'll find that you can come up with creative and innovative ways to take advantage of this powerful system.

Shadow Copies of Shared Folders

The shadow copy feature, new in Windows Server 2003, lets you configure the system to move copies of the contents of shared folders to another (shadow) folder, in order to retain a copy of every document in its current state. The copy process occurs at specific times (the administrator can set the schedule) and captures the contents of the folders at that point in time.

Users continue to work on current versions of existing documents in the original folder, but can access the shadow folder to view previous versions of documents. In addition to satisfying curiosity about earlier incarnations of documents, this means that previous versions of changed documents can be recovered if they were overwritten mistakenly.

To use shadow copies, you must have at least 100MB of free space on the volume. To get started, you enable the feature, create a schedule for copying files from the shared folder to the shadow folder, and provide users with software for viewing shadow copies. All of these tasks are covered in this section.

Enabling Shadow Copies

You can only enable this feature for an entire volume, not for individual shared folders. All shared folders on the volume are included when shadow copies are created. To enable a Windows Server 2003 volume for shadow copies, follow these steps:

1. Right-click the volume's object in My Computer or Windows Explorer and choose Properties from the shortcut menu.

2. Move to the Shadow Copies tab.

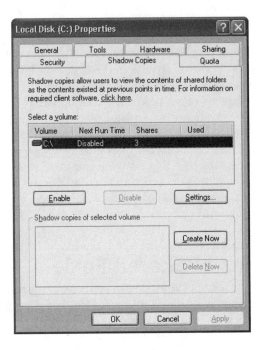

3. Click Enable.

4. Windows displays a message asking you to confirm your action, and informing you that the system will use the default schedule for maintaining shadow copies. You can modify the schedule later, so click Yes.

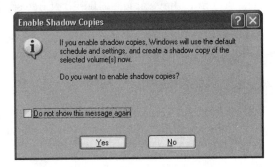

5. It takes a few seconds to create the shadow copies, and then the dialog displays the current (default) statistics:

- Next scheduled time for copying (in this case the first time copies are created)
- The number of shared folders on the volume
- The size allocated to shadow copies

At this point, you've enabled the feature and you're ready to configure the settings and distribute the client-side software.

Whether or not you're planning to change the scheduled times for shadow copies, if you don't want to wait for the next automatic copy, click Create Now. The system copies the contents of shared folders. It doesn't matter if users are working on documents—this isn't a standard copy process and you won't see an error that a file is in use.

Configuring Shadow Copies

To set the size of the shadow and the frequency of copying, click Settings to open the Settings dialog, shown in Figure 16-4.

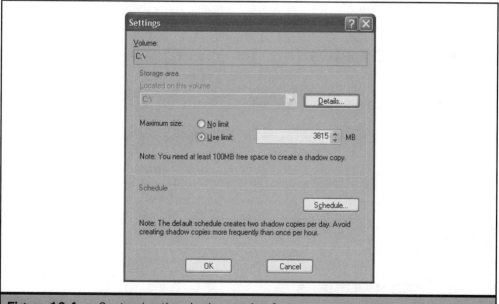

Figure 16-4.   *Customize the shadow copies feature to match user needs.*

Configure the Storage Area

By default, Windows Server 2003 sets the storage area for shadowed copies to about 10 percent of the size of the volume that has shared folders, with a minimum size of 100MB. To see the amount of storage space used by the current collection of shadow copies, click Details.

If the server has two volumes, and only one is enabled for shadow copies, you can save the shadow copies on the other volume. Just select the volume from the drop-down list at the top of the dialog (if the server has only one volume, the drop-down list is grayed out).

You can change the maximum size of the storage area, or dispense with limits altogether. Use the following guidelines to configure the storage size:

- Each shadow copy uses an amount of bytes equal to the total amount of bytes of the copied documents.

- Each time a shadow copy is made, it's saved as a discrete unit. This means that several copies may have similar content, depending on the frequency of your copying schedule.

- When the size limit for storage is reached, the oldest shadow copy is removed to make room for the current copy. If necessary, more than one old shadow copy may be removed to make room for the current copy.

Configure the Schedule

By default, Windows Server 2003 schedules a copy every weekday at 7:00 A.M. and again at noon. You can change the schedule to as many days a week and as many times a day as you wish. To do so, click Settings, then click Schedule to open the dialog shown in Figure 16-5.

The current scheduled copy processes are in the drop-down list at the top of the dialog. To remove a scheduled copy, select it from the list and click Delete.

To add scheduled copies, use the fields in the dialog. Click Advanced if you want to schedule a special copy, or multiple special copies, from a start date to an end date. Your schedule is written to the Windows Server 2003 Task Scheduler.

    Don't schedule copies too often, because you'll probably fill the storage area before documents have had a lot of changes. This can destroy the whole purpose of the feature.

Disabling Shadow Copies

If you no longer want to use disk space for preserving shadow copies, return to the Shadow Copies tab of the volume's Properties dialog, select the volume, and click Disable. All of the current sets of shadow copies are deleted, and all of the settings are removed. The job entry for making shadow copies is removed from the Task Scheduler.

If you're going to remove the volume by repartitioning the drive (usually done to combine the volume with another volume on the same drive), you must first remove

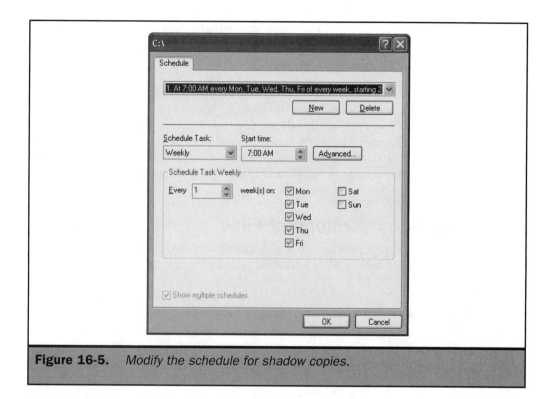

Figure 16-5. *Modify the schedule for shadow copies.*

the job from the Task Scheduler, or disable shadow copies. Otherwise, the event log will fill up with errors about the task being unable to run.

Installing Client Software for Shadow Copies

In the absence of an installed copy of the Previous Versions Client (the name of the client-side software for the shadow copies feature), nobody, including the administrator, can view shadow copies of documents in the usual system windows (My Computer, Windows Explorer, or the Open dialog of an application). The software is preinstalled on Windows Server 2003, but must be installed on the other computers on your network.

Windows Server 2003 includes client software for Windows XP only. For Windows versions Windows 98 SE and later, you can download the software from Microsoft's web site.

The Windows XP client software, twcli.msi, is located in the %SystemRoot%\ System32\clients\twclient\x86 directory on your Windows Server 2003 computer.

You can move the client software to a network sharepoint and notify users to fetch it, e-mail a copy of it to each user who needs it, deploy it using SMS, or use group policies to distribute it. Be sure to explain to users what this feature does, why you're enabling it, and how to use it efficiently.

Installing the software on client computers takes only a few seconds, and no user interaction is required, except to click Finish when the installation is complete. No listing appears on the Programs menus (although a listing for Previous Versions Client appears in the Add or Remove Programs applet in Control Panel). This program doesn't have an executable—instead, after installation, users see an additional tab named Previous Versions in the Properties dialog of all shared folders on a volume that's enabled for shadow copies.

Accessing Previous Versions of Files

On the client side, you can access previous versions of files, working with either an entire shadow copy for a specific date and time, called a *version*, or an individual file within the version.

Working with Versions

To work with a version (a shadow copy instead of an individual file), you must select the version from the Previous Versions tab of the folder's Properties dialog. To get to the folder, mapped drives (which automatically open the folder to reveal the contents) don't work—you must open the folder object in order to view the Properties dialog. My Network Places or Network Neighborhood is the way to go. Because the folder is shared, its object appears when the client opens the Windows Server 2003 computer.

To select a version, right-click the folder object and choose Properties from the shortcut menu. Move to the Previous Versions tab to see the list of versions, as shown in Figure 16-6.

Viewing the Files in the Version   Click View to see a list of the files in the selected version. All the files in the original folder are listed, but there's no way to tell which of those files have been changed.

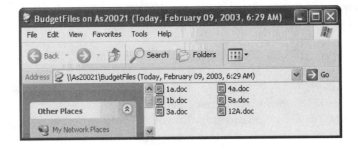

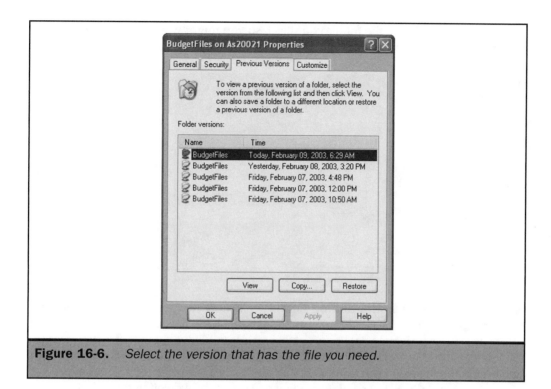

Figure 16-6.   *Select the version that has the file you need.*

Open a file to view its contents; you're looking at the contents as they were when this shadow copy was created. If you want to know whether the file's current version is different, you must open the shared folder and compare the contents. (There's an easier way, covered later in the section "Working With Individual Files.")

You cannot make changes to this copy, because it is read-only. You can, however, use the Save As function to copy the file to another location (by default, the My Documents folder on the local computer).

Copying a Version to Another Location   If you want to work with all the files in a version, select the version and click Copy to open the Copy dialog and select a location.

All the files are copied to the folder you select, so you might want to create a new folder for this special group of files.

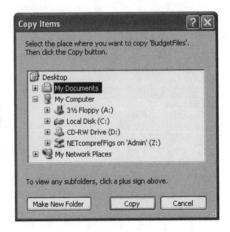

Restoring a Version to the Shared Folder   Clicking Restore copies all the files in the selected version to the original shared folder, replacing the current contents of that folder. This is an extremely dangerous action unless you have some compelling reason to undo the work performed on those files since the selected version was created. The only compelling reason I can think of is that all the files in the shared folder have disappeared, usually as the result of someone inadvertently deleting them.

Working With Individual Files

Most of the time, you'll want to work with individual files in a version, instead of the entire version. Perhaps you want to return to a previous incarnation of the file's contents, or maybe you just want to see the difference in content between the current file and a version that was saved earlier. Here's how to access a previous version of a particular file:

1. Open the shared folder (using a mapped drive, a UNC, or browsing My Network Places/Network Neighborhood).

2. Right-click the file's listing and choose Properties from the shortcut menu.

3. Move to the Previous Versions tab.

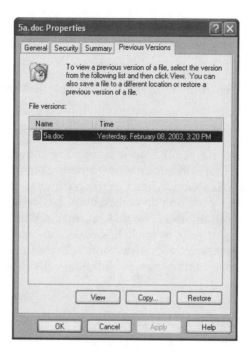

The File Versions list includes only those versions that include a copy of this file—that is, when this version was created, the contents of the file differed from the contents in the shared folder. In fact, there may be no versions listed on the dialog, which indicates one of the following conditions:

- The file hasn't changed when compared to all the versions still on the volume. Remember that older versions may have been deleted to make room for newer shadow copies.

- The file hasn't changed since shadow copies were enabled on the volume.

You can view, copy, or restore the file as described in the previous section, "Working With Versions."

Disk Quotas

Disk quotas provide a method of managing the amount of disk space users can fill. You can limit the amount of disk space available to each user, which is a double-edged sword. On one side, it's a marvelous tool for preventing disk usage from growing so large that you have to keep purchasing drives. On the other side, you're going to spend more time dealing with user complaints and requests for special favors.

Your philosophical approach to disk quotas can take either of two forms:

- **Strict quotas**   Users cannot exceed the allowable disk space
- **Loose quotas**   Permits users to exceed their quotas but tracks usage so you can decide which users to approach about reducing disk usage

The loose quotas choice has another approach you might want to consider, which is what I call the quota-on/quota-off information-gathering paradigm. That sounds more complicated than it is, so I'll explain. When you impose quotas, you can get quick quota reports quite easily. If disk space isn't an immediate and drastic problem, you can use those reports to speak to certain users (the disk hogs) about their disk usage. Then turn off quotas. The next time you want to track disk usage, turn quotas on again to get the quick reports and repeat the conversations (probably with the same users). The advantage to this is that you don't have to run a volume full time with quotas applied (quotas require some overhead).

Requirements for Disk Quotas

The following conditions must exist if you want to apply disk quotas on a volume:

- The volume must be formatted with NTFS.
- To administer quotas, you must be a member of the Administrators group on the local computer where the volume resides (disk quotas can be administered for both local and remote volumes).

File Compression and Disk Quotas

File compression doesn't count. If a user has a quota of 5MB of disk space, that space is filled when 5MB of files have been written to the volume. If file compression is in effect and therefore the 5MB of files occupy 3MB of disk space, it doesn't matter—the user has still reached the 5MB limit. If you use file compression, you might want to make this fact very clear to users to avoid any arguments about the definition of a megabyte of disk space.

Metadata and Disk Quotas

On a volume formatted with NTFS, the system tracks metadata for each file on the volume. The bytes occupied by the metadata (which can be as much as 64K per file) are not counted against the users' quotas.

Volume Structures and Disk Quotas

Quotas are applied to a volume, whether the volume is part of a drive that has multiple volumes or the volume spans multiple physical disks. The folder structure of a volume plays no part in the quotas. Users are free to write to as many folders as they wish (and have access to), and the total space used on the volume is calculated for the quota.

Users who move files from one folder to another on the same volume don't change their space usage. However, users who copy files to a different folder on the same volume double their space usage.

Upgrading Issues

Because quotas track file ownership, you could have some potential problems with existing files if you've upgraded to NTFS. If you upgraded to Windows Server 2003 from Windows 2000/NT 4 with NTFS installed, the previous information about file ownership is upgraded.

However, if you upgraded from a FAT or FAT32 volume, there is no ownership information on files. After the volume is converted to NTFS, all files are owned by the local administrator. This presents no particular problem to the administrator, because disk quotas aren't applied to the local administrators.

However, the user files that were on the volume at the time of conversion don't count against user quotas. When a user accesses or modifies an existing file, the ownership doesn't change. If you don't have a lot of users, or you have a lot of spare time, you could probably change the ownership of each file to reflect its user, but that seems rather excessive. New files that users create count against their quotas, of course.

Planning Default Quotas

When you set quotas, start with a default quota for each volume and then adjust individual user quotas as needed. Setting a tight (low) default quota and then adjusting specific users upwards is far more efficient than the other way around. You can also adjust the default quota when necessary.

Some users require more space than others. For instance, the graphics department creates files that are much larger than those created by the word processing department. The ideal situation is to assign volumes for user types (if you have enough disks and volumes to do so). The volume for the graphics department would require a much higher default quota than the volume for the clerical department.

Once quotas are applied, make sure the local administrator account (which doesn't have a quota imposed) installs all software on the volume. If a user installs software, the software files are owned by the user, and the ownership counts against the user's quota. Most applications are far larger than any quota.

You may decide to make default quotas small if you're not using strict quota rules; that is, you will not stop users from writing to a volume when they exceed their quotas (although you may choose to contact users who exceed their quotas). In that case, you're really using quotas to track disk usage as a preventive measure, in a "kinder and gentler" manner than applying strict enforcement (using the quota limit as a psychological deterrent).

Enabling and Applying Quotas

To begin working with quotas on a volume, right-click the volume in My Computer and choose Properties from the shortcut menu. In the Properties dialog, move to the Quota tab.

Enable Disk Quotas

To enable quotas, select the Enable Quota Management check box. This action makes the other choices on the tab available, as shown in Figure 16-7.

Deny Access When Quota Is Reached

Select Deny Disk Space To Users Exceeding Quota Limit if you want to prevent users from writing to the volume when their allotted disk space is filled. Users will have to clear out files to make room for new ones. The error message the user sees depends on the software, but most programs report that the disk is full.

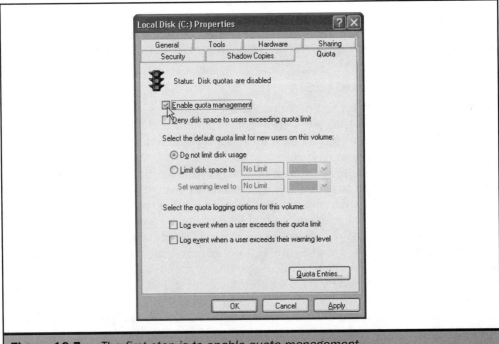

Figure 16-7.   *The first step is to enable quota management.*

If you just want to warn users who are approaching (or have reached) their quota limits, don't select this option.

Set Default Quotas

You can set two values for quotas:

- **Disk quota limit**   The amount of disk space a user is permitted to use
- **Disk quota warning**   The point at which you feel users are getting close enough to the disk quota limit to receive a warning

To enter the quotas, select Limit Disk Space To and enter a number. Then choose the measurement unit from the drop-down list in the measurement box. The measurement units displayed in the drop-down list are created dynamically, and they depend on the size of the volume for which you are enabling quotas. If the volume is less than 1GB, the drop-down list includes only KB and MB. If the volume is larger than 1GB, the drop-down list includes all the available units of measurement. There may be some measurement units that are unfamiliar to you:

- **TB** is terabyte, which is 1000 gigabytes.
- **PB** is petabyte, which is approximately 1000 terabytes (2 to the 50th power bytes).
- **EB** is exabyte, which is one billion gigabytes (2 to the 60th power bytes). Some people refer to an exabyte as a quintillion bytes (1,152,921,504,606,846,976 bytes).

Set Logging Options

You can opt to write an event to the Event Viewer when a user exceeds the quota level, the warning level, or both. The events are written to the System Log of the Event Viewer. They are Information events, and the event type is Disk Event.

Viewing the event isn't terribly helpful. The information includes the user SID instead of the logon name, and the description of the event is "A user hit their quota limit on Volume X" or "A user hit their quota threshold on Volume X". There's no particular advantage to enabling this option; it just fills up the Event Viewer.

When you've configured the options, click OK to enable quotas. The system displays a message explaining it needs to scan the volume to collect information about file ownership, and calculate the current disk usage for each user (except the local administrator). Click OK.

Set Individual Quota Entries

There may be users who should have quotas that are either larger or smaller than the default limit you specified. And there may be users who should not have any limits imposed at all. To customize quota entries for users, click Quota Entries to open the Quota Entries dialog.

By default, the Administrators group is listed and has no limits. To add specific quota entries, choose Quota | New Quota Entry, select users from the Select Users dialog, and then click OK. You can select multiple users as long as all your selections are to receive the same quota limits. When you've completed your selections, click OK to apply the quotas. Set a quota that differs from the default, or turn off quotas for the selected users.

You can also keep an eye on users and quotas in this dialog:

- Click a column heading to sort the list by that column's contents (click again to change the sort order).
- Double-click a listing to edit the quota limits.
- Select a listing and press DELETE to remove the entry. (See the next section, "Deleting User Quota Entries.")

 Technically, you can select groups as well as users when you're assigning quota entries. However, it's difficult to remove them, and removing a user from the quota entries list is not uncommon (users leave or are transferred to other departments or branches).

Deleting User Quota Entries

You can't remove a quota-tracking entry for a user account until all the files owned by that user have been deleted from the volume, moved to another volume, or have had their ownership transferred to another user. You can perform those tasks during the user quota entry deletion process, so that requirement is not overly onerous.

To delete a user from quota entries, open the volume's Properties dialog and move to the Quotas tab. Then click Quota Entries to open the Quota Entries window. Select the user you want to remove from the list and press DELETE. The system asks you to confirm that you want to delete the user listing; click Yes.

The Disk Quota dialog opens, displaying all the files on the volume that belong to the user you're deleting. Select a file, multiple files, or all the files and then take one of these actions:

- Delete the files (you're asked to confirm the deletion).
- Take ownership (the files immediately disappear from the list; no confirmation dialog appears).
- Move the files to another volume (which can be on another computer on the network).

You are not deleting the user; you are merely deleting the user account from quota tracking.

Quota Reports

After the system is scanned, and at any time thereafter, you can check the status of user disk quotas by opening the volume's Properties dialog and moving to the Quota tab.

Click Quota Entries to see the disk space status of the users who access this volume. The status column's icon is a quick indicator of a user's quota level:

- An up arrow in a white circle indicates the user is below the warning level.

- An exclamation point in a yellow triangle indicates the user is over the warning level but below the limit.

- An exclamation point in a red circle indicates the user has reached the limit.

The first time you open the Quota Entries window to view disk space usage, the system does a lookup on each user, resolving the SID to the username. That process takes a bit of time. The list of resolved names is saved to a file, and thereafter the file is loaded so that there's no delay in the display of usernames and statistics. However, that file is outdated if you add users, so you must press F5 to refresh the list.

You can create reports in a host of software applications, using any of several methods. Start by selecting the users you want to include in your report. Your selection actually includes more than the highlighted listings; it also automatically includes the title bar of the window and the column headings.

Use the clipboard to copy the selection into a software application. Whether you paste the clipboard contents into a word processor or a spreadsheet, the listings and the column headings are positioned appropriately (using a table in a word processor).

Open the appropriate software application, and drag the selection to the software window. Again, everything is laid out correctly.

Moving Quota Entries to Another Volume

Suppose a user transfers to another location in the company, or for some other reason is going to use another volume for file services. You can move his or her quota entries to the new volume (to the user, it's like a haunting). The following events characterize a transfer of quota entries:

- The files on the source volume are not transferred.

- The quota levels on the source volume are not removed (the user now has quota levels on two volumes).

There are three methods for transferring a user's quota entries records between volumes:

- Open the Quota Entries window for both volumes and drag the information between volumes.

- Export the information from the source volume to the target volume.

- Export the information from the source volume to a file; then import the file to the target volume.

The Export and Import commands are on the Quota menu. The import/export file has no extension (don't add one), and the format of the file is proprietary to the Quota feature. Microsoft says the extension is hidden, even if you have folders configured to display hidden extensions, but I've examined the file with all sorts of utilities, and I think there's just no extension.

Remote Storage Service

Remote Storage Service (RSS) is a way to extend disk space on a server without adding hard disks. RSS keeps an eye on the amount of free space available on a server volume, and automatically moves infrequently accessed files (the criteria for determining "infrequently" are set by an administrator) to a tape or optical disk when disk usage reaches a level determined by the administrator. When a user needs one of the transferred files, it's fetched from the remote storage media. A placeholder for the file remains on the server, which points to the remote file. RSS runs as a service and uses the Removable Storage Manager (RSM) to access the tapes (RSM is discussed later, in the "Removable Storage Management" section of this chapter). RSS is administered via an MMC snap-in.

Remote Storage data storage is a two-level hierarchy. The upper level, called *local storage*, includes the NTFS volumes of the server running RSS. The lower level, called *remote storage*, is on the tape drive, robotic tape library, or optical disk that is connected to the server computer.

Quick Overview of RSS

Before you start configuring and using RSS, it's a good idea to understand the guidelines and limitations:

- RSS runs only volumes formatted with NTFS.
- Do not use RSS on a server that is part of a cluster (RSS does not fail over to other nodes).
- Disk quotas are unaffected by the actions of RSS. When files are transferred, even though no disk space is actually used, the logical size and the date/time (created, last modified, last accessed) attributes of the file remain unchanged.
- RSS supports all SCSI class optical, 4 mm, 8 mm, and DLT tapes.
- QIC tapes are not supported. Exabyte 8200 tapes do not work properly and are not recommended.
- The media type you specify during installation cannot be changed later.
- You can reconfigure your settings for RSS, but you can't start over if you want to change the basic configuration. (In fact, you can't get the RSS wizard to run again after you've initially installed the service on a drive.)

- File management on an RSS-managed volume must be approached with care. Renaming and deleting files, or moving files to other RSS-managed volumes, interferes with the matchup on the remote media.

- Administrative permissions are required to configure the RSS settings, but normal user permissions apply to the files.

- RSS has its own media pool for tapes, and you must be sure you have a sufficient number of tapes in that pool. You cannot use tapes from another service's media pool for RSS. (See the discussion on media pools later in this chapter.)

Installing RSS

Installing RSS is a two-step process:

1. Install the component.
2. Install the service.

Install the RSS Component

RSS is not installed by default when you install the operating system, so if you didn't select it during setup, you must install the component manually, as follows:

1. Insert the Windows Server 2003 CD in the CD drive, or be sure you have access to the original installation files on a network sharepoint.
2. Open the Add or Remove Programs applet in Control Panel.
3. Click Add/Remove Windows Components.
4. Select the Remote Storage check box, and click Next.
5. After the files are copied, click Finish.
6. Restart the computer.

Install the RSS Service

After the files are installed on the computer, install the service by opening the Remote Storage snap-in from the Administrative Tools menu. Because this is the first time you open the Remote Storage snap-in, the Remote Storage Setup Wizard automatically launches to install and configure RSS.

Click Next on the wizard introductory window to launch a search for your tape system. Then, continue with the wizard to configure RSS services, which includes the following tasks:

- Select the volumes you want to manage.
- Set the free-space level for managed volumes.
- Set the criteria for copying files to tape.

- Select the type of tape to use.
- Set the automatic file-copy schedule.
- Specify the number of media copies.

Tweaking RSS Settings

The settings you establish in the wizard during setup of RSS are for all managed volumes on the computer. If you have more than one managed volume, you may want to create different settings for each. Even if you're managing only one volume, you may find that you need to make changes as you gain experience with RSS. This section covers some guidelines.

To change settings, open the Remote Storage snap-in by choosing Remote Storage from the Administrative Tools menu. When the Remote Storage console opens, expand the console tree to find the object you want to modify.

File Copy Schedule

You can modify the file copy schedule in the Remote Storage snap-in. Right-click the Remote Storage object and choose Change Schedule from the shortcut menu. In the File Copy Schedule dialog, make the changes you require. (Remember that you can create multiple schedules.) The schedules you create are transferred to your Scheduled Tasks folder.

Copy Files Manually

You may find there are times you want to copy files to remote storage before the next scheduled automatic copy process. To accomplish this, open the Remote Storage snap-in and select the Managed Volumes object in the console pane. In the details pane, right-click the volume and choose All Tasks | Copy Files to Remote Storage.

Free Space Settings

To modify the settings for free space on the managed volume, select the Managed Volumes object in the console pane. In the details pane, right-click the volume and choose Settings from the shortcut menu. On the Settings tab, use the arrows in the Desired Free Space section to change the value. When the available space on the volume falls below your setting, RSS removes cached data from files that have been copied to the tape.

Create Free Space Manually

If you need to free up space on the volume immediately, select the Managed Volumes object in the console pane and then right-click the appropriate volume in the details pane. Select All Tasks | Create Free Space from the shortcut menu. All cached data from files that have been copied to RSS media is removed. (If the cached data from local files has already been removed through the normal RSS procedures, you won't gain any additional space.)

Remember that the more cached data you remove from the volume, the more recall activity your users must wait for if they need those files.

File Selection Criteria

You can alter the file selection criteria you set in the RSS wizard at any time in the RSS snap-in. There are two reasons to do this:

- Your current criteria do not produce enough free space on the volume.

- Your current criteria are too aggressive, and your users are complaining that too many files are fetched by recalling them from the tape.

Select the Managed Volumes object in the console pane. Right-click the volume in the details pane and choose Settings from the shortcut menu. You can change the file size value or the last accessed value. In addition, you can set exclusion and inclusion rules by right-clicking the volume in the console pane and choosing Include/Exclude Rules.

RSS predefines some file inclusion and exclusion rules, and some of them can't be changed (which means neither the rule nor its priority can be changed). You can, however, create a new rule by clicking Add. Any rule you create can be edited.

The order of rules (called the rule *priority*) is important, because the first rule that matches a file is used, even if rules that fall later in line also match that file. To change the priority of a rule, select it and use the arrows to move it up or down on the list (raising or lowering the priority).

Media Copies

The remote media that receives the files from local storage is called the *media master set*. If you have the hardware to support it (additional removable drives), RSS can create copies of the media master, which are called the *media copy set*. You can automatically create up to three media copy sets. To accomplish this, right-click the Remote Storage object in the RSS snap-in and choose Properties from the shortcut menu. Move to the Media Copies tab and change the value.

To synchronize the media copy set, right-click the Media object and select Synchronize Media Copies from the shortcut menu. A wizard walks you through the process. You can only synchronize one media copy set at a time. During synchronization, files can't be recalled or managed.

You should prepare sufficient tapes for your media copies in the Remote Storage media pool. However, after using all available media in the Remote Storage media pool, RSS will use media in the Free media pool.

If you reduce the number of media copies, the media is not deallocated. To deallocate the media, you must first delete the media copies. To accomplish this, select the Media object in the console tree. Then, right-click one of the displayed media in the right pane and choose Media Copies. On the Media Copies tab, click Delete Copy X, where X is Copy 1, Copy 2, or Copy 3.

If the media master set becomes corrupted (or disappears), you can re-create it using a media copy. To accomplish this, select the Media object in the console tree and then right-click a media listing and choose Properties. Move to the Recovery tab and select Re-Create Master. Follow the instructions to complete the task.

Validate Stored Files

It's important to make sure that the files on the managed volume point to the right data on the remote media. The validation process checks those links and also updates the statistics for the volume. To configure validation, select Managed Volumes in the console tree. In the right pane, right-click the volume and choose All Tasks | Validate Files from the shortcut menu.

Using the Files Managed by RSS

RSS works by reacting to two different configuration settings: the file selection criteria for copying files to tape, and the amount of free space you mandate for the managed volume.

When a file meets the criteria, it's copied to remote storage. The original data is still stored on the managed volume, and the data is referred to as *cached* data. The difference between cached data and standard file data is a technicality, merely signifying that a file has been copied to the remote media. The file continues to occupy the same amount of disk space. If a user needs the file, it's opened from the volume, and the user doesn't know that the data is considered to be cached. As time goes by, and additional files meet the criteria due to their aging, those files are added to the list of files that are copied to the remote tape and cached locally.

When the free space on the managed volume dips below the size you specified in your configuration setting, RSS removes the cached data from a sufficient number of files to provide the disk space you configured. The file's object remains on the volume, but the file uses no disk space.

When a user wants to use a file that has no cached data on the volume, the process is called a file *recall*. The file is opened by selecting its listing on the volume in the usual way (from an application, My Computer, or Windows Explorer). However, to display the data to the user, the file must be fetched from the remote tape. This takes more time than opening a file directly from the volume. In fact, it can take as long as five minutes to open a file.

When you view the volume from a Windows Server 2003/2000 computer with My Computer or Windows Explorer, the icon for an offline file changes to denote that the file is archived. Legacy Windows systems, including NT 4, do not see the icon.

When a user or application on a Windows XP/2000 computer opens an archived file, a message appears on the screen stating that the file is being recalled from offline storage. Legacy clients do not receive a message and therefore don't know they have to wait a long time for the file (which can cause some problems if you don't explain what's going on).

If a user or application recalls a second file within ten seconds, it's called a *runaway recall.* You can limit the number of runaway recalls a user or application can perform. To set the limit, right-click Remote Storage in the console pane of the RSS snap-in and choose Properties from the shortcut menu. Move to the Recall Limit tab and specify a maximum number of successive recalls.

If you're running virus-checking software or indexing, these applications read files, and those read actions count as recalls. The Findfast tool that is installed by default with Microsoft Office is a classic example. Either stop using the tools (eliminating Findfast is a good idea even if you're not using RSS) or raise the recall limit.

 You can use the Exempt check box to exclude administrators from the recall limit.

Don't delete, move, or modify files that are involved in the RSS copy process. The RSS database will lose track of them. The use of these files should be limited to viewing and printing. If file data needs to be changed, save the file with a new filename.

RSS Backups

Your backup software should back up the following RSS files:

- Files cached on the managed volumes
- The Remote Storage database and other RSS program data files in the %SystemRoot%\System32\RemoteStorage folder

The RSS database is backed up by enabling the System State option in the backup software, if the backup software is running under the context of the Administrators group. If your backup software runs under the context of the Backup Operators group (a common practice), the RSS database is not included with the system state.

If you create media copy sets, that provides a full backup of the RSS-managed files. On a regular basis (in fact, on a daily basis), move a media copy set from the Remote Storage media pool into the Backup media pool. Each time you move a tape from the RS media pool into the Backup media pool, move the previous day's tape back to the RS media pool. This ensures that a restore operation will restore your RSS environment.

Removing RSS

If you decide to discontinue volume management with RSS, you must take a few preliminary steps before removing the feature. First, make sure you have enough room on the volume to recall all the data that's stored offline. If this step requires moving files to another volume, change your settings to avoid additional copies, and go through the steps to perform a manual copy to the offline tape.

Open the Remote Storage snap-in, and select the Managed Volumes object in the console pane. Then, right-click the volume in the details pane and select Remove from the shortcut menu. Go through the Remove Volume Management Wizard to complete the process. During the process, you are given the option to recall all the copied data from storage, which you should do.

Removable Storage Management

Removable Storage Management (RSM) tracks and manages removable media (tapes and discs) and hardware (drives, changers, and jukeboxes). To manage the media, RSM labels and catalogs the tapes and discs. Managing the hardware involves controlling the slots and doors to access and remove the media.

RSM doesn't work alone; it is the media management arm for applications and features that interact with removable media, such as Backup and Remote Storage Services. RSM cannot support more than one computer-removable media connection. All applications that use removable media must run on the same computer that connects to the removable media library. Within the context of RSM, the word "library" means a data storage system that consists of removable media and the hardware that reads and writes to that media. There are two library types:

- Robotic libraries, which are automated multiple-drive devices
- Stand-alone libraries, which are manually loaded single-drive devices

In Windows Server 2003 (and Windows 2000), your ATAPI CD-ROM changer has only a single drive letter assigned. The Removable Storage Manager mounts, dismounts, and manages all the removable media.

Configuring Removable Storage

Removable Storage is part of the Computer Management snap-in, which you reach by right-clicking My Computer and choosing Manage. In the console pane, expand the Storage object, and then expand the Removable Storage object. In addition, there's a preconfigured common console for RSM, named ntmsmgr.msc in %SystemRoot%\ System32. This snap-in contains the same objects as the Removable Storage section of the Computer Management snap-in. Choose Start | Run, enter **ntmsmgr.msc**, and click OK to use this dedicated snap-in.

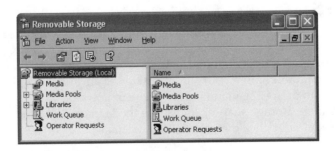

You can view or set the configuration properties for the RSM components by selecting the appropriate object in the console pane. You'll find you spend most of your time working with media (moving media in and out of media pools or ascertaining the state of media) or library management. In the following sections, I'll define and discuss the RSM library and media elements.

Libraries

A *library* is the combination of media and the device used to read and write to that media. There are two types of libraries: robotic and stand-alone. Technically, you could say there's a third library, the offline library. RSM tracks offline media when the media is not contained in a library. The media could be anywhere—in your desk, on a shelf, or in your lunch box. Because RSM tracks offline media, we can say that all media that's currently offline is part of the offline library.

Robotic Libraries

Robotic libraries are automated drives that can hold multiple physical media (tapes or discs). Sometimes these devices are called *changers* or *jukeboxes.* There's usually a robotic subsystem (sometimes called *drive bays*) that moves the media in and out of slots. The slots can be storage slots (the media is parked when not being accessed) or drive slots (the media is the active target). Some robotic libraries have additional hardware components such as doors, cleaning cartridges, bar-code readers, and inject/eject ports. Those additional components are also managed by RSM.

Stand-alone Libraries

Stand-alone libraries are single-drive units that are not automated. The drive holds a single tape or a single CD disc, and the media must be inserted manually.

Taking Inventory of a Robotic Library

You need to let RSM keep inventory for your robotic libraries. This is a two-step process: first you specify the default type of inventory; then you run the inventory.

Setting a Default Inventory Type   To specify the default inventory type for your robotic library, follow these steps:

1. Open the RSM snap-in and expand the Libraries object in the console pane.

2. Right-click the library you want to set an inventory method for, and choose Properties from the shortcut menu.

3. On the General tab, select the inventory method to use as the default: None, Fast, or Full.

   ■ A fast inventory checks for storage slots that have changed status between being occupied and unoccupied.

■ A full inventory with bar-coded media will read bar-code information. For media that lacks bar codes, the media is mounted and RSM reads the on-media identifier.

The selected inventory method is automatically performed each time a library door is accessed. A full inventory is always performed when a mount operation fails, regardless of the inventory type you select. (If you feel it's necessary, you can disable this feature by deselecting the option Perform Full Inventory on Mount Failure.)

Taking Inventory of a Library   To have RSM take inventory of a robotic library, expand the Libraries object in the console pane of the RSM snap-in. Right-click the appropriate library and choose Inventory from the shortcut menu.

Media Pools

All media belongs to a *media pool,* a collection of media that share certain attributes, including media type and management policies. Media pools have a hierarchical structure that starts with the media pool class. There are two classes of media pools:

■ **Application**   Created by software applications for the purpose of grouping and tracking media. In Windows Server 2003, Backup and Remote Storage each maintains an application media pool.

■ **System**   Created and managed by RSM, and include the following pools: Unrecognized, Free, and Import.

Media can be moved from one media pool to another, and that job is always managed by RSM. A media pool can contain media or other media pools. A media pool cannot contain both media and other pools; it is either a single structure or a hierarchical structure. For example, the Free pool could contain media pools for each type of media, but not a hierarchical structure of free media pools.

A library can include media from various media pools, and a single media pool can work with multiple libraries.

Unrecognized Media Pools

Unrecognized media pools hold media that RSM doesn't recognize. This is usually because the media is totally blank and has not yet received an ID from RSM (which occurs when you insert the media in the library). However, media that has an ID that RSM is unable to read or understand also becomes part of the unrecognized media pool. Media in the unrecognized pools is not listed in the RSM database and is therefore not available to applications.

Free Media Pools

Free media pools hold media that are not currently being used by applications. The media is available for use by any application that needs it. It's assumed that any data on the media is not needed, usually because the data is an old backup and would not be useful for a restore procedure.

You can configure RSM to have applications draw media from the Free media pool automatically, whenever an application runs out of media in its own pool. If you don't configure automatic draws from the Free pool, you must move media manually into the Application pool when it's needed.

Import Media Pools

Import media pools contain media that is recognized as a valid media type but has not been used by RSM. Typically, media lands in the Import pool when it is brought to an RSM system from a different RSM system within the organization. You can move media from an Import pool into a Free pool or an Application pool.

Media Identification

To track media and keep its inventory records, RSM identifies each unit of media. There are two identification methods: on-media identifiers and bar codes.

On-Media Identification

On-media identifiers are recorded electronically the first time the media is inserted into a library. The identifier has two parts:

- **The label type**   Identifies the format used to record data. The format is dependent on the type of media.
- **The label ID**   A unique identifier for the specific disc or tape.

Bar Code Identification

If your library supports bar codes, RSM can identify media from the bar codes you supply. Media that use bar codes also receive on-media IDs, and RSM can use either method to identify the tape or disc. Bar codes are easier because you don't have to mount the media in the drive in order to identify it.

Media Formats

RSM uses a *Media Label Library (MLL)* to manage on-media identifiers. An MLL is a DLL that's used to interpret the format of a media label that was written by an application. RSM supports FAT, NTFS, and CDFS for disk media, and MTF (Microsoft Tape Format) for tape media. RSM can discern which application wrote the media label by checking the registered MLLs. Developers who distribute applications that use another media format must provide MLLs.

Media States

The media state is the current operational status of a tape or disc. RSM uses the on-media identifier or the bar code to ascertain the current state. Media states are determined on two levels: physical state and side state.

The *physical* state identifies the current status regarding the media's location and physical use. There are five possible physical states, described in Table 16-1.

The *side* state is the status of the side(s) where data is stored. Every type of media has either one or two sides. For example, magnetic-optical disks have two sides, while tape has a single side. RSM tracks the sides of media, as described in Table 16-2.

An allocation maximum is set by an administrator to control the number of times an application can allocate and deallocate the media. RSM checks the count each time a side is deallocated, and when the maximum is reached, the side is decommissioned. This feature lets administrators prevent media from being used beyond their normal useful life (especially important with tape).

Managing Media Pools

You use the Removable Storage snap-in to manage media pools. You can create a pool, delete a pool, and move media between pools.

Create and Configure a Media Pool

You can create a media pool for an application, either as a new top-level pool or within an existing application pool (but not within the system pools: Free, Import, or Unrecognized).

To create a top-level media pool, right-click the Media Pools object in the console pane and select Create Media Pool from the shortcut menu. To create a media pool within an existing application pool, right-click the existing pool and select Create Media Pool from the shortcut menu.

Physical State	Description
Idle	The media is offline, either in a storage slot (in a robotic device) or physically absent (stored).
In Use	RSM is currently moving the media.
Loaded	The media is mounted in a drive and is available for reading or writing data.
Mounted	The media is in a drive but not yet available for reading or writing data.
Unloaded	The media has been dismounted and is waiting for someone to physically remove it.

Table 16-1. *Descriptions of Media Physical States*

Side State	Description
Allocated	The side is reserved by an application and is not available to any other application.
Available	The side is available for use by an application.
Completed	The side is full.
Decommissioned	The side is not available because it has reached its allocation maximum (see note on allocation maximum).
Imported	The side's label type is recognized. The label ID is not recognized.
Incompatible	The media type is not compatible with the library and should be removed.
Reserved	The side is only available to a specific application. This state applies to two-sided media where one side is allocated.
Unprepared	The side is in a Free media pool and has not yet received a free media label.
Unrecognized	RSM does not recognize the side's label type and ID.

Table 16-2.   *RSM Tracking by Sides*

Configure the new media pool in the Create a New Media Pool Properties dialog, shown in Figure 16-8.

Configure the General tab of the media pool's Properties dialog as follows:

■ Enter a name for the new media pool.

■ Enter a description (optional).

■ In the Media Information section, configure the media pool to hold other media pools, or to hold media.

■ Enter the media type if the pool contains media.

■ Select allocation/deallocation/reallocation options as follows:

　■ Automatically draw media from a Free pool when this media pool runs out of media. Don't select this option if you prefer to move media from a Free pool to this pool manually (using the RSM snap-in).

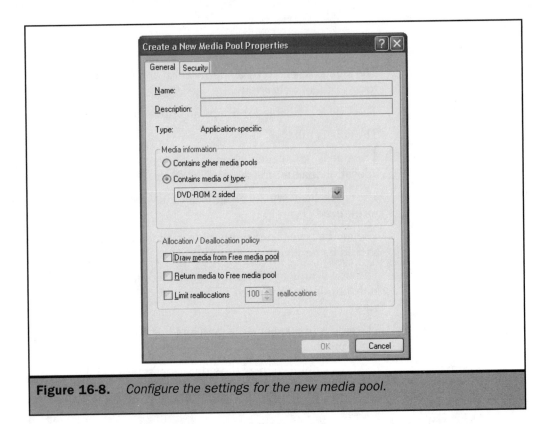

Figure 16-8.   *Configure the settings for the new media pool.*

- Automatically return media to a Free pool when the media is no longer needed by an application. Don't select this option if you prefer to move the media to the Free pool manually.

- Limit the number of times the media can be allocated by other media pools.

Use the Security tab to give permissions to users and groups to manipulate this media pool.

Delete a Media Pool

You can only remove an Application media pool from the Removable Storage snap-in. Expand the console pane to display the media pools, right-click the Application media pool you want to remove, and choose Delete from the shortcut menu. You're asked to confirm your action.

Managing Media

You need to move media between media pools, allocate and deallocate media, and perform other tasks related to keeping RSM well supplied with media.

Moving Media to Another Media Pool

You can drag media from one media pool to another in the Removable Storage snap-in. If either the source or target media pool is in a hierarchy, expand the parent media pool in the console pane. Select the source media pool in the console pane, and drag the media from the details pane of the source media pool object to the target media pool in the console tree.

When you create and configure media pools, if you don't set the option to draw media from and return media to the Free media pool automatically, you must use this manual method of moving the media.

Cleaning Media

RSM keeps records on media-cleaning procedures, so you should use the RSM console when you perform a cleaning operation. The steps you use in the console differ between a stand-alone library and a robotic library.

To clean media in a stand-alone library, manually insert the cleaning cartridge. RSM doesn't do anything about the cleaning process, but it does track whether (and when) media is cleaned. After you clean the drive, notify RSM using the following steps:

1. Open the RSM snap-in.

2. In the console pane, expand the Libraries object to *Applicable Library*\\Drives.

3. In the details pane, right-click the drive and choose Mark As Clean from the shortcut menu.

To clean media in a robotic library, right-click the appropriate library and choose Cleaner Management from the shortcut menu. The Cleaner Management Wizard walks you through the steps (including instructions for inserting a cleaning cartridge).

Managing the Work Queue

RSM can't multitask; it works sequentially, plugging away at one task at a time. If your tape unit has multiple drives and you want RSM to prepare two tapes, it will finish the first tape before beginning the second, even though both tapes are equally accessible.

The work queue displays all requests sent to a library from an application or from Removable Storage.

View the Work Queue

You can keep an eye on the progress of jobs by viewing the Work Queue. To get there, select the Work Queue object in the console pane. The details pane displays the tasks and their states.

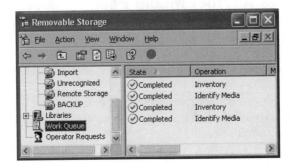

Table 16-3 enumerates the possible states of a job in the work queue.

Cancel or Delete Jobs in the Work Queue

To cancel a job in the work queue, right-click the job's object in the details pane and choose Cancel Request. To delete a job, right-click its object and choose Delete. You can't delete a job that's in progress, except for door openings.

Work State	Description
Completed	The job completed successfully.
Failed	RSM could not complete the job.
In Process	RSM is currently performing the job.
Queued	The job is ready to be carried out, but RSM has not yet begun to operate on it.
Waiting	One or more resources required to complete the job are currently in use.
Cancelled	A user cancelled the job.

Table 16-3. States of Jobs in the Work Queue

Managing Operator Requests

Operator requests are messages that ask you to perform a specific task. The requests can come from RSM, or from a program that is aware of RSM (such as the backup software included with Windows Server 2003). RSM issues an operator request when any of the following events occur:

- An application initiates a mount request for a tape or disk that is offline.

- No media is available online. Usually this occurs when an application requires media, and none exist in the appropriate application media pool (or in a Free media pool, if you've configured RSM to automatically transfer media from the Free media pool to an Application pool).

- A library has experienced a failure, and requires servicing.

- A drive needs cleaning, but no cleaner cartridges are available in the library.

You can either complete or refuse an operator request. When you refuse an operator request, RSM notifies the application that generated the request. By default, RSM stores an operator request in the work queue for 72 hours after you respond to the request.

Click the Operator Requests object in the console pane to view the current requests. As with the items in the Work Queue, you can right-click any request in the details pane and cancel or delete the request.

RSM Tricks and Tips

RSM is quite powerful, but at the same time it requires a commitment to keep on top of it or it won't work properly for you. If you use a tape backup device, RSM is going to become an important part of your professional life.

The trick is to remember that whatever you do with removable media, you must do it through the RSM console. Don't move a tape, clean a tape, throw away a tape, or introduce new tapes without telling RSM.

If you have to restore files from a tape backup, you may encounter a problem with the tape—not a physical problem, but a problem with mounting the tape so its contents or catalog can be read. Sometimes, the backup software may go into a cycle of mounting, cataloging, and dismounting the tape, over and over. This is almost always caused by the fact that the on-media label does not match the RSM database information for the tape that was mounted. The media in the tape library may have been switched with another tape, or placed in the wrong slot. Always use the RSM Eject Media and Inject Media Wizards instead of manually removing and replacing media. This permits RSM to keep track of the media.

If it's too late to heed my advice, and the tape you need for a restore is endlessly cycling, here's the fix: cancel the restore and perform a full inventory of the library. After the inventory, RSM should be able to recognize the tape and mount it correctly.

If all of this makes you long for the days when making a backup required you to manually insert the right tape in the tape drive, and the backup program just checked to see if a tape was there (and didn't care about its day-of-the-week ID or any other "personal information" about the tape), join the club.

Chapter 17

Windows Server 2003 Security

585

There is a common myth that the Windows platform is inherently insecure. This is fundamentally untrue. Windows Server 2003 is one of the most secure operating systems ever developed. It builds on the security of Windows 2000 and extends it. Windows Server 2003 can be made as secure as required if the administrator knows how. This chapter discusses some of the tools and processes for securing the server.

Windows Server 2003 Authentication

Authentication is the verification that a person is who they claim to be, and thus is a fundamental component of Windows Server 2003 security. It confirms the identity of a user attempting to log on to a computer, a network, or a domain. Using Active Directory, Windows Server 2003 supports single sign-on to all network resources. This enables a user to log on to the domain using a single password or smart card and authenticate to any resource in the domain.

Windows Server 2003 supports two primary protocols for authentication:

- **Kerberos V5** The default authentication protocol for Windows 2000, Windows XP, and Windows Server 2003 servers when they are members of an Active Directory domain. It can be used with either a password or a smart card for interactive logon.

- **NTLM** Supported for compatibility with Windows 95, Windows 98, Windows Me, and Windows NT 4, which use NTLM to connect to the network. Computers running Windows Server 2003 use NTLM when connecting to or accessing resources in a Windows NT 4 domain.

NTLM Authentication

Microsoft Windows 9x and Windows NT operating systems cannot use Kerberos, so they use NTLM for authentication in a Windows Server 2003 domain. There are security weaknesses in NTLM that can allow password crackers to decrypt NTLM-protected authentication. To prevent this, NTLM version 2 was developed by Microsoft. Windows 2000 clients and servers, as well as XP, will continue to authenticate with Windows Server 2003 domain controllers using Kerberos regardless of whether NTLM or NTLMv2 is used.

 For more information about enabling NTLMv2 on earlier versions of Windows, see the Microsoft Knowledge Base article 239869, "How to Enable NTLM 2 Authentication for Windows 95/98/2000/NT" at http://support.microsoft.com.

NTLM Telnet Authentication

A feature added to the Windows 2000 telnet Client is NTLM authentication support. It allows a Windows 2000 or Windows Server 2003 telnet client to log on to a Windows

Server 2003 telnet server using NTLM authentication. Users can use their local Windows 2000 username and password or domain account information to access the telnet server. If NTLM authentication is not used, the username and password are sent to the telnet server as plain text. This can then be picked up with a network sniffer. With NTLM authentication, the client uses Windows Server 2003 security for authentication, and the user is not prompted for a username and password. The username and password are passed to the server encrypted. After authentication, all commands are passed as clear text.

> **Note** *Microsoft Terminal Server is a more secure alternative to telnet. Terminal Server can be locked down using many of the same processes for hardening Windows servers.*

Kerberos Overview

The Kerberos authentication protocol provides mutual authentication between clients and servers and between servers. When a user logs on to a domain using a login/ password or a smart card logon, the computer locates an Active Directory server and Kerberos authentication service. Kerberos then issues tickets to allow access to network services. These tickets contain encrypted data, including an encrypted password, that confirms the user's identity to the service.

A primary component of Kerberos is the Key Distribution Center (KDC). The KDC runs on each domain controller as part of Active Directory and stores client passwords and account information. Windows Server 2003 implements the KDC as a domain service and uses the domain's Active Directory as its account database. The Kerberos authentication process involves the following steps:

1. A user on a client system authenticates to the KDC with a password or a smart card.

2. The KDC issues a special ticket-granting ticket (TGT) to the client to allow it to access the ticket-granting service (TGS) on the domain controller.

3. The TGS issues a service ticket to the client.

4. This service ticket confirms the user's identity to the service and the service's identity to the user.

Implementing Kerberos in Windows Server 2003

By default, Kerberos is both transparent and secure in Windows Server 2003. This frees you from worrying about how Kerberos is actually implemented.

> **Note** *The Domain or Enterprise Administrators should not make changes to the default Kerberos implementation without a clear understanding of why these changes are being made and identifying their impact on the domain. Once changes are configured on one domain controller, the settings will replicate to all the other domain controllers. Any modifications to Kerberos policy will affect all the computers in the domain.*

If it is necessary to make a change to the Kerberos policy, do the following:

1. Open Active Directory Users and Computers.

2. In the console tree, right-click the domain.

3. Click Properties, and then click the Group Policy tab.

4. Click Edit.

5. In the console tree, click Kerberos Policy (Computer Configuration/
   Windows Settings/Security Settings/Account Policies/Kerberos Policy).

6. Double-click the Kerberos policy you wish to modify.

7. Modify the policy and then click OK.

There are several Kerberos-related policies that can be modified if absolutely required:

- **Enforce User Login Restrictions** Forces the KDC to check if a user has the "Log on locally" or "Access this computer from the network" user right. If the user does not have one of these rights, the service ticket will not be issued. This policy is enabled by default.

- **Maximum Lifetime That a User Ticket Can Be Renewed** Sets the maximum lifetime of a TGT or a session ticket. Defaults to 7 days.

- **Maximum Service Ticket Lifetime** Sets the number of minutes a Kerberos service ticket is valid. It must be between ten minutes and the setting for "Maximum lifetime for user ticket." Defaults to 600 minutes.

- **Maximum Tolerance for Synchronization of Computer Clocks** Sets the maximum number of minutes by which the KDC and client machines' clocks can differ. The KDC server and workstation clocks should be synchronized as closely as possible. Defaults to five minutes.

- **Maximum User Ticket Lifetime** Determines the number of hours a Kerberos TGT is valid. After this time, a new ticket must be obtained or the old one renewed. Defaults to ten minutes.

There are a few other Kerberos options available. They can be accessed from the Active Directory Users and Computers window by selecting a user and clicking Properties.

- **Smart Card Is Required for Interactive Logon** Requires a user to log on with a smart card. Defaults to disabled.

■ **Use DES Encryption for This Account** Forces the use of 56-bit DES encryption instead of the 128-bit RC4 used in Microsoft Kerberos. Since DES is significantly less secure then RC4, the use of DES is not recommended. This policy defaults to disabled.

While Kerberos provides significant security over earlier authentication protocols, its overall security is still based on the user's password. As a result, poor password policy can undermine the security advantages of Kerberos. One way to overcome this problem is with smart cards.

Implementing Smart Cards

Windows Server 2003, like Windows 2000, supports the use of smart cards for logon. The user's certificate and private key can be stored on the card, so they log in by inserting the smart card into the smart card reader. The computer will then request a personal identification number (PIN) to allow the user to log on to the systems.

The advantages of using smart cards over passwords are as follows:

■ It eliminates the weak password issue in Kerberos. Smart cards provide stronger authentication than passwords because they use encrypted identification.

■ It requires a user to physically posses the smart card to authenticate to the domain.

■ A smart card can be locked after a specific number of unsuccessful PIN inputs. This can prevent dictionary and brute force attacks against the smart card.

Windows Server 2003 uses several policies to define how smart cards log in to a system. The Smart Card Is Required for Interactive Logon policy requires a smart card to interactively log on to a system. When this policy is set, the user cannot use a password to log on to the account. The policy only applies to interactive and network logons, not to remote access logons, which use a different policy. Smart cards are highly recommended for sensitive accounts such as Administrator accounts. The Smart Card Is Required for Interactive Logon policy should not be used when a user must give a logon, password, and domain name to access network resources.

Public Key Infrastructure and Windows Server 2003 Authentication

Windows Server 2003 uses certificates for a variety of functions, such as smart card authentication, web server authentication, secure e-mail, Internet Protocol security, and code signing. A certificate is a digital document issued by an authority to vouch for the identity of a certificate holder. It associates a public key with a person, computer, or service that holds its corresponding private key. A certificate generally includes information about the person or system the certificate is issued to, information about the certificate, and usually information about the certificate authority (CA) who issued the certificate. Certificates generally contain the following information:

- A user's public key
- A piece of identifier information about a user, such as their name and e-mail address
- How long the certificate is valid for
- Information about the certificate issuer
- A digital signature of the issuer that associates a user's public key and their unique identifier information

Note *Although certificates have been available in previous Windows operating systems, they are not widely used as a security mechanism. This may change as more organizations deploy Active Directory.*

Generally, certificates are valid only for a specific period of time that is included within the certificate. Once a certificate's validity period has passed, a new certificate must be requested by the users. When certificates are used, Windows Server 2003 trusts that the certificate issuer has verified the identity of the certificate user. A server designates a certificate issuer as a trusted root authority by placing the issuer's self-signed certificate into the trusted root CA certificate store of the host computer. In Windows Server 2003, Certificate Services is used to create and manage these CAs. The CA is then responsible for establishing and vouching for the identity of certificate holders. You can manage Certificate Services using the Certification Authority MMC console.

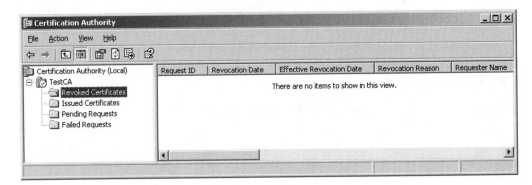

Certificate Templates

A certificate template is the set of rules and settings that are applied to requests for certificates. For each type of certificate, a certificate template must be configured. Certificate templates are customizable in Windows Server 2003 enterprise CAs, and are stored in Active Directory for use by all CAs in the domain. This allows you to choose a default template or modify existing templates in order to create customized templates. There are multiple types of certificate templates in Windows Server 2003:

- **Server Authentication Certificates**   Used to authenticate themselves to clients.
- **Client Authentication Certificates**   Used to authenticate themselves to servers.
- **Code Signing Certificates**   Used to sign active content and applications to ensure that they are from a trusted source.
- **Secure Email Certificates**   Used to sign e-mail messages.
- **Encrypting File System Certificates**   Used to encrypt and decrypt the symmetric key used by Windows Server 2003 Encrypted File System (EFS).
- **File Recovery Certificates**   Used to encrypt and decrypt the symmetric key used for recovering encrypted data by Windows Server 2003 EFS.

Protecting Data Using Windows Server 2003 Encrypting File System

Like Windows 2000 and XP Professional, Windows Server 2003 can protect data using Encrypting File System (EFS) on NTFS-Formatted Drives. It will not work on drives formatted as FAT32. When a file is encrypted, it is given a unique file encryption key to decrypt its data. This encryption key is then encrypted with the user's public key. The file encryption key is also protected by the public key of other users who have been given permission to decrypt the file as well as a designated recovery agent. It is also important to recognize that when EFS-encrypted files are transmitted over the network, they are not secure unless Internet Protocol Security (IPSec) is implemented.

 While the EFS encryption algorithm is considered highly secure, encrypted data can be accessed and read if a hacker can guess the user's or administrator's password. Strong passwords are critical to keeping encrypted data secure.

There are two methods for encrypting folders and files with EFS. The primary way is to encrypt a directory or file with Windows Explorer:

1. Right-click the file or directory.
2. Select Properties | General | Advanced.
3. Select the Encrypt Contents To Secure Data check box.

The data is encrypted automatically and is completely transparent to the user.

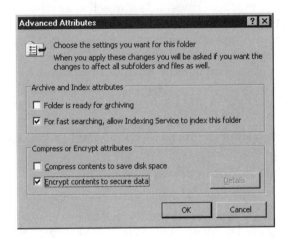

It is also possible to use a program called cipher to encrypt data using EFS. Cipher can be invoked from a command prompt to encrypt files, directories, and subdirectories that are passed to it.

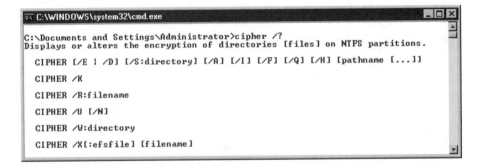

Administrative Issues with EFS

When you back up encrypted files, all files will continue to be encrypted. When restoring the backed up encrypted data, the data will remain encrypted after the restore operation.

One of the key problems with recovery of encrypted data is when a person leaves the company or when the data is requested by law enforcement. This data recovery requires decrypting a file without having the user's private key. To recover an encrypted file, the recovery agent will need to take the following steps:

1. Back up the encrypted files.
2. Move the backed up files to a secure system.

3. Import the files recovery certificate and private key to the secure system.

4. Restore the backup files.

5. Decrypt the files with Windows Explorer or the cipher command.

An administrator can use the Group Policy snap-in to define a data recovery policy for individual computers, domains, or organizational units (OUs). The CA can issue recovery certificates using the MMC Certificates snap-in. In a domain, Windows Server 2003 implements a default recovery policy for the domain when the first domain controller is set up. The domain administrator is designated as the recovery agent.

To change the recovery policy for the local computer:

1. Click Start, and then click Run.

2. Type **mmc**, and then click OK to start the Microsoft Management Console (MMC).

3. On the Console menu, click Add/Remove Snap-ins, and then click Add.

4. Add the Group Policy Object Editor.

5. Under Group Policy Object, make sure that "Local Computer" is displayed and click Finish. Click Close, and then click OK.

6. In Local Computer Policy (Local Computer Policy\Computer Configuration\ Windows Settings\Security Settings\Public Key Policies), right-click Encrypting File System, and then do one of the following:

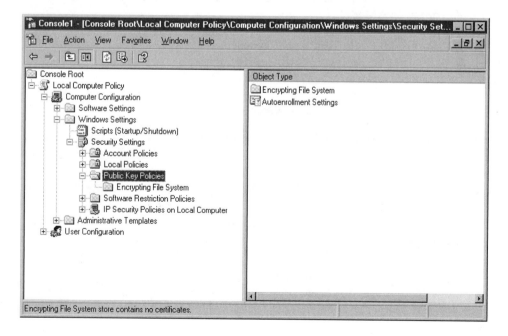

- To designate a user as an additional recovery agent using the Add Recovery Agent Wizard, click Add Data Recovery Agent. Only users who have recovery agent certificates can be designated as recovery agents.

- To allow EFS to work without recovery agents, click All Tasks and then click Do Not Require Data Recovery Agents.

- To delete this EFS policy and every recovery agent, click All Tasks and then click Delete Policy. If you select this option, users can still encrypt files on this computer.

Using the System Key

The system key (SYSKEY) strongly encrypts password files and is installed by default on Windows 2000, XP, and Windows Server 2003 machines. The system key can also protect the following sensitive information:

- Master keys that protect private keys
- Keys for user account passwords stored in Active Directory
- Keys for passwords stored in the registry in the local Security Accounts Manager (SAM) registry key
- Protection keys for LSA secrets
- The key for the Administrator account password used for system recovery startup in Safe Mode

Note *You may have difficulty using a security tool that audits passwords on computers with SYSKEY installed, because SYSKEY-encrypted password files look identical to their unencrypted ones but are currently considered uncrackable.*

SYSKEY can be stored one of three ways:

- In normal mode, or Mode 1, the system key is stored in the registry using a "complex obscuring function" to hide the system key in the registry. This option allows users to restart the computer without having to enter the system key. This is the default configuration for the system key.

- Mode 2 also stores the key in the registry but requires a password to unlock the system key during startup. The system key is generated using an MD5 hashing technique from a password that's up to 128 characters. This password is typed in at startup for the system to boot.

- Mode 3 stores the system key on a floppy disk, which must be inserted during the Windows startup sequence or Windows will not boot. It is inserted when Windows Server 2003 begins the startup sequence, but before users can log on to the system.

Note

If the system key password is forgotten or the floppy disk containing the system key is lost, it is not possible to start the system. The only way to recover the system if the SYSKEY is lost is by using an Emergency Repair Disk (ERD) to restore the registry to a state prior to enabling system key protection. This will lose any changes to the system since then.

To configure system key protection:

1. Type **syskey** at the command prompt.
2. Click Encryption Enabled (if it is not already selected) and then click OK. You will get a reminder that you should create an updated ERD, and you are presented with options for the Account Database. The default option is Mode 1.

3. Click Update.
4. In the Account Database Key dialog, select a key option or change the password, and then click OK.
5. Select the system key option that you want, and then click OK.

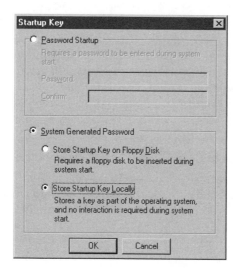

6. Restart the computer.

> **Note** *If the password-derived system key option is used, **SYSKEY** does not enforce a minimum password length.*

When the system restarts, users might be prompted to enter the system key, depending on the key option installed. Windows Server 2003 detects the first use of the system key and generates a new random password encryption key. The password encryption key is protected with the system key, and all account password information is then strongly encrypted.

When SYSKEY is installed, the Windows startup sequence is as follows:

1. Windows Server 2003 obtains the system key, from the registry stored key, the password entry, or a floppy disk.

2. Windows Server 2003 uses the system key to decrypt the master protection key.

3. Windows Server 2003 uses the master protection key to derive the user account password encryption key, which is then used to decrypt the password information in Active Directory or the local SAM registry key.

Use of SYSKEY in the Domain

For computers that are part of a domain, only members of the Domain Admin group can run SYSKEY. For stand-alone computers, local administrators can run SYSKEY.

> **Note** *A computer-generated SYSKEY stored locally on a Primary Domain Controller is not replicated to other domain controllers.*

SYSKEY can be configured independently for each computer in a domain. Each computer can have its own password encryption key and a unique system key. For example, one domain controller might use Mode 3, and another domain controller might use Mode 2.

> **Note** *When there is only a single domain controller, administrators should ensure there is a second domain controller available as a backup until the changes to the first domain controller are complete and verified. It is also recommended to have an up-to-date copy of the ERD for that computer as well.*

Password-Protected Screensavers

A password-protected screensaver enables Windows Server 2003 to automatically lock the screen after a set period of inactivity. This can be a backup when a user or administrator forgets to lock the workstation. Once the computer screen lock is invoked, only the user whose account is currently logged on to the computer or an authorized administrator will be able to unlock it.

To set an automatic screen lock on an individual computer:

1. Right-click the user desktop and select Properties. The Display Properties window appears.

2. Click the Screen Saver tab.

3. Select a screensaver from the Screen Saver drop-down menu.

4. In the Wait box, enter the number of minutes of inactivity that the system must wait before initiating the screensaver (the default of 15 minutes is recommended).

5. Select the On Resume, Password Protect check box.

6. Click OK to set the password-protected screensaver.

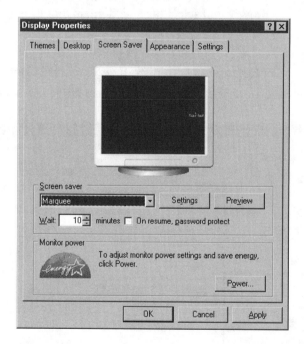

Domain Administrators can enable Active Directory group policy to control whether users will use screensavers and whether they can change screensaver properties.

Here are group policy settings that can affect screensaver functionality:

■ **Hide Screen Saver Tab** Removes the Screen Saver tab from Display in Control Panel.

■ **Screen Saver** Can prevent any screensavers from running.

- **Screen Saver Executable Name** Specifies the screensaver for the user's desktop and prevents changes.
- **Password Protect the Screen Saver** Allows passwords on all screensavers. Disable to prevent passwords from being used on all screensavers.

To make screensaver password locks unavailable to users through group policy, follow these steps:

1. Click Start, and then click Run.
2. Type **mmc**, and then click OK to start the Microsoft Management Console (MMC).
3. On the Console menu, click Add/Remove Snap-ins, and then click Add.
4. Click Group Policy or Local Policy. If this will be an Active Directory policy, click Add, click Browse and select the site, domain, or OU to which you want this policy to apply.
5. Click Close.
6. Expand User Configuration\Administrative Templates\Control Panel\Display.
7. In the right pane, double-click Password protect the screen saver.

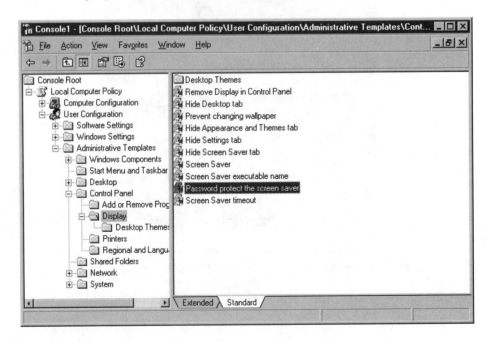

8. Click to select Disable on the Policy tab. This prevents users from setting passwords on screensavers for this computer or domain.

9. Click the Explain tab for information about how to use this policy.

10. Click Apply.

11. Click OK, and then close the MMC.

Internet Protocol Security

IP Security (IPSec) can be used to securely send data between two computers. It is completely transparent to applications since it is implemented at the OSI transport level, allowing applications to communicate using TCP and UDP ports. IPSec has the capability to

■ Provide message confidentiality by encrypting all of the data sent over network connections including remote access connections such as dial-ups.

■ Provide message integrity between two computers by protecting data from unauthorized modification during transmission.

■ Restrict which computers can communicate with one another. Administrators can also restrict communication to specific IP protocols and TCP/UDP ports. IPSec can be used as a limited firewall to block receipt or transmission of specific IP traffic.

■ Prevent replay attacks by ensuring that valid packet data is not reused in order to gain access the network in the future.

Note   *Two of the more common uses of IPSec are as a host-based firewall and to connect two servers separated by a firewall. For example, IPSec can be used to securely pass data between a web server in front of a firewall with a database server behind a firewall on the corporate intranet.*

Windows Server 2003 IPSec policy configuration translates the business IPSec needs into IPSec policies that can be assigned to domain, site, organizational unit (OU), or local machines. It can be implemented by putting the servers in an OU and assigning the IPSec policy to that OU with a rule that requires secured traffic between the servers and all other computers. In Windows Server 2003, the IP Security Monitor in MMC allows administrators to manage IPSec policy issues, including:

■ Create and modify IPSec policy

■ Monitor IPSec information about local computer and remote computers

■ View details about IPSec policies

■ View IPSec filters, statistics, and security associations

The IP Security Policies MMC snap-in can manage IPSec policy centrally for Active Directory members or for local computers. An IPSec policy is made up of a set of filters, filter actions, and rules. A *filter* contains the following:

- A single source IP address or a range of addresses
- A single destination IP address or range of addresses
- An IP protocol, such as TCP, UDP, or "any"
- Source and destination ports

A *filter action* identifies what happens when a filter is invoked. Possible options include allowing the IP traffic to be sent and received without being blocked, blocking the traffic, and negotiating the security protocol to use between systems.

A *rule* associates a filter with a filter action. A mirrored policy applies rules to all packets with the exact reverse of the specified source and destination IP addresses.

> **Caution**   *Windows Server 2003 has a set of predefined IPSec filter lists, filter actions, and default policies. These are only intended to provide an example of IPSec policies. They should not be used without modification. These default policies are defined for computers on intranets because they allow members of an Active Directory domain to receive unsecured traffic.*

To add, edit, or remove IPSec policies, use MMC to open a console containing IP Security Policy Management and then do one of the following:

- **To add a new policy**   Select Action | Create IP Security Policy. Follow the instructions in the IP Security Policy Wizard until the Properties dialog for your new policy appears.
- **To modify an existing policy**   Double-click the policy that you want to modify and make any changes necessary.
- **To remove a policy**   Click the policy that you want to remove, and on the Action menu, click Delete.

If you are adding or modifying a policy, click the General tab, type a unique name in the Name list box, and type a description of the security policy under Description.

To specify how often the IPSec Policy Agent checks for updates, type a value in Check for policy changes every *number* minute(s).

If you have special requirements for the security of the key exchange, click Settings, click the Rules tab, and create or modify any necessary rules for the policy. Activate or deactivate rules as needed.

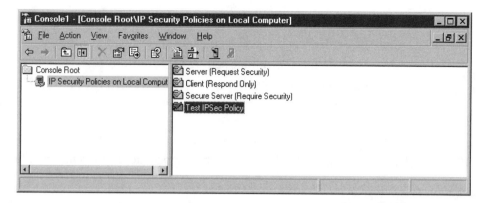

 Filters are the most important part of IPSec policy for a computer protected by IPSec. If the filters are not properly configured in either client or server policies, or if the IP addresses change, then the protection IPSec provides may be lost.

To add, edit, or remove IPSec filters:

1. Use MMC to open a console containing IP Security Policies.

2. Double-click the policy that you want to modify.

3. Double-click the IP Security rule that contains the IP filter list you want to modify.

4. On the IP Filter List tab, double-click the IP filter list that contains the IPSec filter you want to modify.

5. In the IP Filter List dialog, do one of the following:

   ■ To add a filter, click Add.

   ■ To modify an existing filter, select the filter that you want to modify, and then click Edit.

   ■ To remove an existing filter, select the filter that you want to remove, and then click Remove.

6. In IP Filter List dialog, do one of the following:

   ■ To use the IP Filter Wizard to create a filter, confirm that the Use Add Wizard check box is selected, and then click Add.

   ■ To create a filter manually, clear the Use Add Wizard check box, and then click Add.

   ■ To modify an existing filter, select the filter that you want to modify, and then click Edit.

7. On the Addresses tab, select the Source Address.

8. Click Destination Address and repeat Step 7 for the destination address.

9. Under Mirrored, select the appropriate setting:

   ■ To automatically create two filters based on the filter settings, one for traffic to the destination and one for traffic from the destination, select the Mirrored check box.

   ■ To create a single filter based on the filter settings, clear the Mirrored check box.

10. On the Description tab, in the Description box, type a description for this filter.

IPSec Monitor Snap-In

In Windows 2000, the IP Security Monitor was a stand-alone executable program called IPSecmon.exe. In Windows Server 2003, IP Security Monitor is implemented as a MMC snap-in that allows you to do the following:

■ Monitor IPSec information for both local and remote computers.

■ View details about active IPSec policies, including the name, description, date last modified, store, path, OU, and Group Policy Object name.

■ View IP filters information.

■ View IPSec statistics.

■ View main mode and quick mode security associations.

■ Search for filters based on source or destination IP address.

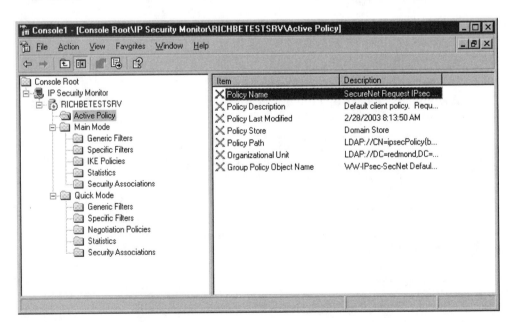

Local Security Policies

Security policies are critical to implementing secure Windows Server 2003 servers and secure domains. Administrators can control security policy on local and remote computers, including password policies, account lockout policies, Kerberos policies, auditing policies, user rights, and other policies. These security policies can be managed by editing policies on a local computer, OU, or domain as well as by applying security template files (files that end in .inf). Local Security Policy settings can be set on stand-alone computers or be applied to domain members. Within an Active Directory domain, the Domain Security Policy settings will take precedence over Local Security Policy settings.

Both Microsoft and the National Security Agency (NSA) offer security template files that can secure Windows, servers, workstations, and applications. These should be used with great caution and only after extensive testing. They can keep many applications and server configurations from working properly after installation.

To modify the Local Security Policy:

1. Log on to the computer with administrative rights.
2. Select Start | Programs | Administrative Tools | Local Security Policy. This opens the Local Security Settings console.

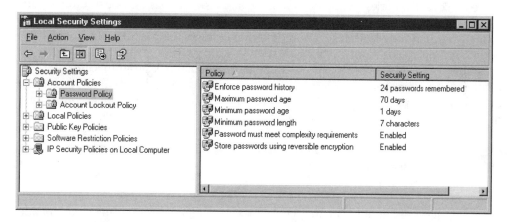

Local Security Account Policies

Windows Server 2003 uses account policies to manage the two major account authentication features:

■ **Password policy**   Determines settings for implementing user password management functions.

■ **Account lockout policy**   Determines when and for how long an account will be locked out of the system in case of user misauthentication.

- **Enforce Password History**   Should be set to remember 12 passwords.
- **Maximum Password Age**   Sets the length of time before users need to change their password. Should be set to 45-90 days.
- **Minimum Password Age**   Sets the minimum length of time users must keep a password before they can change it. Should be set to one day.
- **Minimum Password Length**   Sets the minimum number of characters required for user passwords. Should be set to require a password of at least eight characters. Each additional character in a password significantly increases the difficulty of breaking the password.
- **Password Must Meet Complexity Requirements**   Forces the use of strong passwords and thus should be Enabled. This requires a password with at least three of the following four character sets: uppercase letters, lowercase letters, numbers, and nonalphanumeric characters.

Weak user and administrator passwords are one of the leading causes of servers being hacked. If a hacker can guess the Domain Administrators password, they will "own" the entire domain.

Account Lockout Policies

There are several theories on implementing account lockout policies. One recommendation is that account lockout should not be implemented because if the password policies are properly configured, no attacker should be able to guess the password in a reasonable period of time. In addition, enabling account lockout policies greatly increases the possibility of a denial of service occurring if automated attack programs are used to attempt to compromise the server. These programs often test a small number of commonly used passwords, and can result in the lockout of some or all accounts on the server (except the Administrator account, which cannot be locked out).

There are a number of worms that attempt to log on to open network shares by guessing a small number of passwords for the Administrator account. Once they log on, they drop back doors that allow hackers into the system.

If you decide to implement an account lockout policy, here are some recommended policy settings:

- **Account Lockout Duration**   Should be 0, which requires an administrator to unlock the account. This policy locks the account for a specified period of time after invalid password attempts.

- **Account Lockout Threshold**   Should lock out accounts after five bad login attempts.
- **Reset Account Lockout Counter After**   Should be set to 30 minutes. This policy sets how long the lockout threshold is maintained before being reset.

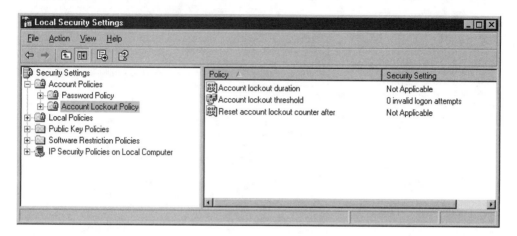

Local Policies

Local policies allow administrators to implement security settings that apply to individual computers or users. The Local Policies section can be used to configure:

- **User rights assignment**   Covers a variety of policies that identify the types of actions individual users or groups can perform. How they are implemented will vary by site and computer.
- **Security options**   Manage various security settings for the computer. How these options are implemented depends on the site environment and how the server is being used.
- **Audit policy**   Determines which security events are logged in to the security event log on the computer. The Windows Security log is managed through the Event Viewer MMC snap-in.

There are a number of *security options* that you can implement in Windows Server 2003. How these options are configured depends heavily on the server environment and how the server is being used. For example, a domain controller might have different options than an Internet-facing web server. There are several of these policies that you might want to review and perhaps implement. Two of the most important are renaming the Administrator and Guest accounts.

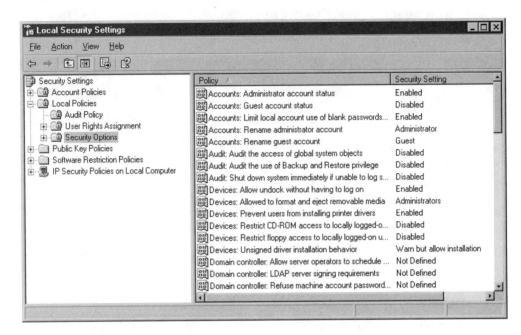

The following security policies can be set to increase security of local and domain member computers:

- **Set Additional Restrictions for Anonymous Connections**   Disables the ability of anonymous users to enumerate SAM accounts and shares. This makes it harder to identify accounts that can be compromised. This policy should be Enabled.

- **Disable Shutdown Without Logon**   Prevents users from shutting down the computer without first authenticating to the system. This policy should be Disabled.

- **Clear Virtual Memory Page File When System Shuts Down**   Removes the virtual memory pagefile when the system is shut down. This ensures that any information remaining in the pagefile is not available to the next user that logs on to the machine. This policy should be Enabled.

- **Disable CTRL+ALT+DEL Required for Logon**   Makes it easier to spoof a user login session. The default setting of this option is Disabled and should remain so. *Do not enable this option!*

- **Do Not Display Last User Name on Logon Screen**   Removes the name of the last user from the login session. This then requires an attacker to guess both the user ID and password. This policy should be Enabled.

- **Implement an Authorized Usage Warning**   Implements an interactive logon screen to display a logon banner with a title and warning. Administrators can set a message title and message text.

- **Rename Administrator Account**   Reduces the chances of successful attacks by forcing a potential hacker to guess the password and user ID of the Administrator account. Administrators can set the new name for the Administrator account.

- **Rename Guest Account**   Reduces the chances of successful attacks by forcing a potential hacker to guess the password and user ID of the Guest account. Administrators can set the new name for the Guest account.

Implementing Auditing

Auditing is a primary tool for administrators to identify and track potential security problems, ensure user accountability, and provide evidence of security breaches. Implementing an auditing policy requires you to determine which events and objects need to be audited. The most common types of events that are audited include:

- Users logging on and logging off from the system
- Changes to user accounts and groups
- User access to sensitive objects, such as files and folders
- Policy changes

Note   *Event log auditing is one of the most effective ways to determine if a server has been hacked.*

To audit Windows Server 2003 effectively, you should establish an audit strategy that defines the following:

- Which server security events should be audited.

- The maximum size and retention period for the Windows Security log. These can be set in the Event Viewer (select Start | Settings | Control Panel | Administrative Tools | Event Viewer, right-click the specific log, and click Properties).

- Define which objects, such as files and directories, must be monitored. Administrators should not audit more objects than necessary, since it could cause audit logs to fill up very rapidly.

- Deploy Auditing Policy with the Local Security Policy tool (Start | Settings | Control Panel | Administrative Tools | Local Security Policy) on a stand-alone machine, or with Group Policy on a domain.

- Review the security logs regularly. Auditing is only valuable if the logs are checked for security breaches. The following are the locations of the Windows Server 2003 logs:

  - %SYSTEMROOT%\system32\config\SysEvent.Evt
  - %SYSTEMROOT%\system32\config\SecEvent.Evt
  - %SYSTEMROOT%\system32\config\AppEvent.Evt

- Update the auditing policy as necessary. After reviewing the logs for a period of time, it may be necessary to collect more or less information.

To enable local Windows security auditing through the Local Security Policy:

1. Log on as an Administrator to Windows Server 2003.

2. Select Start | Settings | Control Panel.

3. Double-click Administrative Tools.

4. Double-click Local Security Policy to start the Local Security Settings MMC snap-in.

5. Double-click Local Policies to expand it, and then double-click Audit Policy.

6. In the right pane, double-click the policy that you want to enable or disable.

7. Click the Success checkbox and Fail checkbox.

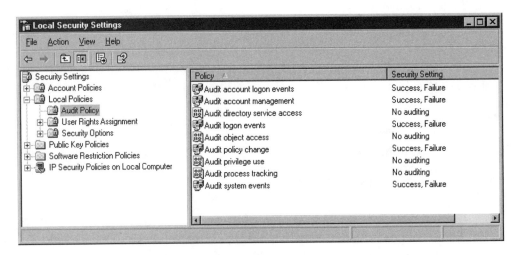

To enable security auditing through the MMC:

1. Log on as an Administrator to Windows Server 2003.

2. Select Start | Run, type **mmc**, and then click OK.

3. Add Group Policy.

4. In the Select Group Policy Object box, click Local Computer, click Finish, click Close, and then click OK.

5. Expand Local Computer Policy\Computer Configuration\Windows Settings\Security Settings\Local Policies, and then click Audit Policy.

6. In the right pane, double-click the policy that you want to enable or disable.

7. Click the Success checkbox and Fail checkbox.

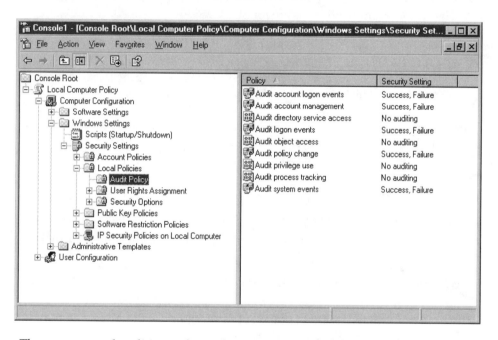

There are several auditing policies that can be implemented to increase Windows Server 2003 security:

- **Audit Account Logon Events**   Audits logon events associated with user authentication. The Audit recommendations are for SUCCESS and FAILURE.

- **Audit Account Management**   Audits any event that involves account management, such as account creation, account lockout, and account deletion. The Audit recommendations are for SUCCESS and FAILURE.

- **Audit Directory Service Access**   Enables auditing of access to Active Directory objects. The Audit recommendations are for SUCCESS and FAILURE.

- **Audit Logon Events**   Audits logon events occurring on the system this policy is applied to. The Audit recommendations are for SUCCESS and FAILURE.

- **Audit Object Access** Enables auditing of access to all auditable objects such as file system and registry objects. The Audit recommendations are for SUCCESS and FAILURE.
- **Audit Policy Change** Defines whether to audit changes to user rights assignment policies, audit policies, or trust policies. The Audit recommendations are for SUCCESS.
- **Audit System Events** Audits events such as system shutdown, system start, or events affecting the system and/or security logs, such as clearing the logs. The Audit recommendations are for SUCCESS.

Note *The most important events that should be monitored are Audit Logon Events, which will tell who tried to log on, Audit Policy Change, which will tell if a policy change has been made, and Audit System Events, which can identify unusual actions on the computer. These audit events are often used to identify computer hacks against a system.*

After setting up auditing to detect and record security access to files or folders, you can track users who access certain objects and analyze security breaches. The audit trail can show who performed the actions and who tried to perform actions that are not permitted.

To set up auditing on a file or folder:

1. Start Windows Explorer and then locate the file or folder that you want to audit.
2. Right-click the file or folder, click Properties, and then click the Security tab.
3. Click Advanced, and then click the Auditing tab.
4. Determine the type of Auditing change to be made:
   - To set up auditing for a new group or user, click Add. In the Name box, type the name of the user that you want to audit, or use the Advanced button to query for a specific user.
   - To view or change auditing for an existing group or user, click the name, and then click View/Edit.
   - To remove auditing for an existing group or user, click the name, and then click Remove.
5. Under Access, click Successful, Failed, or both depending on the type of access that you want to audit.
6. If you want to prevent files and subfolders in a folder from inheriting these audit features, select the Apply these auditing entries checkbox.

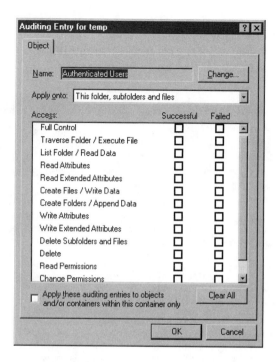

You can view IPSec Policy Agent events in the audit log and IPSec driver events in the system log. To enable IPSec driver event logging, set the HKEY_LOCAL_MACHINE\ System\CurrentControlSet\Services\IPSec\DiagnosticMode registry setting to 1 and restart the computer. The IPSec driver only writes events to the system log once an hour.

Detecting Security Breaches Through Auditing of Logs

Unauthorized access attempts in the Windows Security log can be seen as warning or error log entries. To detect possible security problems, review the Windows Security log:

1. Select Start | Settings | Control Panel.
2. Double-click Administrative Tools, and then double-click Computer Management.
3. Expand System Tools, and then expand Event Viewer.
4. Click Security.
5. Inspect the logs for suspicious security events, including the following events:
   - Invalid logon attempts
   - Unsuccessful use of privileges

- Unsuccessful attempts to access and modify .bat or .cmd files
- Attempts to alter security privileges or the audit log
- Attempts to shut down the server

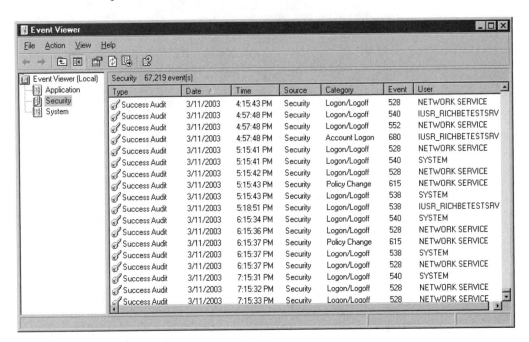

Protecting Event Logs

It is important to limit access to the event logs to protect them from modification. An attacker may try to modify the security logs, disable auditing during an attack, or clear the security log to prevent detection.

 A completely empty security log, when security auditing is enabled, may indicate that the server was hacked and that the hacker was trying to cover his tracks.

The event logs can be assigned access rights to limit the users who can read the files. By default, the Everyone group can read these files. To ensure that the event log entries are protected, you should take steps to protect the security of the event logs:

- Remove the access rights of the Everyone group and restrict access to members of the Administrators and System groups.
- Define a policy for the storage, overwriting, and maintenance of all event logs. The policy should define all required event log settings and be enforced by Group Policy.

- Ensure that the policy includes how to deal with full event logs, especially the security log. It is recommended that a full security log require the shutdown of the server if possible.

- Enable the security policy settings to prevent local Guest accounts from accessing the system, application, and security logs.

- Ensure that the system events are audited for both success and failure to determine if any attempts are made to erase the contents of the security log.

- All administrators that have the ability to view or modify audit settings must use complex passwords or two-factor authentication methods, such as smart card logon, to prevent attacks against these accounts to gain access to audit information.

Trust Relationships Between Domains

A domain trust is a relationship between two domains that enables users in one domain to be authenticated by a domain controller in another domain. With Windows Server 2003, account authentication between domains is enabled by two-way, transitive trusts based on Kerberos. This allows users and computers to be authenticated between any domain in the domain tree or forest. These trust relationships are automatically created between parent and child domains when a new domain is created in a domain tree. In a forest, a trust relationship is automatically created between the forest root domain and the root domain of each domain tree added to the forest.

Domain trusts can pose a major security concern. Normally, a security threat is limited to a specific domain at a time. A security compromise on a domain with trust relationships can put all its partner domains at risk. For example, If a high-level account is compromised on one domain, it could be used to hack other trusted domains.

Before an account can be granted access to resources by a domain controller of another domain, Windows Server 2003 must check if that domain has a trust relationship with the first domain. To do this, Windows Server 2003 computes a trust path between the two domain controllers. A *trust path* is the set of domain trust relationships that must be traversed by Windows Server 2003 security to pass authentication requests between any two domains.

Note   *When a user is authenticated by a trusting domain controller, this does not automatically give the user access to resources in that domain. The user's access is still determined by the rights and permissions granted to that user account by the domain administrator for the trusting domain.*

Explicit trusts are trust relationships between domains that administrators create rather than trusts created during installation of a domain controller. Administrators create and manage explicit trusts using the MMC Active Directory Domains and Trusts.

There are two kinds of explicit domain trusts: external trusts and shortcut trusts. External trusts enable user authentication to a domain outside of a forest, whereas shortcut trusts shorten the trust path in a complex forest.

External trusts create trust relationships between domains in different forests. An external trust allows user authentication to a domain that is not part of a trust path of a forest. Although all external trusts are one-way nontransitive trusts, two external trusts can be combined to create a two-way trust relationship.

> **Note** *In Windows NT, trusts were limited to the two domains involved in the trust, and the trust relationship was always one-way. When upgrading a Windows NT domain to Windows Server 2003, the existing one-way trust relationships between that domain and any other domains are maintained. If you are installing a new Windows Server 2003 domain and want trust relationships with Windows NT domains, you must create external trusts with those domains.*

Shortcut trusts are two-way transitive trusts that shorten the path between domains within a forest for authentication. For example, shortcut trusts are often used between two domain trees in a forest.

> **Note** *To create an explicit trust, the administrator must have a user account with permission to create trusts in each domain. Each trust is assigned a password that must be known to the administrators of both domains.*

To create an explicit domain trust between two domains:

1. Select Start | Programs | Administrative Tools | Active Directory Domains and Trusts.
2. In the console tree, right-click the domain node for the domain you want to administer, and then click Properties.
3. Click the Trusts tab.
4. Depending on your requirements, click either Domains trusted by this domain or Domains that trust this domain, and then click Add.
5. If the domain to be added is a Windows Server 2003 domain, type the full DNS name of the domain. Or, if it is an NT domain, type the domain name.
6. Type the password for this trust, and confirm the password.
7. Repeat this procedure on the other domain in the explicit trust relationship.

Patch Management

Keeping Windows Server 2003 patched with the latest software releases is critical to keeping the box secured. If the system is not patched, all the other attempts to secure Windows Server 2003 are wasted.

Software companies release patches to fix code or configuration problems. These problems are sometimes security related and can allow malicious users to take advantage of security holes or vulnerabilities. Once a vulnerability has been made public, attackers will often try to exploit this hole in order to compromise systems. Generally, software companies release these security patches as soon as possible to make their customers as secure as possible.

It's common to use the terms patch, service pack, and hotfix interchangeably to mean a software update, but each has a specific definition:

- **Service packs**   Keep the product current, and correct known problems after the product was released. There are separate service packs for each product but the same service pack will generally work for different versions of the same product. Service packs are cumulative, so each new service pack contains previous service packs as well as new fixes since the last service pack.

- **Hotfixes**   Code patches for products that are provided to individual customers who have critical problems with no other workaround. Hotfixes do not undergo extensive regression testing and are very problem-specific. Groups of hotfixes are often rolled into service packs.

- **Security patches**   Designed specifically to eliminate security vulnerabilities. They are similar to hotfixes but primarily are released to keep systems secure. Failure to keep Windows Server 2003 current with security patches leaves it highly vulnerable to viruses and being hacked.

With all updates, you should weigh the risks and benefits of deploying them. You should also do testing of each update before deploying it to a production environment. Microsoft has developed free tools for determining if a system is patched.

Microsoft Network Security Hotfix Checker (HFNETCHK)

HFNETCHK is a command-line utility that allows you to check whether a workstation or server is up to date with all of its security patches. MBSA V1.1, which was released in December 2002, replaces the stand-alone HFNETCHK tool with an equivalent program Mbsacli.exe.

Administrators who are currently using HFNETCHK can get the same information by typing the following command from the folder where MBSA 1.1 was installed:
`Mbsacli.exe /hf`.

Mbsacli.exe, the HFNETCHK replacement, can be used to check the patch status of Windows Server 2003, Windows NT 4, Windows 2000, and Windows XP, as well as hotfixes for Internet Information Server (IIS) 4.0, IIS 5.0, SQL Server 7.0, SQL Server 2000, Microsoft Data Engine (MSDE), Exchange Server 5.5, Exchange Server 2000, Windows Media Player, and Internet Explorer 5.01 or later.

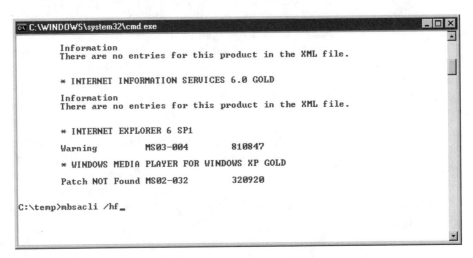

Microsoft Baseline Security Analyzer (MBSA)

MBSA is a free graphical security tool that scans Windows computers for common security misconfigurations and generates a security report for each computer that it scans. MBSA runs on Windows Server 2003, Windows 2000, and Windows XP computers. It only scans for security vulnerabilities on Windows Server 2003, Windows NT 4, Windows 2000, and Windows XP computers. MBSA scans for common security misconfigurations in Microsoft Windows, Microsoft IIS, Microsoft SQL Server, Microsoft Internet Explorer (IE), and Microsoft Office. MBSA also scans for missing security updates in Microsoft Windows, IIS, SQL Server, IE, Windows Media Player (WMP), Exchange Server, and Exchange 2000 Server. It requires Administrative privileges to run a security scan against a machine.

MBSA, Mbsacli.exe, and the old HFNETCHK all use an XML file directly downloaded from the Microsoft web site that contains a list of the latest hotfixes that should be installed on the system. They will use a local XML file if there is no connection to the Internet, but it could be out of date and leave a system insecure even if it says that it is patched. When MBSA or Mbsacli.exe is run, it will always try to obtain the latest copy of the XML file.

The XML file, MSSECURE.XML, contains the security bulletin name and title, and detailed data about product-specific security hotfixes, including:

- The files in each hotfix package along with their file versions and checksums
- Registry keys that the hotfix applies

- Information about which patches replace other patches
- Associated Microsoft Knowledge Base article number

MBSA Scanning Options

MBSA can be used as a free, very limited, vulnerability-assessment tool with the capability to do the following:

- Scan one or more Windows Server 2003, Windows NT 4, Windows 2000, and Windows XP machines.
- Check for Windows operating system vulnerabilities.
- Check for IIS vulnerabilities.
- Check for SQL Server vulnerabilities. The tool checks for vulnerabilities on each instance of SQL Server that it finds on the computer.
- Check for weak passwords and common password vulnerabilities. MBSA password checks can add Security log entries if auditing is enabled. MBSA will reset any account lockout policies that are detected, so it will not lock out any user accounts during the password check, but this check is not performed on domain controllers.
- Check for missing security updates.

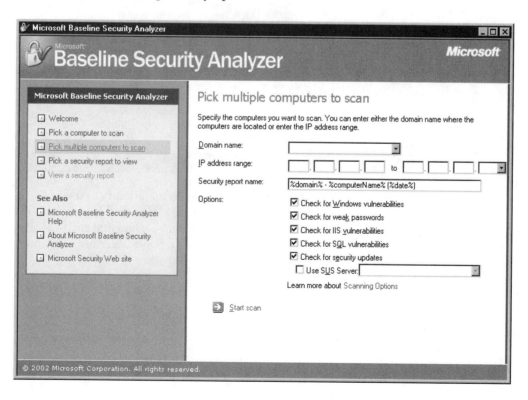

An MBSA security scan stores the output reports in individual XML files for each computer scanned in the %userprofile%\SecurityScans folder. These can be viewed through MBSA Scan reports.

A known issue with MBSA is that when a non-security hotfix is applied to a machine after a security hotfix, MBSA may say that the security hotfix is missing. The computer will still be secure even though MBSA says it is not. This will be fixed in the next release of MBSA.

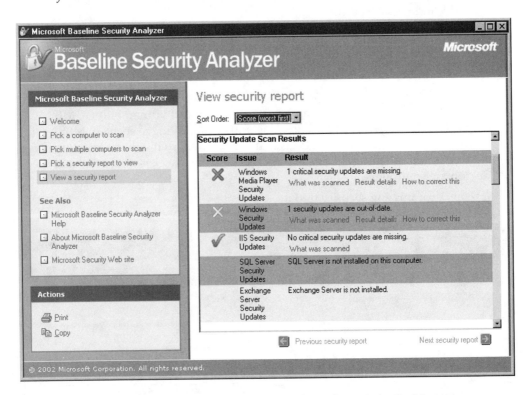

Another way to determine whether hotfixes have been installed is to use Regedit32 to look in the registry under the HKLM\Software\Microsoft\Windows NT\ Currentversion\hotfix key. Every new hotfix installed will have a key that corresponds to the article in the Microsoft Knowledge Base for that hotfix. Some older hotfixes and hotfixes for some applications may not show up here.

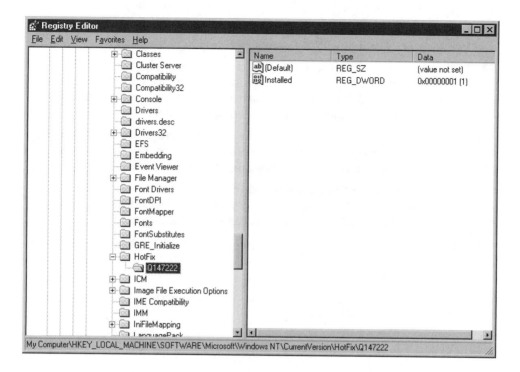

Checklist

Here is a general checklist for keeping Windows Server 2003 secure:

- Keep antivirus software current. There are thousands of viruses, with an average of five new ones found every day. Viruses not only can damage the computer but also can leave it vulnerable to being hacked.

- Subscribe to Microsoft Security Notification Service to be notified of the latest Microsoft security patches: www.microsoft.com/technet/security/bulletin/notify.asp.

- Implement a system for managing patches. Organizations should have a process for testing and deploying new security patches soon after they are released.

- Review the logs on a regular basis. Look for indications of intrusions.

  - Check the Application, System, Security, and IIS (if IIS is installed) logs.

  - Ensure that administrators can recognize what an attack looks like.

- Implement regular network monitoring to look for intrusions and hacker activity.

- Run regular security scans with MBSA against all Windows Server 2003, Windows NT 4, Windows 2000 clients and servers, as well as XP.

- Lock down your web servers with tools such as IISlockdown/URLSCAN. You can find them at http://www.microsoft.com/windows2000/downloads/recommended/iislockdown/default.asp and http://www.microsoft.com/windows2000/downloads/recommended/urlscan/default.asp.

- Review the Microsoft security guidelines to implement secure configurations for your environment: www.microsoft.com/technet/security/tools/tools. These guides can be very useful even if they are not Windows Server 2003 specific.

- Review the NSA security guides for additional ideas on securing your Windows environment at http://nsa2.www.conxion.com/win2k/index.html. Be aware that installing the NSA .inf files may break your applications.

- Have third-party organizations do regular security audits and assessments of your network and server environment.

The
Complete
Reference

Windows
Server
2003

Chapter 18

Domain Controllers

If you're moving to Windows Server 2003 from Windows NT, you're going to love the way domain controllers are installed, and the way they do their jobs. Microsoft has separated the process of creating domains and domain controllers from the operating system installation process. In Windows NT, you had to decide whether a computer would be a domain controller during setup, and then you couldn't create additional (backup) domain controllers until the PDC was up and running, and the new computers could communicate with it over the network.

Now you can perform straightforward vanilla installations of Windows Server 2003 and then, after you've made sure the servers boot properly and have no problems, you can begin the tasks of creating DCs and other system servers. In fact, if you're upgrading hardware equipment when you upgrade the operating system, you can have your favorite hardware supplier preinstall Windows Server 2003 without worrying about naming and configuring domain controllers.

A Windows Server 2003 network doesn't have PDC and BDCs; rather, it has domain controllers, and all domain controllers are more or less equal (you can specify roles for domain controllers, but generally speaking, a domain controller is a domain controller). This means that if you're taking a DC down for service or maintenance, or a DC just goes down, you don't have the complicated and annoying hassle of demoting and promoting PDCs and BDCs to keep your network going.

In this chapter, I'll go over some of the common approaches to moving Windows Server 2003 DCs into your network. I can't cover every scenario, because the possible permutations and combinations are too vast (new domains, upgrades of existing domains from Windows 2000 or Windows NT, mixed domains, adding domains to existing forests, adding DCs to existing domains, and so on). However, the overview presented in this chapter should provide sufficient information for you to plan and implement your rollout of Windows Server 2003.

Creating a New Domain

When you install the first domain controller in your organization, you are also installing the first instance of your enterprise hierarchy:

- **The first domain** A domain is a collection of objects (computers, users, and groups) as defined by an administrator. All of these objects share a common directory database (Active Directory) and security policies. In addition, a domain may have security relationships with other domains.

- **The first forest** A forest is one or more domains that share the same schema (definitions for classes and attributes), site and replication information, and searchable components (a *global catalog*). Domains in the same forest can be linked by trust relationships.

- **The first site** A site is essentially a TCP/IP subnet. You can set up additional sites, which can be located locally or remotely (such as across a WAN).

Chapter 19 has detailed explanations and instructions about working with these components of your enterprise hierarchy.

Planning DC Deployment

The number of DCs you create is dependent on the size of your enterprise, and your own attitudes about speed and failover. It's possible, for a single LAN on a single subnet, to run your company on a single DC. But it's risky. Installing a second DC means that authentication, access to network resources, and other user requirements can continue if a DC goes down. In addition, if you have a great many users, having multiple DCs reduces the authentication burden of a single DC, especially if many users shut down their computers at night and then restart them and log on to the network at 9:00 A.M.

If your enterprise operates in multiple sites, you should create at least one DC in each site (having a second DC for failover is even better). To log on, computers and users need a DC, and if the DC is in a different site, the logon process can take a long time.

Keep your DCs physically secure, in locked rooms if possible. This isn't just a hedge against damage done by miscreants; it's a safety measure to protect your enterprise against accidental damage by your own users.

Installing Active Directory

The thing that distinguishes a domain controller from other system servers is the presence of Active Directory. To turn any Windows Server 2003 computer into a domain controller, install Active Directory. (The server must be running NTFS; if it isn't, before you install AD, you must run convert.exe to change the file system from FAT to NTFS.)

This is all accomplished with the help of wizards, but prompts and actions differ depending on whether this is the first DC or an additional DC for the domain, and whether DNS services are available at the time you install the DC. I'll cover some of the common permutations and combinations in the following sections.

Active Directory and DNS

When you install the first DC in a new domain, you encounter a problem—the need to examine and solve the eternal puzzle, "which comes first, the chicken or the egg?" You can't install Active Directory unless you have DNS running, and you can't install DNS unless you have a domain. Fun, huh?

The Active Directory Installation Wizard automatically tries to locate an authoritative DNS server from its list of configured DNS servers that will accept a dynamic update of a service (SRV) resource record. If found, the records for the DC will be registered automatically with the DNS server after the DC is rebooted.

For the first DC in a new domain, it's probable that no suitable DNS server is located. As a result, the wizard automatically adds DNS to the roles being installed on this computer. The server's preferred DNS setting is configured to be itself. This is a workable solution, because after you set up additional DNS servers, you can remove DNS from this DC.

As an alternative, you can set up a DNS server first, but because it won't be integrated with the AD (because you haven't yet installed the AD), the data for the DNS zone will be a flat file. This doesn't mean the new DC won't recognize the fact that DNS is installed, but it does have an effect on DNS security. A flat file DNS zone asks no questions and imposes no restrictions. Any device that attempts to register a name is allowed to do so, even if it's replacing a previously registered same name. No permissions are examined or enforced on the DNS database, so anybody can mess with it. However, after you've established your domain and DCs, you can convert a flat file zone to an AD-integrated zone (see Chapter 12 for information about setting up and configuring DNS).

Installing the First DC in a New Domain

To install AD, open Manage Your Server from the Start menu, and click Add or Remove a Role to launch the Configure Your Server Wizard. In the Server Role window, select Domain Controller (Active Directory) to open the Active Directory Installation Wizard. Click Next to move through the wizard, using the following guidelines to set up your first DC:

1. In the Domain Controller Type window, choose Domain Controller For A New Domain.

2. In the Create New Domain window, click Domain in a new forest.

3. In the New Domain Name page, enter the fully qualified domain name (FQDN) for the new domain. (That is, enter *companyname*.com, not *companyname*.)

4. In the NetBIOS Domain Name window, verify the NetBIOS name (not the FQDN).

5. In the Database and Log Folders window, accept the location for the database and log folders, or click Browse to choose a different location if you have some reason to prefer another folder.

6. In the Shared System Volume window, accept the location of the Sysvol folder, or click Browse to choose a different location.

7. In the DNS Registration Diagnostics window, verify whether an existing DNS server will be authoritative for this forest, or, if no DNS server exists, select the option to install and configure DNS on this server.

8. In the Permissions window, select one of the following permissions options (depending on the Windows versions of the client computers that will access this DC):

   ■ Permissions compatible with pre-Windows 2000 server operating systems

   ■ Permissions compatible only with Windows 2000 or Windows Server 2003 operating systems

9. Review the Summary window, and if you need to change anything, click Back to reconfigure your options. If everything is right, click Next to begin the installation.

When all the files have been copied to your hard drive, restart the computer.

Installing Additional DCs in a New Domain

You can add as many additional DCs to your domain as you deem necessary. If you upgrade an existing member server to a DC, remember that many configuration options for that server will disappear when it becomes a DC. For example, local user accounts and cryptography keys are removed during the upgrade to DC. If this member server had been storing files with EFS, you must remove the encryption. In fact, after removing the encryption, you should move the files to another computer.

To create and configure additional DCs in your new domain, launch the Active Directory Installation Wizard as described in the previous section. Then move through the wizard, using the following directions:

1. In the Domain Controller Type window, choose Additional Domain Controller For An Existing Domain.

2. In the Network Credentials window, type the username, password, and user domain of the user account you want to use for this operation.

3. In the Additional Domain Controller window, enter the full DNS name of the existing domain for which this server will become a DC.

4. In the Database and Log Folders window, accept the location for the database and log folders, or click Browse to choose a location other than the default.

5. In the Shared System Volume window, accept the location of the Sysvol folder, or click Browse to choose a different location.

6. In the Directory Services Restore Mode Administrator Password window, enter and confirm the password you want to assign to this server's Administrators account. (This account is used when the computer is started in Directory Services Restore Mode.)

7. Review the Summary page, and if your settings are correct, click Next to begin the installation. Click Back if you want to change any settings.

The system configuration is adapted to meet the requirements of a DC, and the first replication is initiated. After the data is transferred (which can take some time, so if the computer is in a secure location, go get some coffee), click Finish on the last wizard window and restart the computer. When the system reboots, the Configure Your Server Wizard appears, announcing that the computer is now a domain controller. Click Finish to close the wizard, or click one of the links in the window to learn more about maintaining domain controllers.

Creating Additional DCs by Restoring a Backup

You can create additional Windows Server 2003 DCs in the same domain as an existing DC quickly, by restoring the backup of a working Windows Server 2003 DC. It takes only three steps (which I'll go over in detail in the following sections):

1. Back up the system state of an existing Windows Server 2003 DC (I'll call it ServerOne) in the same domain.

2. Restore the system state to an alternate location, which is the Windows Server 2003 computer you want to turn into a DC (I'll call it ServerTwo).

3. Promote the target server (in this case, ServerTwo) to a DC by entering **DCPROMO /adv** at the command line.

This shortcut works for all scenarios: installing a new Windows Server 2003 domain, upgrading a Windows 2000 domain, and upgrading a Windows NT domain. As long as you've installed Windows Server 2003 on a computer, you can turn that computer into a DC with this method.

This is extremely useful if your domain has multiple sites, and your DCs replicate over a WAN, which is never as fast as communicating over Ethernet cable. The first replication seems to take forever when a new DC is established in a remote site. This method eliminates that first replication, and subsequent replications handle only changes (which doesn't take very long).

The following sections describe the guidelines you need to follow for this method of creating DCs.

Back Up the System State

Start Ntbackup.exe (from the Administrative Tools menu, or from the Run dialog) and make the following choices in the wizard windows:

1. Choose Back Up Files and Settings.

2. Choose Let Me Choose What To Back Up.

3. Select the System State option.

4. Select a location and a name for the backup file. I used a network sharepoint and named the file DCmodel.bkf (backup files have the extension .bkf).

5. Click Finish.

Ntbackup backs up the system state to the location you specified. You'll need access to the backup on the target computers, so it's easiest to use a network share, or burn the backup file onto a CD-R disc.

Restore the System State to the Target Computer

To restore the system state to the Windows Server 2003 computer you want to turn into a DC, go to that computer (which must have access to the backup file you created on the source computer). Start Ntbackup.exe on this computer, and use the following choices as you step through the wizard:

1. Choose Restore Files and Settings.

2. Catalog the file, and point to the location of the backup file.

3. Select the System State check box.

4. Click the Advanced button.

5. Choose Alternate Location from the drop-down list, and enter a location on the local hard drive (for example, you could create a directory named ADRestore on drive C).

6. Choose the option Replace Existing Files.

7. Select the options Restore Security Settings and Preserve Existing Volume Mount Points.

8. Click Finish.

Ntbackup restores the system state into five subdirectories in the location you specified in the wizard. The names of the directories match the names of the components of the system state, to wit:

- Active Directory (the database and log files)
- Sysvol (policies and scripts)
- Boot Files
- Registry
- COM+ Class Registration Database

When you run DCPROMO with the new /adv switch, the program looks for these subdirectories.

Run DC Promo

In the Run dialog, enter **dcpromo /adv** to launch the Active Directory Installation Wizard. Use the following instructions to make your choices in each window of the wizard:

1. Choose Additional Domain Controller for Exiting Domain.

2. Choose From These Restored Backup Files, and point to the location on the local drive into which you restored the backup. This is where the five subdirectories are located.

3. If the source DC held the global catalog, a wizard window appears to ask if you want to put the global catalog on this DC. You can choose Yes or No, depending on your own configuration plans. The process of creating a DC is actually a bit faster if you select Yes, but you may have decided to keep the global catalog on only one DC.

4. Enter the credentials for performing this operation (Administrator name and password).

5. Enter the name of the domain in which this DC will operate. It must be the same domain that the source DC is a member of.

6. Enter the locations for the AD database and logs (accepting the default locations is usually best).

7. Enter the location for SYSVOL (again, the default location is the best choice).

8. Enter the Administrator password to use if this computer ever has to be started in Directory Services Restore Mode.

9. Click Finish.

Dcpromo promotes the server to a DC, using the data in the restored files, which means you don't have to wait for this new DC to replicate every object in the AD from the existing DC. If any objects have been changed, added, or deleted since you began this process, the next replication will let the new DC catch up in a matter of seconds.

When the process is finished, restart the computer. You can delete the folders that hold the restored backup.

Upgrading Windows 2000 Domains

If you are upgrading Windows 2000 DCs to Windows Server 2003, or adding Windows Server 2003 DCs to a Windows 2000 domain, you have to prepare the domain (and the forest in which it resides) first, because of the difference in the schema between the Windows 2000 and Windows Server 2003 Active Directory. After that, installing and configuring the Windows Server 2003 Active Directory is rather simple.

 All of your Windows 2000 DCs must be running Service Pack 2 or higher.

 *Before beginning the upgrade of a Windows 2000 DC, you should check upgrade compatibility and copy updated Setup files by running **winnt32 /checkupgradeonly** from the Windows Server 2003 CD, or from a network sharepoint.*

Preparing the Forest and Domain

To prepare for the Windows 2000 to Windows Server 2003 upgrade, you must first prepare AD with adprep.exe, a command-line tool you can find in the i386 directory on the Windows Server 2003 CD. To accomplish this task, you can either take a Windows Server 2003 CD to the Windows 2000 DCs or put the i386 directory on a network sharepoint. You update your system by first updating the forest, then the domain(s):

■ The forest update is run on the schema master.

■ The domain update is run on the infrastructure master.

For most systems, the schema master and the infrastructure master are the same computer. (See "Understanding DC Roles," later in this chapter, to learn about roles.)

Upgrade the Forest

Since AD upgrades are top-down processes, start with the forest. In order to do this, take the following steps on the schema master computer:

1. Back up the schema master, including the system state.

2. Disconnect the schema master from the network.

3. Open a command prompt and move to the location of the Windows Server 2003 i386 directory (either the CD or the network sharepoint).

4. Enter **adprep /forestprep**.

After adprep.exe has finished, check for errors as follows:

Note any errors displayed by adprep.exe during execution. The errors are specific, and it's easy to identify what has to be corrected. Frequently the error message points out the steps needed to correct the problem. Take any necessary steps before moving ahead with upgrading the domain.

Check the System log of Event Viewer to see if any errors connected to the upgrade appear, or run a diagnostic tool such as Dcdiag. (If you see replication errors while the DC is disconnected from the network, that's a normal occurrence and isn't connected to adprep.exe.) If error messages indicate a significant problem, restore the schema master from the backup, and correct the configuration of the DC in order to run adprep /forestprep successfully.

If no errors occur, reconnect the schema master computer to the network. If the schema master is a different computer from the infrastructure master, wait for the changes made by adprep.exe to replicate from the schema master to the infrastructure master. Wait about a half hour if the schema master and infrastructure master are on the same LAN. Wait longer (half a day or a full day) if the computers are not on the same site.

 If you try to perform the domain upgrade on the infrastructure master before the changes from the forest upgrade are replicated, adprep.exe will display an error message to notify you that not enough time has elapsed to perform the domain upgrade.

Upgrade the Domain

After the schema master has replicated its changes to the other DCs, you can upgrade the domain by opening a command prompt on the infrastructure master and entering **adprep /domainprep**. Check for errors, as described in the previous section on upgrading the forest, and take any needed correctional steps.

Wait for the DC to replicate throughout the enterprise, which could take a few hours, or a full day, depending on the geographical configuration of your infrastructure.

Upgrade the Windows 2000 DCs

After the domain and forest have been prepared, you have two easy tasks to perform to upgrade each Windows 2000 DC to Windows Server 2003:

1. Run Setup.exe from the Windows Server 2003 CD or a network sharepoint to upgrade the operating system to Windows Server 2003.

2. After the operating system is installed, log on to the computer and run the Active Directory Installation Wizard (which appears automatically).

After you install the first DC in a domain, if you need additional DCs in the same domain, you can alternatively use the method of restoring the system state of the existing DC to another Windows Server 2003 computer. See the section "Creating Additional DCs by Restoring a Backup," earlier in this chapter.

Upgrading Windows NT 4 Domains

Before you start upgrading your Windows NT 4 DCs to Windows Server 2003, you need to understand some basic rules:

- DNS is required (see the next section, "DNS Decisions").
- The functional level of your AD (both forest and domain) can be manipulated until you've fully upgraded the enterprise. (See the section "Domain and Forest Functionality," later in the chapter.)

In addition, of course, you must understand and plan your AD hierarchy, which is a vastly different networking paradigm than you experienced in a Windows NT network.

DNS Decisions

DNS is required for Active Directory, and if you haven't been running DNS on your Windows NT 4 networks, you have two ways to remedy this missing ingredient:

- Configure DNS servers and set up DNS services for your Windows NT 4 network before upgrading.
- Install DNS on the first Windows Server 2003 DC you install during the upgrade, and then redistribute DNS services as discussed earlier in this chapter.

Note *If you install (or you previously installed) DNS on your Windows NT network, it's important to know that Windows NT DNS does not support dynamic updates, but Windows 2003/2000 DNS does.*

Domain and Forest Functionality

The phrase "domain and forest functionality" refers to the scope of Active Directory features you have available in your enterprise. The basis of functionality depends on the Windows versions of your DCs. For large enterprises, it's unrealistic to think that you'll upgrade every DC to Windows Server 2003 in one night, or even one weekend, presenting a whole new enterprise to your administrators and users when they return to work.

IT professionals also refer to the functionality level as "mode," a word that was frequently heard when Windows 2000 was released. At that time, upgraders referred to "mixed mode" (networks with DCs running Windows 2000 and Windows NT 4 BDCs still functioning on the network) and "native mode" (all DCs running Windows 2000). Mixed-mode enterprises could not take advantage of some AD features that were only available in native mode. For example, universal groups, nested groups, and the ability to move security principals (SIDs) between domains were only available in native mode.

The functionality levels available with Windows Server 2003 are more complex, and are divided between domain functionality and forest functionality (which was not an issue with Windows 2000 modes).

 You can view the current levels of your Windows Server 2003 domain in the Active Directory Domains and Trusts snap-in. Right-click the forest or domain object in the console pane and choose Properties. The current level is displayed on the General tab.

Domain Functionality

Domain functionality enables certain features on a specific domain. Four domain functional levels are available, depending on the Windows versions of the DCs in the domain.

Domain Functionality Level	Windows Versions on Domain DCs
Windows 2000 mixed	Windows NT 4
	Windows 2000
	Windows Server 2003
Windows 2000 native	Windows 2000
	Windows Server 2003
Windows Server 2003 interim	Windows NT 4
	Windows Server 2003
Windows Server 2003	Windows Server 2003

It's important to understand that the domain functionality level isn't a passive setting that the operating system settles itself into depending on what it finds. Instead, administrators set the level (and change it as the DCs are upgraded). During the upgrade to Windows Server 2003 of the first DC in your Windows NT 4 domain, you're asked to set the domain functionality level (the default is Windows 2000 mixed).

When you change (raise) the domain functional level, DCs running earlier versions of Windows can no longer be attached to the domain. For example, if you raise the domain functional level to Windows 2000 native, DCs running Windows NT 4 cannot be part of the domain.

Forest Functionality

Forest functionality enables AD features for all the domains within your forest. The following three forest functional levels are available:

Forest Functionality Level	Windows Versions on Forest DCs
Windows 2000	Windows 2000 Windows Server 2003
Windows Server 2003 interim	Windows NT 4 Windows Server 2003
Windows Server 2003	Windows Server 2003

When you upgrade your first Windows NT 4 domain to a new Windows Server 2003 forest, the domain functional level is Windows Server 2003 interim. Once the forest functional level has been raised, DCs running Windows NT 4 cannot be introduced into the forest.

Upgrading the DCs

It's been my experience, and that of other administrators I talked to, that the upgrade to Windows Server 2003 from Windows NT 4 is almost always uneventful. However, before beginning, you must take some preliminary steps:

- Be sure you've installed SP5 on all DCs in the domain.
- Back up all DCs.
- After replication of the accounts database to your BDCs, remove one of those BDCs from the LAN.

The first two items are mandatory, whereas the third item is my way of dealing with my own need to have a fallback scenario in case of a problem (it's safer to be pessimistic). It's not difficult to promote the BDC to a PDC, take the original (now upgraded) PDC off the LAN, and plug the cable of the previously removed BDC (now a PDC) back into the hub. Users can log in and work.

Upgrade the PDC

Start by upgrading the PDC. This is just an upgrade in the operating system, and the installation of the AD (which is what turns the computer into a DC) occurs afterwards. Use the Windows Server 2003 CD, or run Setup.exe from a network sharepoint. After the operating system is installed, when Windows Server 2003 reboots, the Active Directory Installation Wizard launches to walk you through the process of turning the computer into a domain controller.

The wizard requires that you join an existing domain tree or a forest, or create a new domain tree or forest. If you decide to join an existing domain tree, you reference the desired parent domain during the upgrade process. If you're creating a new child domain, a transitive trust relationship is established with the parent domain. Eventually, the parent domain DC replicates all schema and configuration information to this new child domain controller.

The existing Security Accounts Manager (SAM) object is copied from the registry to the new data store.

During the upgrade process, the wizard creates the necessary container objects for the accounts and groups from the Windows NT domain. (The container objects are named Users, Computers, and Builtin and you can see them in the Active Directory Users and Computers snap-in.)

Existing Windows NT 4 groups are located in different containers, depending on the nature of the group. Windows NT 4 built-in local groups (such as Administrators and Server Operators) are located in the Builtin container. Windows NT 4 global groups (such as Domain Admins) and any user-created groups (both local and global) are located in the Users container.

Upgrade the BDCs

After you've upgraded the PDC, you can proceed to upgrade all the BDCs (except the BDC you removed from the network as a fallback system). When all the BDCs are upgraded, and the system is running properly, reconnect the "savior" BDC to the network and upgrade it.

Understanding DC Roles

When Windows 2000 was first released, a great deal of discussion was generated about the fact that the PDC/BDC paradigm of NT 4 was no longer an administrative fact of life. Since the PDC/BDC rules were clunky and annoyingly complicated when a PDC went down or needed maintenance, this was good news. Along with all of these pronouncements was an oft-repeated statement that "all domain controllers are equal." This is not quite true, because all domain controllers do not have to be equal. Instead, a very logical set of roles exists to make it easier and more efficient to maintain your enterprise through Active Directory. The following five distinct roles are required to maintain a forest and domain(s), and you can assign roles to specific DCs, and assign multiple roles to a single DC:

- Schema master (forest role)
- Domain naming master (forest role)
- Relative ID (RID) master (domain role)
- Primary Domain Controller (PDC) emulator master (domain role)
- Infrastructure master (domain role)

These are all called operations master *roles, but administrators who deployed Windows 2000 during the beta period tend to call them* flexible single master operations (FSMO) *roles, which was Microsoft's original terminology. Microsoft changed the terminology to* operations master roles, *but some of us just can't break the habit of saying* fizz-mo. *Probably the easiest solution is to say "roles," and we'll all know what we're talking about.*

Replication: The Motivation for Roles

Windows NT ran on the single-master replication model, in which one DC stores the only modifiable copy of the directory (the role assigned to the PDC), and all the other DCs (the PDCs) store backup copies they receive through replication. The PDC was the only place you could modify the SAM. After replicating the SAM to BDCs, users could log on and be authenticated at a BDC, but changes in settings had to be sent directly to the PDC. If the PDC was across a WAN, making changes to domain objects was a slow process. If the WAN was down, changes couldn't be made at all. This can be a problem, because lots of changes take place on a domain. Users, computers, and groups are occasionally added to the domain, and user passwords are changed frequently.

Windows Server 2003 (and Windows 2000) supports the multimaster replication model, in which any DC can accept changes to the domain's structure and objects (making each DC a *master*). The changes are replicated to all the other DCs in the domain.

The multimaster approach to gathering information and replicating it is responsible for the impression that, starting with Windows 2000, all DCs are created equal. But if you think about it, it's not terribly efficient to have a pure multimaster domain. It's more work than necessary to replicate everything all over the place. And, sometimes it can be dangerous. For example, if two members of the IT department, working at different DCs, create objects with the same name but different configuration settings, the resulting changes in the AD database are conflicting.

To make the multimaster paradigm more efficient, you can assign roles. Assigning a role to a DC means that for this particular role, while all DCs are equal, this DC is "more equal than others" (that amusing phrase isn't original, and if I remember correctly, it's from George Orwell's satiric novel *Animal Farm*).

Assigning Roles

When you install the first Windows Server 2003 DC and create the first forest and domain, that DC has all the roles for the forest and the domain. As you add DCs to the domain, that doesn't change. When you add domains to the forest, the first DC in the domain has all the domain roles, and adding DCs doesn't change that fact.

Windows does not apply any form of intelligence, nor any automatic configuration efforts, to split roles among DCs. You must manually assign roles to DCs, and you can split the roles among as few or as many DCs as you wish. The configuration of your own enterprise is the guideline you use to perform these tasks. In the following sections, as I discuss each role, I'll also tell you how to assign the role to a particular DC.

Don't change roles in an automatic fashion—there's no theoretical "keep it balanced" paradigm here. This is one of those tasks that you perform only when needed, and your guiding principles are "keep it simple" and "if it ain't broke, don't fix it." Only change roles if it makes sense. For instance, if a DC with multiple roles is noticeably getting slower, transfer roles to other DCs. Or, if most of the administrators who manage and manipulate the enterprise are located at one site, but the forest roles are on a DC at another site, move the forest roles to DCs nearer the administrators, so work doesn't have to be done across a WAN.

Schema Master

The schema master is a forest role, and it's in charge of all updates and modifications to the schema. (Since the AD is a database, you can think of the schema as the field definitions of the database.) There can be only one schema master in the forest.

You can view and modify the schema, although it's unusual for administrators to make changes. Commonly, the schema is modified by adding objects for software applications, and detailed information about working with the schema is available from Microsoft through the MSDN program.

Install the Schema Snap-in

To view the schema, and to determine which DC in the forest has the role of schema master, you need to install the Active Directory Schema snap-in.

To install the snap-in so that you can install it in an MMC, open a command prompt and enter **regsvr32 schmmgmt.dll**, to register the snap-in. The system displays a success message. Click OK to clear the message, then exit the command window.

Load the Schema Snap-in in an MMC

To view the schema for your forest, you must load the snap-in in a MMC, using the following steps:

1. Choose Start | Run, type **mmc /a**, and click OK to open an MMC in author mode.

2. In the MMC, choose File | Add/Remove Snap-in to open the Add/Remove Snap-in dialog.

3. Click Add to open the Add Standalone Snap-in dialog.

4. Select Active Directory Schema, click Add, and then click Close (or double-click Active Directory Schema, and click Close) to return to the Add/Remove Snap-in dialog.

5. Click OK to load the snap-in into the console pane.

It's a good idea to save this console (so you don't have to go through all the steps to add the snap-in again), which you can do by choosing File | Save. Choose a filename that's relevant (such as schema). The system automatically adds the extension .msc. The saved console is forever available on the Administrative Tools submenu of the All Programs menu, so you don't have to open the Run box to use it.

When the snap-in loads, its object in the console pane specifies the name of the DC that holds the schema.

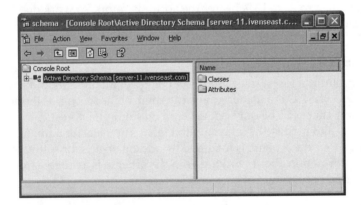

You can expand the schema object to examine the classes and attributes, which are rather complicated objects. It's beyond the scope of this book to discuss modifying or adding schema objects, because that task is best left to experienced programmers. Incidentally, adding objects to the schema is called "extending the schema."

Transfer the Schema Master Role to Another DC

If you're a member of the Schema Admins group, you can move the schema master role among DCs. You can perform this task from any Windows Server 2003 computer; you don't have to work at the DC.

Start by opening the schema MMC you saved (covered in the previous paragraphs). Then, follow these steps to transfer the role to another DC:

1. In the console pane, right-click the Active Directory Schema object and choose Change Domain Controller from the shortcut menu.

2. Click Specify Name and enter the name of the DC to which you want to transfer the schema master role. You can enter the NetBIOS name (Windows will automatically apply the FQDN).

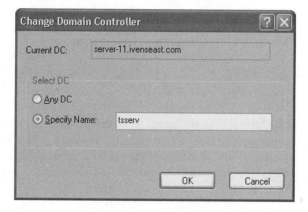

3. Click OK to return to the console, where the new server's name appears in the name of the Active Directory Schema object.

4. In the console pane, right-click the Active Directory Schema object again, and choose Operations Master to open the Change Schema Master dialog.

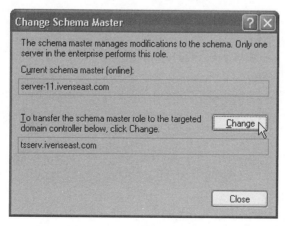

5. Click Change. If the Change button isn't accessible, you don't have the appropriate permissions to make this change. Add yourself to the Schema Admins group, log off and log on again, and return to this dialog.

6. Confirm the change, click OK to dismiss the message announcing success, and click Close.

The schema role is transferred.

Domain Naming Master

The domain naming master is a forest role, and it's in charge of the addition or deletion of domains in the forest. You can only have one domain naming master in the forest. You can create or remove domains from any DC, but the "keeper of the data" is the DC performing the domain naming master role, and it accepts or rejects your actions. This prevents administrators working at different DCs from creating a new domain with the same name but different configuration settings. First one in wins.

   A domain naming master in a forest set to Windows Server 2003 functional level is not required to be enabled as a global catalog. This is a change from Windows 2000.

The way you transfer the role of the domain naming master to another DC differs depending upon whether you're working at the current domain naming master or at the DC you want to turn into the domain naming master. However, in either case, you must be a member of the Domain Admins group (if you have only one domain in the forest) or the Enterprise Admins group (if you have multiple domains in the forest).

Transfer the Domain Naming Master Role Using the Current Role Holder

If you're working at the DC that is currently handling the role of domain naming master, follow these steps:

1. Open Active Directory Domains and Trusts from the Administrative Tools menu.

2. In the console pane, right-click Active Directory Domains and Trusts and choose Connect to Domain Controller to open the Connect to Domain Controller dialog (see Figure 18-1).

3. To select a different domain for this task, click Browse and select the domain.

4. Enter the name of the target DC, or select the name from the list of DCs.

5. Click OK.

6. In the console tree, right-click Active Directory Domains and Trusts again, and choose Operations Master to open the Change Operations Master dialog.

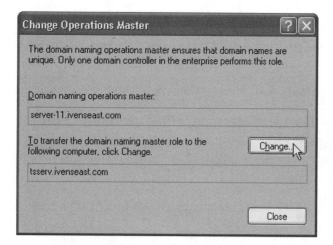

Figure 18-1. *Choose a domain and the DC in that domain that you want to act as the domain naming master.*

7. Click Change.

8. Confirm the change, click OK to dismiss the message announcing success, and click Close.

The domain naming master role is now transferred to the target computer.

Transfer the Domain Naming Master Role Using the New Role Holder

If you're working at the DC that you want to transfer the role to, it takes fewer steps to effect the role transfer:

1. Open Active Directory Domains and Trusts from the Administrative Tools menu.

2. Right-click Active Directory Domains and Trusts and choose Operations Master.

3. In the Change Operations Manager dialog, the name of the current domain naming master is displayed, and the system assumes you want to transfer the role to the current DC.

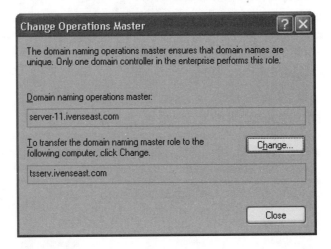

4. Click Change.

5. Confirm the change, click OK to dismiss the message announcing success, and click Close.

The domain naming master role is now transferred to the local computer.

Relative ID Master

This is a domain role, and you can only have one relative ID (RID) master in each domain. The RID master is the keeper of the pool of unique security IDs (SIDs). As discussed earlier in this chapter, administrators can create new user and computer objects on any

DC. When these new objects are created, they are assigned a SID that is created from multiple parts:

- A set of identifiers linked to the domain (all objects in the domain have the same domain identifiers)
- A set of identifiers linked to the new object, called a relative ID (RID), which is randomly generated

To make sure all objects have SIDs with unique RIDs, you need a single source for RIDs, and that's what the RID master does.

The RID master isn't contacted each time you create a new object; instead, it hands out pools of RIDs (500 RIDs at a time) to every DC. Just before a DC runs out of RIDs, it asks the RID master for 500 more. This means the RID master isn't contacted constantly, so its work doesn't impact network bandwidth on a daily basis. Of course, this lack of constant contact also means it's uncommon to face the need to move the RID master role to another, less busy, DC. However, if you have some reason to transfer the role to another DC in the same domain, you can perform the task from the current RID master, or from the DC to which you want to transfer the role.

Transfer the RID Master Role Using the Current Role Holder

To transfer the RID master role while working at the current role holder, follow these steps:

1. Open Active Directory Users and Computers.
2. In the console pane, right-click Active Directory Users and Computers and choose Connect to Domain Controller.
3. Enter the name of the target DC or select it from the list of available domain controllers.
4. Click OK.
5. In the console pane, right-click Active Directory Users and Computers again, and choose All Tasks | Operations Masters.
6. In the Operations Masters dialog, click the RID tab.
7. Click Change.
8. Confirm the change, click OK to dismiss the message announcing success, and click Close.

The RID master role is now transferred to the target computer.

Transfer the RID Master Role Using the New Role Holder

If you're working at the DC that you want to receive the role of RID master, use these steps to move the role from the current role holder:

1. Open Active Directory Users and Computers.

2. In the console pane, right-click Active Directory Users and Computers and choose All Tasks | Operations Masters.

3. In the Operations Masters dialog, click the RID tab.

4. Click Change.

5. Confirm the change, click OK to dismiss the message announcing success, and click Close.

The RID master role is now transferred to the local computer.

PDC Emulator Master

The Primary Domain Controller (PDC) emulator master is a domain role, and there's one permitted for each domain in your forest. You must be a member of the Domain Admins group to manipulate the PDC emulator master. The PDC emulator master role is rather interesting, because it changes some of its responsibilities, depending on the functional level of the domain in which it's working.

PDC Emulator Master in a Mixed Windows Version Network

Until your network is running entirely with Windows versions that don't need a PDC, the DC that's designated as the PDC emulator master pretends to be a PDC, and acts as if it were part of a network ruled by a PDC and BDCs (hence the name of the role). If you haven't yet replaced all the NT 4 DCs on your network, the remaining NT 4 DCs (all BDCs) won't accept account changes and will insist on finding a PDC to make those changes. In addition, an NT 4 BDC will access this emulated PDC when it needs to update the SAM. If you need to establish a trust with an NT 4 network, the NT 4 network won't "talk" to any computer that isn't a PDC. NT 4 is trained that way, and you can't teach an old dog new tricks.

But the need for a PDC emulator goes further than that, and continues to be needed even after you've eliminated all the NT 4 DCs from your system. Client computers may require the services of a PDC. For example, Network Neighborhood and My Network Places use "browsing" functions, and require the election of a "master browser" (a computer that tracks the names of all the computers on the network so they can be displayed in these network folders). Because the PDC is, by default, the master browser, having a PDC emulator master to assume this task is a lot easier than going through all the steps required to change the way the master browser is elected.

PDC Emulator Master in a Windows Server 2003/ Windows 2000 Network

Even when your network is composed entirely of computers running Windows 2000/ XP/2003 Server, the PDC emulator master continues to serve a useful purpose. In addition to continuing to provide master browser services, it also provides the important function of "instant replication." While most AD changes are replicated around your enterprise at regularly scheduled intervals, one change you make to the AD is marked "urgent delivery" and is replicated immediately. That change is a user's password change. As soon as a password is changed on any DC in the enterprise, the DC that accepted the password change contacts the PDC emulator master and records the change. The next scheduled replication is irrelevant.

If a user attempts to log on with this new password to a DC other than the one that originally accepted the change, that DC may not yet have been through a replication process. When the password doesn't match, before denying the user the right to log on, the DC contacts the PDC emulator master to ask, "Anything new on this guy?" The PDC emulator master answers, "Yep, new password, here it is, and if this is the password he entered, let him on."

The advantage of the PDC emulator master is really appreciated by administrators who support users in multiple sites. For example, suppose you have a user who was away from the office when her password expired, and the domain is configured to insist that a user must log on to change passwords. Or, suppose you have a forgetful user who continuously typed wrong passwords until the tolerance for a lockout was met. The user is in your East Overcoat, Iowa branch office, and the administrators are in the Denver, Colorado office. Without the clever intervention of a PDC emulator master, after entering a new password in the user's record (in Active Directory Users and Computers), in the Denver office, you'd have to wait until the next replication before the new password reached the authenticating DC in East Overcoat. Even if you manually forced a replication, replicating over a WAN can be a slow process, and your user is unable to do her job for some time. Also, if you support roaming users in a system that insists on regular password changes, you can easily see the advantage of a PDC emulator master.

Forestwide Time Synchronization

Perhaps the important (and most misunderstood) role of the PDC emulator master is its responsibility for synchronizing time across the forest. Windows 2000/XP/2003 Server computers are configured to check with a time server periodically to make sure their time synchronizes with the time on the time server. The PDC emulator master is the authoritative time server for the forest.

While synchronized clocks are obviously handy for making sure time stamps on documents and database entries are accurate, the reason for synchronizing time in a Windows Server 2003 or Windows 2000 network is far more important than that, because it's tied in with the security of your enterprise. Kerberos uses synchronized time as one of the checkpoints before allowing users to access network resources. Kerberos operates under the philosophy that if your computer clock has a different time than the clock on the network computer you're accessing, you're an intruder.

For information on the time services required in your enterprise, see the section "W32Time" later in this chapter. After you learn about the importance of time services, you'll know that if you transfer the PDC emulator master role to another DC, you also need to configure the new DC for time synchronization with an outside authoritative time source.

Transfer the PDC Emulator Master Role Using the Current Role Holder

To transfer the PDC emulator master role while working at the current role holder, follow these steps:

1. Open Active Directory Users and Computers.

2. In the console pane, right-click Active Directory Users and Computers and choose Connect to Domain Controller.

3. Enter the name of the target DC or select it from the list of available domain controllers.

4. Click OK.

5. In the console pane, right-click Active Directory Users and Computers again, and choose All Tasks | Operations Masters.

6. In the Operations Masters dialog, click the PDC tab.

7. Click Change.

8. Confirm the change, click OK to dismiss the message announcing success, and click Close.

The PDC emulator master role is now transferred to the target computer.

Transfer the PDC Emulator Master Role at the New Role Holder

If you're working at the DC that you want to receive the role of PDC emulator master, use these steps to move the role from the current role holder:

1. Open Active Directory Users and Computers.

2. In the console pane, right-click Active Directory Users and Computers and choose All Tasks | Operations Masters.

3. In the Operations Masters dialog, click the PDC tab.

4. Click Change.

5. Confirm the change, click OK to dismiss the message announcing success, and click Close.

The PDC emulator master role is now transferred to the local computer.

Infrastructure Master

The infrastructure master is a domain role, and there is a single infrastructure master for each domain. You must be a member of the Domain Admins group to manipulate the settings. The infrastructure master is responsible for keeping track of objects in its domain, and providing that information to all the DCs in the domain. To do so, it compares its data with the global catalog, and when there's a difference, it requests an update from the global catalog. (The global catalog receives regular updates of objects in all domains through replication, so the global catalog data is always up to date.)

In essence, the data that's kept on the infrastructure master is a domain catalog. And therein lies a potential problem, because the global catalog takes precedence, and if it resides on the DC that's acting as an infrastructure master, the domain data is never replicated to the other DCs in the domain.

You don't have to worry about this if you have only one domain, and only one DC in that domain (because the global catalog *is* the domain catalog). Also, if all the domain controllers in a domain are hosting the global catalog, all of the domain controllers will have the current data and it doesn't matter which domain controller holds the infrastructure master role. For information on the global catalog, see the section "Global Catalog," later in this chapter.

Transfer the Infrastructure Master Role Using the Current Role Holder

To transfer the infrastructure master role while working at the current role holder, follow these steps:

1. Open Active Directory Users and Computers.

2. In the console pane, right-click Active Directory Users and Computers and choose Connect to Domain Controller.

3. Enter the name of the target DC or select it from the list of available domain controllers.

4. Click OK.

5. In the console pane, right-click Active Directory Users and Computers again, and choose All Tasks | Operations Masters.

6. In the Operations Masters dialog, click the Infrastructure tab.

7. Click Change.

8. Confirm the change, click OK to dismiss the message announcing success, and click Close.

The infrastructure master role is now transferred to the target computer.

Transfer the Infrastructure Master Role at the New Role Holder

If you're working at the DC that you want to receive the role of infrastructure master, use these steps to move the role from the current role holder:

1. Open Active Directory Users and Computers.

2. In the console pane, right-click Active Directory Users and Computers and choose All Tasks | Operations Masters.

3. In the Operations Masters dialog, click the Infrastructure tab.

4. Click Change.

5. Confirm the change, click OK to dismiss the message announcing success, and click Close.

The infrastructure master role is now transferred to the local computer.

W32Time

Windows Server 2003 includes the Windows time service (W32Time), which makes sure that all Windows 2000/XP/2003 computers on your network have synchronized clocks. This isn't a trivial feature, because Kerberos security and other network-wide features are linked to the time service.

Kerberos authentication fails if the clock time of the client computer and the authenticating DC are more than five minutes apart. This interval is called the Maximum Tolerance for Synchronization of Computer Clocks. You can use group policy to change this value, but doing so weakens network security. (Kerberos policies are in the Default Domain Policy at Computer Configuration\Windows Settings\Security Settings\Account Policies\Kerberos Policy.)

Replication also depends on accurate time stamps, because the replication process uses "latest change" to determine whether to replicate data. What's more important, however, is the fact that if the time difference between two DCs is greater than the Kerberos Maximum Tolerance for Synchronization of Computer Clocks, authentication between DCs fails, and that failure means replication processes won't run.

Just as important, computers with different times can wreak havoc on data file writes. Inaccurate time stamps can compromise functions such as synchronizing offline files and working with collaborative documents.

Understanding the Time Synchronization Hierarchy

Within your enterprise, time synchronization is configured on a hierarchical basis, so every computer on the network doesn't have to check its clock against one computer. At the top of the hierarchy is the *authoritative time server*, selected as follows:

- For a domain, the authoritative time server is the PDC emulator master.

- If you have multiple domains, the PDC emulator master of the first domain you created in the forest is the authoritative time server for the forest.

All Windows Server 2003 and Windows 2000 DCs are on the second level, and they sync their clocks to the authoritative time server. All member servers and workstations running Windows 2000 or later automatically sync their clocks to the DC that authenticates them.

Windows Server 2003 (and Windows 2000) offers the chance to put another time server at the very top of the hierarchy—an outside clock that is deemed to be perfectly accurate. You can have your authoritative time server sync its clock to that clock. See the section "Using an External Time Server," later in this chapter, to learn how to find and connect to an external clock.

Understanding the Synchronization Process

As computers running Windows 2000 and later log on to the domain, the Windows time service checks the time on an appropriate computer to determine the *target time*, which is the time the computer wants to match on its own clock. For DCs, the target time is the time on the authoritative time server. For all other computers, the target time is the time on the authenticating DC.

If the target time doesn't match the time on the local clock, the logging-on computer takes the following steps to adjust its own clock:

■ If the target time is later than local time, W32Time automatically sets the local time to the target time.

■ If the target time is earlier than local time by three minutes or less, W32Time slews (the time service jargon for "slows") the local clock until the times match.

■ If the target time is more than three minutes behind the local time, W32Time automatically resets the local time to the target time.

Time synchronization isn't only a logon process—the computers continue to synchronize clocks periodically. The computers connect to their time source computers once each *period*, and each computer defines its period in the following manner:

■ The initial period is 45 minutes.

■ If the time synchronization is successful three consecutive times using the 45 minute period, the new period becomes eight hours.

■ If the time doesn't sync three consecutive times, the period remains at 45 minutes and the process of defining the period continues until three successful synchs are accomplished.

■ If, after the period has been changed to eight hours, the time doesn't sync three consecutive times, the period is changed to 45 minutes and the process begins again.

Before attempting to sync time, the computer that's setting time exchanges a data packet with the computer that's providing the time. The purpose of the data packet exchange is to measure the latency (delay in communications) between the computers. That latency is taken into consideration when the clock times are compared. This means that time services over a WAN are as efficient as those services performed over a LAN.

Synchronizing Downlevel Computers

Downlevel Windows computers don't have the W32Time service, so there are no automatic checks for time synchronization available. That's not a threat to authentication or connectivity, because Kerberos doesn't authenticate these computers. However, for the purpose of accurate time stamps on documents, or database records, it's a good idea to try to keep the clocks of downlevel computers as close to the rest of the network clocks as possible.

Downlevel computers can manually synchronize their clocks to an already-synchronized clock by using the following command:

net time \\\\<*ComputerName*> /set /yes

where:

<*ComputerName*> is the name of a computer within the domain that you believe has an accurate clock.

/set instructs the computer to sync time (instead of just checking the time of the remote computer).

/yes confirms that the time on the remote computer should be written to the local computer.

You can enter this command in a batch file and place a shortcut to the batch file in the Startup folder of the Programs menu to synchronize time every time the computer starts up, or you can place a shortcut to the command on the desktop and let users synchronize time at will.

In addition, if your network is operating among sites in different time zones, don't worry—Windows automatically adjusts for time zones (as long as you correctly configured your computers for their local time zones).

Using an External Time Server

It doesn't matter to your network services (such as Kerberos) whether the clocks are accurate in terms of the current time of the outside world; it only matters that they're synchronized among themselves within the tolerance permitted. However, as long as all the computer clocks on your network are synchronizing themselves, it's a nice touch to make sure their clocks match the rest of the world.

You can assure your clock times are accurate by letting your authoritative time server sync its clock to an external clock that's known to be accurate. Then, as your enterprise computers sync their times through the hierarchy, every clock in the system will be accurate.

You have two ways to let your authoritative time server sync its time to make sure its clock matches the real world: buy a doohickey that performs this task, such as an atomic clock device that gets signals from satellites, which you can attach to your authoritative time server; or use the Internet to access an external clock with accurate time. I'm making an assumption about the choice you make, so for the rest of this section I'll discuss the Internet option.

Locating an External Time Server

Time servers are available around the world, and are maintained in a hierarchy. Primary (stratum 1) servers are the most accurate, but secondary (stratum 2) servers are generally either synchronized perfectly with stratum 1 servers or are only slightly off the clock ticks of the stratum 1 servers. The difference between stratum 1 and stratum 2 servers is never more than a few nanoseconds, which you certainly won't notice (nor care about).

- A list of stratum 1 servers is at www.eecis.udel.edu/~mills/ntp/clock1a.html.
- A list of stratum 2 servers is at www.eecis.udel.edu/~mills/ntp/clock2a.htm.

Stratum 1 time servers are frequently very busy and can time out before synchronizing your authoritative time server, so it's always a good idea to select a stratum 2 server as your external time source.

Each list contains the NTP time servers available for public access, including any restrictions on their use (for example, some time server sites require you to notify them that you're using their clock). The lists are sorted by country code. You can only select time servers that use the Simple Network Time Protocol (which is the protocol used by the Windows time services), and these servers are marked as "NTP Servers."

If you don't want to search, Microsoft offers the following suggestions for external time servers (all of which are open-access servers, which means you don't have to ask permission):

- time.windows.com
- time.nist.gov
- ntp2.usno.navy.mil
- tock.usno.navy.mil

Configuring Synchronization with an External Time Server

The only computer in your enterprise that can access an external time server is your authoritative time server (the PDC emulator master). To set up time synchronization with an external NTP time clock, enter the following command from a command prompt:

net time /setsntp:*server_list*

where *server_list* is one or more addresses for NTP time servers.

The advantage of entering a list of target external servers is that if one server isn't available, the authoritative time server tries to contact the next server on the list. Separate each address with a space, and enclose the entire list within quotation marks (for example: net time /setsntp:"time.windows.com time.nist.gov").

 You can enter the IP addresses for the external servers instead of URLs, but if the site moves to a different IP address, you won't follow it.

You only have to enter this command once, because the system writes the list of NTP time servers to the registry, to let your authoritative time server synchronize its clock to the external source automatically. The addresses you specify in the command are saved as a unit, which is replaced in its entirety if you enter the command again. This means that if you want to add another address, you must enter the command as a full list, including both the original and new addresses. On the other hand, if you enjoy the danger of working in the registry, you could add a new address directly in HKEY_LOCAL_MACHINE\SYSTEM\CurrentControlSet\Services\W32Time\Parameters.

To see the current NTP server list, enter **net time /querysntp** at a command prompt on your authoritative time server. The system returns the address(es) of the external time servers.

Caution *Make sure the date on your authoritative time server is correct, because some Internet clocks won't provide information to a computer that has the wrong date.*

W32Time Event Log Entries

One of the annoying problems with the Windows time service is its lack of overt warnings. If your authoritative time server fails to get a time sync from an Internet clock, no warning message displays. The same is true when your DCs fail to get a time sync from the authoritative server, or your network computers fail to sync with their authenticating DCs.

However, Event Viewer reports problems with the time service, although many of the warnings and errors are vague, so it's not always easy to figure out what's going on. W32Time error messages appear in the System log with the source W32Time (click the Source column heading to sort the log by source).

If the authoritative time server isn't available and you experience DC replication problems, you might not realize that the problem lies with the time service. If you see an event with the text "The RPC server is unavailable," a time synchronization failure is the likely source.

If a Windows 2000 or later client can't find a DC for authentication, the client can log on anyway, because the system caches authentication credentials by default. However, the time synchronization process fails, which causes W32Time to log event ID 11, "The NTP Server didn't respond," in the System log.

On the authoritative time server, if you see the warning event "Event ID 11, The NTP server didn't respond," you probably have one of the following problems:

- The Internet time server is no longer available.
- Your proxy server may be interfering with access to the Internet time server.

If the Internet time server isn't available, locate another server, and use the **net time /setsntp** command to specify its address.

If you're running Windows proxy server, the authoritative time server is probably prohibited from accessing the Internet time server. The Windows time service runs under the local system account on the internal server, and the Access Control feature in the proxy server will not give that account access to data exchanges over the Internet. Use one of the following cures:

- Disable the Access Control feature for the Winsock proxy by clearing the Enable Access Control check box on the Permissions tab of the Properties dialog of the Winsock Proxy service in IIS Manager.
- Set the authoritative time server to access the proxy server for its NTP server, and configure the proxy to point to the external server.

Global Catalog

Because the discussions of domain controller roles and jobs in this chapter included references to global catalogs, it seems appropriate to present an overview of this feature. By overview, I mean I'll briefly explain what a global catalog does, and how you can enable or disable it on a DC. I'll not get into a discussion of adding objects and attributes to the global catalog, because that topic is beyond the scope of this book. However, if you've been running Windows 2000, and you're familiar with this process, you'll welcome the change in Windows Server 2003 that changes replication after new objects are added—only the changes are replicated, not the full global catalog.

The global catalog is a directory database of AD objects in the forest. As you can imagine, for a large enterprise, the size of the global catalog is enormous, and even for smaller companies, the size can be quite substantial.

On any given domain controller that holds a copy, the global catalog has a full copy of all objects in the directory for its host domain, and a partial copy of all objects for all the other domains in the forest. Those partial copies include the objects that are most commonly used in user search operations, which gives you efficient searches across the forest without weighing down the network with constant queries to all the domain controllers in the forest.

Global Catalog Searches

When a user performs a search for a user, a printer, or any other resource in the forest, the search takes place in a global catalog. The search request is routed to the default global catalog port 3268, and then sent to a global catalog for resolution. If the DC holding the global catalog has the result, it returns it. If the target of the search is in another domain, and the object isn't in the DC's partial catalog, the DC queries the DC holding the global catalog of the other domain, and returns the results to the user.

Global Catalog Authentication Tasks

If a user logs on to a computer in one domain using a logon name for a user in another domain, the authenticating DC doesn't have knowledge of the account, and contacts a global catalog. The global catalog resolves the logon name to a user principal name (UPN), which is the user's account in the form *UserName@domain.company* (for example, billg@executives.microsoft.com). Because the UPN reveals the domain in which the user account resides, the authenticating DC can allow the user to log on.

Global Catalogs Maintain Universal Groups

In a multidomain environment, global group memberships are stored in each domain, but universal group memberships are stored only in a global catalog. (Remember that universal groups are only available when domains are set to Windows 2000 native domain functional level or higher.)

When a user who belongs to a universal group logs on to any domain, the global catalog provides universal group membership information for the user's account at logon. That information is not available from any domain-object-based database.

Universal Group Membership Caching

Windows Server 2003 has improved the way universal group membership works when authenticating users. The first time a member of a universal group logs on, the universal group membership information that's obtained from the global catalog is cached. In subsequent logons, the authenticating Windows Server 2003 DC obtains the universal group membership information from its local cache. For remote-site users, where the global catalog isn't on the site, this saves a great deal of time and bandwidth. And, of course, it means universal group members can continue to log on if the connection to the global catalog is unavailable.

Windows Server 2003 DCs check the global catalog every eight hours to update its cached information, and can update as many as 500 universal group memberships with one update request. This is frequently faster and more efficient than putting a global catalog on the site, because replication of the global catalog is a time-consuming process. (See Chapter 19 to learn about replication of AD, including the global catalog.)

Local caching is not enabled by default, so if you want to enable this feature on Windows Server 2003 DCs that have a slow connection to the global catalog, use the following steps:

1. Open Active Directory Sites and Services from the Administrative Tools menu.

2. In the console pane, select the target Site object.

3. In the details pane, right-click the NTDS Settings object and choose Properties.

4. Select the check box labeled Enable Universal Group Membership Caching.

NTDS Site Settings Properties   [?][X]

Site Settings | Object | Security

NTDS Site Settings

Description: [   ]

[Change Schedule...]

Inter-Site Topology Generator

Server: [TSSERV   ]

Site: [Default-First-Site   ]

Universal Group Membership Caching

[✓] Enable Universal Group Membership Caching

Refresh cache from: [<Default>   ▼]

[OK   ] [Cancel] [Apply]

5. In the Refresh Cache From field, either select a site from the drop-down list or accept <Default> to refresh the cache from the nearest site that has a global catalog.

Enabling/Disabling Global Catalog on a DC

You can enable or disable the global catalog on a DC, which means you're specifying whether or not a particular DC should hold a copy. By default, the first DC in the first domain in the forest holds the global catalog, but you might want to move the global catalog to another DC (one that's less busy or has more disk space). In addition, you might want to enable a DC in a remote site to hold a copy, so the DC doesn't have to authenticate or resolve global objects across a slow WAN connection. Use the following steps to enable or disable the global catalog on a DC:

1. Open Active Directory Sites and Services from the Administrative Tools menu.

2. Expand the objects in the console pane to \Sites*TargetSite*\Servers\ *TargetDomainController*.

3. In the details pane, right-click the NTDS Settings object and choose Properties.

4. In the Global Catalog check box, add a check mark to enable the global catalog, or clear the check box to disable the global catalog (after you've enabled another DC, and waited for the global catalog to be installed).

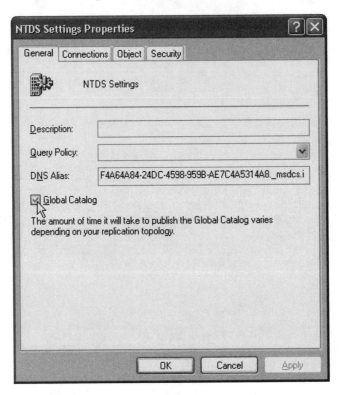

The
Complete
Reference

Chapter 19

Understanding
Active Directory

Active Directory is the database of the Windows Server 2003 platform. Active Directory contains information about objects such as printers, network accounts, groups, servers, and printers as well as other information about the domain. Active Directory is supported on Windows Server 2003, Enterprise Edition, and Datacenter Edition. Active Directory cannot be installed on Windows 2003 Web Edition servers.

Active Directory provides a hierarchical structure for the administrator to organize the objects in their domain. The proper planning of the directory structure can allow the administrator to simplify the delegation of administration and ease the management of desktop systems.

Because AD is a Lightweight Directory Access Protocol (LDAP) database, you can conduct queries on objects contained in the directory. Tools are provided to allow you to apply filters to your queries, helping you to narrow down your searches to find the information you need.

This chapter describes the structure of Active Directory and provides you with some strategies on structuring your own Active Directory database. It also covers how to create queries and use the tools provided by Active Directory Users and Computers to find information.

Active Directory Structure

Active Directory provides you with a hierarchical structure for organizing objects contained in your domain. Objects can be users, printers, and groups, for example. Chapter 18 discussed running DCPROMO to promote your Windows 2003 member server to a domain controller. After running DCPROMO, your server will have a default install of Active Directory.

Active Directory Users and Computers

Active Directory Users and Computers is your interface for managing Active Directory objects such as users, computers, and groups. To view your install of Active Directory, select Start | Programs | Administrative Tools | Active Directory Users and Computers (see Figure 19-1).

Active Directory Users and Computers looks similar to Windows Explorer. It has folder icons and objects contained in the folders. These folders are known as organizational units (OUs) and containers. OUs are the folders with the book icon in the middle. AD comes with a default OU of Domain Controllers. Containers are the folders that do not have any icon.

Organizational Units

OUs are objects in Active Directory that can be user defined and to which a group policy can be applied. By default, AD contains the Domain Controllers OU, which contains all domain controllers within your domain. Every time you run DCPROMO

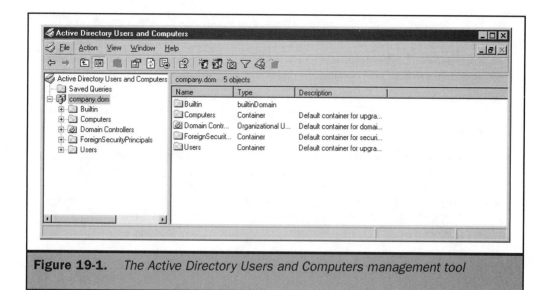

Figure 19-1.   *The Active Directory Users and Computers management tool*

on a member server within a domain, that computer account will be moved into the Domain Controllers OU.

An administrator can also create OUs. Usually, OUs are created to simplify administrative control of the domain. To create an OU:

1. Right-click the node for which you wish to create an OU (for example the domain node), and select New | Organizational Unit.

2. In the New Object – Organizational Unit dialog, type the name of your OU. In this example, Sales is used.

3. Click the OK button.

4. The dialog closes and you see the newly created OU underneath the domain node.

You can create and nest OUs underneath your new OU, but it usually is not recommended to go over five levels deep when creating your OU structure.

Containers

Containers are created by Windows Server 2003 for various reasons. By default the following containers are created:

- **Builtin**   Contains several default domain local groups (which are discussed further in Chapter 20).

- **Computers**   By default, when you add a computer to your domain, the computer account is located in the Computers container. You can move the computer accounts at a later time if you wish to organize them in an OU created by you.

■ **ForeignSecurityPrincipals** Contains proxy objects for your domain to interact with NT 4 and below domains as well as foreign domains outside your forest.

■ **Users** Default area for Windows accounts; when migrating from an NT 4 domain, your user accounts will be located here. You can move the user accounts to other OUs if you want.

If you select View | Advanced Features in Active Directory Users and Computers, you should see the following additional containers:

■ **LostAndFound** Contains objects that were deleted in the domain if the object was moved to an OU or container that was deleted before the directory was replicated.

■ **NTDS Quotas** Several new technologies have been added to Windows Server 2003 by being able to set quotas on Active Directory objects. This container stores information about the directory services quotas.

■ **Program Data** A new container for Windows Server 2003 for storing authorization manager policies for applications.

■ **System** Holds several child containers:

  ■ **AdminSDHolder** Used to control permissions of user accounts that are members of the built-in Administrators or Domain Admins groups.

  ■ **ComPartitionSets** Used in application development, contains information for COM+ partition sets, which allow users in a domain to access application services provide by the COM+ application.

  ■ **Default Domain Policy** Contains the default security groups and permissions for your domain.

  ■ **Dfs-Configuration** Contains information on the fault-tolerant Distributed File System. See Chapter 16 for more information on DFS.

  ■ **DomainUpdates** If you performed an update from Windows NT or Windows 2000 to Windows Server 2003, containers will be created here.

  ■ **File Replication Service** Provides information for scheduling the replication of the System Volume (SYSVOL) for your domain.

  ■ **FileLinks** Used by the Distributed Link Tracking service for tracking information on files that have been moved to different NTFS volumes.

  ■ **IP Security** Contains the IPSec policies for your domain that provide secure network communications between systems.

  ■ **Meetings** Used for holding information pertaining to Microsoft NetMeeting meetings.

- **MicrosoftDNS** Active Directory integrated DNS zones are stored in this container. All zone records are stored here and then replicated to other DNS servers for the same AD zone in the domain. For more information on AD integrated DNS, refer to Chapter 12.

- **Policies** Contains the Group Policy Objects (GPOs) for your domain. Read Chapter 22 for more information on GPOs.

- **RAS and IAS Servers Access Check** Contains information on Remote Access Services and Internet Authentication Services for your domain.

- **RpcServices** Remote Procedure Call Name Service for looking up domains that are pre–Windows 2000.

- **Winsock Services** Socket-based services which use the Registration and Resolution Protocol are published in this container.

- **WMIPolicy** Contains Windows Management Instrumentation GPOs for your domain. WMI Filters are only applied to Windows XP and later.

Active Directory Objects

Another item contained in Active Directory are objects. Objects are placed within the OUs and containers within Active Directory. You can place objects within a particular OU and then define a group policy on that OU to ease administrative tasks or control the computer environment. Examples of objects are printers, user accounts, computer accounts, and security groups.

LDAP and Active Directory

Active Directory can be queried using the Lightweight Directory Access Protocol (LDAP), which is supported by several platforms. LDAP specifies a naming path that defines any particular Active Directory object, OU, or container. The naming paths used to access Active Directory are described in this section.

Distinguished Names

Every object within Active Directory has its own distinguished name (DN). The DN defines a full LDAP path to get to a particular Active Directory object. A DN contains the following path attributes:

- **Domain Component (DC)** Used to define a component of the DNS name of an Active Directory object

- **Organizational Unit (OU)** An organizational unit

- **Common Name (CN)** An object other than a DC or OU; for example, a CN could be used to define a computer or user account

The following is an example of what the DN of the Active Directory OU Domain Controllers in the fictitious domain company.dom would look like:

```
OU=Domain Controllers, DC=company,DC=dom
```

So, what does this DN describe? By looking at the DN, you can tell that the OU of Domain Controllers is in the domain company.dom.

As another example, suppose you have an OU structure of Sales underneath the domain of company.dom. Under the Sales OU, you have another OU called West. Within the West OU, you have a user account called Mary Smith. This account would be accessed using the following DN:

```
CN=Mary Smith,OU=West,OU=Sales, DC=company,DC=dom
```

You can see that the DN works from the bottom of the Active Directory path, starting at the object and working its way up to the domain root.

Relative Distinguished Names

The relative distinguished name of the LDAP path contains the information about an Active Directory object in the context of the current path you are focused on. From the previous example of obtaining an object using the DN, in which you had the user account Mary Smith, the DN was

```
CN=Mary Smith,OU=West,OU=Sales, DC=company,DC=dom
```

The relative distinguished name for this object would be

```
CN=Mary Smith
```

Planning Your Active Directory Structure

You should take very seriously the planning of your AD structure. Having a well-structured directory can ease administrative tasks and allow you to delegate control of objects. This section discusses some things you should consider when creating your AD structure.

Centralized or Decentralized Administrative Control

How is the information services support for your organization configured? Some organizations have a large centralized IT staff who administer Active Directory. Other organizations are spread out and have some technical support on location. In an environment in which you have decentralized administration, you may want to configure your directory structure in a way that makes it easier to delegate administrative tasks to the local administrators.

Delegation of Control Wizard

Using the Delegation of Control Wizard, you can select a particular OU and delegate administrative control of that OU. This allows you to allow administrative authority to those who know their area of responsibility.

Say, for example, that you have a division that employs temporary staff. The people they hire do not stay long with the company. The division may have several resources they like to restrict by group membership and allow access to those people. The division may have several resources for which they would like to restrict access to the temporary staff using a group policy or implementing security.

Use the following procedure to run and delegate administrative control of a particular OU:

1. Right-click the OU and select the Delegation of Control Wizard from the context menu.

2. Click the Next button and you will see another dialog allowing you to add groups and/or users to delegate control to. Click the Add button to add the groups or users to the wizard. Click the Next button to get to the next dialog.

3. In the Task to Delegate dialog, you can select which common tasks you wish to delegate to the selected user and/or group accounts:

   - Create, delete, and manage user accounts
   - Reset user passwords and force password change at next logon
   - Read all user information
   - Create, delete, and manage groups
   - Modify the membership of a group
   - Manage Group Policy links
   - Generate Resultant Set of Policy (Planning)
   - Generate Resultant Set of Policy (Logging)
   - Create, delete, and manage inetOrgPerson accounts
   - Reset inetOrgPerson passwords and force password change at next logon
   - Read all inetOrgPerson information

4. In addition to common tasks, you can also define custom tasks to delegate. By selecting the Custom option and clicking the Next button, you are presented with a large number of Active Directory objects and what type of task you want the selected delegates to be able to do on these objects.

5. If you selected Custom, you can then apply the appropriate permissions on the selected objects.

Creating Custom MMC Consoles

Once you complete the Delegation of Control Wizard, the selected groups should then be able to perform administrative tasks. You can create custom Microsoft Management Consoles (MMCs) and then distribute them to the individuals you delegated authority to. By creating custom MMCs, you can customize the administrative interface to the objects so that the delegated administrators only see what they have permission to administer.

In the following procedure we will create a custom MMC for displaying and allowing access to a specific OU in Active Directory.

1. To create a custom MMC, select Start | Run and enter **mmc** in the Run dialog.

2. The MMC will open with the default title of Console1. To create a console to manage a specific OU, select File | Add/Remove Snap-In.

3. In Add/Remove Snap-In dialog, click the Add button.

4. In the Add Standalone Snap-in dialog, select Active Directory Users and Computers, and click the Add button.

5. Click the Close button in the Add Standalone Snap-in dialog to return to the Add/Remove Snap-in dialog.

6. You should see the snap-in appear in the Add/Remove Snap-in dialog. Click the OK button to return to the MMC.

7. Expand the Active Directory Users and Computers snap-in and drill down to the OU you wish to create the MMC for.

8. Right-click the OU and select New Window From Here. This opens a new console window with just your selected OU in focus. Close the original window behind your new window so only the selected OU's window remains.

9. Select File | Options to open the Options dialog.

10. In the Options dialog, enter a friendly name for your MMC, and select a mode from the Console Mode drop-down list. In this example, select User mode—limited access, single window.

11. Click OK, close the console, and save your changes.

You should now see your new console in the Administrative Tools program group. If you open the console, you will be in user mode and see what your delegated administrator will see. You can e-mail this console to the administrator and they will see only what they need to in order to administer their OU.

 If you create and distribute custom consoles, you must ensure that the person you send the console to has the appropriate snap-ins installed on their machine first.

Creating MMC Taskpads

Custom consoles are fine for administrative tasks, but they still require some understanding of using an application like Active Directory Users and Computers. There may be instances where you wish to delegate control of an AD object to a nontechnical person. Windows Server 2003 provides a way to create taskpad views for administrative tasks. Custom taskpads allow you to create and expose just the administrative function required for the delegated administrator. The interface is very intuitive and similar to using a web page. The following exercise describes how to create a custom taskpad for resetting a password for a user account in the example Sales OU:

1. To create a custom MMC, select Start | Run and enter **mmc** in the Run dialog.

2. The MMC will open with the default title of Console1. To create a console to manage a specific OU, select File | Add/Remove Snap-In.

3. In the Add/Remove Snap-In dialog, click the Add button.

4. In the Add Standalone Snap-in dialog, select Active Directory Users and Computers from the list, and click the Add button.

5. Click the Close button in the Add Standalone Snap-in dialog to return to the Add/Remove Snap-in dialog.

6. You should see the snap-in appear in the Add/Remove Snap-in dialog. Click the OK button to return to the MMC.

7. Expand the Active Directory Users and Computers snap-in and drill down to the OU you wish to create the MMC for.

8. Right-click the OU and select New Window From Here. This opens a new console window with just your selected OU in focus. Close the original window behind your new window so only the selected OU's window remains.

9. Right-click the OU and select New Taskpad View. The New Taskpad View Wizard appears. Click the Next button to begin the wizard.

10. This dialog is for selecting how you wish your taskpad to look. You can select:

   - **Vertical List**   Creates a vertical listing of AD objects in the OU of focus

   - **Horizontal List**   Creates a horizontal listing of AD objects contained in the selected OU

   - **No List**   Does not list the objects, just icons for executing defined tasks

11. For this example, select Vertical List and click the Next button.

12. Select the scope of the task. You can select all the tree items that are the same type as the selected tree items, or the selected tree items. Select the Selected tree item radio button and click Next.

13. Provide a name and description for your taskpad and click Next. Click Finish to complete this step of the wizard.

14. When the New Task Wizard dialog appears, click Next to begin the wizard.

15. Select a command type; for this exercise, select "menu command" in order to allow reset of passwords of accounts.

16. In the Shortcut Menu Command dialog, make sure a user account is in focus in the left pane; in the right pane, there will be commands that affect the current object in focus. Select All Tasks | Reset Password from the right pane and click Next.

17. Provide a name and description for the newly created task. Click the Next button.

18. In the Task Icon dialog, select an icon that you want to represent this task and then click Next.

19. In the Completing Task Wizard dialog, click Finish to complete the wizard and go back to the MMC.

After completing these wizards, you should see a vertical listing of the objects in the selected OU. Click the object and you should see the new icon representing the reset password command. Customize the look of the taskpad and then save the console as you did in the previous exercise. Now you can distribute the taskpad as you would a custom console.

Geographical Location

If your organization is administered based on geographical location, then you may want to structure AD to reflect this. Say, for example, you have multiple facilities in Europe where a single IT person is the administrator for the location. You could structure AD so that you have a Europe OU and then delegate control of the OU to the IT support in that location.

Organizational Structure

You may have an organization that is divided up by divisions or departments that all have their own support personnel who wish to manage their AD objects. For instance, suppose the finance department has one individual responsible for administering all finance operations in the organization regardless of location. You could create an OU structure that would have a Finance OU and then delegate control on that OU.

You may also need to deploy an application via a group policy so that all users in Finance have a particular accounting package; having an OU structure based upon function rather than location may help facilitate this.

Mixed Organizational Structure

In some cases, you will need to structure Active Directory using a combination of both location and function. For example, you could create a structure that has function and then location nested under the functional OU. Just remember for the sake of easing administration and simplicity that you should not go more than five levels deep when creating OUs.

Searching Active Directory

Now that you have an OU structure in place, have created your objects, and have placed your objects in the appropriate OUs, how do you find the information contained in Active Directory? Windows Server 2003 provides you with excellent search tools to build queries to find information contained in the directory.

Active Directory Users and Computers

Active Directory Users and Computers in Windows XP and subsequent operating systems contain a node used for creating saved queries. You can create queries, save them, and export your search results. To create a query:

1. Open Active Directory Users and Computers from the Administrative Tools menu in Windows Server 2003.

2. At the top of the left pane, right-click Saved Queries and select New | Query.

3. In the New Query dialog, enter a name for your query and description.

4. In the middle of the New Query dialog, you can select the query root for your search; by default, this will be the domain root. You can click the Browse button to select another root for your search; for example, you can select an OU to begin your search on. The more restrictive you are with selecting just the specific root you want to search, the faster your search will execute.

5. Click the Define Query button.

6. In the Find Common Queries dialog (see Figure 19-2), you can create filters on objects in order to find your information.

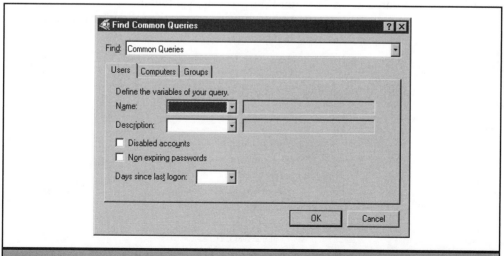

Figure 19-2.   *Creating a filter to find information in Active Directory*

Once you have the Find Common Queries dialog open, you can select a variety of options to build filters for your search. There are three tabs you can select from: User, Computers, and Groups. Within each of these tabs, you can conduct basic searches on the objects, such as disabled accounts. In addition, you can select Custom Search from the Find drop-down list box, which allows you to create filters on the various attributes on the directory objects.

After creating your search, you can then save the search for viewing and exporting at any time.

Using Windows Search

Most of your users will not have access to Active Directory Users and Computers. In absence of this, they can use the Search feature of Windows XP to search Active Directory. Selecting Start | Search opens a search window that allows you to search for computers, printers, and users on your network.

Maintaining Active Directory

You may encounter instances in which you need to repair or modify information contained in your Active Directory. Windows Server 2003 provides you with a couple of tools you should be aware of as an administrator: NTDSUtil and DCDiag.

NTDSUtil

NTDSUtil is a command-line tool for modifying and managing your Active Directory structure. This tool is primarily used for database maintenance on Active Directory, for removing metadata information contained in AD and controlling single-master operations. NTDSUtil.exe is located in the %SystemRoot%\System32 folder.

To start NTDSUtil, open a command prompt and enter the following command:

```
ntdsutil
```

You can type **help** at the prompt to view the options available:

```
ntdsutil: help
?                            - Show this help information
Authoritative restore        - Authoritatively restore the DIT database
Configurable Settings        - Manage configurable settings
Domain management            - Prepare for new domain creation
Files                        - Manage NTDS database files
Help                         - Show this help information
LDAP policies                - Manage LDAP protocol policies
```

```
Metadata cleanup            - Clean up objects of decommissioned servers
Popups %s                   - (en/dis)able popups with "on" or "off"
Quit                        - Quit the utility
Roles                       - Manage NTDS role owner tokens
Security account management - Manage Security Account Database - Duplicate SID Cleanup
Semantic database analysis  - Semantic Checker
Set DSRM Password           - Reset directory service restore mode administrator account password

ntdsutil:
```

Each one of these options sends you down a different administrative path. Some options are not available when you are currently logged in normally to the operating system. For example, the Authoritative restore option is only available when logging in to the system using Directory Services Restore Mode.

Covering every aspect of NTDSUtil is beyond the scope of this chapter. You can find more information on NTDSUtil by searching the Microsoft Knowledge Base.

Note   *Be careful using NTDSUtil. This tool is for modifying Active Directory. Make sure you know exactly how to perform the operation or you could make changes that adversely affect your AD.*

DCDiag

DCDiag is a command-line utility for monitoring your Active Directory. You can install DCDiag by executing the Support Tools installation on the Server 2003 installation CD in the <cdroot>\Support\Tools directory.

Once you install the support tools, you can then run DCDiag. When you execute DCDiag, it will run several diagnostics on your Active Directory:

```
C:\Documents and Settings\Administrator>dcdiag
Domain Controller Diagnosis
Performing initial setup:
   Done gathering initial info.

Doing initial required tests
   Testing server: Default-First-Site-Name\SERVER2003
      Starting test: Connectivity
         ...................... SERVER2003 passed test Connectivity
Doing primary tests
   Testing server: Default-First-Site-Name\SERVER2003
      Starting test: Replications
```

```
..................... SERVER2003 passed test Replications
    Starting test: NCSecDesc
..................... SERVER2003 passed test NCSecDesc
    Starting test: NetLogons
..................... SERVER2003 passed test NetLogons
    Starting test: Advertising
..................... SERVER2003 passed test Advertising
    Starting test: KnowsOfRoleHolders
..................... SERVER2003 passed test KnowsOfRoleHolders
    Starting test: RidManager
..................... SERVER2003 passed test RidManager
    Starting test: MachineAccount
..................... SERVER2003 passed test MachineAccount
    Starting test: Services
..................... SERVER2003 passed test Services
    Starting test: ObjectsReplicated

..................... SERVER2003 passed test ObjectsReplicated

    Starting test: frssysvol
..................... SERVER2003 passed test frssysvol
    Starting test: frsevent
..................... SERVER2003 passed test frsevent
    Starting test: kccevent
..................... SERVER2003 passed test kccevent
    Starting test: systemlog
..................... SERVER2003 passed test systemlog
    Starting test: VerifyReferences
..................... SERVER2003 passed test VerifyReferences

Running partition tests on : ForestDnsZones
    Starting test: CrossRefValidation
..................... ForestDnsZones passed test CrossRefValidation
    Starting test: CheckSDRefDom
..................... ForestDnsZones passed test CheckSDRefDom

Running partition tests on : DomainDnsZones
    Starting test: CrossRefValidation
..................... DomainDnsZones passed test CrossRefValidation

    Starting test: CheckSDRefDom
..................... DomainDnsZones passed test CheckSDRefDom

Running partition tests on : Schema
    Starting test: CrossRefValidation
..................... Schema passed test CrossRefValidation
```

```
Starting test: CheckSDRefDom
       ...................... Schema passed test CheckSDRefDom

  Running partition tests on : Configuration
     Starting test: CrossRefValidation
       ...................... Configuration passed test CrossRefValidation

     Starting test: CheckSDRefDom
       ...................... Configuration passed test CheckSDRefDom

  Running partition tests on : company
     Starting test: CrossRefValidation
       ...................... company passed test CrossRefValidation
     Starting test: CheckSDRefDom
       ...................... company passed test CheckSDRefDom

  Running enterprise tests on : company.dom
     Starting test: Intersite
       ...................... company.dom passed test Intersite
     Starting test: FsmoCheck
       ...................... company.dom passed test FsmoCheck
```

As you can see from the output of running DCDiag, everything in the domain appears to be running correctly. If a problem exists with AD, DCDiag should display an error.

If I force an error by disabling DNS on the server, DCDiag will report back on the error:

```
Doing initial required tests
   Testing server: Default-First-Site-Name\SERVER2003
      Starting test: Connectivity
         The host 65fc42b7-0020-4c4e-9ba5-d241450ee25c._msdcs.company.dom could not
be resolved to an IP address.  Check the DNS server, DHCP, server name, etc
Although the Guid DNS name 65fc42b7-0020-4c4e-9ba5-d241450ee25c._msdcs.company.dom)
couldn't be resolved, the server name (server2003.company.dom) resolved to the IP
address (192.168.65.129) and was pingable.  Check that the IP address is registered
correctly with the DNS server.
         ...................... SERVER2003 failed test Connectivity

Doing primary tests

   Testing server: Default-First-Site-Name\SERVER2003
      Skipping all tests, because server SERVER2003 is not responding to directory
service requests
```

As you can see, DCDiag is an excellent tool to start with when troubleshooting errors with Active Directory.

Active Directory Sites and Services

We have our Active Directory structure in place, global catalog servers defined; now we have to configure our Sites and Services to replicate this information across our forest. Active Directory Users and Computers, you can define the logical structure of your domain. AD Sites and Services focuses on the physical structure of your network and defines how replication of the Active Directory takes place.

Creating a Site Structure

When you do an install of the first domain controller in the forest, the forest is configured with only a single site. Open Active Directory Sites and Services and expand the Sites node, and you should see the Default-First-Site-Name (see Figure 19-3).

The newly created server will be listed in this site. A site is a network with a highly available and high bandwidth connection, such as a LAN. As you add additional servers in your forest, if they are distributed across WAN links, you will want to modify AD Sites and Services to account for the WAN structure. By creating this structure, you will optimize your replication. To create a site for a new location, use the following procedure:

1. In Active Directory Sites and Services, expand the Sites node, right-click the node, and select New Site.

2. In the New Object – Site dialog, provide a name for your site: for example, "NewYork" (note that spaces are not allowed). Then, select the DEFAULTIPSITELINK (we'll go over site links in the next section, "Inter-Site Transports"). Click the OK button to finish.

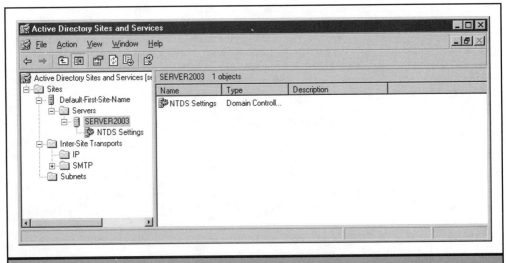

Figure 19-3. *Active Directory Sites and Services management console*

3. If you want, you can rename the Default-First-Site-Name to something else by right-clicking the site and selecting Rename. For example, rename it Chicago. Since you selected DEFAULTIPSITELINK as your site link, you may want to rename this to NewYork-Chicago to make it easier for viewing.

4. Expand the Inter-Site Transports node, expand the IP node, right-click DEFAULTIPSITELINK, select Rename, and rename it NewYork-Chicago.

Inter-Site Transports

Inter-Site Transports are how you define a path for replication in Active Directory. In the preceding example, you created an Inter-Site Transport between New York and Chicago; this would directly relate to a WAN link between these two locations. Inter-Site Transports can be either IP or SMTP. Each transport would be used based upon the link connecting the sites:

- **Reliable leased line**   In this case, where you know the line will be available the majority of the time, the recommended transport mechanism for replication would be IP. IP is recommended to use whenever possible for replication of Active Directory.

- **Unreliable link**   If you know that the line is unreliable and may go down periodically, you may opt to use SMTP as your transport mechanism. To use SMTP, you need to install Certificate Services to encrypt and verify the Active Directory replication.

Expand the Inter-Site Transports node, expand the IP node, and then right-click a site link. Choose Properties to open the Properties dialog for that transport. Under the General tab, you have the following options:

- **Description**   You can type in a short description to be displayed.

- **Sites in the link and not in the link**   In these two panes, you can select or remove the sites that you wish to replicate using this link.

- **Cost**   Comes into play when you have two or more links connecting sites. For example, suppose you have a T1 connecting two sites, New York and Chicago, and an ISDN link that connects Chicago and Seattle. You can set the cost of the ISDN link higher and the T1 lower so that replication occurs using the T1 as the replication path rather than the ISDN link.

- **Replication schedule**   You can specify the interval between replication and the time you wish replication to occur. For example, you may wish to have a lower rate of replication during business hours in order to reduce traffic during heavy times.

As mentioned, when configuring your cost, you may want to have redundant links between sites. For example, some topologies have a hub-and-spoke WAN, where there is a centralized data center and each site has one link to the central data center. You could also have a mesh network, where you have links between multiple sites. You could have New York connected to Chicago, Chicago connected to Seattle, and Seattle connected to New York. This type of network provides multiple paths for AD replication.

Subnets

Subnets define your physical network segments. You then associate the subnets with a particular site. A site can have multiple subnets. When you install the first domain controller in your forest, there will not be any sites configured. You must go into Active Directory Sites and Services and define your network segments. To define a subnet:

1. Right-click the subnets node and select New Subnet from the context menu.

2. In the New Object – Subnet dialog, enter an IP address and subnet mask for your LAN. This dialog box will accept variable-length subnet masks; note the CIDR notation appears when you type in your subnet mask.

3. Once you define you network, click a site to associate the network to it. Click the OK button to complete the configuration.

Defining sites, subnets, and transports is vital to ensuring that replication and authentication work correctly on your domain. For example, when a user logs on to the network and receives an IP address, the computer will query DNS to see which site the computer is in and then authenticate it against a domain controller in a site that is associated with a subnet that client is currently in. Global catalog searches are first performed within a site that the client is in. Many other features of Active Directory are dependent on how Active Directory Sites and Services is configured, so ensure that you take the time to configure it correctly.

Services

In this section we will cover the Services piece of Sites and Services. Right-click the top level of the Active Directory Sites and Services node and select View | Services Node. By default, the Services node is not displayed (very rarely would you need to administer objects contained within this node).

If you expand the Services node, you will see additional nodes that contain information for services running on your network:

- **MsmqServices** Contains information pertaining to Microsoft Messaging Queue services.
- **NetServices** Contains information on various network services, such as DHCP
- **Public Key Services** Manages certificate services
- **RRAS** Contains information pertaining to Routing and Remote Access Services
- **Windows NT** Contains information for domain-based services

More services nodes may appear based on applications you install that are "site aware" and can take advantage of the WAN topology, such as Exchange Server. You also can run the Delegation of Control Wizard on them, enabling you to distribute administration of the various services.

Tools for Maintaining and Troubleshooting Sites and Services

There may be occasions when something with your domain is not working correctly. Many problems can happen due to Active Directory not replicating information across all sites. In this section we will discuss some of the tools available for diagnosing problems that can occur within your domain.

Replmon

Replmon is a graphical tool for monitoring replication between sites. Replmon is installed when you install the Support Tools, as described earlier in the "DCDiag" section. Running **replmon** at the command prompt opens the Active Directory Replication Monitor window, shown in Figure 19-4.

By right-clicking the root node, you can select a server to monitor. This opens a dialog in which you can define a server to be monitored. Once you make the connection, you can do a variety of tasks:

- **Update the Status**   Displays any errors in the right pane and displays the current status for the selected server

- **Check Replication Topology**   Displays in graphical format direct replication partners of the selected controller

- **Synchronize Each Directory Partition with All Servers**   Sends out a message to server to initiate replication across the domain

- **Generate Status Report**   Allows you to export a status report to a log file on the computer

- **Show Domain Controllers in the Domain**   Displays all domain controllers within the domain currently in focus

- **Show Replication Topologies**   Displays all replication paths to the various sites within your forest

- **Show Group Policy Object Status**   Displays the status of GPOs within the forest

- **Show Current Performance Status**   Provides performance information for your forest replication

- **Show Global Catalog Servers in the Enterprise**   Displays any servers within the forest configured as a Global Catalog server

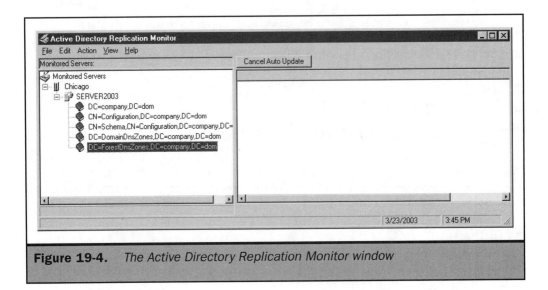

Figure 19-4. *The Active Directory Replication Monitor window*

- **Show Bridgehead Servers** Displays servers used as bridgehead servers; bridgehead servers are the preferred replication server for a particular site

- **Show Trust Relationships** Displays trust relationships for the forest. Trusts are explained in more detail latter in this chapter

- **Show Attribute Meta-Data for Active Directory Object** Displays any meta-data for the forest objects

Under the Action menu, you can also search the entire forest for domain controllers with replication errors.

As you can tell, replmon should be in every administrator's toolbox, because it provides several tools for monitoring your Active Directory.

Netdiag

Netdiag is another tool located under Support Tools on the installation CD. You can use dcdiag and replmon, mentioned previously in this chapter, to find errors, but you should also be aware of the netdiag tool. Network diagnostics performs several network tests and reports back any errors it finds. Just open a command prompt and type:

```
C:\Documents and Settings\Administrator>netdiag
.................................
    Computer Name: SERVER2003
    DNS Host Name: server2003.company.dom
    System info : Windows 2000 Server (Build 3718)
    Processor : x86 Family 6 Model 11 Stepping 1, GenuineIntel
```

```
    List of installed hotfixes :
        Q147222
Netcard queries test . . . . . . . : Passed
Per interface results:
    Adapter : Local Area Connection
        Netcard queries test . . . : Passed
        Host Name. . . . . . . . . : server2003
        IP Address . . . . . . . . : 192.168.65.129
        Subnet Mask. . . . . . . . : 255.255.255.0
        Default Gateway. . . . . . : 192.168.65.2
        Dns Servers. . . . . . . . : 192.168.65.129
        AutoConfiguration results. . . . . . : Passed
        Default gateway test . . . : Passed
        NetBT name test. . . . . . : Passed
        [WARNING] At least one of the <00> 'WorkStation Service', <03> 'Messenger
Service', <20> 'WINS' names is missing.
            No remote names have been found.
        WINS service test. . . . . : Skipped
            There are no WINS servers configured for this interface.
Global results:
Domain membership test . . . . . . : Passed
NetBT transports test. . . . . . . : Passed
    List of NetBt transports currently configured:
        NetBT_Tcpip_{C19E851C-C540-4E6C-A9C2-5AD7AB351712}
    1 NetBt transport currently configured.
Autonet address test . . . . . . . : Passed
IP loopback ping test. . . . . . . : Passed
Default gateway test . . . . . . . : Passed
NetBT name test. . . . . . . . . . : Passed
    [WARNING] You don't have a single interface with the <00> 'WorkStation
Service', <03> 'Messenger Service', <20> 'WINS' names defined.
Winsock test . . . . . . . . . . . : Passed
DNS test . . . . . . . . . . . . . : Passed
    PASS - All the DNS entries for DC are registered on DNS server
'192.168.65.129'.
Redir and Browser test . . . . . . : Passed
    List of NetBt transports currently bound to the Redir
        NetBT_Tcpip_{C19E851C-C540-4E6C-A9C2-5AD7AB351712}
    The redir is bound to 1 NetBt transport.
    List of NetBt transports currently bound to the browser
        NetBT_Tcpip_{C19E851C-C540-4E6C-A9C2-5AD7AB351712}
    The browser is bound to 1 NetBt transport.
DC discovery test. . . . . . . . . : Passed
DC list test . . . . . . . . . . . : Passed
Trust relationship test. . . . . . : Skipped
Kerberos test. . . . . . . . . . . : Passed
LDAP test. . . . . . . . . . . . . : Passed
```

```
Bindings test. . . . . . . . . . : Passed
WAN configuration test . . . . . . : Skipped
    No active remote access connections.
Modem diagnostics test . . . . . . : Passed
IP Security test . . . . . . . . . : Skipped
    Note: run "netsh ipsec dynamic show /?" for more detailed information
The command completed successfully
```

As you can see, netdiag performs a comprehensive list of network diagnostics on your machine. If an error shows up in the list, you should consult the Microsoft Knowledge Base for information on the specific error message.

Active Directory Domains and Trusts

Active Directory Domains and Trusts is where you can view, create, modify, and verify trusts for your forest. Trusts enable users from one domain to be authenticated by the trusting domain. Once a user account can be authenticated, you can then provide access to resources within the trusting domain.

The following is a list of the various types of trusts in Windows Server 2003:

- **Domain root trust**   Occurs between two different domain roots within the same forest. Figure 19-5 shows a domain root trust between two trees: company.dom and domain2.dom.

- **Parent-child trust**   Occurs within the same domain name space. In Figure 19-5, under the root company.dom domain is the sales domain. The trust that occurs between the two is the parent-child trust. Within an Active Directory forest, trusts are both two-way and transitive. Transitive trusts mean that within a domain tree, as in Figure 19-5, we have a child domain of finance.company.dom, the finance domain trusts the parent domain; company.com, since trusts are transitive we don't need to configure a trust in order for sales.company.dom to access resources in finance.company.dom. Since both the sales.company.dom and finance .company.dom trust the parent domain, company.dom, this trust will pass through all domains within the domain tree.

- **Shortcut trust**   For the transitive trust to work throughout the domain and forest, the trust has to be checked up through the domain tree. You can create a shortcut trust, which reduces the amount of time needed to check the trust path. By manually creating a shortcut trust in Active Directory Domains and Trusts, you reduce the amount of time required to authenticate access to resources.

- **Forest trust**   A new kind of trust with Windows Server 2003; allows one forest to trust all domains within another forest transitively. For example say we have our company.dom domain from previous examples, and there is another child domain within the company.dom domain called sales.company.dom. If we configure a forest-level trust with another forest called external.dom, then sales.company.dom will pass the transitive trust up through the forest root and to the other trusted forest. You can configure this trust as transitive, two-way, or one-way.

■ **Realm trust** By adding a Kerberos realm trust, you can enable trusts with a non-Windows Kerberos version 5 realm. As in other external trusts, this can be transitive or nontransitive, two-way or one-way.

The following exercise adds a trust to an existing domain:

1. Select Start | Programs | Administrative Tools | Active Directory Domains and Trusts.

2. Expand the top node of Active Directory Domains and Trusts to view all domains within your forest. Right-click the domain that you want to add the trust to and select Properties.

3. In the Domain Properties dialog, click the Trusts tab to view the trusts for your domain.

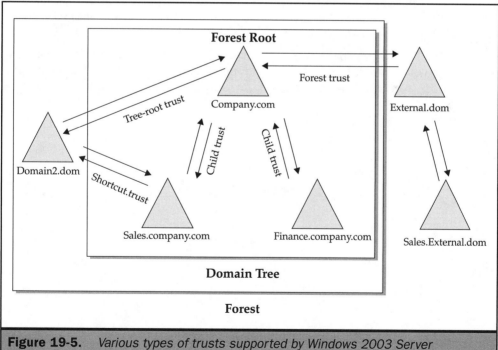

Figure 19-5.   *Various types of trusts supported by Windows 2003 Server*

4. Click the New Trust button to start the New Trust Wizard, and click the Next button.

5. In the Trust Name dialog, enter either the NetBIOS name or DNS name of the domain you wish to create the trust with. Click the Next button to continue.

6. Select the type of trust you want this to be:

   ■ **Two-way** Users from your domain will be able to be authenticated and use resources in the trusted domain; users in the other domain will be authenticated in your domain and be able to use resources in your domain.

   ■ **One-way Incoming** Users in your domain can be authenticated in the other domain and access resources in that domain.

   ■ **One-way Outgoing** Users in the other domain can be authenticated by your domain and access resources within the domain.

7. Click the Next button to open the Sides of Trust dialog. Specify if you wish to create the trust in your domain or both domains, provided you have the appropriate permissions. Click Next to continue.

8. In the Outgoing Trust Authentication Level dialog, specify the scope of the trust; you can select either Domain-wide authentication, which allows all users from the other domain to access resources in your domain, or Selective Authentication, which requires you to specify the user's access once you have established the trust. Click Next to continue.

9. In the Trust Password dialog, enter a password for verifying the new trust; this password has to be entered on both domains to establish the trust. Click Next to continue and view the summary of the task you just performed.

Chapter 20

Managing Groups
and OUs

679

Groups and organizational units provide a logical and easy way to manage your domain, especially the security of your network resources. If you're coming to Windows Server 2003 from Windows NT, you understand the definition of a group, but you'll find vast changes in the way groups work in Windows Server 2003.

OUs are an entirely new concept to Windows NT administrators, but this feature is easy to understand and use, and you'll appreciate the way OUs help you manage your domains.

In this chapter, I'll discuss the way these two features work, and how you can use them to administer and secure your enterprise.

Windows Server 2003 Groups

A *group* is collection of objects, such as users, computers, contacts, and even other groups. Windows Server 2003 has a hierarchy of group types, starting at the top with the following two types:

- Distribution groups, which are used only for e-mail distribution.
- Security groups, which are used to grant permissions to resources (and can also be used as e-mail distribution lists).

The security groups for domains can be further classified by type and scope, such as domain local, global, and universal, and I'll cover those distinctions in this chapter.

Local Groups

When you install a Windows Server 2003 computer as a member server (instead of as a domain controller), a number of local groups are automatically created. If you add certain roles to the computer, additional groups are created so that you can let users perform the tasks associated with those roles. For example, if you make the computer a DHCP server, local groups are created for administering and using DHCP services.

Distribution Groups

Except for this paragraph, I'm not going to spend time on distribution groups in this chapter (or in this book). A distribution group is used solely for e-mail distribution, and is used only by e-mail applications such as Microsoft Exchange Server. A distribution group has no relationship to security, and cannot be referenced in discretionary access control lists (DACLs) when you are setting up permissions on resources.

You can populate the default local groups with members. You can also create new local groups for the computer, if you want to give a certain group of users specific rights to perform tasks that aren't covered by the default group.

Remember that local groups exist to give their members rights to perform actions on local computers. Most of the time, your Windows Server 2003 computer is playing a role in a domain, and it would be unusual to have to set up a complex set of users and groups to run the computer.

Remember also that the purpose of groups is to limit user actions on the server, not to provide the right to perform actions. Most local groups have no members, which doesn't mean that nobody can perform the tasks permitted by group membership—it means no user has had her rights limited by that group. Members in groups with more rights (for example, Administrators) already have the right to perform the tasks.

Default Local Groups

You can view the default groups in the Groups folder located in the Local Users and Groups Microsoft Management snap-in (see Figure 20-1). To open the snap-in, right-click My Computer and choose Manage from the shortcut menu. Then expand the Local Users and Groups object in the console pane, and select the Groups object.

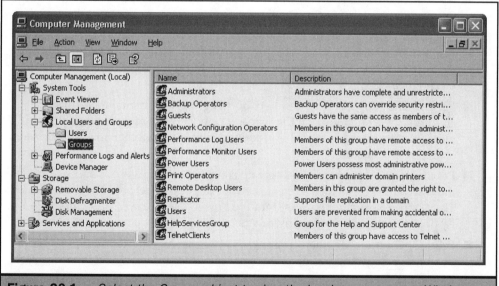

Figure 20-1.   *Select the Groups object to view the local groups on your Windows Server 2003 computer.*

The following local groups exist on a member server running Windows Server 2003:

- **Administrators**   Members of this group have unrestricted rights to manipulate and manage the computer locally, or remotely. By default, the local Administrator and any member of the Domain Admins group are members of the group.

- **Backup Operators**   Members can log on locally or remotely, back up and restore folders and files, and shut down the computer. Note that group members can back up and restore folders and files for which they may not have regular access permissions, but the backup/restore group membership takes precedence over those rights. By default, the group has no members.

- **Guests**   Only the Guest account is a member of this group, but the Guest account is disabled by default in Windows Server 2003. Members of the group have no default rights or permissions. If you enable the Guest account, and a guest logs on to the computer, a temporary profile is created at logon, and deleted at logoff.

- **HelpServicesGroup**   This group exists to set permissions for support applications, and the only member is the account associated with installed support applications, such as Remote Assistance. Don't add users to this group.

- **Network Configuration Operators**   Members of this group can make changes to network (TCP/IP) settings, and can renew and release TCP/IP addresses if the computer is a DHCP server. By default, the group has no members.

- **Performance Monitor Users**   Members of this group can monitor (view) performance counters on this server locally and remotely. By default, this group has no members.

- **Performance Log Users**   Members of this group can manage performance counters, logs, and alerts on the server locally and remotely. By default, the only member of the group is the NT Authority\Network Service (an interactive system user, not a real user).

- **Power Users**   Members of this group can create user accounts and manipulate those accounts. They can also create new local groups, and populate those groups. They can add or remove users from the Power Users, Users, and Guests groups. By default, the group has no members.

- **Print Operators**   Members of this group can manage printers and print queues. By default, the group has no members.

- **Remote Desktop Users**   Members of this group can log on to this server remotely. To learn how to enable remote desktop features and add users to this group, read Chapter 3.

- **Replicator**   The Replicator group supports replication functions. The only member of the group is a domain user account that's needed for the Replicator services of a domain controller. Don't add user accounts to this group.

- **Users** Members of this group can perform basic tasks, such as running applications and using printers. Group members can't create shares or printers (but they can connect to network printers to install them locally). Any user account created in the domain is a member of this group.

- **TelnetClients** Members of this group can use the Telnet Server service on this computer, if it's running. By default, Telnet Server service is disabled.

Adding Members to Local Groups

You can add objects to any group. Those objects can be local users, domain users, or even other local or domain groups. To add members to a group, follow these steps:

1. Right-click My Computer and choose Manage to open the local Computer Management snap-in.

2. Expand the Local Users and Groups object in the console pane.

3. Select the Groups object to display the local groups in the details pane.

4. Double-click the listing of the group to which you want to add members, to open the group's Properties dialog.

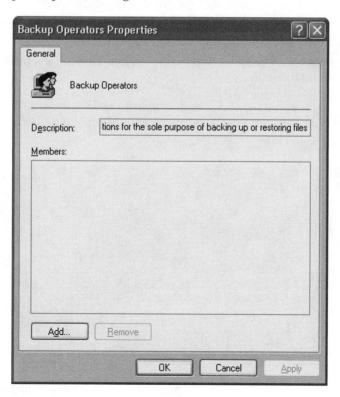

5. Click Add to open the Select Users, Computers, or Groups dialog.

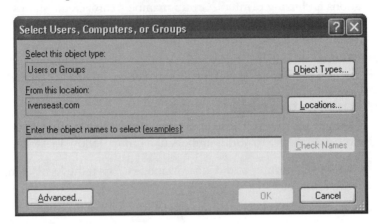

6. Find the appropriate objects, using the following guidelines:

■ Click Object Types to choose one or more types of member(s) to add to the group. The options include Computer, User, and Group.

■ Click Locations to choose the local computer or the domain as the place from which to select the new member(s).

■ Enter the object name(s), separating each name with a semicolon, or click Advanced to initiate a search.

If you enter names directly, click Check Names to make sure you've entered them accurately. You can enter logon names of users, and the system will convert them to fully qualified domain names (FQDNs).

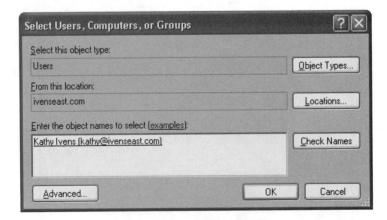

Click OK when you've finished adding members. The group's membership list appears in its Properties dialog (see Figure 20-2).

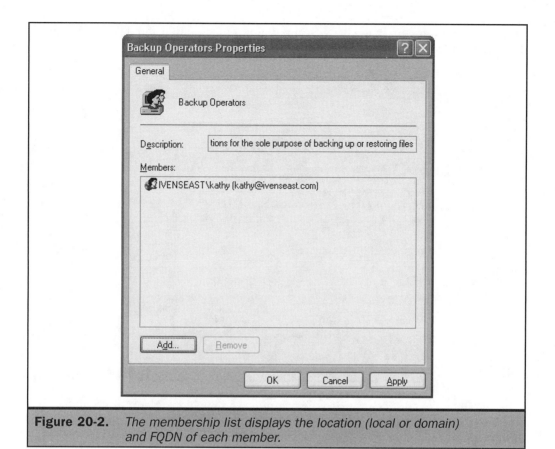

Figure 20-2.   *The membership list displays the location (local or domain)
and FQDN of each member.*

Creating Local Groups

If you're using your Windows Server 2003 computer for some special function or
application, you may need to enable special permissions to perform tasks. It's frequently
a good idea to create a group for these tasks, and populate it with the appropriate
members. For most of the roles you can assign a computer, the system automatically
creates a group to administer the role. For example, if you make the computer a DHCP
server, appropriate groups are added to the computer.

To create a new group, open the Computer Management snap-in using the steps
described in the previous section. Right-click the Groups container and choose New Group

from the shortcut menu. In the New Group dialog, enter a name and description, and then click Add to populate the group with members.

Click Create to add the group to the computer. A new blank New Group dialog opens so that you can create another group. When you're finished creating local groups, click Close.

Domain Groups

Domain groups are part of Active Directory, and can exist in the root domain of a forest, in any domain in the forest, or in an OU. A Windows Server 2003 computer that is a DC automatically creates the default groups for the domain. You administer domain groups in the Active Directory Users and Computers snap-in, which is on the Administrative Tools menu of the DC.

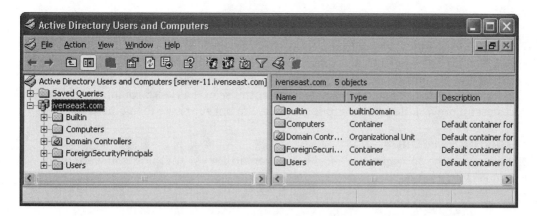

You can manipulate domain groups by adding members to existing groups, or by creating new groups, using the same procedures described for local groups.

One thing to remember about domain groups is that you can only use them to set permissions on system resources. You cannot apply group policies to groups—group policies are applied to domains, sites, and OUs. This is one of the most frustrating things about group policies, because it defies logic.

Understanding Group Scopes

Windows Server 2003 characterizes groups by a scope that identifies the extent to which the group is applied in the domain tree or forest. There are three group scopes: global, domain local, and universal.

Global Groups

If you're moving to Windows Server 2003 from Windows NT, the concept of a global group isn't new. Global groups can contain user accounts from the domain, and other global groups from the domain. In addition, you can put a global group into a local group for a member server in the same domain, or in any trusted domain.

This means you can use a global group as a sort of "traveling army of administrators." Populate the global group with the appropriate members, and then put that group into a local computer group in the domain, or in a trusted domain, to let those members administer member servers (or workstations, for that matter).

Domain Local Groups

Domain local groups were introduced in Windows 2000. They can include among their membership user accounts, and other domain local groups from the same domain. You can use these groups to assign permissions to members within a domain.

Because it's totally based in a single domain, this scope has less flexibility (and therefore less useful power) than global groups. In fact, I'm not sure I see the point of them.

Universal Groups

Universal is the "powerhouse" scope. You can do almost anything you want with a universal group:

- Populate it with global groups from any domain in the forest.
- Make it a member of any local (computer) group.
- Populate it with other universal groups.

This means that once you've populated your universal groups with the appropriate members, you can manage all the parts of your enterprise by giving the universal groups rights to perform tasks, and giving the group members the appropriate permissions on resources.

Once you understand the power of universal groups, you realize that the most efficient way to manage your enterprise is with universal groups, and there's no reason to have any other type of group. Beware, though, because there are two catches.

First, you cannot have universal groups while your enterprise is running in mixed mode. *Mixed mode* means that Windows NT DCs still exist within your enterprise, and Windows NT has no ability to handle this scope. The best reason I can think of to upgrade all of your Windows NT DCs is to gain the advantage of universal groups. There are two modes above mixed mode:

- **Native mode**   Your enterprise DCs are running Windows 2000 and/or Windows Server 2003.
- **Windows Server 2003**   Your enterprise DCs are running Windows Server 2003.

Second, the way universal groups are replicated across the DCs in your enterprise may create some problems. When you replicate a universal group to DCs that hold the global catalog (typically, one on each site), both the group names and the names of all the members of each group are replicated. If you have nested universal groups, replication could take a very long time, especially if you're replicating across slow connections. Therefore, use universal groups sparingly, for best results.

By contrast, global group replication involves only the name of the group, and replication is limited to the home domain of the group. Domain local groups aren't replicated at all (in my opinion, that's just another limitation that gives me a reason to eschew their use).

Changing Scopes

When you create a group, it's a global group by default. If your enterprise is not running in mixed mode, you can change the scope of a group you create as follows:

- **Global to universal**   The global group cannot be nested in another global group; it must exist as a top-level group.

- **Domain local to universal**   The domain local group must have only users as members, not other domain local groups.

- **Universal to global**   The universal group cannot have another universal group as a member.

- **Universal to domain local**   There are no restrictions for this change.

Default Domain Groups

When you install AD on a Windows Server 2003 computer (creating a DC), the system automatically installs a number of groups. Use the Active Directory Users and Computers snap-in to view and manipulate domain groups.

Some of the groups are in the Builtin container (which contains only groups), and some of the groups are in the Users container (which contains user and group accounts).

Groups in the Builtin Container

In this section, I'll give you a brief overview of the groups that you find in the Builtin container. Your own domain may contain additional groups, depending on the configuration of the domain or the DC.

Account Operators   Members of this group can create, modify, and delete accounts for users, groups, and computers located in the Users container, the Computers container, and OUs (but not the built-in Domain Controllers OU). However, members of this group can't modify the Administrators or the Domain Admins groups, nor modify the accounts of any members of those groups. Members of this group can log on locally to all DCs in the domain and can also shut them down.

Administrators   Members of this group have full control of all DCs in the domain. By default, the Administrator account and the Domain Admins and Enterprise Admins groups are members.

Backup Operators   Members can back up and restore files on all DCs in the domain, regardless of their own permissions on those files. Members can also log on to all DCs, and shut them down.

Guests   Members of this group have no default rights. Both the Guest account (which is disabled by default) and the Domain Guests group (in the Users container) are members.

Incoming Forest Trust Builders   This group only appears in the forest root domain. Members can create one-way, incoming forest trusts to the forest root domain.

Network Configuration Operators   Members of this group can make changes to network (TCP/IP) settings, and can renew and release IP addresses on DCs.

Performance Monitor Users   Members can monitor (view) performance counters on DCs, either interactively or remotely.

Performance Log Users   Members can manage performance counters, logs, and alerts on DCs interactively or remotely.

Pre-Windows 2000 Compatible Access   Members have read access on all users and groups in the domain. This group exists to provide backward compatibility for computers running Windows NT 4 and earlier. By default, the special identity Everyone is a member of this group. (For more information about special identities, see "Special Identities" later in this chapter.) Only add users to this group if they are running Windows NT 4 or earlier.

Print Operators   Members can manage domain printers.

Remote Desktop Users   Members can remotely log on to DCs in the domain with the Remote Desktop client software. See Chapter 3 to learn about the remote desktop feature.

Replicator   This group is used by the File Replication service on domain DCs. Don't add users to the group.

Server Operators   Members have the following powers on DCs:

- Create and delete shared resources
- Start and stop some services
- Back up and restore files
- Format drives
- Shut down the computer
- Only add users who know what they're doing

Users   Members can perform most common tasks (run applications, use local and network printers). By default, the Domain Users and Authenticated Users groups are members of this group (which means that any user account you create in the domain is automatically a member of the Users group).

Groups in the Users Container

The groups covered in this section are located in the Users container in the AD Users and Computers snap-in. In addition to these groups, you may have other groups in your Users container. For example, if your DC is a DNS server, you'll have several groups configured to manage DNS.

Cert Publishers   Members can publish certificates for users and computers.

Domain Admins   Members have full control of the domain. By default, this group is a member of the Administrators group on all DCs, all workstations in the domain, and all member servers in the domain. The Administrator account is automatically a member of this group, and you shouldn't add other users unless they have experience and expertise.

Domain Computers   This group contains all workstations and member servers on the domain.

Domain Controllers   This group contains all domain controllers in the domain.

Domain Guests   This group contains all domain guests.

Domain Users   This group contains all domain users, which means that any user account created in the domain is a member.

Enterprise Admins   This group only appears in the forest root domain. Members have full control of all domains in the forest, and the group is a member of the Administrators group on all DCs in the forest. By default, the Administrator account is a member of this group, and you shouldn't add any user who isn't expert and experienced in enterprise network issues.

Group Policy Creator Owners   Members can modify group policies in the domain. By default, the Administrator account is a member of this group, and you should only add users who understand the power and consequences of applying group policies.

Schema Admins   This group only appears in the forest root domain. Members can modify the Active Directory schema across the forest. By default, the Administrator account is a member, and you should add only users who have expertise in Active Directory. See Chapter 19 for a discussion of the schema.

Special Identities

Your domain also has groups that you can't manipulate. You can't view or modify the membership, you can't see the group in the AD Users and Computers snap-in, and the groups have no scope. You can only see these groups when you're setting permissions on network resources.

These groups are called *special identities* and Windows uses them to represent different users at different times, depending on the circumstances. The membership is temporary and transient. For example, the Everyone group represents all currently logged-on network users, including guests and users from other domains.

The following special groups exist:

- **Anonymous Logon**   Users and services that access a computer and its resources through the network without using an account name, password, or domain name. On computers running Windows NT and earlier, the Anonymous Logon group is a member of the Everyone group by default. However, in Windows Server 2003 (and Windows 2000), the Anonymous Logon group is not a member of the Everyone group.

- **Everyone**   All current network users, including guests and users from other domains. Any user who logs on to the network is automatically a member of the Everyone group.

- **Network**   Users currently accessing a given resource over the network (instead of locally at the computer that holds the resource). Any user that accesses a resource over the network is automatically a member of the Network group.

- **Interactive**   Any user currently logged on to a particular computer and accessing a given resource on that computer (the opposite of Network). Any user working locally who accesses a resource on the computer is automatically a member of the Interactive group.

Using Groups for Permissions

Groups inherently provide rights to perform tasks, but you can also configure permissions on resources with groups. Resource permissions can also be given to individual users, but most of the time it's more efficient to use a group. Then, just make sure that any users who need the permissions are members of the group.

Folders, printers, and other shared resources on NTFS volumes have default permissions for users and groups. Most of the time, the permissions on system folders (those directories created during installation) don't need changing. However, folders you create to install software on your Windows Server 2003 computers need to be configured for the users who access the software, as well as administrators who need to manage those folders.

Folder Permissions

By default, when you create a folder on a Windows Server 2003 computer, permissions are granted to local users. You can view the default permissions on the Security tab of the folder's Properties dialog. For example, Figure 20-3 shows the default permissions for a folder named Regmon on the computer named AS20021.

Select each group or user to see the Allow/Deny permissions for that user. If you need to add users or groups to the list, click Add. If you need to edit the permissions of listed users and groups, click Advanced.

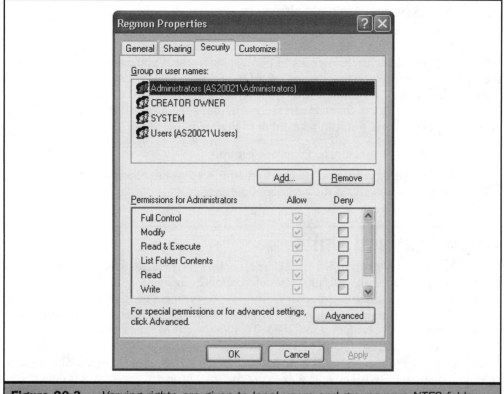

Figure 20-3. *Varying rights are given to local users and groups on a NTFS folder.*

The users and groups with permissions on the folder are local to the computer. Most of the time, system servers like your Windows Server 2003 computer aren't used by an interactive user, except for maintenance tasks. Servers in an enterprise usually exist to service network users who are working from their own, remote workstations.

However, if users are working in software directly at the computer, the existing permissions should suffice. The default permissions for the local Users group are Read & Execute, List Folder Contents, and Read. For common applications such as word processors and spreadsheets, where users write documents to their own documents folders (either a Home folder on a server, or locally), these permissions are usually sufficient. If the application is a database, and the files are in the same folder as the software, you should edit the Users group permissions to permit Write and Modify rights.

Shared Resource Permissions

If your Windows Server 2003 computer is serving the role of providing services to users on the network, sharing a folder automatically creates the permissions needed by those users. A shared folder has its own set of permissions, which you can view by clicking the Permissions button on the Sharing tab of the folder's Properties dialog.

By default, when you share a folder, the Everyone group is given Read permissions on the folder. For folders that contain software, that's usually sufficient. If users need additional permissions, you can take either of the following steps:

- Increase the rights for the Everyone group.
- Add domain groups you created for just this purpose, populated with the users and groups who need the additional permissions.

Organizational Units

An OU has a specialized role within AD: it's a boundary you create when the common boundaries don't suffice. An OU organizes objects in a domain into a logical administrative group, rather than a security group or a group representing a geographical entity, such as a site. An OU is the smallest unit you can use to apply group policies, and to delegate responsibility.

The theory is interesting and logical—move objects into an OU, and take advantage of the fact that Windows lets you create hierarchies of OUs. A parent, some children, and some grandchildren—what an easy way to use the "trickle down" theory of administration.

Don't rush to do this. I've seen too many administrators lose track of who lived where in their OU structures. Administrative tasks and group policies fall through the cracks or are applied multiple times against the same objects, because when objects end up buried deep in multiple OUs, they get lost, and frequently are re-established and duplicated.

When it comes to OUs, I offer some advice based on watching the errors and confusion of others:

- *Move slowly.* Add OUs when you absolutely need them, not when you theoretically believe "hey, it might be a good idea to create an OU" for some group of objects.
- *Keep it flat.* Don't start out with hierarchical OUs. If you build your hierarchies later, out of need, you're more likely to understand the relationships and use them properly.

Also, remember the difference between OUs and groups: the real difference is in the security paradigm—group policies vs. permissions. If you have a group of users or computers that needs restrictions applied to tasks, and a group policy meets that need, create an OU. If you have a group of users or computers that needs special permissions on folders in order to run applications or manipulate data, create a group.

Create an OU

To create an OU, open Active Directory Users and Computers and follow these steps:

1. Right-click the parent object for this OU in the console pane. If this is the first OU, the domain is the parent object. After this, you can use the domain or an existing OU as the parent object.

2. Choose New | Organizational Unit from the shortcut menu to open the New Object-Organizational Unit dialog.

3. Enter a name for the new OU.

4. Click OK.

The new OU appears in the details pane when you select its parent in the console pane. If you want the OU to display a description in the AD Users and Computers snap-in, right-click its icon in either the console pane or the details pane, and choose Properties. In the General tab, enter the information you want to maintain about this OU (Figure 20-4 shows information about an OU named Lab).

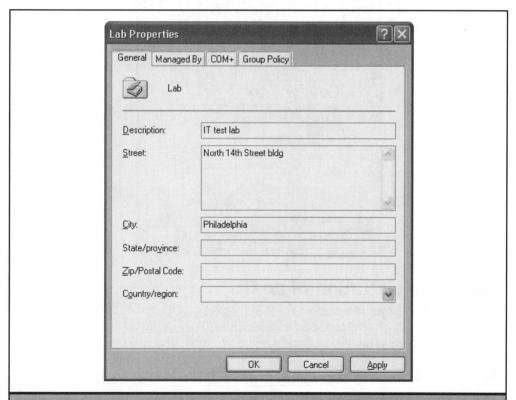

Figure 20-4.   *Enter a description and other information about the OU as needed.*

Locate Objects in an OU

You can populate an OU with users, computers, groups, or other OUs. However, good planning demands a thoughtful approach, and you should use your company's organization as the blueprint. For example, if your company tends to deal with organization matters by "thinking" in terms of departments, you might want to use the primary object associated with departments. Usually, if departments are a physical division (a floor or a building), and if each department operates on the same LAN or subnet, putting computers into an OU for the department is probably the best decision.

On the other hand, if you want to manage group policies differently for executives than for regular employees, it might be best to populate the OU with groups or users. In fact, in this case, it would probably be most efficient to create a new group in the OU for the users you want to manage. That way, you could manage resource permissions and group policies together, and also delegate the administration of the OU.

To move an existing object, such as a computer, into an OU, right-click the object (or multiple objects you select by holding down the CTRL key) and choose Move from the shortcut menu. In the Move dialog, select the target OU.

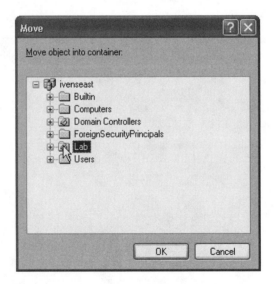

Delegate Administration of an OU

Quite a few administrators have told me that they create OUs solely for the purpose of delegating the work of administering the enterprise. They organize their OUs to match the way the company is organized, and delegate administrative tasks to members of the IT department in a logical fashion. For example, if a company is organized by building floors, the delegated administrator occupies a desk on the appropriate floor.

To delegate control of an OU, right-click the OU's object in the console pane and choose Delegate Control from the shortcut menu. This launches the Delegation of Control Wizard. Click Next in the opening window to proceed.

In the next window, click Add to open the Select Users, Computers, or Groups dialog. Use the selection options in the dialog to choose an object type (commonly a user, but if you've created a group of users with administrative rights, you can select that group). Also choose a location (usually the domain) from which to select the delegate. To search for the target name using filters, click Advanced. If you know the name of the user or group you want to assign to this OU, you can type in the name without searching for it. When your list of delegates is complete, click Next.

Note *You're not limited to one delegated administrator; you can name multiple administrators for an OU.*

In the next window, select the tasks you want to assign to the delegate (see Figure 20-5). The more tasks you assign, the more efficient your delegation scheme is, as long as your

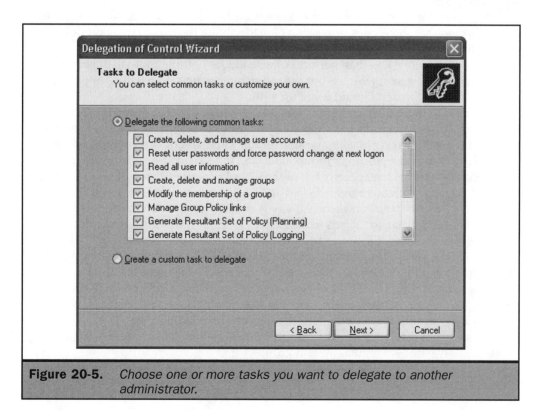

Figure 20-5. *Choose one or more tasks you want to delegate to another administrator.*

delegate has sufficient knowledge and training to perform the tasks properly. When you're finished, click Next.

Note *The wizard also offers the option to create a custom task, but the tasks offered aren't well suited for administering an OU.*

The next wizard window offers a summary of your selections. Click Back if you want to redo anything, otherwise click Finish.

Managing Delegations

You can't track or manage delegations. There is no function built into Windows Server 2003 to tell you whether an OU has been turned over to a delegated administrator. Therefore, you must keep track of your delegation tasks outside the AD. Create a spreadsheet, a database, a binder, or even a bunch of post-it notes. The bad news gets worse—there's also no tool for modifying the delegated tasks if you change your mind about the scope of those tasks.

Delegation management is a major missing ingredient in Active Directory, but I found a workaround that sometimes provides a clue to solving the mystery: "Did I delegate administration of this OU, and if so, to whom?"

My workaround is less than perfect because it does nothing more than help you make an educated guess, which is not the same thing as finding reliable, empirical evidence. But it's the best I could come up with.

My workaround, however, isn't efficacious unless you've delegated the OU to an individual user, or to a group you created. If you used an existing administrative group, you'll never get the answer to your question for this information. To see why, keep reading.

The trick is to find a person or group that sticks out like the proverbial sore thumb in the Permissions list on the Security tab of the OU's Properties dialog. If you're trying to follow along, and you've just right-clicked an OU and chosen Properties, you're probably not seeing a Security tab. Don't worry, there is one; it's just hidden from you by default. To reveal the Security tab for objects in the Active Directory Users and Computers snap-in, choose View | Advanced Features from the MMC menu bar.

With Advanced Features enabled, right-click an OU, choose Properties, and you'll see the Security tab. Figure 20-6 shows the Security tab of the OU named Lab. You can see that a username appears in the list of users and groups that have permissions on this OU. This is a clue! If you created a group, and its name appears in the permissions list, that's a clue too! By default, the system gives permissions to default groups. (Open an OU for which you've not delegated administration, or create a new OU to use as a standard—you'll see only names of regular system groups.)

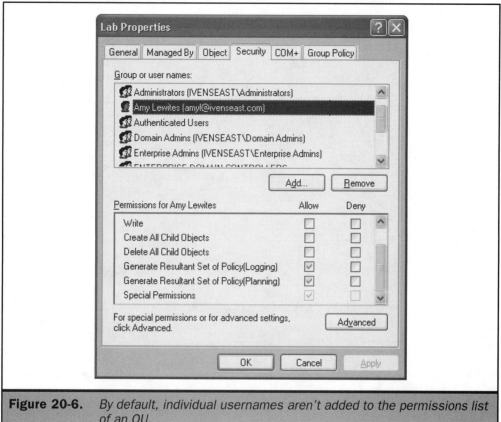

Figure 20-6.   *By default, individual usernames aren't added to the permissions list of an OU.*

The Security tab also provides the opportunity to remove a delegated administrator, or to modify the tasks the delegated administrator can perform:

- To remove the delegation, select the delegate's name and click Remove.
- To modify the scope of the delegated tasks, select the delegate's name and click Advanced. In the Advanced Security Settings dialog, select any listing that contains the delegate's name, and click Edit. Then make any changes you wish to.

The
Complete
Reference

Chapter 21

Managing Users
and Logons

In any secure environment, you need a method to identify and authenticate users. In order to protect local systems and network servers alike from unauthorized access, an operating system has to require that a user have a preexisting set of credentials before being permitted to access local and network resources. In Windows Server 2003, user accounts serve that purpose.

Understanding User Accounts

A user account provides a username and password that a person uses to log on to either the local computer or the domain. In addition, the user account, particularly in Active Directory, serves to identify the user with data such as full name, e-mail address, phone number, department, address, and other data fields you may opt to use. User accounts also serve as a means for granting permissions to a user, applying logon scripts, assigning profiles and home directories, and linking other working environment properties for the user.

Local Accounts

Local accounts are created and stored in a computer's security database. Local accounts are most often used in a workgroup environment to provide logon capability for users of the local computer. However, local accounts also can be used to secure local resources that other users in the workgroup want to access. These other users connect to the resource across the LAN using a username and password stored on the computer where the resource resides (the account must have been granted permissions to the resource). As the number of workstations grows, however, local accounts and workgroups become impractical for controlling access to local resources. The answer is to switch to a domain environment and domain accounts.

In some cases, your Windows Server 2003 server may be used for a special purpose, not as a central location for client services. Perhaps you maintain a database that is designed to be accessible locally only, or you keep sensitive information on the server. In those situations, you'll want to create user accounts for those employees who are designated for access.

Domain Accounts

A domain account's information is stored on the domain controllers for a given domain. Rather than being localized to a specific computer, domain accounts offer privileges across the domain. Unless the domain account restricts a user from doing so, the user can log on from any workstation in the domain. Once the user is logged on, the domain account can grant the user permissions to both local and shared network resources, depending on the permissions that are granted for each resource. In Windows Server 2003, domain accounts are stored and managed in AD. The main advantage to using domain accounts is that they provide centralized administration and security.

Groups

Although you could grant permissions to users on a user-by-user basis, it would be a real pain to do it if you had more than a few users. Imagine trying to grant permissions to a network folder individually to 3000 or more users.

A group, as the name implies, is a group of users. You don't put user accounts into groups; instead, user accounts are assigned membership in groups—groups don't actually contain anything. Instead, user accounts are assigned membership in a group. That distinction may seem to fall under the category "too fine a point," but it's the only way I can think of to make it clear that a user can belong to multiple groups.

Groups can be nested in one another, so that a group can contain other groups in addition to users. Groups come in four flavors, depending on the type of logical network structure you're using. For more information on groups, see Chapter 20.

Managing Domain Accounts

On the domain, accounts represent a physical entity such as a computer or a person, and user accounts can also be used as dedicated service accounts for applications that require this feature. User accounts, computer accounts, and groups are all *security principals*. Security principals are directory objects that are automatically assigned security IDs (SIDs), which are used to access resources on the domain.

The two most important uses of an account are to authenticate the identity of a user, and to authorize or deny access to resources on the domain. Authentication enables users to log on to computers and domains with an identity that has been authenticated by the domain. Access to domain resources is authorized (or denied) based on the permissions given to the user (usually via membership in one or more groups).

Built-in Domain Accounts

In Active Directory, the Users container holds the three built-in user accounts: Administrator, Guest, and HelpAssistant. These built-in user accounts are created automatically when you create the domain. Each of these built-in accounts has a different set of permissions.

Administrator Account

The Administrator account has Full Control permissions for all resources on the domain, and can assign permissions to domain users. By default, the Administrator account is a member of the following groups:

- Administrators
- Domain Admins
- Enterprise Admins

- Group Policy Creator Owners
- Schema Admins

You can't delete the Administrator account, nor can you remove it from the Administrators group. However, you can rename or disable this account, which some administrators do in order to make it difficult for malicious users to try to gain access to a DC by using the account. Then, those administrators log on with user accounts that have membership in the same groups listed here to administer the domain.

If you disable the Administrator account, you can still use the account to access the DC when necessary, by booting the DC into Safe Mode (the Administrator account is always available in Safe Mode). See "Renaming Accounts" and "Disabling and Enabling Accounts" later in this chapter for more information about those functions.

Guest Account

The Guest account is for letting people who do not have an account in the domain log on to the domain. Additionally, a user whose account is disabled (not deleted) can log on with the Guest account. The Guest account doesn't have to have a password, and you can set permissions for the Guest account, just as you can for any user account. The Guest account is a member of the Guests and Domain Guests groups.

Having told you about when and how the Guest account can be used, I'll point out that in Windows Server 2003, the Guest account is disabled by default. Unless you have some urgent reason to use the account, it's a good idea to keep it that way.

HelpAssistant Account

This account, which is used during a Remote Assistance session, is automatically created when you request Remote Assistance. The account is created and managed by the Remote Desktop Help Session Manager service, and has limited permissions on the computer.

Domain User Accounts

Domain user accounts are created in Active Directory, working at a DC. Open Active Directory Users and Computers, and expand the appropriate domain (if more than one domain exists). Unlike Windows NT, Windows Server 2003 separates the processes involved in creating users. First, you create the user and the associated password, and then, in a separate step, you configure the user details, including group memberships.

Creating a Domain User Account

To create a new domain user, right-click the Users container and choose New | User to open the New Object-User dialog, shown in Figure 21-1. (As you type the first name, the initial, and the last name, Windows Server 2003 automatically fills out the Full name field.)

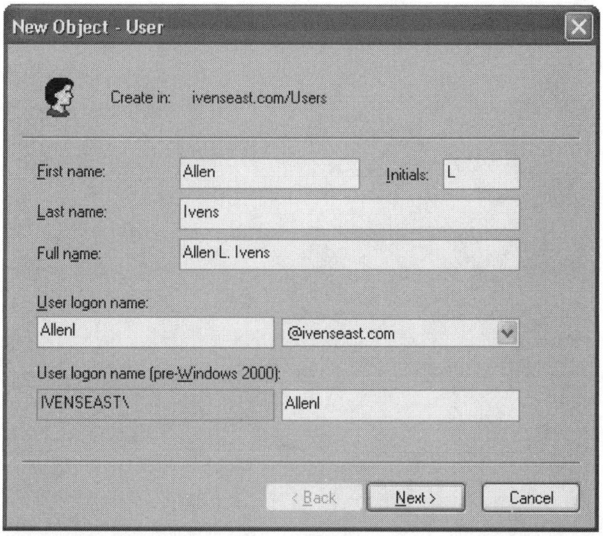

Figure 21-1.   *Creating a user starts with entering basic information.*

Enter the user's logon name. You should come up with a naming scheme that provides consistency throughout your organization. For example, you might use the first initial of the first name plus the last name, the full first name plus the first few characters of the user's last name, a pattern of firstname.lastname, or some other paradigm you can follow throughout the enterprise.

Add a user principal name (UPN) suffix to the logon name. The dialog displays the available UPN suffixes in a drop-down list. Until you create additional UPNs, the drop-down list shows the current domain suffix. See the section "Managing UPNs," later in this chapter, for more information.

You can also enter a username for logging on to the domain from computers running Windows 9x/NT. Windows Server 2003 assumes the same name, which is usually appropriate, but you can specify a different logon name if desired.

Click Next to configure the user's password (see Figure 21-2). By default, Windows Server 2003 forces the user to change the password during the next logon process. This means you can use a standard company password for each new user, and then let the user create her own password the first time she logs on. Select the password option you want to impose on this user.

Click Next to see a summary of your choices, and then click Finish to create the user in AD. (More information on passwords is in the section "Passwords," later in this chapter.)

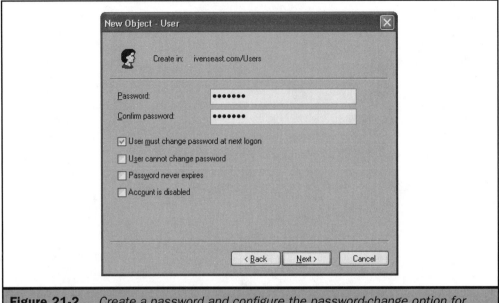

Figure 21-2.   *Create a password and configure the password-change option for this user.*

Configuring Properties for a User Account

To configure or modify the properties for a domain user, select the Users container in the console pane to display the list of users in the details pane. Then, double-click the user listing you want to configure. As you can see in Figure 21-3, you have a copious number of configuration categories.

I'm not going to discuss each tab in the Properties dialog, because many of them are self-explanatory. Several tabs are covered in this and other chapters as I cover user settings for different features. For example, information about home folders, profiles, logon scripts, and password options is found later in this chapter. The Member Of tab, which controls the user's group membership, is covered in Chapter 20.

Copying a User Account

After you've filled in configuration options for a user, you can copy the user's settings to another, new, username to avoid having to configure the new user from scratch. In the details pane of the Users container, right-click the username you want to use as the source, and choose Copy. The Copy Object-User dialog opens, which is a blank new user dialog. Enter the new user's information and password options as described in the preceding paragraphs.

The best way to use the copying feature is to create a series of template user accounts to cover the variety of settings you might want to apply to new users. For example, you can create a user named Power, with membership in the Power Users group, with

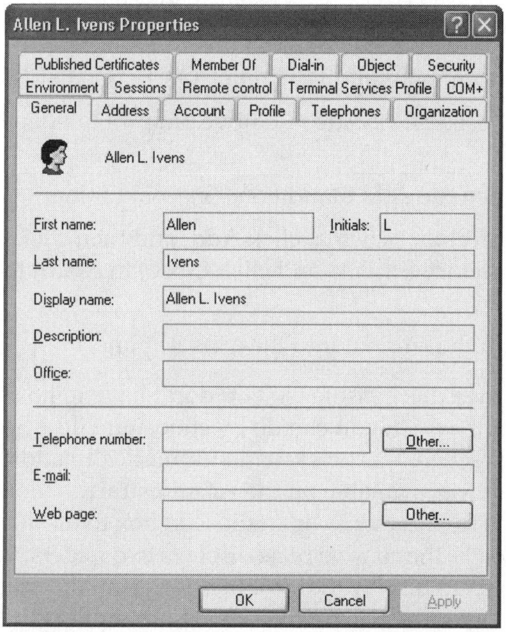

Figure 21-3.   *You can maintain detailed information about each user in the Properties dialog.*

unlimited logon hours, and other attributes. Then, create another user named Regular, with lower-level settings. Perhaps a user named DialIn, with preconfigured settings on the Dial In tab, is appropriate for your company. Then, as you create new users, just select the appropriate template user to copy from.

By default, the commonly used attributes (logon hours, workstation restrictions, home directory, account expiration restrictions, and so on) are copied. However, you can add other attributes for automatic copying, or prevent certain attributes from being copied, by modifying the Active Directory Schema.

Modifying the Schema for Copying User Properties

The schema is a forest-wide database of class objects and attributes for all the objects in the AD. (See Chapter 18 for more information on the schema, and on the DC that fulfills the role of Schema Master.) You can use the schema to modify the user attributes that are marked for automatic copying when you copy users.

Unlike Windows 2000, Windows Server 2003 does not preinstall the schema snap-in, so you must install it before you can use it. To install the schema snap-in, open a command window and enter **regsvr32 schmmgmt.dll**, to register the snap-in. The system displays a success message. Click OK to clear the message, then exit the command window. Then, load the snap-in in an MMC, using the following steps:

1. Choose Start | Run, type **mmc**, and click OK to open an MMC in author mode.

2. In the MMC, choose File | Add/Remove Snap-in to open the Add/Remove Snap-in dialog.

3. Click Add to open the Add Standalone Snap-in dialog.

4. Select Active Directory Schema, click Add, and then click Close (or double-click Active Directory Schema and click Close) to return to the Add/Remove Snap-in dialog.

5. Click OK to load the snap-in into the console pane.

It's a good idea to save this console (so you don't have to go through all the steps to add the snap-in again), which you can do by choosing File | Save. Choose a filename that's relevant (such as schema). The system automatically adds the extension .msc. The saved console is forever available on the Administrative Tools submenu of the All Programs menu, so you don't have to open the Run box to use it.

When the snap-in loads, the console pane displays two folders: Classes and Attributes. Select the Attributes object to display the attributes for your AD objects. Not all of them are user attributes, and unfortunately no column exists to indicate whether an attribute is a user-class attribute. However, many of the attribute names provide a clue.

Right-click an attribute listing and choose Properties from the shortcut menu to display the attribute's Properties dialog. The way to tell whether an attribute is available for automatic copying when creating new users is to look for the option Attribute is copied when duplicating a user. For example, Figure 21-4 shows the Properties for LogonHours, which is copied by default. If you want to set restrictions on logon hours on a user-by-user basis, then deselect the option. On the other hand, if you find an attribute that isn't already marked for copying, and want to make it a global attribute for all new users, then select the option.

Renaming Accounts

You can rename a user account by selecting its listing and pressing F2 (or by right-clicking the listing and choosing Rename from the shortcut menu). The listing is highlighted so you can type a new name.

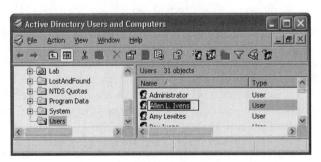

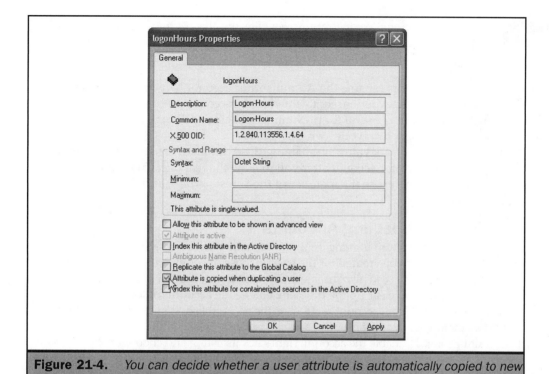

Figure 21-4.   *You can decide whether a user attribute is automatically copied to new users by selecting or deselecting that option.*

After you enter the new name, press ENTER to open the Rename User dialog, where you can make further changes to the user's listing (for example, you may also want to change the logon name).

Renaming an account doesn't require changing any other settings. The renamed account keeps its SID, so all the other account data, such as password, group memberships, profile settings, permissions, and so on, are retained.

Many administrators rename the Administrator account, which is a good security tactic. While advanced, experienced, talented hackers could probably get past this subterfuge, it's extremely useful for preventing malicious actions by less sophisticated hackers, including people in your own user group.

To enhance the security value of renaming the Administrator account, consider creating an Administrator account after you rename the real one. Create an account named Administrator, make it a member of the Guests group, and disable the account (covered next).

Disabling and Enabling Accounts

To prevent an account from logging on to the domain, you can disable it, which is useful for template accounts you created for the sole purpose of copying them when creating a new user. However, you can also disable an account if you think it's been compromised in some way. After you clear up the problem, enable the account for logon.

To disable or enable an account, right-click the account listing in the details pane of Active Directory Users and Computers and choose Disable Account. A red X appears over the account listing. To enable the account, right-click its listing and choose Enable Account.

Managing UPNs

When you create a domain user account, you specify a *user principal name,* or UPN. A UPN comprises a prefix and suffix separated by the @ sign. The prefix is the logon name, and the suffix identifies the user's logon domain. With a username of kathy and a domain of ivenseast.com, the UPN would be kathy@ivenseast.com.

While the UPN suffix is intended to identify the logon domain, it doesn't have to be a valid DNS domain. Instead, you can create any suffix to simplify logon or administration. For example, let's say your IT department is headquartered on a certain floor of the building. You've created an OU for the department so you can apply appropriate group policies. You might want to create a UPN suffix for users who are members of that department. You can do this for any OU, or for any company department/division.

To create a UPN suffix, follow these steps:

1. Open Active Directory Domains and Trusts from the Administrative Tools menu.

2. In the console pane, right-click the listing for Active Directory Domains and Trusts at the top of the left pane, and choose Properties from the shortcut menu. This opens the Properties dialog shown in Figure 21-5, which has one tab: UPN Suffixes.

3. Enter the name of the new UPN, click Add, and then click OK.

The new UPN appears in the UPN drop-down list when you're creating a new user, and in the Accounts tab of the Properties dialog for an existing user (so you can edit the UPN).

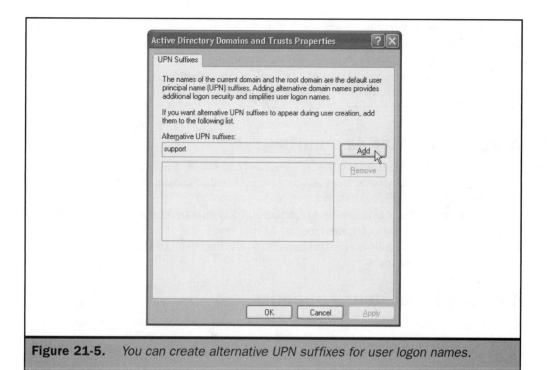

Figure 21-5. *You can create alternative UPN suffixes for user logon names.*

Managing Local User Accounts

Local user account administration takes place in the Computer Management snap-in, which you open by right-clicking My Computer and choosing Manage from the shortcut menu. In the console pane, expand the Local Users and Groups object, and select Users to display the local user accounts in the details pane.

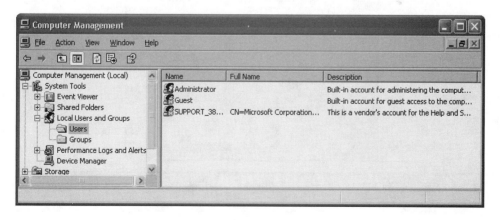

Only member servers have local users; you cannot manage local users on a Windows Server 2003 computer that's acting as a DC. In fact, on a DC, the Local Users and Groups object doesn't appear in the Computer Management snap-in.

Like domains, local computers have built-in accounts, and you can add new local accounts and make them members of local groups. Chapter 20 has information about managing local groups.

Creating Local User Accounts

To create a new local account, right-click the Users object in the console pane and choose New User. In the New User dialog (see Figure 21-6), enter the user's logon name, full name, an optional description, and a password.

If you want to change the password options, you must first deselect the option User must change password at next logon. At that point, the other password options are accessible. Click Create to finish. Then create another user, or click Close if you're finished creating local users.

Configuring Local User Accounts

Double-click a user listing to open the Properties dialog, where you can configure the user's settings. As you can see in Figure 21-7, compared to domain user account options, there are far fewer tabs for local user configuration options.

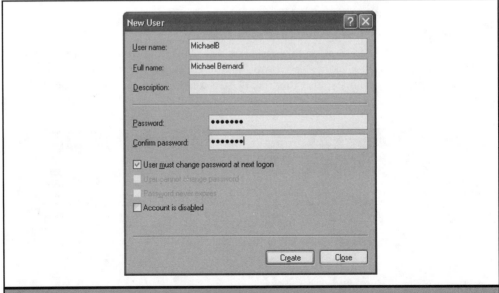

Figure 21-6. *The dialog for a new local user has fewer fields than the dialog for a domain user.*

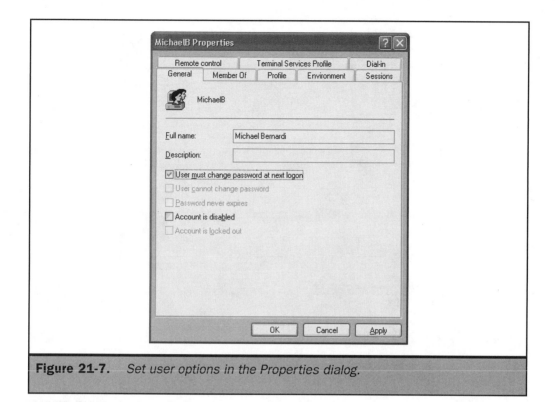

Figure 21-7.   *Set user options in the Properties dialog.*

Local Group Membership

To make a local user a member of a group, click the Member Of tab on the user's Properties dialog. By default, all local users are members of the Users group. Click Add if you want to provide additional group memberships for this user. Enter the name of the group if you know it, or click Advanced and then click Find Now to browse the list of groups (see Figure 21-8).

Remember that when you're working with local users, settings are geared to the local computer—for instance, when you want to make a local user a member of a group, your choice of groups includes only local groups.

Local Profiles

A local user has a profile, and you can configure that profile in the Profile tab of the user's Properties dialog. Just as with domain users, a profile contains a home folder and a logon script. (Profiles for domain users are covered in the section "User Profiles," later in this chapter; also see "Home Folders" in this chapter.)

Every user who logs on to a Windows Server 2003 computer has a My Documents folder, and this usually works well as a home directory when the user is working locally. You can, however, use the options in the Profile tab to set a different local home directory.

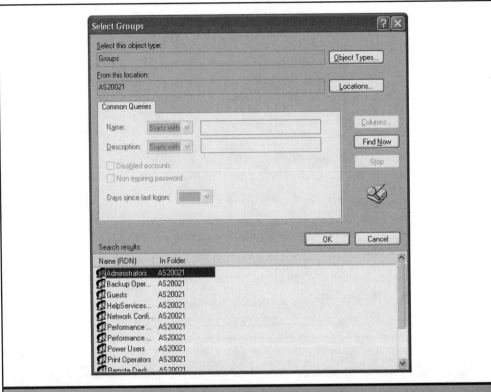

Figure 21-8. Group membership is restricted to local groups.

 The Profile tab offers the option to map a drive to a network share, but this doesn't work when the user logs on to the local computer—that option is only for the user's domain profile.

You can also assign a logon script, but this is uncommon for a local logon—you might want to consider creating a batch file and loading it in the Startup folder of the All Programs menu.

Overview of the Logon Process

Windows Server 2003 prompts for Username and Password during logon, and the user either selects the local computer or chooses a domain from the Log On To drop-down list.

Local Logon

If the user specifies the local computer name in the Log On To drop-down list box, Windows Server 2003 checks the local security database for a valid, matching account.

The logon succeeds if the specified account is found and the password the user entered matches the password for the account.

Domain Logon

If the user chooses a domain in the drop-down list, Windows Server 2003 uses the AD to process the logon request. The Net Logon service sends a DNS name query to the DNS servers, looking for the nearest DC. The specific DNS query has the following characteristics:

- Query type: SRV (service locator resource record)
- Query name: _ldap._tcp.*domain_name*

This discussion assumes the logon is initiated from a computer running Windows Server 2003, Windows XP/2000, or a legacy version of Windows with the Active Directory client installed. If the logon is initiated from a computer running an earlier version of Windows without the AD client, the DC cannot check the AD, and the authentication process is different.

For example, if the user is trying to log on to the domain ivenseast.com, Windows Server 2003 sends a DNS name query of the type SRV, looking for the name _ldap._tcp .ivenseast.com. The DNS server responds with the DNS names of the closest DCs belonging to the domain ivenseast.com, along with their IP addresses.

Using the IP addresses, Windows Server 2003 attempts to contact each DC deemed close enough to be appropriate, to see if the DC is up and running. The first DC to respond is used for the logon process. Net Logon then caches the DC information so that any future requests from that computer do not attempt to repeat the same location search process.

The DC checks the AD for the user account information of the user trying to log on. If the account and password are valid and the security settings allow that account to log on from that computer, the DC authorizes the logon.

Logon to Trusted Domains

In a trust relationship, the trusting domain trusts users and groups from the trusted domain. This enables users to log on in the trusting domain. When a user logs on to a trusting domain, she specifies the domain where her user account resides. Windows Server 2003 passes the logon request to the specified domain, which authenticates the logon request and grants logon if the account and domain relationship permits it.

Remote Logon

Remote Access Service (RAS) enables a user to log on to a domain through a remote connection such as a dial-up account or dedicated WAN connection. Remote logon happens in much the same way as a local or local domain logon. The logon request is passed through the RAS server to the DC for the specified account's domain, which authenticates the request, passing the information to the RAS server to allow or deny logon. See Chapter 13 to learn about RAS.

Authentication

Authentication is the basis of system security, confirming the identity of users who want to log on to a domain and access network resources. Windows Server 2003 enables single sign-on to all network resources, which means a user can log on to the domain and thereafter authenticate to any computer in the domain.

Windows Server 2003 supports a number of authentication protocols, including protocols designed for logging on to secure web sites, and over dial-up connections. In this section, I'll discuss standard user network interactive authentication processes: Kerberos V5 and NTLM.

Kerberos

As discussed in more depth in Chapter 17, Windows Server 2003 uses the Kerberos V5 authentication protocol as the default authentication protocol. For user logons, Kerberos works with passwords and smart cards, and it is the primary security protocol for authentication within a domain. Kerberos is also used to verify network services, and this ability to perform dual verification is known as *mutual authentication*.

Kerberos issues tickets for accessing network services, and the tickets hold encrypted data (including an encrypted password) that authenticates a user's identity to any network service. Once the user has entered a password, or used a smart card, the rest of the authentication process is invisible.

Chapter 17 includes information on configuring, maintaining, and troubleshooting Kerberos authentication.

NTLM

NTLM is the authentication protocol for transactions when at least one computer involved in the transaction is running Windows NT 4. Windows Server 2003, like Windows 2000, supports NTLM authentication. It's important to remember that this doesn't just mean it's possible for Windows NT 4 computers to authenticate when accessing a Windows Server 2003 computer—it also works the other way around. Windows Server 2003 supports NTLM in both directions, and therefore will use NTLM when accessing a resource on a computer running Windows NT 4. Following are some of the possible scenarios on your network in which NTLM support kicks in:

- A Windows Server 2003/Windows 2000/Windows XP computer authenticating to a Windows NT 4 domain controller
- A Windows NT 4 Workstation client authenticating to a Windows Server 2003/ Windows 2000 DC
- Users in a Windows NT 4 domain authenticating to a Windows Server 2003/ Windows 2000 domain
- A Windows NT 4 Workstation client authenticating to a Windows NT 4 DC

NTLM was introduced with Windows NT, and was referred to as Windows NT challenge/response authentication. In addition to authenticating users and passwords, NTLM supported encryption and signing. Windows NT also supported LAN Manager (LM) authentication, for downlevel (Windows 9*x*) clients.

In response to frequent reports of hackers gaining access to passwords, Microsoft enhanced the security of NTLM, introducing NTLM version 2 (usually called NTLM 2), with Service Pack 4 for Windows NT 4.

Windows Server 2003 supports NTLM 2 automatically for Windows NT computers on the network. If you still have Windows 9*x* clients, install the AD client on those computers, to enable them to authenticate using NTLM 2.

Dsclient.msi, the AD client (the technical name is *directory service client*), is not included on the Windows Server 2003 CD. You can download the client from Microsoft's web site. If you're moving to Windows Server 2003 from Windows 2000, Dsclient.msi is on the Windows 2000 Server CD in the \Clients\Win9x folder.

Passwords

Administrators and help desk professionals spend a great deal of time working with password problems. Users forget passwords, password change procedures don't work properly, and users complain about the complexity level you've required for passwords. It's like a haunting—password problems and complaints are a daily fact of life for administrators.

Most of us let users create their own passwords, and it's a good idea to distribute guidelines for this task. You can present your definition of a good password, along with some suggested rules (you could call them absolute rules, but some are difficult to enforce).

The best password is one that's unassociated with the user, because an intruder who knows the user could possibly crack such a password. An employee who keeps a picture of his dog on his desk is highly likely to use his dog's name as his password.

On the other hand, a password that has no association for the user may be eminently forgettable. Users solve this problem in a number of amusing ways, ranging from writing their passwords on sticky notes that they affix to their monitors, to leaving notes in an unlocked desk drawer.

New Password Requirements

Windows Server 2003 has a new feature that checks the complexity of the password for the Administrator account during installation of the operating system. If the password is blank, or doesn't meet complexity requirements, a dialog appears to warn you how dangerous it is to use a null or weak password for the Administrator account.

In fact, on the subject of passwords, Windows Server 2003 goes further, by preventing access to certain features if a user doesn't have a password:

- If you leave the Administrator password blank (a *null* password), you cannot access the account over the network.

- Any user with a blank password is denied access to remote control administrative features. That means your own user logon, which gives you administrative permissions (because you don't use the Administrator account, of course), won't let you perform administrative tasks across the network if the account has a null password.

Strong Passwords

A strong password contains alphabet characters, numbers, and special characters (, . ; : * % & !) or at least two of those three categories. However, many users have difficulty remembering such involved passwords, and I'll bet your help desk personnel can attest to that fact. One suggestion you could make is to tell users to merge unrelated adjectives and nouns, such as *sillyrug* or *smartsink*. It's even more effective to use that scheme if you place a number or special character between the adjective and the noun.

Password-cracking software keeps getting more sophisticated, and weak passwords fall victim to those tools in a split second. With enough time, of course, the automated methods employed by password-cracking software can crack any password. However, strong passwords provide a stronger defense against malicious intruders.

You can enforce the use of strong passwords with a group policy (covered in the next section).

Windows Server 2003 passwords can contain as many as 127 characters, but computers running Windows 9x cannot handle passwords that are longer than 14 characters. Don't assign long passwords to users working from these downlevel computers, or to roaming users who might have to log on from Windows 9x computers.

Domain Password Policies

Beyond making rules and suggestions for your users to enhance security, you have the assistance of the rules available in the form of policies in Windows Server 2003, which are the subject of this section.

You should carefully examine and think about the available password policies in Windows Server 2003, because your users (and therefore, your IT department) are going to live with the results on a daily basis.

Password policies are only available for the domain, not for an OU. Configure password policies for the domain in the Group Policy Editor, at Computer Configuration\Windows Settings\Security Settings\Account Policies\Password Policy.

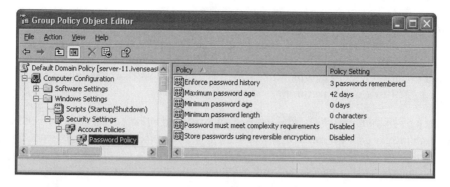

Password Policies and User Password Settings

Regardless of the domain policies you put into effect, password options you set for individual users on the Account tab of the user's Properties dialog override domain policies. This makes it easier to set up new users, because during setup you can enter any password, regardless of the rules imposed by your policies. Then, when the user changes her password, the policies kick in. Of course, this means you must always select the option User must change password at next logon, to make sure your security settings are met.

This also means that you can exclude certain users from password policies, by entering a password that doesn't match your policy settings and selecting the option Password never expires.

Enforce Password History

This policy lets you specify the number of unique new passwords that a user has to use before he can reuse a previously used password. By default, the policy is defined, requiring three unique passwords before reusing a password. The acceptable values are any number between 0 and 24 passwords. This policy enables administrators to enhance security by ensuring that old passwords are not reused continually. If password changes are required, some users constantly alternate between password A and password B. If either of those passwords is learned (or stolen), the next time the user switches to the compromised password, the person who has learned the password could log on. Requiring multiple unique passwords before repeating a previously used password lessens the possibility that a miscreant could log on as this user.

Maximum Password Age

This policy determines the number of days a password can be used before the user must change it. The allowable values are numbers between 1 and 999. The default value is 0, which means passwords never expire. If you set the maximum password age for any value except 0, make sure the minimum password age (covered next) is less than the number you set for the maximum password age. However, if you leave the maximum password age at 0, the minimum password age can be any value between 0 and 998 days.

Minimum Password Age

This policy defines the number of days a password must be used before the user can change it. You can set any value between 1 and 998, or leave the default value of 0 if you want to allow changes at will. Make sure this value is less than the value of maximum password age (unless maximum password age is set to 0).

Be sure to configure the minimum password age for a value greater than 0 if you're enabling the policy to enforce password history. Without a minimum password age, users can cycle through passwords repeatedly every day to get to their favorite old passwords, which undoes what you're trying to do with the password history policy.

Minimum Password Length

This policy determines the minimum number of characters that a password can have. You can set a value between 1 and 14 characters. If you leave the default setting of 0, you're essentially telling users it's okay to skip passwords, because without a minimum length, a blank password is permitted (blank passwords are often referred to as *null passwords*).

Password Must Meet Complexity Requirements

This is where you can get serious about security in passwords. Enabling this policy means you're imposing *strong passwords*. All passwords must meet the following requirements:

- It cannot contain part (or all) of the user's account name
- It must contain at least six characters
- It must contain characters from three of the following four categories:
    - English uppercase characters (A through Z)
    - English lowercase characters (a through z)
    - Base 10 digits (0 through 9)
    - Nonalphabetic characters (for example, !, $, #, %)

Bad Password Lockouts

Enabling a lockout policy means that a user account is locked out of the network if an incorrect password is entered a specific number of times, over a specified period. This can help you prevent attackers who are guessing a user's password from gaining access to your network.

However, before you embrace this security feature, consider the price you'll pay when the user who is locked out is an employee who either forgot her password or is a sloppy typist. That scenario is the most common cause of a lockout. If a lockout policy is in effect, you have two remedies when a legitimate user is locked out:

- Let the user wait until the specified amount of time has passed to cause the lockout to be released. This is undesirable because the user produces no work for the company. In addition, if the user cannot remember the password, starting a series of "guesses" later won't solve the problem.

- Stop what you're doing and perform the steps required to release the lock manually. This is a pain.

You can enable and configure lockouts for a domain, an OU, or a local computer.

Configuring Lockouts for a Domain or an OU

To enable and configure lockouts for a domain, or for an OU, open the GPE and expand the console pane to Computer Configuration\Windows Settings\Security Settings\Account Policies\Account Lockout Policy. In the details pane, configure the policies, as described in this section. You can configure the policies in any order, and as soon as you configure one policy, the system automatically sets the other two policies, using options that are appropriate. You can change the automatic settings by opening the policy and setting your own, preferred, values.

Account Lockout Duration   This is the number of minutes a locked out account stays locked before it is automatically unlocked. The available range for automatic unlocking is 1 minute through 99,999 minutes. Enable the policy, and set the duration to 0 to specify that the account must be unlocked manually by an administrator.

Account Lockout Threshold   This is the number of failed logon attempts required to lock the account. The acceptable values are a number between 1 and 999. If you set the value to 0, the account is never locked out. Failed passwords on workstations or member servers that have been locked either using CTRL-ALT-DELETE or by launching a password-protected screen saver also count as a failed logon attempt.

Reset Account Lockout Counter After   This is the number of minutes that must elapse after a failed logon before the failed logon attempt counter is reset to 0 bad logon attempts. Set a number of minutes between 1 and 99,999. This setting must be less than, or equal to, the setting for account lockout threshold.

Configure Lockouts for a Computer

To enable and configure lockouts for a computer (workstation or member server), open the Local Security Policy snap-in from the Administrative Tools menu. In the console pane, expand the objects to reach Account Policies\Account Lockout Policy. In the details pane, configure the settings as described in the previous section.

Unlocking a Locked Account

When a user's account is locked, Windows Server 2003 displays the following message: "Unable to log you on because your account has been locked out, please contact your administrator."

When contacted by this user, who will be either embarrassed or angry (depending on his personality type), you need to unlock the account. However, if the user cannot remember the password and is going to continue to guess, and therefore cause the account to lock again, unlocking the account does help. You must also reset the password and give the user the new password.

Resetting a User Password   To reset a user's password, right-click the user's listing in Active Directory Users and Computers, and choose Reset Password. (For a local account, use the Computer Management (Local) snap-in.) Enter the new password, confirm it, and click OK. You can also select the option User must change password at next logon.

Resetting a user's password has some negative side-effects. The following user information is lost:

- All files that the user encrypted
- Internet passwords that are saved on the local computer
- E-mail messages that are encrypted with the user's public key

For local computer accounts, you can create and use a password reset disk, which prevents the loss of user information. See the upcoming section "Password Reset Disks."

Unlocking a Locked Account   To unlock a locked account, double-click the user's listing in Active Directory Users and Computers and move to the Account tab. (For a local account, use the Computer Management (Local) snap-in.) A check mark appears in the check box next to the setting labeled The account is locked out. Click the check box to remove the check mark, and click OK.

Password Reset Disks

For a local computer account (a user who logs on to the local computer instead of the domain), Windows Server 2003 has a feature called a password reset disk. You can use the disk to reset a forgotten password.

Creating a Password Reset Disk

You can create a password reset disk for any existing local computer account, using the following steps:

1. Put a blank disk into the floppy disk drive.
2. Press CTRL-ALT-DEL, and click Change Password.
3. Enter the username of the account for which you're creating a password reset disk.
4. In Log on to, select the local computer from the drop-down list.
5. Don't change the password.
6. Click Backup to launch the Forgotten Password Wizard.
7. Enter the current password for this user.
8. When the reset disk is complete, click Next, then click Finish.
9. Label the disk and store it in a secure place.

The password disk has a single file, named userkey.psw. You do not have to create a new reset disk when the user's password changes.

Resetting a Password with the Reset Disk

If a user forgets his password, the password disk can reset the password so the user is able to log on to the computer. Take the following steps to use the reset disk:

1. At the Welcome to Windows dialog, press CTRL-ALT-DELETE to open the Log On to Windows dialog.

2. Enter the username and select the local computer in the Log on to field.

3. Click OK without entering the password (or enter a bad password if you want to make one last guess).

4. The Logon Failed dialog appears, which includes an invitation to use a password reset disk, if one exists.

5. Click Reset and insert your password reset disk into the floppy drive.

6. Follow the prompts in the Password Reset Wizard to create a new password (and also fill in a password hint to help you remember this one).

7. Log on to the computer with the new password.

Store the password reset disk in a safe place, in case you need it to reset your password again.

User Profiles

A user profile is a group of settings that define a user's working environment. Windows Server 2003 uses the profile to build the user's working environment at logon. Typical user profile settings include desktop configuration, menu contents, Control Panel settings, network printer connections, and so on.

Several types of profiles are available, and you can use any combination of profiles throughout your enterprise in order to serve your users' needs. In this section, I'll go over the profile types:

- Local
- Roaming
- Mandatory

How Password Disks Work

The Forgotten Password Wizard creates a security key pair: a public key and a private key. The private key is written to the password reset disk. The public key encrypts the local user's password on the computer. If a user has to use the disk (because she forget her password for the local computer account), the private key on the disk is used to decrypt the current password. The user is prompted to create a new password, which is encrypted with the public key. No user data is lost because, essentially, the user is only changing her password.

Local Profiles

Windows Server 2003 creates a local profile the first time each user logs on to a computer. Each user's profile is stored in the folder \Documents and Settings*User*, where *User* is the user's logon name (see Figure 21-9). The registry file portion of a user profile is a cached copy of the HKEY_CURRENT_USER portion of the registry, stored as Ntuser.dat. The user-specific directory structure makes up the rest of the profile. Ntuser.dat defines the computer's hardware, installed software, and working environment settings. The directory structure and the shortcuts therein determine the user's desktop and application environments.

Table 21-1 describes the specific contents of the directory structure as they relate to the user's profile.

Configuring the Default User Profile

The first time a user logs on to a Windows Server 2003 computer, the system creates the directory hierarchy for the user. To populate the folders and create a profile, Windows copies the contents of the Default User folder to the user's profile folders—and therein lies administrative control over a user's initial profile.

Customize the Local Default User Profile

You can tinker with the default user profile to design the profile presented to each user who logs on to a computer. Log on to the computer (don't use the Administrator account), and

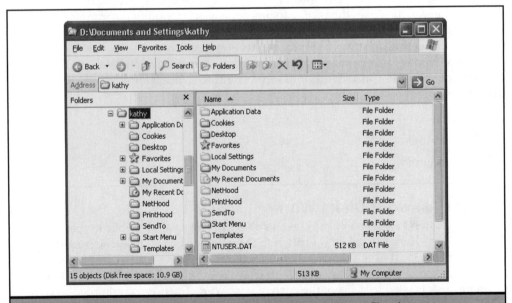

Figure 21-9.   *The user's directory structure contains the profile elements.*

Folder	Contents
Application Data	Data saved by applications
Cookies	User information and preferences from Internet sites
Desktop	Desktop objects
Favorites	Shortcuts to favorite locations on the Internet
Local Settings	Application data, history, and temporary files
My Documents	User documents
My Recent Documents	Shortcuts to recently used documents
NetHood	Shortcuts to My Network Places objects
PrintHood	Shortcuts to printer folder objects
SendTo	Shortcuts to document "Send To" targets
Start Menu	Shortcuts to program listings
Templates	User templates

Table 21-1.   *Locations of Profile Components*

install software, create desktop shortcuts, install a printer, configure a Send To target, and so on. Now you can provide any or all of those profile components to the profiles of users who will eventually log on to the computer, by including them in the Default User profile. Use the following steps to accomplish this:

1. Log on as Administrator.
2. Right-click My Computer and choose Properties from the shortcut menu to open the System Properties dialog.
3. Move to the Advanced tab.
4. In the User Profiles section of the dialog, click Settings.
5. Select the user who installed software and performed other tasks described here.
6. Click Copy to, and enter \Documents and Settings\Default User as the target folder (or click Browse and select that folder).
7. In the Permitted to use section of the dialog, click Change.
8. Type **Everyone** in the Enter the object name to select field.

9. Click OK to see a summary of your selections.

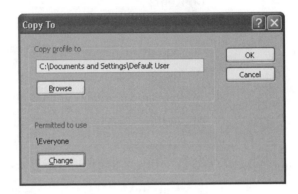

10. Click OK and confirm the copy procedure.

 The Copy to button is not accessible for the current logged-on user's profile, which is why you have to create the profile as one user, and copy it as another user.

Roaming Profiles

A roaming profile is stored on a server. The profile is loaded to the local computer from the server whenever a user logs on to the network, regardless of which computer the user logs on from. Any changes the user makes to configuration settings are saved back to the profile on the server.

In order to provide roaming profiles, you need to create a share for these profiles on a server. Here are the guidelines:

- You don't have to use a domain controller; any server accessible to users will suffice. I name my folder Profiles (in a wild display of my creative tendencies) and also use the name Profiles for the share (you use the share name, not the folder name, when you enable roaming profiles for users).
- Set permissions on the share to Full Control for Everyone.
- The shared folder cannot be configured for EFS.
- The shared folder's volume should not be configured for Disk Quotas— if it is, be sure it's a large volume and all users have large quotas.

Configuring Roaming Profiles for Users

To tell the system that the user logging on to the domain has a roaming profile, you configure the user's account in the Active Directory Users and Computers snap-in. Here are the steps to accomplish this:

1. Double-click the user's listing to open the Properties dialog.

2. Move to the Profile tab.

3. Enter the UNC to the Profiles folder, using the share name, not the folder name, and ending with the username. The username subfolder does not have to exist; it's created when the roaming profile is created on the server.

How Roaming Profiles Are Created on the Server

The way the roaming user's profile is created on the server depends on the circumstances under which the user is logging on to the domain. When the user logs on, Windows checks the user's account to see if a user profile path exits. If it does (because you entered it in the Profile tab as described in the previous section), the system looks for the user's profile subfolder in the specified profile folder:

- If the subfolder doesn't exist, and the computer from which the user is logging on has a local profile for him, his profile subfolder is created on the server and the local profile becomes the profile written to the server.

- If the subfolder doesn't exist, and the computer from which the user is logging on doesn't have a local profile for him, his profile subfolder is created on the server, and the default user profile on the local computer becomes the profile written to the server.

- If the subfolder exists, it means that either of these two scenarios occurred previously (this is not the first logon since you enabled roaming profiles for this user), or it means that you prepopulated the user's profile subfolder (covered next).

Prepopulating a Roaming Profile

Earlier in this chapter, I discussed the fact that you can copy a local profile to the local default user profile, to make the default user profile match the configuration options you'd prefer. You can also copy a local profile to the Profiles folder on the server that's holding user profiles:

- If the roaming user has a local profile on a workstation, copy that profile to the server. Then, when you enable roaming profiles for the user, and he logs on to the domain from any other computer, his own profile becomes his roaming profile. (You don't need to perform this task if you make sure that after you enable roaming profiles for the user, the user logs on to the domain from a computer that has a local profile for him—in that case, the profile is copied automatically.)

- If the roaming user doesn't have a local profile on a workstation, copy another, suitable, profile to the server for the roaming user.

Perform these tasks before you enable roaming profiles for the user. Otherwise, if the user logs on to the domain before you've prepopulated the server-based profile, the local computer will automatically create the server profile as described earlier.

 A "suitable" profile means the software and utilities listed on menus exist on every computer from which the roaming user might log on to the domain.

To perform either task, take the following steps:

1. Log on as Administrator.
2. Right-click My Computer and choose Properties to open the System Properties dialog.
3. Move to the Advanced tab.
4. In the User Profiles section of the dialog, click Settings.
5. Select the user profile you want to use for the roaming user (use the roaming user's local profile if one exists, or choose another profile).
6. Click Copy to, enter the UNC to the server-based Profiles folder, and include the user's logon name as the last subfolder in the path.
7. In the Permitted to use section of the dialog, click Change.
8. Type the user's logon name in the Enter the object name to select field.
9. Click OK to see a summary of your selections.
10. Click OK.

When you enable roaming profiles for this user on the DC, be sure to use the same UNC path, so the username subfolder matches the target of your copy action.

New Group Policies for Roaming Profiles

Windows Server 2003 has added new policies for roaming profiles to the Group Policy Editor. In addition, the GPs for profiles are now in their own containers (in Windows 2000, the GPs for profiles were in the Logon container) as follows:

■ Computer Configuration\Administrative Templates\System\User Profiles
■ User Configuration\Administrative Templates\System\User Profiles

These policies, which are self-explanatory, add power and controls to your administration of roaming profiles.

Roaming Profiles for Downlevel Clients

All of the discussion in this section assumes servers and workstations running Windows 2000 or later. You can also set roaming profiles for users who log on to the domain from Windows 9x computers, but the configuration and the execution differ.

Create a separate server-side folder for roaming profiles for Windows 9x clients, and use that UNC when configuring users for roaming profiles in AD.

On the client computers, open the Passwords applet in Control Panel and move to the User Profiles tab. Select the option Users can customize their preferences and desktop settings. Then select either or both of the options you want to include in the roaming profiles:

■ Include desktop icons and Network Neighborhood
■ Include Start menu and Program groups

Remember that you have to reboot Windows 9*x* computers after making this change (in fact, you have to reboot Windows 9*x* computers after making almost any change, which is why we've all learned to love Windows XP).

Mandatory Profiles

A mandatory profile is a roaming profile that can't be changed. Even though users may change some settings during a session, the changes aren't saved back to the server-based profile and won't be available the next time the user logs on to the network. Administrators, however, can make changes to mandatory user profiles. Because mandatory profiles can't be changed to reflect individual user settings, they can be applied to groups of users.

As handy as all this may seem at first glance, I personally advise administrators to avoid the use of mandatory profiles, because they're fraught with problems. Indeed, I've rarely seen a set of circumstances that calls out for mandatory profiles. You have hundreds of group policies available to prevent users from making changes to their environment, and that's a far safer approach than using mandatory profiles. However, in case you have some cogent reason to implement mandatory profiles that I haven't thought of, I'll go over this feature.

Mandatory profiles are very much like roaming profiles; in fact, they really are roaming profiles. However, the profile must exist in the user's server-based profile subfolder before the user logs on, because the client workstation can't write the profile to the server.

When you create the user's profile subdirectory, you must actually create the subdirectory on the server, because the workstation can't do this automatically as it can with roaming profiles. Configure permissions for Read and Execute.

In addition, you must add the extension .man to the last component of the UNC. For example, if you were creating a regular roaming profile, you'd format the UNC in the user's Properties dialog as \\Server\ProfileFolder*UserName*. For a mandatory profile, the UNC format is \\Server\ProfileFolder*UserName*.man.

After you copy a profile to the user's subfolder, rename the hive file, NTUSER.DAT, to NTUSER.MAN, which makes it read-only. The .man extension on the subfolder alerts Windows Server 2003 to the fact that the profile is mandatory, which, in turn, makes

---

Problems with Unavailable Servers

The most common problem with roaming profiles is that the server that holds a user's profile isn't available at logon. When that happens, Windows loads the locally cached copy of the profile. If the user has not logged on to the computer before, the system creates a new temporary profile. Temporary profiles are deleted at the end of each session. Changes made by the user to their desktop settings and files are lost when the user logs off.

If the server becomes available while the user is working, it doesn't matter. Changes the user makes to the profile aren't uploaded to the server at logoff. The rule of thumb is "if not available at logon, not available at logoff."

Windows Server 2003 refuse to let a user log on to the domain if the server that holds the profile is unavailable. Users who are configured for roaming profiles can use a local profile to log on, but mandatory profile users can't. The local computer issues a message telling the user he can't log on to the domain because his mandatory profile isn't available. (See what I mean by "fraught with problems"?)

Home Folders

A home folder is a directory you designate as the container for user documents. On a domain, this is usually a server-based directory, which facilitates backing up user data. Servers are usually backed up regularly, whereas local workstations are almost never backed up, even if you threaten your users. You can also create home folders for users on their local workstations, but the My Documents folder usually fills that role.

Server-based home folders are created for individual users under a pre-created share. For example, create a folder named Users, with a share name Users, and give the Everyone group Full Control permissions. Then you can add subfolders for users (\\Server\Users*UserName*).

Adding Home Folders to Profiles

To establish a home folder for a user, open the user's Properties dialog in Active Directory Users and Computers. Move to the Profiles tab (see Figure 21-10), select the Connect option (which is actually an automatic drive mapping), specify a drive letter, and then enter the UNC.

By default, Windows Server 2003 specifies drive Z: for home folders, but some old-time administrators (including me) follow the early tradition of mapping home folders to drive H:.

If the last section of the path (the username) doesn't exist, it's created immediately. This differs from the creation of the *username* part of the path for roaming profiles, which isn't created on the server until the user logs on to the domain.

It's important to look at the home folder paradigm and make decisions about using this feature for some or all users. The big advantage to home folders is server-based user documents, which means you can be sure you're backing up your company's documents.

For roaming users, you automatically gain the advantage of server-based documents, because the profile that's downloaded to the local computer during logon contains the user's My Documents folder. When the user logs off, the profile is written back to the server, including the My Documents folder and its contents. However, if you use home folders, when roaming users log on to the domain, they don't have to wait for the My Documents folder (and all its contents) to be copied to the local computer. Instead, a pointer to the server-based home folder is part of the profile, making logon and logoff processes much faster (and saving you any worries about disk space on the local computer).

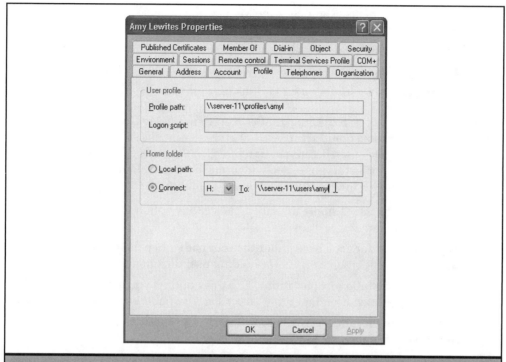

Figure 21-10.   *Connect a drive letter to a server-based folder for the home folder.*

Redirecting Documents to the Home Folder

When a user who is not roaming has a server-based home folder, the mapped drive appears in My Computer, and the command prompt in a command window is for the mapped drive. However, software continues to save to My Documents, which is a local folder. You need to redirect My Documents to the home folder, and you have a variety of methods available.

Manually Redirect My Documents

If you only have a handful of users who are not roaming, and they have home folders, you can instruct those users to redirect the location of their My Documents folders. The instructions are quite easy: right-click the My Documents folder, choose Properties, and then change the location in the Target field to the home folder (the drive letter). Windows asks if you want to transfer existing documents to the new location. Click Yes.

Use Group Policies to Redirect My Documents

Instead of letting users redirect their My Document folders manually, you can use a group policy to manage redirection. Open the GPE for the domain, or for an OU that contains the target users, and go to User Configuration\Windows Settings\Folder

Redirection\My Documents. Right-click the My Documents object in the console pane to open its Properties dialog, with the Target tab in the foreground (see Figure 21-11).

The Setting field has a drop-down list with the following choices:

- Basic: Redirect everyone's folder to the same location
- Advanced: Specify locations for various user groups

Basic Redirection   Basic redirection results in every user's My Documents folder being redirected to the same sharepoint. Then, below that sharepoint, the system automatically creates subfolders for each user. Because basic redirection targets one server, it works best in a small network, or for an OU populated with users in the same location.

In the Target folder location field, select one of the following options:

- **Redirect to the user's home directory**   Select this option if you've created home folders for your users.
- **Create a folder for each user under the root path**   Use this option after you've created a sharepoint on a server for holding user documents.
- **Redirect to the following location**   Use this option if you already have subfolders for each user. Enter the *%username%* variable as the end of the UNC.
- **Redirect to the local userprofile location**   Reverses any of the other selections and copies the data back to the user's local profile.

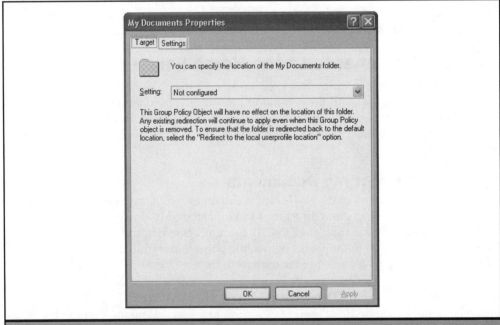

Figure 21-11.   *You can redirect users' My Documents folders with a group policy.*

On the Settings tab, shown in Figure 21-12, configure the target folder by making the appropriate selections.

- **Grant the user exclusive rights to My Documents** This setting, which is selected by default, sets permissions for the *%username%* only, keeping everyone else out (including administrators). If you, as an administrator, want to get into the folder, you have to take ownership of the subdirectory. Deselecting this option sets permissions as determined by inheritance (which depend on the permissions you set when you created the parent folder).

- **Move the contents of My Documents to the new location** Selected by default, this option does exactly what it says it does. The next time the user logs on to the domain, her documents are automatically moved (not copied) to the target folder. This happens whether the user is a local or roaming user.

- **Policy Removal** This option lets you select what happens when the policy no longer applies. There's not really an expectation that you'll return to the GPE and discard your policies on direction; instead, this option exists because the system assumes you're applying the policy to an OU. Your selections here determine what happens to a user you move out of this OU.

- **My Pictures Preferences** Use this option to determine whether the My Pictures subfolder is affected by the policy.

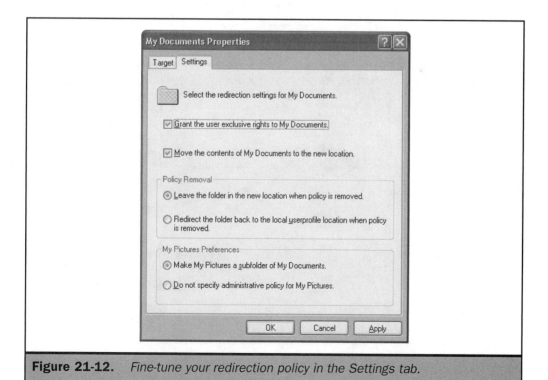

Figure 21-12. *Fine-tune your redirection policy in the Settings tab.*

Advanced Redirection   Advanced redirection is for larger enterprises, where you want to be able to target specific servers based on location, or on groups. If you've created security groups that are related to departments (for instance, an accounting group), this feature works beautifully. When you select this redirection option, the dialog displays a Security Group Membership box (see Figure 21-13).

Click Add to select a group and specify the target sharepoint. Repeat for each group and sharepoint you want to use for this policy.

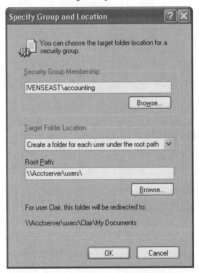

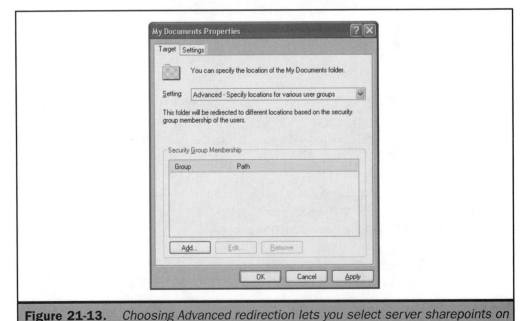

Figure 21-13.   *Choosing Advanced redirection lets you select server sharepoints on a group-by-group basis.*

Logon Scripts

Logon scripts are optional programs (a batch file, a command file, or vbs script) you can use to configure the work environment for users. The scripts run automatically during logon. To make this feature work, you must set a path to a logon script in the user's Properties dialog (on the Profile tab) or apply a Group Policy for logon scripts.

Enable Logon Scripts in User Properties

Use the Profile tab of the user's Properties dialog to assign logon scripts you've created. Enter the filename (for instance, accntg.bat) in the Logon script field. Then, during logon, the authenticating DC locates the logon script and runs it.

By default, the DC looks for the file in %SystemRoot%\SYSVOL\sysvol\ *DomainName*\scripts, so that's where you save the script file. However, if you want to put your logon scripts in a different location on the DC, you must enter a relative path before the filename (for instance \Accnt\accntg.bat), to tell the DC where to look for your script.

 It doesn't matter which DC authenticates a user, because Windows Server 2003 uses File Replication Service (FRS) to replicate logon scripts to every DC in a domain.

Enable Logon Scripts with a Group Policy

After you create the script and save it in the NETLOGON share (%SystemRoot%\ SYSVOL\sysvol*DomainName*\scripts), you can use a Group Policy to enable logon scripts, applying the policy to domains or OUs. In the GPE, expand the console pane to User Configuration\Windows Settings\Scripts (Logon/Logoff). Select Logon in the details pane to open the Logon Properties dialog, then click Add.

In the Add a Script dialog, type the path to the script in the Script Name field, or click Browse to search for the script file. In the Script Parameters field, type any parameters that you want to add.

 You can also write and assign logoff scripts using the same approach.

The
Complete
Reference

Chapter 22

Using Group Policy to Manage Server and Client Machines

If you're familiar with Windows 2000 Group Policy, you'll find few significant changes in Windows Server 2003 Group Policy. You'll also be pleased to learn that Microsoft is releasing a new tool shortly after release of Windows Server 2003 called the Group Policy Management Console (GPMC), an MMC snap-in and command-line tool that really simplifies using Group Policy. If you're moving to Windows Server 2003 from Windows NT 4.0, you'll find Group Policy to be very different than system policy—in good ways.

In this chapter, we'll discuss in overview terms how you can use Windows Server 2003 Group Policy to help manage and secure your clients and servers, and also how you can centrally manage Group Policy deployments, operations, and troubleshooting by using GPMC. We'll assume that you're either upgrading from Windows NT 4.0 or else new to using GPMC, and present most Group Policy operations from the perspective of GPMC.

If you intend to use Group Policy, make sure to buy one of the complete deployment and administrative guides for Windows Server 2003 Group Policy, which detail all the features and operations described in this chapter, as well as hardcore information such as scripting GPMC operations. Also be sure to carefully read the Windows Server 2003 Group Policy online help for complete information about the management and security settings available through Group Policy.

Group Policy Basics

Group Policy is an Active Directory–enabled tool for centrally managing users and configuring computers running Microsoft Windows Server 2003, Microsoft Windows 2000, or Microsoft Windows XP Professional. It is built into those operating systems, ready to use across your entire organization as soon as you install Active Directory. You use Group Policy to define automated configurations for groups of users and computers, including many registry-based settings, software installation options, logon and logoff scripts, folder redirection, Remote Installation Services (RIS), Internet Explorer Maintenance, and a wide range of security settings. Use Group Policy to help manage server computers as well as clients, using many settings made especially for servers.

Table 22-1 shows how you can use the various Group Policy features, listed in the order you'll encounter them in the Group Policy Object Editor (GPOE) MMC snap-in. We'll walk you through each of these Group Policy extensions later in this chapter.

Group Policy works by enforcing the configuration settings you save in a Group Policy object (GPO), which is linked to the Active Directory object of your choosing. A GPO is a stored collection of Group Policy settings that not only configures client and server computers but also supplies users with software, redirected folders, files and folders for offline use, user profiles for when they roam—all totaling several hundred options. GPOs let you centrally manage computers and users in terms of where they

Group Policy Feature	Description
Software Installation	Centrally install, update, and remove software
Remote Installation Services	Manage Remote Installation Services
Scripts (Startup/Shutdown)	Apply scripts during user logon/logoff and computer startup/shutdown
Security Settings	Manage security
Folder Redirection	Establish seamlessly redirected server folders to manage users' files and folders
Internet Explorer Maintenance	Manage Internet Explorer
Offline Files and Folders	Enable users to work with network files even when they're not connected to the network
Roaming User Profiles	Manage user profiles
Administrative Templates	Manage computers and users via registry-based settings

Table 22-1.   *Group Policy Features for Management*

are in an Active Directory structure, such as a domain or organizational unit (OU), and where you linked GPOs within that structure.

Make sure you have a good handle on your Active Directory structure, including where the users and computers you plan to manage are within your structure, before you set about creating GPOs.

Group Policy works like this: At each restart, user logon, or manually forced Group Policy refresh, each GPO's settings are applied to that user and computer. Each setting within the GPO is evaluated by the target computers, using the hierarchical nature of Active Directory, as described in "Group Policy Processing and Inheritance," later in this chapter.

So you set a user or computer configuration only one time, and then rely on Windows XP, Windows 2000, or Windows Server 2003 to enforce your configuration on all client computers until you change it. From then on, Group Policy settings continue to be enforced automatically, and they take precedence over registry or UI preferences that users set and alter without your intervention. Whenever there's a conflict—say, you enforce a specific Internet Explorer configuration, and a local user sets different preferences—Group Policy overwrites the local preferences at logon, at restart, during a normally scheduled refresh, or whenever you force a Group Policy refresh.

All the Group Policy settings in the Administrative Templates Group Policy extension actually write to special Group Policy sections of the registry. Settings configured elsewhere by using GPOE (such as Software Installation, Security Settings, or Scripts) use varying methods of applying their features. By using GPOE, you can set the machine registry, specify network paths to server shares or automatic software downloads, and so on—all from a single management interface that automatically reapplies these settings on a regular schedule. By using the free Group Policy Management Console (GPMC), you can centrally manage all aspects of Group Policy—including creating GPOs, linking GPOs, delegating Group Policy management, and adding Group Policy–delivered scripts—except for actually configuring GPOs. But you can even launch the GPOE from within GPMC by selecting a GPO and then selecting Edit.

Several GPOs can be linked to a single site, domain, or OU, and a single GPO can be linked to any number of sites, domains, or OUs. By linking GPOs to Active Directory sites, domains, and OUs, you can deliver Group Policy settings to as broad or as narrow a portion of the organization as you want. In other words, you can create a single GPO that manages every computer and user in your company, or else you can create a GPO for every OU to provide different configurations for each of those OUs. Additionally, you can do both and depend on how Group Policy is applied according to your Active Directory hierarchy. I describe how you can take advantage of this overwriting feature of Group Policy in "Group Policy Processing and Inheritance," later in this chapter.

Each Group Policy setting is described in detail in GPOE when you use the Extended view, which is the default behavior; if it's not enabled, click the Extended tab to see this view. Otherwise, the text appears on the Properties screen under the Explain tab of the Group Policy setting. If you want to take a look at all the descriptions in one place, you can open the associated Windows online help files directly using the command line by typing **hh** and then the help filename. Table 22-2 lists the Group Policy–related help files available in Windows Server 2003.

On a computer running Windows XP Professional, you see settings for Windows 2000 and Windows XP Professional only. On a computer running Windows Server 2003, you see settings for Windows 2000, Windows XP Professional, and Windows Server 2003. These help files often have links to the other help files listed here, so you needn't keep returning to the command line after you've launched one of these.

Because many settings (and some .chm help files) are not available by default on Windows XP, install Windows Help from the Windows Server 2003 installation CD onto any administrative computers running Windows XP Professional.

Requirements for Using Group Policy

Back in the days of Windows NT, Windows computers were managed by using system policy or by permanently "tattooing" the registry of your clients. System policy is based on registry settings set when you use the System Policy Editor, Poledit.exe. From Windows 2000 on, Group Policy added much greater flexibility for management, plus

Settings Covered in Help File	Help Filename(s)
Most Administrative Templates	system.chm
Security Settings	secsetconcepts.chm, spolsconcepts.chm, secsettings.chm
Security Templates	sceconcepts.chm
Group Policy Management Console	spconcepts.chm, gpmc.chm
Software Restriction Policies	safer.chm, saferconcepts.chm
NetMeeting Settings	conf1.chm
Settings for Internet Explorer	inetres.chm
Wireless Network (IEEE 802.11) Policies	infrared.chm
Offline Files and Folders	offlinefolders.chm
Automatic Updates	wuau.chm
Windows Media Player Settings	wmplayer.chm

Table 22-2. *Windows Server 2003 Group Policy–Related Help Files*

you can more easily clean up after yourself by simply unlinking GPOs from Active Directory containers, by getting rid of old GPOs, or by creating new ones that apply their settings later in the processing cycle (and thus overwrite the earlier settings).

First of all, if you're going to use Group Policy, remember that target clients and servers must be running Windows 2000 (Professional or Server), Windows XP Professional, or Windows Server 2003. If you have older machines on your network, they are unaffected by Group Policy.

Because Group Policy works with fully qualified domain names, you need to have DNS running in your forest, not just NetBIOS, in order to correctly process Group Policy. Also, because client or destination computers must be able to ping your network's domain controllers, do not turn off the ICMP protocol. If destination computers cannot ping the domain controllers, Group Policy processing will fail.

To use Group Policy, you need to use Active Directory. You can use Group Policy to manage server computers as well as client computers; in fact, Group Policy has many settings specific to server computers. If you don't build an Active Directory structure, you cannot use most Group Policy–related features (though you can configure local Group Policy objects on a time-consuming, per-machine basis), and you certainly can't use Group Policy to centrally manage computers and users.

Be sure to base your Group Policy deployment on your Active Directory structure, especially the geographical location of sites and the physical placement of domain controllers. Specifically, consider replication speed, because complex GPOs can get pretty big. In other words, don't try to use one GPO across the oceans. Plan accordingly, which means creating new GPOs for each OU in a domain that spans sites, or copying those GPOs to distant sites, domains, and OUs using the Group Policy Management Console (GPMC).

Only domain or enterprise administrators can create and link GPOs, though you can delegate this task to other users. For more information about delegating Group Policy tasks, see "Delegating Group Policy Management" in this chapter.

New user and computer accounts are created in the CN=Users and CN=Computers containers by default. It is not possible to apply Group Policy directly to these containers. However, two new tools are included with Windows Server 2003 to take care of this: Redirusr.exe (for user accounts) and Redircomp.exe (for computer accounts). These apply Group Policy to new user and computer accounts. You can find them in <windir>\ system32. Run Redirusr.exe and Redircomp.exe once for each domain, and specify in which OUs you want new user and computer accounts to be created. You can then manage these accounts with Group Policy. Microsoft recommends that you link high-secure GPOs to OUs that you use for new accounts. The Microsoft Knowledge Base article Q324949, "Redirecting the Users and Computers Containers in Windows Server 2003 Domains," provides more information on using these tools and for redirecting new accounts.

You might already be thinking (or have heard) that Group Policy is difficult to manage—ironic that a management tool should be tough to manage! Though Group Policy can save you a lot of time and heartache for configuring many computers at once, especially over time, Group Policy itself isn't the easiest tool to use out of the box. Microsoft has heard our cries and created GPMC, an MMC snap-in and command-line tool that makes using Group Policy much easier. Make sure you download GPMC from the Microsoft web site before going any farther: http://www.microsoft.com/ windowsserver2003/gpmc/default.mspx.

Interoperability with Older Operating Systems

There's no reason not to use the newest Group Policy settings that come with Windows Server 2003 administrative templates (.adm files), because not only do they support the newest operating systems, they also support operating systems back to Windows 2000. If you apply a Windows Server 2003 GPO to, say, a Windows 2000 machine where a setting isn't supported, literally nothing will happen, good or bad. The Windows 2000 machine simply ignores that setting. You can see which settings are supported on which systems by selecting a setting in GPOE, then checking what it says under Requirements.

If your organization uses all kinds of Windows systems, you'll need to take several things into account before using Group Policy.

First of all, machines running Windows NT, Windows 95, Windows 98, or Windows XP Home Edition cannot process GPOs. If any of these systems are part of an Active Directory container, they are unaffected by normal Group Policy Administrative Templates settings, as well as most Group Policy–related settings. Use system policy to manage those computers, even in later Active Directory domains, even when you've linked GPOs to those domains.

Machines running Windows 2000, Windows XP Professional, or Windows Server 2003 all support Group Policy. You can use either Windows 2000 or Windows Server 2003 GPOs to manage these machines, but using later GPOs offer more versatility. Just keep an eye on which settings are supported on which systems so that you won't have any surprises when a configuration that worked for Windows XP Professional doesn't work on Windows 2000.

To use Group Policy to its fullest, both computer and user accounts should be located in Windows 2000 or Windows Server 2003 domains, preferably the latter if you want to use the newest Windows Server 2003 Group Policy features. When a *computer* account is in a Windows NT domain, and the *user* account is in a Windows 2000 or Windows Server 2003 domain, only *computer* system policy is processed when the user logs on. After logon, only the user portion of a Group Policy configuration is applied. When a *user* account is in a Windows NT domain, system policy is the only set of policies processed for that account.

Conversely, when the *computer* account is in a Windows 2000 or Windows Server 2003 domain, and the *user* account is in a Windows NT domain, the computer portion of Group Policy is processed during startup. When the user logs on, *user* system policy is applied.

Finally, when both the computer and user accounts are part of a Windows NT domain, only system policy is applied, even if the machines are running Windows 2000, Windows XP, or Windows Server 2003.

Group Policy Processing and Inheritance

Before you start putting together GPOs and linking them to your Active Directory structure, you need to think about how Group Policy processes, and how inheritance within this hierarchical structure affects which settings are applied to users and computers. In fact, a thorough understanding of this processing and inheritance gives you much more management power and makes Group Policy even more flexible and targeted.

GPOs can be linked to (from highest to lowest) sites, domains, or OUs; in fact, you can link a single GPO to all three levels by using GPMC, or simply save it and then link it separately to each as unique GPOs. You can also link as many GPOs to a single site, domain, or OU as you need for your management purposes.

GPOs are inherited within Active Directory and are cumulative. They also affect all computers and users in the linked Active Directory container. A Windows 2000, Windows XP Professional, or Windows Server 2003 client processes GPOs in the following order:

1. Local Group Policy object (LGPO), configured per machine

2. GPOs linked to sites

3. GPOs linked to domains

4. GPOs linked to OUs

    a. GPOs linked to parent OUs

    b. GPOs linked to child OUs

    c. GPOs linked to child OUs within those child OUs, and so on, to a maximum depth of 64 Active Directory levels

That is, the first settings applied at startup or logon come from the LGPO, which you configure per machine—though why bother if you're using Group Policy, except to apply some pretty darned specific settings to a particular user's machine, say, an executive who requires something no one else gets (and then you better make sure that setting isn't overwritten by a later-processed GPO). After the LGPO, then the site-linked GPOs are processed, then the domain-linked GPOs, then the parent-OU- linked GPOs, and finally the varying levels of child-OU-linked GPOs within those parents.

For example, let's say you link three GPOs, one to the site (GPO1), one to a domain in that site (GPO2), and one to an OU in that domain in that site (GPO3), and you also configure a machine with an LGPO. To make it more interesting, let's say some settings configure the computers in conflicting ways (say, with different desktops or security settings). Upon startup, the client first processes the LGPO, and then it processes GPO1, then GPO2, then GPO3. Whatever's in GPO3 takes precedence over whatever was processed in GPO2, and that over GPO1, and that over the LGPO, so you need to keep a close eye on what GPOs your organization uses, which settings might conflict (that is, overwrite earlier-processed settings), and test new GPOs before sending them into your production environment. If you link multiple GPOs to the same OU, you can specify the processing order of those GPOs, adding yet another level of control.

Use Group Policy Modeling and Group Policy Results, described later in this chapter, to see if you've introduced any conflicts when linking a new GPO.

As you might have guessed, GPOs linked lower in an Active Directory hierarchy do not affect computer and user accounts higher in the hierarchy. For example, if the NYHR OU is below the New York Users OU, and you link a GPO to the NYHR OU, the computer and user objects in the New York Users OU are not affected by the GPO.

A GPO linked to a site provides those settings to all domains (per forest) within that site and is inherited by all domains and OUs within that site according to the Active Directory hierarchy. That is, each domain controller replicates a newly linked GPO on the normal replication schedule, so you might see some delay before site-linked GPO's settings are fully implemented.

A GPO linked to a domain provides those settings to all users and computers in that domain and is inherited by all OUs within that domain. If a domain spans multiple sites, the GPO replicates to distant domain controllers using your intersite replication schedule; try avoid this situation if at all possible. Obviously, domain-linked GPOs aren't inherited across domains; you can, however, link the same GPO to multiple domains. Such GPOs apply from the GPO's source domain to clients in the linked domain at logon or startup. Again, try to simply duplicate a GPO per domain, and then link these duplicates within their local domains.

A couple of special GPOs are linked to each domain when the first domain controller in the domain is installed and when the administrator first logs on. They are the Default Domain Policy GPO and Default Domain Controller Policy GPO. These GPOs contain domain Account Policy, Password Policy, Account Lockout Policy, and Kerberos Policy, enforced by the domain controller computers. Don't modify or delete these GPOs.

A GPO linked to an OU provides those settings to all users and computers in that OU and is inherited by all users and computers in any child OUs within the linked OU. Linking GPOs to OUs can really help target settings to specific groups, departments, or sets of users organized by these low-level Active Directory containers. For example, you might group all your New York Human Resources users in a single OU called NYHR, the OU from our previous example, which is a child of the New York Users OU. By linking a GPO with settings specific to that group defined by the OU, you can provide them with the software, security settings, and desktops they need for their jobs while everyone else in the domain gets a domain-linked GPO that doesn't provide the software or desktop delivered to them.

When GPO Processing Occurs

Group Policy extensions are called by Winlogon during the following events:

- **Computer startup**   This is when the Computer Configuration portion of a GPO is processed.

- **Logon**   This is when the User Configuration portion of a GPO is processed.

- **During the Group Policy background refresh**   Both the Computer Configuration and User Configuration portions of a GPO are processed at this time. The default refresh period is 90 minutes, with an additional (randomized) offset of 0–30 minutes either direction to help defeat people working against your enforced configurations and to avoid a lot of computers downloading the GPO simultaneously, thus creating a lot of network traffic. You can specify the background refresh to be anywhere from 0 (seven seconds) to 45 days. Don't use the very short refresh rates unless you're running tests in a lab environment, because you'll see heavy network traffic. Also, don't use very long refresh rates, because users might reconfigure their machines during the interim, defeating the purpose of your centralized configuration. For obvious reasons, the Folder Redirection and Software Installation extensions do not process during a background refresh, only during startup and logon.

- **When you run the Gpudpate.exe tool**   This manually refreshes both the Computer Configuration and the User Configuration of a GPO, say, when you're troubleshooting Group Policy or need to enforce new settings without having to wait for the background refresh. You can specify a number of parameters for Gpupdate.exe to control which settings are refreshed and how they are refreshed. To see the complete list of Gpupdate.exe parameters, use the **gpupdate /?** switch. Computers will restart if any GPO extensions contain settings that work only at computer startup, such as Folder Redirection and Software Installation, so be careful how and when you use this tool.

Filtering Group Policy

You can use filtering on a GPO so that it applies only to members of specific groups, or to control how GPOs are applied. By taking advantage of Active Directory hierarchy processing and then using Security and WMI Filtering, you can really target GPO settings and control their behavior without having to create and manage a huge number of GPOs.

Security Filtering

You use Security Filtering to specify which security principals in a linked Active Directory container get a GPO's settings. You cannot use Security Filtering per Group Policy setting, only per complete GPO.

To filter a GPO by security group, add a group to the Security Filtering section on the Scope tab of a GPO in GPMC. In the Enter The Object Name To Select box, enter the name of the security group, user, or computer that you want to add to the Security Filter.

See the GPMC online help for more details about how to use Security Filtering.

WMI Filtering

You use Windows Management Instrumentation (WMI) Filtering to control where GPOs are applied. You can link a GPO to one WMI Filter, which is evaluated on the client during GPO processing. If the WMI Filter evaluates to *true*, the GPO applies. WMI Filters are ignored by Windows 2000 or older machines, so GPOs are always applied on them, regardless of WMI Filtering. WMI can provide you with data about a computer, such as hardware configuration, available disk space, installed software, user settings, registry information, and much more.

You can use WMI Filtering only if you have at least one Windows Server 2003 domain controller in the domain. Otherwise, you won't see the WMI Filtering section on the Scope tab for GPOs and the WMI Filtering item under the domain in GPMC.

See the GPMC online help for more details about how to use WMI Filtering.

Group Policy Objects

The Group Policy settings that you create are contained in a GPO, which then delivers those settings to users and computers in the linked Active Directory container(s). GPOs are stored on a per-domain basis. Information contained within a GPO is stored in a Group Policy container in Active Directory, and a Group Policy template on the Sysvol of each domain controller. Each of these has a different replication schedule and method. Be sure to read the Group Policy online help for detailed troubleshooting information involving these replication issues.

The second type of GPO is the LGPO (local GPO), which exists on every computer whether or not you configure it. LGPOs aren't linked to any Active Directory containers. Unless you have very specific configuration needs on specific computers, you needn't worry about LGPOs. They don't have nearly as many options, either.

GPOs get bigger—and use more network bandwidth—as the number of settings and scripts they contain grows. Also, the more GPOs you link within your organization, the more bandwidth you'll use, though that's less important than the number of settings and scripts delivered by each GPO. LGPOs do not affect network bandwidth.

To create a GPO using the free GPMC, right-click Group Policy Objects in the domain where you want to create it, and then click New.

Editing Group Policy Objects

It's easy to create and edit a GPO, but not so easy to determine how you'll configure all those hundreds of options. After you've opened your newly created GPO, you select one of those settings; if it's in the Administrative Templates section of the GPO, you'll see the setting's description right there in the GPOE Extended View. Figure 22-1 shows the GPOE opened to show many of the available extensions. The user clicked the System portion of Administrative Templates in the User Configuration, and then right-clicked the System setting Prevent Access to the Command Prompt so that Properties is ready to launch.

To edit a new GPO, right-click a GPO in GPMC, click Edit, and then use the GPOE snap-in. If you haven't installed GPMC, you can also launch GPOE directly from the

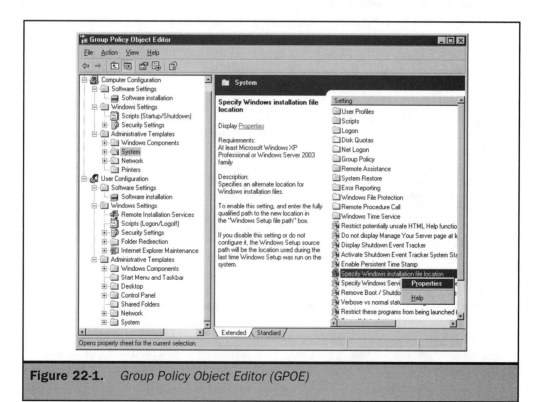

Figure 22-1. *Group Policy Object Editor (GPOE)*

command line by typing **Gpedit.msc** after you've added it by using the Add/Remove Snap-In feature of the Microsoft Management Console (MMC). When you edit a GPO, your changes affect all linked containers.

To edit a GPO, you must have Edit permissions on the GPO that you want to edit. To edit GPO-delivered IPSec settings, you must be a Domain Administrator.

To configure a setting in a GPO, open the Properties window by either double-clicking the setting, clicking the Properties link in the description, or right-clicking the setting and then selecting Properties. This opens the configuration window for that setting. Most settings offer the choices of Not Configured, Enabled, and Disabled, though some require you to type information into a text box or provide other details. The setting's configuration window also provides the Explain text for the setting, including which operating systems or Windows components the setting is "Supported On"—that is, what's the oldest OS or Windows component (such as which version of Windows Media Player or Internet Explorer) that recognizes the setting. Remember that it's okay to use GPOs with settings not supported on some machines contained in the linked site, domain, or OU; they simply won't recognize or be affected by those settings.

Group Policy Settings

We will not go into each and every Group Policy setting available, because that would require a book all by itself, and you can see detailed information about the configurable settings by opening any of the Windows online help files listed in Table 22-2. However, we will walk you through all of the extensions in both Computer and User Configuration categories. These extensions are the built-in mechanisms that apply configuration changes. We'll also describe how to load more templates and let you know how to create your own custom templates.

Several Group Policy client-side extensions are preinstalled on the target machines, so you needn't load those. Client-side extensions are installed and registered as .dll files on clients during Windows installation. To trigger Group Policy processing on a target machine, Winlogon calls these .dll files using the client-side extension settings contained in the Winlogon registry subkey. Table 22-3 lists the extensions and their associated files.

All of this is wrapped up in each GPO by a mechanism called Group Policy. Let's walk through your options now.

Computer Configuration

This portion of a GPO contains the settings that configure computers in the Active Directory container that is linked to the GPO. These settings affect all users on that computer. Figure 22-2 shows Computer Configuration opened to reveal all of your configuration options for this node. Note that I chopped the screenshot in half and set the halves side by side so that you can see all the options on a single printed page.

Now we'll go through the groups of settings available in Computer Configuration.

Group Policy Client-Side Extension	Filename
Software Installation	Appmgmts.dll
Scripts (Startup/Shutdown)	Gptext.dll
Security Settings	Scecli.dll
IPSec	Scecli.dll
Folder Redirection	Fdeploy.dll
Disk Quotas	Dskquota.dll
EFS Recovery	Gptext.dll
Internet Explorer Maintenance	Iedkcs32.dll
Administrative Templates	Userenv.dll

Table 22-3. *Group Policy Extension Files*

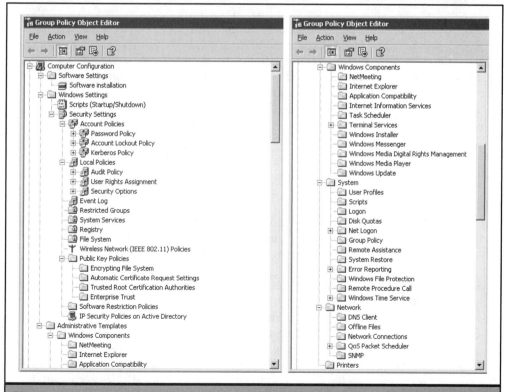

Figure 22-2. *Computer Configuration portion of Group Policy*

Software Settings

This node contains the Software Installation extension. It also contains software settings that apply to computers regardless of who logs on to them. This folder might also contain other settings placed there by the software packages you deploy through Group Policy.

Software Installation   You use the Software Installation extension to centrally deploy, patch, upgrade, and remove software applications without having to visit each machine or hope that users load, patch, or upgrade their needed software. You assign applications to a computer to provide that computer's users with reliable access to the applications they need. These applications also show up in Add Or Remove Programs.

If you assign a software package to computers in a site, domain, or OU, the software is available to users at the next restart or logon. The application can also be fully installed by the user from the Start menu, from Add Or Remove Programs, from a desktop shortcut, or by opening a document (on demand) with a filename extension associated with the application.

Only the local or network administrator can remove the software, though a user can repair the software. A user can temporarily remove the software and then later choose to reinstall it. However, by using Group Policy, you make sure that assigned applications are available on demand, regardless of whether users remove them, and that the applications are available again the next time the user logs on or starts the computer.

The Software Installation extension of Group Policy uses Windows Installer–based software packages (.msi files). If you need to deploy non–Windows Installer software packages, you'll use special packaging software to create the necessary .msi files, or else create simple text-based .zap files. Windows Installer .msi files offer many advantages over .zap files, so use those whenever possible.

After you assign software to computers in a site, domain, or OU, the software automatically installs the next time the computer restarts or a user logs on. After installation, you don't need to worry about users uninstalling it (only the local or network administrator can remove it), though a user can repair it using the Repair feature in Add Or Remove Programs.

Windows Settings

Windows Settings are available in the Computer Configuration and User Configuration nodes in GPOE. Computer Configuration Windows Settings apply to all users of the target computer. This node includes two extensions: Security Settings and Scripts.

Scripts   You can use Group Policy–delivered scripts to automate computer startup and shutdown by using the Scripts extension to specify startup and shutdown scripts. These scripts run with Local System permissions.

For Windows Server 2003 and Windows 2000 GPOs, you can scope the scripts using inheritance, WMI Filtering, and Security Filtering, as described earlier in this chapter.

Windows Server 2003 includes Windows Script Host (WSH) support, a language-independent scripting host for 32-bit Windows platforms that includes both Visual

Basic Scripting Edition (.vbs files) and JScript (.js files), as well as WSH files (.swf files). WSH is included in Windows Server 2003 and Windows 2000. You can use WSH to run .wsf, .vbs, and .js scripts directly on a client or in the command console by double-clicking a script file, or by typing the script at the command prompt.

You can use any language supported by WSH to create scripts. There's lots of software-vendor WSH support for scripting languages such as Perl, JavaScript, and batch files (.bat and .cmd).

When you configure the Scripts extension of Group Policy, you create new scripts stored in the appropriate folder at <windir>\System32\GroupPolicy\Machine\Scripts\. To configure a script in a GPO, open the Properties window by either double-clicking the setting, clicking the Properties link in the description, or right-clicking the setting and then selecting Properties. This opens the configuration window for that setting.

Security Settings   You use Security Settings to configure protect computers and your entire network. You can specify security for your site, domain, or any level of OU. Table 22-4 shows the types of settings available by using the Group Policy Security Settings extension in the Computer Configuration node.

As you can see, you can use the Group Policy Security Settings extension to deliver and enforce a wide variety of security configurations for Windows XP Professional,

Security Setting Type	Description
Account Policies	Control and manage Password policy, Account Lockout policy, and Kerberos policy. Applied only at domain level. If configured at site or OU level, they are not processed or applied.
Local Policies	Control and manage Auditing policy, User Rights assignment, and Security options.
Public Key Policies	Control and manage Encrypting File System, Automatic Certificate Request settings, Trusted Root Certification Authorities, and Enterprise Trust settings. Also enables Enterprise Trust policy to automatically enroll users in certificate programs.
Event Log	Contains System and Security Event Log settings. Controls settings such as the size and storage for Application, Security, and System Event logs.
Restricted Groups	Control and enforce membership of security-sensitive groups, as well as define to which additional groups a security-sensitive group belongs.

Table 22-4.   *Types of Computer Configuration Security Settings Available with Group Policy*

Security Setting Type	Description
System Services	Control startup mode and access permissions for system services.
Registry	Configure security permissions for registry keys, including access control, audit, and ownership.
File System	Configure security permissions for folders and files, including access control, audit, and ownership.
Software Restriction Policies	Identify programs running on computers, and control their ability to run. By default, Software Restriction Policies allow all software to run with User permissions. You can configure this so that no software is allowed to run regardless of user rights.
Wireless Network (IEEE 802.11) Policies	Configure settings for the Wireless Configuration Service, which operates installed IEEE 802.11 wireless network adapters.
IPSec Policies	Configure Client Policy, Secure Server Policy, and Server Policy, and propagate IPSec configurations to computer accounts managed by the GPO. Only one IPSec policy can be assigned in a GPO. Note that IPSec is also its own MMC snap-in.

Table 22-4. *Types of Computer Configuration Security Settings Available with Group Policy* (continued)

Windows 2000, and Windows Server 2003 machines. These security policies are applied to computers whenever a GPO is processed that is linked to the Active Directory container where the machine lives. Some settings don't take effect until after restart. To check which GPOs containing security settings were applied during the last policy update, see the local policy cache in <windir>\security\templates\policies\gpt*.*. Each file represents a security template in one GPO, and the GUID for the GPO is stored in the file.

Security Settings enhance existing security tools such as the rest of Group Policy and the Security tabs on the Properties windows of files, folders, Active Directory objects, and so on. Note that Security Settings might tattoo the registry even if the setting is no longer configured in the GPO that applied it or the GPO was removed or unlinked.

Administrative Templates

What most people think about when they hear the term "Group Policy" are the administrative templates that centrally configure the registry of clients. This extension is where the registry-based administrative templates (.adm files) live in Group Policy. Some 700 unique settings are available through using .adm files.

Windows Components   These settings allow you to configure settings for operating system components, such as NetMeeting, Internet Explorer, and Terminal Services.

System   These settings allow you to configure various system components to control features such as disk quotas, script and logon behavior, and error reporting. Disk quotas limit how much disk space that users' special folders can fill.

Network   These settings allow you to configure components of the operating system that connect a client machine to a network. This includes the ability to specify a primary DNS suffix and prevent users from changing it. You can also configure Offline Files and the Simple Network Management Protocol (SNMP) service in this section.

Printers   This section contains many settings for managing network printer configurations and publishing options.

User Configuration

This portion of a GPO contains the settings that configure users in the Active Directory container that is linked to the GPO. Figure 22-3 shows User Configuration opened to reveal all of your configuration options for this node. Note that I chopped the screenshot in half and set the halves side by side so that you can see all the options on a single printed page.

Now we'll walk through the groups of settings available in User Configuration.

Software Settings

This node contains the Software Installation extension. It also contains software settings that apply to users regardless of which machine they use. This folder might also contain other settings placed there by the software packages you deploy through Group Policy.

Software Installation   You use the Software Installation extension to centrally deploy, patch, upgrade, and remove software applications without having to visit each machine or hope that users load, patch, or upgrade their needed software. You assign or publish applications to users to provide them with reliable access to the applications they need. These applications also show up in Add Or Remove Programs for user-initiated repair, removal (if published), or reinstallation.

Software published to users in a site, domain, or OU can be installed by opening an associated document (if you selected Auto-Install), or by using Add Or Remove

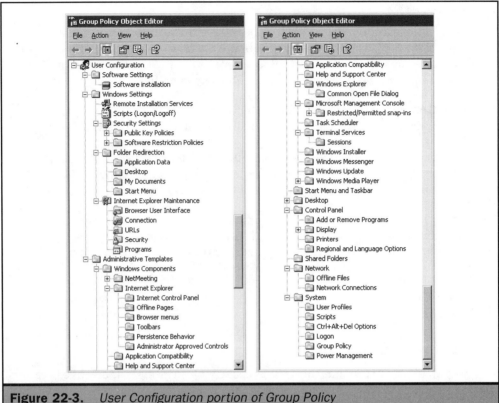

Figure 22-3.   *User Configuration portion of Group Policy*

Programs to install the software. If you link a GPO to deploy software and want the software to be immediately available, refresh the GPO before the application appears in Add Or Remove Programs. The user can remove the software, and then later choose to reinstall it, by using Add Or Remove Programs.

Software assigned to users in a site, domain, or OU automatically installs at the next restart or logon. After installation, you don't need to worry about users uninstalling it (only the local or network administrator can remove it), though a user can repair it using the Repair feature in Add Or Remove Programs.

The Software Installation extension of Group Policy uses Windows Installer–based software packages (.msi files). If you need to deploy non–Windows Installer software packages, you'll use special packaging software to create the necessary .msi files, or else create simple text-based .zap files. Windows Installer .msi files offer many advantages over .zap files, so use those whenever possible.

Windows Settings

Windows Settings are available in the Computer Configuration and User Configuration nodes in GPOE. User Configuration Windows Settings apply to all users regardless of which computer they use. This node also contains five extensions: Remote Installation Services, Scripts (startup, shutdown, logon, and logoff), Security Settings, Folder Redirection, and Internet Explorer Maintenance.

Remote Installation Services   You can use Group Policy to control whether the user of a Remote Installation Services (RIS)–configured machine must supply a computer name during installation, whether the remote installation attempt should be restarted if it fails, and whether users have access to tools before the operating system is installed. A GPO can support the choices that the Client Installation Wizard displays when using RIS for operating system installation.

Scripts   You can use Group Policy–delivered scripts to automate user logon and logoff by using the Scripts extension to specify logon and logoff scripts. These scripts run with User permissions. For Windows Server 2003 and Windows 2000 GPOs, you can scope the scripts using inheritance, WMI Filtering, and Security Filtering, as described earlier in this chapter.

Windows Server 2003 includes Windows Script Host (WSH) support, a language-independent scripting host for 32-bit Windows platforms that includes both Visual Basic Scripting Edition (.vbs files) and JScript (.js files), as well as WSH files (.swf files). WSH is included in Windows Server 2003 and Windows 2000. You can use WSH to run .wsf, .vbs, and .js scripts directly on a client or in the command console by double-clicking a script file, or by typing the script at the command prompt.

You can use any language supported by WSH to create scripts. There's lots of software-vendor WSH support for scripting languages such as Perl, JavaScript, and batch files (.bat and .cmd).

When you configure the Scripts extension of Group Policy, you create new scripts stored in the appropriate folder at <windir>\System32\GroupPolicy\Machine\Scripts\. To configure a script in a GPO, open the Properties window by either double-clicking the setting, clicking the Properties link in the description, or right-clicking the setting and then selecting Properties. This opens the configuration window for that setting.

Security Settings   You use Security Settings to configure protection for computers and your entire network. You can specify security for your site, domain, or any level of OU. Table 22-5 shows the types of settings available by using the Group Policy Security Settings extension in the User Configuration node.

You can use Public Key Policies to do the following:

■ Make computers submit a certificate request to enterprise certification authorities and install the issued certificate. The Automatic Certificate Request Settings GPO setting controls this behavior.

■ Create and distribute a certificate trust list. The Enterprise Trust GPO setting controls this behavior.

■ Establish common trusted root certification authorities. The Trusted Root Certification Authorities GPO setting controls this behavior. You might not need to use this setting for Microsoft root certification authorities in a domain, because all users and computers in the forest might trust them by default by installing a Microsoft certification authority. Use this setting to establish trust in a root certification authority that is not a part of your organization or a trusted root certification authority.

■ If necessary, configure root and NTAUTH trust policies for the domain. You configure this on the Properties page of the Public Key Policies node.

■ Add encrypted data recovery agents, and change encrypted data recovery behavior. The Encrypted File System GPO setting controls this behavior.

You do not normally need to use these Public Key Policies to deploy a public key infrastructure, but these settings provide added control for establishing trusts, issuing certificates, and deploying the Encrypted File System.

Software Restriction Policies consist of rules that determine what programs are allowed to run, and also specify exceptions to the rules. You can configure Security Levels, set Additional Rules, set Enforcement, specify Designated File Types Properties, and identify Trusted Publishers Properties. The rules identify software applications and specify whether the application is allowed to run providing descriptive text with each rule to help communicate why the rule was created. A software restriction policy supports four rules to identify software, as shown in Table 22-6.

Security Setting Type	Description
Public Key Policies	Control and manage Encrypting File System, Automatic Certificate Request settings, Trusted Root Certification Authorities, and Enterprise Trust settings. Also enables Enterprise Trust policy to automatically enroll users in certificate programs.
Software Restriction Policies	Identify programs running on computers, and control their ability to run. By default, Software Restriction Policies allow all software to run with User permissions. You can configure this so that no software is allowed to run regardless of user rights.

Table 22-5. *Types of User Configuration Security Settings Available with Group Policy*

Rule	Description
Certificate Rule	Identify a set of scripts that can be run anywhere
Hash Rule	Allow or disallow a specific version of a program
Internet Zone Rule	Allow software to be installed from trusted Internet zone sites
Path Rule (with environment variables)	Identify a program that is always installed in the same place
Path Rule (registry)	Identify an antivirus program that can be installed anywhere on a client computer
Path Rule (server)	Identify a set of scripts on the server
Path Rule (with wildcards)	Identify a set of scripts on a set of servers, disallow certain filename extensions from running, or disallow specific programs from running

Table 22-6.   *Software Restriction Policy Rules*

By combining the Security Settings extension in both the Computer and User Configuration nodes, you can use Group Policy to deliver and enforce a wide variety of security configurations for Windows XP Professional, Windows 2000, and Windows Server 2003 machines. These security policies are applied to computers whenever a GPO is processed that is linked to the Active Directory container where the user is a member. Some settings don't take effect until after restart or logon. To check which GPOs containing security settings were applied during the last policy update, see the local policy cache in <windir>\security\templates\policies\gpt*.*. Each file represents a security template in one GPO, and the GUID for the GPO is stored in the file.

Security Settings enhance existing security tools such as the rest of Group Policy and the Security tabs on the Properties windows of files, folders, Active Directory objects, and so on. Note that Security Settings might tattoo the registry even if the setting is no longer configured in the GPO that applied it or the GPO was removed or unlinked.

Folder Redirection   By redirecting files from local machines to a network share, you can back them up as part of your routine rather than depend on users to take any action to safeguard their data. Group Policy provides Folder Redirection settings for redirecting special folders to network shares. Each Folder Redirection option has advanced options that provide fine-control that takes into account Security Group membership. For more information about specific procedures, see Use Folder Redirection. The special folders you can redirect include

- My Documents
- My Documents\My Pictures (whether or not My Documents is redirected, or you can redirect it within My Documents, the default behavior)
- Desktop
- Application Data (when you also enable the Group Policy setting that controls the behavior of Application Data with client-side caching)
- Start Menu (if redirected, its subfolders always redirect, as well)

When you enable Roaming User Profiles, only the *path* to My Documents is part of the roaming user profile, not the folder itself. This keeps your network from having to copy the files up and down between client and server during logon and logoff. Even if a user logs on to various computers on the network, his or her documents are always available.

When you enable Offline Files, users can access redirected folders even when they are not connected to the network. You'll find this handy if you have a lot of laptops, roaming users, or a power failure. Offline Files works with any local or remote drive that a user accesses offline. Offline Files does not depend on Folder Redirection, though they work well together. If a user goes offline, an Offline Files icon appears in the system tray (lower-right part of the Taskbar), and users are notified with a pop-up.

If a remote worker and a user on the network both make changes to the same file, the newly connected user has the option of saving the offline version of the file to the network, keeping the other version, or saving both.

Internet Explorer Maintenance   Group Policy supports the administration and customization of Microsoft Internet Explorer for clients running Windows 2000, Windows XP Professional, and Windows Server 2003. The Internet Explorer Maintenance extension contains settings for configuring Internet Explorer. Use these Internet Explorer settings to manage things such as security zones, proxy settings, search, and temporary Internet files.

Administrative Templates

What most people think about when they hear the term "Group Policy" are the administrative templates that centrally configure the registry of clients. This extension is where the registry-based administrative templates (.adm files) live in Group Policy. Some 700 unique settings are available through using .adm files.

Windows Components   Use these settings to configure the following Windows operating system components:

- NetMeeting
- Internet Explorer

- Windows Explorer
- Microsoft Management Console
- Task Scheduler
- Terminal Services
- Windows Installer
- Windows Messenger
- Windows Update
- Windows Media Player

Start Menu and Taskbar   Use these settings to configure, add, remove, and disable parts of the Start menu, taskbar, and notification area/system tray. You have nearly 50 settings to choose from here.

Desktop   Use these settings to manage client desktops, including Active Desktop settings, My Documents and My Computer icons, and many other options. You can also use settings here to manage how users interact with Active Directory.

Control Panel   Use these settings to configure users' Control Panel, including Add/ Remove Programs visibility and behavior, screen savers and related password-protected screensavers, language options, and user access to Control Panel.

Shared Folder   Use these settings to allow shared folders or DFS roots to be published.

Network   Use these settings to configure components of the operating system that connect a client machine to a network. This includes the ability to specify a primary DNS suffix and prevent users from changing it. You can also configure Offline Files from here. Many Network Connections settings are also available here.

System   Use these settings to control the behavior of features such as User Profiles, Scripts, CTRL+ALT+DEL Options, Logon, Group Policy, Power Management, and many other items, including Windows Automatic Updates.

Custom Templates

By default, you have access to more than 700 Group Policy settings. Even so, you might need to create additional policy settings to support a new piece of software your organization has purchased, or if you want to manage registry settings not configurable through existing Group Policy settings. You can perform these tasks three ways:

- **Add administrative templates already in Windows**   Some .adm files are available only by adding them using GPOE.

- **Create new Group Policy extensions**   Before you do this, read up on advanced Group Policy literature.
- **Create client-side extensions**   Again, not a beginner strategy, but also available for building versatile GPOs.

Some applications write and install their own, additional extensions (both Group Policy extensions and client-side extensions) to expand the management capabilities of GPOs.

You won't usually need to create new extensions, because the existing options are very versatile and complete. However, if an application or feature looks for policy settings in the registry, you might want to create a new .adm file to manage it and then import the new .adm template into the Administrative Templates extension. They are essentially text files that you create with a basic text editor such as Notepad, and saved with the .adm filename extension. Take a look at an advanced book on Group Policy for details about creating custom .adm files, but once you get a hang of it, they're pretty simple to create and customize. Read the Platform SDK: Policies and Profiles to get details about .adm template syntax.

A related note about loading other .adm templates: Those located in <windir>\Inf, which aren't loaded into Administrative Templates, really exist only to support system policy, and they tattoo the registry. Don't use these .adm files unless you can't avoid it.

Using GPMC to Manage Group Policy

GPMC is a new, free tool that unifies Group Policy management, even across forests. Use GPMC to manage all your GPOs, WMI filters, delegation, and Group Policy–related permissions. GPMC consists of a set of scriptable interfaces for managing Group Policy and an MMC snap-in, which includes Group Policy tools such as GPOE, RSoP, and Active Directory Users and Computers, and many other tools. GPMC runs Windows Server 2003 or Windows XP Professional, Service Pack 1 or later. It can manage Windows Server 2003 and Windows 2000 Active Directory domains, but it won't run from a Windows 2000 machine. You can use drag-and-drop in GPMC, which makes using it for managing GPOs even simpler.

Figure 22-4 shows the GPMC user interface.

Read the online GPMC help for step-by-step information about using GPMC to deploy and manage Group Policy, which is available only by downloading GPMC.

To open GPMC, go to Start | Programs | Administrative Tools | Group Policy Management. To download the free GPMC, go to the Microsoft web site: http://www.microsoft.com/windowsserver2003/gpmc/default.mspx.

Creating Group Policy Objects

To create an unlinked GPO, expand the GPMC console tree until you see Group Policy Objects in the container for which you want to create a new GPO. Right-click Group Policy Objects, and then click New. In the New GPO dialog box, specify a name for the

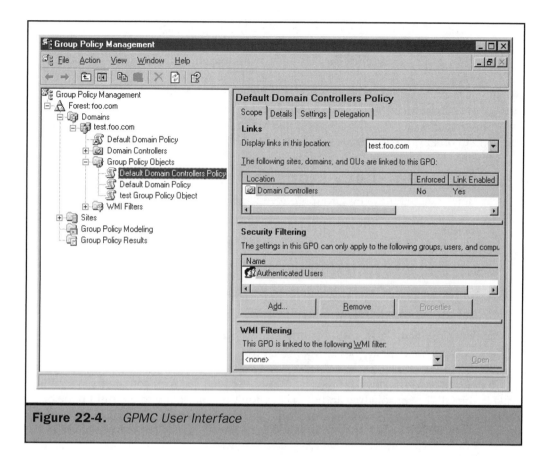

Figure 22-4.   *GPMC User Interface*

new GPO, and then click OK. Now that you've created a new GPO, you can customize it to suit your client and server needs. To edit a GPO, in the GPMC console tree, right-click the GPO you want to edit, and then click Edit. This starts the GPOE snap-in, which we walked through earlier in this chapter.

You can select Create And Link A GPO Here—that is, to any Active Directory object visible in the GPMC console tree—but that will only cause you pain. New GPOs try to enforce their settings right away, so always create unlinked GPOs, configure them as needed, and then test them in a non-production environment before linking them to production Active Directory containers.

Linking Group Policy Objects to Active Directory Containers

Once your GPO is tested and ready to go, you need to link it to Active Directory containers before it can have any effect. To link a GPO, right-click the Active Directory container to which you want to link, and then click Link An Existing GPO Here. Drag a GPO from the Group Policy Objects node to the OU. This drag-and-drop functionality works only within the same domain.

To unlink a GPO, right-click the GPO you want to unlink. In the details window, click the Scope tab. In the Links section, right-click the Active Directory object from which you want to unlink. Select Delete Link from the list. When you delete a GPO, you are prompted to delete this GPO and all links to it in this domain. This does not delete links to this GPO from *other* domains. Make sure you remove those links from this GPO to other domains, as well, before deleting this GPO.

Delegating Group Policy Management

You can delegate the following Group Policy tasks:

- Creating GPOs
- Managing GPOs
- Read-only access to GPOs
- Managing Group Policy links per Active Directory container
- Performing Group Policy modeling
- Reading Group Policy results data
- Creating, managing, and editing WMI filters for GPOs

To delegate permissions for linking GPOs to Active Directory containers, click the node in the GPMC console tree and then click the Delegation tab in the right pane of GPMC. Several items are listed here, so right-click the one whose permissions you want to change, and then select Link GPOs, Perform Group Policy Modeling Analyses, or Read Group Policy Results Data. You can also configure custom permissions by clicking Advanced and then selecting the object whose permissions you want to change.

To edit a GPO, you need the following permissions on the GPO set to Allow: Read, Write, Create All Child Objects, and Delete All Child Objects. GPMC sets all of these permissions when you grant the Edit permission. Be sure to read the online GPMC help for full details about how to delegate GPMC and GPOE management.

Group Policy Modeling

GPMC uses Resultant Set of Policy (RSoP) features, though they work a little differently in GPMC. The Group Policy Modeling Wizard simulates the net effect of GPOs and provides RSoP data before you link them to your network. You can view this RSoP report to see GPO interaction and troubleshoot potential problems before they happen. The report is available in the Settings tab of the right GPMC pane after you select a GPO.

To run Group Policy modeling, you need at least one Windows Server 2003 domain controller, and you need to be granted the Perform Group Policy Modeling analyses permission on the Active Directory container where you want to run the analysis. You run the wizard by right-clicking Group Policy Modeling (or an Active Directory container), and then selecting Group Policy Modeling Wizard. If you run Group Policy modeling from an Active Directory container, the wizard fills in the Container fields for user and computer; otherwise, you need to fill in the items requested by the wizard.

The results are saved as a query under Group Policy Modeling. To permanently save the results, right-click the query, and then click Save Report.

You can see which GPO delivered each setting under Winning GPO. You can see information such as which GPO's settings did not succeed by right-clicking the Group Policy Modeling item, and then selecting Advanced View. Each setting provides a Precedence tab for further troubleshooting. Because Group Policy modeling doesn't evaluate LGPOs, you will see a difference between the simulation and the actual results if you've configured LGPOs.

Group Policy Results

The Group Policy Results Wizard reports which Group Policy settings are applied to a user or computer by gathering RSoP data from a target machine. The target must have Windows XP Professional or Windows Server 2003. You can view this RSoP report to troubleshoot existing GPOs. The report is available in the Settings and Summary tabs of the right GPMC pane after you select a GPO.

You can remotely access Group Policy results data rather than walking around to each affected machine, but first you need the Remotely Access Group Policy Results Data permission on the Active Directory container where the user or computer lives, or you must be a Local Administrator and have network connectivity to the target machine. To delegate Group Policy results, the Windows Server 2003 schema must exist in the Active Directory—you don't need a Windows Server 2003 domain controller. To install this schema, run **ADPrep /forestprep** on any Windows 2000 or later domain controller in the domain.

After the wizard runs, the results are saved as a query under Group Policy Results, and they display how Group Policy is applied to the target. To permanently save the results, right-click the query, and then click Save Report. You can see which GPO delivered each setting under Winning GPO.

Backing Up Group Policy Objects

GPMC makes it easy to regularly back up all of your GPOs. You can back up GPOs to any local computer or network folder where you have Write access. Always use GPMC to work with this backup folder (either the GPMC MMC snap-in or by scripting). You can interact with backed-up GPOs by using the Import and Restore GPMC operations. Use the following procedure to back up GPOs:

1. In GPMC, right-click the GPO you want to back up, and then click Back Up.

2. In the Backup Group Policy Object box, type the path to the backup folder. You can also click Browse, then locate the folder.

3. Provide information for the GPO that you want to back up, and then click Backup. When that's done, click OK.

Importing GPO Settings

A very useful GPMC feature is the ability to import settings from existing GPOs into a new GPO. To import GPO settings, right-click the GPO you want to import settings into, and then click Import Settings. Walk through the Import Settings Wizard regarding the backed-up GPO whose settings you want to import, and then click Finish.

Restoring Backed-Up Group Policy Objects

Using GPMC, you can restore a backed-up GPO to the same domain from which it was backed up. You cannot restore a GPO into a domain different from the GPO's original domain; use the other GPMC operations described before to do that. To restore a backed-up GPO, right-click the GPO you want to restore and then click Restore From Backup. Walk through the Restore Group Policy Object Wizard regarding the backed-up GPO you want to restore, and then click Finish.

Copying Group Policy Objects

You can use GPMC to copy GPOs from the same domain or even across domains. When you copy a GPO, GPMC creates a new GPO. It's a really simple operation: either copy and paste or drag and drop the GPO you want to copy—that's it! Well, it's not quite that simple if you're copying across domains, because you'll likely also want to copy the DACLs on the GPO to ensure that the new GPO contains the same Security Filtering and delegation configuration as the original GPO. If you are copying between OUs within a domain, click Use The Default DACL For New GPOs or Preserve The Existing DACL, and then click OK. Also, because settings in a GPO are often specific to a domain (such as network paths), you'll likely want to use migration tables, as described next.

Migrating GPO Settings

GPMC makes it easy to migrate a standard GPO across domains. Settings in a GPO are often specific to a domain, so GPMC uses migration tables. Migration tables are XML files with the filename extension .migtable. Creating and using migration tables are advanced Group Policy operations, so be sure to read the "Migrating GPOs Across Domains by Using GPMC" white paper on the Microsoft GPMC web site: http://www.microsoft.com/windowsserver2003/gpmc/default.mspx.

Scripting GPMC Operations

GPMC provides a comprehensive set of COM interfaces for scripting all GPMC operations except editing GPOs. You can see sample scripts that use these interfaces after you've installed GPMC in the \Program Files\GPMC\Scripts\ folder. All of the scripts run from the command line. Running a script with the /? switch displays the usage for that script.

The sample scripts echo output to the command window and must be executed by using cscript.exe. If cscript.exe is not your default scripting host, you will need to explicitly specify cscript.exe on the command line. For example, type **d: \Program Files\GPMC\ Scripts>cscript ListAllGPOs.wsf**. Type **cscript //<drive>:cscript** at a command line to make cscript the default scripting host.

Many of the sample scripts rely on a library of common helper functions contained in the file Lib_CommonGPMCFunctions.js. If you copy these scripts to another location, you must also copy this library file to that location in order for the script samples to work.

Read the Platform SDK: Group Policy Management Console for complete information about scripting GPMC interfaces.

The
Complete
Reference

Windows
Server
2003

Chapter 23

Network Software Installation

Windows Server 2003 expands on the strong tool sets available with Windows 2000 Server for software installation over networks and management support. These tools prove to be valuable time savers and serve to provide the standardization that defines secure and highly available Windows 2003 environments. Some sites and companies are not going to implement Microsoft SMS (System Management Server) and can take advantage of Intellimirror Application setup and publishing technologies available with Windows 2003 and Remote Installation Services for operating systems deployment and complete image delivery.

The tools and technologies available for network software installation are Intellimirror and RIS (Remote Installation Services). Additionally, some new features focus on movement of a user's data to a new computer. This is the User State Migration tool, which is new to the Windows Server 2003 family.

However, many other new Windows 2003 tools and techniques fall under the network software installation area, although they may not appear to qualify. Some great new tools exist that don't necessary install software but restrict it! They are covered by the brand new software restriction policy, which provides for policies that will disallow software installation and use in your environment, including restricting Internet site use.

Windows Update is significantly enhanced, even employing the ability to access Windows update sites during install. This is another method of software deployment, but in secure and closed environments Internet access is not an option, so Microsoft has released an important tool to take advantage of Windows 2003's Automatic Update capability, which is Software Update Services. This is not a Windows 2003 feature, but it is certainly a server product to help take advantage of Windows 2003's Automatic Update features within secure networks.

Windows Web Server 2003 will not have the capability to serve as a RIS server given the operating system's role limiting it to Web Server and Web Services operations. The features and techniques outlined in this chapter relate to Windows Server 2003, Windows 2003 Enterprise Server, and Windows 2003 Data Center Server.

Table 23-1 identifies what is new in this area in the Windows 2003 platform, not found in Windows 2000. All of these features are assumed new for Windows NT 4.0 Server platforms.

RIS represents the most significant tool within Windows 2003 for network operating system software deployment. Accordingly, we will focus on it first and then cover in detail the remaining options for software deployment and management over a Windows 2003 network:

- Intellimirror/group policy distribution of software using Active Directory
- Software restriction policy
- User State Migration tool

The role of each of these technologies is explored in detail; they are then combined to represent extensions of Windows 2003 management techniques to users, computers, and the Windows Server 2003 environment.

Network Software Installation Service	New Features
Remote Installation Services	Supports the following target clients: Windows XP Professional/Home Windows Server 2003 (all flavors)
	Advanced control over the answer files used for installation
	Access to network files while in recovery mode
Group Policy Software Distribution	Advanced deployment options to enable or disable availability of 32-bit and 64-bit computers
	Enable or disable default publication of OLE class information about a software package
	Can now enforce assigned applications at the time of deployment
Intellimirror	Application publishing at time of use or first logon to Windows 2003 Active Directory–based network

Table 23-1.   *New Features in Windows Server 2003*

Remote Installation Services

RIS is designed to deploy operating systems and images of operating systems. RIS is enhanced in Windows 2003 by addressing the deployment of Windows 2003/Windows 2000 Server flavors and Windows XP. RIS as provided with Windows 2000 would not image or support the roll-out of Windows 2000 Server products without considerable tweaking. Support for the primary Microsoft Server network operating systems is a huge enhancement for RIS and one that will offer a rapid way to provide base images or flat image installation for the critical server tiers of operating systems. If you have Windows NT 4.0 as a primary server network operating system, unfortunately, there is no support provided by Microsoft within the RIS set of technologies.

RIS employs a distinct technical architecture composed of the following tiers:

1. **Network infrastructure**   Minimal requirements are Active Directory, DNS, and DHCP. DHCP is adjusted to support the TCP/IP address assignment required for RIS-based PXE boot clients, using TFTP.

2. **Remote boot technology**   PXE (Pre-Boot Execution Environment) is required for network interface cards for client machines to boot up to a RIS server for

operating system load. This is an industry standard, and most network interface cards manufactured since 1999 include this technology. Microsoft RIS also provides an application to create boot disks for RIS.

3. **RIS installation images** RIS supports creation and deployment of two types of images:

   ■ **Flat Image** An image created directly from the operating system CDs using an answer file

   ■ **RIPrep Image** An image created directly from a setup system employing all software and settings required, similar to a Norton Ghost image

Table 23-2 describes the operating systems supported with their image types.

This exciting new capability allows more flexibility than before in today's highly demanding IT environments, where server creation and deployment represent daily tasks in some business environments. Let's jump in and review the setup of RIS and deploy some operating systems via the network.

Setup of Remote Installation Software

RIS setup is accomplished via the Add/Remove Windows Components section of the Add/Remove software applet within the control pane (see Figure 23-1). RIS install is required prior to planning the image and deployment process. When installing RIS, remember that the following requirements must be met prior to attempting RIS operations:

1. An Active Directory domain must exist (you don't have to install RIS on a domain controller). The RIS host must be a member server of the AD forest or domain it is supporting.

2. You will have to reboot upon installation of RIS on the intended RIS server.

3. Place the RIS server(s) within appropriate subnets to ensure you can service clients in PXE boot mode. If PXE cards are not available, the RIS application Rbfg.exe created when RIS is installed will create a boot disk for your network adapter to allow a RIS boot. Bootp operations can cross subnets if routers within your organization are configured to pass Bootp broadcasts.

4. Network interface cards must be capable of conducting PXE boot operations, PXE ROM Version 1.0 or greater.

5. DNS and DHCP must be functional and configured to support PXE boot operations. Specific adjustments are required that we review in this section. Also remember to enable the Bootp clients table so that the RIS clients' Bootp requests will appear in your DHCP MMC views. The DHCP server, like any Windows 2003–based DHCP server, must be authorized prior to use.

6. Another implementation factor that dictates RIS use is that the target computers must be new—that is, no upgrades will work—and RIS will target only the C or first fixed drive of the system.

Operating System	Flat Image	RIPrep Image
Windows XP Professional	X	X
Windows Server 2003, Standard Edition	X	X
Windows Server 2003, Web Edition	X	X
Windows Server 2003, Enterprise Edition	X	X
64-bit version of Windows Server 2003, Enterprise Edition	X	
Windows 2000 Professional	X	X
Windows 2000 Server (without IIS Only)	X	X
Windows 2000 Advanced Server (without IIS Only)	X	X

Table 23-2. *Operating Systems Within RIS*

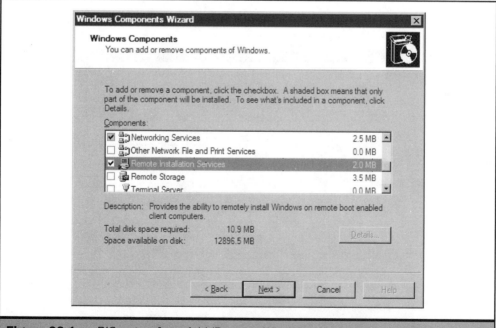

Figure 23-1. *RIS setup from Add/Remove Windows Components*

Once RIS is installed on the server(s) you have designated, a new applet will appear in the Administrative Tools program group, called Remote Installation Services Setup. This applet will help you complete the steps required to set up RIS services, before you begin the image preparation process for deploying images.

The RIS Services Setup applet is a guide to ensuring RIS is ready to accept PXE-based clients for imaging and operating system configuration. Clicking the RIS Icon in the Administrative Tools program group addresses the primary areas of RIS setup.

The first key configuration component is the folder Structure, or location for images (see Figure 23-2). You will use an NTFS 5.0 volume that is separate from the Operating System volume. That is, you cannot use the same disk for RIS image files storage that the operating system is installed on. This is an important support point that provides flexibility for the following options:

1. The image storage becomes portable, especially when using a SAN (storage area network).

2. RIS servers can be changed at need within the domain by simply reattaching the NTFS volumes holding RIS images to the new server. Thus if your primary RIS server suffered an operating system or other core failure, the NTFS volume holding the RIS images can be moved.

3. Network drive shares are not supported, which is fine because this indicates that network latency would not become a factor in image deployment speed.

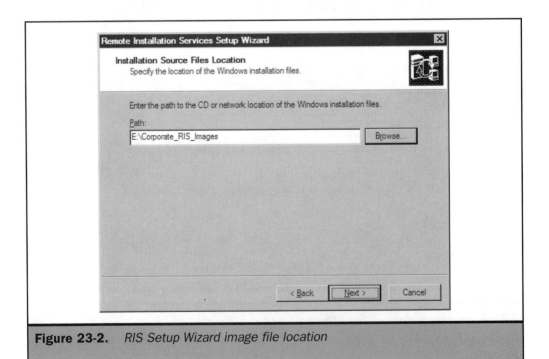

Figure 23-2. *RIS Setup Wizard image file location*

4. Multihomed RIS servers will fail to accept PXE 2.0 or higher clients, and thus a single NIC installation is required to ensure servicing of all clients.

The identified RIS server can install the host images in two ways. The first RIS installation method is the flat image, or a conditioned unattended installation that provides for operating system installation. The second RIS installation method is the RIPrep method, which will image an entire system. Figure 23-2 indicates the dialogue for placement of RIS images.

Flat Image Technique

The RIS Wizard applet is designed to incorporate a flat image setup. The dialog in the wizard is very simple and leads you through the location of the source files and the desired directory location for the source on the RIS data partition. It also turns the RIS server on to listen for RIS client requests forwarded from the DHCP server. This method is akin to an unattended installation and will call winnt.exe with an appended unattended setup file. The installation will actually automate the unattended process, dramatically reducing prep time to deploy operating systems. This method is especially effective when integrating new hardware that will require a new Windows XP load, for instance, to ensure that driver sets and hardware configuration are correct.

When using the RIPrep method, you will also first image the target host with the Flat Image technique so that when you load applications and customize, it will be an original RIS installed application. Figure 23-3 shows installation in progress.

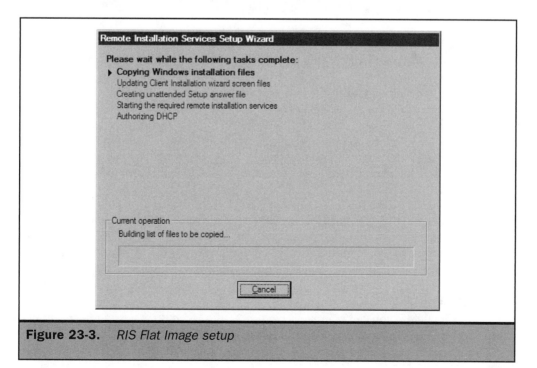

Figure 23-3. *RIS Flat Image setup*

Once the flat image collection process is complete, a client can connect to the RIS server during a PXE boot and will receive a menu that describes the available operating system installations. The description provided in the Flat Image applet is what is advertised.

RIPrep Setup

The RIPrep method allows creation of actual images of servers, desktops, and notebooks. This image is stored by the RIS server in the same directory structure as the Flat Image files. A description is also added to the RIPrep image so that selection is available on the client-based RIS menu. The RIPrep host may contain multiple software or server applications already preloaded and configured and is a much more through deployment than just the Flat Image technique.

The RIPrep data collection technique is located within the executable file Riprep.exe, located in the path %windir%\system32\reminstl. This application provides the dialog to create a RIPrep image that is then used on the RIS server. The application is similar to the previous SYSPREP/RIPrep available with Windows 2000, in that it is executed on the Windows host planned as the reference. Windows 2003 RIPrep now supports Windows XP and the Windows Server 2003 line of operating systems.

To complete a RIPrep of Windows 2003, load Windows 2003 on a server and then execute RIPrep from that server, using the UNC to the command on the RIS server. For example: \\london\risshare$\riprep. The file share on the RIS server contains the riprep.exe application that begins the dialog, allowing the imaging of the computer that is already set up. This image is then stored on the RIS server for use in deploying premade or imaged Microsoft operating systems.

RIS Client Procedures

The RIS client is the key to loading the operating systems. The first step, which is simple but sometimes overlooked, is changing the boot order for the personal computer or server slated for loading, with the network adapter as the first boot device. Upon reboot, the client will contact the RIS server to request a network service boot. Then RIS menu will appear upon pressing F12, which provides the options to either install a new operating system or access the RIS tools for maintenance. Pressing F12 will start the client operating system installation wizard. This method will also work for the RIS client boot disk for computers that do not have a PXE DHCP-capable network interface card.

Security should be established in an Active Directory account to allow insertion of new computers into the domain. The account logged in to the RIS Setup menu should have these rights. A recommended technique is to configure the OU for new computers into the RIS setup and then conduct an Active Directory rights delegation to the specified RIS service account to allow insertion of new computers into the respective OU.

RIS Management

Once RIS is installed, you can manage it via the Active Directory Users and Computers MMC snap-in. The management capabilities provide multiple functions to include verifying that RIS servers are working, image addition, viewing current clients in session, turning RIS services on and off, and making decisions on naming conventions for new computers along with location of the computer accounts. RIS also provides the capability to select an OU or location within the Active Directory zone for the created computer accounts from RIS imaging or flat image load operations.

A great new feature is RIS services check which provides a quick report as to whether or not RIS is listening and ready to service clients. Additionally this check queries the DHCP services in use to ensure RIS clients are supported.

RIS uses single-instance storage technology to provide that identical files are not duplicated in storage in the RIS directories, but once the same file is identified in multiple locations then a parse point is created with a pointer to the actual file. This reduces the amount of disk space required for multiple images of the same operating system or source files. In Windows 2000, the SIS process, and particularly SIS Groveler, which searches a partition for multiple instances of a file, was applied to the entire partition in which RIS files were located. In Windows 2003, and since Windows 2000/SP3, only the directory RIS files are in is affected by the SIS Groveler. Some RIS management options are shown in Figures 23-4 and 23-5.

RIS for Managing Your Windows 2003 Environment

RIS technology is now easy and practical technology for you to use. This section suggests a practical framework for corporate use of RIS and methods to tie in other technologies we will visit under the rubric of network software installation.

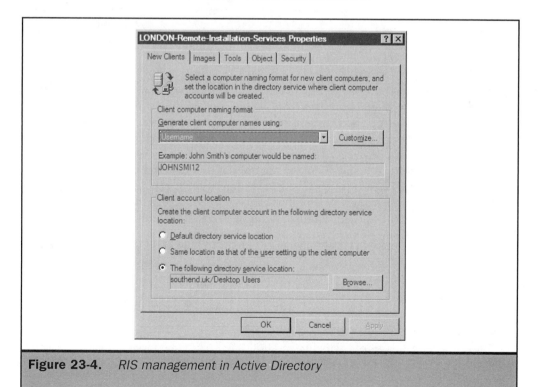

Figure 23-4.   *RIS management in Active Directory*

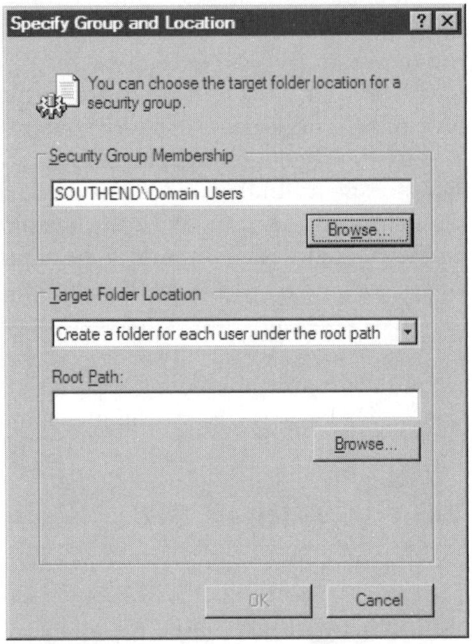

Figure 23-5. *RIS management options*

Maintaining standards and a well-managed computing environment is a key corporate goal. The object is to provide security, manageability, and of course availability by having systems with similar setups and the ability to create those setups as needed. The Windows 2003 or Windows 2000 server is the primary building block of most computing environments, probably including your own if you are reading or referring to this book.

Most security exploits take advantage not only of lack of security patches but also of misconfigured or inconsistent server standards, especially in Internet DMZ environments. A simple framework to attack this problem is provided in the next section. If Microsoft SQL Servers running Windows 2000 in a web services DMZ that faces the Internet require minimal software for security, RIS is the tool to ensure the consistency of server loads. Many administrators have had to bring up a service with multiple servers on an emergency basis, and they may choose to load them by hand. RIS can alleviate this problem and induce consistency and standards into the Windows 2003/ 2000 load process.

RIS Solution Framework

The following tasks are sample planning and building/deploying tasks in which RIS is the key technology; they will show you how to deploy server and desktop images as required.

Establish a RIS reference server and workstation; these will serve as the corporate or company "GOLD" standard. Any required core changes, such as an operating system change or new security standards that may require extensive changes can be updated on the "GOLD" platform after testing. Windows 2003/Windows 2000 plug-and-play technology allows some flexibility in that the "GOLD" server and workstation may not be identical to deployed hardware. For example, given that the corporate server standard for web servers is a dual-processor 1.4 GHz Pentium III, with 2GB of RAM, two hardware-mirrored 72GB drives, and a Gigabit Ethernet NIC, if the latest server uses 1.8 GHz processors then the same RISprep image will work in most cases. At some point for substantial hardware changes, the isolated "GOLD" reference workstation and servers would require an upgrade to track with new servers introduced in the environment.

New server installations with Windows 2003/Windows 2000 should receive a RISprep image from your RIS environment, based on your "GOLD" corporate standard, which is maintained in the isolated server and workstations just described.

The RIS instance in your AD environment will also help you to become more effective. If you require ten additional web servers to meet some load demands or capacity change—Victoria's Secret webcast is a good example—RIS is the solution; it will allow ten simultaneous web server loads, not just one load at a time.

RIS environments are very supportive of information technology staff training and proficiency. Often senior team members can establish standards and rely on RIS to ensure they are implemented, yet junior team members can view and gain understanding of the standards without necessarily having to design them.

The other Windows 2003 technologies providing network software installation work in conjunction with RIS. Software delivery and software publishing via Active Directory can add the finishing touches to any RIS installation.

Intellimirror and Active Directory Software Installation and Maintenance

Intellimirror and use of group policies in Active Directory to distribute software are key features of Windows 2003 management and are excellent follow-on or enhancement technologies for RIS use in the Windows 2003 environment. Settings required are held in Active Directory group policies and can affect objects in forests, domains, or sites. The technology name is quite descriptive, as this feature of Active Directory is designed to mirror settings for a user from one computer to the next.

Intellimirror allows the establishment of settings for either a computer or a user based on the established group policy. The attraction is that this is a superb software distribution mechanism that can ensure software requirements and standards are met in an automated fashion. Intellimirror also addresses the constant administrative overhead of managing customers' data and user-specific settings, especially in a fluid environment, such as a call center where customers may use any computer available. Key management areas in Intellimirror are as follows:

- User data management
- User settings management
- Software installation and maintenance

The underlying management technology supporting Intellimirror and software distribution is the group policy management capability within Active Directory. As this is such an important element in making Intellimirror or GPO (Group Policy Object) software distribution work, Microsoft has included a new MMC snap-in within the Windows 2003 Server platform called the Group Policy Management Console. This provides a new capability to back up and restore GPOs, which becomes extremely essential for porting test GPOs from an offline sandbox Active Directory install to production. Additionally, this new MMC will manage GPOs across forests if a trust is in place, taking advantage of Windows 2003's new cross-forest transitive trust-based capability. This cross-forest support extends to a capability to permit a person to log on to a system in the trusting forest and receive policies from their own forest.

The complexity that exists when setting up multiple GPOs and then measuring the effect on customer performance has led to the inclusion of the new RSOP (Resultant Set of Policy) tool. This tool allows the modeling of RSOPs to actually view policies a client may inherit in terms of multiple GPOs acting from the site, domain, or OU level.

Intellimirror

Intellimirror is implemented through group policy and allows management of users and computers with specific settings available to the GPO templates included with Windows 2003. Intellimirror is implemented via the Computer/Software/User sections of Active Directory group policies that are applied at various locations within the Active Directory zones. The zones include organizational units, sites, domains, and forests. GPO management and the other elements composing Active Directory are addressed extensively in this text, and we will not rehash them here but focus on putting Intellimirror to work.

Intellimirror is implemented either via Windows Scripting components or primarily through a policy template setup within the Active Directory or GPMC (Group Policy Management Console). Intellimirror settings generally reflect normal business drivers or needs, such as laptop/notebook/mobile users, users that change computers often but need to have transportable settings with them, and rollouts of new software packages or shortcuts to specific corporate applications.

Each GPO that is constructed allows creation of settings that apply to either the computer or the user. Most Intellimirror-specific settings are normally made within the user section of the Group Policy Object Editor and then linked to the required organizational unit.

The GPO Editors (see Figure 23-6) allow construction of group policies specifying Intellimirror settings from scratch, or predefined templates are available.

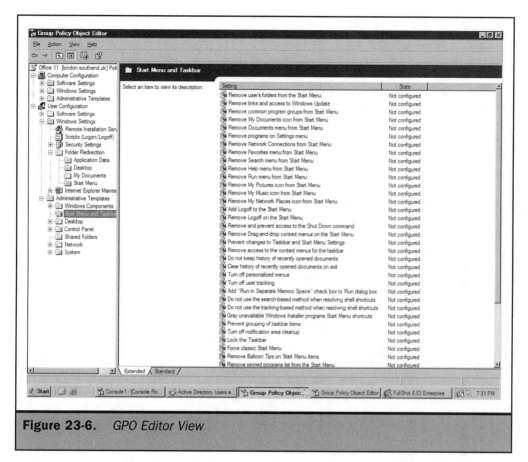

Figure 23-6.   *GPO Editor View*

User Data Management

Intellimirror addresses the range of settings available to manage customers' desktops. A key function is the redirection of the user's data and other specific desktop settings. The uniqueness of a Windows XP system is defined within the users settings in the Documents and Settings folder normally located on the root volume of the Windows XP system. Intellimirror in conjunction with Active Directory and Roaming Profiles can redirect any portion of a user's definitions as expressed in the Documents and Settings user profile to any other computer. For notebook or mobile users, this becomes especially important, as a person may move from a desktop to a notebook but require the same data on each system.

The areas for user data management and folder redirection are:

1. Application data
2. The Desktop

3. My Documents

4. The Start menu

Although these areas don't qualify as network software installation, they are in a sense an install because the Start menu, the Desktop, and application data may indeed be bits moved across the wire to satisfy a Intellimirror policy established for these settings. Even though Active Directory is playing a large role in supporting Intellimirror operations, network home directories or file shares for each user are required, as they are actually the redirection point. Windows 2003 builds on this feature set by allowing GPO decisions to redirect to the same location for all users, sometimes in the form of \\homeserver\user$, wherein the user's name is substituted within this UNC, or by allowing specification of redirection to location based on the security groups in which a person is a member. So a security group called Real Secure may redirect all clients to the share. This is an enhancement of the Windows 2003 GPO implementation of point \\realsecureserver\ user$r supporting Intellimirror.

User Setting Management

The User Setting Management capability of Intellimirror technologies is designed to use the power of a group policy to control key elements of what a user can and can't do within a Windows session on either a Windows 2000, Windows XP, or Windows 2003 server platform. These settings apply to either the user or the computer and can range from items such as the operating system's desktop color to what core control panel applets are available for a user to adjust.

Figure 23-6 shows some of the available settings. Chapter 22 addresses these settings in detail and describes what combinations exist to create custom group policy templates.

Software Installation and Maintenance

Software installation and maintenance is the primary feature of Intellimirror focused on in this chapter. Software installation is configured and managed from the Group Policy Editor within the Active Directory Users and Computers MMC. Software installations can either apply to the computer or follow a roaming user to multiple computers. In some cases, core corporate applications that are required for every user in the company may be applied as a GPO to computers and then address custom software to either OUs that contain functional groups or specific users in the case of custom software used by a few. The key as in all GPO design and employment is not to encumber a user with the application of so much software or so many GPOs that logons actually can become latent and problematic.

The Resultant Set of Policies tool new to Windows 2003 provides administrators with the capability to model possible GPOs prior to using them in a production environment. This tool covers a user's inclusive GPO policies and assists in evaluating GPO performance (see Figure 23-7). This tool should become your default check prior to use of GPOs to ensure group policy application to users at the time of logon is performing and the user's result of policies is what is expected.

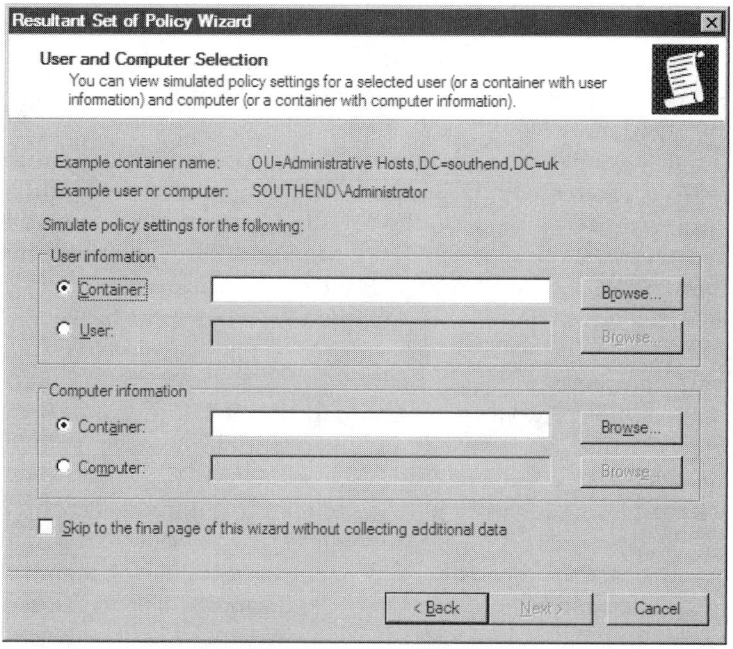

Figure 23-7.   *Intellimirror user settings management*

Several considerations exist for software installation. Best planning practices to consider for inclusion of software for GPO distribution are:

- **Source of the software**   (Should be on a UNC-based file share that does not change. As you might expect, if the UNC contained in the GPO setup changes, then the package being distributed breaks.) Additionally, some applications, given how their MSI packages are formed, require an installation first to an admin or network share. One clear example is Office XP or Office 11.

- **Point at which software is installed**   This is key, as performance is important. Use of a GPO after RIS setup is a great way to deliver software, as a user may not actually be on the system yet.

- **Flavors of applications**   Applications installed are available in two flavors: assigned or published. The distinction is that published applications are available for users to install, and this GPO setting can apply only to users, while assigned applications are installed regardless of need.

Software distribution is conducted using the Software Installation section of the User or Computer section of the Group Policy Editor. Software packages should expose an MSI (Microsoft Installer) package as shown by the Software Installation Wizard. The

MSI or application, if required, should already exist in an installed fashion on a network share point, and access in the dialog is via UNC. Once the MSI package is accessed, then a list of options appears that allows decisions about the GPO software package settings and, of course, which users or computers receive the package according to the OU in which the GPO is assigned.

Software installation options once you attach to the required MSI are either published, assigned, or covered in an advanced section addressing other options, such as security, upgrades to the package once installed, modifications required via some MSI transforms files, and deployment options. Figure 23-8 shows a few of the options available in the Advanced Options area of the software package's properties.

Software installations changed from published to assigned can be installed on logon.

The application event log of clients receiving software installations records the success or failure of software packages distributed.

Software distribution is not the simplest of Intellimirror operations but one that pays management dividends, especially for breadth applications that don't require the complexity level of an installation like Microsoft Office XP.

The collection of technologies composing Intellimirror provides the opportunity for plenty of lights-out management for environments using Windows 2003 Active Directory services and group policies. For network software installation, the Intellimirror component of Software Installation and Maintenance provides the mechanism to distribute software

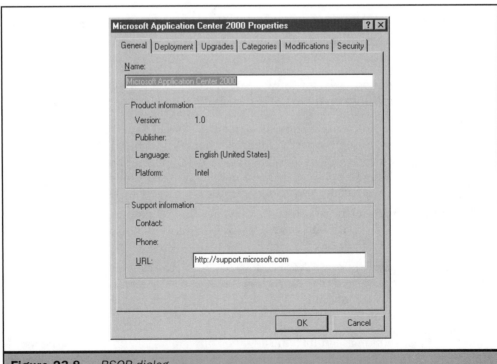

Figure 23-8.   *RSOP dialog*

in an unattended fashion, provide software for use by customers in a selective fashion, and ensure compliance with licensing regulations by using the objects in organizational units to provide snap counts of installed licenses by computer or user.

Software Restriction Policies

A completely new way to manage software in a network environment with Windows 2003 is capability to restrict software. Software restrictions, as the name implies, do not support software installation but enforce restrictions on code or software that you do not support in your environment. Do you want your customers to play Solitaire or not? This feature supports security and can prevent illegal use of software. This feature is not present in Windows 2000 and is a cornerstone of the Microsoft commitment to secure computing environments.

The software restriction policy builds on previous zone-type security methods that existed in Internet Explorer. The following zone types are supported and implemented via a Group Policy Object:

- Hash rules
- Certificate rules
- Path rules
- Internet Zone rules

One challenge facing many companies is that Internet access is required for a number of jobs and so personnel can download programs and applications, as port 80 is a commonly allowed port to support HTTP traffic on the World Wide Web. The software restriction policy can enforce firewall, proxy servers, and other measures in place to secure untrusted Internet-based traffic, as illustrated in Figure 23-9. The Internet Zone rule would allow disabling all Internet site access for sites not listed in the actual trusted zones or web sites setting. This is tantamount to disabling entire Internet sites. This is a powerful new security feature implemented via GPOs but providing protection from untrusted software.

The software restriction settings are contained in the standard Group Policy Editor and are accessed under the security settings for either a user or computers. The software restriction element for defining policies for paths brings an entirely new dimension for security, in that one can effectively restrict access to paths. In the case of task workers that may work in Windows 2003 Terminal Server environments, path policies become critical. Figure 23-10 shows a sample policy construction of paths placed to support a lockdown of a task worker in a terminal server environment.

Software restrictions originally released with Windows XP for local use and with Windows Server 2003 are now applicable to Active Directory sites, domains, and organizational units. This is a powerful new tool in an administrator's tool set to secure a Windows 2003 computing environment.

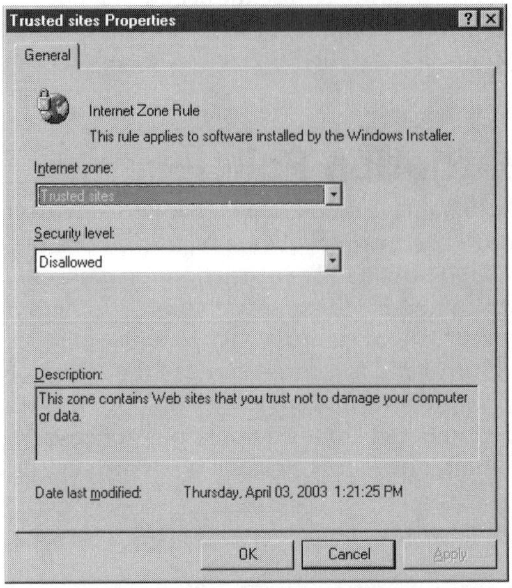

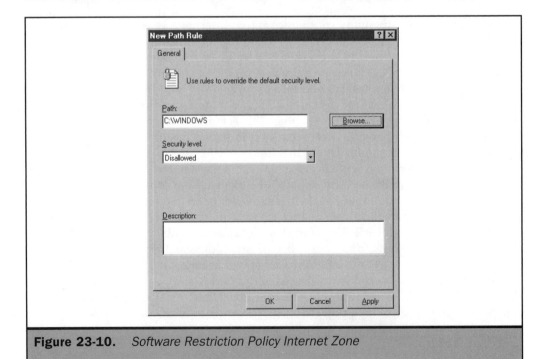

Figure 23-9. *Software Installation dialog for Advanced Options*

Figure 23-10. *Software Restriction Policy Internet Zone*

The Complete Reference

Chapter 24

Clustering

rom its roots in the Wolfpack Project at Microsoft, clustering has matured into an important part of any enterprise Windows implementation. This chapter examines Microsoft's latest cluster offerings and describes how they can be used to scale and extend your Windows Server 2003 network.

A *cluster* can most easily be defined as a group of individual servers that work together as a single system. Software and clients see the cluster as a single entity, and the cluster is managed as a single unit. Clustering is used to ensure high availability for mission-critical applications, manageability for 24/7 implementations, and scalability for large enterprise solutions. Two clustering technologies are available in Microsoft Windows Server 2003:

- **Network Load Balancing (NLB)**   Primarily intended to balance incoming TCP/IP traffic. NLB is commonly used for web servers.
- **Server Clusters**   Implemented to provide failover services among the clustered computers. The Cluster service is commonly used for database applications.

You can't use both on the same server, but you can use the two cluster solutions together to gain complementary functions—for example, making a database application available to web site visitors.

Note *Microsoft also offers a third clustering technology, Component Load Balancing (CLB) clusters. This technology is a feature of Microsoft Application Center 2000, and is not included in any version of Windows Server 2003. CLB clusters enable COM+ applications to be distributed across multiple servers, ensuring application scalability and high availability.*

Network Load Balancing Clusters

Network Load Balancing (NLB) is a software solution used by Microsoft Windows clustering to scale the performance of IP-based programs by distributing client requests among the multiple servers within the cluster. NLB is most often used to enhance the performance and availability of web-based applications, but can also enhance a variety of IP-based applications within your enterprise.

Note *Network Load Balancing in its current form first appeared in Windows 2000 Server as a redesigned replacement for Windows Load Balancing Service (WLBS) in Windows NT 4. However, you'll find that references to the original WLBS aren't entirely gone— for example, the command-line management program, wlbs.exe, still exists for backward compatibility.*

NLB is a part of the following Windows Server 2003 versions:

- Standard Edition
- Enterprise Edition

- Datacenter Edition
- Web Edition

Network Load Balancing Advantages

Using Network Load Balancing, clusters of up to 32 hosts can be created over which client requests can be distributed. NLB is enhanced in Windows Server 2003, allowing you to create multiple virtual NLB clusters on the same server by configuring NLB on more than one NIC, and by configuring more than one load-balanced cluster IP address on a single NIC. Availability and scalability are NLB's two key benefits for applications.

Availability

A key advantage of NLB is the high availability it offers enterprise applications. The cluster software can automatically reallocate the distribution of client requests in the event of server failure. To accomplish this, the cluster and the individual servers within the cluster monitor each other's health. Multicast or broadcast messages are exchanged among the servers, and between each server and the cluster.

If the status of a server (or multiple servers) within the cluster changes, the active servers launch a process called *convergence* to determine which servers are still active, and to agree about how the application workload will be allocated among them. By default, NLB detects the loss of a cluster member within five seconds, and completes convergence within the next five seconds. While convergence is taking place, each node of the cluster continues to process application packets according to the rules in place before convergence began.

If convergence is triggered by the loss of a member server, the application requests that would have been processed by the downed server go unfulfilled until its requests are reassigned at the completion of convergence. The user, or the application—but not NLB—is responsible for handling this error condition in the interim.

If an additional host server is added to the cluster, this same convergence process permits the new host to receive its share of traffic. This makes expansion of the cluster completely transparent to both clients and applications.

Scalability

NLB provides two levels of scalability:

- **Scalable activity**   Additional users and traffic are managed smoothly by the constant distribution of requests to give all clients equal access to the application or service.

- **Scalable system**   Additional components (servers or processors) can be added to the cluster.

Manageability

Administration of Network Load Balancing is efficient, because the cluster is managed as a single unit from a single control point (which can be remote). Administrators manage the cluster with shell commands and scripts to start, stop, and manipulate the cluster. In addition, the ability to take individual servers offline without disturbing the cluster's performance makes maintenance and OS upgrades easier.

NLB Architecture

Network Load Balancing runs as a Windows networking driver, and the operations of the driver are transparent to the TCP/IP stack. All computers in the cluster can be addressed by the cluster's IP address. However, each computer also maintains its own unique, dedicated IP address. Microsoft implemented NLB as a network driver that operates between the network card driver and the IP stack. All members of an NLB cluster must reside on the same IP subnet, so that client requests directed to the cluster IP address can be processed by all members of the cluster.

An algorithm determined during cluster convergence allows each node of the cluster to determine whether or not to process a client request. The processing node sends the packet up the IP protocol stack, and all other nodes discard the packet. Each host can be configured with a specific load percentage, or the load can be distributed equally among all the hosts.

NLB intercepts only TCP and UDP packets. Packets of other IP protocols are passed up the protocol stack and are processed by all the NLB cluster nodes.

Hardware and Protocols

NLB is built to provide clustering support for TCP/IP-based server programs. This, of course, requires TCP/IP to be the default protocol for the system. The NLB version in Windows Server 2003 operates on FDDI or Ethernet-based LANs within the cluster.

You can enhance NLB performance by installing two network adapters in each host. NLB uses one network adapter for the client-to-cluster traffic, and the other for all other network traffic (including cluster communications). The additional IP addresses assigned to the NICs are automatically detected.

Incoming client requests are mapped to cluster hosts via a distributed algorithm. When a packet arrives, every host performs the mapping simultaneously. This allows a quick determination of which host should handle the packet. This simultaneous filtering algorithm is more efficient for packet handling than are programs that use centralized load-balancing algorithms. Centralized filtering involves the modification and retransmission of packets, which can add latency. Simultaneous filtering, on the other hand, provides a high aggregate bandwidth.

NLB controls the distribution on a per-connection basis for TCP, and a per-datagram basis for UDP, by filtering the incoming traffic before anything gets to the TCP/IP protocol software. Only the TCP and UDP protocols within TCP/IP are handled, and all controls are applied on a per-port basis.

 Some point-to-point TCP/IP programs, most notably ping, will produce duplicate responses when targeting the cluster's IP address. To avoid this, use the dedicated IP address for the host you're pinging.

NLB can be configured to handle the cluster traffic more precisely by using features such as port rules or affinity. See the section "Installing and Configuring Network Load Balancing," later in this chapter, for more information.

Virtual Clusters

Network Load Balancing in Windows Server 2003 is enhanced with support for virtual load-balanced clusters. You create a virtual cluster by enabling NLB on more than one NIC in a server, or by assigning multiple IP addresses to the same NLB-enabled NIC. Since each IP address can correspond to a different web site or application, judicious use of virtual clusters and their port rules allows you to control the way different web applications are distributed between physical load-balanced servers.

Virtual clusters have the following properties:

■ Each IP address defines a distinct virtual cluster, and a physical server can host only a single instance of a virtual cluster. (A physical server can't have the same IP address assigned to more than one NIC.)

■ Each virtual cluster can be comprised of a different combination of physical servers.

■ A port rule can act on behalf of all the virtual clusters defined for a NIC, or be assigned to a single virtual cluster.

Application Configuration

There are several ways to configure applications on an NLB cluster. The cluster can be configured in such a way that a copy of a server-based program runs on every host; or the application can be run on one host, sending all client requests to that host instead of distributing the load throughout the cluster. This decision depends on the type of application. For instance, applications that require centralization, such as Microsoft Exchange Server, belong on a single host. In addition, writes to a database can be sent to a dedicated database server within the system. If databases are load-balanced in a cluster, each cluster node must have its own copy of the data. Updates to the contents of the database tables have to be synchronized by being merged offline at regular intervals. Most of the time, however, mission-critical databases are deployed in a server cluster environment that's designed for failover, instead of a NLB environment (see "Server Clusters," later in this chapter).

Pure NLB is best suited for noncentralized data storage, or for applications that don't accept data from clients accessing the server—that is, read-only TCP or UDP-based applications. Web sites are an ideal candidate for NLB because it is easy to provide each host with a current copy of the pages (which are usually static) to make sure that high-volume traffic is handled with ease and speed. For web clients who need access to a database, the web servers can direct the requests to a database server. Other good candidates for NLB are the following:

■ HTTP, HTTPS, FTP, TFTP, and SMTP over TCP/IP

■ HTTP over SSL—port 443

- FTP—port 21, port 20, ports 1024–65, and port 535
- SMTP—port 25
- Terminal Services—port 3389
- Web servers (such as Microsoft Internet Information Services)—port 80
- Web servers using round-robin DNS
- Virtual private network servers
- Streaming media servers

Software applications can be deployed on an NLB cluster as long as multiple instances of the application can run simultaneously without error or harm.

Application Servers and Stateful Connections

There are two kinds of client-host connections for application servers, and they're usually described with the term *stateful connection*:

- **Interclient state** Updates are synchronized with transactions performed for other clients. An example is the update of the inventory database on an e-commerce site, after the sale of goods to a client connection.

- **Intraclient state** The state is maintained for a specific client throughout a session, such as the sale of products (usually involving a shopping cart process) at an e-commerce site. In fact, at most e-commerce sites, the shopping cart process can span multiple separate connections from the same client.

NLB works best when it is used to provide scalability for stateless front-end services (a standard HTTP web application, for example), even if those front-end services access a shared back-end database server.

NLB should never be used with interclient stateful connections. The applications that use this stateful connection type aren't designed to permit multiple instances of connections that access a shared database and simultaneously synchronize updates.

NLB can be used to scale intraclient state applications, even within a session that spans multiple connections. With one of the options for client affinity enabled, NLB directs all TCP connections to the same cluster host, which permits the session state to be maintained in host memory. (Client/server applications that embed the state within cookies or send it to a back-end database don't require client affinity.)

Installing and Configuring Network Load Balancing

NLB is a service bound to a NIC, and is installed automatically—but not enabled—when you install a NIC under any of the versions of Windows Server that includes NLB as a feature. Configuration parameters are established through the Network Load Balancing Properties dialog, and the settings are written to the registry.

New in Windows Server 2003 is an enhanced NLB configuration and management tool—nlbmgr.exe. Because the NLB Properties dialog method is common to Windows Server 2003 and earlier versions, I'll describe it first, and talk about using nlbmgr.exe later in this chapter, in the section "Using Nlbmgr.exe to Configure Clusters and Nodes."

Installing the NLB Service in the NLB Properties Dialog

Right-click the Local Area Connection icon on which you want to run NLB, and choose Properties. If the computer has multiple NICs, each NIC has its own Local Area Connection icon.

In the Properties dialog, Network Load Balancing is listed as a component. Click the check box to place a check mark in it to enable the service (see Figure 24-1).

If Network Load Balancing isn't listed in the Properties dialog (which usually means it was specifically uninstalled), click the Install button and choose Service as the type of network component. Then click Add and install Network Load Balancing. Microsoft recommends that you not uninstall Network Load Balancing, even if you choose not to enable it, because its removal can have negative consequences.

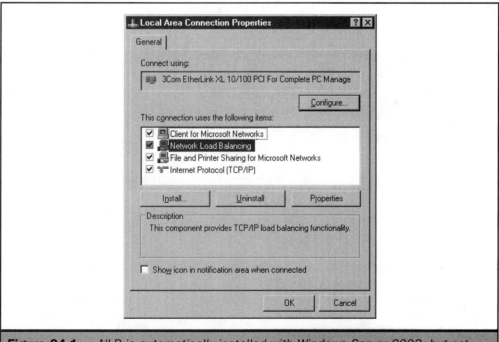

Figure 24-1.   *NLB is automatically installed with Windows Server 2003, but not activated until you put a check mark in its check box.*

With Network Load Balancing selected, choose Properties to open the Network Load Balancing Properties dialog, which has three tabs: Cluster Parameters, Host Parameters, and Port Rules.

Setting Cluster Parameters for Network Load Balancing

The Cluster Parameters tab, shown in Figure 24-2, has options that apply to the entire cluster. Configure the cluster parameters for each host in the cluster, using the guidelines discussed in this section.

Primary IP Address   Enter the cluster's primary IP address, using standard Internet dotted notation. The address is a virtual IP address because it's the one that's used for the cluster as a whole. You must use the same address for all the hosts in the cluster.

Subnet Mask   Enter the subnet mask, which is linked to the IP address you just entered (for instance, 255.255.255.0).

Cluster's Full Internet Name   Enter the cluster's full Internet name, for example, nlbcluster.admin911.com. This name is applied to the cluster as a whole, and should be the same for all the hosts in the cluster. The name must also be resolvable to the cluster's primary IP address through a DNS server or the HOSTS file.

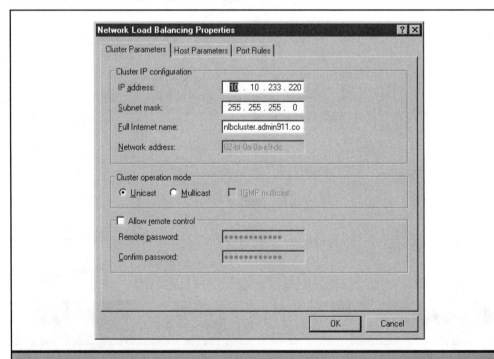

Figure 24-2.   *NLB cluster parameters are the same on all nodes of the cluster.*

Cluster's Network Address   NLB automatically generates the network address (MAC address) for the NIC that will handle client-to-cluster traffic, based on the cluster's primary IP address. If multicast support is enabled, NLB uses a locally administered address that is also a multicast MAC address.

Cluster Operation Mode   Specify multicast or unicast mode. In either mode, NLB will use the cluster IP address to generate a locally administered MAC address.

In unicast mode, NLB generates a unicast MAC address that it uses in place of the NIC's hardware MAC address. This address is used for packets sent from the cluster IP address, and for packets from other IP addresses configured for the NLB NIC. Because the network stack will never send a packet out to the network wire if it is addressed to a MAC address that is on its own computer, nodes of the same NLB cluster can't communicate with one another using the load-balanced NIC if they're in unicast mode. Unicast mode requires that each cluster node have a second NIC if the nodes need to access one another for reasons other than the NLB service.

If multicast mode is enabled, NLB continues to use the NIC's hardware MAC address with the node's dedicated (unique) IP address, so the cluster nodes can access one another using the load-balanced NIC. However, NLB generates a multicast MAC address for cluster operations. This means that the cluster's primary (unicast) IP address will resolve to this multicast MAC address as part of the ARP protocol.

Take care before enabling multicast mode. Many firewalls and routers—including Cisco routers —fail to add this entry to their ARP cache, causing client communications to the cluster to fail unless you implement a workaround (described next). For this reason, unicast mode is NLB's default mode of operation, even though multicast mode is the preferred mode of operation.

If clients are accessing a cluster operating in multicast mode via a router, the router must accept an ARP reply that has one MAC address in the payload of the ARP structure, but appears to arrive from a station with another MAC address (as seen in the Ethernet header). Additionally, the router must be able to accept an ARP reply that has a multicast MAC address in the payload of the ARP structure. If the router cannot meet these requirements, you may be able to add a static ARP entry to the router or firewall upstream from the cluster to support the resolution of unicast IP addresses to multicast MAC addresses.

    If the NIC does not permit changes to the MAC address, you'll have to replace the NIC with one that does. This is a hardware requirement for NLB in unicast mode.

In unicast mode, it's best to use two NICs, dedicating one to client-to-cluster traffic and one to node-specific traffic. Otherwise, the performance level of the cluster suffers.

    You cannot mix multicast and unicast mode in a NLB cluster.

New IGMP Multicast Mode IGMP Multicast is a multicast-mode option new to Windows Server 2003. This new option is designed to eliminate switch flooding caused by multicast traffic. *Switch flooding* occurs when a switch doesn't know which switch port services a particular MAC address, and so needs to send the packet to all switch ports. This, of course, means you've lost the advantages of a switch over a hub.

The Internet Group Management Protocol (IGMP) allows IP hosts to report their multicast group membership to neighboring routers and switches. A layer 3 switch is aware of upper-level network protocols and addresses (like IP), in addition to the layer 2 hardware-level protocols and related MAC addresses. When NLB cluster nodes connect to the network through a layer 3 switch, IGMP reduces traffic through the switch by informing the switch which ports connect to members of the multicast group. To use the IGMP Multicast option effectively, the cluster nodes must connect to the network through a switch that supports IGMP Monitoring. Periodically (once a minute by default) each NLB cluster node sends an IGMP Join message, informing network equipment upstream that it is a member of the cluster's IGMP group.

If you enable IGMP Multicast support, the associated multicast IP address must be a valid Class D IP address—that is, an address in the range 224.0.0.0 to 239.255.255.255.

Remote Password You can supply a remote password for accessing the cluster from a remote Windows Server 2003 computer. This password is used for authentication by the nlb.exe cluster control program (it is not used when controlling the cluster operations from the cluster host). Remote operations from nlb.exe require the /passw parameter on the command line, along with the password, to perform control operations on the cluster.

To eliminate the need for a password, clear both the Remote Password and Confirm Password fields.

If remote control is enabled, it is important to secure the cluster, because it is possible for intruders to take advantage of the environment through the remote-control ports. Use a firewall to control access to the Network Load Balancing UDP control ports (the ports that receive the remote-control commands). By default, these are ports 1717 and 2504 at the cluster IP address. Better yet, use nlbmgr.exe or a WMI-based management tool instead of nlb.exe in remote-control mode.

Nlb.exe remote-control commands don't work properly when IPSec encrypts the packets.

Host Parameters

The Host Parameters tab of the Network Load Balancing Properties dialog offers options that apply to the host in question. This section presents guidelines for configuring this (and every other) host computer in the cluster. Figure 24-3 shows the available Host Parameters configuration options.

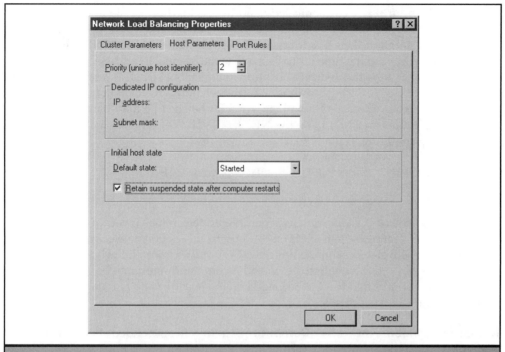

Figure 24-3. *Each node of an NLB cluster must have a unique Priority, but need not have a dedicated IP address.*

Priority (Unique Host ID) The priority ID is this host's priority for handling default network traffic for TCP and UDP ports that are not specifically configured in the Port Rules tab (covered in the next section). The priority is unique to this host, and is used for convergence.

The value can range between 1 and 32, where 32 is the maximum number of hosts allowed in a NLB cluster. The highest priority is 1, and higher numbers indicate lower priorities. Each host in the cluster must have a unique priority ID.

If a host within the cluster fails, the convergence process must know which of the remaining hosts can handle the traffic for the offline host. The host with the highest priority is selected, and if that host fails, the host with the highest priority among the remaining hosts steps in. This system provides some fault tolerance for the NLB cluster.

Keep records about the priority that is assigned for each host. If a new host is added to the cluster, and it is configured with a conflicted priority, the new host will not be able to join the cluster (the event log reports the problem).

Dedicated IP Address The dedicated IP address is this host's unique IP address, and it's used for network traffic that's unrelated to the cluster. Enter the address in standard Internet dotted notation. This IP address is used to address each host individually, so it must be unique. Most of the time it's easiest to use the original IP address, because that's unique to the host. Enter the dedicated IP address and subnet mask as a static IP address.

When operating NLB in unicast mode with a second NIC for non-cluster traffic, it is a good practice to leave this field blank, forcing the use of a load-balanced NIC for cluster traffic. Remember to update the NIC's TCP/IP Properties to include only the addresses you configure in the NIC's NLB Properties.

 The dedicated IP address cannot be a DHCP-obtained address.

Initial Cluster State The Initial State parameter determines whether NLB should start when the operating system loads on this host. If this option is selected (by clicking the check box), NLB starts each time Windows Server 2003 boots. If the box is unchecked, then hosts can join and leave the cluster via NLB command-line controls. This is useful if there are other services that need to be loaded on the host (usually manually) before bringing the host into the cluster.

Retain Suspended State after Computer Starts In suspended state, a host or a cluster performs no application processing, and responds only to Resume and Query commands. By default, rebooting a server hosting a suspended cluster member will cause the cluster member to rejoin the cluster and resume processing. Checking the box causes suspended clusters to retain suspended state through a server reboot.

Port Rules

Port rules help determine the way the cluster traffic is handled for each port, which makes it easier to configure and control clusters. The method by which a port handles network traffic is referred to as its *filtering mode*. The Port Rules tab, shown in Figure 24-4, displays current port rules.

Clicking the Add or Edit button brings up the dialog shown in Figure 24-5, where you can create or modify port rules.

You create a port rule by specifying a set of configuration parameters that define the filtering mode. Each rule contains the following parameters:

- The TCP or UDP port range to which the rule applies
- The protocol for which the rule applies (TCP, UDP, or both)
- The filtering mode that determines the way the cluster allocates traffic to the members of the cluster for the port range and protocols you're configuring
- Optionally, a selection for client affinity

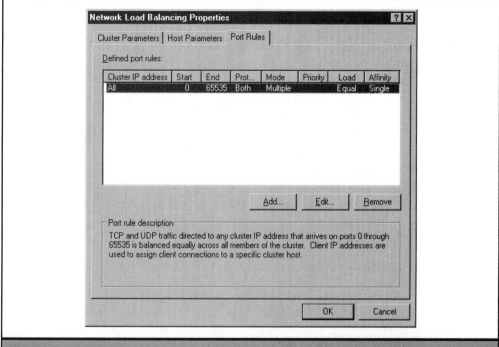

Figure 24-4.   *The default port rule enables Single affinity and equal load weights for all TCP and UCP ports.*

The number and type of rules that are created on one host must be duplicated on every other host in the cluster. If a host attempts to join the cluster without being configured with identical port rules, the host will not be accepted as a member of the cluster.

Upon installation, NLB includes a port rule directing NLB to process ports 0–65535 for both TCP and UDP, equally distributing the load between all NLB cluster nodes, and specifying Single affinity to cause the same NLB cluster node to process all packets from the same IP address.

NLB filters packets for all TCP and UDP ports. The NLB cluster node with the lowest-numbered host ID becomes the default node, and processes all packets for which no port rule applies.

The following sections present the guidelines for using the Port Rules tab to create a port rule.

Port Range   Specify the TCP/UDP port range that the port rule covers. Any port numbers in the range 0 to 65,535 are supported (and that range is also the default). To specify a single port, enter the same starting and ending port number.

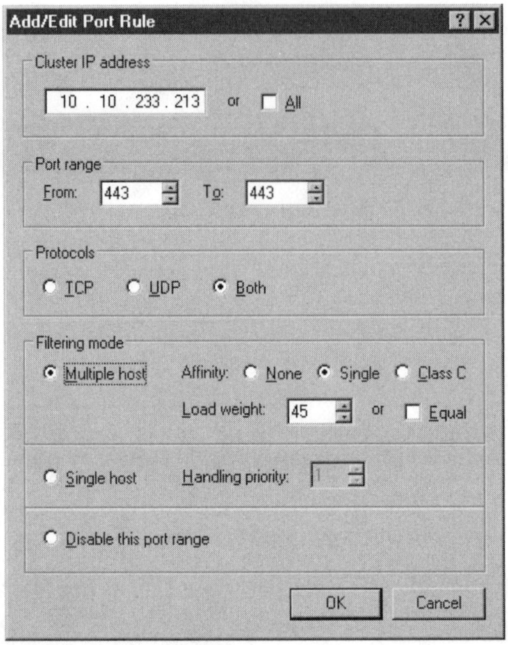

Figure 24-5. *The Add/Edit Port Rule window allows you to assign a port rule to a single virtual cluster, or to all the NIC's clusters.*

Protocols   Select the specific TCP/IP protocol that the port rule covers (TCP, UDP, or both). The network traffic for the protocol that is named here will be the only traffic that is affected by this rule. All other traffic will be handled using the default filtering mode.

Filtering Mode   To specify that multiple hosts in the cluster will handle network traffic for this port rule, select the Multiple Hosts option. By distributing the load among multiple hosts, you gain fault tolerance as well as scaled performance. The filter mode also presents the option of deciding whether the load should be distributed equally among the hosts in the cluster or a specific host should handle a specific percentage of the load.

Select Single Host to specify that network traffic for the port rule should be handled by a single host in the cluster, according to a priority that is set. This priority overrides the host priority ID for this port's traffic.

Select Disabled to specify that the network traffic for this port rule should be blocked. This is a simple way to build a firewall to prevent network access to a specific range of ports.

Changing a port rule to Disabled for an active host or for the cluster as a whole immediately blocks all traffic for the rule's port range. Using nlb.exe to drain a rule blocks new connections, but allows existing sessions to continue.

Affinity   *Client affinity* determines the way NLB allocates incoming traffic to cluster nodes. Its primary purpose is to support applications that require all requests from the same client computer be processed by the same NLB server—applications that maintain some kind of client state information on the server. The allocation algorithm uses portions of the source IP address in the packet to determine which member server will process the packet.

When you have a small population of application users, or your application users work from behind a firewall that implements Network Address Translation (NAT), selecting Single or Class C affinity can cause an uneven distribution of requests to cluster nodes.

Select None to specify that NLB should not direct multiple requests from the same client to the same cluster host. This option causes NLB's hashing algorithm to use the full 4 bytes of the sender's IP address along with the TCP or UDP source port when choosing the NLB node to process a packet. Since TCP/UDP changes the source port with nearly every request, selecting None gives all cluster nodes a chance to process packets from any given client computer.

Select Single (the default setting) to specify that multiple requests from the same source IP address should be directed to the same cluster host. With Single affinity, NLB's hashing algorithm ignores the source TCP or UDP port. Affinity has a negative effect on performance, but under certain circumstances this is outweighed by the efficiency provided to the client making the multiple requests. For example, if each request from a client is connected to a cookie, keeping the client at the same host is more efficient (in fact, it's a necessity). Secure HTTP applications (HTTPS on TCP Port 443) require Single affinity.

Class C affinity provides affinity for a group instead of a single-client IP address. Selecting this option directs multiple requests from the same TCP/IP Class C address range to the same host. With this configuration, clients that use multiple proxy servers are treated in the same manner that individual client IP addresses are handled under Single affinity. When a client who is accessing the cluster through multiple proxy servers makes multiple requests, each request appears to originate from a different computer. If all of the client's proxy servers are located within the same Class C address range (usually a safe assumption), enabling the Class C option means that client sessions are handled similarly to Single affinity.

Load Weight   In Multiple Hosts filtering mode, you can use the Load Weight parameter to specify the percentage of traffic a host should handle for the associated port rule. To prevent the host from receiving network traffic, specify 0. To specify a percentage, use a value between 1 and 100.

As each host is configured, the total of the individual Load Weight parameters does not have to add up to 100 percent. The actual traffic load is computed dynamically, using the host's load weight specification divided by the total of the cluster's load. Insistence on a constant value of 100 percent for all load weights would not work because hosts occasionally enter or leave the cluster.

Equal Load Distribution   Use the Equal Load Distribution option to specify that a host participates in equally balanced traffic, in multiple-host filtering mode, for the associated port rule.

Handling Priority   The handling priority is used if single-host filtering mode is utilized, and it specifies the host's priority level for traffic for this port rule. The host with the highest handling priority for a rule will handle all of the traffic for that rule. Enter a value between 1 and X, where X is the number of hosts. Each host must have a unique value for this parameter. The value 1 is the highest priority.

Configuring TCP/IP for Network Load Balancing

The TCP/IP properties for the NIC that is used for NLB must also be configured during setup of NLB. Defining a cluster or dedicated IP address within the NLB Properties pages does not automatically define the address to the TCP/IP protocol stack. The following entries must be the same in both the NLB configuration and the TCP/IP configuration:

- Dedicated IP address (must be static, not DHCP assigned). Make no entry if you have configured all 0's for the dedicated IP address on NLB's Host Parameters page.
- Cluster IP address.

Using Nlbmgr.exe to Configure Clusters and Nodes

Configuring NLB from the Network Load Balancing Properties page on each cluster node can be time consuming. Ensuring that port rules are consistent on all cluster nodes can be problematic. The Network Load Balancing Manager (nlbmgr.exe) addresses both issues.

NLB Manager allows you to create new Windows Server 2003–based clusters, and to add nodes to existing clusters. The program also allows you to create port rules, and to deploy rules to all cluster nodes at the same time.

NLB Manager can run on Windows XP Professional or Windows Server 2003 to create and manage NLB clusters on Windows Server 2003 systems. NLB Manager is located in the Administrative Tools package (\i386\adminpak.msi) on the Windows Server 2003 installation CD.

While the Windows 2000–based NLB nodes can interoperate with Windows Server 2003–based NLB nodes, NLB Manager only works with pure Windows Server 2003 NLB clusters.

While the NLB cluster installation and configuration concepts are similar whether you use NLB Manager or configure each server using the Network Load Balancing Properties dialog, the procedure is different in one key aspect. When configuring servers individually using the NLB Properties dialog, you must reenter the configuration parameters on each server. Using NLB Manager, you first define the properties of the cluster, and then configure individual servers by adding them to the cluster. In the act of adding a server to a cluster, NLB Manager configures the server with the predefined settings. Using NLB Manager eliminates the possibility that you might have servers that won't converge with the cluster because of differences in one or more parameters.

 When your NLB cluster uses unicast mode, and one or more of the cluster member servers has only a single NIC, you must run NLB Manager from a computer that is not a member of the cluster. Unicast mode NLB cluster member servers configured with a single NIC cannot communicate with one another in the normal fashion, because they all use the same MAC address.

When you choose to use NLB Manager to configure and manage an NLB cluster, you should use it consistently. Forgo the temptation to make simple changes using the NLB Properties dialog, because doing so can result in one or more servers with a configuration that prevents them from converging successfully with the cluster.

Create a Cluster with NLB Manager

When you use NLB Manager to create a cluster, you must first define cluster parameters and port rules, and then add nodes to the cluster. To create a cluster, follow these steps:

1. Start NLB Manager by running nlbmgr.exe from a command prompt or from the Start | Run menu item.

2. Open the Cluster menu and select New (see Figure 24-6).

3. Fill in the Cluster Parameters and Port Rules panels as you would if you were working directly through the Properties dialogs. Notice that you are not able to enter host-specific information at this time.

4. Click OK to complete the definition of cluster-level parameters.

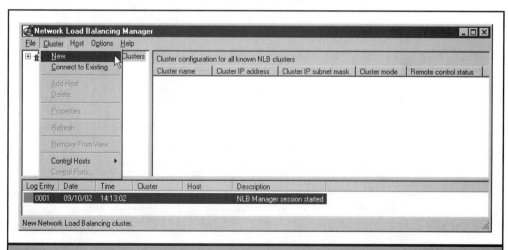

Figure 24-6. *Use NLB Manager to create, modify, and manage NLB cluster configurations.*

Add Nodes to the Cluster with NLB Manager

With the cluster elements common to all nodes complete, NLB Manager walks you through the rest of the processes, starting by asking you to designate the first server you want to add to the cluster. Use the following steps to complete this process:

1. Enter the server name and click Connect. NLB Manager prompts you for credentials. Supply the username in fully qualified format (*domain\username* or *servername\username*, not just *username*).

2. NLB Manager displays the NICs it discovers on the server, and asks you to select one (see Figure 24-7).

3. In the Host Parameters page (similar to the NLB Properties Host configuration dialog), supply the requested information, and click Next.

NLB Manager updates both the NLB properties and the TCP/IP properties of the target server, and brings the cluster online. Upon completion, it displays the results and the status of the cluster in the original cluster management window, as shown in Figure 24-8.

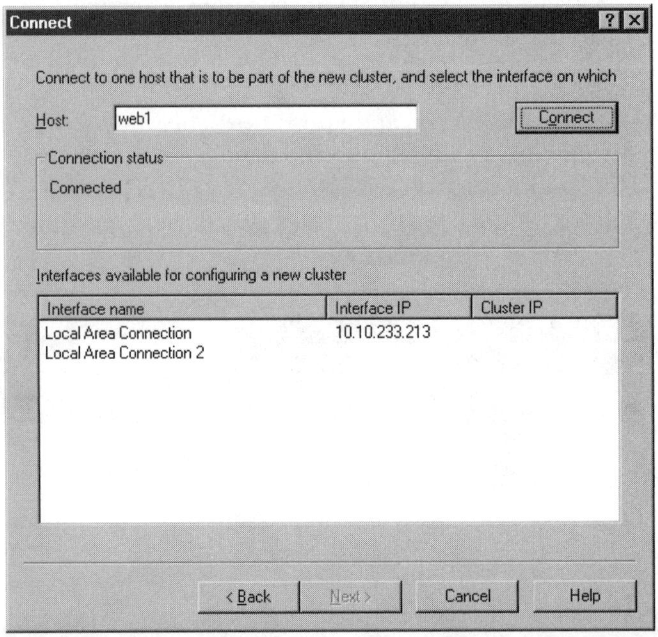

Figure 24-7.   *Select the network interface for this NLB cluster member.*

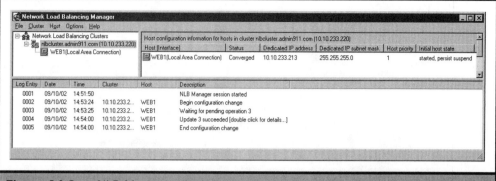

Figure 24-8. *NLB Manager displays the current status of all monitored clusters, and logs the success or failure of NLB cluster management tasks.*

To add additional hosts to the cluster, right-click the cluster name and select Add Host To Cluster. Alternatively, you can highlight the cluster name, and then choose Cluster | Add Host To Cluster from the menu bar. NLB Manager then guides you through the steps enumerated in the previous paragraphs.

Modifying Cluster and Host Parameters Using NLB Manager

NLB Manager allows you to modify the configuration of the cluster as a whole, or of the individual cluster hosts.

To modify cluster parameters, open the Cluster Properties dialog, either by right-clicking the cluster name and selecting Properties or by selecting the cluster name and then choosing Cluster | Properties. To modify cluster properties, make the appropriate changes and click OK. NLB Manager will stop cluster operations, make changes to individual cluster nodes, and then restart the nodes in their initial default state.

To modify cluster host parameters, open the Host Properties dialog from its shortcut menu, or from the Host menu after selecting the desired host. The Host Properties dialog has four tabs, as shown in Figure 24-9. NLB Manager allows you to modify parameters on the Host Parameters tab, and to modify the handling priority for any single host type rules. All other information is display only, and not modifiable from the Host Properties dialog.

Administering Network Load Balancing

After you've completed all the setup chores, managing NLB clusters on a day to day basis isn't onerous. You can check the status of the cluster and its hosts to avoid serious problems, or perform maintenance tasks to resolve problems.

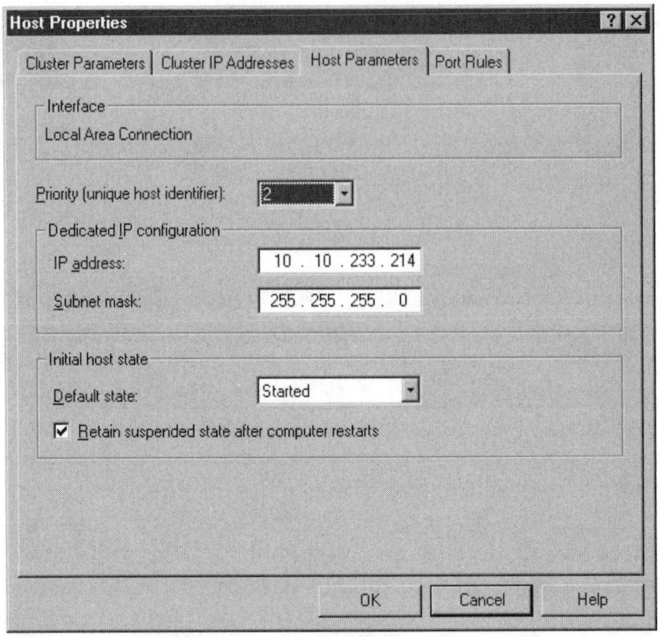

Figure 24-9. *You can modify configuration settings in the Host Properties dialog.*

You have two tools available for administering your NLB clusters: NLB Manager, and nlb.exe, both of which are discussed in the following sections.

Administering NLB with NLB Manager

Using NLB Manager, you can fully control operations of a cluster and individual cluster hosts. Right-clicking either the cluster name or an individual cluster host allows you to select either the Control Host(s) or the Control Ports option.

As shown in Figure 24-10, the Control Hosts menu allows you to Start, Stop, Drainstop, Suspend, or Resume a host or all hosts in a cluster.

The Control Ports dialog allows you to Enable, Disable, or Drain an individual rule for a single host, or for all hosts in the cluster (see Figure 24-11).

Managing the Network Load Balancing Cluster Using Nlb.exe

After NLB has been installed and configured, its operations can be controlled (and some parameter settings can be modified) with the Network Load Balancing control program, nlb.exe.

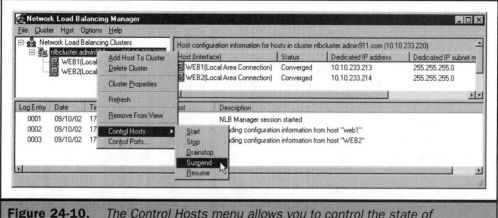

Figure 24-10. *The Control Hosts menu allows you to control the state of cluster hosts.*

You can use nlb.exe, located in the %SystemRoot%\System32 folder, from cluster hosts or from any remote Windows Server 2003 computer that can access the cluster over a LAN or WAN. Nlb.exe is a shell-based program, which allows administrators to write and execute command-line scripts to simplify administration.

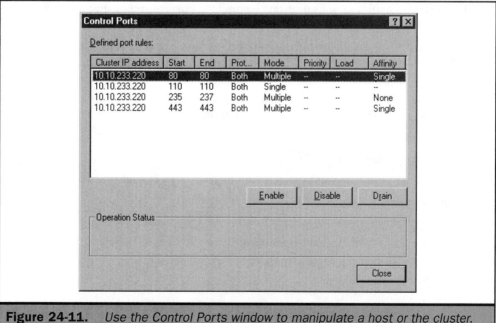

Figure 24-11. *Use the Control Ports window to manipulate a host or the cluster.*

Caution   *Nlb.exe cannot be used to modify the parameters of a host from a remote computer, although you can view information about a remote computer.*

The syntax for nlb.exe is

nlb *<command>* [*<cluster>*[:*<host>*] [/passw [*<password>*]] [/port *<port>*]]

where:

command is one of the supported commands (listed next) and the following parameters are used when accessing a cluster from a remote computer:

- **cluster** is the cluster primary IP address.
- **host** is the IP address of a host in the cluster (if omitted, all hosts).
- **/passw *<password>*** is the password for remote access.
- **/port *<port>*** is the cluster's remote-control UDP port.

Following are the available commands:

- **ip2mac *<cluster>***   Converts cluster IP address to cluster MAC address.
- **reload**   Reloads parameters from the registry; acts on the local machine only.
- **query**   Queries to see which hosts are currently part of the cluster.
- **display**   Displays configuration parameters, current status, and recent event log messages; displays local machine information only.
- **suspend**   Suspends control of cluster operations; stops cluster host operations. Suspended cluster hosts will ignore all other cluster control commands except Resume (and Query).
- **resume**   Resumes control of cluster operations; does not restart a suspended cluster, but rather only allows it to accept other control commands.
- **start**   Starts cluster operations.
- **stop**   Stops cluster operations.
- **drainstop**   Ends all existing connections and stops cluster operations.
- **enable *<port>* | all**   Enables traffic for *<port>* rule or all ports.
- **disable *<port>* | all**   Disables all traffic for *<port>* rule or all ports.
- **drain *<port>* | all**   Disables new traffic for *<port>* rule or all ports.
- **igmp *<enable | disable>* *<cluster IP>***   Enables or disables IGMP Multicast support for the cluster.

Server Clusters

The other component in Windows Clustering is *server clusters*. The goal behind server clusters differs slightly from that of Network Load Balancing. Server cluster functionality focuses more on providing high availability and manageability to your Windows Server 2003 network environment, whereas NLB works primarily on providing high reliability and performance. Server cluster functionality provides high availability to applications that are impractical or impossible to run on more than one server, like many database applications.

Server clusters ensure system availability by enabling failover technology from one node to another. The cluster software automatically moves processes and resources from a failed system to the remaining systems in the cluster. The Cluster Service is available in Enterprise Edition and Datacenter Edition of Windows Server 2003 (both of which support eight-node clusters).

Server Cluster Architecture

Like NLB, a server cluster is a group of computers that work together as a single entity. Both Enterprise Edition and Datacenter Edition of Windows Server 2003 support eight-node clusters. (Windows 2000 Advanced Server supports two computers in a server cluster, and Windows 2000 Datacenter Server supports four computers.)

In a server cluster, each computer in the server cluster is called a *node,* and each node is equally responsible for maintaining server and application availability. In addition, a common set of storage devices is attached to every node by way of a shared bus. This allows effective ownership of the storage device to move to another node in the cluster when responsibility for processing applications that reside on the storage device moves from one node to another. This is known as *shared nothing* architecture, because resources used by clustered applications are never accessed by more than one node at a time. This architecture ensures that a node gives up ownership of a resource before that resource is acquired and used by another cluster node.

Server clusters offer centralized management of the systems. Since server clusters work as a single entity, so should the management software work as if it were managing a single system. This streamlines the process of accessing and managing server clusters so that you can work more effectively and efficiently.

Failover and Failback

Server clusters provide high availability by ensuring that applications and nodes are constantly accessible. If a node or application were to go offline (either planned or unplanned downtime), another node in the server cluster would immediately take over the responsibilities. This process is known as *failover.*

Failover   Failover is one of the many features of server clusters that differentiate it from NLB. Failover occurs when either an application or a node experiences a failure. For instance, when a hardware resource on a node causes the system to crash, another node in the server cluster domain immediately takes control (and becomes the *recovery node*).

The recovery node first takes ownership of the failed node's resources. Dependent resources are taken offline before the resources on which they depend are taken offline. The Cluster Service does this by using the Resource Monitor to communicate with the resource DLL that manages the resource (see the section "The Resource Monitor," later in this chapter). If the resource can't be contacted or brought offline gracefully, it is terminated abruptly. Once the resources are offline, the recovery node then begins to take ownership of the resources, assumes the IP address of the downed node, and, finally, automatically starts providing the services of the downed node to clients by bringing resources and services back online.

Application failure, although a very similar process, goes through a slightly different procedure from that of node failure. After detecting the application failure, the node can first try to restart the application. If that effort is unsuccessful, the node initiates failover so that the other node in the server cluster starts the application.

There are two very important things to remember concerning failover:

- Failover is only truly useful if the node recovering the application can adequately service the additional workload. Since unplanned failures are rarely, if ever, predictable, you should equip all nodes so that they can easily accommodate workloads upon failure.

- The failover process is entirely customizable. You can use Cluster Administrator to define policies and procedures for failover. For example, you can define application dependencies—whether or not an application failure invokes application restart on the same node—and failback policies.

Failback   After failover, a recovery node (or nodes) is hosting services from a node or application that has gone offline. You should always consider this failover solution as temporary, because usually it results in resources becoming strained. As a result, you should try to get the application or node back online as soon as possible.

The mechanism for restoring the original configuration is called *failback*. Failback is essentially failover in reverse. It automatically balances the workload when the application or node becomes available again.

Server Cluster Operation Modes

There are two basic operation modes for Windows Server 2003 clusters within your network environment. These modes are not to be confused with the clustering scenarios that clustering can provide to your environment. Rather, they are the underlying mechanisms that allow server clusters to be versatile in your environment.

The following two operation modes are supported by Windows Server 2003 clusters:

- **Active/active clustering** The most productive and efficient operational mode that you can use. In this mode, all nodes are operating under workloads (they're servicing clients), and they're able to provide recovery services for any application or node that goes offline. The benefit is that hardware resources are used more efficiently. In other words, resources aren't wasted by sitting idle and waiting for an application or node to go offline.

- **Active/passive clustering** Used to provide the highest level of availability, stability, and performance. In this mode, one node is actively providing services while the other is sitting idle waiting for the active application or node to go offline. Although this mode provides the highest level of security for your Windows Server 2003 cluster, the downside is that you are wasting valuable resources.

Server Cluster Hardware Components

The hardware components required by the server cluster provides another differentiating factor between server clusters and NLB. Simply put, there are heavier resource requirements to support the functionality of server clusters (that is, failover, failback, and active/active clustering). The following sections detail the fundamental hardware components needed to create and support a server cluster.

Nodes As mentioned earlier, a server cluster is comprised of two or more individual computer systems (nodes) that work as a single entity. Client computers see and use server clusters as a single resource. Before a server can become a node and participate in the server cluster, it must meet the following prerequisites:

- The server must be running Windows Server 2003 Enterprise Edition or Datacenter Edition.

- The server must be a member of a domain, not a workgroup.

- The server must have the Cluster Service installed and running.

- The server must be attached to one or more shared storage mediums. See "Shared Storage Devices," later in this chapter, for more information.

 Place all servers that will be server cluster nodes in their own Active Directory OU, to isolate them from group policies that may be in effect for other servers.

Once these prerequisites are met, the server can actively participate with other members of a server cluster. The nodes, by definition, have the following properties:

- Since every node in the server cluster is attached to one or more shared storage devices, each of them shares the data stored on those devices.

■ Each node detects the presence of other nodes in the server cluster through an interconnect. An *interconnect* is typically a high-speed connection that is attached to each node. Nodes don't have to have a separate interconnect apart from their NIC that connects them with the rest of the Windows Server 2003 network environment. However, a separate interconnect is highly recommended.

Note   *Nodes participating in a server cluster can also detect when nodes are joining or leaving the server cluster. This detection ability is responsible for detecting both system and application failures.*

A node's participation within the server cluster can fluctuate. Table 24-1 lists the five possible operational states for a node. A node can only be in one state at a time.

Shared Storage Devices   All nodes participating in a server cluster share one or more storage devices, as illustrated in the diagram in Figure 24-12. These storage devices use a shared SCSI bus to connect to two nodes in the server cluster.

If you want to support more than two nodes (up to eight nodes), you must install fibre channel storage. Windows Server 2003 Enterprise Edition and Datacenter Edition support a wide range of SCSI hardware manufacturers, but I highly recommend that you consult the Hardware Compatibility List (HCL) before you attempt to create a server cluster. Microsoft officially supports only cluster-certified combinations of servers and storage. See www.microsoft.com/hcl for a list of supported systems.

Tip   *You'll save yourself a huge amount of time if you make sure that the SCSI devices are operating properly before you begin creating the cluster.*

State	Description
Down	The node isn't operational within the server cluster, due to a system or application failure, or planned maintenance.
Joining	The node is becoming a member of the server cluster domain.
Paused	Shared resources are tied up, so the node is temporarily waiting for resources to be freed.
Up	The node is active and operational within the server cluster.
Unknown	The node's state of operation can't be determined.

Table 24-1.   *Operational States for a Node*

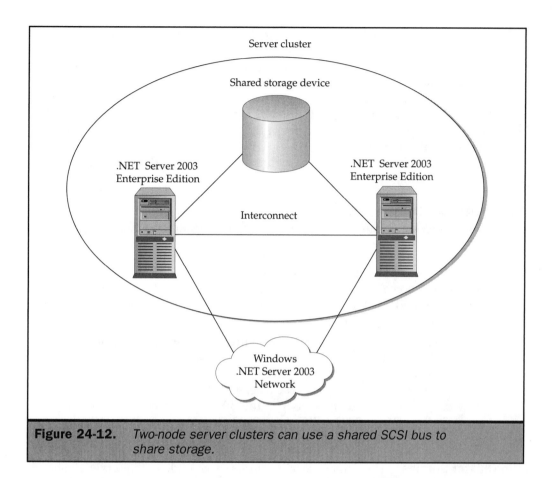

Figure 24-12.   *Two-node server clusters can use a shared SCSI bus to share storage.*

The storage devices themselves store any data that the nodes need to share, and also store all of the server cluster's configuration and resource information. Only one node can take temporary ownership of the data contained in the shared storage device or devices, which prevents resource conflicts.

Note   *For additional fault tolerance, you should use Redundant Array of Independent Disks (RAID) 5. RAID 5 stripes data among three or more disks in the array and keeps parity information to improve performance and reduce the risk of losing data due to disk subsystem failures.*

Interconnects   An interconnect is the physical medium used for server cluster communications. An interconnect can be either the NIC that is used for communication with the rest of the network (receives incoming client requests) or another NIC that is dedicated to serving server cluster communications. For improved performance and redundancy, use a dedicated NIC for cluster communication, and a second NIC for communicating with the rest of the network.

Two NICs in each node isn't a requirement, but it's certainly the recommended configuration. The reasoning is rather straightforward. First, network traffic that is generated between two nodes won't be negatively affected by other traffic circulating the network. Most importantly, however, you're reducing the number of single points of failure in the server cluster. Isn't this one of the primary reasons why you're using server clusters in the first place?

Clusnet.sys, the cluster network driver, runs on each node and manages the server cluster communications.

Software Components

Several software components make up server clusters; they fall into two categories:

- **Clustering software**   Describes the software components that are required for the server cluster to operate. This software enables communication between nodes, detection of application or node operational status, the transfer of resource operations, and much more. The two main components for clustering software are the Resource Monitor and the Cluster Service.

- **Administrative software**   Gives you control and manageability over the server cluster so that you can configure and monitor it. There are two main components within the administrative software category: Cluster Administrator and a command-line utility called cluster.exe. Cluster Administrator doesn't necessary have to be run on a node in the cluster; it can be run remotely from any Windows Server 2003 or Windows 2000 computer as well as a Windows NT 4 computer with Service Pack 3 or later installed.

The Cluster Service   The Cluster service runs on each node in the server cluster. It is the heart of the server cluster, controlling all of the server cluster activity. More specifically, the Cluster service controls the following activities:

- Manages all server cluster objects including nodes (for example, the node that it is installed on), shared storage devices, and configuration information (for example, a node's IP address or computer name).

- Facilitates and coordinates communication with other Cluster services in the server cluster domain, including when a node joins or is removed from the server cluster.

- Detects application and node failures, and initiates failover operations. This may include trying to restart an application as well as distributing workloads to another node in the server cluster.

- Manages event notification.

The Resource Monitor   Any physical or logical component (most of which were previously mentioned) within a server cluster is considered a resource by the Cluster service. To increase the manageability aspects of the server cluster, a Resource Monitor is used to aid communication between the Cluster service and the cluster resources.

Resource Monitors are various software components that serve as a liaison between the Cluster service and server cluster resources. A Resource Monitor allows these resources to run separately from each other, and from the Cluster service. The separation of resources promotes reliability, availability, and scalability for the server cluster. For instance, if a resource fails, it doesn't affect the operability of the Cluster service. Also, the Resource Monitor is used to watch over the Cluster service, so that if it fails, the Resource Monitor can respond by taking all of the node's resources offline.

The Resource Monitor doesn't invoke any server cluster operations, with two exceptions: to gather status reports from the Cluster service or resources, and to take all of the node's resources offline when the Cluster service fails. When the Resource Monitor communicates with a resource, it's actually communicating with the resource's *resource DLL*. The resource DLL can be viewed as the interface to the resource. Take, for example, a resource where an event has occurred. The resource DLL must report this event to the Cluster service. This is when the Resource Monitor steps in; it essentially takes the message and makes sure that the Cluster service is notified.

Cluster Administrator   Cluster Administrator is the primary tool for administering and configuring server cluster objects such as nodes, groups, and other resources. It's installed by default on every node in the cluster, but it can also be installed on any computer with Windows Server 2003, Windows 2000, or Windows NT 4 with Service Pack 3 or higher. This allows you to manage the server cluster without having to actually be physically located at one of the nodes.

The Cluster Administrator program is found the Administrative Tools menu on Windows Server 2003 Standard Edition, Enterprise Edition, and Datacenter Edition (but not Web Edition) installations.

 You install Cluster Administrator on Windows XP Professional systems when installing \i386\adminpak.msi from a Server 2003 installation CD.

The Command-Line Cluster Utility   Cluster.exe gives you the ability to manage the cluster from the Command prompt or from a script that calls cluster.exe. This tool can be run on Windows Server 2003, Windows 2000, or Windows NT 4 with Service Pack 3 or higher computer.

Before you begin using cluster.exe, you need to learn the following important syntax rules:

- Use quotation marks around all names that contain spaces and special characters.
- For Boolean values (True and False), specify 1 for True and 0 for False.

- If you don't specify a server cluster name or use a period (.), it is assumed that you are working from and specifying the local server cluster.

- Cluster.exe processes options from left to right, and if an option fails, the command will stop executing at the failed option.

- Use double quotation marks (") in a string that has two consecutive double quotation marks (" ").

The syntax for cluster.exe depends on what you're trying to manage. Table 24-2 describes the various objects you can manage, with their corresponding basic syntax.

To display the options for any of the basic syntax definitions in Table 24-2, enter cluster.exe /? or cluster.exe /help at the command prompt.

Logical and Physical Cluster Components

The Cluster service manages applications by controlling logical and physical cluster components.

Logical Components   The Cluster service manages a variety of logical components, including the following:

- **Virtual server**   Consists of a servername together with groups of resources needed to run a clustered application. The virtual server is the clients' view of the clustered server, as the clients are unaware of which cluster node is hosting the virtual server.

Object	Basic Syntax
Cluster	cluster [[/cluster:]*cluster_name*] /*option*
Cluster node	cluster [[/cluster:]*cluster_name*] **node** *node_name* /*option*
Cluster group	cluster [[/cluster:]*cluster_name*] **group** *group_name* [/**node:***node_name*] /*option*
Cluster network	cluster [[/cluster:]*cluster name*] **network** *network name* /*option*
Cluster netinterface	cluster [[/cluster:]*cluster name*] **netinterface** /**node:** *node name* / **network:** *network name* /*option*
Cluster resource	cluster [[/cluster:]*cluster_name*] **resource** *resource_name* /*option*
Cluster resourcetype	cluster [[/cluster:]*cluster_name*] **resourcetype** *resource_type_display_name* /*option*

Table 24-2.   *Basic Syntax for Cluster.exe*

- **Resources**   The basic elements managed by the Cluster service. The definition of any given resource may correspond to a physical device (such as a disk drive) or a logical entity (such as an IP address, a service, or a name). Resources have attributes that, among other things, specify which nodes are allowed to bring the resource online, along with the prerequisites that a cluster node must have online before it may bring the given resource online.

- **Groups**   A collection of resources, and any specific resource may belong to only one group at a time. During failover and failback, the Cluster service moves a group from one cluster node to another, ensuring that all the resources of a group are offline to the old cluster node before any of the resources are brought online on the new cluster node. An operation performed on a group affects all of the resources within the group.

Physical Components   Physical components support the cluster's logical components, and include the following:

- **Nodes**   A server that is a member of the cluster. A node is said to be online when the server is running, the Cluster service is running on it, and the node is in communication with other online nodes.

- **Cluster disks**   Logical disks (either individual physical disks or RAID volumes) that reside on a shared bus accessible by all the nodes of the cluster. Cluster disks host application data. When you are preparing cluster disks, be sure to configure them as basic disks, not dynamic disks.

- **Quorum resource**   A disk drive on a shared bus that is not a member of any failover group. The Cluster service places management data and the recovery log on the quorum resource, and uses it to arbitrate control of the cluster. The quorum resource on a shared bus disk drive must be configured as a Basic disk, not a Dynamic disk.

- **Heartbeats**   IP packets exchanged regularly by cluster nodes. When a node fails to receive a heartbeat packet from another node, it assumes that the nonsending node has failed. An active node then initiates the failover process.

Using Server Clusters in Your Environment

Planning the way that server clusters will fit into your Windows Server 2003 network environment is a crucial step. Don't skip any part of planning before you begin implementation. Unfortunately, too many administrators give short shrift to planning, and the results vary from disastrous to a cluster that doesn't really benefit the enterprise.

There are several predefined implementation variations to choose from, and you should make your choices by asking yourself the follow questions:

- *What are you trying to support?* File and print services, web services, and applications are just a few of the things that you can support with server clusters. Your answer has a tremendous impact on the model that you'll follow.

- *What level of high availability, scalability, reliability, and performance do you need?* The models that Microsoft presents (see the next section) vary in the type of services offered. In other words, one model may offer the highest degree of availability while not offering much in terms of scalability.

- *What, if any, budget constraints do you have?* 'Nuff said.

This following section describes the configuration models that Microsoft suggests you consider. For simplicity, I'll discuss these models as if you were planning two nodes in your cluster. Keeping in mind the questions just covered, review each model to see which one is more appropriate for your Windows Server 2003 network environment.

Hot-Spare Cluster Model

The hot-spare cluster model, illustrated in Figure 24-13, is also called the active/passive model because not all the hardware resources are being used simultaneously. As a result, this model provides the highest level of availability.

In the hot-spare model, one node in the server cluster services all requests for resources. The other node sits idle until the active node fails. You can think of this paradigm as a dedicated backup.

Typically, the passive node uses the same hardware configuration as the active node. That way, if a failure occurs, the passive node can quickly take its place and provide the same services.

The primary advantage to this model is that it provides the highest level of availability without sacrificing performance levels. You should consider using this model for your most critical applications and services. Of course, since I'm including the budget among the questions to ask yourself, remember that you must be willing to spend the extra money on a node that sits idle for much of the duration of its life.

Active/Active Cluster Model

The active/active cluster model represents two nodes in a server cluster that are working simultaneously (see Figure 24-14). Each node is responsible for its own server cluster resources until a failover occurs. When one node fails, the surviving node assumes the resources of the failed node.

This active/active model is designed to provide the same level of high availability as the hot-spare cluster model. However, after a failure, performance can be compromised if the surviving node's capacity to handle the additional workload isn't adequate. For this reason, it is key to size each node so that it can adequately handle the double workload (another budget consideration).

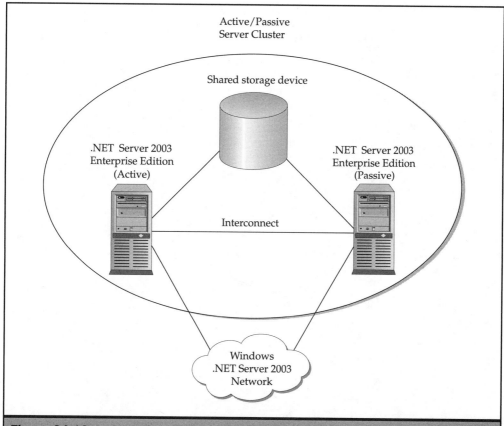

Active/Passive
Server Cluster

Shared storage device

.NET Server 2003
Enterprise Edition
(Active)

.NET Server 2003
Enterprise Edition
(Passive)

Interconnect

Windows
.NET Server 2003
Network

Figure 24-13. *An active/passive cluster model uses the second node only when the primary node fails.*

Hybrid Configuration

The hybrid configuration model represents a configuration where one or more applications run on cluster nodes outside the control of the Cluster service, while one or more applications are under the control of the Cluster service. For example, the Cluster service may control an instance of SQL Server, while DNS may run outside the context of the Cluster service. Should the node fail, SQL Server would fail over to another online node, while DNS would not.

Single-Node Configuration

In a single-node configuration, you install Cluster service on a single computer, and define one or more virtual servers within the cluster. This configuration provides none of the usual high-availability benefits of server clusters, but it does have some administrative

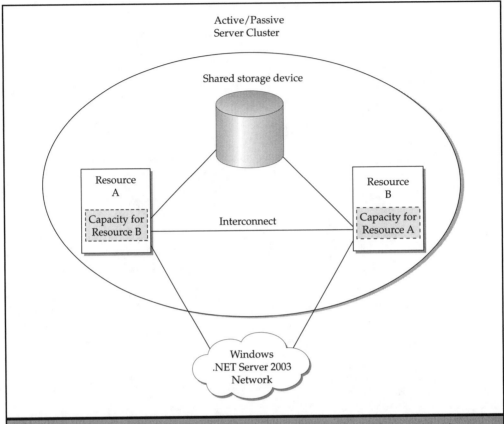

Figure 24-14. *In the active/active model, both nodes host different virtual servers, and use excess capacity to take on the role of the other when the other falls.*

benefits. For example, you could define two virtual servers on a single node cluster, each serving different departments. Should the need for higher availability or additional server resources arise, you add a second node to the cluster. Meanwhile, the client's view of the server resource doesn't change. You can install a single-node configuration on a server that lacks a shared storage bus, but you should configure the server with a SCSI or Fibre Channel bus initially to allow for the addition of another node to the cluster at a later date.

Installing Cluster Service

Installation is the culmination of your planning and design efforts. You must install Cluster service on one node at a time. If you launch the operating system on multiple nodes before you have Cluster service running on the first node, the disks involved in the cluster could become corrupted. After you have completed and verified the physical installation of your cluster, including the shared storage bus, quorum resource, shared disks, heartbeat NIC, and client access NIC, shut down all the unconfigured cluster nodes except the node that you're installing.

Since most applications that run under the control of the Cluster service are cluster-aware, don't install the application on cluster nodes until after you have installed Cluster service on all nodes.

Creating a New Cluster

All cluster nodes must be members of the same domain. To create a new cluster, launch Windows Server 2003 Enterprise Edition or Datacenter Edition on the first target node, and make sure that all other computers connected to the shared storage bus are powered down. Then install the first cluster node using the following steps:

1. Open the Cluster Administrator program from the Administrative Tools menu. Choose Create New Cluster from the Action list box.

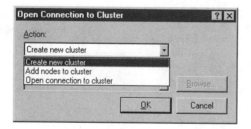

2. In the New Server Cluster Wizard, click Next at the Welcome screen to get started.

3. In the next wizard window, enter the cluster name, and verify the domain name, as shown in Figure 24-15. Then click Next.

4. In the next window, enter the name of the computer that will be the first node of the new cluster, and click Next.

5. The next window displays the progress as the wizard analyzes the required components (see Figure 24-16). When the analysis is complete, if an error appears, click View Log and correct the errors you find in the log file, then start again. If no error appears, click Next to continue.

6. In the next window, enter the IP address for the cluster, and click Next. This is the IP address that all the cluster management tools will use to manipulate this cluster.

7. In the next window (see Figure 24-17), enter the name and password for the cluster's service account, which is the security context within which Cluster service will run. The account must already exist in the domain (in the same domain that the servers belong to), but it doesn't need elevated domain privileges, because the wizard will automatically grant it the rights and privileges that it needs. Click Next to continue.

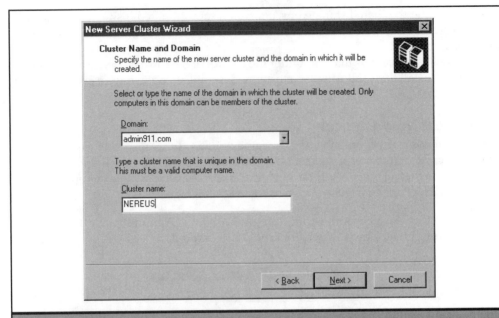

Figure 24-15.   *Each cluster must have a name, and all of its nodes must be members of the same domain.*

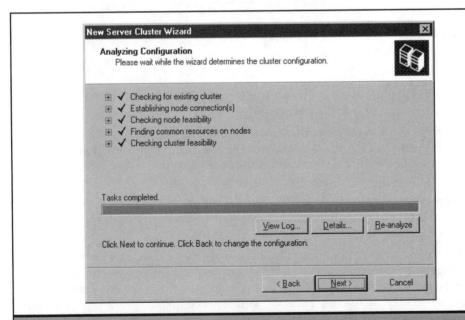

Figure 24-16.   *The Create New Cluster Wizard examines the server to be sure it has what is needed to be a cluster node.*

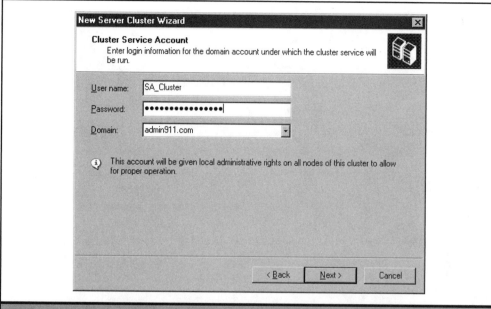

Figure 24-17. *The Cluster service account must be a domain account, not a local computer account.*

8. The wizard displays a summary of the cluster configuration it has created (see Figure 24-18). Scroll through the list to make sure it contains the configuration options you want. Notice that the wizard automatically selected an available disk drive to be your quorum resource, but it may not have selected the drive you planned to make your quorum resource.

9. To select a different drive as your quorum resource, click the Quorum button and select the drive you want to use. Then click Next.

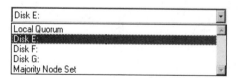

10. The wizard completes the node configuration and reports the results. Verify that the installation completed successfully (see the next section, "Fixing Configuration Errors"), and click Next to continue.

11. Click Finish on the final screen to exit the Create New Cluster Wizard.

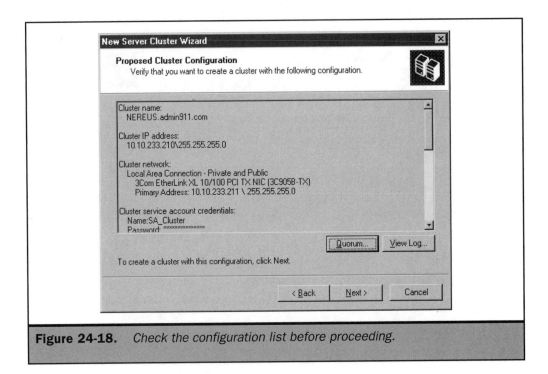

Figure 24-18. *Check the configuration list before proceeding.*

Fixing Configuration Errors

When the Create New Cluster Wizard completes the node configuration, it displays a red plus sign for a configuration option that has a serious problem, and a yellow warning triangle if noncritical errors occur. If you see an error icon, expand the installation progress log by clicking the small black plus sign on the left. You'll see that some errors can be corrected after the wizard finishes creating the cluster. Other, more serious, errors must be corrected before you exit the wizard, by using the Back button to return to the configuration steps.

Figure 24-19 shows an error that is corrected post-installation. This particular error was an error in the cluster name. I originally chose a name that was the same as the NetBIOS name for another domain on the network, which is a definite no-no. To correct the problem, I used cluster.exe at the node to rename the cluster, reran the Create New Cluster Wizard, specifying the new, legal name, and then restarted the Cluster service.

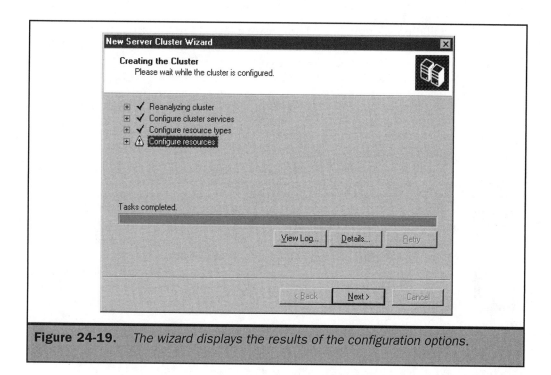

Figure 24-19.   *The wizard displays the results of the configuration options.*

Using Cluster Administrator

Cluster Administrator connects to the new cluster, and displays its status.

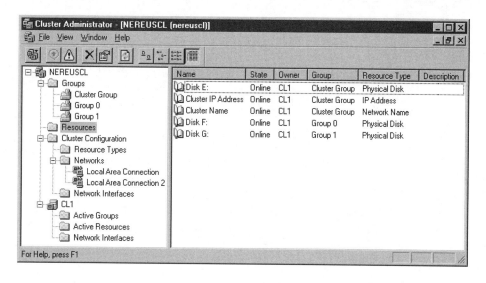

During installation, all network adapters are enabled for both private cluster communications and for public communication to the cluster. If you installed a network adapter on a private network that you want to dedicate to private cluster communication, use Cluster Administrator to open the adapter's Properties dialog. Then reconfigure the adapter to allow only private cluster communication.

Make sure the service runs without error on this node before beginning the installation process on the next node. Should you need more detailed information to diagnose an installation problem, the installation wizard creates a log file at %SystemRoot%\system32\logfiles\cluster\ClCfgSrv.log.

Adding Nodes to an Existing Cluster

You follow a similar procedure to add additional nodes to your cluster. Begin by ensuring that the first cluster node is powered on and operating normally. Then, power on the server that you wish to configure as the next cluster node, and open Cluster Administrator. Right-click the name of your cluster and select New | Node from the shortcut menu to launch the Add Cluster Computers Wizard. Follow the wizard to complete your configuration of additional nodes, one node at a time. In each case, be sure that the computer and the Cluster service are running without error before adding the next node.

Test the Cluster

When you have at least two nodes installed, you can test the cluster by moving a group. Moving a group transfers control of the group—and the execution of any applications that are a part of the group—to a different node of the cluster. Open Cluster Administrator, right-click the group name, and select Move Group from the shortcut menu. Cluster Administrator performs the following actions:

1. Forces the Cluster service to take the resources that comprise the group offline.

2. Causes the Cluster service on another node to bring those resources online.

Figure 24-20 shows the results after moving a group from node CL1 to CL2.

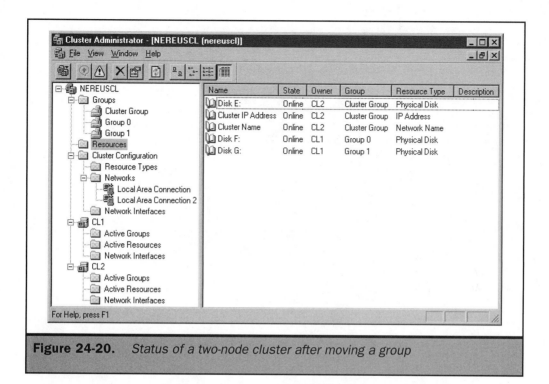

Figure 24-20. *Status of a two-node cluster after moving a group*

Setting Up Applications

The procedures for installing applications on a cluster vary from application to application, and detailed instructions are therefore beyond the scope of this book. In general, when you install a cluster-aware application on a server running the Cluster service, the application's setup routines offer you cluster-related installation options. Research each application's requirements for running in a clustered environment before attempting to install the application.

Chapter 25

Tweaking and
Optimizing Performance

Tweaking and optimizing performance is often a misunderstood concept so it's common for administrators to pay little attention to optimization. Maintaining a Windows Server 2003 environment is challenging enough without having to consider performance aspects. Performance optimization or tweaking is typically done when a problem such as slow logons or other performance glitches arise.

Ironically, performance optimization can significantly reduce administrators' workloads and help them get an edge over the daily grind. Combined with capacity planning, performance optimization can be used to head off problems before they become significant issues. It can assist administrators in establishing baseline metrics on which to gauge how the network or system operates. Future performance measurements can be compared to those baselines to determine how to streamline performance. Performance optimization can also be used to handle tasks, such as how to size a system, when to upgrade, and when to segment workloads.

No matter the circumstances, you can see how performance optimization and capacity planning affect you, your environment, and users' perceptions. So how can you change users' perceptions? How can you create or maintain a reliable, efficient Windows Server 2003 environment and minimize or eliminate fire fighting? These questions and many more are addressed in this chapter. By no means will this chapter be your savior for all computing problems, but it will give you a solid understanding of why you need to adhere to performance optimization and capacity planning procedures. The beauty of these procedures is that they can be applied to small environments and scale well into enterprise-level systems.

Examining Performance Optimization

Performance optimization has matured over the years for Windows-based environments into a way to make systems run faster, handle bigger workloads, and ensure reliability, availability, and serviceability of computer resources. Engineers and administrators responsible for systems can appreciate the need for proactive monitoring to provide adequate support to end users and the business structure.

With the increasing popularity of Windows systems in the business world, the responsibilities now placed on Windows Server 2003 are far greater than those placed on its predecessors, Windows NT and Windows 2000. As a result, performance optimization is crucial to the successful management of your environment.

Performance optimization coupled with capacity planning is one of the most important and most difficult responsibilities you face with both small- and large-scale Windows Server 2003 environments. It requires a combination of disciplines and can always be improved upon because work habits and environments continually change. Performance optimization encompasses many aspects of systems management, performance management, deductive reasoning, and forecasting. However, there is more to performance optimization than just using formulas or statistical information. You must use your subjective, creative, and intuitive insight in addition to relying on purely analytical solutions.

When faced with performance optimization aspects, it's important to apply the focus of the business along with technical principles so that the organization as a whole benefits. Just because a system can perform operations blazingly fast doesn't necessarily mean that the organization is adequately serviced or that resources are properly used. Some key questions to keep in mind while tweaking or optimizing performance are the following:

- How quickly can a task be accomplished?
- How much work can be performed?
- What costs are associated with different business strategies?
- Is the system used effectively and efficiently?

Performance optimization combined with capacity planning enables you to stay one step ahead of your system and anticipate future resource requirements by evaluating existing system behavior. It also helps define the overall system by establishing baseline performance values and then, through trend and pattern analysis, providing valuable insight into where the system is heading. It is an invaluable aid for uncovering both current and potential bottlenecks. Properly implemented performance optimization procedures can reveal how specific system management activities (software and hardware upgrades, changes in network topologies, and so on) may affect performance, future resource requirements, and budgeting strategies. Performance optimization allows you to attend to performance issues proactively instead of retroactively.

Establishing Service Levels and Goals

Performance optimization seeks to balance resources and workloads. It is extremely difficult to provide just the right amount of computing power for the tasks to be performed. If a system is powerful but underutilized, then a lot of resources are of little value and a waste of money. On the other hand, if a system cannot handle the workload, then tasks or transactions are delayed, opportunities are lost, costs increase, and the user (or customer) perceives a problem. Thus, a primary goal of performance optimization is *balance*.

Performance optimization involves working with unknown or immeasurable aspects of a system, such as the number of transactions the system will need to perform in the next few months or years. Other issues may relate to administration workload capacity, such as the number of system administrators that will be needed to maintain the operability of the company's database server. All of these questions are related to performance optimization and capacity planning methodologies, and their answers cannot be predicted with complete accuracy. Estimating future resource requirements is not an easy task. However, performance optimization provides a process in which you can establish benchmarks and analyze characteristics of present system resource utilization and use these to make predictions about future needs. Your level of understanding and control of your system needs is limited; to achieve a balance between capacity and workload, you must gain as much understanding and control of the environment as possible. Controlling the aspects that are within your reach greatly increases your chances of successfully maintaining the reliability, serviceability, and availability of your system.

To begin proactively managing your system, it is important to establish *system-wide policies and procedures*. Policies and procedures help define service levels and shape users' expectations. Once these are defined, you can easily begin characterizing workloads, which will, in turn, help you define the *baseline performance values* needed to gauge the health of your system. For instance, you can define a service level agreement that states that response times for a particular system will be three seconds or less.

Establishing Policies and Procedures

The policies and procedures you decide to implement depend entirely on your network environment. The process of defining levels of service and objectives for your system gives you a certain level of control over the system's resources. Without this level of control, it is difficult to understand a system's intricacies much less manage and optimize system performance. Policies and procedures also help you winnow out empirical data and transform it into information that you can use to determine current as well as future capacity requirements. In essence, policies and procedures define how the system is supposed to be used, establishing guidelines to help users understand that they can't always have total freedom to use system resources any way they see fit. In a system where policies and procedures are working successfully and where network throughput suddenly slows to a crawl, you can assume that the reason is not, for instance, that some people were playing a multiuser network game or that a few individuals were sending enormous e-mail attachments to everyone throughout the company.

Consider establishing two sets of policies and procedures: one set that you communicate to users, and one set that the information systems (IS) department and systems support staff use internally. For example, policies and procedures for users might include a limitation on the size of e-mail attachments and discouragement of the use of beta products (other than ones internally developed) on your network. Internal policies or procedures might include rules that all backups should be completed by 5 A.M. each workday and that routine system maintenance (server refreshes, driver updates, and so on) should be performed on Saturday mornings between 6 and 9 A.M. The following list provides additional examples of policies and procedures that might be applied to your environment:

- Specify that computing resources are intended for business use only—that is, that no gaming or personal use of computers is allowed.

- Specify that only certain applications are supported and allowed on the network.

- Establish space quotas on private home directories while enforcing these policies through quota management software provided within Windows Server 2003.

- Establish replication intervals for certain databases.

- Specify that users must follow a set of steps to receive technical support.

It's important to understand what users expect from the system. This can be determined through interviews, questionnaires, and the like.

Establishing Baseline Values

By now you may be asking, "What do I do to begin performance monitoring?" or "How do I size a new Windows Server 2003 network or server?" In fact, you've already begun the process by defining policies and procedures, which cut down the amount of empirical data that you face. The next preparatory step for performance optimization is establishing baseline values so you can monitor performance. You need a starting point to which you can compare results. In determining baseline values, you deal with a lot of hard facts (statistical representations of system performance), but there are also a few variables that require your judgment and intuition. These variables are workload characterization, benchmarks, vendor-supplied information, and of course, your data collection results. Later on you can compare the baseline with the current metrics to troubleshoot, perform trend analyses, and more.

Workload Characterization

Identifying the *workloads* of a system can be an extremely challenging task, in part because resources often intertwine among different workloads and vary in processing time as well as in the amount of data being processed. Workloads are grouped, or characterized, according to the type of work being performed and the resources used. The following list shows how workloads can be characterized:

- Department function (research and development, manufacturing, and so on)
- Volume of work performed
- Batch processing
- Real-time processing
- Service requests needing attention within a specified time
- Online transactions

Once you have identified your system's workloads, you can determine the resource requirements for each and plan accordingly. This process will also help you understand the performance levels the workloads expect and demand from the system. For example, some workloads may be more memory intensive than processor intensive.

Benchmarks and Vendor-supplied Information

Benchmarks are values that are used to measure the performance of products such as processors, video cards, hard disk drives, applications, and entire systems. They are among the most sought-after performance indicators in the computer industry. Almost every company in the computer industry uses these values to compare itself to the competition. As you might suspect, benchmarks are used heavily in sales and marketing, but their real purpose is to indicate the levels of performance you can expect when using the product.

Most benchmarks are provided by the vendors themselves, but they can originate from other sources, such as magazines, benchmark organizations, and in-house testing labs. Table 2-1 lists organizations that provide benchmark statistics and tools for evaluating product performance. Benchmarks can be of great value in your decision-making process but they should not be your only source for evaluating and measuring performance. When consulting benchmark results during capacity planning, use them as guidelines only and use care in their interpretation.

Data Collection: What Is Being Monitored

Each Windows Server 2003 system has components that the Performance snap-in can monitor. These components can be hardware or software components that perform tasks or support workloads. Many of these components have indicators that reflect certain aspects of their functionality that can be accurately measured in terms of the rate at which tasks are accomplished. For example, the Network Segment: Total bytes received/second counter shows you the number of bytes placed on the Windows Server 2003 system by the network subsystem. All collected data comes from the counters that the Performance snap-in monitors.

Objects

In Windows Server 2003 systems, many of the components that comprise an entire system are grouped into *objects* based on their characteristics. For example, anything pertaining to the processor is located in the Processor object, and anything pertaining to memory is located in the Memory object. Objects are grouped according to functionality or association within the system. They can represent logical mechanisms, such as processes, or physical entities, such as hard disk drives.

The number of objects isn't limited to what Windows Server 2003 provides. All Microsoft BackOffice products have objects that can be evaluated and tracked by the Performance snap-in or similar performance monitoring tools. Objects can also be created by third-party vendors, so that you, as an IT professional, can use a tool like

Organization Name	Web Address
Transaction Processing Performance Council	www.tpc.org
Computer Measurement Group	www.cmg.org

Table 25-1. *Organizations That Provide Benchmarks*

the Performance snap-in to monitor your own components. Microsoft has purposely chosen to let outside vendors create objects and counters specific to their own applications or devices that these tools can read.

The number of objects present on a system depends on the system configuration. For instance, Internet Information Server counters won't be present if the system isn't running that application. However, a few of the common objects that can be found in every system are the following:

- Cache
- Logical disk
- Memory
- Paging file
- Physical disk
- Process
- Processor
- Server
- System
- Thread

Counters

Each object contains *counters*. Counters typically provide information about use, throughput, queue length, and so on for a particular object. For example, all counters pertaining to the paging file are contained in the Paging File object. Performance optimization tools use the counters within an object to collect data. The information gathered from these counters is then displayed in the tool's window or dumped into a data file.

Instances

If your system has more than one similar component (two hard drives, four processors, and so on), each one is considered an instance of that component. Each instance in the system has an associated counter that measures its individual performance. Counters with multiple instances also have an instance for the combined instances.

Performance Monitoring Tools

A growing number of tools are available for collecting and analyzing system data and forecasting system capacity on the Windows Server 2003 platform. Microsoft offers some useful utilities that are either built into Windows Server 2003 or sold as separate products that can be used to collect and analyze data. These include Task Manager,

Network Monitor, and Performance snap-in (also known as Performance Monitor), which are built into the operating system, as well as Microsoft Operations Manager (MOM) and Systems Management Server (SMS), which are stand-alone products. Data collected from these applications can be exported to other applications, such as Microsoft Excel or Access, for storage and analysis.

Task Manager

The Windows Server 2003 Task Manager provides multifaceted functionality. It allows you to monitor system activity in real time and to view processor, memory, application, and process status information. You can switch to other running applications or processes, and you can easily end a task or process.

To start using Task Manager, you can use any of the following three methods:

- Right-click the taskbar and select Task Manager.

- Press CTRL-SHIFT-ESC.

- Press CTRL-ALT-DELETE and then click Task Manager.

When you execute Task Manager, the screen that you see in Figure 25-1 will appear.

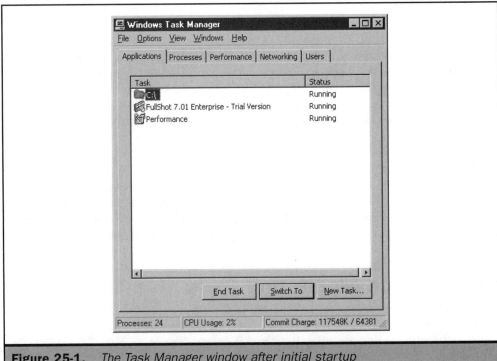

Figure 25-1.   *The Task Manager window after initial startup*

This window contains five tabs—Applications, Processes, Performance, Networking, and Users—that you can toggle among. In addition, a status bar at the bottom of the window displays the number of running processes and the percentage of CPU and memory used.

Task Manager presents valuable real-time performance information that can help you determine what processes or applications are problematic and give you an overall picture of the health of your system. Unfortunately, its limitations, such as its inability to store collected performance information and the breadth of its monitoring capabilities, do not make it a prime candidate for performance optimization purposes. Moreover, it can give you information pertaining to the local machine only. You must be physically at the machine to gauge performance with Task Manager.

Network Monitor

There are two flavors of Network Monitor that can be used to check network performance. One is packaged within Windows Server 2003, and the other is a component of SMS. Both versions have the same interface, as shown in Figure 25-2, and many functional components, but there are a few differences in what they can monitor.

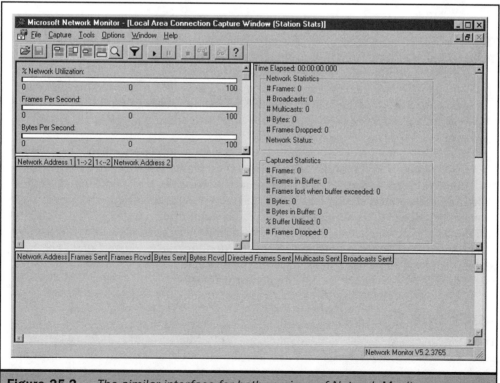

Figure 25-2.   *The similar interface for both versions of Network Monitor*

Network Monitor, built into Windows Server 2003, is intended to monitor only the network activity on the local machine. For security reasons, you cannot capture traffic on remote machines. Network Monitor can, however, capture all frame types traveling into or away from the local machine.

To install Network Monitor, do the following:

1. Choose Start | All Programs | Control Panel | Add or Remove Programs.

2. Select Add or Remove Windows Components.

3. Highlight Management and Monitoring Tools and then click Details.

4. Select Network Monitor Tools and then click OK.

5. Click Next and then click Finish when the installation is complete.

To use Network Monitor, simply select it from the Start | Administrative Tools menu.

The SMS version of Network Monitor is essentially an enhanced version of the one integrated into Windows Server 2003. The primary difference between them is that the SMS version can run promiscuously throughout the network and monitor remote machines. In addition to monitoring remote machines, it can find routers present on the network, monitor the traffic circulating through the network, and resolve addresses from names.

Caution   *The SMS version of Network Monitor presents possible security risks because of the nature of its monitoring techniques and privileges. It can monitor network traffic traveling into and away from remote machines. Any sensitive data that Network Monitor captures could possibly be revealed. Consequently, it is imperative that you limit the number of administrators or IS staff members who can use this version of Network Monitor.*

The SMS version of Network Monitor coincides more with performance optimization objectives because it can monitor several machines at once from a centralized location. Using the Windows Server 2003 version limits the scope of your monitoring and data collection. It also forces you to install management and monitoring tools on every machine that needs to be monitored. This results in additional memory requirements and processing power for each machine. For performance optimization and capacity planning purposes, the SMS version of Network Monitor is an excellent tool for providing real-time network analysis and establishing historical network performance statistics that can be used to examine the health of your network.

Performance Snap-in

The Performance Microsoft Management Console (MMC) snap-in is the most commonly used performance monitoring tool, both because it is bundled with the operating system and because it allows you to monitor every system object that has measurable counters associated with it. The Performance snap-in has two tools: System Monitor and Performance Logs and Alerts. The Performance snap-in is located within the Administrative Tools group on the Start menu. Figure 25-3 shows the System Monitor startup screen.

The Performance snap-in is an excellent tool because it allows you to analyze data through charts, reports, and logs that you can save for future scrutiny. This chapter assumes that you will use the Performance snap-in as your performance optimization tool since it is available to everyone running Windows Server 2003 and its principles can be applied to other utilities.

Charting Performance with System Monitor

Counter statistics can be monitored in real time with System Monitor. The results of the collected data appear in a histogram (bar chart) or graph. The graph format is the default format for System Monitor and it produces a chart that looks something like an electrocardiogram used for monitoring a heartbeat. The charting format you choose is determined mainly by personal preference. You may find one format more suitable than others for viewing your system.

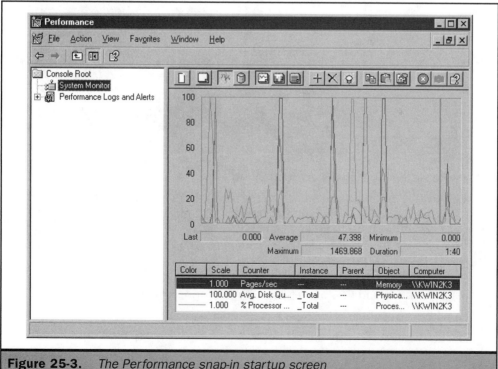

Figure 25-3.   *The Performance snap-in startup screen*

To add counters to view in real time after opening the Performance snap-in from the Start | Administrative Tools menu, follow these steps:

1. Ensure that the System Monitor in the left pane is selected and then click the + button in the right pane to add counters to monitor.

2. If you want to monitor a remote machine, enter the UNC name of the computer in the Add Counters window.

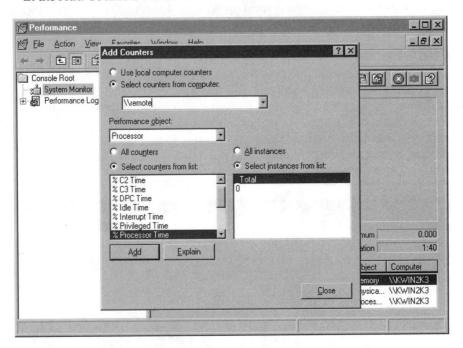

3. Choose the object you want to monitor.

4. Select the desired counters within the object; you can also select the All Counters option to select all the counters for a given object.

  If you're not sure whether to add a certain counter, click Explain to gain a better understanding of the particular counter.

5. Click Add to add the counter to your monitoring scheme.

6. Add more counters if desired.

7. Click Close when you are finished.

  You can highlight an individual counter by selecting the counter and pressing CTRL-H. There's also an easier way now with System Monitor: just select the counter you want to highlight and click the highlight button in the right pane. This helps you differentiate that counter from the rest.

Toggling Views The default view for System Monitor is the graph format. However, you can easily switch to histogram or report viewing. Using the button bar, you can choose among any of these formats. For instance, you can click the View Report button to view the real-time data in a report format, as shown in Figure 25-4.

Performance Logs and Alerts

Working in conjunction with System Monitor is the Performance Logs and Alerts service. It stores the data it collects in a data file, or log. Logged data isn't viewed in real time, so logging provides a historical perspective on system performance. Logging is the preferred approach in performance optimization because it makes it easier to interpret trends or patterns in system performance. It also provides a mechanism for storing data in a convenient format for future scrutiny. You can use System Monitor to replay the cataloged performance data, or you can easily export it to other applications.

Because Performance Logs and Alerts runs as a service, you don't have to be logged on to collect vital system statistics.

Performance Logs and Alerts serves three functions: it monitors counters, collects event traces, and provides an alerting mechanism. These three functions can be found by expanding Performance Logs and Alerts in the Performance snap-in.

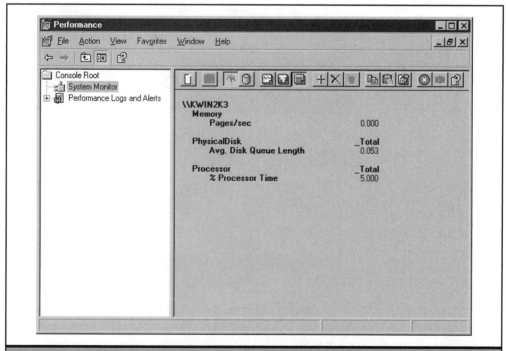

Figure 25-4. *Viewing real-time data with the report format*

Working with Counter Logs

Counter logs allow you to record system activity or usage statistics for local and remote machines. In addition to starting and stopping the Performance Logs and Alerts service manually, you can also configure the service to start and stop automatically or to log data continuously.

Note *You can log data from individual counters or entire objects. This provides the flexibility to keep the amount of data you're logging to a minimum.*

To begin logging activity using the counter logs, follow these steps:

1. Start the Performance snap-in by selecting Performance from the Start | Administrative Tools menu.

2. Expand Performance Logs and Alerts and then select Counter Logs.

3. Choose New Log Settings from the Action menu, or right-click in the right pane and select New Log Settings. You'll be asked to supply a name for the log.

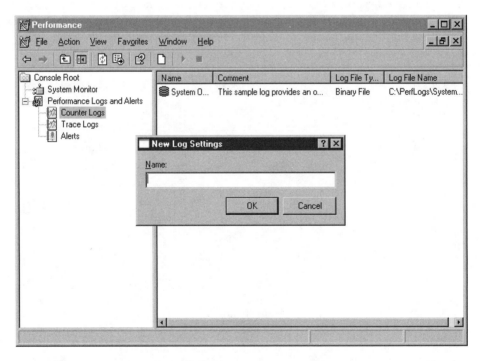

4. After you name the log, click OK; a properties window for the new log file appears, as shown in Figure 25-5. On the General tab, click Add Counters or Add Objects depending upon what you want to monitor.

5. In the Add Objects or Add Counters window, add what you want to monitor by clicking the Add button. When you're done adding all of the objects or counters, click Close to return to the Counter Log's properties window.

6. Specify the snapshot interval (the default is 15 seconds).

7. On the Log Files tab, you can specify the location of the log files or the name of the log file by clicking the Configure button. Also, you can specify how to end log filenames, the file format of the log file, and any log file size restrictions. See the following "Log Files Tab" section for more information.

8. The Schedule tab lets you specify more options for starting and stopping the log file. You can also specify the action to take when the log file closes. See the "Schedule Tab" section later in this chapter for more information.

Log Files Tab   As mentioned in Step 7 in the preceding list, the Log Files tab (see Figure 25-6) offers many options. These options are important because they not only can affect your monitoring methodology, but some can also affect your system's performance.

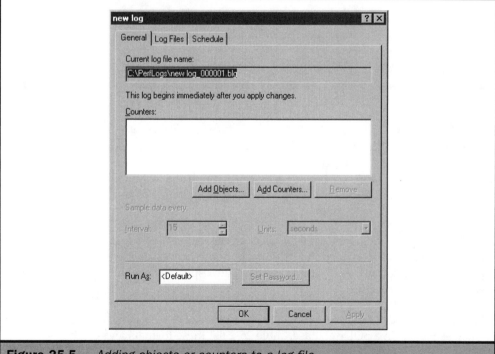

Figure 25-5.   *Adding objects or counters to a log file*

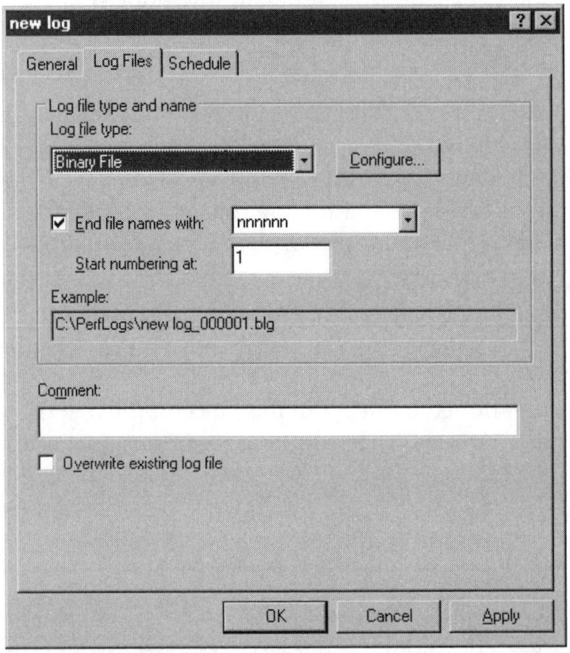

Figure 25-6. *The Log Files tab*

Log File Location   By default, Performance Logs and Alerts stores all log files in the %Systemroot%\PerfLogs directory. This directory should be immediately changed to another disk drive. Both Windows Server 2003 and monitoring processes are competing against one another for resources by using the same drive. Moving the entire disk I/O associated with counter log writes to the drive frees valuable resources and enables your system to function more efficiently.

End File Names   A convenient way to keep track of log files is to end the log filename with a number or a date. The default configuration enables this feature, and we highly recommend that you use this naming mechanism, especially if you're considering creating sequential log files.

File Type   Log files can now be saved in two types of text format, two types of binary format, as well as in a SQL database. Table 25-2 list these formats and gives a brief description of each.

Log File Size   The log file size setting enables you to control the growth of log files. Here are some of the benefits of using this feature:

- Controlling the size of the log files makes them easier to manage.
- You reduce the chances of running out of disk space.
- Limited data collection is easier to analyze.

Note | *Windows Server 2003 supports log file sizes beyond 1GB. You may also append these log files to keep performance data contiguous.*

Schedule Tab   As mentioned earlier, the Schedule tab (see Figure 25-7) has a variety of options that control the starting and stopping of the log file as well as options that become effective when the log file stops.

Of course, you can always manually start and stop a log file using the CD-player-like buttons located in the Counter Logs pane, but the real advantage of the Schedule tab comes when you configure automatic start and stops. In the Stop log section, you can specify when to stop the log in seconds, minutes, hours, or days. You can also opt to stop the log file at a specific time and date, or when it reaches a specified capacity if using the Binary Circular File format.

Also located in the Stop log section of the Schedule tab are options to start a new log when a log file closes and to run a command.

Log File Format	Description
Text File – CSV	Comma-delimited file. This file format can easily be read by spreadsheets such as Microsoft Excel.
Text File – TSV	Tab-delimited file. This file format is suitable for viewing with spreadsheet and database programs.
Binary File	This format refers to a sequential, binary format that uses the .blg extension. Use this file format when creating multiple sequential logs.
Binary Circular File	This format refers to a circular, binary format that uses the .blg extension. After the log file reaches its capacity, it will begin to overwrite data starting from the beginning of the file.
SQL Database	Storing performance data in a SQL database can be an extremely useful format for retrieving the specific information that you need. Also, it should be used when monitoring multiple computers and collecting large amounts of data.

Table 25-2.   *Logging Formats*

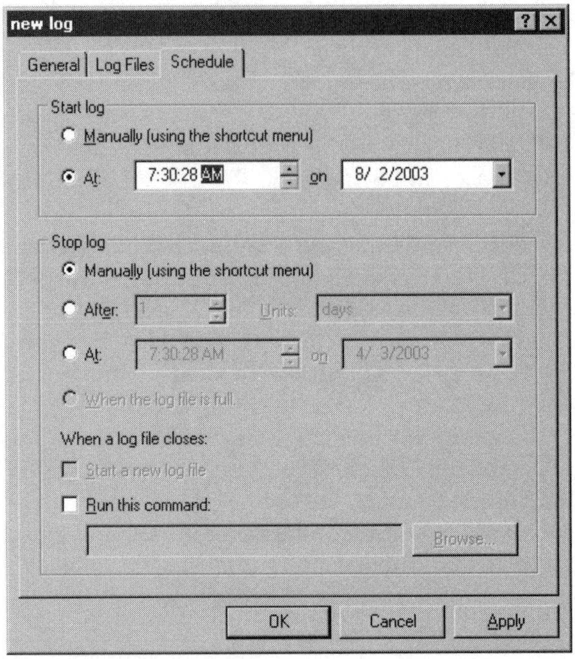

Figure 25-7. *The Schedule tab*

Creating Sequential Logs   You can now more easily manage log files by creating sequential logs. Sequential logs are useful because you can keep separate log files for specified periods of time. For instance, if you want to create a log file for each day of the week, you can easily do so by creating sequential logs.

There are a few important points to remember when you configure Performance Logs and Alerts to create sequential logs:

- Use the End file names with check box on the Log Files tab and choose the Numbers format unless you're confident that the maximum capacity you specified won't be reached.
- Use the binary format.
- On the Schedule tab, at the bottom of the Stop log section, choose Start a new log file.

Working with Trace Logs

Trace logs record data when an event from the operating system or an application occurs. Events are classified as either system provider events or non-system provider events. Examples of system provider events include, but aren't limited to, the following:

- Hard disk I/O
- Process creations and deletions
- Thread creations and deletions
- TCP/IP errors
- Page faults

Trace logs differ from counter logs in the type of data they collect as well as in the frequency of the data collection. Trace logs monitor events continuously instead of at intervals.

The process of creating a trace log is very similar to that for creating a counter log, explained earlier in the "Working with Counter Logs" section. To create a trace log, click Trace Log under Performance Logs and Alerts in the left pane of the Performance window, and then right-click in the right pane and select New Log Settings. Name the log file; the trace log properties window appears.

In the trace log properties window, shown in Figure 25-8, notice the similarities with the counter log properties window. The General tab is slightly different, and there is an additional tab called Advanced. The Log Files and Schedule tabs are identical to the ones for the counter log.

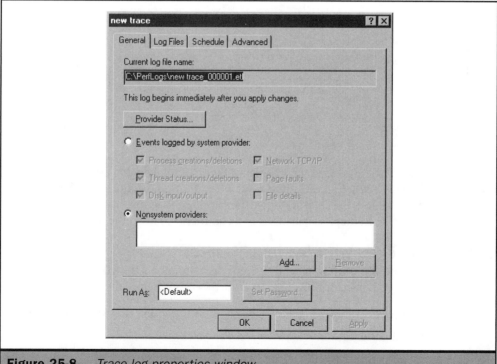

Figure 25-8. *Trace log properties window*

General Tab   At the top of the General tab, you can see that the log filename ends in .etl. You then see the available system and non-system providers that you can monitor. By selecting Events logged by system provider, you can choose events by selecting the check boxes beside them. The Page faults and File details events are not checked by default because they tend to produce a tremendous amount of data. If you plan to monitor these events, Microsoft recommends monitoring them for a maximum of two hours at a time.

Click the Provider Status button to display a list of the current providers and their status (enabled and running or stopped).

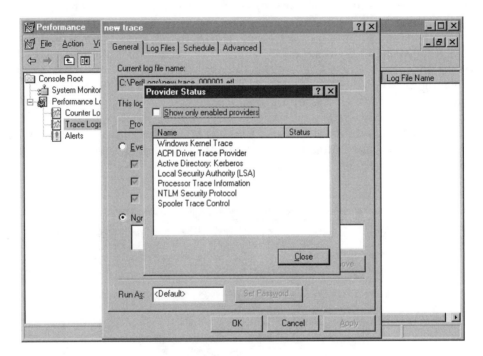

Advanced Tab   The Advanced tab, shown in Figure 25-9, lets you configure buffer settings. Data that is being logged is first transferred to memory buffers before the data is written to the trace log. By default, the buffers are filled to capacity before the data is written to the log file. In most scenarios, it is recommend to keep the default settings.

Viewing Log Files with System Monitor

Once you have a log file containing raw system performance data, you can retrieve and analyze the data that has been collected. To view a log file, follow these steps:

1. In the left pane of the Performance snap-in window, select System Monitor.

2. In the right pane, right-click and select Properties.

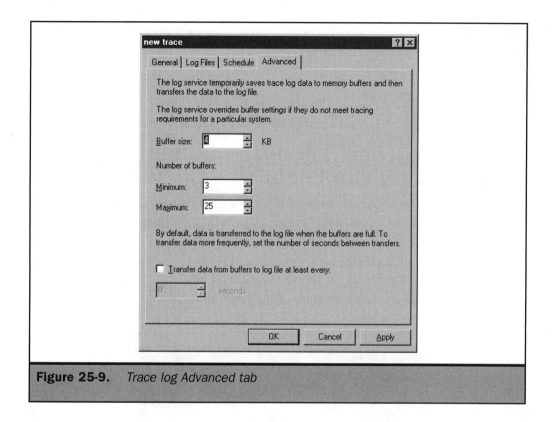

Figure 25-9. *Trace log Advanced tab*

3. On the Source tab, either click Log files and then click Add to locate the log file you want to view or click Database to specify a SQL database. Click OK when you've selected the log file.

4. You can either click OK to view the entire log file or click the Time Range button to specify the time you want to view.

5. At this point, you can also switch to the Data tab and select the counters you want to view.

Working with Alerts

Alerts can be set on any available counter to notify the administrator when a specified condition occurs, such as when processor use exceeds 90 percent. If a counter exceeds or falls below the value that you specify, the Performance Logs and Alerts service triggers an alert that logs the event and can also trigger another event, such as sending a notification message, starting a performance data log, or running a program.

Make sure that the Alerter service is running before trying to configure an alert log. Also, if you plan to send notifications when an alert is triggered, make sure that the Messenger service is started.

To create an alert, do the following:

1. In the left pane of the Performance snap-in window, click Alerts under Performance Logs and Alerts.
2. Right-click in the right pane and select New Alert Settings.
3. Name the alert and click OK.
4. On the General tab, you can optionally add a comment to identify the alert.
5. Click Add to display the Add Counters window, and add the counters that you want to monitor. Click Close when you're done.
6. For each counter that you want to monitor, specify the condition that will trigger an alert, as shown in Figure 25-10.
7. Set the snapshot interval (the default is every 5 seconds).

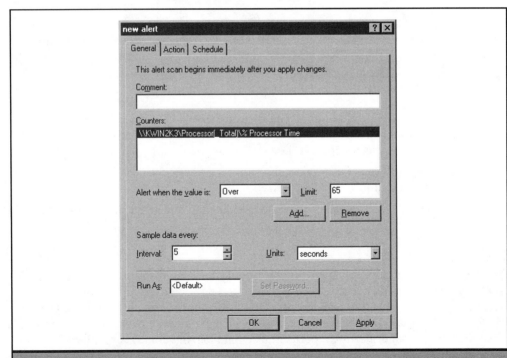

Figure 25-10. *Specifying alert conditions*

8. Select the Action tab and choose the events that will occur when an alert is triggered (see Figure 25-11). Note that any action specified here will apply to all counters being monitored in this alert log. If you want to have different actions for different counters, you'll need to create separate alert logs.

Select the Schedule tab to modify the start and stop times for alert logging.

Third-Party Utilities

In addition to the Microsoft tool set, a number of third-party capacity planning utilities are available for Windows Server 2003. Some of these tools are listed in Table 25-3.

These products commonly provide a means for collecting, analyzing, storing, and reporting statistical system information much as Windows Server 2003's Performance snap-in does. Most, if not all, of the products also incorporate enhancements such as scheduling or graphical reporting capabilities. Some even integrate innovative functionality that promises to automate many aspects of performance optimization. For example, some of the more advanced programs, such as PATROL, perform historical trend analysis and incorporate decision-support models to help you predict future system use.

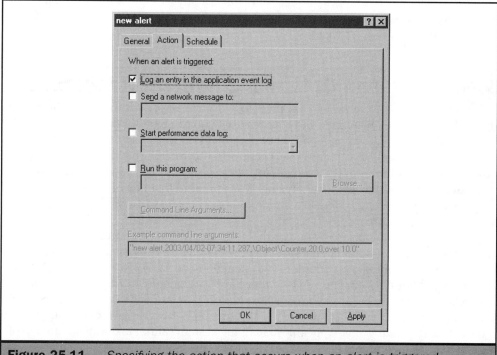

Figure 25-11.   *Specifying the action that occurs when an alert is triggered*

Utility Name	Company
HP OpenView	Hewlett Packard Web site: www.openview.hp.com/
Unicenter TNG	Computer Associates Web site: www.cai.com/unicenter/
PerfMan	Information Systems Web site: www.infosysman.com/
PATROL	BMC Software Web site: www.bmc.com/products/

Table 25-3. *Third-Party Monitoring Tools*

Whether third-party products add enhanced storage features or GUI enhancements, most are superior in overall functionality to Windows Server 2003's Performance snap-in. However, there are advantages (for example, trend analysis, ease of use, and reporting) and disadvantages (such as cost and complexity) to using these utilities instead of the free, built-in utility.

Monitoring and Optimizing System Resources

You can monitor numerous system resources for the purpose of performance optimization. In fact, there are so many objects and counters that you can monitor that you can quickly become overwhelmed with the amount of data that you collect. If you do not carefully choose what to monitor, you may collect so much information that the data will be of little use. Large amounts of data can be unwieldy and can cause you to spend most of your time organizing instead of analyzing. Keep in mind that one of the key concepts behind capacity planning is *efficiency*. Tailor your monitoring to the server's configuration as accurately as possible.

There are a few important resources that you should always monitor for every server: the memory, processor, disk subsystem, and network subsystem. These resources are the four most common contributors to system bottlenecks. A *bottleneck* is the slowest component of your system and can be either hardware or software. Bottlenecks limit a system's performance because your system runs only as fast as its slowest resource. For example, a file server may be equipped with a gigabit network interface card (NIC), but if the disk subsystem is relatively antiquated, the system cannot take full advantage of the network throughput provided by the NIC. There are also residual effects of bottlenecks, such as the underconsumption of hardware resources. Resources may not be utilized because the system is trying to compensate for the bottleneck.

In addition, the way a Windows Server 2003 server is configured functionally influences the resources or services that you should consider monitoring. For example, the most common Windows Server 2003 configurations enable database, file, and print sharing, application sharing, domain controller functions, and a number of other functions. You may want to monitor the effects of replication and synchronization on domain controllers, but not for an application for file and print servers. It is important to monitor the most common contributors to system bottlenecks as well as those that pertain to the particular server configuration.

This section discusses specific counters you should monitor for each common contributor to bottlenecks. Note, however, that there are many other counters that you should consider monitoring in addition to the ones described here. This section is intended to give you a baseline or an absolute minimum number of counters to start your monitoring process.

Monitoring Memory

Of the four common contributors to bottlenecks, memory is usually the first resource to cause performance degradation. This is simply because Windows Server 2003 tends to devour memory. Fortunately, adding more memory is also the easiest and most economical way to upgrade performance. Figure 25-12 shows System Monitor's screen for monitoring memory counters in real time.

Memory has many significant counters associated with it. However, the two counters that should always be monitored are Page Faults/sec and Pages/sec. These indicate whether the system is configured with the proper amount of RAM.

A page fault occurs when a process requires code or data that is not in its *working set*. A working set is the amount of committed memory for a process or application. The Page Faults/sec counter includes both hard faults (those that require disk access) and soft faults (where the faulted page is found elsewhere in memory). Most systems can handle a large number of soft faults without sacrificing performance. However, hard faults can cause significant delays because of hard disk access times. Even the seek and transfer rates of the fastest drive available on the market are slow compared to memory speeds. The enormous latency associated with hard page faults should immediately convince you to configure the system with as much RAM as possible.

The Pages/sec counter reflects the number of pages read from or written to disk to resolve hard page faults. Hard page faults occur when a process requires code or data that is not in its working set or elsewhere in memory. The code or data must be found and retrieved from disk. This counter is the primary indicator of *thrashing* (relying too much on the hard disk drive for virtual memory) and excessive paging. Microsoft states that if the Pages/sec value is consistently above 5, you should suspect that your system may have insufficient memory. When this value is consistently above 20, you may begin to notice slower performance because of insufficient memory.

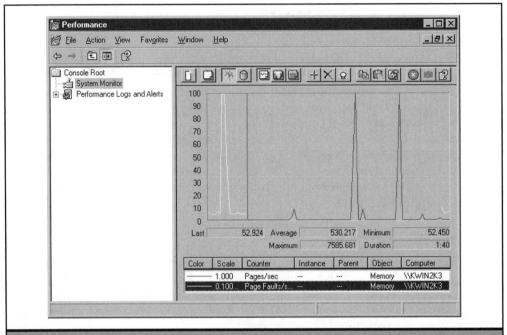

Figure 25-12. *System Monitor monitoring memory counters in real time*

Monitoring the Processor

The processor is often the first resource analyzed when there is a noticeable decrease in system performance. For performance optimization purposes, there are two significant counters to monitor in the processor object: % Processor Time and Interrupts/sec. The % Processor Time counter indicates the percentage of overall processor utilization. If more than one processor exists on the system, an instance for each one is included along with a total (combined) value counter. If the % Processor Time counter sustains a processor use rate of 50 percent or greater for long periods of time, you should consider upgrading. When the average processor time consistently exceeds 65 percent utilization, users may notice a degradation in performance that will not be tolerable.

The Interrupts/sec counter is also a good indicator of processor utilization. It indicates the number of device interrupts that the processor is handling per second. The device interrupt can be hardware or software driven and can reach high values into the thousands. Some ways to improve performance include off-loading some services to another, less-used server, adding another processor, upgrading the existing processor, clustering, and distributing the load to an entirely new machine.

Monitoring the Disk Subsystem

The disk subsystem consists of two main types of resources: hard disk drives and hard disk controllers. The Performance snap-in does not have an object directly associated with the hard disk controller because the values given in the Physical and Logical Disk objects accurately represent disk subsystem performance.

> **Note** *Both the Physical and Logical Disk objects are enabled by default.*

Today, virtually every system component is more powerful than ever, and this is true for components within the disk subsystem as well. As a result, the effects of disk subsystem performance objects are becoming increasingly negligible and, depending on your system configuration, perhaps even unnoticeable.

Windows Server 2003 also gives you flexibility in starting and stopping disk subsystem objects. You can use **diskperf -y** to enable disk counters, **diskperf -y \\mycomputer** to enable them on remote machines, or **diskperf -n** to disable them just as you could prior to Windows Server 2003. Where the flexibility comes in is in the ability to enable the Logical Disk and Physical Disk objects separately. To specify the object that you want to activate or deactivate, include a **d** for the Physical Disk object or a **v** for the Logical Disk object. For instance, to begin viewing Logical Disk statistics, you must re-enable the Logical Disk performance object with the command **diskperf –yv**.

The best, but certainly not necessarily the only, disk performance counters to monitor for performance optimization are % Disk Time and Avg. Disk Queue Length. The % Disk Time counter monitors the amount of elapsed time that the selected physical or logical drive spends servicing read and write requests. Avg. Disk Queue Length indicates the number of outstanding requests (requests not yet serviced) on the physical or logical drive. This value is an instantaneous measurement rather than an average over a specified interval, but it still accurately represents the number of delays the drive is experiencing. The request delays experienced by the drive can be calculated by subtracting the number of spindles on the disk from the Avg. Disk Queue Length measurement. If the delay is frequently greater than 2, then the disks are degrading performance.

Monitoring Network Performance

Because of its many components, the network subsystem is one of the most complicated subsystems to monitor for bottlenecks. Protocols, NICs, network applications, and physical topologies all play important roles in your network. To further complicate matters, your environment may implement multiple protocol stacks. Therefore, the network performance counters you should monitor vary depending upon your system's configuration.

The important information to gain from monitoring network subsystem components is the amount of network activity and throughput. When monitoring network subsystem components, you should use other network monitoring tools in addition to the

Performance snap-in. For example, consider using Network Monitor (either the built-in or SMS version) or a systems management application such as MOM. Using these tools together broadens the scope of monitoring and more accurately represents what is occurring within your network infrastructure.

This discussion of performance optimization for the network subsystem focuses on TCP/IP. Saying that Windows Server 2003 relies heavily on this protocol is an understatement. The counters for TCP/IP are added to the system after the protocol is installed and include counters for Internet Protocol version 6 (IPv6).

There are many significant counters within the objects related to TCP/IP that you should consider monitoring. Two important counters to use for TCP/IP monitoring pertain to the NIC object. They are the Bytes Total/sec and the Output Queue Length counters. The Bytes Total/sec counter indicates the amount of inbound and outbound TCP/IP traffic experienced by your server. The Output Queue Length counter indicates whether there are congestion or contention problems on your NIC. If the Output Queue Length value is consistently above 2, check the Bytes Total/sec counter for abnormally high values. High values for both counters suggest that there is a bottleneck in your network subsystem, and it may be time to upgrade your server network components.

There are many other counters that need to be monitored and consulted before you can accurately pinpoint the cause of abnormal counter values or network performance degradation. For example, were the abnormal Bytes Total/sec and Output Queue Length values the result of a temporary burst in network activity or unusually high collision rates? If you know that the collision rate is greater than 10 percent, then the problem may be the performance of the overall network and not just the Windows Server 2003 server in question.

Controlling System Resources

Throughout this chapter, we've analyzed various ways to monitor and utilize system performance data. Although monitoring or analyzing performance data is necessary to more accurately tweak or otherwise tune system performance, it does not provide a direct way to control the resources that you're monitoring. As such, Microsoft has developed an MMC snap-in called Windows System Resource Monitor (WSRM) to give that level of control in today's systems.

Windows System Resource Monitor

WSRM, shown in Figure 25-13, is a utility that can be used with Windows Server 2003 Enterprise or Datacenter Editions. It gives you additional control over system resources and processes. You can use WSRM to control applications, services, and process resource utilization (e.g. processor utilization, memory usage, and processor affinity).

To control or protect system resources and utilization, ceiling values for applications, services, or processes are set using policies. These policies are customizable so that you can easily apply different standards to different systems. In addition to setting the

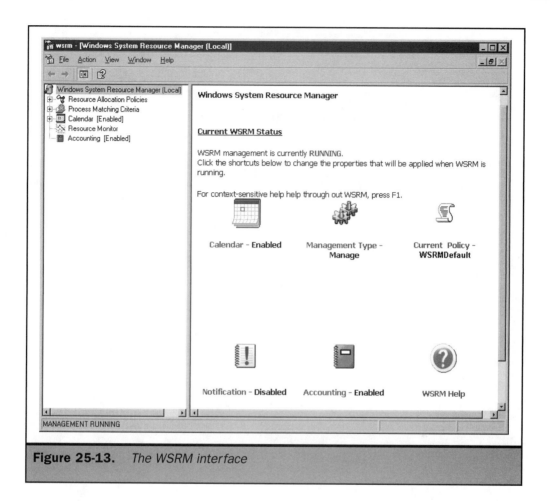

Figure 25-13.   *The WSRM interface*

utilization limitations, you also can take into account scheduling considerations. So, for example, you can limit a specific application to using only 25 percent of processor utilization during peak hours of the business day. WSRM manages its own scheduling through the built-in calendar function.

WSRM is especially useful for systems serving multiple functional roles (gone are the days when you should install and configure only one type of workload or role per system). The different functionalities may compete for system resources in order to complete the tasks at hand. If an application, service, or process associated with a particular server role is susceptible to dominating system resources, WSRM can step in and ensure that the policy boundaries are not exceeded.

The
Complete
Reference

Chapter 26

Disaster Planning
and Recovery

D rives die, motherboards go to computer la-la land, users destroy files, and floods, fires, and all sorts of other disasters occur with frightening regularity. You can't bring your enterprise back unless you have an efficient, workable plan for disaster recovery.

In this chapter, I'll discuss some of the Windows Server 2003 tools you need to know about in order to make sure you can bring a computer, or your company's entire system, back after a disaster.

Backup

Backing up isn't just a hedge against disasters; it's also protection for recovering from mistakes. Backups are used to restore files that were accidentally deleted as often as they're used to recover from disk disasters.

New Backup Features

If you're migrating to Windows Server 2003 from Windows NT, you'll find that new functions have been added to the backup feature (most of which were added in Windows 2000). In this section, I'll go over those new functions.

Volume Shadow Copy

Brand new in Windows Server 2003, a volume shadow copy is an "at the moment" copy of the volume being backed up, which is helpful when applications are keeping files open. The shadow copy includes open files and files that are being used by the system. This means users can continue to access the system while the backup utility is running, without risking loss of data.

This feature is implemented by the Volume Shadow Copy service (VSS). This service provides new backup functionality, and includes new APIs that are available to software companies that want to use the service. The Volume Shadow Copy service notifies programs and services that a backup is about to occur, and applications that are VSS-aware prepare for the backup by flushing caches and log files. Check the documentation for applications that you're running on your Windows Server 2003 computer to see if they're VSS-aware. If they're not, use the software's recommendations for backing up the data.

Windows Server 2003 includes a command-line tool, vssadmin.exe, that you can use to manage this service. Detailed documentation for this tool is available in the Windows Server 2003 Help and Support Center, but some of the commonly used command syntax follows:

- Enter **vssadmin list providers** to display the name, type, provider ID, and version of all installed shadow copy providers.
- Enter **vssadmin list shadows** to list the existing volume shadow copies.
- Enter **vssadmin list volumes** to list volumes that are eligible for creating shadow copies.

Multiple Target Media Types

Rejoice! Finally, you can back up files to storage devices in addition to tape drives. This long-overdue feature means you can use any of the following target media types:

- Tape
- Removable disk
- Hard drive (logical drive, another physical hard drive, and so on)
- Recordable CD-ROM

To find removable disks that work with Windows Backup, check the following manufacturers: Iomega (www.iomega.com) for Zip drives and Network Attached Storage (NAS) drives; Linksys (www.linksys.com) for Network Attached Storage (NAS) drives.

Support for QIC and other floppy-based tape drives has been dropped.

Backup/Restore the System State

Backup includes the ability to back up and restore the Windows System State. The components that comprise the System State differ depending on the server's role in the enterprise.

System State for All Servers   The following components comprise the System State for all Windows Server 2003 computers:

- Registry
- COM+ Class Registration database
- Boot files including the system files
- IIS Metadirectory (if IIS is installed)
- System files that are under Windows File Protection

System State for Servers with Special Roles   In addition to the components that are part of the System State for all servers, the following servers that have special roles have additional components in their System States:

Server Role	Components
Certificate Server	Certificate Services database
Domain Controller	Active Directory; SYSVOL directory
Cluster Server	Resource registry checkpoints; quorum resource recovery log (contains cluster database information)

If a domain controller is running DNS, the Active Directory portion of the System State contains the DS-integrated DNS zone data. The non-DS-integrated DNS zone data, which is saved as .dns files in %SystemRoot%\System32\DNS, is part of the boot volume, so it's included in your backup if you run a Normal backup type.

Backup of Protected System Files

Windows 2000 and later provides Windows File Protection service as a way to avoid losing important system files by overwriting or deleting them. The Windows File Protection service operates by maintaining catalog files, located in %SystemRoot%\System32\catroot\{F750E6C3-38EE-11D1-85E5-00C04FC295EE}.

In Windows NT 4 and earlier, you could selectively back up and restore operating system files in the same manner as you would back up data files. This meant you could configure incremental backup and restore operations for most of the operating system files.

Starting with Windows 2000, you cannot perform an incremental restore of operating system files. Instead, system files are backed up and restored as a single entity. If you configure your backup program to back up the System State, that selection automatically backs up protected system files.

Integration with Remote Storage Services

Remote Storage is a Windows Server 2003 feature that lets you store data on tape or magneto-optical disks in a library and provide users access to that data. This means you can free up disk space for data that is old and infrequently used, and make that data available via a library of archived files.

Integration with Task Scheduler

When you configure the backup application for automated processing, the schedule can be accessed through Task Scheduler.

Backup Storage Media Managed Separately

The target media is handled by the Removable Storage Manager (RSM), which is part of Windows Server 2003. The service creates libraries of removable media and organizes everything for easy access.

Fault-Tolerant Disk Configuration Is Not Backed Up

Windows NT stored information about fault-tolerant disk settings in the registry. Therefore, when you backed up the registry, you had a way to restore the settings. However, starting with Windows 2000 Server, the Fault Tolerant Disk state is stored in hidden sectors right on the disk, and cannot be backed up. Therefore, keep accurate records on the configuration of your fault-tolerant disks (including stripe sets, mirrors, and volume sets) because you'll have to reconfigure these settings before you perform a restore operation.

Backup Permissions Issues

To back up all the folders and files on a computer, you must be a member of the Administrators group or the Backup Operators group. If you are not a member of either of those groups, you can only back up files and folders that meet the following criteria:

- You own the files and folders you want to back up
- You have one or more of the following permission levels for the files and folders you want to back up:
  - Read & Execute
  - Modify
  - Full Control

Disk Quotas and Backup Files

If you are operating under a disk quota, and you are backing up to a hard drive, you must make sure your disk quota doesn't restrict your ability to save the backup file. You can check whether you have any disk quota restrictions by right-clicking the disk you want to save data to, clicking Properties, and then clicking the Quota tab.

 More information about disk quotas is available in Chapter 16.

Backup Types

Windows Backup offers five specific backup types to choose from:

- **Normal**   Backs up all the selected files, and clears the Archive attribute (marks the files on the disk to indicate they have been backed up).
- **Copy**   Backs up all the selected files but does not clear the Archive attribute.
- **Incremental**   Looks at the selected files and only backs up those that have changed since the last backup. For the files that are backed up, the Archive attribute is cleared.
- **Differential**   Only backs up files that have changed since the last backup, but does not clear the Archive attribute.
- **Daily**   Backs up those files that have been modified or added today. The Archive attribute is not cleared.

The only use I can think of for a Daily backup type is to back up the files you were working on today, so that you can take them home to continue your work.

Backing Up

To launch the backup application, open the System Tools submenu on the Accessories menu and select Backup. The Backup or Restore Wizard, shown in Figure 26-1, opens.

You can use the wizard, which means going through the wizard's windows, answering questions, and setting the options for the backup job, one window at a time. Alternatively, you can jump right to the program windows to do the same thing. The latter is faster, and you get there by clicking the Advanced Mode link to open the Backup Utility program window, shown in Figure 26-2.

If you always want to use Advanced Mode, on the opening wizard window, deselect the option Always Start in Wizard Mode the next time you run the program.

Configure the Backup Software

Before you run the first backup, it's a good idea to configure the way you want the software to work when you back up or restore. To accomplish this, choose Tools | Options to open the Options dialog, in which you configure default options and the behavior of the software.

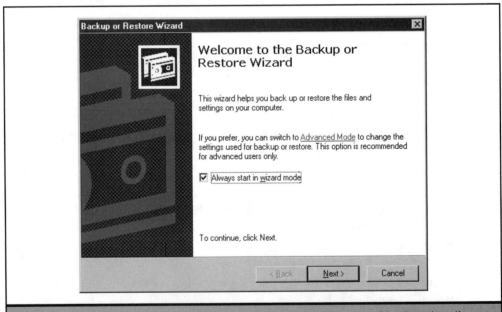

Figure 26-1. *Backup opens with a wizard, but you can opt to skip the wizard's walk-through approach.*

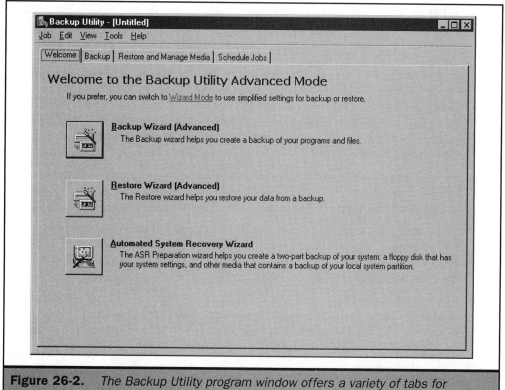

Figure 26-2. *The Backup Utility program window offers a variety of tabs for configuring and launching tasks.*

General Tab Settings

On the General tab, select or deselect the following features:

■ **Compute selection information before backup and restore operations**   The system will calculate the number of folders and files in your backup selection, and the disk space they need, before beginning the operation. For backing up, this is only necessary if the drive(s) you're backing up is much larger than the capacity of your target media and you want to know how many tapes or disks you'll need. For restoring, this is only necessary if you're restoring to a drive that already contains data.

■ **Use the catalogs on the media to speed up building restore catalogs on disk**   When you restore a backup, the system builds a catalog on the target disk before restoring files from the backup media. If the media catalog is damaged, or you have a multitape backup and the tape that holds the catalog is missing, you won't be able to use this option. Instead, the software scans your backup media to build the on-disk catalog from scratch.

- **Verify data after the backup completes** Selecting this option causes a verification process between the target media and the hard drive after the backup is completed. However, the process is little more than making sure that the backup software can read the file on the target media. This is not the same thing as a file-by-file comparison that ensures the backed-up version of a file is exactly the same as the original file. However, if the backup software can't read the file, it's frequently an indication that there's a problem with the media or even the type of media. While this makes an interesting test, a more definitive test is to create a small backup and restore it, and then make sure everything on the drive is the same as it was before the restore.

- **Back up the contents of mounted drives** If you're using mounted drives, this ensures that the data on the mounted drive is backed up. Deselecting this option means that only the path information about the mounted drive is backed up.

- **Show alert message when I start the Backup Utility and Removable Storage is not running** Select this option to receive a warning if the Removable Storage service isn't running. This is only necessary if your target media is handled by the Removable Storage service, which means tape or optical disk.

- **Show alert message when I start the Backup Utility and there is recognizable media available** Select this option if you use media that is handled by the Removable Storage service and you want to know if and when there is new media available in the media pool.

- **Show alert message when new media is inserted** Select this option if you use media that is handled by the Removable Storage service and you want to know that new media has been inserted in the target device.

- **Always allow use of recognizable media without prompting** Select this option if you use media that is handled by the Removable Storage service and you want to automatically move new media that's been detected by the service from the available pool to the media pool used by Backup.

Restore Tab Settings

The configuration items on the Restore tab apply to partial restores, not recovery from a disk disaster in which you're rebuilding your system on a new disk. Select the default behavior for restoring files that already exist on the disk, choosing from the following:

- Don't replace existing files.
- Replace existing files when the files on the disk are older than the files on the restore media.
- Always replace the file on my computer.

The first option is the safest, of course. However, remember that you are only setting the default configuration, and when you actually restore, you're offered a chance to change the defaults.

Backup Type Tab Settings

Use the drop-down list in this tab to select the default backup type (all five types are described in the "Backup Types" section, earlier in this chapter). This setting only sets the default for your backup session, and you can change the type when you perform a backup.

Backup Log Tab Settings

Choose the option for logging the backup operation. You have the following choices:

- **Detailed**   Logs the names of every backed-up file and folder.
- **Summary**   Logs the major processes, including the time the backup began and a list of any files that couldn't be backed up.
- **None**   Means no log is kept.

Backup logs are named backup*XX*.log (where *XX* starts with 01) and are kept in the directory \Documents and Settings\<*LoggedOnUserName*>\Local Settings\Application Data\Microsoft\Windows NT\NTBackup\data. Unlike Windows Backup in Windows NT, you cannot change the location.

Exclude Files Tab Settings

The Exclude Files tab displays a list of files that are excluded from the backup (see Figure 26-3). You can add files to that list and apply the new exclusions to the computer (regardless of the logged-on user), or to backups that are made while you're logged on.

- To exclude files for all users, click the Add New button under the section for Files Excluded For All Users.
- To exclude files in backups you make, click the Add New button under the section Files Excluded for *UserName*.

 If other users perform backups on this computer, and they want to create their own sets of excluded files, they must log on to create that excluded file set.

The excluded files list is written to the registry at HKEY_LOCAL_MACHINE\ System\CurrentControlSet\Control\BackupRestore\FilesNotToBackup. As a result, these files are excluded regardless of whether you're using Windows Backup or a third-party application.

Create a Backup Job

Begin your backup by launching the Backup Wizard or by moving to the Backup tab to manually establish the settings for your backup.

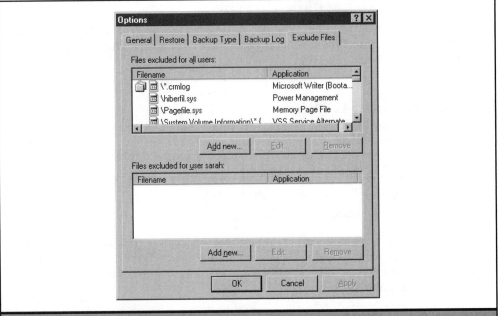

Figure 26-3. *Exclude file types you don't want to back up.*

If you use the wizard, first use the Backup tab to check (or change) the target in the Backup Media or Filename field.

The wizard offers three choices:

- A full backup (everything on the computer)
- Selected files (you select the drives, folders, and files to back up from a tree of the system hierarchy)
- System State only

If you don't use the wizard, preferring to use Advanced Mode to configure the backup manually, go to the Backup tab and select the folders and files that you want to include in the backup. The Backup tab displays a tree of the system hierarchy, and you can expand it to include the objects you want to back up (see Figure 26-4). Your pointer turns into a check mark and deposits a check mark with every click. Clicking again in a check box toggles the check mark off. Click the check box next to an object to select it. Click the drive or folder object to display its contents in the right pane.

Remember to select the System State for the local computer (you cannot back up the System State on a remote computer).

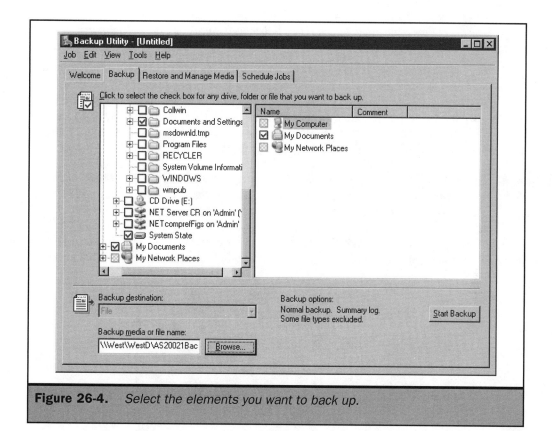

Figure 26-4. *Select the elements you want to back up.*

If you are using Removable Storage to manage media, or you are using Remote Storage to store data, back up the following folders to make sure all of your Remote Storage and Removable Storage data can be restored:

- *Systemroot*\System32\Ntmsdata
- *Systemroot*\System32\Remotestorage

There are two options available for selecting storage media (the Backup Media or File Name field at the bottom of the Backup tab window):

- **Back up to a file on a drive**   A drive can be a hard disk or any other type of removable or nonremovable media. If you're using a drive, enter the path and filename (you can use a UNC), or click Browse to select the target drive.

- **Back up to a tape device**   The tape device option is available only if the system detects a tape device on the computer. If you choose to use the tape device, the media is managed by the Removable Storage system.

Note *The file option is always available, even if there is a tape device on the computer.*

If you want to save these configuration options, choose Job | Save Selections to retain the selections and options you've created as a backup selection file. Give the file a name (the system automatically adds the .bks extension). You can load this job any time you want to use it (choose Job | Load Selections), and you can also create and save additional backup jobs with different file and folder selections. However, you don't have to save your selections in order to perform a backup of the files you've selected.

Tip *You can use a saved backup selection file to specify the files and folders to back up if you want to run backups from the command line. See the section "Use Backup Batch Files," later in this chapter.*

Click Start Backup when you've finished making your selections. The Backup Job Information dialog appears, prompting for additional information about this backup job.

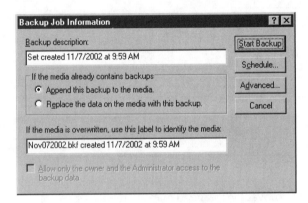

Click the Advanced button to see additional configuration options for this backup job.

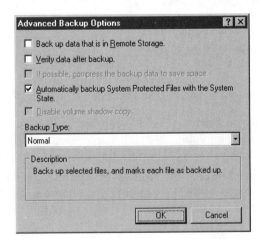

Volume Shadow Copy is enabled by default for the built-in backup application. If you're backing up a computer that doesn't require this feature, deselect the option, to save the space and processing burden it imposes. If you selected the System State as one of the components to back up, however, the option Disable Volume Shadow Copy is inaccessible. Click OK when you're finished configuring the advanced backup options, to return to the Backup Job Information dialog. Click Start Backup to begin the backup.

Schedule a Backup

If you'd prefer to schedule the backup to run at a later time (it's automatically added to your Scheduled Tasks list), click the Schedule button in the Backup Job Information dialog. If you haven't saved the selection file, a message displays to tell you that you have to save your selections before you can schedule a backup. Click Yes to perform the task, and enter a name for this set of options in the Save Selections dialog.

The system prompts for account information, and by default the current user is displayed. You can instead enter the name and password for the username under which you want this backup to run. However, if you enter a different username and password, you must be aware of the following rules:

- The user you specify must have the appropriate rights to perform a backup.
- The user becomes the owner of the backup set.

In the Schedule Job Options dialog, enter a job name for the backup—this is the name that appears in the Scheduled Tasks window—and click OK. Then click Properties and configure the Schedule Job dialog (see Figure 26-5).

You can accept the default configuration specification to run this job once, but notice that the scheduled time is set for right now—in fact, if you've spent a moment looking at the dialog, or thinking about it, the time is past. Enter the correct time, or change the schedule to make this backup job a regularly scheduled event. When you click OK, the backup job moves to the Scheduled Tasks folder. (For detailed information on using the Task Scheduler for scheduled tasks, see Chapter 8.)

Use Backup Batch Files

If you're comfortable with the command line, you can run your backup procedures via a batch file, with the ntbackup command. Before you use the command line, open the GUI backup application and create the list of files and folders you want to back up, and save those settings in a .bks file. In addition, use the Options dialog to set global configuration options.

When you use the ntbackup command, the following switches default to the settings you configured in the GUI application (unless you specifically change them in the command line): **/V /R /L /M /RS /HC**. If you create multiple GUI configurations,

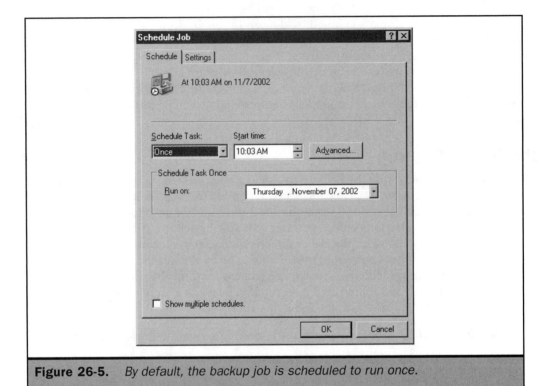

Figure 26-5. *By default, the backup job is scheduled to run once.*

you can create multiple backup batch files. Use the Task Scheduler to automate the launching of your backup batch files. The syntax for ntbackup is

> **ntbackup backup [systemstate]** *"@bks file name"* **/J** {*"job name"*} [**/P** {*"pool name"*}]
> [**/G** {*"guid name"*}] [**/T** { *"tape name"*}] [**/N** {*"media name"*}] [**/F** {*"file name"*}] [**/D**
> {*"set description"*}] [**/DS** {*"server name"*}] [**/IS** {*"server name"*}] [**/A**] [**/V:**{**yes** | **no**}]
> [**/R:**{**yes** | **no**}] [**/L:**{**f** | **s** | **n**}] [**/M** {*backup type*}] [**/RS:**{**yes** | **no**}] [**/HC:**{**on** | **off**}]
> [**/SNAP:**{**on** | **off**}]

where:

systemstate specifies that you want to back up the System State (the backup type will be forced to Normal or Copy).

@bks filename is the name of the backup selection file (.bks file) you want to use for this backup (the @ character must precede the name of the backup selection file). You must create the file using the GUI version of Backup.

/J {*"job name"*} is the job name for the log file.

/P {*"pool name"*} is the media pool from which you want to draw media. (Using this switch precludes the use of the following switches: **/A /G /F /T**.)

/G {*"guid name"*} uses the tape with the specified GUID. (If you use this switch, you cannot use the **/P** switch.)

/T {*"tape name"*} uses the tape with the specified tape name. (If you use this switch, you cannot use the **/P** switch.)

/N {*"media name"*} specifies a new tape name. (If you use this switch, you cannot use the **/A** switch.)

/F {*"file name"*} is the path and filename for the backup file. (If you use this switch, you cannot use any of the following switches: **/P /G /T**.)

/D {*"set description"*} is the label for each backup set.

/DS {*"server name"*} backs up the directory service file for the specified Microsoft Exchange Server.

/IS {*"server name"*} backs up the Information Store file for the specified Microsoft Exchange Server.

/A backs up using an append operation. (Either **/G** or **/T** must be used in conjunction with this switch. You cannot use this switch in conjunction with **/P**.)

/V:{yes | no} specifies whether to verify the data after the backup is complete.

/R:{yes | no} restricts access to this tape to the owner or to members of the Administrators group.

/L:{f | s | n} specifies the type of log file (**f**=full, **s**=summary, **n**=none).

/M {*backup type*} specifies the backup type: Normal, Copy, Differential, Incremental, or Daily.

/RS:{yes | no} backs up the migrated data files located in Remote Storage. The **/RS** switch is not required to back up the local Removable Storage database (contains the Remote Storage placeholder files). When you back up the %SystemRoot% folder, ntbackup automatically backs up the Removable Storage database as well.

/HC:{on | off} specifies whether to use hardware compression on the tape drive (if it's available).

/SNAP:{on | off} specifies whether or not the backup is a volume snapshot.

Working with Removable Storage Manager

You'll find some complications inherent in the Windows Server 2003 backup utility if you back up to tape devices. The need to manage tape media with the Removable Storage Manager (RSM) and the media pool has made backing up to tape more complex. If you're migrating from Windows NT 4, especially if you used batch files to back up, you're probably going to have mixed emotions about the new features in the backup utility.

For many organizations, tapes used to be merely another media form, and backups wrote to whatever tape was in the tape drive. Any employee could mount a tape, change a tape, and remove a tape from the drive. For example, if every Wednesday someone inserted the tape labeled "Wednesday" before leaving for the day, the IT department was assured a middle-of-the-night automated backup would be written to the right tape. There were only two requirements for success:

- The employee who inserted the tape in the drive had to be able to read (at least the days of the week).

- The automated backup commands included the appropriate instructions regarding overwriting or appending.

This is no longer the case. In fact, your Windows NT 4 backup batch files won't work in Windows Server 2003, because they don't contain the switches that control the target media.

RSM provides robust features for organizations that need a method of tracking and controlling removable media. However, using RSM means that tapes can no longer be casually placed in a tape drive. Tapes must be prepared, named, assigned to media pools, and otherwise manipulated via RSM.

Given all of this, here are some guidelines for preventing problems when backing up to tape:

- Be sure to prepare a sufficient number of tapes for your backup before starting the backup (you can't just grab another tape if you need it). Use the Computer Management functions to move them into the Backup pool or the Import pool (if Backup sees a tape in the Import pool, it will ask if you want to import it).

- Use physical labels on tapes to duplicate the tape's RSM information.

- Keep a manual log book of tapes, indicating when they were last used, in order to make sure you can successfully restore if you have a disk disaster. Alternatively (or additionally), you can configure Backup to write a detailed log, and then print the logs and store them.

See Chapter 16 for detailed information on using Removable Storage Manager.

Restore

You must use the GUI backup application to restore files you backed up, whether you used the GUI or the command line to perform the backup operation. There is no restore operation available via the command line.

The backup type you selected when you backed up your files affects the restore method, so when you are faced with a restore operation, the first step is to identify the backup files you need:

- If you always perform a Normal backup type, you need only the last backup.

- If you perform Differential backups, you need the last Normal backup and the last Differential backup.

- If you perform Incremental backups, you need the last Normal backup and every Incremental backup since the last Normal backup. The Incremental backups must be restored in the same order in which they were created.

Restore Files and Folders

To restore files and folders, open the Backup software and decide whether you want to use the Restore Wizard or manually configure the restore operation. If you opt to use the wizard, click Next and select Restore Files and Settings. Then follow the prompts to complete the operation (the options you face are the same options I'll cover in this section as I go through a manual restore procedure).

Note   *This section covers regular files and folders, not the System State files, which are restored with special procedures (discussed later in this chapter).*

For a manual restore, click the Restore and Manage Media tab. The left pane displays a tree view of your backup sets, and you can expand a set to select individual folders and files, or select the set itself to restore the entire contents (see Figure 26-6).

In the left pane, select the check box next to the backup set, drives, or folders you want to restore. If you only want to restore one or more specific files, expand the appropriate folder and then select the check box next to each file in the right pane.

Set Restore Options

When you're restoring folders and files, you have some options about the way you want to accomplish the task.

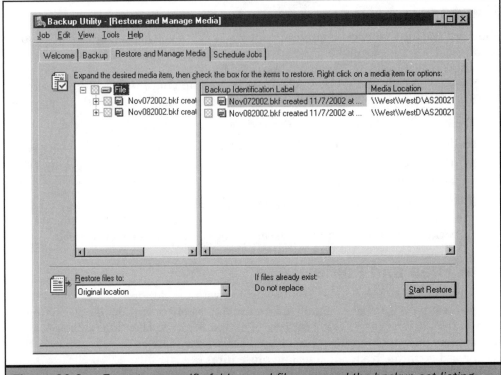

Figure 26-6. *To restore specific folders and files, expand the backup set listing.*

File Location Options

On the Restore and Manage Media tab, use the Restore Files To text box in the lower-left corner to specify the target location for the files you restore. The drop-down list offers three choices:

- **Original location** Restores to the original folder(s). Use this option when you're restoring folders or files that have been corrupted or inadvertently deleted.

- **Alternate location** Restores to a folder that you designate. Use this option to restore older files that you may need, but you want to make sure you don't overwrite any existing files. The original folder structure is retained in the alternate folder.

■ **Single folder**   Restores all files to a single folder. The only time to use this option is when you know you've lost a file on the drive and you can't find it in the backup folder you thought it was in (or you don't have time to search for it). This option doesn't transfer folders, so the original folder structure is lost. All the files are dumped into the target folder.

File Replacement Options

Select Options from the Tools menu and go to the Restore tab to specify the conditions for restoring files.

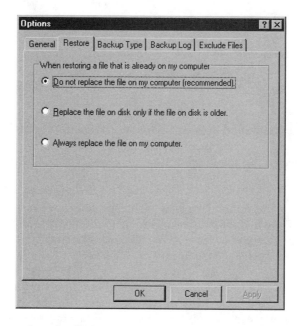

The options you select depend on your reason for restoring files. If you're replacing files that have been corrupted, you want the backup files restored even if the filenames already exist on the drive and have a newer date. Perhaps the file was fine yesterday and you backed it up, but today something awful has happened to the file while you were using it. If you're restoring after a major disk disaster, you need all the files.

Excluded Files Options

Certain files that may be on the backup set are not restored, and you can add to the list in the Exclude Files tab of the Options dialog. The default excluded files are written to the registry in HKEY_LOCAL_MACHINE\SYSTEM\CurrentControlSet\Control\ BackupRestore\KeysNotToRestore and those files won't be restored whether you use Windows Backup or a third-party application.

Advanced Options

After you've set your configuration options, click Start Restore. A Confirm Restore message box opens to offer the opportunity to set advanced configuration settings before beginning the file transfer. Click Advanced to see the available options.

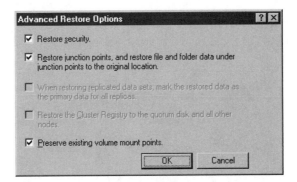

The advanced configuration options are for special circumstances, which I'll describe in this section. (Depending on the circumstances, some of the options may be inaccessible.) When you have selected the advanced options you need, click OK and then OK again to begin restoring files.

Restore Security   This option is only available for data you backed up from a volume formatted with NTFS, which you are restoring to a volume formatted with NTFS. The security information attached to the restored file includes security access permissions, audit entries, and file/folder ownership.

Restore Junction Points   The option, whose full name is Restore Junction Points, And Restore File And Folder Data Under Junction Points To The Original Location, is only important if your system has either of the following configurations:

- You used the linkd command to create junction points, and you want to restore both the junction points and the data to which they point. Otherwise, the junction points are restored as directories, and the data they point to won't be available.

- You are restoring a mounted drive, and you want to restore its data (rather than restore only the folder containing the mounted drive).

Mark Replicated Data as Primary   If you're restoring replicated data, the option When Restoring Replicated Data Sets, Mark The Restored Data As The Primary Data For All Replicas, is important if you're restoring data (Active Directory) that's involved in File Replication Services (FRS). See the upcoming section "Restoring Domain Controllers."

If you don't select this option, the FRS data you restore will be overwritten by replication, because it will be older than the data on the other participating servers.

Selecting the option causes Windows Server 2003 to mark the data as newer than that on the other servers.

Restore the Cluster Register to the Quorum Disk and All Other Nodes   This option restores the server's cluster quorum database and then replicates it to all nodes in the cluster.

Preserve Existing Volume Mount Points   Use this option when you're restoring an existing (previously formatted and used) drive, to tell Windows Server 2003 to restore the volume mount points you backed up. Don't use this option if you're restoring data to a whole new configuration, in which you've applied a new configuration (even if it resembles the old configuration), due to installation of a new drive.

Restoring Domain Controllers

Restoring domain controllers requires special considerations and special steps. You cannot perform this task remotely; you must do this work at the DC. There are three types of restore operations available for DCs:

- Primary
- Normal (nonauthoritative)
- Authoritative

Restore System Services

When you're restoring a DC, you're restoring the system services (SYSVOL and Active Directory) to the System State folder of the DC. This can only be accomplished by booting into Directory Services Restore Mode (which is a form of Safe Mode). To accomplish this, restart the computer and press F8 to force the display of operating system menu choices. From the list of boot options, select Directory Services Restore Mode. Here's what to expect:

- A message appears: "The system is booting in safemode – Directory Services Repair."
- Select Windows Server 2003 as the operating system to start.
- The words "safe mode" appear in the four corners of your screen.
- Message boxes appear (Preparing Network Connections, Applying Security).
- The standard Welcome to Windows dialog that tells you to "Press CTRL-ALT-DELETE to begin" appears.
- You press CTRL-ALT-DEL and log on as the local Administrator.
- A message box appears to explain that Windows is running in Safe Mode, giving details about the variety of things you may want to try to get your computer to boot normally. Click OK.

■ The desktop appears with the four Safe Mode text announcements in the corners. Use the Start menu to open Backup and perform a restore procedure, either with the wizard or manually.

Choosing a Restore Type for a DC

The type of restore you perform for a DC depends on the state of the data you backed up in relation to the data on the other DCs in the domain. To make your decision, you have to understand how DCs replicate data.

When AD data is replicated, the operating system uses update sequence numbers to determine which data set is the most recent. This ensures that older data never overwrites newer data. At the end of the replication process, the OS assigns new update sequence numbers to keep track of new/old data. When you back up the System State on a DC, the current update sequence number (USN) is backed up as part of the data.

Primary Restore

Select primary restore (the option discussed earlier in this section) when you're either restoring a stand-alone DC, or restoring the first replica set (and you'll later restore all the DCs in the domain). You cannot perform a primary restore if one or more replica sets have already been restored to other DCs.

Normal (Nonauthoritative) Restore

This is just a regular restore action. Use this when you're restoring a DC to join other, working, DCs. AD is restored with its original update sequence number. Because the sequence number is outdated (lower than the current sequence numbers on the other DCs), the AD database will be overwritten during the next replication event, and the DC you're restoring will catch up with the domain data. This is a nonauthoritative restore, and it is appropriate when you want the restored data to be replaced by replicated AD data from another DC. Nonauthoritative restores are the way to go when you're replacing a DC after a crash or a hardware upgrade, and you want the computer to catch up during the next replication.

Authoritative Restore

Suppose your AD database has become corrupt, and the corrupt data has been replicated to the other DCs. After you restore the System State, with its pristine precorruption data, the update sequence number will be much lower than the update sequence numbers on the other DCs. During the next replication, your clean data will be overwritten by the corrupt data.

To avoid this, you need to run an *authoritative restore*, which forces the restored data to be replicated to the other DCs. During the process of an authoritative restore, the system resets the update sequence number to make sure the restored data is seen as the "latest and greatest" data set.

The definition of "corrupted" includes (and is frequently caused by) a mistaken deletion of one or more important objects in the AD.

To create an authoritative restore, you must run the ntdsutil utility (located in the %SystemRoot%\System32 folder) after restoring the System State data, and before restarting the server. Ntdsutil lets you mark Active Directory objects for an authoritative restore. This really means that an object's update sequence number is changed to make it higher than any other update sequence number in the Active Directory replication system. The data with the highest sequence number is the data that's replicated throughout the organization. Ntdsutil adds 100,000 to the sequence number it finds in the restored data.

Here's how to use the ntdsutil utility:

1. While you're still in Directory Services Restore Safe Mode (after restoring), open a command window.

2. Enter **ntdsutil**.

3. The system displays ntdsutil:.

4. Enter **authoritative restore**.

Ntdsutil changes the sequence number. Now you can restart the server and boot normally. The restored System State data will become the source for the next replication procedure.

Restore System State to a Different Location

Depending on the reason you're restoring data, you may want to restore the System State to a different location during the restore process. For example, you may have had a problem that requires you to restore only the local computer (local files and settings, unrelated to the computer's role as a DC).

When you restore the System State data to an alternate location, only the registry files, SYSVOL directory files, and system boot files are restored to the alternate location. Windows Server 2003 does not restore Active Directory, the directory services database, the Certificate Services database, or other domain-based databases when you indicate an alternate location. Therefore, if the problem that caused you to restore is only with the local computer, use an alternate location during the restore process and then copy the files to the System State folder. The system services (AD, and so on) in the System State folder won't be replaced with the earlier data on the backup.

Note *Even if you opt to restore the System State to an alternate location, you must follow the steps previously described for restoring in Directory Services Restore Mode.*

Recovery Console

The best thing about the Recovery Console, which was introduced in Windows 2000, is that it works. In addition, it's easy to use and logical. Microsoft finally gave us a disaster recovery tool we can count on! This is a command-line program for repairing an OS installation, and it works on both FAT and NTFS file systems.

When you're working in the Recovery Console, you can stop and start services, repair the Master Boot Record (MBR), read and write data on a local hard drive, copy data (such as a corrupt or missing system file) from a floppy disk or CD-ROM, and perform other command-line tasks.

You can enter the Recovery Console when you need it by launching it from the Windows Server 2003 CD, or you can preinstall it as a defense against the day you have a failure.

It's a good idea to preinstall the Recovery Console on important servers, as well as on the workstations of your IT personnel. Those are the computers you need to get up and running quickly when they fall victim to problems, and preinstalling this tool means you won't have to spend time finding the Windows Server 2003 CD or stepping through the processes required to access the Recovery Console from the CD.

Access the Recovery Console from the CD

If you don't preinstall the Recovery Console, use the Windows Server 2003 CD as your lifesaver when the operating system either doesn't boot at all or boots with so many error messages that it's clear you have a problem.

Start by booting your computer to the CD (you may have to change your BIOS settings during startup to do this) and let Setup begin. When you're asked if you want to continue installing the operating system, press ENTER to continue. Setup loads files as if it were performing a standard installation. When that function ends, a Welcome to Setup message appears on your screen. The message displays three options:

- To set up Windows, press ENTER.
- To repair Windows, press R.
- To quit Setup, press F3.

Press R to start the Recovery Console. The Recovery Console operates in text mode, and the screen displays a numbered list of operating system directories. Unless you're dual-booting, there's only one listing (usually C:\Windows).

Enter the number next to the Windows Server 2003 installation you want to log on to in order to make repairs, and press ENTER. You must press a number before pressing ENTER, even if only one listing appears. If you press ENTER without entering a number, the system reboots and you get to start over again.

Note *Mirrored volumes appear twice in the Recovery Console list of Windows installations, but each entry has the same drive letter, so they're the same installation. Any changes you make in the Recovery Console will be mirrored.*

The Recovery Console automatically logs on the administrator, so type the local administrator's password and press ENTER. (You're logging on as the local Administrator account, not as a domain administrator.)

Because you perform a logon to get to the Recovery Console, this feature won't work if the Security Accounts Manager (SAM) hive is corrupt or missing. In that case, you'll have to reinstall the operating system.

You're at a command prompt in the %SystemRoot% directory, and you can enter the Recovery Console commands required to perform the repair tasks (covered later in this section).

Preinstall the Recovery Console

You can preinstall the Recovery Console so that it's always available when you need it. You should perform this task on all the computers in your enterprise that are considered mission-critical. You have to decide on your own definition of "mission-critical," but usually this refers to any computers that have to be repaired quickly to avoid chaos, such as DCs, servers that provide services to client users, your own workstation, and the workstations of IT staff members.

To preinstall the Recovery Console, put the Windows Server 2003 CD in the CD-ROM drive. Choose Start | Run and enter *d*:\i386\winnt32.exe /cmdcons (where *d* is the drive letter for the CD-ROM drive). You can also use a UNC to install the Recovery Console from a network share point.

The system prompts you to confirm installation. Clicking Yes starts the installation procedure. Setup copies the appropriate files to your hard drive, and then displays a message indicating that the Recovery Console has been successfully installed. You must restart the computer to finish the process.

You cannot preinstall the Recovery Console on a mirrored volume. If the computer on which you're preinstalling the Recovery Console has a mirrored volume, you must first break the mirror. Install the Recovery Console, and then reestablish the mirrored volume. You also cannot preinstall the Recovery Console on an Itanium computer. You must use the CD version.

Hereafter, during startup, you'll see a menu choice for the Recovery Console. Use the DOWNARROW to select the Recovery Console menu option, which produces the Administrator logon.

Using the Recovery Console

When you use the Recovery Console, you're working at a special command prompt, which is not the same as the usual Windows Server 2003 command prompt. The Recovery Console has its own command interpreter.

Rules for Using the Recovery Console

By default, several rules are in effect while you're working in the Recovery Console, the most important of which are the following:

■ You can only access %SystemRoot% and its subdirectories for the installation you logged on to in Recovery Console.

■ You cannot get to the drive root, nor to other folders such as Program Files, Documents, and Settings, nor to the %SystemRoot% of another Windows installation.

■ You cannot copy a file from the hard drive to removable media.

■ You can change these rules—see the section "Changing the Rules for Recovery Console," later in this chapter.

Recovery Console Commands

A limited number of commands are available to you when you're working in the Recovery Console. Many of the commands are also available in the standard Windows command console, but most of the time the commands have different parameters or the parameters have a different meaning in the Recovery Console than they do when you're working in Windows. For that reason, it's worth going over the commands and the way their parameters work in the Recovery Console.

Attrib   Use the attrib command to change attributes on a single file or subdirectory. The syntax is

attrib *filename | directoryname*

Batch   Use the batch command to execute commands specified in a text file, using this syntax:

batch *inputfile [outputfile]*

where:

inputfile is the text file that contains the commands.

outputfile holds the output of the commands (if omitted, output displays to the screen).

CD (Chdir)   In the Recovery Console, CD operates only within the system directories of the current Windows installation, removable media, the root directory of any hard disk partition, or the local installation sources.

Chkdsk   You can use chkdsk in the Recovery Console to check for, and repair, bad sectors on the drive. Chkdsk uses the following syntax:

chkdsk [/p] | [/r]

where:

/p checks the drive even if the drive is not flagged dirty.

/r locates bad sectors and recovers any readable information (implies /p).

Chkdsk requires autochk.exe, and automatically looks for it in the startup (boot) directory. If it cannot be found, chkdsk looks for the Windows Server 2003 Setup CD. If the installation CD cannot be found, chkdsk prompts the user for the location of autochk.exe, which is %SystemRoot%\System32.

Cls   Enter **cls** to clear the screen.

Copy   Use the copy command to copy a single file to a target location, with the following limitations:

- The target cannot be removable media.
- You cannot use wildcards.

Copying a compressed file from the Windows Server 2003 Setup CD to the local drive automatically decompresses the file.

Del (Delete)   In Recovery Console, you can only use the del command against a single file; it does not support wildcards. The command operates within the system directories of the Windows installation you selected when you entered the Recovery Console, removable media, and the root directory of any hard disk partition.

Dir   Use the dir command to display a list of all files in the current directory. The system automatically includes hidden and system files.

Disable   Use the disable command to disable a Windows system service or driver. The command takes the following syntax:

Disable servicename.

When you enter the command, the system displays the original startup type of the service before changing it to SERVICE_DISABLED. You should note the original startup type, so that you can enable the service again (see the upcoming description of the enable command).

Diskpart   Use diskpart to manage partitions on hard disk volumes, using the following syntax:

Diskpart [/add | /delete] [*device-name* | *drive-name* | *partition-name*] [*size*]

where:

/add creates a new partition.

/delete deletes an existing partition.

device-name is the device name for a new partition (for example, \Device\HardDisk1).

drive-name is the drive letter for a partition you're deleting (for example, D:).

partition-name is the partition-based name for a partition you're deleting (can be used in place of the *drive-name* argument; for example, \Device\HardDisk0\Partition1).

size is the size of the new partition, in megabytes.

Enable   Use the enable command to enable or re-enable a Windows system service or driver. The command uses the following syntax:

enable *servicename* [*start_type*]

where:

servicename is the name of the service or driver you want to enable.

start_type is the startup type for the service, using one of the following:

- SERVICE_BOOT_START
- SERVICE_SYSTEM_START
- SERVICE_AUTO_START
- SERVICE_DEMAND_START

Exit   Use the exit command to quit the Recovery Console. The computer automatically reboots.

Expand   Use the expand command to expand a compressed file or a cabinet (.cab) file. The command is commonly used to extract drivers, and it uses the following syntax:

Expand *source* [*/f:filespec*] [*destination*] [**/y**]

Expand *source* [*/f:filespec*] **/d**

where:

source is the file you want to expand, if the source is a single file. No wildcard characters are permitted.

destination is the target directory for the extracted file. If omitted, the current directory is used. The destination directory cannot be on removable media.

/y specifies an automatic confirmation before overwriting an existing file.

/f:*filespec* is required if the source contains more than one file, usually multiple files from the same .cab file. Wildcards are permitted.

/d displays a list of the files in the source cabinet file. No files are expanded or copied.

Fixboot   Use the fixboot command to write a new boot sector on the system partition. The command uses the following syntax:

fixboot [*drive***:]**

Fixmbr   Use fixmbr to repair the MBR code of the boot partition. The command uses the syntax:

fixmbr [*device-name***]**

where:

device-name specifies the device that needs a new MBR.

You can obtain the *device-name* with the map command (see map). Omitting the *device-name* parameter writes a new MBR to the boot device (the drive that holds the system files for the Windows installation you're working in).

If the system is suspicious about the condition of the *device-name*, you're given a warning and asked if you wish to continue. Suspicions are aroused if the partition table signature seems to be invalid, or nonstandard. Unless the reason you entered the Recovery Console is that you were having a problem accessing drives, do not continue. Writing a new MBR could damage the partition table, making the partition inaccessible.

Format   Use the format command to format a disk, using the following syntax:

format [*drive***:] [/q] [/fs:***file-system***]**

where:

Drive: is the drive you want to format. You cannot specify a floppy drive.

/q specifies a quick format, which does not check the drive for bad spots.

/fs:*file-system* specifies the file system to use, using one of the following choices:

- FAT
- FAT32
- NTFS

Help   Use the help command to obtain information about the Recovery Console commands. Use the following syntax:

help [*command***]**

If no command is specified, the system displays all the commands supported in the Recovery Console.

You can also get help on a specific command by entering **command /?**

Listsvc Use the listsvc command to display all the available services and drivers on the computer.

Logon Use the logon command to log on to a different installation of Windows after you've entered the Recovery Console for the Windows installation you originally chose. Entering the command displays all the Windows installations on the computer. Choosing an installation prompts you for the local administrator password for that installation.

If you enter the wrong password three times, the Recovery Console automatically issues an exit command and reboots the computer.

Map Use the map command to display the device mappings, the type of file system, and the size of the disks on the computer. You need this information to use the fixboot and fixmbr commands. The syntax is

map [arc]

where:

arc specifies the use of Advanced RISC Computing names instead of standard device names.

ARC paths are the format for specifying devices in the boot.ini file. Refer to Chapter 5 for information about boot.ini and the ARC path format.

MD (Mkdir) Use the MD command to create a new directory or subdirectory. In the Recovery Console, this command operates only within the following areas:

- System directories of the current Windows installation (the installation you logged on to)
- Removable media
- The root directory of any hard disk partition

More Use the more command to display a text file to the screen. The syntax is

more [*filename*]

where:

filename is the complete path to the file (unless the file is in the local directory).

net use Use this command to map a network share to a drive letter. The syntax for net use is

net use [*ComputerName**ShareName* [**/user:**[*DomainName*\]*UserName*] *password*] | [*drive letter:*] [**/d**]

where:

*ComputerName**ShareName* is the name of the server and the shared resource.

/user: is the username you want to use to connect to the share.

DomainName is the name of a domain that can validate the user.

UserName is the username with which to log on.

Password is the password required to access the shared resource (if omitted, and if the share requires a password, the system prompts for the password).

/d disconnects the mapped drive.

| Note | *If ComputerName has blank characters, enclose the entire computer name from the double backslash (\\) to the end of the computer name in quotation marks.* |

RD (Rmdir) Use RD to delete an empty directory. You cannot use wildcards. The command operates only within the following areas:

- System directories of the Windows installation you logged on to when you entered the Recovery Console
- Removable media
- Root directory of any hard disk partition, or the local installation sources

Ren (Rename) Use the ren command to change the name of a file, using the following syntax:

ren [*drive:*] [*path*] *filename1 filename2*

You can only use the command on a single file, and you cannot use wildcards. You cannot specify a different path for *filename2*.

Set Use the set command to display and set the Recovery Console environment variables. You must enable the use of the Recovery Console set command via Group Policy Security Templates. See the following section, "Changing the Rules for Recovery Console."

Systemroot   Use the systemroot command to set the current directory to the %SystemRoot% directory of the Windows installation you logged on to when you entered the Recovery Console.

Type   Use the type command to display a text file. The syntax is

type *filename*

Changing the Rules for Recovery Console

Feeling hemmed in by the rules and restrictions that are imposed by the Recovery Console? Well, break out and change them. Microsoft has built in an escape hatch if you're ready to step out of the confines proscribed by the default Recovery Console environment. Before you leap, however, take a moment to remember that you're playing around with some very powerful commands, and your playing field is the section of the computer that contains the heart of the operating system. If you widen your power, you widen your ability to do damage.

Set Policies to Enable Recovery Console Environment Changes

You can expand the power of the Recovery Console, by eliminating the strictures built into the environment. The reversals are accomplished via the set command, which you can use to change the rules. You should think about giving yourself additional power for any computer in which you've preinstalled the Recovery Console.

You can use the set command to change the environment in the Recovery Console (instead of just using the command to view the rules), but you must enable that feature. This is done by changing the computer's security policies (which means you have to enable the feature on a working computer, before you need the Recovery Console). Use these steps to change the computer's policies:

1. Enter **mmc** in the Run dialog to open an MMC console.

2. Choose File | Add/Remove Snap-in to open the Add/Remove Snap-in window.

3. Click Add to open the Add Standalone Snap-in window.

4. Select Group Policy Object Editor, and click Add to open the Select Group Policy Object window (which is a wizard).

5. Choose Local Computer (if it isn't already displayed), and click Finish to return to the Add Standalone Snap-in window.

6. Click Close to return to the Add/Remove Snap-in window, and click OK to return to the MMC console.

7. Expand the Local Computer Policy object to Computer Configuration\ Windows Settings\Security Settings\Local Policies\Security Options.

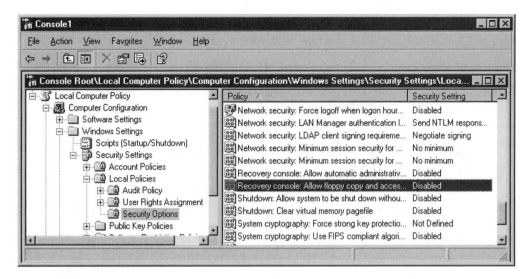

8. In the right pane, double-click the policy named Recovery Console: Allow Floppy Copy And Access To All Drives And Folders.

9. Select Enabled, and click OK.

You should save the console, so you don't have to load the snap-in again from scratch if you want to make changes. To do so, choose File | Save and name the console file appropriately (I use RecConsole). Windows Server 2003 adds the .msc extension automatically, and by default saves the console in the \Documents and Settings\ *YourUserName*\Start Menu\Programs\Administrative Tools folder.

If you want to load this console again, use one of these actions:

■ Enter **mmc\path***filename*.**msc** in the Run dialog of the Start menu (substitute the name you gave the console for *filename*).

■ Enter **mmc** to open a blank console. Then choose File | Open and select your saved console.

The Group Policy snap-in offers another policy in the right pane, called Allow Automatic Administrative Logon, which eliminates the need to enter the local administrator password in order to enter the Recovery Console. I'd be careful about enabling this policy, because you'd have to name the console file "a disaster waiting to happen." Some user (one of those users who knows enough to be dangerous) could access the Recovery Console and dive right in. Requiring a password to enter the Recovery Console is safer.

Incidentally, if you've configured this policy for the domain, it overrides any policy you set for the local computer. It would be unusual for an administrator to set a domain policy for the Recovery Console, but I mention it just in case.

Now that you've changed the security policy for the Recovery Console, you can change the rules when you're working in the Recovery Console.

Change the Recovery Console Environment

Before you start changing the rules, you should know and understand them. Entering **set** at the Recovery Console command prompt displays the current environment settings. Until you change them, the environment has the following settings:

- AllowWildCards = FALSE (prevents wildcard support for commands such as copy and del)
- AllowAllPaths = FALSE (prevents access to directories and subdirectories outside of the system installation that was selected when you entered the Recovery Console)
- AllowRemovableMedia = FALSE (prevents access to removable media as a target for copying files)
- NoCopyPrompt = FALSE (forces prompting for confirmation when overwriting an existing file)

To change any of the rules, use the set command with the following syntax:

set *variable=string*

where:

variable is a rule.

string is the setting for the rule, and is either TRUE or FALSE—to widen your power, change the string to TRUE.

For example, to allow access to all the directories on the computer, instead of being limited to the directories under %SystemRoot%, enter **set AllowAllPaths=TRUE**.

Uninstalling the Recovery Console

If you preinstalled the Recovery Console, you can easily uninstall it. Uninstalling the Recovery Console makes sense if you give the computer to another user, or if multiple users have access to a computer. The trick is to avoid letting a user who falls into that "knows enough to be dangerous" category into the Recovery Console.

Take the following actions to remove the Recovery console from a computer:

1. Delete the \Cmdcons directory from the root of the boot partition.
2. Delete the file named cmldr from the root directory of the boot partition.
3. Edit Boot.ini to delete the Recovery Console line.

Automated System Recovery (ASR)

Floppy disk–based recovery procedures have become more and more difficult to implement in Windows. The last "workable" (and I use the term loosely) floppy disk recovery process was the Emergency Repair Disk (ERD) in Windows NT 4. Windows 2000 also contained the ERD, but the size of the data files made it far less useful than its predecessor. (Okay, I'll say it: It was useless.)

During the beta test period of Windows 2000, a feature called Automated System Recovery was available, but those of us who tried to use it faced repeated failures (and transmitted our resulting bug reports to Microsoft). Before the retail version of Windows 2000 was released, ASR had been dropped from the feature set. It's back, and it works (and I use the term loosely).

ASR is a "last resort" procedure, useful only when you cannot get your Windows Server 2003 to start (not even via Safe Mode, Last Known Good Configuration, or the Recovery Console). It's the function you should think of after you think "It looks as if I have to reformat my drive and reinstall Windows," and then reject that solution. (However, don't reject that solution too quickly; I've found it to be a better solution than using ASR sometimes, because ASR reinstates a registry that's no longer accurate.)

Like the ERD, you create the ASR floppy from the Windows Backup application. Unlike the ERD, the ASR feature requires you to create a related backup of the files required to start Windows. You can store this backup on a local tape drive or a locally attached removable disk.

The locally attached tape drive or removable disk device may only work during an ASR restore if it works with native Windows drivers. If you used the Have Disk option to install the device, the system may not be able to access your backup data during an ASR restore.

Create an ASR Recovery System

To create an ASR recovery system, open the Backup program, and click Advanced Mode to move to the Backup Utility program window. Click the Automated System Recovery Wizard button, which launches the ASR wizard.

The wizard asks you to specify the location of the system file backup. After you do so, click Finish. The wizard opens the Backup Progress dialog, to display the progress as it performs the following tasks:

- Creates a shadow copy of the files you'll need to use the ASR recovery option, including System State, system services, and all disks associated with the operating system components.

- Writes hard disk configuration information (disk signatures, partition table information, and volume data) to a floppy disk.

When the files are written, you can view a report of the backup by clicking the Report button on the Backup Progress dialog. To see the contents of the ASR floppy disk, select the floppy drive in My Computer or Windows Explorer. All the files on the floppy disk can be viewed with Notepad.

The ASR backup is called a *set,* because the floppy disk and the backup file you created are linked. You cannot use the floppy disk to recover the system with a different backup file. Be sure to label the floppy disk carefully, making sure you note the filename for the backup file to which it's linked.

 The %SystemRoot%\Repair directory holds copies of the two .sif files that are placed on the floppy disk. The log file exists only on the floppy disk.

Recover a System with ASR

If all efforts to boot the computer fail, and you decide to use the ASR feature to recover, you'll need the following:

- Your ASR floppy disk
- The ASR System State backup you made
- Your Windows Server 2003 CD

Boot to the Windows Server 2003 CD. Almost immediately, a message appears at the bottom of the screen telling you to press F6 to install your own SCSI drivers. That message is replaced by one telling you to press F2 to use the ASR. Pressing F2 displays a message to insert your ASR floppy disk and press any key. Setup continues by loading the setup files, so the process looks like a standard installation for a few minutes. When the files are loaded, Setup displays the following message:

```
To restore the configuration of your system, Setup must delete and recreate all the
partitions on the disks listed below.
CAUTION: All data present on these disks will be lost.
Do you want to continue recreating the partitions?
To continue, press C. Partitions on all the disks listed below will be deleted.
To quit Setup, Press F3. No changes will be made to any of the disks on the system.
```

Pressing C begins the attempt to recover your system. Follow the prompts and hope for the best. If the cause of your problem is in the hard drive or its controller, this won't work...but neither would any other recovery method. Remember that this is not an installation, so you cannot make changes to partitions, partition sizes, or any other basic components.

ASR reads the disk configuration settings from the floppy, and restores all of the disk signatures, volumes, and partitions required for booting. ASR tries to restore all of the disk configuration information, but that's not always successful.

ASR then uses the Windows Server 2003 CD to install a minimal installation of the operating system, following which ASR automatically restores your system from the backup created by the ASR wizard.

Creating Boot Disks

If your Windows Server 2003 computer won't start, and you think it's because some of the boot files may be corrupted, you can try to boot the computer with a floppy disk that's configured for this purpose. Then you can repair any corrupted files that may be the cause of boot failure. The boot disk will work regardless of the file system (FAT, FAT32, or NTFS).

To create a bootable floppy disk, you need to format the disk by entering **format a:** at a command prompt of a computer running Windows Server 2003, Windows XP, Windows 2000, or Windows NT.

Copy ntldr and ntdetect.com to the floppy disk. You can find these files on the Windows Server 2003 CD, in the i386 folder.

The floppy disk also requires a boot.ini file, which you can create from scratch or copy from another Windows Server 2003 computer that has the same hardware and operating system configuration. By "hardware and operating system configuration," I mean that the computers must have the following characteristics in common:

- The hard drive controller type must be the same: SCSI or IDE.
- The Windows files (%SystemRoot%) must be on the same drive or partition (either drive/partition 0 or drive/partition 1).
- The Windows files must be contained in a folder with the same name (the default system folder name is Windows).

If your boot drive is SCSI, the floppy disk also requires the driver for the SCSI controller, which you must rename to ntbootdd.sys.

See Chapter 5 for detailed information about the boot process (and troubleshooting that process).

STOP Errors: Blue Screen of Death

STOP! When you see this word on a computer screen (a blue screen with white text), you're facing the Blue Screen of Death, the dreaded BSOD, the appalling Fatal Error. The computer, of course, has stopped dead in its tracks; no mouse or keyboard action can initiate a response, and only the power button works (unless you've configured the computer to reboot automatically when this happens).

Note *Another term for a STOP Error is "bugcheck," and these are the "official" terms. However, these events are affectionately called BSODs by system administrators.*

Encountering BSODs is an experience unique to Windows administrators, and in older versions of Windows the scare came with the display of General Protection Fault on the screen. In my Novell NetWare consulting days, I shuddered when I saw ABEND, and during my experience with UNIX, I'd want to leave the room when I saw Kernel Panic errors. Regardless of the platform, computer-stopping errors are a fact of life for all system administrators.

This section is a general overview of BSOD management techniques, designed to give you an idea of the process of dealing with crashes you may encounter as part of the "fun" of being a system administrator.

What Causes a BSOD?

A computer crash is actually a protective maneuver, designed to stop a malfunctioning process from doing even more damage once it has begun to misbehave. The misbehavior takes the form of an illegal action—usually, a process does something it's not supposed to do. Examples of illegal actions include an attempt to write data to a read-only memory page or an attempt to read data from a memory address that isn't mapped.

Most of the time, the offending code is part of a device driver. That's why Microsoft has moved to the paradigm of certifying and protecting device drivers. Sometimes, however, it's not the programmer's fault; for instance, the code could be interacting with memory in a proper and legal fashion, but the memory is corrupt.

Whatever the cause, there's a possibility that the system could be victimized by the "domino theory," as problems lead to additional problems, corrupting parts of the system that were not directly affected by the original problem. To prevent that possibility from becoming a reality, the operating system is designed to STOP.

 The function that invokes the crash is KeBugCheckEx(). It's hard to find information about this function in the normal places you look for explanations (help files, the Microsoft Knowledge Base), but one source I know of for documentation is the Windows DDK.

Preparing for BSODs

Even though you cannot do anything when a BSOD appears (except power down and power up again if you haven't configured the computer to reboot automatically after a STOP error), you can prepare your system to provide information about BSODs so that you (probably with the help of a Microsoft support person) can resolve the problem.

Configure System Recovery Options

To configure your computer's behavior when a BSOD occurs, open the System Properties dialog (right-click My Computer and choose Properties). Move to the Advanced tab and click the Settings button in the Startup and Recovery section to see the Startup and Recovery dialog. The System Failure section of the dialog offers the settings you want to examine. By default, all the options in the System Failure section of the dialog are selected (see Figure 26-7):

- **Write an event to the system log**   Specifies whether Windows will write event information to the System Log in Event Viewer when the computer encounters a STOP error. This option is grayed out for all versions of Windows Server 2003 (and Windows 2000 Server), because you can't deselect it. For client computers (Windows XP Professional/2000 Professional), you can deselect this option, but it's not a good idea because the information could be useful. In fact, I'm guessing that Microsoft forced the event write because the support personnel got frustrated too often during support sessions in which they needed the information in the event to diagnose a failure, and heard "Oh, I turned that off."

- **Send an administrative alert**   Specifies whether you want to send a message to administrators when the computer encounters a STOP error. See the section "Configuring Administrative Alerts," later in this chapter.

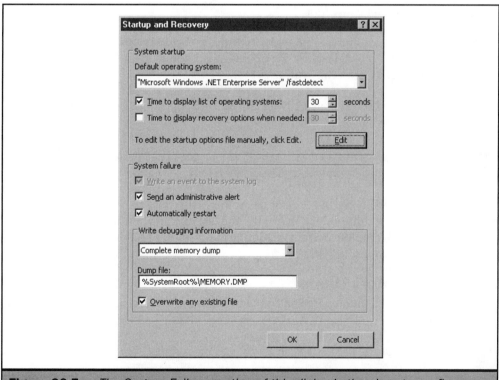

Figure 26-7.   *The System Failure section of this dialog is the place to configure recovery options.*

■ **Automatically restart** Configures the computer to perform a reboot when a BSOD occurs. Of course, if the problem that caused the BSOD is serious, the computer may not be able to restart, but quite often a reboot is successful. This option is rather important for servers, because if the computer can reboot without error, clients can regain the use of the server's resources more quickly.

Configuring the Dump File Type

One important decision is the type of memory dump you want to kick off when a BSOD occurs. The kernel dumps the contents of system memory to a file specified in the Startup and Recovery dialog (by default, %SystemRoot%\memory.dmp), and you can select the type and amount of information that's written. These choices are new if you're migrating to Windows Server 2003 from Windows NT—Windows NT had an "all or nothing" attitude about memory dumps. The choices, discussed in the following sections, are the following:

■ Complete Memory Dump (same as Windows NT)

■ Kernel Memory Dump

■ Small Memory Dump

If you change the option for the type of dump, you must reboot the computer to have the settings take effect, because the operating system reads the registry at startup to determine the behavior of this feature.

The drop-down list also includes None as a memory dump type. I suspect you can figure out its meaning, so I'm not discussing it.

To take advantage of the dump file, your paging file must be on the boot volume. If you've moved the paging file to another volume, move it back.

In addition to specifying the type of dump file, you must also specify whether or not you want the next dump file to overwrite the last one. It's best to select this option if you're using the Complete Memory Dump option so that you don't use up all the free space on the drive.

Complete Memory Dump

A complete memory dump records all the contents in system memory at the point that the system stops.

Actually, the size of the dump file is limited to 2GB, but that should be sufficient.

To use a complete memory dump, your paging file must be as large as the amount of physical RAM, plus 1MB. The extra megabyte is required because the system writes a header in addition to dumping the contents of memory. The header has a crash dump signature, and also specifies the values of several kernel variables. The header information doesn't really need a full megabyte of space, but the system sizes your paging file in increments of megabytes.

If and when another BSOD occurs, the previous file is overwritten. Therefore, rename the dump file after you reboot, or in the Recovery Console (if it becomes necessary to enter the Recovery Console as a result of the problem).

Kernel Memory Dump

A kernel memory dump writes only the contents of the kernel memory. This includes memory that's allocated to the kernel, the HAL, the kernel-mode drivers, and any other kernel-mode programs. The file is smaller, so the process of writing the information is faster.

Usually, information in kernel memory reveals enough data to determine the cause of the disaster. BSODs arise from problems that occur during kernel-mode execution, so user-mode application data (which is included in a complete memory dump) isn't usually necessary when you're trying to diagnose the reason for the crash.

This dump file type requires a paging file that's one-third the size of physical memory; however, the minimum requirement is 50MB. If and when another BSOD occurs, the previous file is overwritten. Therefore, as soon as possible, rename the file.

Small Memory Dump

A small memory dump (also called a *minidump*) is limited to 64KB, so it writes much less information than the other two dump file options. However, the data written to the dump file has a reasonably good chance of revealing the source of the problem (it's essentially the same information that the system displays to the screen). The information in the dump includes the BSOD error and code, a list of currently loaded drivers, information about the process and thread that was executing at the time of the crash, and information about recently used functions. This option requires a paging file of at least 2MB.

Dump files from small dumps don't overwrite any previous dump files. The files are located in %SystemRoot%\minidump, and the filename is in the form mini*mm-dd-yy-nn*.dmp (*nn* is the dump number for the same date, in case you experience more than one BSOD a day).

Configuring Administrative Alerts

The process of setting up administrative alerts for BSODs is Microsoft's version of the classic cat and mouse game, in which the mouse is harder to catch each time you actually capture it, so your moments of success become fewer and less frequent. With each version of Windows, it's harder to find a method for sending an administrative alert when a server crashes.

When you select the option to send an alert from the Startup and Recovery dialog, you run into a small problem—no tool exists to perform this task. The dialog should have a button that's labeled Configure Alert, and clicking it should let you perform the tasks necessary to send alerts. But that would take away the fun that Microsoft's programmers are having as they make their cat and mouse game more difficult to win.

In Windows NT, it's easy to set up these alerts—open the Server applet in Control Panel, click Alerts, and add the names of alert recipients.

In Windows 2000, no applet exists, no MMC-based administrative tool is available, and no dialog box offers this function. However, as a friendly aid to users playing the "configure alerts cat and mouse game," Microsoft inserted an updated version of a Windows NT tool in %SystemRoot%\System32—Server Manager (the filename is srvmgr.exe). Actually, it's a new version of Windows NT Server Manager. You can use it on Windows 2000 Server versions to set up administrative alerts for crashes. In addition, in Windows 2000 server versions, the Messenger and Alerter services (required for sending alerts) are started automatically during startup.

In Windows Server 2003, all the same ingredients are missing as went missing in Windows 2000, but this time, the programmers got more serious about winning the game—srvmgr.exe is not included in the OS. In addition, the Messenger and Alerter services are disabled by default.

I have figured out how to send administrative alerts in Windows Server 2003 following a BSOD, and therefore I declare myself the winner of the cat and mouse game. I have no idea if my solution is the one that *really* wins the game (assuming there's a panel awarding prizes at Microsoft), but it works, so I announce Victory!

Enable the Messenger and Alerter Services on the Server

To enable the Messenger and Alerter services on the server, you first must change the startup values for the Messenger and Alerter services so that they start automatically when the operating system starts. To accomplish this, open the Services snap-in from the Administrative Tools menu and double-click the listing for each service. Figure 26-8 shows the Properties dialog for the Alerter service.

Choose Automatic from the Startup Type drop-down list, and click Apply. Then click Start to start the service immediately (so you don't have to restart the computer to start the service). Click OK to close the Properties dialog.

> **Note**   *The Alerter service is started by default in Windows Server 2003 and Windows 2000 Server, but not in Windows XP Professional or Windows 2000 Professional. If you want to send an alert when a Windows XP Professional/2000 Professional computer crashes, use the Services snap-in to configure the Alerter service for automatic startup.*

Specify Alert Recipients

You must tell Windows Server 2003 the names of the recipients when an alert is transmitted, which you accomplish by changing the registry. Open Regedit and travel to the HKEY_LOCAL_MACHINE\System\CurrentControlSet\Services\Alerter\ Parameters subkey. In the right pane, double-click the data item named AlertNames, and add the names of all the computers and users on the network that should see

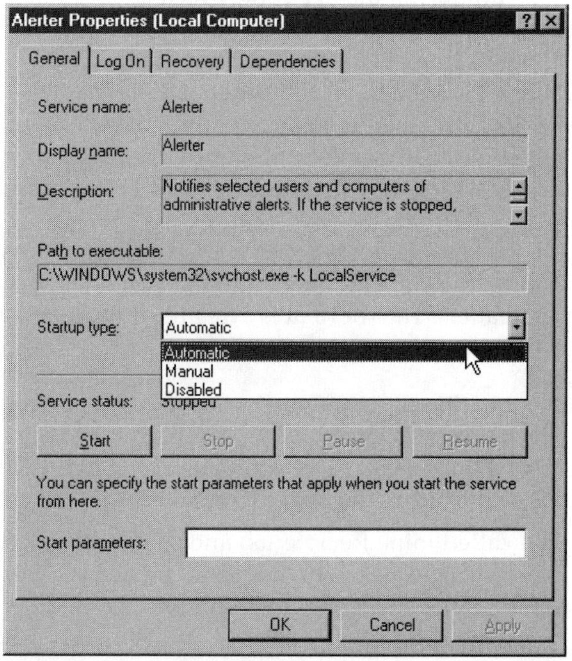

Figure 26-8.   *Changing the startup type for the Messenger and Alerter services*

a pop-up message when the server experiences a BSOD. Put each computer or username on its own line.

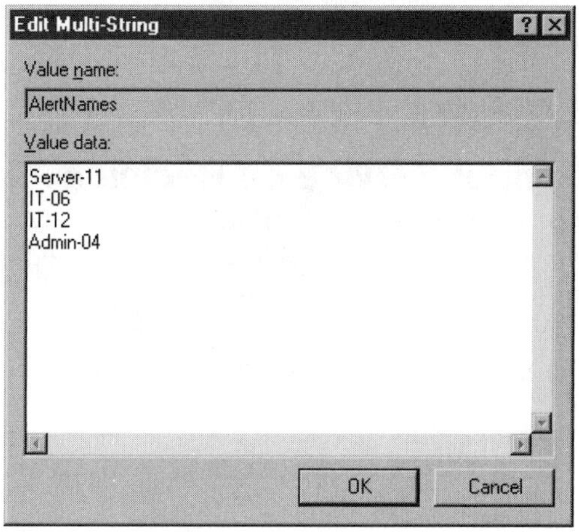

Every name must be unique on the network, which means that if you create a list of all computer names and all usernames, you have no duplicates. You probably already know that computer names must be unique and usernames must be unique, but you may not realize that a combination of all computer and usernames must also contain no duplicates. If you have a user named ivens, you cannot have a computer named ivens.

The best approach is to list all the users in your IT department, and/or all the computers that are regularly used by members of your IT department (including yourself, of course).

After you configure the first Windows Server 2003 computer, you can use a shortcut to add the recipient names to other computers running Windows Server 2003 (or Windows 2000, for that matter). The shortcut is a .reg file that automatically adds the recipient names to all the computers you want to monitor for crashes. Here's how:

1. Open regedit.exe on the computer you just configured for recipient names, and export the subkey (HKEY_LOCAL_MACHINE\System\CurrentControlSet\Services\Alerter\Parameters) by selecting its object in the left pane and choosing File | Export from the Regedit menu bar.

2. Name the file (I called mine Recipients) and save it. Windows saves the file as a registry file (with the extension .reg) and, by default, locates it in the My Documents folder of the current logged-on user.

3. You can distribute the resulting .reg file via e-mail, or place the file in a network share. To merge the settings into the target computer's registry, just double-click the .reg file, which produces a message asking you if you're sure you want to merge data into the registry.

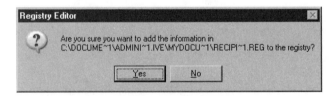

4. Click Yes. Windows displays a success message. Click OK to clear it.

Enable the Messenger Service on Recipient Computers

In order to see an alert pop up that's sent from the server, the receiving computer must have the Messenger service running. (The Alerter service needs to be running only on computers that are sending alerts, whereas the Messenger service is required for both sending and receiving.) On Windows 2000 (Professional or Server) and Windows XP, the default startup type of the Messenger service is Automatic, so you shouldn't have to take any action (I'm assuming the IT personnel are all working at computers running Windows 2000 or Windows XP).

 There isn't any way to turn on alerts specifically for BSODs. Alerts are Boolean, so if you or your computer is a recipient, be prepared to receive pop-ups and hear beeps whenever any unexpected event occurs on the machine for which you've configured alerts.

Testing the Configuration with a BSOD

It's a good idea to make sure everything you've done to prepare for resolving problems that cause a BSOD will actually work. Microsoft provides a way to force a BSOD without doing any harm to your system. You can perform this test to see whether alerts, dump files, and Event Viewer logs respond properly.

Understanding Crashes

Before forcing a BSOD on a computer, you should have some understanding about what's going to happen, so you know if your preparation efforts covered all bases. This section is a brief overview of how the dump process works.

When you configure the options discussed in the previous sections, Windows Server 2003 writes the settings to the registry. In addition to the registry item that contains the names of recipients of alerts (discussed in the preceding section), the registry also holds the settings for the recovery options you selected. That data is in the registry subkey HKEY_LOCAL_MACHINE\SYSTEM\CurrentControlSet\Control\CrashControl.

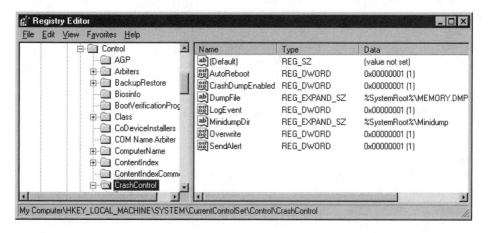

During startup, Windows Server 2003 reads the data items in this subkey and prepares the system to match the behavior indicated by the values of the data items.

CrashDumpEnabled is checked for the type of dump file:

- 0 specifies no dump
- 1 specifies a Complete Memory Dump
- 2 specifies a Kernel Memory Dump
- 3 specifies a Small Memory Dump

During startup, the system also creates a map of the disk blocks that the paging file uses, and saves that information in memory. In addition, the system identifies the driver that manages the boot volume, and also identifies the services and structures that must exist in order to perform disk I/O in the face of a BSOD.

When a crash occurs, the kernel checks these components and, if they're intact, calls disk and driver I/O functions that exist solely for the purpose of dumping memory when the system crashes. The crash-specific I/O functions are independent, and they don't need or use normal running kernel services. Being outside of the kernel means that any damage done to the kernel or the drivers during the crash doesn't prevent the I/O function from running. The kernel writes the contents of memory to the paging file's sector map, which means the I/O process doesn't need file-system drivers.

When you restart the computer, Session Manager (\%SystemRoot%\System32\ smss.exe) initializes the system's paging file (this is a normal procedure; refer to Chapter 5 for information about the startup process). One of the functions involved in initializing the paging file is to check to see if a paging file already exists, has data, and has a dump header. If those conditions are true, when Session Manager launches the logon manager (\%SystemRoot%\System32\winlogon.exe) to start the Winlogon process, Session Manager also tells Winlogon that a crash dump exists. Winlogon then automatically executes savedump.exe, which is located in %SystemRoot%\System32.

Savedump.exe looks at the dump header to determine which crash response actions must be performed. If the header indicates that a memory dump exists, savedump.exe copies the contents of the paging file to the crash dump filename you specified in the Startup and Recovery Options dialog. During the copying process, the operating system can't use the part of the paging file that contains the crash dump, so you lose some virtual memory. (If you see a pop-up error message about the system being low on virtual memory, don't worry about it.) After the paging file contents are copied to the dump file, the operating system's memory manager releases the part of the paging file that held the dump data. Also, after copying the data to the dump file, savedump.exe performs any other options specified in the Startup and Recovery Options dialog, such as sending out administrative alerts or writing an event to the System log.

The important thread through all of this is that all the recovery options you've configured occur during the next startup, not at the time the computer crashes. This is why it's important to configure the computer to reboot automatically after a crash.

Otherwise, you won't be sent an alert at your own workstation, and the only way you'll know that a server has crashed is when you happen to pass by the computer and see a blue screen.

Forcing a BSOD

Microsoft has built a feature into Windows Server 2003 (and Windows 2000) that forces a computer to crash and produce a BSOD. Setting it up and using it is easy, and a great way to test your recovery configuration settings. To force a BSOD, you need to make a registry change, and then invoke the keystrokes that combine with the new registry setting to crash the computer.

Configuring a Forced BSOD

To set up a computer so it responds to a forced BSOD, open Regedit and travel to the HKEY_LOCAL_MACHINE\SYSTEM\CurrentControlSet\Services\i8042prt\ Parameters subkey. (The i8042prt key controls the keyboard and mouse ports, and the Parameters subkey contains their basic settings.) Add a new REG_DWORD item named CrashOnCtrlScroll to the subkey, and give it a value of 1. Restart the computer to put the new settings into effect (the operating system only reads this subkey at startup).

Crashing the Computer on Purpose

When the computer is up and running again, don't load software (technically you could, but there's no point in crashing your computer with software open—you might do some damage to an application).

Hold down the right CTRL key and press the SCROLL LOCK key twice (this doesn't work if you use the left CTRL key). You should see a blue screen with the following STOP message:

```
*** STOP: 0x000000E2 (0x00000000,0x00000000,0x00000000,0x00000000)
A problem has been detected and Windows has been shut down to
prevent damage to your computer.
The end-user manually generated the crashdump.
```

There's more to the message, but that's the important part. It looks so real, it's scary, isn't it?

You should also see a message indicating that the contents of memory are being written to disk, and an increasing number that represents the disk write. If you configured the computer to reboot after a STOP message, it should do so (otherwise, start the computer again manually). During the reboot, if you configured alerts, the computers and/or users who are the designated recipients should receive a message during OS startup (just before the user logon process starts).

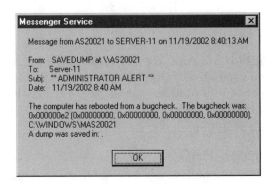

Investigating a BSOD

To eliminate the cause of a BSOD, you have to figure out what provoked it. The scope of the data you collect is a result of the options you selected for recovery functions. Testing the recovery components after a forced BSOD is a good way to see if you should change options (perhaps you don't need a complete memory dump, or perhaps a minidump doesn't provide enough information).

  After you test your recovery efforts, it's probably a good idea to delete the registry item you added for forcing BSODs, or change its value to 0 (which disables the function).

Take Notes on the STOP Error

Sometimes the contents of the STOP message that appears on the screen (the BSOD itself) can provide enough information to determine the cause of the crash. The first line of the STOP message uses the following format:

STOP stop code identifier (parameter1 parameter2 parameter3 parameter4)

The stop code identifier is a hex value, which indicates the general cause of the crash. Each of the four parameters has its own meaning, providing additional information to help you narrow down the specifics of the stop code identifier. For example, many STOP screens have parameters that include the following:

- The first parameter is the memory address that was referenced by the problematic module/driver.

- The second parameter is the IRQL that the system used to access the memory address referenced in the first parameter.

- The third parameter is the type of memory access that was made, and the last number is interpreted as follows: 1=Write; 0=Read.

- The fourth parameter is the instruction address that tried to access the memory address.

The second line of the STOP screen contains the descriptive text that's linked to the stop code's identifier. If you invoked the deliberate crash described earlier in this chapter, you see the text "The end-user manually generated the crashdump."

Of course, that's not the code identifier and text you see when you have a real system crash. The text is usually something like UNEXPECTED_KERNEL_MODE_TRAP, or IRQL_NOT_LESS_OR_EQUAL.

You can frequently find specific information by searching the Microsoft Knowledge Base for the stop code identifier, or the text that's connected to the identifier. Or, you can call Microsoft support in the hope that this data is sufficient to analyze the problem.

Check the Event Log

Check the System Log of the Event Viewer to see the bugcheck code error, and information about the dump file.

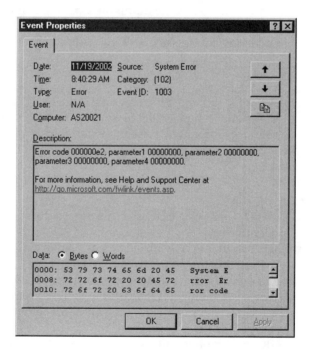

Verify the Dump File

Check the contents of %SystemRoot% to make sure the dump file memory.dmp exists. Rename the file, using a .dmp extension, so that if you have another crash, you won't lose the information to an overwrite. If you specified a small dump file, check the %SystemRoot%\Minidump subdirectory for a file named for the date of the dump.

Sometimes the system doesn't save a dump file, even though you're sure you configured the recovery options correctly. The most likely causes for this failure are that the volume you specified for the dump file didn't have enough free space or that the paging file was too small. In either case, the event record in the System Log of the Event Viewer indicates that no dump file was saved.

A badly written disk driver might not invoke the dump I/O routines that the system requires in order to perform a dump. Believe it or not, such disk drivers weren't all that rare in previous versions of Windows. The "digitally signed drivers" feature in Windows Server 2003 guarantees that Microsoft has checked the code, and one of Microsoft's standards is that the driver includes crash dump support.

Send the File to Microsoft Support

If you call Microsoft support, and they can't give you a solution by interpreting the STOP code message, they may ask you to send the dump file via e-mail, or by uploading the file to an ftp site. Compress the file before you e-mail it or upload it. (The dump file is filled with "air" so it compresses to a file size that's much smaller than the original file.)

Common STOP Errors

In this section, I'll present a list of the most common STOP errors, including brief explanations of their causes and, when available, some suggested solutions. I've deemed these errors "common" because I've seen them referred to multiple times in discussion lists, or because somebody at Microsoft told me that numerous support calls involve these errors.

0x0000000A

Descriptive text: IRQL_NOT_LESS_OR_EQUAL. This error occurs when a driver has used an improper memory address.

Usually this error appears after you've installed a driver. Restart the computer and press F8 to access the Advanced Options menu. Select Last Known Good Configuration. If this works, you need to contact the manufacturer for a good driver.

If the error appears when upgrading to Windows Server 2003 from another operating system, check to see whether the computer is running antivirus software. If so, disable it and see if that resolves the problem.

If the error appears during a fresh installation of Windows 2000, you may be running into a hardware incompatibility problem. Make sure the computer and all peripherals that the installation process discovers are on the Hardware Compatibility List (HCL).

0x0000001E

Descriptive text: KMODE_EXCEPTION_NOT_HANDLED. This error occurs when a kernel-mode program generates an illegal process that the error handler could not handle.

This is a very general error and can be difficult to track down without further information. Microsoft support personnel can usually help you pinpoint the problem by using the parameters attached to the STOP message. The first parameter is the exception code, which is usually helpful for gaining information about the errant process; the other parameters help determine the location of the problem (for example, memory address).

    Check the Event Viewer to see if the event entry names a driver.

If you installed hardware or drivers (or both) immediately before encountering this error, restart the computer using the Last Known Good Configuration option. Then, of course, fix the problem by obtaining a valid driver or removing the incompatible hardware component.

If you run into this error during installation, you may have a hardware compatibility issue, so check the computer and its peripherals against the HCL.

0x00000024

Descriptive text: NTFS_FILE_SYSTEM. This error indicates that a problem occurred with the driver for the NTFS file system (ntfs.sys) while it was permitting a read or write.

    The first parameter contains the name of the source file, and the line number within that file that caused the STOP error. The high 16 bits (the first four hexadecimal digits following 0x) identify the source file. The lower 16 bits (the last four hex digits) identify the source line in the file where the STOP occurred.

The most common causes for this STOP error include the following:

- **Bad spots on the disk**   Run chkdsk /f (see Chapter 11 to learn about running chkdsk.exe).

- **A problem with antivirus software**   Disable the software and restart the computer to see if the problem goes away.

- **Depleted nonpaged pool memory**   Increase the RAM in the computer.

0x0000002E

Descriptive text: DATA_BUS_ERROR. This is almost always a hardware error, and most frequently a parity error in memory.

If you see this error after adding RAM to the machine, remove the new RAM. It's also possible that existing RAM has gone bad, in which case you should run a diagnostic program to examine RAM.

Other known causes for this error are problems with a hard disk (run chkdsk /f) or bad drivers (boot into Last Known Good Configuration).

0x00000050

Descriptive text: PAGE_FAULT_IN_NONPAGED_AREA. This is almost always an indication of a hardware error, and the most common cause is defective RAM on the system board, in the L2 RAM cache, or on a video controller.

If you added any hardware to the system immediately before encountering this error (even if it wasn't RAM), remove it to see if the error occurs again. If not, use a hardware diagnostics program to examine RAM. Other, less common causes for this error include antivirus software (disable it) and a hard disk that's having problems (run chkdsk /f).

0x00000058

Descriptive text: FTDISK_INTERNAL_ERROR. This error occurs when you boot a mirrored system from the wrong partition.

If you break the mirror, and then revive the primary partition, and then encounter this STOP error, the primary partition has an error. Unfortunately, almost everyone who encounters this crash reports that everything seemed correct, and the primary partition clearly seemed bootable, and yet the system crashed.

Boot from a floppy disk with the ARC path in boot.ini pointing to the shadow. (Refer to Chapter 5 to learn how to create a boot disk with a customized boot.ini file.) Break the mirror, configure a new boot and system partition, and create a new mirror.

0x0000007A

Descriptive text: KERNEL_DATA_INPAGE_ERROR. This error occurs when a requested page of kernel data in the paging file could not be read into memory. A number of scenarios cause this error, and the following are the most common causes:

- Bad blocks on a drive (run chkdsk /f)
- Bad RAM (use a diagnostic tool to check RAM)
- Improper SCSI cabling/termination (if the pagefile is on a SCSI drive)

0x0000007B

Descriptive text: INACCESSIBLE_BOOT_DEVICE. This error means that the system partition is not available to the boot process.

You can't debug this error, and any configuration options you've set for recovery (for example, dump files) are irrelevant because none of the drivers and processes that perform these tasks are loaded when the error occurs.

This crash usually occurs during OS installation, or after installing a new disk or a new disk driver. However, a boot sector virus can also cause this STOP error.

I always go for the easiest fix first (keeping my fingers crossed throughout the process), so try a DOS-based virus detection program that runs from a bootable floppy. If that doesn't work, you need to reinstall the operating system. Of course, make sure that any hardware or driver you installed appears on the HCL.

0x0000007F

Descriptive text: UNEXPECTED_KERNEL_MODE_TRAP. The most common cause of this STOP error is hardware failure.

This error usually occurs after you've installed new hardware, including RAM. You must remove the hardware and reboot to prove this theory. If you haven't just installed new hardware, then an existing hardware component has probably failed.

This error can also appear after you install a new driver for existing hardware. If that's the case, use one of the recovery options to replace the driver, or boot to the Last Known Good Configuration option.

0x00000076

Descriptive text: PROCESS_HAS_LOCKED_PAGES. This error means a driver locked memory pages during I/O, and then failed to release the lock (a really bad programming error).

While the parameters that appear on the error message may help support personnel identify the pages that were locked, they don't identify the driver that caused the problem. You can track down the offender by configuring your system to save stack traces. Then, the next time the driver causes this crash, you'll see STOP error 0x000000CB, which provides more information. To configure stack trace saves, use any registry editor to go to the HKEY_LOCAL_MACHINE\SYSTEM\CurrentControlSet\Control\Session Manager\Memory Management subkey. Create a new REG_DWORD data item named TrackLockedPages and set the value to 1. You must reboot the computer to put the setting into effect.

0x00000077

Descriptive text: KERNEL_STACK_INPAGE_ERROR. This error occurs when a requested page of kernel data in the paging file cannot be called into memory.

The most common cause of this error is a bad block on a hard disk (run chkdsk /f). Other common causes include virus infection and bad RAM.

0x00000079

Descriptive text: MISMATCHED_HAL. This error means a mismatch between the Hardware Abstraction Layer (hal.dll) or ntoskrnle.exe, and the installed OS kernel or the machine's hardware configuration.

While it sounds like this error couldn't occur outside of the installation process, it does—and usually because somebody decided to update either ntoskrnl.exe or the HAL file.

Ntoskrnl.exe is a bit tricky, because on the CD (or in a downloaded update) there are two copies of this file:

- ntoskrnl.exe, which is for single-processor systems
- ntkrnlmp.exe, which is for multiprocessor systems

During installation, Setup uses the appropriate file, but no matter which file is used, it's named ntoskrnl.exe on your local system partition (it's located in %SystemRoot%\System32). If Setup finds multiple processors, it uses ntkrnlmp.exe and renames the file to ntoskrnl.exe after it's transferred to the local computer.

A similar situation exists with the HAL. Multiple HALs exist on the installation CD, and Setup determines which is the appropriate file. That file is transferred to the hard drive and renamed hal.ddl.

Given these facts, image the havoc wreaked when somebody decides to "update" a file, or fix a "problem" by transferring a file from the CD to the hard drive. It happens more often than you'd think. The solution is to determine the right file and transfer it, renaming it appropriately. Failing that (it's not easy deciding which HAL should become hal.dll), run setup.exe and choose the Repair option.

0xC000021A

Descriptive text: STATUS_SYSTEM_PROCESS_TERMINATED. This error appears when a user mode subsystem fails, and the system must switch to kernel mode. Because the operating system can't mount, or run, without user mode subsystems (such as winlogon), the system crashes.

 The fact that this crash is related to user mode subsystems means you can't investigate the problem with kernel debugging tools.

This crash almost always occurs as a result of problems with third-party software, usually drivers.

- If you just installed a device driver, reboot with the Last Known Good Configuration option.
- If the problem is a software application, try booting to Safe Mode, and then remove the software from the system.

 If the software is a utility that runs at startup, you may have to use the Recovery Console to remove the software files.

0xC0000221

Descriptive text: STATUS_IMAGE_CHECKSUM_MISMATCH. This error occurs when a system driver or .dll file is corrupt.

If the BSOD displays the name of the corrupted file, try booting to Safe Mode with Command Prompt, and then copy the file from the Windows Server 2003 CD. If the file is compressed, you must use the expand command to expand it as you transfer it. Personally, I find it easier to go into the Recovery Console to perform this task, because the copy command in the Recovery Console automatically expands compressed files (and wouldn't it be nice if the "regular" copy command did that when the source file is a compressed installation file?).

If the BSOD doesn't display the name of the corrupted file, run Setup and choose Repair to replace any and all damaged system files.

Windows Error Reporting

The Windows error reporting feature lets you collect information about serious errors and examine reports that may provide a clue to the cause. This provides a way to determine whether there are patterns for computers that crash or hang, which is useful for repairing problems and for setting up a disaster prevention plan.

The feature includes the ability to send the reports to Microsoft for analysis and assistance. You can also send the reports to a sharepoint on your network so that you can track operating system errors in an effort to uncover the causes.

Windows error reporting is part of the Event Tracker feature (which is also discussed in Chapter 18). You can configure error reporting for both operating system errors and application errors. The error reporting feature uses the following definitions of "error":

- An operating system error occurs when you generate a BSOD, or have an unplanned shutdown (a dirty shutdown).

- An application error occurs when a program stops responding and either closes automatically or is closed by a user (generally via Task Manager).

With error reporting, whenever the operating system encounters a BSOD or an unplanned shutdown, information about the error is written to a log file. The next time a user with administrator rights logs on, an error reporting dialog appears. The dialog includes three fields:

- **Choose a Reason** Select from a drop-down list that includes the following choices:
    - Other (unplanned)
    - Other Failure: System Unresponsive
    - System Failure: Stop error

- Security issue

- Power Failure: Cord Unplugged

- Power Failure: Environment

- **Problem ID**   Enter text to identify this event.

- **Comment**   Enter text to explain what occurred immediately preceding the event (if you know).

After an operating system error occurs, the Event Viewer System log has the information you recorded in the dialog.

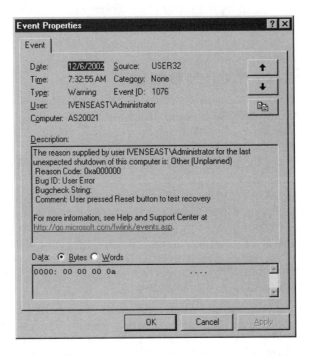

Enable Error Reporting in System Properties

By default, Windows Server 2003 enables error reporting for both operating system and application failures. Error reporting is enabled/disabled in the System Properties dialog, which you can open by right-clicking My Computer and choosing Properties.

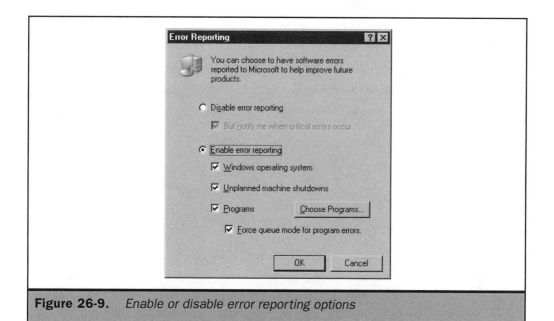

Figure 26-9.   *Enable or disable error reporting options*

Go to the Advanced tab and click Error Reporting to see the Error Reporting dialog, shown in Figure 26-9.

You can disable error reporting if you have a cogent reason for this decision, but it's not a good idea to take this step for network servers. If you decide to disable error reporting, you can select the option But Notify Me When Critical Errors Occur, to have Windows notify you when an operating system error occurs. This, however, does not provide an opportunity to track the circumstances that might have caused the error, so it's not helpful for preventing errors in the future.

With error reporting enabled, you can choose the error types you want to track, including or excluding operating system errors and application errors. The following configuration options are available for operating system errors:

- **Windows operating system**   Enables error tracking when a BSOD occurs.

- **Unplanned machine shutdowns**   Enables error tracking when a machine is powered down via the power button or the reset button, without using the Shut Down command.

For application errors, select Programs. If you want to track only specific applications, click Choose Programs and narrow or expand the list of reporting applications in the Choose Programs dialog.

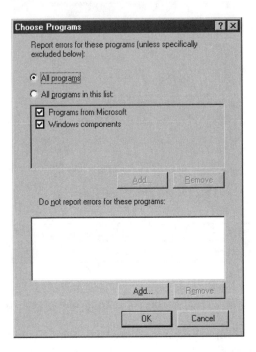

To alter the list of applications included in error reporting, select All Programs In This List. Then take any of the following steps to configure application error reporting:

- Deselect Programs From Microsoft to eliminate applications from error reporting.
- Deselect Windows Components to eliminate programs that are operating system components from error reporting.
- Click Add, and then enter the path to the executable file for an application you want to include in error reporting (or use the Browse button to find the application).

If you want to specifically exclude one or more applications from error reporting, click the Add button at the bottom of the dialog, and then enter the path to the executable file, or click Browse to locate the application.

The option Force Queue Mode For Program Errors refers to the way error reports are displayed. Queue mode displays the ten most recent errors, each in its own window. This lets you pick the errors you want to keep a record of, or send to Microsoft.

Enable Error Reporting in Group Policies

You can also set up error reporting by applying group policies, which offer the additional features you need if you want to send reports to Microsoft or to a network sharepoint. To open the local group policy add-in, choose Start | Run, type **gpedit.mmc**, and click OK. Expand the console pane to Local Computer Policy\Computer Configuration\ Administrative Templates\System\Error Reporting (see Figure 26-10).

The policies are all "not configured," which means that the options set in the System Properties dialog are the current settings. Using group policies to set options for error reporting overrides settings in the System Properties dialog.

The following sections explain the group policies that are available for error reporting.

Display Error Notification

This setting specifies whether users are given the opportunity to report an error. Unlike the configuration options in the System Properties dialog, which only offer error reporting to users who have administrative permissions, this policy applies to any users. After an error, the next user to log on is notified that an error occurred and is given access to details about the error. If the Report Errors setting (covered next) is also enabled, the user can determine whether to report the error. You can disable this setting on servers that don't have interactive users.

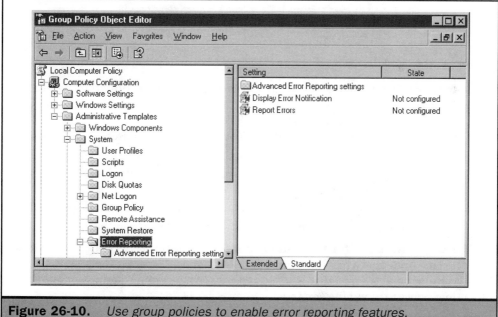

Figure 26-10.   *Use group policies to enable error reporting features.*

Report Errors

This policy controls whether errors are reported to Microsoft or to a corporate file share.

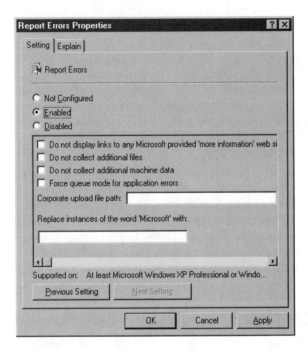

After you enable the policy, the following options are available:

- **Do not display links to any Microsoft provided 'more information' web sites** Controls whether users see links to Microsoft web sites that may have more information about the error message. Select this option if the computer doesn't have an Internet connection, or if you just want to prevent users from traveling to the Microsoft web site.

- **Do not collect additional files** Prevents the collection of additional files to be included in error reports.

- **Do not collect additional machine data** Prevents the system from collecting information about the machine for inclusion in the error reports.

- **Force queue mode for application errors** Means the user is not given the option to create a report when an application error occurs. The error is placed in a queue directory, and the next user who logs on with administrative permissions is offered the chance to report the error.

- **Corporate upload file path** A UNC path to a network sharepoint that collects error reports.

■ **Replace instances of the word 'Microsoft' with** Provides a search-and-replace function for the contents of the error notification dialogs. You can enter your own text (usually your company name) to customize the text in error reporting dialogs.

When you create a network share to collect reports, be sure to click the Permissions button on the Sharing tab and make sure Everyone has Full Control permissions so users can write to the share.

Advanced Error Reporting Settings

Select the Advanced Error Reporting settings object in the console pane to display the available policies, shown in Figure 26-11 and described next:

■ **Default application reporting settings** Offers the option to report application errors. You can select Microsoft applications, Windows components, or both.

■ **List of applications to always report errors** Offers a way to list specific applications for which you want to enable error reporting.

■ **List of applications to never report errors** Offers a way to list specific applications for which you don't want error reporting enabled.

■ **Report operating system errors** Enables error reporting for STOP errors (BSODs).

■ **Report unplanned shutdown events** Enables error reporting when the computer has a dirty shutdown.

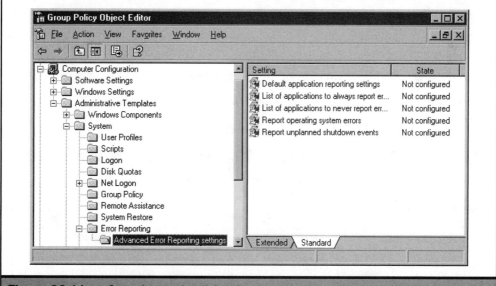

Figure 26-11. *Set advanced policies for the error reporting feature.*

Sending Reports

Most of the time, administrators configure the error reporting feature to send reports to a network sharepoint. After examining the report, an administrator can decide whether it's necessary to forward the report to Microsoft in order to gain technical support to resolve the problem.

When a user logs on after a computer crash, a message dialog such as the one shown in Figure 26-12 appears. To send the error report, click the button labeled Send Error Report.

Collecting and Viewing Reports

If you've used group policies to send error reports to a network sharepoint, each error produces a set of subfolders:

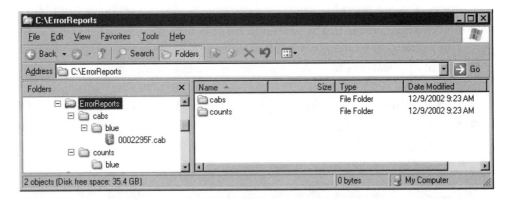

- ■ **Cabs** Holds the files that contain information about the error. These are cabinet files that must be extracted in order to read the contents.

- ■ **Counts** Tracks the number of files that have been delivered to the cabs folder.

After a BSOD, you can examine the files by selecting the cabinet file to display its contents in the right pane.

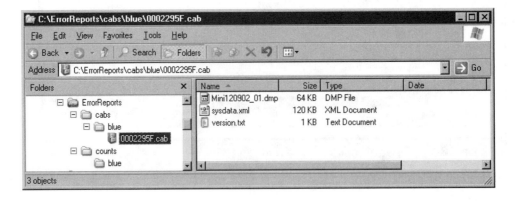

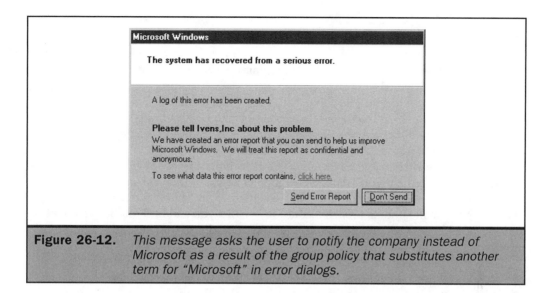

Figure 26-12. *This message asks the user to notify the company instead of Microsoft as a result of the group policy that substitutes another term for "Microsoft" in error dialogs.*

To open a cabinet file, indicate the location to use for extracting the file. You can navigate through the top-level locations to select a specific folder for the extracted files, or you can create a new folder to hold these files.

Unless you configured a group policy to omit sending system files with the error report, the memory dump file is sent to the sharepoint (see the section "Configuring the Dump File Type" earlier in this chapter). To read a dump file, you must download the appropriate application from Microsoft's support site.

Chkdsk

NTFS is a recoverable file system that uses transaction logging and recovery techniques to ensure the consistency of a volume's metadata. An NTFS format creates a set of files to hold the data used to implement the file system structure. NTFS reserves the first 16 records of the Master File Table (MFT) to hold information about these files, and that information is called metadata. Metadata is the data stored on a volume in order to support and manage the file system format, including the data that defines the placement of files and directories on the volume.

NTFS uses transaction logs to record I/O transactions, and then writes the transaction to disk from the cache. If you've used Exchange Server or other transaction-log-based applications, you're probably familiar with this paradigm. (Microsoft has a number of informative white papers on this technology, which you can find on the Microsoft TechNet site.) The write includes the user's data, in addition to the location and other metafile information that's held in the MFT.

If the system fails before the permanent write process completes (generally because of a dirty shutdown due to power failure or user error), NTFS counts on recovery tools, particularly chkdsk.exe, to fix the metadata in the MFT. The recovery tools do not repair or replace user data, only the MFT.

Chkdsk

One of the most important tools for repairing an NTFS volume is chkdsk.exe, a command-line tool that performs disk analysis and disk recovery tasks. (Chkdsk.exe also runs on FAT file systems, but I'm assuming you're using NTFS on all your servers.) In addition to performing repair operations on operating system files, chkdsk also deals with the physical problems on a disk by identifying bad sectors so that the operating system won't attempt to write data to those sectors.

When you run chkdsk from the command line or from the GUI (for example, from a disk's Properties dialog), the program calls .dlls (untfs.dll for NTFS volumes, and ufat.dll for FAT volumes). However, if chkdsk is scheduled to run at the next boot, or automatically runs at bootup after a dirty shutdown, it uses autochk.exe, which is a binary module that contains the verification code for chkdsk. Regardless of the "helper files" it uses, chkdsk performs the same tasks.

Running Chkdsk Manually

You can run chkdsk from the Windows Server 2003 GUI, or from the command line. To use the GUI, right-click a drive's icon in My Computer or Windows Explorer and choose Properties. Move to the Tools tab and click Check Now in the Error-checking section of the dialog. Then choose whether you want to check the file system only or also check the drive for bad sectors.

If you're invoking chkdsk on a system volume, Windows cannot perform the operation, because the volume is in use. A dialog appears to ask whether you want to check the volume during the next boot (see the upcoming section "Autochk.exe").

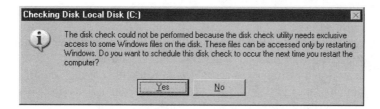

If you're trying to check a nonsystem volume, you're offered the opportunity to dismount the volume (which closes all open handles to the volume). If you don't want to dismount the volume, the same dialog that appears when you try to check a system drive is displayed, so you can opt to run chkdsk on the volume during the next boot.

To run chkdsk from the command line, use the following syntax:

chkdsk [*Volume*:][[*Path*] *FileName*] [**/f**] [**/v**] [**/r**] [**/x**] [**/i**] [**/c**] [**/l**[:*Size*]]

where:

/f fixes errors on the disk, which requires that the disk be locked. If chkdsk cannot lock the drive, a message appears to ask if you want to check the drive the next time you restart the computer.

/v runs chkdsk in verbose mode, displaying the name of each file as the disk is checked.

/r locates bad sectors and recovers readable information, which requires locking the disk.

/x forces the volume to dismount first, if necessary. All open handles to the drive are invalidated, and the **/f** switch is automatically invoked.

/i is used only with NTFS. This switch performs an index-only check on NTFS volumes. This takes less time than a full chkdsk operation and can be performed interactively.

/c is used only with NTFS. This switch skips checking of cycles within the folder structure, which reduces the amount of time needed to run chkdsk. This switch will not fix problems arising from cycles within the folder structure, but those problems aren't very common.

/l[:*Size*] is used only with NTFS. This switch changes the size of the log file to the size you specify. If you omit the *Size* parameter, **/l** displays the current size.

Note *The /c, /x, and /i switches were first introduced in Windows 2000, so they're new to you if you're upgrading from Windows NT.*

Autochk.exe

Autochk.exe controls the behavior of chkdsk when chkdsk runs at bootup, either because it has been manually scheduled to run during the next boot or is run automatically during the next boot due to the presence of a "dirty bit" on the volume.

The default switch for autochk is an asterisk (autochk *), which means "check for a dirty bit and run chkdsk if you find one." When you have a dirty shutdown, the system records the fact by writing a bit to the system files, where the kernel will find it during the next boot. Autochk then automatically launches chkdsk /f.

When you attempt to run chkdsk on a locked disk, and respond Yes when asked whether you want to run chckdsk during the next boot, the value **autocheck autochk /p\??\C:** is added to the BootExecute registry item in HKEY_LOCAL_MACHINE\ System\CurrentControlSet\Control\Session Manager.

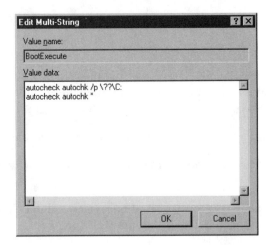

To force chkdsk to run, the system does not set the "dirty bit" on the volume; instead, it adds this value to the registry item, which the OS kernel reads during startup.

If you change your mind after you tell the system to run chkdsk on the next boot, open Regedit, go to the subkey referenced here, and change the value of the BootExecute registry item to remove the value autocheck autochk /p\??\C:. Be sure to leave the value autochk * intact.

Chkntfs.exe

Every time the operating system boots, the kernel calls autochk.exe to scan all volumes to see if a volume dirty bit is set. If a dirty bit exists, autochk performs an immediate chkdsk /f on that volume. However, it isn't an automatic given that a dirty shutdown causes file system errors that need to be repaired by chkdsk. For very large volumes, chkdsk could take hours to complete its tasks, so it's often practical to run chkdsk manually when the computer isn't needed by users.

You can use the command-line utility chkntfs.exe to control chkdsk, using the following syntax:

chkntfs *volume*: [**/d**] [**/t**[:*time*]] [**/x** *volume*:] [**/c** *volume*:]

where:

volume: specifies the drive letter (followed by a colon), mount point, or volume name. Using this switch displays a message that identifies the file system of the specified volume, and also displays a message indicating whether the volume has a dirty bit.

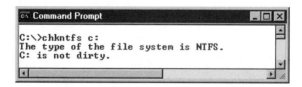

/d restores all **chkntfs** default settings, including checking all volumes for a dirty bit during operating system startup.

/t[:*time*] changes the autochk.exe initiation countdown time to the amount of time you specify. It you don't specify *:time*, the **/t** switch displays the current countdown time.

/x *volume*: excludes the specified volume from being checked when the computer starts, even if the volume is marked with a dirty bit. This switch overwrites the previous entry every time you use it, so if you want to exclude multiple volumes, you must list all of them in one command. For example, to exclude both C: and D:, enter **chkntfs /x c: d:**.

/c *volume*: schedules the specified volume to be checked the next time the computer starts. To use this switch, you must reset the defaults to clear any previous chkntfs commands, exclude all volumes from being checked, and then schedule automatic file checking on the target volume. For example, to schedule automatic file checking on E:, enter the following commands:

```
chkntfs /d (resets defaults)
chkntfs /x c: d: e: (excludes automatic checking on all volumes)
chkntfs /c e: (schedules automatic checking on e:)
```

The Complete Reference

Appendix

Internet Information Services 6 (IIS 6)

925

If you're planning to use Windows Server 2003 for hosting web sites and dynamic web applications, you'll find that there have been some significant changes to Internet Information Services (IIS) in the new platform. Version 6 of IIS includes enhancements in the areas of security, reliability, scalability, manageability, and performance. Understanding these changes is important if you want to get the most out of the new version.

We've relegated the discussion of IIS to an appendix because in Windows Server 2003, IIS is usually an optional component that is not installed by default. The exception is Web Edition, which installs IIS and many of its subcomponents by default. Web Edition is a specialized product that is only available preinstalled through OEM channels, so our focus here is on Standard and Enterprise Editions of Windows Server 2003.

New Features of IIS 6

We'll begin with a brief overview of the new features of IIS 6, focusing on improvements in architecture, security, and manageability. After that we'll explain how to perform basic tasks such as creating and configuring web sites and applications, including how to implement the various new features supported by the platform.

If after reading this appendix you want to learn more about IIS 6, get a copy of IIS 6 Administration *from McGraw-Hill/Osborne, which includes comprehensive coverage of all aspects of IIS 6 and numerous walkthroughs for hands-on practice in administering the new platform.*

Enhanced Architecture

Perhaps the most radical change in this version of IIS is the architecture. The previous version—IIS 5 on the Windows 2000 Server platform—allowed web applications to run in any of three different levels of application protection:

- **Low (IIS Process)**   The application runs in process, that is, with the core IIS Admin (inetinfo.exe) process itself.
- **Medium (Pooled)**   The application runs with other applications as a pooled process within a COM+ host process named dllhost.exe.
- **High (Isolated)**   The application runs out-of-process alone within its own host process dllhost.exe.

The IIS 5 model had the following limitations:

- If an application with low protection failed, it could cause inetinfo.exe to hang, thus bringing down the entire web server.
- Applications with high protection had high overhead and performed poorly compared to pooled applications.

- Only one pool of applications was supported, limiting the scalability of the server for hosting web applications.

To address this limitation, the architecture of IIS 6 has been redesigned so that all applications run as pooled processes, with multiple pools being supported instead of just one. This means that user-developed code does not run in process, so faulty applications can no longer bring down the web server. Let's see how all this works.

Isolation Modes

IIS 6 has a dual architecture that can run in one of two modes:

- **IIS 5 isolation mode**   This mode emulates IIS 5 so that applications developed for the earlier Windows 2000 Server platform can run without problems on Windows Server 2003.
- **Worker process isolation mode**   This mode supports all the architectural enhancements of IIS 6, including application pools, web gardens, health monitoring, worker process recycling, and processor affinity.

If you perform a clean installation of Windows Server 2003 and then install the IIS 6 components, your server will run in worker process isolation mode. If you upgrade a Windows 2000 Server machine running IIS 5, your server will run in IIS 5 isolation mode. If you decide to perform an upgrade, test your web applications after the upgrade; if they run properly, change to worker process isolation mode to take advantage of the new features in this mode.

Application Pools

In IIS 5, applications ran by default with Medium (Pooled) protection within a host process called svchost.exe. In IIS 6 in worker process isolation mode, applications can be grouped together into multiple pools called application pools, with each application pool serviced by one or more worker processes (instances of w3wp.exe). Each application pool can be configured separately, and applications can be moved from one pool to another. The result is increased reliability because a failed application can only affect other applications within the same pool and not applications in other pools.

Kernel Mode Queuing

To improve the performance of IIS, handling of HTTP requests has been moved to a new kernel mode component called the HTTP Listener (http.sys), which resides within the TCP/IP stack of the server. Incoming requests are queued for handling, with each application pool having its own separate queue. This increases the reliability of IIS because incoming requests continue to be queued even if an application fails. Once the application is brought online again, requests are drawn from the queue and nothing is lost.

 Note   *IIS logging is now performed at the kernel level, using http.sys for increased performance.*

Web Gardens

Another new feature of IIS 6 is support for web gardens. A web garden is an application pool serviced by multiple worker processes that share the load and provide fault tolerance in case one process terminates unexpectedly. Web gardens also increase the scalability of IIS 6, allowing a single server to simultaneously host thousands of applications and making it an excellent hosting platform for service provider environments.

Worker Process Recycling

Applications sometimes contain faulty code that causes memory leaks and other error conditions. To keep such applications running, earlier versions of IIS had to be rebooted periodically; in IIS 6 a new feature called *worker process recycling* eliminates this need. Administrators can configure the worker process servicing a buggy application to restart periodically to prevent memory leaks from reaching a critical level and crashing the application. Recycling can also be configured to start a new worker process before the old process is terminated, a feature called *overlapped recycling* that ensures uninterrupted service from the client's perspective.

Demand Start and Idle Time Out

To conserve valuable processor and memory resources, IIS 6 implements demand start. With this feature, the worker process associated with an application pool is not started until the application receives the first HTTP request. IIS 6 also supports idle time out, a feature that shuts down idle worker processes after a configurable time interval to release unused resources for other processes to use.

Health Monitoring, Orphaning, and Rapid Fail Protection

Worker processes are managed by the Web Administration Service (WAS), a new feature of IIS 6 that is implemented as a component of the WWW Service. In addition to recycling worker processes, WAS pings worker processes periodically to monitor their health. When a worker process is blocked and fails to respond, WAS terminates the process and starts a new one to replace it. Alternatively, WAS can be configured to leave the unresponsive process running while WAS starts a replacement. This is useful in a development scenario where a debugger could be connected to the orphaned process to determine what went wrong. If an application is so buggy that its worker process hangs repeatedly, a feature called *rapid fail protection* can be used to take the application pool out of service until the problem is resolved.

Processor Affinity

An additional feature of IIS 6 is enhanced support for symmetric multiprocessing (SMP) hardware platforms. Using processor affinity, individual worker processes can be assigned to specific CPUs to increase performance for large mission-critical applications.

XML Metabase

The metabase, the file that stores IIS configuration information, has been changed from its binary format in earlier versions to a plain-text XML file in IIS 6. This change makes the metabase easier to edit (you can use a simple text editor like Notepad) and results in faster restart times for IIS. The metabase also includes the following new features:

- **Edit-while-running**   The capability to edit the metabase directly while IIS is running.

- **Metabase history**   A feature that tracks all changes made to the metabase and simplifies restoring IIS when you make configuration errors.

- **Server-independent backup**   By creating a password-protected backup of the metabase, you can copy an entire IIS configuration to another machine, enabling you to easily clone IIS configurations for faster deployment.

Enhanced Security

Security is the second biggest improvement in IIS 6 over previous versions. IIS is no longer installed by default during a clean installation of the operating system; when you do install IIS, it is configured by default in a locked-down state that allows only static content to be served. Before you can serve clients dynamic content, you must enable features like ASP, ASP.NET, CGI, and ISAPI so that web applications will run. This means that you can enable only the components you need and leave the others disabled, which is a big improvement in security for the platform. Dynamic content features are enabled or disabled using the new Web Service Extensions (WSE) node in IIS Manager, which we'll look at shortly.

Other Security Improvements

The new platform includes other improvements in security:

- The low-privileged NetworkService identity is used as the default context in which worker processes run, as opposed to the high-privileged LocalSystem account used by svchost.exe in IIS 5.

- The account under which worker processes run can be configured manually, which enables administrators to employ separate security contexts for different application pools to provide greater security and reliability.

- Support is included for two new authentication methods: advanced digest authentication, which can work through firewalls and proxy servers, and .NET Passport authentication, which allows users to use Passport as a single sign-on service for web services running on IIS.

- Requests for files with unknown extensions are now rejected by default, though wildcard mappings can also be configured to handle such extensions.

■ Anonymous users can no longer run executables, like cmd.exe, that are located within the system folder.

■ Anonymous users are denied write access to web content by default (the IUSR_*computername* account has the Deny Write permission configured).

■ Group Policy can be used to prevent users from installing IIS on machines they have access to.

Enhanced Manageability

In addition to the IIS Manager console in Administrative Tools, there are a number of other ways to efficiently manage IIS 6 machines:

■ **Remote Desktop**   Previously known on the Windows 2000 Server platform as Terminal Services in Remote Administration Mode, Remote Desktop is installed by default on Windows Server 2003 and can be enabled by selecting a single checkbox on the Remote tab of the System utility in Control Panel. Remote Desktop was discussed in Chapter 3 of this book.

■ **Web Interface for Server Administration (WISA)**   By installing the Remote Administration (HTML) component of IIS 6, you can use a web browser like Internet Explorer to administer many aspects of IIS (and some general aspects of Windows Server 2003) from remote locations. WISA is implemented as an ASP application and is installed by default on Web Edition.

■ **Windows Management Instrumentation (WMI)**   IIS 6 includes a built-in WMI provider that allows you to write scripts for managing most aspects of IIS from the command line. A number of such scripts are included with IIS 6 in the \system32 folder and can be used for creating web and FTP sites, creating virtual directories, enabling or disabling web service extensions, creating metabase backups, and more. You can run these scripts from a command-line session on the IIS machine; from a remote machine using Remote Desktop; or using Telnet.

Common Administration Tasks

Let's look at how to perform some basic administration tasks on IIS 6 and implement many of the new features supported by the platform.

Install IIS

The easiest way to install IIS is to use the Manage Your Server page, which automatically opens whenever you boot your computer. If this page is not open you can open it and install IIS by adding the Application Server role. To add the Application Server role, follow these steps:

1. Insert the Windows Server 2003 product CD into the CD-ROM drive to make the Setup files available.

2. Click Start and select Manage Your Server from the top of the Start menu.

3. Click the Add or Remove a Role link to open the Configure Your Server Wizard.

4. Click Next to test the network connection.

5. Select Application Server (IIS, ASP.NET) from the list of available roles and click Next.

6. Select optional IIS components like ASP.NET or FrontPage Server Extensions if you want to install these as well.

7. Click Next to review the summary of components you are about to install.

8. Click Next to install and configure IIS on your machine.

Manage IIS

Once IIS is installed you can manage it by either:

- Clicking the Manage This Application Server link in Manage Your Server, which opens an Application Server console containing snap-ins for .NET Framework 1.1 Configuration, Internet Information Services (IIS) Manager, and Component Services

- Selecting Internet Information Services (IIS) Manager from Administrative Tools to open the IIS Manager console by itself

To perform the remaining tasks discussed in this appendix, we'll use the second approach and assume that IIS Manager (see Figure A-1) is already open.

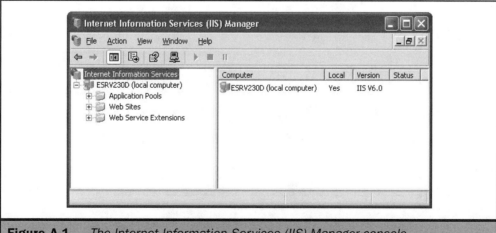

Figure A-1.   *The Internet Information Services (IIS) Manager console*

Enable Web Service Extensions

By default, when you install IIS it can only serve clients static content. If you plan to host dynamic content such as Active Server Pages (ASP) applications, you must enable the associated DLLs to support that content. For example, to enable the ASP extension so that you can host and run ASP applications on your server, follow these steps:

1. Select Web Service Extensions node under the IIS server node (see Figure A-2).

2. With the Extended tab selected, select the Active Server Pages extension from the list.

3. Click Allow.

Create a Web Site

Although you can use the Default Web Site for hosting ASP or ASP.NET applications, it's generally better to create new web sites for these applications. (Reserve the Default Web Site, which listens on all unassigned IP addresses, for hosting a sample under construction page that displays your company logo and contact information.) Before you create the new sites, make sure you have assigned the necessary additional IP

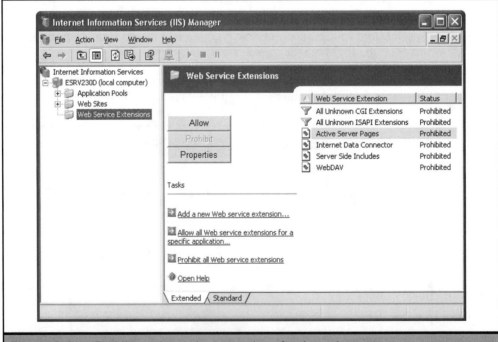

Figure A-2.   *Enabling web service extensions for dynamic content*

addresses to your server (unless you plan to use host header names for identifying your web sites to clients).

To create a new web site using IIS Manager, follow these steps:

1. Right-click on the Web Sites node and select New | Web Site.

2. Click Next at the opening screen of the Web Site Creation Wizard.

3. Type a descriptive name like Sample Web Site in the Description box and click Next.

4. Select a unique IP address for the site or specify a host header name and click Next.

5. Select a content directory for the site or create a new one. If you don't want anonymous users to have access to your site, clear the checkbox. Then, click Next.

6. Specify web permissions for the site. By default Read and Run Scripts are allowed and all others are denied. Note that web permissions are different from NTFS permissions and apply equally to all clients that access the site (don't forget to configure proper NTFS permissions on your content directory afterwards to secure your site's content).

7. Click Next and then Finish.

The newly created web site is now visible in IIS Manager (see Figure A-3). We'll add some content to our site in a moment.

Tip   *You can also create a new site using the iisweb.vbs script found in \system32.*

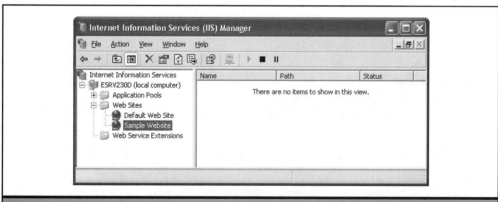

Figure A-3.   *New web site called Sample Web Site*

Configure a Web Site

Once you've created your site, you can configure it by opening its properties sheet. Just right-click on the node for the site and select Properties (see Figure A-4). Then use the various tabs on this sheet for configuring web site identity, connection limits, logging, bandwidth throttling, home directory, web permissions, application settings, default documents, authentication methods, IP address restrictions, custom error messages, and more. For a comprehensive explanation of the various web site configuration options, see *IIS 6 Administration* from McGraw-Hill/Osborne.

Create an Application

Let's create a simple ASP application that does something we can test, such as display the current time on the server. The following script will do just this:

```
<html>
<head>
<title>Sample ASP Application</title>
</head>
<body>
<%
Dim strMessage
strMessage = "Sample ASP Application"
Response.Write (strMessage)
Response.Write ("<hr>")
Response.Write ("The time is " & Time())
%>
</body>
</html>
```

Type the preceding script into Notepad and save it with the name **default.asp** in the home directory you specified for your new web site. Refresh the view in IIS Manager by pressing F5, right-click on the Sample Web Site node, and then select Browse to test whether the application works (see Figure A-5).

By default IIS configures the new application to have the same name as the Default Application, so let's change this:

1. Right-click on the Sample Web Site node and select Properties.

2. Select the Home Directory tab.

3. Delete Default Application and replace it with **Sample Application**. Then, click Apply.

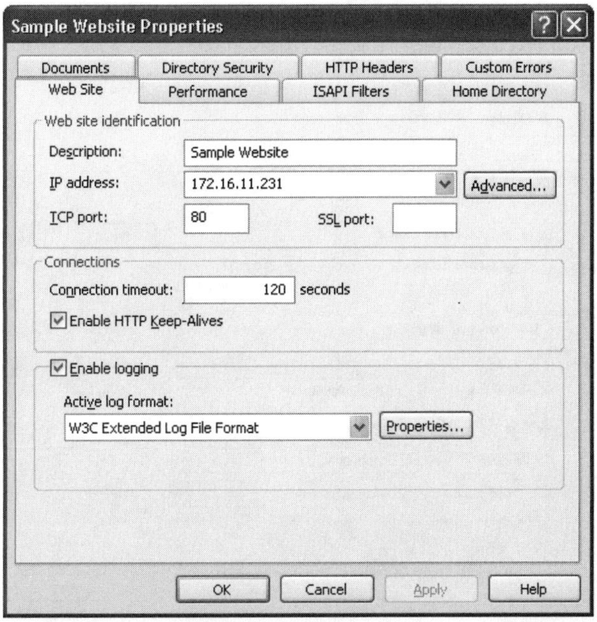

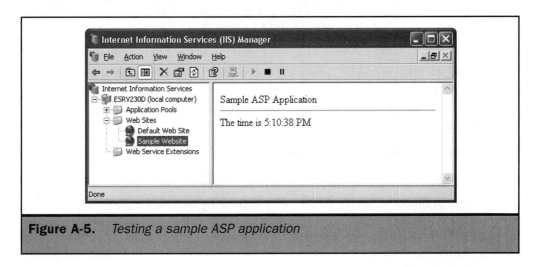

Figure A-4.   *Configuring a web site*

You now have an ASP application named Sample Application whose application starting point is the root directory of the Sample Web Site (see Figure A-6).

Figure A-5.   *Testing a sample ASP application*

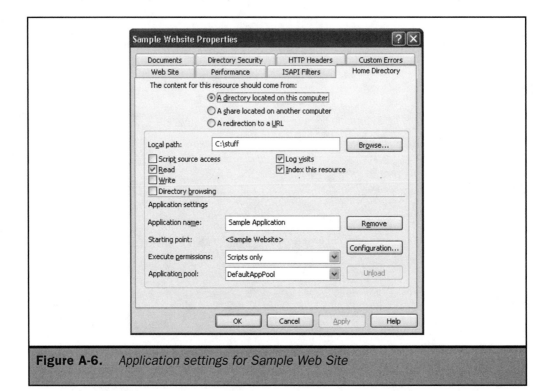

Figure A-6. *Application settings for Sample Web Site*

Create an Application Pool

Let's isolate the new application by placing it in a separate application pool. When IIS is running in worker process isolation mode it has a default application pool named DefaultAppPool. If we select this pool in IIS Manager we will have two applications running in it (see Figure A-7):

- The Default Application whose starting point is the root directory of the Default Web Site
- The new Sample Application whose starting point is the root directory of the Sample Web Site

To create a new application pool named Second Pool, follow these steps:

1. Right-click on the Application Pools node and select New | Application Pool.

2. Type **Second Pool** as the ID for the new pool. By default the pool will be assigned generic settings that you can configure later (or you can choose to inherit the settings of an existing pool like the DefaultAppPool instead).

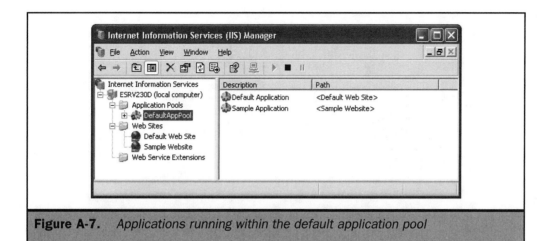

Figure A-7.   *Applications running within the default application pool*

3. Click OK. The new pool is created and appears under the Application Pools node in IIS Manager.

Now let's move the Sample Application to Second Pool:

1. Right-click on the Sample Web Site node and select Properties.

2. Select the Home Directory tab.

3. Change the setting "Application pool" from DefaultAppPool to Second Pool.

4. Click OK.

IIS Manager should now display the Sample Application within the Second Pool (see Figure A-8).

Having moved the application to a separate pool, let's configure recycling, health monitoring, rapid fail protection, idle time out, and other features of the application pool. The following sections walk you through these procedures.

Configure Recycling

To configure recycling of all worker processes servicing applications within the Second Pool, follow these steps:

1. Right-click on the Second Pool node under Application Pools and select Properties.

2. Select the Recycling tab (see Figure A-9).

3. Configure recycling settings as desired.

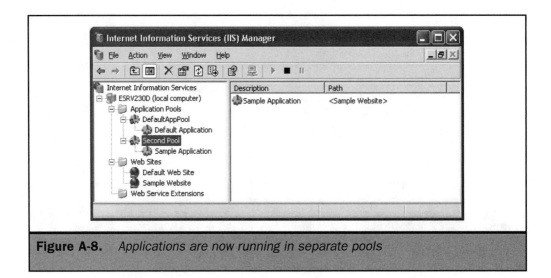

Figure A-8.   *Applications are now running in separate pools*

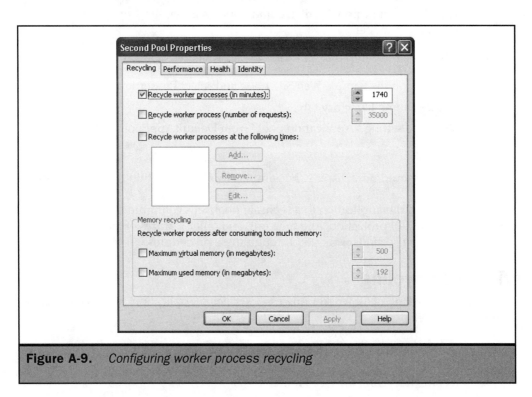

Figure A-9.   *Configuring worker process recycling*

Note that you can initiate worker process recycling based on the following parameters:

- Time interval since last recycle event
- Number of requests serviced
- At specified times
- When too much memory has been consumed (memory leak)

You can also force recycling to occur at any time by right-clicking on the application pool and selecting Recycle.

Configure Idle Time Out

To configure worker processes to shut down after they've been idle for a period of time, follow these steps:

1. Right-click on the Second Pool node under Application Pools and select Properties.

2. Select the Performance tab (see Figure A-10).

3. Configure idle time out as desired.

By default, worker processes are shut down after being idle for 20 minutes so that memory and processor resources on the machine can be reclaimed for other applications.

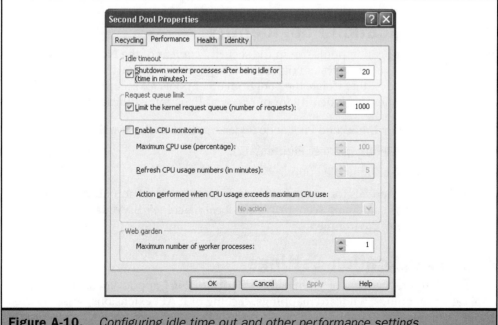

Figure A-10. *Configuring idle time out and other performance settings*

Create a Web Garden

By default, IIS creates one worker process to service applications within each application pool. If your application is resource intensive or you want to provide fault tolerance for its operation, you can create a web garden, an application pool serviced by multiple worker processes. To create a web garden, follow these steps:

1. Right-click on the Second Pool node under Application Pools and select Properties.
2. Select the Performance tab (see Figure A-10 again).
3. Under Web Garden change the number of worker processes servicing the pool to the desired number.

Configure Health Monitoring

By default, health monitoring is enabled on all application pools, with IIS pinging worker processes to ensure they're working. You can enable or disable this feature on the Health tab by following these steps:

1. Right-click on the Second Pool node under Application Pools and select Properties.
2. Select the Health tab (see Figure A-11).
3. Select or clear the checkbox to enable or disable health monitoring for the pool.

You can also use the Health tab to configure settings for rapid fail protection.

Configure Application Pool Identity

By default, all application pools run in the security context of the NetworkService identity, which has very few system rights. You may want to change this for a particular pool, for example to further isolate the pool from other pools for security reasons. To change the application pool identity for our Second Pool, follow these steps:

1. Right-click on the Second Pool node under Application Pools and select Properties.
2. Select the Identity tab (see Figure A-12).
3. Select the Configurable option.
4. Specify credentials for an account or browse to select an account from Active Directory (in a domain scenario) or the local machine's SAM database (in a workgroup environment).

Configure Application Settings

You can configure a variety of settings for ASP or ASP.NET applications, including application mappings, wildcard mappings, caching of ISAPI extensions, session state, buffering, parent paths, and debugging and script error settings. It's beyond the scope

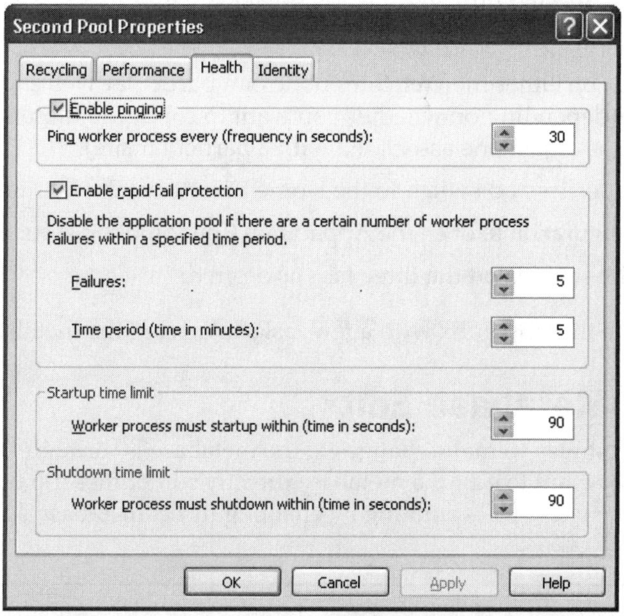

Figure A-11.   *Configuring health monitoring and rapid fail protection*

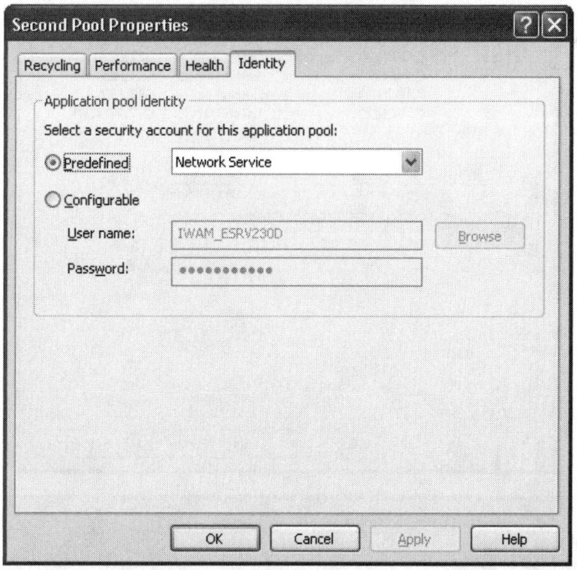

Figure A-12.   *Configuring application pool identity*

of this appendix to discuss how these work, but so you know how to access these settings try this:

1. Right-click on either the Web Sites node or a particular web site node in IIS Manager (depending on whether you want to configure these settings for all applications or just one associated with a particular site).

2. Select Properties and switch to the Home Directory tab (see Figure A-6 again).

3. Click Configuration to open the Application Configuration sheet (see Figure A-13).

4. Modify the settings on the three tabs as desired.

We'll conclude this appendix with a few tasks involving the metabase.

Enable Direct Metabase Edit

Although the safest way to make changes to the metabase is through the IIS Manager interface, you may want to edit the metabase directly sometimes. IIS 6 allows you to do this in real time while IIS is running by enabling direct metabase editing (also called

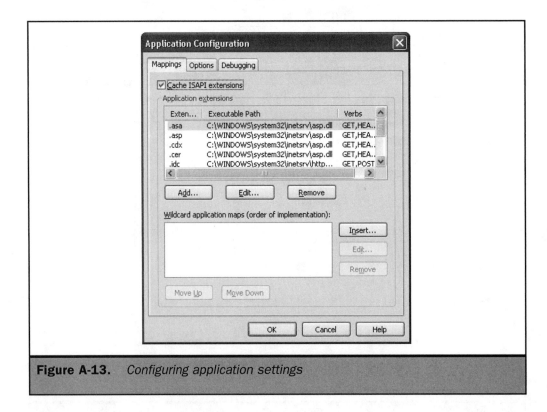

Figure A-13. *Configuring application settings*

edit-while-running) on your server. To enable direct metabase editing, follow these steps:

1. Right-click on the node in IIS Manager that represents the server itself.
2. Select Properties to open the properties sheet for the server.
3. Select the checkbox labeled Enable Direct Metabase Edit (see Figure A-14).
4. Click OK.

You can also do this from the command line by editing the metabase itself, but you must use the iisreset command to briefly stop and start IIS, which results in service interruption. To enable edit-while-running from the command line, follow these steps:

1. Open a command-prompt window and use iisreset to stop all IIS services:

```
C:\ >iisreset /stop
Attempting stop...
Internet services successfully stopped
```

2. Use Windows Explorer to find the metabase configuration file Metabase.xml in the \system32\Inetsrv directory.

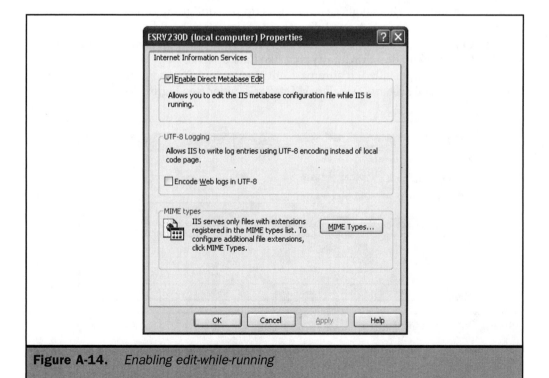

Figure A-14.   *Enabling edit-while-running*

3. Right-click on Metabase.xml and select Open With | Notepad.

4. Find the line `EnableEditWhileRunning="0"` and change this to `EnableEditWhileRunning="1"`.

5. Save the changes to Metabase.xml.

6. Return to the command prompt and use iisreset to start IIS again:

```
C:\ >iisreset /start
Attempting start...
Internet services successfully started
```

Note that the iisreset command can also be used to restart remote IIS machines from the command line. Type **iisreset /?** for full syntax for this command.

Only experienced administrators should edit the metabase directly, as a single error in XML syntax may prevent IIS services from starting.

Back Up the Metabase

IIS 6 automatically creates metabase backups in the form of history files, but you should also manually back up the metabase periodically to ensure recovery from a system failure. Note that backing up the metabase only backs up IIS configuration information, and not actual web site content. A good disaster recovery plan should also include regular backups of all data on your server, including its system state information. To do this, use Windows Backup or a third-party tool like Backup Exec from Veritas.

When IIS is first installed, it automatically creates an initial configuration backup and saves it in the \system32\Inetsrv\MetaBack folder (see Figure A-15). If needed,

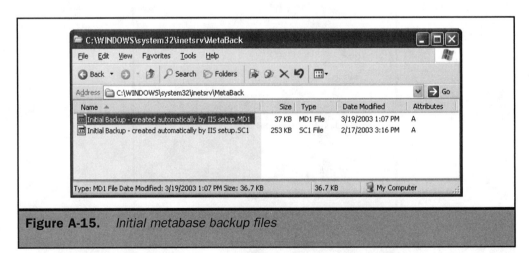

Figure A-15. *Initial metabase backup files*

you can use this backup later to restore IIS to its immediate post-installation state. Note that two files are backed up:

- The metabase configuration file (Metabase.xml) is backed up as an *.MD1 file.
- The metabase schema file (Mbschema.xml) is backed up as an *.SC1 file.

To manually back up the metabase at any time using IIS Manager, follow these steps:

1. Right-click on the node in IIS Manager that represents the server itself.
2. Select All Tasks | Backup/Restore Configuration.
3. All existing metabase backups are displayed in the Configuration Backup/ Restore dialog box (see Figure A-16), including

   - The initial configuration backups that were automatically created when you installed IIS and saved in the \Inetsrv\MetaBack folder
   - Any backups you manually created, also saved in the \Inetsrv\MetaBack folder
   - Metabase history files created automatically by IIS and saved in the \Inetsrv\History folder

   The list of backups displayed in the Configuration Backup/Restore dialog box is thus a merge of the contents of the History and MetaBack folders.

4. Click Create Backup and specify a name for your backup set. You can also optionally specify a password, which is required if you plan to restore your metabase backup on a different machine.
5. Click OK to create the new backup. The result is an *.MD0 and an *.SC0 file located in the MetaBack folder.

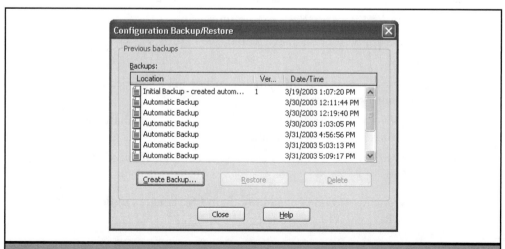

Figure A-16. *Configuration Backup/Restore displaying metabase backups*

Note that the initial configuration backup created automatically when IIS is installed is not encrypted; therefore it is useless if your server fatally crashes and you have to reinstall the operating system on it. Immediately after installing the IIS components on your machine, you should manually create a second, encrypted configuration backup. Creating encrypted backups takes longer than unencrypted ones, and the metabase is locked during the backup process to prevent modifications from occurring.

You can also back up the metabase using the iisback.vbs script found in the \system32 folder:

```
C:\>iisback /backup /b mybackup190303 /e mypassword
Connecting to server ...Done.
Backup mybackup190303 version NEXT_VERSION has been CREATED.
You can also use iisback.vbs to list the backups you've created: \
C:\>iisback /list
Connecting to server ...Done.
Backup Name                           Version #      Date/Time
==================================================
Initial Backup - created automatically by IIS setup 1 3/19/2003 1:07:20 PM
mybackup190303                          0               3/19/2003 4:30:23 PM
```

Restore the Metabase

It's easy to restore the metabase from the backup we've just created. To verify that it works we need to make a change, so delete the Sample Web Site you created earlier by right-clicking on its node in IIS Manager and choosing Delete. Now follow these steps:

1. Right-click on the node in IIS Manager that represents the server itself.

2. Select All Tasks | Backup/Restore Configuration.

3. Select the backup you previously created (see Figure A-17).

4. Click Restore.

5. A message will appear indicating that IIS needs to be stopped and that a restore may take some time. Click OK.

6. If you specified a password when you backed up the metabase previously, you'll be prompted to enter it again during the restore.

7. When you are notified that the operation has completed successfully, click OK and then Close.

Your Sample Web Site should be visible again in IIS Manager, indicating that the restore was successful.

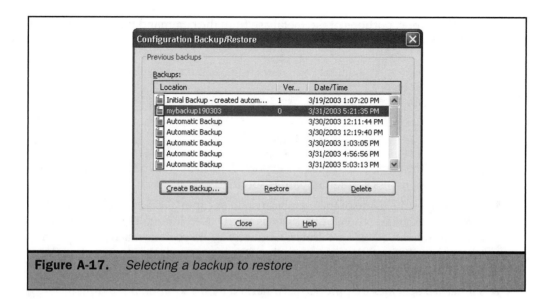

Figure A-17.   *Selecting a backup to restore*

 You can also use the preceding procedure to restore from a history file.

Export the Metabase

You can export and import selected portions of the metabase such as the configuration information for a specific web site or virtual directory or even the configuration of all web sites on your machine. The exported file will be an XML file that can later be imported back into your machine or into another machine with IIS 6 installed. You can also use the export feature to create a metabase template to copy or "clone" web site configurations to multiple IIS machines so that they all have the same configuration.

Note, however, that metabase export is not intended to replace regular backups of the metabase. This is because metabase export can be used only to back up the metabase configuration file and not the metabase schema file. Furthermore, metabase export files do not include encrypted properties present in metabase backup files.

To use IIS Manager to export the configuration of your Sample Web Site, follow these steps:

1. Right-click the Sample Web Site and select All Tasks | Save Configuration to a File.

2. Specify a name for the export file and select the encryption option so you can later try importing the file into a different IIS 6 machine.

3. Click OK.

You can also export portions of the metabase from the command line using the iiscnfg.vbs script as follows:

```
C:\>iiscnfg /export /f test.xml /sp /lm/w3svc/1226210006 /inherited /children
Connecting to server ...Done.
Configuration exported from /lm/w3svc/1 to file export_test_2.xml.
```

The syntax of this command is as follows:

- /f assigns the name text.xml to the export file, which is saved by default in the C: drive root unless a different path is specified.

- /sp specifies the name of the metabase node to export, which here is /lm/ w3svc/1226210006 where 1226210006 is the ID used internally to identify the Sample Web Site (this is generated randomly by IIS so your machine may show something different). You can view the IDs for your web sites by selecting the Web Sites node in IIS Manager.

- /inherited specifies that properties inherited by the location node from its parent node should explicitly be included in the export file.

- /children specifies that subkeys should be recursively added to the export file.

Import the Metabase

To import your previously created metabase export file to the same machine, first delete the Sample Web Site for testing purposes, and then follow these steps:

1. Right-click the Web Sites node and select New | Web Site From File.
2. Click Browse in the Import Configuration dialog box and select the export file you created earlier.
3. Click Read File. Sample Web Site should appear in the Location listbox.
4. Select Sample Web Site and click OK.
5. Enter the password you used to encrypt the export file and click OK.
6. The Sample Web Site should appear in IIS Manager in a stopped state. To start it, right-click on its node and select Start.

Importing a metabase export file to a different machine is a little more complicated, as you must first perform the following tasks:

- Change or remove any machine-specific information from the export file.
- Create any necessary folders on the target machine such as home directories for each web site being imported.

- Modify any file system paths in metabase properties if these are different on the target machine.

- Delete any properties referencing IUSR or IWAM accounts (they will be different on the target computer).

- Delete any AdminACL properties (they are machine-specific and cannot be manually modified).

- Delete any properties specifying passwords (they are machine-specific and cannot be manually modified).

Note   *You can also use iiscnfg.vbs to import a metabase export file.*

Index

Symbols and Numbers

" (double quotation marks), using with cluster.exe utility, 814

* (asterisk), using with autochk.exe program, 922

- (hyphen), using with .reg files, 127

/?, getting help on commands with, 886

/? switch, running scripts with, 764–765

/4 parameter for dir command, description of, 215

: (colon) in registry path, meaning of, 125

= (equal sign) in registry path, meaning of, 125

[] (square brackets) in .reg files, meaning of, 125

\ (backslash) in registry path, meaning of, 125

0-3 dump types, explanations of, 902

1-7 values for DHCP message types, explanations of, 385

0x0000000A STOP error, explanation of, 906

0x0000001E STOP error, explanation of, 907

0x00000024 STOP error, explanation of, 907

0x0000002E STOP error, explanation of, 907–908

0x00000050 STOP error, explanation of, 908

0x00000058 STOP error, explanation of, 908

0x00000076 STOP error, explanation of, 909

0x00000077 STOP error, explanation of, 909

0x00000079 STOP error, explanation of, 909–1401

0x0000007A STO error, explanation of, 908

0x0000007B STOP error, explanation of, 908–909

0x0000007F STOP error, explanation of, 909

0xC000021A STOP error, explanation of, 910

0xC0000221 STOP error, explanation of, 911

2003 DNS. *See also* DNS (Domain Name System)
client-side registry entries in, 405–410
improvements made to, 402–405

A

A and AAAA records in DNS, explanations of, 399–400

A parameter
in multi() syntax, 159
in scsi() syntax, 160
in x86 ARC path statements, 158

/A parameter for dir command, description of, 214

/a parameter of Winnt.exe, explanation of, 26–27

/A switch for del or erase commands, description of, 214

AAAA resource record type in IPv6, explanation of, 338

ABRs (area border routers), role in OSPF routing protocol, 431–432

access methods
ADSL (Asymmetric Digital Subscriber Line), 443
ATM (Asynchronous Transfer Mode), 444
ISDN (Integrated Services Digital Network), 442–443
for RRAS (Routing and Remote Access Service), 442–444
X.25, 443

C

U

V

INTERNATIONAL CONTACT INFORMATION

AUSTRALIA
McGraw-Hill Book Company Australia Pty. Ltd.
TEL +61-2-9900-1800
FAX +61-2-9878-8881
http://www.mcgraw-hill.com.au
books-it_sydney@mcgraw-hill.com

CANADA
McGraw-Hill Ryerson Ltd.
TEL +905-430-5000
FAX +905-430-5020
http://www.mcgraw-hill.ca

GREECE, MIDDLE EAST, & AFRICA
(Excluding South Africa)
McGraw-Hill Hellas
TEL +30-210-6560-990
TEL +30-210-6560-993
TEL +30-210-6560-994
FAX +30-210-6545-525

MEXICO (Also serving Latin America)
McGraw-Hill Interamericana Editores S.A. de C.V.
TEL +525-117-1583
FAX +525-117-1589
http://www.mcgraw-hill.com.mx
fernando_castellanos@mcgraw-hill.com

SINGAPORE (Serving Asia)
McGraw-Hill Book Company
TEL +65-6863-1580
FAX +65-6862-3354
http://www.mcgraw-hill.com.sg
mghasia@mcgraw-hill.com

SOUTH AFRICA
McGraw-Hill South Africa
TEL +27-11-622-7512
FAX +27-11-622-9045
robyn_swanepoel@mcgraw-hill.com

SPAIN
McGraw-Hill/Interamericana de España, S.A.U.
TEL +34-91-180-3000
FAX +34-91-372-8513
http://www.mcgraw-hill.es
professional@mcgraw-hill.es

UNITED KINGDOM, NORTHERN, EASTERN, & CENTRAL EUROPE
McGraw-Hill Education Europe
TEL +44-1-628-502500
FAX +44-1-628-770224
http://www.mcgraw-hill.co.uk
computing_europe@mcgraw-hill.com

ALL OTHER INQUIRIES Contact:
McGraw-Hill/Osborne
TEL +1-510-420-7700
FAX +1-510-420-7703
http://www.osborne.com
omg_international@mcgraw-hill.com

Complete References

Herbert Schildt
0-07-213485-2

Jeffery R. Shapiro
0-07-213381-3

Chris H. Pappas & William
H. Murray, III
0-07-212958-1

Herbert Schildt
0-07-213084-9

Ron Ben-Natan & Ori Sasson
0-07-222394-4

Arthur Griffith
0-07-222405-3

For the answers to everything related to your technology, drill as deeply as you please into our Complete Reference series. Written by topical authorities, these comprehensive resources offer a full range of knowledge, including extensive product information, theory, step-by-step tutorials, sample projects, and helpful appendixes.

Osborne
www.osborne.com

For more information on these and other Osborne books, visit our Web site at www.osborne.com